D1086604

Bible Commentary

by

E. M. Zerr

Volume I

Genesis—Ruth

© **Guardian of Truth Foundation 2006.** All rights reserved. No part of this book may be reproduced in any form without written permission from the publisher. Printed in the United States of America.

ISBN 1-58427-181-7

Guardian of Truth Foundation
P.O. Box 9670
Bowling Green, Kentucky 42102
www.truthbooks.net
1-800-428-0121

Foreword: The E.M. Zerr Bible Commentaries

Cecil Willis

Reprinted From *Truth Magazine* XX:26 (June 24, 1976), pp. 3-5

The Cogdill Foundation, which publishes *Truth Magazine*, has obtained exclusive publication rights to the six volume *Bible Commentary* written by Brother E.M. Zerr. . . .

Information About E.M. Zerr

Brother Zerr was quite well-known among a group of very conservative brethren, but he may not have been known among brethren in general. Hence, a little information concerning him is here given. Edward Michael Zerr was born October 15, 1877 in Strassburg, Illinois, but his family soon thereafter moved to Missouri. He was the second of six children born to Lawrence and Mary (Manning) Zerr. Brother Zerr's father was reared as a Catholic, but after he married Mary Manning, he obeyed the gospel. At the age of seventeen, young Edward was immersed into Christ in Grand River, near Bosworth, Missouri.

In June, 1897 young Brother E.M. Zerr received a letter from A. L. Gepford asking him to go to Green Valley, Illinois, and to preach in his stead. His first sermon was entitled, "My Responsibility as a Preacher of the Gospel, and Your Responsibility as Hearers." In the years between delivery of this first sermon on July 3, 1897, and the delivery of his last sermon on October 25, 1959, Brother Zerr preached about 8,000 sermons, from California to Connecticut, and from Washington to Arizona. It is noteworthy that his last sermon was built around Matt. 13:44, and was entitled "Full Surrender." Brother Zerr preached the gospel for a little over 60 years.

Among the brethren with whom Brother Zerr was most frequently associated, it was then common to have protracted periods of concentrated Bible studies, commonly referred to as "Bible Readings." Young Brother Zerr attended a three month "Bible Reading" conducted by the well-known teacher, A.M. Morris, in 1899. During this study which was conducted at

Hillsboro, Henry County, Indiana, Brother Zerr stayed in the home of a farmer named John Hill. After leaving the John and Matilda Hill farm, "E.M." began correspondence with their daughter, Carrie. The following year, while attending a "Bible Reading" conducted by Daniel Sommer in Indianapolis, "E.M." and Carrie were married, on September 27, 1900. The newlyweds took up residence in New Castle, Indiana, where their four children were born, one of whom died in infancy.

In 1911, Brother A.W. Harvey arranged for Brother Zerr to conduct a "Bible Reading" which continued for several months at Palmyra, Indiana. These "Bible Readings" usually consisted of two two-hour sessions daily. Young Brother Zerr's special ability as a teacher was soon recognized, and he continued to conduct such studies among churches of Christ for 48 years. Edward M. Zerr died February 22, 1960, having been in a coma for four months following an automobile accident at Martinsville, Indiana. His body was laid to rest in the little country cemetery at Hillsboro, Indiana, near the church building in which he had attended his first "Bible Reading."

Brother Zerr's Writings

In addition to his oral teaching and preaching, Brother Zerr was a prolific writer. He was a regular contributor to several religious periodicals. Brother Zerr also composed the music and lyrics of several religious songs. Two of these, "The True Riches," and "I Come to Thee," may be found in the widely used song book, *Sacred Selections.*

One of the books written by Brother Zerr is entitled *Historical Quotations*, and consists of the gleanings from 40,000 pages of ancient history and other critical sources which he read over a period of twenty years. These quotations are intended to explain and to confirm the prophetic and other technical statements of the Bible. Another book, a 434 page hard-cover binding, consists of a study course containing 16,000 Bible questions. This book, *New Testament Questions*, has at least 50 questions on each chapter of the New Testament. A smaller book, *Bible Reading Notes,* consists of some of the copious notes which Brother Zerr made in connection with the "Bible Readings" which he conducted. But the crowning success of his efforts was the writing of his six volume commentary on the whole Bible.

These six volumes were published between 1947 and 1955. Brother Zerr has the unique distinction, so far as is known to this writer, of being the only member of the church to write a commentary on the entire Bible. Many other brethren have written excellent and valuable commentaries on various books of the Bible, but no other brother has written on the entire Bible.

The writing of this commentary consumed more than seven years of full-time labor. In order that he might devote himself without interruption to this herculean effort, Brother Zerr was supported by the Newcastle church during this seven year period. It is unfortunate, in this writer's judgment, that other competent men have not been entirely freed of other duties that they might give themselves to such mammoth writing assignments. Through *Bible Commentary*, Brother E.M. Zerr, though dead since 1960, will continue to do what he liked best to do—conduct "Bible Readings" for many years to come. The current printing is the fifth printing of the Old Testament section (four volumes) of the commentary, and the sixth printing of the New Testament section (two volumes).

Many Christians spend but little money on available helps in Bible study. Some own perhaps only a *Cruden's Concordance*, a Bible dictionary of some kind, and then *Johnson's Notes*. It would be interesting to know how many copies of B.W. Johnson's *The People's New Testament Commentary With Notes* have been sold. If I were to hazard a guess, it would be that at least 1,000,000 copies of this superficial commentary have been sold. *Johnson's Notes* contains the printing of the entire New Testament text in both King James Version and the English Revised Version (the predecessor to the American Standard Version), and his comments, all contained in two volumes. In fact, a single volume edition also is available. Thus one is buying two copies of the New Testament, and B. W. Johnson's *Notes*, in one or two volumes. So necessarily, *Johnson's Notes* are very brief.

If brethren somehow could be made acquainted with Brother Zerr's *Bible Commentary*, it is possible that it could be as widely used as has been *Johnson's Notes*, first published in 1889. Brother Zerr printed very little of the Bible text in his commentary. He assumed you would have your own Bible nearby. To have printed in the commentary the entire Bible would have required at least three other volumes. While it would have been helpful to have the Bible text printed by the comments, this unnecessary luxury would have been very expensive, since we all have copies of the Scriptures already. Furthermore, Brother Zerr intended that one be compelled to use his Bible, in order that his commentary never supplant the Sacred text.

A Word of Caution

I am sure that Brother Zerr, were he yet living, would advise me to remind you that his *Bible Commentary* is only that of a man, though a studious man he was. In fact, in the "Preface" to this set of books, just such a word of warning is sounded by Brother Zerr. The only book which we recommend without reservation is the Bible! But Bible commentaries, when viewed merely as the results of many years of study by scholarly men, can be very helpful to one.

Brother Zerr spent his life-time working among those brethren who have stood opposed to "located preachers" and to "Bible Colleges." However, he has not "featured" these distinctive views in his *Bible Commentary*. If one did not know of these positions held by Brother Zerr, he might not even detect the references to them in the commentary. However, I want to call such references to your attention. Along with the opposition to "located preachers," Brother Zerr also held a position commonly referred to as "Evangelistic Oversight." This position declares that until a congregation has qualified elders appointed, each congregation should be under the oversight of some evangelist. With these positions, this writer cannot agree. References to these positions will be found in his comments on Acts 20:28; Eph. 3:10; 3:21; 4:11; 1 Tim. 5:21; 2 Tim. 4:5, and perhaps in a few other places that do not now come to memory. Brother Zerr also took the position that a woman should never cut or even trim her hair. His comments on this position will be found at 1 Cor. 11:1-16.

But aside from a very few such positions with which many of us would disagree, Brother Zerr's *Bible Commentary* can be very helpful. Some restoration period writers of widely used commentaries held some rather bizarre positions regarding the millennium. Brethren scruple not to use *Barnes' Notes*, in spite of his repeated injection of Calvinism, and *Clark's Commentary*, in spite of his Methodist teaching.

Brother Zerr's *Bible Commentary* is far superior to *Johnson's Notes*. Though there are some extraordinarily good volumes in the well-known Gospel Advocate commentaries, there also are some notoriously weak volumes in this widely used set. Viewed from the point of consistent quality, Brother Zerr's *Bible Commentary* is superior to the Gospel Advocate set. Some brethren whom I consider to be superior exegetes of the Word have highly recommended Zerr's *Bible Commentary* and have praised the splendid and incisive way in which he has handled even those "hard to be understood" sections of God's Word.

Our recommendation regarding E.M. Zerr's six volume commentary can be paraphrased from the words of a well-known television commercial: "Try it; you'll like it!"

PREFACE

In presenting the reading public a Bible Commentary, I do not come as a competitor of other commentators, as to scholarship and knowledge of world affairs. I have not traveled in foreign countries, nor learned the technical principles of the various languages so much used in the production of works in this field. On questions depending on such information, the authors of present day volumes are evidently qualified to write, and the correctness of their statements is not necessarily questioned. It has been my aim to consult their works when desired, and avail myself of the information offered by their scholarship and labors. I have also depended on such works of reference as Young and Strong have given in their concordances. The lexicons of Thayer, Robinson, Liddell and Scott, and others, have been consulted in the examination of the original languages of the Old and New Testaments. Using such sources of information for critical purposes, and my own study and learning of the Sacred Text for purposes of the doctrine of the Bible, it has been my controlling object to write a Bible Commentary, as detailed and thorough as my ability permits.

The body of the text will not be found in this book. The student will be required to have his Bible always at hand; thus this work cannot be substituted for that volume. This plan also conserves space that would not be used to any great advantage if taken for the mere printing of the text.

In view of the preceding paragraph, some further explanation will be offered. The beginning of each paragraph will be a reference to a verse or verses of the chapter under consideration, such as Verse 1, in the first chapter of Genesis. The particular word or words of that paragraph to be given attention in the commentary will be printed in italics, as *in the beginning,* with the comments thereon following immediately. Where no words of any given passage are in italics the comments are on the paragraph as a whole.

The Old Testament was written, generally in Hebrew, and the New Testament in Greek. When the original language is offered to the student, it will be printed in small capitals, as RESITH in the Old Testament, and ARCHE in the New Testament. These are the original words spelled out with English letters. That will enable the student to examine them in the lexicons, and other critical works, even though he is not a Hebrew or Greek scholar.

Among the critical and other works consulted in compiling this commentary are the following: Young's *Analytical Concordance*; Strong's *Exhaustive Concordance*; Thayer's *Greek-English Lexicon*; Robinson's *Greek Lexicon*; Grove's *Greek Lexicon*; Greenfield's *Greek Lexicon*; Donnegan's *Greek Lexicon*; Westcott and Horte's *Greek Lexicon;* Liddell and Scott's *Greek Lexicon; Ancient Monarchies*, by George Rawlinson; Mommsen's *History of Rome*; Josephus' *History of the Jews*; Myers' *Ancient History*; *Decline and Fall of The Roman Empire*, by Edward Gibbon; Jones' *Church History*; Eusebius' *Church History*; and many others too numerous to mention.

It has been my constant purpose to avoid speculation. I have offered no explanation based on mere guesswork. In all instances where I was not sure I understood the passage, no comment was made. My sole aim has been to encourage a more complete understanding of the Sacred Volume. If such is accomplished I will consider myself fully repaid for all the time and labor expended.

The Author.

Bible Commentary

GENESIS 1

Verse 1. *In the beginning.* This expression is not used with reference to time, but to the order of events. It is as if it read, "In the first place—to begin with", etc. The word for *beginning* is RESHITH and has been rendered in the A. V. by the following words: beginning, chief, chiefest, first, firstfruits, first part, first time, principal thing. Strong defines the word, "The first, in place, time, order or rank (specifically, a firstfruit)." The writer is telling the reader that creation of the material world began with the creation of the heaven and the earth. The time or date when this occurred is not considered here. The word *heaven* is from SHAWMEH and defined by Strong thus, "from an unused root meaning, to be lofty; the sky (as aloft; the dual perhaps alluding to the visible arch in which the clouds move, as well as to the higher ether where the celestial bodies revolve)." In other words, according to Strong the word refers to the first heaven, where the birds fly, and the second heaven, the place of the planets. The word here is in the singular but should be plural just as it is rendered in 2: 1 since it is used with reference to the two regions described in the definition. See notes at verses 6, 20.

Verse 2. *Without form.* This is from TOHUW and one word used by Strong to define it is "desolation." The word *void* is from BOHUW and is defined by Strong to mean "to be empty." Thus the expression could well be rendered "earth was desolate and empty." This is more reasonable since we cannot conceive anything that exists at all as not having any form. Yet we could easily understand how it could be desolate and empty, which was the real condition before the Creator began to arrange it by the six days of the creation. *Darkness.* Since darkness is a negative condition it would exist without creative act. *Deep.* This is from TEHOM and means the sea. *Waters.* As the original condition was water the theory that the earth was at first a ball of fire is false. *Moved.* This is from the same word as "flutter" in Deut. 32: 11.

Verse 3. *And God said.* Note this expression used here and on the five following days. It is the only recorded means used by the Creator to bring about his purpose regarding his works outside of man. His word was all that was used and all that was necessary. This agrees with Psa. 33: 6, 9; Heb. 11: 3. *Let there be light.* Read 2 Cor. 4: 6. It should be noted that light is here a created fact although the sun and other planets had not been created. This means that light is a substance and not the "effect" of the vibratory motion of the sun on the eye as taught by "science."

Verse 4. *God divided the light from the darkness.* Thus it was that God controlled the light which he had created by his miraculous power, thus giving alternations of light and darkness. After the sun and other lights were created he then ordained them as means by which these alternations were to be accomplished.

Verse 5. Let it be noted that just one evening and one morning are mentioned as forming one day. That is the order of nature now. Thus we see that the "six days of creation" were six periods of days just as we know them now. This being so we cannot accept the speculation that they were periods of several years as the so-called scientists teach. Such would require more than one evening and one morning.

Verse 6. *Firmament.* This is from RAQIA and defined thus by Strong, "An expanse, i. e., the firmament or (apparently) visible arch of the sky." It is thus the region that contains the first and second heavens. See v. 20. Also 2 Cor. 12: 2.

Verse 7. Here we see that in the disposal of the water at the creation, part of it was sent upward. This agrees with the reference here given to Psa. 148: 4 and also with 7: 11. The great abundance of water in the time of Noah would not necessarily require creation of it but only the suspension of this firmament, letting this water come back to its former place around the earth. Compare with "the windows of heaven were opened" in Gen. 7: 11.

Verses 9, 10. Having disposed of the bulk of water above the earth, God next brings a portion of the earth's surface to be above the water thus making a place for land life to subsist.

Verses 11, 12. It should be observed here that in God's arrangement, all fruit plants were to reproduce through their own seed and that the fruit of each seed was to be its kind. The theory that "seedlings" are inferior and that seeds will not bring the same kind of fruit as the original contradicts this statement of Moses. If a fruit seed today will not reproduce after its kind it is because something has been done to interfere with God's law of plant reproduction.

Verse 14. *Signs.* From OWTH and one of Strong's words for it is "evidence." See Psa. 19: 1. Does not mean anything like the so-called signs of those who do their planting "according to the sign." *To divide the day from the night.* See verse 4.

Verses 15, 16. Here we see the sun and other bodies were created some four days after the earth. The theory of "scientists" that the earth is a portion of the sun, having been thrown off from it, is false.

Verses 17-19. (Purpose of God in making these planets is said here to be to "give light upon the earth," not to make or originate light as is taught. This light was already in existence from the first day. See note at verse 3. It should be further noted that in stating the uses for which these heavenly bodies were made nothing is said about their being made to furnish a place for living beings.

Verse 20. If this verse should seem to contradict 2: 19 as to the source of material for the fowl, note the same subject in verse 22 is worded "let fowl multiply," etc. This shows the verse here intends only to tell us the proper breeding place of fish and fowl; the one in the waters and the other in the air, and not any direct reference to the creation of the first parent. *Heaven.* As a chain for the three heavens, underscore the word here and write: 1st heaven. See Gen. 22: 17 for the 2nd. Also see 2 Cor. 12: 2.

Verse 21. The word *whales* is from TANNIYN and defined by Strong as "a marine or land monster." Note also here as in the case of the vegetable kingdom, everything was to bring forth "after its kind."

Verse 22. The word *fill* is from the same word as *replenish.* Verse 28. *Let fowl.* See note on this verse at verse 20.

Verses 24, 25. Same law of reproduction after its kind that was given regarding creatures of the sea and air. This law is still observed in the animal kingdom and is a standing refutation of the evolutionary theory of reproduction.

Verse 26. *Us* and *our.* God and the Word were associated in Creation. See John 1: 3; Eph. 3: 9; Col. 1: 16.

Verse 27. The word *man* is used in its general sense and refers to both sexes. That man is made in the image of God as to his body is seen from the idea that in direct connection with the statement that man was made in the image of God it is stated that he made *them,* male and female. Since the body of man is the only part of him that has sex it follows that the image of God refers to his body.

Verse 28. *Replenish.* This is from the same word as "fill" verse 22 and has no idea of a second reproduction as the letters *re* have been erroneously interpreted. These letters do not form a syllable prefix but are simply a part of the body of the word which means to "fill." Let it also be noted that man is to subdue the earth. He is commanded in the New Testament not to abuse this world nor to permit interest therein to interfere with his more important interests of the soul; but, when kept within these restrictions, man may discover and "invent" and use the various properties of nature for his profit and enjoyment.

Verses 29, 30. At this time man was not given the flesh of animals to eat. No reason is assigned for this in the scripture. And if *every green herb* was given him for meat it would appear that the poisonous plants had not yet been created. Evidently they were brought forth along with the "thorns and thistles" of 3: 18.

Verse 31. Everything which God made was pronounced *very good.* And since this is pronouncement of excellence as to the state of created things in the beginning, we cannot accept the theory of evolutionists that they were crude in the beginning and then afterwards attained to a very good condition through long periods of time.

GENESIS 2

Verse 1. *Heavens.* Note the word is in the plural. See explanation at 1: 1.

Verse 2. *Ended* and *rested.* Since both these words are used in the same relation to God's creative work we must know they express the same thought. One does not always rest in the sense of relaxing from weariness or toil, but it is just as often used in the sense of a pause. God paused in his creative work. Attention is called also to the way it is expressed in the following verse. There it says that in the seventh day God "had rested," etc. This gives the idea of reflection and that the work being considered had all been completed when the seventh day came. This does away with the quibble that God must have done some work on the seventh day as it says that on it he ended his work. The complete thought is that he "had ended" it.

Verse 3. *Sanctified.* This is from QADASH and Strong defines it "a primitive root; to be (causate, make, pronounce or observe as) clean (ceremonially or morally)." This shows the word to mean that the day was set apart ceremonially and not that anything was done to its natural character since such a thing as a day could not be said to be either holy or unholy as to its character. There is no such thing as a holy day except as it pertains to what is done on that day.

Verse 4. *Generations.* This is from TOWLDAH and one definition Strong gives of it is "history." Thus the expression means "this is the history," etc.

Verses 5, 6. This is a summing up of some of God's work. The writer is referring to conditions before and after the plants and animals, including man, were made. And since it had not rained upon the earth and since there was no man to till the ground, it could not be concluded that these plants came up through natural inducement of moisture nor as the result of man's labor. And, since there was not a man to till the ground even though there was moisture in the form of mist, there should be a man to take over this duty. Hence the important statement soon to follow.

Verse 7. In this great work God did not merely speak man into existence as he did his other works, but honored the man by forming him with his own personal act. This verse should be studied in connection with other passages in the Bible which will be cited in this paragraph. 1 Thess. 5: 23 tells us that man has three parts. The verse under consideration mentions only two of these parts, the body and soul. Then, as soon as that much of "man" was created God created, immediately and simultaneously, the spirit (Zech. 12:1), thus completing the triune being. Word *breath* is from SHAMAH and defined by Strong as follows: "a puff, i. e., wind, angry or vital breath, divine inspiration, intellectually or concretely, an animal." Hence, since the breath introduced into the nostrils of this man is the same as that which makes other animals alive, it required that man, made in the image of his Creator, should have something else added to lift him above the other order of living beings. Therefore God created this spirit within him.

Verse 8. *Eden.* This was the name of a region of such a character as to be a place of pleasure. The garden was in this region and thus it was not the garden that was named Eden, but the region in which it was located. Further information on this place will be offered at verses below.

Verse 9. We see in this verse that the fact of being pleasant to the sight did not put a tree in the forbidden class. For, after mention of this fact pertaining to the trees in general the writer says "also" and then tells of the two special ones now so famous. There was nothing evil in the one tree itself but the eating of it would bring knowledge of good and evil. The significant idea in this expression is that it mentions both good and evil. Only one conclusion is possible, and that is that it brought knowledge of evil as distinguished from good. It would have been better for man not to have known anything but good. It was the possession of knowledge of good *and* evil that was the occasion of trouble.

Verses 10-14. The word "heads" here is evidently used figuratively since a river would not have four heads after having formed a river of stated existence. It might have formed a delta but would not form various heads. But it could be said that the region called Eden was supplied with four streams which is doubtless the thought of the writer. The modern Tigris corresponds to Hiddekel while Euphrates is the river of the same name as now. Incidentally, since we now know the location of these streams we can thus locate the general site of the famous garden.

Verse 15. This verse shows that man was not intended to be idle. Neither was the vegetation of the garden to be miraculously cared for. Then, as now, man was expected to be a worker with God in the enjoyment of divine blessings.

Verses 16, 17. *Thou shalt surely die.* The marginal rendering here is "dying, thou shalt die." The thought is that in the day they ate of that tree they would become subject to death. That was to be true both physically and spiritually. In a physical sense, in the day they ate they were driven from access to the tree of life, and immediately they began to die since they no longer had access to the tree of life which was the only thing that could have perpetuated their physical life. Then, since death spiritually also means separation, they immediately died since they were on that very day separated from God by their sin.

Verse 18. One reason it was not good for the man to be alone was that, in God's plan for filling the earth with his kind it was to require opposite parties. And also, in order that the creature who was made in the image of the Creator might be prosperous and happy while living on the earth he was to be a social being and this required society which would be impossible with only one kind of human being. *Help.* This means an aid or helper in the same sense as we speak of a worker having a helper. Of course an electric mechanic would want a helper suitable for his needs and thus not one that would be needed by some other kind of mechanic. Even so, the man being the kind he was and with the kind of expected future, he would need a helper suited for his social and reproductive needs. Thus, God declared he would make this man such a helper, hence we have *meet.* This is from NEGED and is thus defined by Strong: "a front, i. e., part opposite; specifically a counterpart, or mate." At first it might seem inappropriate to have a helper that is counterpart or opposite. But when it is remembered that this helper is for the special purpose of reproduction it will be clear. For instance, it would be of no help in arranging a mechanical effect to place one bolt with another. But a counterpart, one opposite, would be a help. Hence the bolt must be helped by the part that fits over the bolt. And so in reproduction, the principal purpose of the man, a counterpart, an opposite, is necessary to constitute a helper suitable for the man's needs. An appropriate wording of the passage would be "I will make him a helper suitable for his needs."

Verse 19. Since there were vast numbers of these living creatures it would require inspiration to be able to name them. This is why the significant statement that whatsoever Adam called the creatures, that was its name. We should not be surprised at seeing indication of Adam's being inspired. He was to be a type of the second Adam (Christ, 1 Cor. 15: 45) and so it was proper to demonstrate his power.

Verse 20. Explained in remarks at verse 18.

Verses 21, 22. In taking a part of the first Adam from which to make his helper God caused a deep sleep to come over him. In taking a part of the second Adam (his blood) from which to make his helper, God caused a deep sleep to come over him. It was the sleep of death. For Christ was dead when his blood was shed. The significant coincidence is that in each case the side of the man was opened.

Verse 23. *Flesh of my flesh.* This shows that both flesh and bone were taken from the man. Bone represents structure and the flesh the formation of the body.

Verse 24. From Matt. 19: 5 we learn the language of this in Genesis is that of God and not Adam as it might seem. And in Mark 10: 7 Jesus repeats the same words as his own. This fleshly relation is the original and only Biblical basis of the marriage instituton. When a male and female are thus joined they are by that act made one flesh and that union cannot be dissolved except by a similar act of one of the partes with a third party. This is why fornication is the scriptural, and the only scriptural basis for remarriage of an innocent party to a third party. *Leave his father and his mother.* When a male is old enough to perform the marriage act he is old enough, according to God, to leave his parents and become married. Lawmakers who arbitrarily set an age limit for marriage legally, without parental consent, would do well to study the above.

Verse 25. From the ideas set forth in 3: 7 and notes it would appear here that the writer means simply to say that the man and woman had not yet taken any notice of the fact that they were naked.

GENESIS 3

Verse 1. *Subtil.* This is from ARUWM and is defined as "cunning." *Beast.* This is from CHAY which has a wide variety of renderings in the A.V. Its outstanding idea is, a living creature. The passage might read "than any living creature of the field." He is here seen to be able to talk with man's language. He is here used as agent of the devil because of his cunning manner.

The devil has possessed superhuman power in the past. See Ex. 8: 18, 19. Here the magicians failed to produce the lice even after having performed the two previous signs. And when they failed this time they explained it by saying "this is the finger of God." Now it is evident that the word "this" refers to the transaction as a whole about the lice and in which they failed. If their failure to produce the lice while Aaron succeeded and if their explanation is that the finger of God accounts for it, then they are acknowledging that their work was not by the finger of God. And if not, and since man alone could not have done what they had been doing at two previous plagues, then it had to be by the finger of the devil. God has at different times suffered evil characters to accomplish the superhuman in order to accomplish some special end of His. See the case of the woman of Endor with Saul in 1 Sam. 28: 12. The behavior and expressions of the woman showed that she had not previously been able to perform the deeds she professed to perform, hence her shock at the happenings on this occasion. This shows that God used this evil woman this time to work a certain result and for that purpose suffered her to have this evil power. And so all the above is to account for the power of the devil exerted through the serpent.

Verses 2, 3. Here the woman truthfully repeats the law that God gave her as to the trees of the garden. This shows that her disobedience afterward could not be laid to any misunderstanding or failure of memory as to what God had said. And yet Paul says the woman was deceived. (1 Tim. 2: 14.) Therefore her deception came by allowing the devil to distract her attention to a one-sided consideration, as follows:

Verse 4. By adding the word "not" to what God had done the meaning of the whole statement was changed. And this was not wholly untrue as will be seen, and that is wherein lay the deception. Since a person can die in one sense and still live in another that gave the devil an opportunity to deceive by playing on the word. See next.

Verse 5. *Shall be as gods knowing good and evil.* See verse 22 where God himself stated the same thing which shows the devil stated some truth. And since a person who is like a god would not be considered as dead, the devil got through with his deception on the woman.

Verse 6. *When the woman saw.* This expression shows that the woman had not taken any special notice of the tree before. Evidently, when God had warned them in such strong terms about the tree, even not to even touch it, she had abstained from interest in the tree as far as possible and thus was taking a safe course. But the wiles of the devil had awakened in her an interest in the forbidden thing and then it was that she saw what had escaped her notice before. *Food, eyes, wise.* See 1 John 2: 16. The apostle says that the lust of the eyes, the lust of the flesh and the pride of life are all that there is in the world. Those three points of temptation are present in this case. They had the effect desired by Satan. He tried the same three points on Christ in Matt. 4: 1-11 but failed. The record states that the devil then left him. We ask why? The answer is because he had no other points of temptation to use since he had used these three which John says are all that are in the world. Notice that nothing is said about the deception of Adam here. And this is as stated by Paul in passage cited at verses 2, 3 above. He ate merely on the effect of association.

Verse 7. *Opened.* This is from PAQACH and defined by Strong "a primitive root; to open (the senses, especially the eyes); figuratively, to be observant." *Knew.* This is from YADA and in 18 places is rendered "perceive." So the passage as a whole means that they had their attention called to the conditions and perceived or took notice that they were naked. This caused their feeling of shame and their use of fig leaves to cover their nakedness. In last verse of previous chapter it is stated that the man and woman were not ashamed even though naked. But that was because they had not had their attention called to it as it is in the verse here under consideration.

Verse 8. Since a voice does not walk we must take this verse to mean that, as God was walking in the garden, they heard his voice. *Hid themselves.* Since according to Psa. 139: 7-13 and other passages it is impossible really to hide from God, we must take this to mean that Adam intended and tried to hide. But the writer speaks as if he did so. This teaches the principle that a man will be charged with his evil desires and attempts whether he succeeds or not. It is as bad in God's sight to desire and think evil as to perform it. See Mark 7: 20-22.

Verses 9-11. There could not have been any fault found against the man and woman for being naked for that was the way God left them when created. But the knowledge of their being so indicated that something was wrong. That they had obtained such knowledge unlawfully since God did not intend for them to have it. Hence the question that was asked of them.

Verse 12. It may be said that it was like the nature of a man to blame his sin on some one else. But that is just as true of woman. The reason in both cases is that it is according to human nature to justify one's own conduct by hiding behind another.

Verse 13. In this verse we have the truthful statement of the woman. But while it was the truth she was not excused for her conduct. She was destined to be punished for her act as will be seen below.

Verses 14, 15. Much speculation has been done on this noted passage. But one of the accepted principles of interpretation of language is that all statements are to be interpreted literally when the factual context will permit. To force a strained and figurative meaning into a passage in order to establish a cherished theory is as much to be regretted as is any other false teaching. To begin with, this is not a "star of hope" offered to man as is popularly preached, because God was not talking to the man at all when he said these words. As far as we know Adam and Eve never knew God had told these words. He was talking to the devil and it was a threat and not a "promise." Well, it is literally true that a special enmity exists between mankind and serpents. It is also true that the serpent once used his feet for traveling and under certain conditions, such as being exposed to heat, those feet in a reverted condition may be seen. And as part of his punishment he was to lose the use of these organs and be compelled to get down into the dust. See Micah 7: 17. Josephus was the celebrated Jewish historian and certainly understood the significance of their language. This is what he says about this circumstance. "He also deprived the serpent of speech, out of indignation at his malicious disposition towards Adam. Besides this, he inserted poison under his tongue, and made him an enemy of man; and suggested to them that they should direct their strokes against his head, that being the place wherein lay his malicious designs toward men, and it being easiest to take vengeance on him that way. And when he had deprived him of the use of his feet, and made him go rolling all along, and dragging himself upon the ground." Josephus, Ant. 1-1-4. Another thing to be noticed, God said "I will put enmity," etc. Now according to the popular speculation on this circumstance God did not mean the woman and the snake at all, but meant Jesus and the devil. But that will not do. If it were said that a man "will put" a fence between himself and his neighbor that means that no fence is there at present. And if the statement that God "will put" enmity between the devil and Christ be the proper conclusion, then the enmity had not yet existed. But that would not be true because that very enmity did already exist. See Rev. 12: 9 and Luke 10: 18. This shows that the devil was already at enmity with Christ before this scene with Adam and that was the very reason he wished to get in his evil work against God's work. And so it would be out of harmony with the sense and facts to speak of "putting" enmity, using the future tense, when that enmity already existed and had for some time. If a speaker wishes to make his own comparisons from this circumstance in order to have a subject for discourse he may do so, but he should not offer it as the meaning Moses had in the passage.

Verse 16. To begin with in discussing this, another noted passage, let it be remembered that the whole verse is on the subject of reproduction and the necessary factors of sexual relations pertaining to it. God said he would greatly multiply. One cannot multiply with only a multiplier. There must be something to multiply and that something must already be in existence. That something in this case consisted in *sorrow and conception*. The first of these words is from a Hebrew word that means pain. So that the expression means that her pain and conception was to be multiplied. This shows that a certain amount of pain and discomfort was to accompany childbirth as the original plan of God. But now it is to be multiplied. Incidently, this makes us know that all modern so-called painless methods of childbirth are attempts to set aside the declaration of God. Now we are not told just what means God was to use in bringing about this increase of conception. That is, we do not know all of the means. But we can assuredly point to one fact that resulted in such increase. That is the fact set forth in verse 21. The covering of the man and woman and the continuous requirement of God all through the ages regarding the subject of modesty, is related to this subject of increase of human reproduction. The reader is here requested to read the account of David and Bathsheba in 2 Samuel 11. Here is an account of one child that was conceived and born that would not have been had woman always been unclothed. It says the woman was "beautiful to look upon." But had woman always been unclothed previously, the fact of seeing her taking a bath would not have affected his sex nature. The sexes, having always lived in that unclothed manner would have been so accustomed to the appearance of each other that nothing would have been left to the imagination to stir the sex impulse. In that case the only condition that would have urged the male to approach the female would have been the physical accumulation of the male seed that would call for outlet in the mutual relation. But with the female form kept covered, the imagination of the male reacted upon his nature and thus caused his desire for the relation. And hence, further, in the intimacies of married life, the privilege of carrying out these imaginations results in the more frequent desire for the reproductive relation. *Thy desire shall be to thy husband.* Since this verse is all on the same subject we must conclude this to mean that the woman's sexual desire must be subject to that of the husband. It does not affect this conclusion any to say that man is thus given an opportunity to abuse his privileges. One wrong does not condemn the authority of law. The New Testament gives special attention to husbands who abuse this law, but that does not release the woman from the consequences of the scene in the garden.

Verses 17-19. Since God here punishes man with thorns and thistles it is clear that such plants were not created at the start. See notes at 1: 29, 30. Without wishing to speculate on this place it is enough to say that while man would have been required to work the ground for his living even had he not sinned, yet it would have always been a success and no hindrance. Now he must toil in the face of obstacles which would bring the sweat out on his body. *Dust thou art.* The word for dust here as also in 2:7 and other places is from APHAR and defined by Strong thus. "Dust (as powdered or gray); hence clay, earth, mud." So we are not bound to think of it as the dry grains of the earth as is the common idea, but think of it as something of fine grain and also suitable for plastic use. Of this material the man was formed but made to be alive according to 2: 7. Very logically then, when the life leaves the body it will return to its former state and become this dust or earth again.

Verse 20. At the time this occurred no one was living but Adam and Eve. But since we have seen that Adam was enabled to name the other living creatures and that he must have had inspiration to do so (see 2: 19, 20), we can understand how he could here have given to his wife the name appropriate to her destiny as the first mother.

Verse 21. This is explained at verse 16.

Verse 22. In this verse the Lord made the same statement the serpent made in his conversation with the woman as seen in 1: 26. Not that the man had become equal to his Creator in all respects, but in the matter of this knowledge that was unlawful for him to have. *Eat and live forever.* Had man been permitted to eat of the tree of life even after his sin, he would have lived forever, but in sin. It would have been tragic to live forever in sin, hence God is going to prevent that.

Verses 23, 24. Man is now sent forth to till the ground and thus begins the sentence imposed on him in verses 17-19. *Drove out the man.* This explains the statement in Romans 8: 20. In that passage the "creature" is mankind in general but specifically applying at first to the first man. Since God drove the man out Paul says he was not going out willingly. The "vanity" in Romans means "frailty" and refers to his being subject to death after having been separated from the tree of life. And by placing the cherubims in service the guard would be perpetual since these creatures do not die. *Keep.* This is from SHAMAR and defined "a primitive root; properly to hedge about (as with thorns), i. e., guard; generally to protect, attend to."—Strong. *Way.* This is from DEREK and Strong defines is "a road (as trodden)"; And notice it says God placed the guard at the east of the garden, not merely at the "gate" of the garden as is so commonly stated. But, while the garden was in a place described as delightful, yet there was a way or road leading to it and this entire road was thus guarded.

GENESIS 4

Verse 1. *Knew*. Referring to Num. 31: 17; Judg. 19: 25; 1 Sam. 1: 19 and various other places we learn this use of the word is a Biblical way of referring to the relations of the two sexes. *Gotten a man from the Lord*. We do not know how long after the events of chapter one until the man and woman began living as husband and wife. We do know that they were in that chapter commanded to multiply. But without any previous experience or history of others, there would be nothing in even the sexual desire to suggest to the couple that their act would result in offspring. But God has never told man to do or accomplish any result without informing him as to the means. Therefore, we have the necessary inference that when he commanded the pair to reproduce he also told them how it was to be accomplished. That the man had been given a counterpart of himself for the purpose of reproduction and hence this was his provision for obeying the command to multiply. Therefore it was natural for Eve to explain the coming of the child to be from the Lord.

Verse 2. Note that in one short verse we have the statement of the birth, growth to maturity and establishment of an occupation of life. This shows the brief nature of the Bible against the complaint that is sometimes heard, namely, that the Bible is such a long drawn out volume and thus so tedious. It is rather the most concise, yet thorough document in all literature.

Verses 3-5. In this particular place we are not told why God respected the offering of Abel but rejected that of Cain. But other passages will give us light. In Heb. 11: 4 we are told Abel offered his sacrifice "by faith." And in Rom. 10: 17 we are told that faith comes by hearing the word of God. Then, since Abel offered his sacrifice by faith and since faith comes by hearing the word of God, we conclude that the word of God had told them what to offer. Abel offered what he had been told to offer while Cain offered something else. It is not a question of whether the ground product that Cain offered was a good quality but the trouble was that God had not told him to offer that at all, but to offer an offering from the animals.

Verses 6, 7. This passage taken as a whole means that had Cain been doing the thing he should he would have been blessed of God. And since he was the older of the two brothers he would have had priority over the other. But since he was disobedient, the responsibility for sin was laid at his door.

Verse 8. Cain selected a time when they were not in presence of others to slay his brother. That this was his plan is seen by the falsehood he uttered to the Lord in the following verse.

Verse 9. He not only falsified about the whereabouts of his brother, but offered as defense the idea that he was not his brother's keeper. Many people have since taken that attitude. When they are urged to do something for the sake of others and it is something they do not wish to bother about, they will offer the same thing in one form or another. They will speak as if they will not be to blame if others do not look after themselves. But, while it is true that a man's neglect to take proper care of his own interests will be charged up against himself, it is also true that others who could have done something about it but did not will also be to blame.

Verse 10. *Blood crieth*. By considering verses 15, 24 Paul says the blood of Christ "speaketh better things than that of Abel." That is because the blood of Christ speaks or cries for mercy while the blood of Abel cried for vengeance.

Verses 11, 12. *From the earth*. This does not mean that Cain was to be sent away in the sense of out of the earth for the last line says he is to be a fugitive *in* the earth. But it means that his punishment was to be produced from or by the earth. That would be accomplished by the failure of the earth to yield to him the expected fruit of his labor. Yes, this same ground that kindly received the innocent blood of his murdered brother would be his instrument of punishment. *Fugitive*. This is from a word that means to be unsettled and not be allowed to have any abiding place. He was to be tossed to and fro and become the object of hatred wherever he went. He would not be permitted to dwell in any desired locality that would have God represented in any favorable circumstance. In this sense was he to be banished from God. Cain understood this to be the meaning of the language of God as expressed by him in following.

Verse 13, 14. The last word of this

passage is used as including Cain and his descendents since no one man could be slain more than once. But he understood that on account of his wandering, uncertain manner of life, the public would consider him in about the same way they would a vicious beast and seek to slay him. But God did not wish to have that extent of punishment imposed on him. See following paragraph.

Verse 15. *Mark.* This is from UWTH and Strong defines it as "a signal (literally or figuratively), as a flag, beacon, monument, omen, prodigy, evidence." From this we see that the mark placed on Cain was not necessarily some physical blemish stamped on his body as is the popular impression. What it was we do not know, only, there was some kind of unusual sign or token placed in his hands for use in identifying him with the implied information to the public that no one was to molest him bodily. And that if anyone did so molest him, vengeance might be taken on the would-be attacker.

Verse 16. *From the presence.* See notes on verses 11, 12.

Verse 17. *Knew his wife.* Consult the references given at verse 1. This merely means that at this place Cain and his wife had intimate relations with the result that a son, Enoch, was born. Since Adam and Eve were the first human pair and to be the ancestors of all other human beings, the conclusion is inevitable that Cain's wife was his sister. Whatever objections that came later against such intimate marriage might indicate, at this early stage of man's existence God would overrule all obstacles.

Verses 18-22. This is a simple statement of the rapid production of Cain's son and grandsons and of their developing into various trades.

Verses 23, 24. *To my hurt.* The marginal reading is "in my hurt." The idea is that a man had made an attempt on Lamech's life and he had defended himself by slaying his would-be murderer. He justifies himself by referring to the protection that had been offered Cain. If Cain, the man so wicked as to be banished from the presence of God, was entitled to veangeful treatment of his attackers, certainly Lamech who is not under any such demotion would be entitled to much more protection.

Verse 25, 26. Note the marginal reference here gives us "call themselves *by* the name of the Lord." This is significant. Since Cain has been banished from the peaceful presence of the Lord it would be considered that his seed could not claim much nearness of relation with the Lord. By the same token, the descendents of Seth, the one taking the place of righteous Abel who was slain, would feel entitled to call themselves by His name. This, then, is doubtless the beginning of recognition of two distinct classes of human beings referred to in 6: 1 and which will be considered in its proper connection.

GENESIS 5

Verse 1. *Generations.* This is from TOLDAH and Strong defines it "descent, i. e., family; (figuratively) history." The statement means that it is the family history, as to descent, of Adam. *Adam.* The Hebrew word here is spelled the same as the English and defined as follows. "To show blood (in the face), i. e., flush or turn rosy: ruddy, i. e., a human being (an individual or the species, mankind, etc.)."

Verse 2. *Adam.* See previous verse. Also in Josephus, Ant. i-i-2 we are told the original color of the earth was red. This would account for the coincident of the name of the first man being the same as a word that means "red." *Their name.* Since the writer is speaking of the human species it is significant that the plural pronoun refers to the same common name. And since this first Adam (see 1 Cor. 15: 45) was a type of Christ the second Adam, it was fitting that the name be used in common. This agrees with the idea that both the second Adam and his partners should have a name of common meaning namely, Christ-Christians.

Verses 3-32. It is thought as well to group these verses into one paragraph since most of the comments will be on the passage as a whole. Mention will be made of the eleven lineal descendants from Adam commonly referred to as the Patriarchs. They are Adam (mentioned in verse 2), Seth, v. 3; Enos, v. 6; Cainan, v. 9; Mahalaleel, v. 12; Jared, v. 15; Enoch, v. 18; Methuselah, v. 21; Lamech, v. 25; Noah, v. 29; Shem, v. 32. These formed the immediate and lineal line from the first man down to the time of the flood in the time of Noah. *Enoch walked with God* in verse 24 refers to his life before being taken to heaven. This is evident from the language of Paul in Heb. 11: 5 where he says that Enoch had the testimony of pleasing God "before his translation." The three sons of Noah were not triplets, hence the language in last verse means that Noah was the age of 500 years in round numbers when his three sons were brought into the world. Also, the brothers are not named in the order of their birth. In Gen. 10: 21 it speaks of Japheth and calls him the "elder." This is from GADOL and Strong defines the word here as follows. "Great (in any sense); hence older; also insolent." But this is not to be wondered at. It frequently happens in the Bible that members of a family will be named or regarded in the order of their importance and not always in the order of birth. As instances, Jacob and Esau, Ephraim and Manasseh, Abram, Nahor and Haran.

GENESIS 6

Verses 1, 2. *Sons of God.* See comments at 4: 25, 26. From all considerations at hand the conclusion is that these sons of God are the descendants of Seth while the daughters of men are the descendants of Cain. It was not the Lord's wish that the two classes of people should intermarry. But then, as well as now, the will of God is not always carried out by human beings. This seems to be specially true when the animal nature of the man is being entertained. So here they made wives of women who met their choice instead of the ones who met the favor of God. And when God's people marry those who are not God's people there is sure to be trouble. That is a statement of rule that has been and always will be true.

Verse 3. *Strive.* This is from DUWN and defined thus. "To rule; by implication to judge (as umpire); also to strive (as at law)."—Strong. The verse here means that God will not keep up his pleading with them indefinitely. He will, however, continue this for a period of 120 years. And this period of grace was the time when God was still endeavoring to bring the people to repentance through the preaching of Noah. It is mentioned in 1 Peter 3: 18-20 and 2 Peter 2: 5. God and Christ directed the Holy Spirit to inspire Noah in those days so that he could preach to the people. In this way God was striving or pleading with them to repent. But this period of probation was to last only 120 years.

Verse 4. *Giants.* This is from NEPHIL and defined thus. "Properly a feller, i. e., a bully or tyrant."—Strong. *Renown.* This is from SHEM and the same authority defines it as follows: "Shame; a primitive word—perhaps from 7760 through the idea of definite and conspicuous position; compare 8064—; an appelation as a mark or memorial of individuality." With these critical explanations the verse is very clear. The offspring of these men with the women of strong personal physical character, since it says they were fair, would naturally be more athletic than otherwise. So these men were not giants in the sense of stature, but, as the definition gives, they were strong physically and also, since they where the offspring of parents who were more carnal than spiritual, they became tyranical and of the nature of a bully. And all this explodes the speculative theory advanced by some that the "sons of God" above meant angels from heaven. In the first place, Jesus says of such persons that they do not marry (Mark 12: 25), and thus would not cohabit with human females. And if they did, their offspring would not be like the ones described in the present passage.

Verse 5. If men had given themselves over to their carnal lusts in the selection of wives it might be expected that their general life would be one of like character.

Verses 6, 7. *Repented the Lord.* The universal meaning of repentance is *change.* The scriptures clearly teach that God does not repent as man repents, yet he repents. Hence we must look for the explanation in some definition that is true of both, at least in some sense. Well, we have that common definition in the word *change.* Whether it is the case of God or of a man that repentance takes place, we must expect to find that a change has taken place. Hence, the definition that is true of man is that when he repents he *changes* his will. When God repents he wills a *change.* Now in the present instance, when it repented God that he had made man on the earth, it means that he willed a change in conditions. Hence he is going to remove man from the earth and in that way would bring about the *change* which is the fundamental meaning of repentance.

Verse 8. We are not told anything about the personal character of the sons and families of Noah. It simply says that Noah found grace or favor with God. Now we know this was under the Patriarchal Dispensation when the father or chief father as the word patriarch means, counted for the rest of the family. And thus we always see the name of Noah as outstanding in this instance. On this thought the reader is requested to read 2 Peter 2:5. Here the A.V. says "Noah the eighth" while Robinson's Greek Lexicon renders it "Noah and seven others." At any rate, the outstanding idea is that Noah was the one whose signal righteousness brought favor from God for the family.

Verse 9. *Generations.* This is the same word as explained at v: 1, which see. *Walked.* This is from HALAK and defined thus. "A primitive root; to walk (in a great variety of applications, literally and figuratively)"—Strong. As an indication of the general meaning of the word I shall here set down a number of the words used to translate it in the A.V. Behave, be conversant, follow, move, and many others. The meaning is that Noah's life was pleasing to God.

Verse 10. As to the relative ages of these sons see explanation at the end of chap. 5.

Verses 11-13. *Earth.* As the earth literally would not be thought of as corrupt morally we should seek for some other use of the word as used in this paragraph. The word is from ERETS and Strong defines it as follows. "From an unused root probably meaning to be firm; the earth (at large, or partitively [in part] a land)." The word has been rendered by country, field, land, nations, world. From this it would appear to be used as referring to life on the earth and especially that part of life dominated by the human beings. *Flesh.* This is from BASAR and one of the words used by Strong to define it is a word that means "modesty." So, with these critical data the meaning of the whole paragraph is that man had become so immodest and immoral that his entire influence was toward the vile. This would naturally result in an abused use of everything which God had created and placed in the hands of man. And this presented a general picture of violence and perversion of the original will of God. And in deciding to clear the earth of these wicked human beings it was just as well to remove the other living creatures also since their widespread existence would not serve any good purposes. Hence God's decree to wipe it all from the face of the earth except that which was entitled to live and whatever would also be needed for the use of those persons entitled to live.

Verse 14. *Gopher.* This is the only place in the Bible this word is used. Strong says it is apparently the cypress. *Rooms.* From QEN and defined "a nest (as fixed), sometimes including the nestlings; figuratively a chamber or dwelling."—Strong. This word is rendered "nest" in following places: Num. 24: 21; Deut. 22: 6; Job 29: 18. *Pitch.* This is from KOPHER and defined by Strong "properly a cover, i. e. (literally) a village (as covered in); specifically, bitumen (as used for coating)." The nature of this substance is to prevent water or other liquids from going through. The quibble might be made that since God is all-powerful he could have kept the water from saturating the walls of the ark without any such natural means. That is true. But this is just another instance of the many where we see that God uses the cooperation of man in carrying out his great plans. Christ could have healed the blind man without the use of clay and the elders with spiritual gifts might have healed the sick without oil. Likewise, the prophet could have fed the widow without the use of her small supply of meal and oil. But it is the will of God to require man to do something for his own good.

Verse 15. *Cubit.* This word is used several times in the scriptures and seems to be somewhat indefinite except that it is known to be a unit of measure. Most tables describe it as being the length of the forearm below the elbow. From this the general amount of the cubit as used in the Bible is 18 inches.

Verse 16. *Window.* This word at this place is from TSOHAR and defined by Strong "a light (i. e., window); dual double light, i. e., noon." But in 8: 6, where the same window is meant, the word is CHALLOWN and defined "a window (as perforated)." Next let us examine *above.* This is from MAHAL and Strong gives us "properly the upper part, used only adverbially with prefix upward, above, overhead, from the top, etc." Now then with this information concerning the leading words in this verse we can conclude the meaning of the verse as a whole. Since a cubit is about 18 inches it would be unreasonable to think that the verse means to tell us the size of this window. While God could cause enough light to go through a pin puncture to serve all needs if he wished, yet it is not in keeping with his rule of propriety to do so. But since the outstanding thought of the original word for "above" is upward, from the top, etc., it now seems plain that the verse means that the window was so arranged that it was elevated above the common level of the roof of the ark to the distance of a cubit. Then, since one part of the definition of the word for "window" is that it was something perforated, and since that was the day before transparent glass, the conclusion is that the sides of this "window" were perforated to admit light and ventilation. The length and breadth of this window are not being considered here by the writer. The word *stories* is not in the original, but the words lower, second and third are. And since the ark is the principal subject of the verse we should conclude that the word stories is necessarily implied. This will also correspond with the three classes of living creatures to occupy the ark, which are man, clean and unclean animals.

Verses 17-19. Attention is invited in this paragraph to the designation of the things that were to be destroyed to be "wherein is the breath of life." But more will be said on this matter at 7:22.

Verse 20. As far as this verse goes the word "two" applies to the sex pair, male and female. Additional thoughts on it will be given in chapter 7.

Verses 21, 22. Note the prescription that it was the food "that is eaten" that was to be taken in. This implies that some things that could be eaten might not have been so used. This will specially apply to the matter of animal flesh.

GENESIS 7

Verses 1-3. Here is where we see the further instructions about what living beings were to be taken in. The clean were to be taken in by sevens which means seven pairs and the unclean one pair, and each of these pairs was to consist in the male and female. Since no record is here given us as to what constituted clean and unclean we are forced to conclude that God instructed Noah verbally about this. One purpose for taking these things into the ark is expressed in last of this paragraph to be "to keep seed alive upon the face of the earth." And we will learn later that man was to be given flesh to eat, also would be called on to make animal sacrifices to God. But in both these uses only the clean would be accepted. Hence the seven of the clean required to be taken in while only one pair of the unclean.

Verses 4, 5. "Yet seven days" and it was to rain forty days and forty nights. Of course this means that when forty days had come the rain would start and continue for that long a period. And we note here that Noah did as was told which means that at the end of this paragraph Noah is in the ark although it is to be seven days yet till the rain starts.

Verse 6. This means it was in the year that would make him that many years of age. See verse 11 below.

Verses 7-9. Comments on this paragraph are same as on verses 1-3 above.

Verse 10. *After seven days.* This was seven days after Noah had entered the ark.

Verses 11-16. This gives the exact date when the rain began to fall which was the 17th day of 2nd month of Noah's 600th year of life. Therefore the date he entered the ark was the 10th day of that month. *Windows of heaven were opened.* See notes at chapter 1: 7.

Verses 17-21. So-called scientists claim the Bible does not teach that the water was over the entire earth. That only the comparatively small portion, the part where man was living, was covered. But the statement is that the waters were over all the high hills "under the whole heaven." Since the entire earth has some hills on it the conclusion is that the whole earth was covered. *Fifteen cubits upward.* That is, the water extended upward from the tops of the highest hills that distance. So whatever is the height of the highest hill, by adding 15 cubits to that we will have the depth of the water at the lowest place.

Verse 22. The use of such words as "nostrils" and "breath of life" and "dry land" shows that only land animals entered the ark. That was because the other creatures were not in any danger from the flood. Had God wanted to destroy the fish he would have used some other means since water is their natural element.

Verse 23. *Living.* This is from CHAY and Strong defines it "alive; hence raw (flesh); fresh (plant, water, year), strong; also life whether literally or figuratively." So the context would have to be referred to in determining in any given case whether the living thing being considered is plant or animal. And the context in this case is right in the verse because it mentions animal things only. This would leave us with the thought that plant life was not all destroyed. And this agrees with the statement in 8: 11 that the dove came in with an olive leaf. This could not have been propagated from the provisions of Noah in the ark for he had not left the ark as yet. Besides, there would not have been time enough for that kind of development.

Verse 24. *Prevailed.* Means they remained at their height that long.

GENESIS 8

Verse 1. *Remembered.* God never forgets anything in the sense of letting it slip his mind as is the case with man. But one word in the definition of the original here is to "recognize." It means that God now took notice and was not going to leave Noah and his group in the ark as in a prison. He was now ready to dispel the water as it has accomplished its purpose on the wickedness of the earth so that Noah could again occupy the land. *Asswaged.* This is the same meaning as "abated" in verses 3, 8.

Verse 2. See comments at chapter 1: 7.

Verse 3. *Returned* and *continually.* Both these are from the same original and the central word in the definition is "retreat" without any specific designation as to where the retreat reached. But the context in chapter 1: 7; 7: 11 and verse 2 here would tell us they retreated to their former places, namely, the deep or sea, and heaven.

Verse 4. *Ararat.* This original word is also rendered Armenia in the A. V. Notice the statement is that the ark rested on the mountains. Since it would not rest twice nor in two places at once we should not refer to the resting place of the ark as on any particular mountain as is popularly expressed. The principal thought is that it was in that country and also that it rested on a mountain. This accounts for the fact that the ark ceased floating a number of months before they left it. The ground generally must become dry before Noah could leave the ark.

Verse 5. The waters continued to abate after the ark rested on a mountain and by the first day of tenth month the mountain tops were *seen.* This is from RAAH and defined by Strong "a primitive root; to see, literally or figuratively." From verses 7, 11 it indicates that Noah had not yet seen the ground. Therefore we would be left with the figurative part of the definition of the word and would read it as if it said the tops of the mountains were visible without regard to whether any human actually saw them.

Verse 6. *Opened the window.* See comments at chapter 6: 16. If the window was made as there described it would be clear as to how Noah would open this place. It would be on the side of the window which would be the natural place to make an outlet.

Verse 7. *To and fro.* The last of these words is from SHUWB and thus defined by Strong: "a primitive root; to turn back (hence, away) transitively or intransitively, literally or figuratively, (not necessarily with the idea of return to the starting point): generally to retreat." Since the word does not necessarily mean that the returning was to the place of starting we would not get the idea the raven returned to the ark. This would be a strange conduct for Noah to have the raven leaving the ark and then returning to it, and keeping this up till the waters had dried up. In that case no occasion would have been present for sending the dove on this reconnaissance mission. But the raven, being tireless on the wing, continued its flight until the waters were abated. This made it necessary for Noah to send out the other bird.

Verses 8, 9. The raven not having reappeared Noah makes another inquiry by the use of the dove. The statements in this paragraph do not contradict that of verse 5. The tops of the mountains would not necessarily be in many places and thus not close enough to the ark to provide a resting place for the dove. Therefore, not being such a hardy bird, would be compelled to return to the ark.

Verses 10-12. The olive leaf in the mouth of the dove would not mean that the earth was entirely dried, only abated. And the existence of the olive leaf indicates that vegetation was not to be destroyed by the flood. See comments on this point at 7: 23. The failure of the dove to return after the third flight showed that the earth was practically clear of the flood.

Verse 13. *Covering.* This is from

MIKCEH and Strong defines it "a covering, i. e., weather-boarding." The nearest we can safely come to the meaning of this statement is that at some place accessible for Noah a part used for protection against the weather was so constructed that it could be removed. It could not have been the same as the window, for, had it been so, he could have looked to see the "face of the ground" at the time he sent the birds out. So, recalling that God shut him in before the waters began to come (see 7: 16), it is a necessary inference that he would not be privileged to open any part of the exterior of the ark until God so directed him. That was done here.

Verse 14. The earth was dry in the year 601 of Noah's life, second month, twenty-seventh day. In year 600, second month, 17th day of his life the flood started according to 7: 11, and according to 7:4, 10 Noah entered the ark seven days before the rain satrted. Then he entered the ark the 10th day of second month of 600th year of his life and left the ark 27th day of second month of 601st year. Therefore he was in the ark a year and 17 days.

Verses 15-19. Nothing new in this paragraph but it is well to note again that only things with flesh or that crept are mentioned which again reminds us that vegetation was not all to be destroyed by the flood.

Verse 20. This is the first time that an altar is mentioned by name although we know that one was used by Abel since he offered an acceptable sacrifice. Note also that the clean creatures were the ones offered which shows us the propriety of his having taken a greater number of the clean than the unclean into the ark.

Verse 21. *From his youth.* Attention is called to the point in human life that evil is charged against individuals. This opposes the doctrine of fatalists who teach that mankind is depraved from birth.

Verse 22. A popular speculation of prophecy is that the time is to be when we can not tell difference between summer and winter. This verse declares that the usual seasons will continue as long as the earth stands. The existence of the famine in Egypt and other places does not contradict this verse. It does not say that no famine will ever come. It only says that the seasons and the planting and reaping times will always recur. That was true in spite of those local famines. Furthermore, while it was said that the famine in the days of Joseph affected the whole earth, that was a miraculous famine and provision was made for it by an overproduction through the seven previous years.

GENESIS 9

Verse 1. This verse is a repetition of the command given the first man and wife as it is written in 1: 28. The command to replenish the earth, not merely a certain locality, would require that they spread abroad as reproduction progressed. And this will explain some of the mistakes made by the people recorded in 11th chapter.

Verse 2. The fall of man did not alter the condition of subjugation of the lower orders of creation under man as has been taught. For this is practically the same as was declared in the first chapter. Besides, Jas. 3: 7 states that such subjugation had taken place in the time of that writer. The only way that a member of the lower order can overcome the human is through its superior physical strength, while man does not effect his control over the beasts by his physical strength but by his intellect. This is one unanswerable argument in favor of the complete superiority of man in spite of the theory of evolutionists.

Verse 3. This is the first instance that we read of the privilege given to man to eat the flesh of animals. We have no information in the scriptures as to why this is.

Verses 4, 5. Whether it be man or beast, the blood is the life. This forms the basis or a part of the basis for various commandments. The first one mentioned is in the paragraph under consideration. It is even stated here that vengeance is to be had on beasts that cause the death of a man. This law was made still more specific as seen in Ex. 21: 28. And the executioner is pointed out here to be the "man's brother." Of course it will be seen in numerous instances as we pursue our study of the Bible that a man's brother is not confined to the strict fleshly relation usually meant in this expression, but whoever is his nearest kin.

Verse 6. Here we have the law of capital punishment proclaimed for the first time. This law has never been repealed by the Lord. Not only does God here state that said punishment is to be meted out to a murderer but no other punishment was ever given by divine law for said crime. It is a well established principle of justice that all law must have some motive for its existence. And as long as that basis is in existence that law is in force. In this case the basis for the law is the fact that man is made in the image of God. This is unavoidably set forth by the word FOR in direct connection with the law. If this capital law had been based on some later date, then the law would not be permanent. But it is as true as it ever was that man is still made in the image of God. If positive proof in the scriptures were thought necessary it will be seen in the following: 1 Cor. 11: 7; Col. 3: 10; Jas. 3: 9. Since then it is still true that man is made in the image of God it is still the law of God that the murderer should be put to death. Not only so, but this punishment is to be administered by *man*, not God. It is so stated in the verse under consideration. It is claimed that capital punishment was under the Old Testament law but not in force now. In the first place, this punishment was decreed long before the law of Moses was given. Besides, it is not a law that is of the character to be affected by any certain dispensation of time or religion. But even granting the above argument (?), it still will not hold against the plain teaching found in the New Testament. In Romans 13: 4 Paul speaks about an officer of the law of the government and calls him the minister of God. Here he states that "he beareth not the sword in vain." Now any one knows that there is only one use for the sword and that is to take life. And yet this very officer who bears the sword to take life is said by the apostle to be a minister of God. Therefore Paul here endorses the law of capital punishment. Furthermore, in Acts 25: 11 this same Paul uses these words: "If I be an offender, or have committed any thing worthy of death, I refuse not to die." Now if Paul had not favored capital punishment he could not have referred to the possibility of doing any thing worthy of death. And even had he not endorsed such a form of punishment and they were determined to administer it to him, he could have said that he could not prevent it. But he could have refused his submission. But he did not merely say that he would expect to die if they decided he was worthy, but said he would not refuse to die. That is the same as consenting to it beforehand, provided he had done anything worthy of death. Therefore it is plainly taught even in the New Testament that capital punishment is God's form of punishment for a murderer.

Verse 8. See comments at verse 1.

Verses 9-17. These verses are grouped into one paragraph because they have to do with one subject, that of the covenant between God and man never again to bring another destruction by water. And the word that is the center of controversy is the word *set*. The question is whether God here created the rainbow for the first time or that it had been already in existence but used here for the first time for the special purpose stated. I am sure the former is the correct view and shall give my reasons. First, I shall give the original word which is NATHAN and defined thus: "a primitive root; to give, used with great latitude of application (put, make, etc.)"—Strong. Among the different words in the A. V. used to translate it are the following: appoint, 11 times; give, 1023 times; make, 108 times; set, 101 times; yield, 14 times. Some of these words indicate the thought of its being used for this special purpose while others indicate that of its being made or created for the purpose. This also agrees with Strong's definition which admits both put and make. Therefore, the subject must be considered from the standpoint of logical reasoning. To insist that the rainbow was already in existence because it is a law of nature is to say that God had to establish all the law of nature at the same time. But that would be assuming the very point in controversy. We might as well argue that thorns and thistles were created at the same time with all other plants since they are a product today of nature. And yet we know from chapter 3: 17, 18 that they were not created until after the first sin of man. Again, it is suggested that it had not rained before this time and thus the bow, while a natural appearance now was something new at the time of Noah. But in that case the cloud would also have been something new. Yet the language indicates that the cloud was already a phenomenon that had been seen before. Notice it says, "when I bring a cloud over the earth, that the bow shall be seen in the cloud." Had the whole thing been unseen before it would have called for a statement something as follows: "I will create a cloud and also a bow so that you may remember my covenant not to destroy the earth again by a flood." But if the cloud was created so as to bring the bow, then by not bringing the cloud at all, no need would have existed for a sign of assurance against a flood, for nothing would have been in their sight to even suggest the possibility of a flood. And if no cloud had existed as yet and God had kept the vegetation alive through some miraculous application of moisture, then what call was there for the changing of his plan?

Verses 18, 19. Mention is made here of the fact that Ham was the father of Canaan. This doubtless is given to the reader as a "tip" for the coming importance of this man

Verses 20-23. See notes at 2: 25, 3: 7; 3: 21. From those instances it can be known what had become the established principle of modesty as to the body of the male as well as the female. Thus it was considered improper to take advantage of one's shameful exposure of himself. The mere fact that Ham saw the condition of his father as one might have done unavoidably was not what condemned him. But the first definition of the word NAGAD which is the word for "told" is "a primitive root; properly to front, i. e., stand boldly out opposite"—Strong. And this definition would evidently be apt in this case since Ham could have taken the same precautions of modesty that his brothers did. But he did not and only went to them with the story after having left his father's shameful condition unchanged. This conduct, which was in defiance of the principle of modesty that God set forth in the case of Adam, doubtless was what brought upon him and his descendants the terrible curse which soon follows.

Verse 24. The fact that enough time has passed since coming out of the ark for grapes to grow and the juice be allowed to ferment is another example of the brevity of the Biblical accounts. And no blame seems to be attached to Noah for having become so drunken from it that he was in the sleep or stupor caused by the wine. No teaching had yet been given on the subject that we know of. Furthermore, since he was in his tent, the place of his own privacy, he could not be justly accused of complete indifference in the matter. At least, the most that can safely be said that the circumstances justify is that he was allowing himself to be more careless than he would have done, even though he is in a place where he had a right to be, and this was because of the wine. And all of this was no reason for Ham's conduct which not only showed disrespect for his father, but irreverence for the teaching of God in the example of the first man.

Verse 25. This is under the Patriarchal Dispensation in which the father of the family represented the authority of God. His predictions and instructions were therefore inspired. (See on this point 20: 7.) Therefore we are to take the statements he made here as inspired. Note also that nothing is said directly about Ham but instead it was about his descendants as represented coming through his most prominent son which was Canaan. *Brethren.* This is from ACH and defined "a primitive root; a brother (used in the widest sense of literal relationship and metaphorical affinity or resemblance)"—Strong. Thus we are to understand Noah to mean those nations of the world which, like Canaan, came from a common stock, Noah, who is now the sole remaining head of the races to follow. *Servant of servants.* A glance at next chapter will show us that the inferior nations sprang from Canaan including the people called Canaanites and Sodomites and also related to the Ethiopians and other African tribes. The prediction of Noah is that the descendants of Ham will be seen in the attitude of serfdom toward other races. Present day conditions support this conclusion as may be observed at every prominent instance of the subjugation and servile demeanor of the Negro.

Verses 26, 27. Shem became the ancestor of the Jewish people while Japheth came to represent the better grades of the nations generally referred to as Gentiles. And the prediction in verse 27 is significant. For fifteen hundred years the Gentiles were shut out from the society of the Jews in their religious relationship. But at last the barrier was taken down and both Jews and Gentiles (descendants of Japheth and Shem) came together. See Eph. 2: 13, 14; 3: 6.

Verse 28, 29. This is simply a brief summing up of the great life of a great man who outlived the first man by twenty years.

GENESIS 10

Verse 1. *Generations.* For the definition of this word see at 2: 4. The great point of interest in this whole chapter is that it gives prophetically as well as historically, the names of the principal nations that came from Noah. Some of the names came to have other forms than those given here which may be discovered by reading secular history. The reader is recommended to read a volume by George Rawlinson on this matter. The title of the volume is *Origin of Nations.* In this work the author traces, through dependable history, the origin of various nations and shows them to to have started from the very sources set forth in this chapter. It is a strong showing for the truth of the statements of Moses and is helpful for the instruction of the student of Holy Writ. It is not questioned by lovers of the Bible as to whether the narratives therein are true. Yet it is wholesome reading to find that whenever secular history deals with subject matter presented also in the Bible that it always corroborates that divine volume. The student is therefore advised to procure said treatise for this chapter.

Verse 2. The modern names that correspond to most of the names in this verse will here be subjoined to them. This information is based on the History of Rawlinson referred to in previous paragraph. *Gomer*—Celts. *Magog*—Slavs. *Javan*—Greek. *Madai*—Medes. *Tiras*—German.

Verses 3-5. *Gentiles* and *nations.* Both these words are from GOI and this word has been rendered in the A. V. as follows. Gentile, 30 times; heathen, 142; nation, 373; people, 11. From this it should be understood that the word Gentile does not always denote the opposite of Jew as is so generally thought. There were Gentiles before any Jew was known. But because of the wide latitude of meaning of the word, after there did come a people restricted to one common head and which came to be called Jews, then the term Gentiles was to be understood as being any of the peoples of the earth outside the Jews.

Verses 6, 7. The name *Cush* is from the same Hebrew word as Ethiopia. Therefore, the people referred to as the sons of Cush, and the Ethiopians, are the same. *Mizraim.* This means "upper and lower Egypt." Therefore the people of that area are meant when the name Mizraim is named. *Canaan.* From this man came the people forming one of the most noted heathen nations of the country west of the Jordan and generally referred to in terms of reproach.

Verses 8, 9. Although verse 7 above starts out with "And the sons of Cush," with a number of names following, yet that of Nimrod is not mentioned. Evidently it was reserved for special mention which we have in the present paragraph. This was because he became noted in history for two facts. He became a mighty hunter before the Lord, and the other is in the following verse.

Verse 10. *Babel.* This is from the same word as Babylon and is defined as follows: "Confusion; Babel (i. e., Babylon), including Babylonia and the Babylonian empire"—Strong. The fact that Nimrod was the founder of the famous community here named explains the prominence given him in this and preceding paragraph. *Shinar.* This is the name of a plain in the region of Babylonia.

Verse 11. *Asshur.* He was the founder of the Assyrian Empire with its capital at Nineveh. This power became an enemy of Babylon. But when it reached its height a mighty officer by name Nabopolassar (father of Nebuchadnezzar), revolted from his lord and founded the later Babylonian Empire. See Myers' *Ancient History,* pp. 66, 72.

Verses 12-14. The chief reason for calling attention to this passage is that Philistim is mentioned, and he was the founder of the Philistines.

Verses 15-20. Principal name mentioned in this paragraph is *Jebusite.* By reference to Josh. 15: 63 we learn this was a name for the inhabitants of Jerusalem.

Verses 21-31. *Eber.* According to Josephus, Ant. 1-6-4, this name came to be the origin of the word Hebrews which is one of the names applied to the people of the Jews.

Verse 32. By beginning and ending this chapter with a verse that cites the reader to the family history of Noah, the importance of that piece of history is emphasized. I have not said anything special about many of the names recorded in this chapter. This is not because I don't think they had any importance, for they did or else they would not have been given space in a book as concise as the Bible. But their importance to us is not always shown and hence nothing much can be said of them without speculation.

GENESIS 11

Verse 1. *Language.* This is from SAPHAH and defined "the lip (as a natural boundary); by implication, language"—Strong. *Speech.* This is from DABAR and defined as "a word; by implication a matter (as spoken of) or thing; adverbially, a cause"—Strong. Thus the two words used together as they are in this verse have almost the same meaning. Yet the fact of their both being used together calls our attention to a special idea in the definition of the latter one, that of "adverbially, a cause." This means that the one "lip" spoken of signified that not only did the people use the one language, but they were interested in one cause. That cause will appear in a statement and scheme soon to follow.

Verse 2. *From the east.* The marginal reading here gives us "eastward." Not much importance is attached to this distinction, yet the marginal theory has something worth considering. A look at the map would show the region of Ararat, the place where Noah disembarked, as being more westward than otherwise, of the plain of Shinar, the place where the events of the present actions took place. And the naming of Shinar as the place of present events connects it with the statements in 10: 9-11. It is noteworthy that Nimrod was the founder of Babel. This was stated in previous chapter as a related fact of Nimrod although the work was not done until the present chapter. And it is worthy of note that Nimrod, the mighty hunter, and founder of the great city and people of Babylon, was a part of the family "tree" of Ham.

Verse 3. *Burn them thoroughly.* The student of history and geography will learn that brick made and used in the south countries, such as Egypt and in the south parts of the U. S. were not always burned. Instead, they were made into the form of adobe. This was permissible because of the small amount of rainfall there. It would not necessarily be different in seasons in the place where people were now pausing. But the fact of their intending to build a tower of such great height would make it necessary to burn the brick in order to withstand the physical pressure exerted on them. *Slime.* This is from CHEMAR and defined as "bitumen"—Strong. It was of the nature of asphalt except of somewhat harder nature.

Verse 4. *Unto heaven.* These people did not know anything about "heaven" as the abode of God for that region is not visible to the natural eye and no one would ever think of trying to reach it by a material means. But the reader is asked to consult notes at 1: 6, 20 and see the meaning of this word as used regarding the material universe. The sky or atmosphere was the place these people had in mind. Their idea was to build a tower so high that, as a boy might exclaim regarding the height of his kite, reached up to the sky. Their motives for such a scheme are given in latter part of the verse. They wanted to make a name for themselves, and also wished to avoid being scattered over the earth. But in this last motive they thought to contravene the command of God as given in 1: 28 and repeated to Noah in 9: 1. For it would be impossible to fill the earth with their kind unless they spread out over the earth.

Verses 5, 6. *Lord came down.* God does not personally come away from the heaven of his dwelling place. But when it is said that he goes or comes to places on this earth, it means he is represented by an angel. See 18: 21 where it says of the Lord "I will go down now" in reference to the report of the wickedness of Sodom. This was done through the angels as will be seen in 19: 1. And thus in the case now considered, God proposes to visit the place of this rebellion through his divine representative. And all this is in keeping with the principle of God's dealings with man. He does not propose to know that man fears him until it is shown by his works. See 22: 12. On the same principle of justice, he will not accuse man of wrong doing until the case has been investigated and then decided upon testimony. *People is one.* Here is a divine tribute to the strength of unity. As long as people are united in their aims and works they are encouraged to succeed. This is indicated by the statement in the close of this paragraph. And it is no less true today that unity will accomplish what cannot be accomplished otherwise. For this consideration compare John 17: 21.

Verse 7. *Us.* For this see note at 1: 26. *Confound their language.* The first word in this citation is from a word that means "to mix." The result of mixing their language was to put an end to their scheme. It is another principle of fact and truth that is acknowledged all through the sacred teachings. If all of God's people speak the same thing they will be able to accomplish the work God requires. Hence the command that they be of the same mind and judgment. The reader is earnestly requested to consult the following. Rom. 12: 16; 1 Cor. 1: 10; Rom. 15: 6.

Verses 8, 9. This is one instance where confusion was a good thing. It is always right to confuse evil doers in their evil attempts. And here is the historic circumstance that gives us the name and significance of Babel or Babylon. And hence the reason for referring to the confused condition of the religious world as Babylon.

Verses 10-26. This large number of verses are thus grouped on the same principle as was done in chapter 5. The importance of the names mentioned is not ignored but as it is another place where the family history (designated by the word *generations*) is the burden of the passage, we will here be concerned chiefly in pointing out the place where each name is recorded that forms the family tree. This will now be done by naming the verse and the man in couplets. Shem and Arphaxed; 10. Salah; 12. Eber; 14. Peleg; 16. Reu; 18. Serug; 20. Nahor; 22. Tereh; 24. Abram; 26. Abram is mentioned first of the three sons of Terah because of his importance. He was not the oldest. In verse 26 Terah was 70 when he became a father. But he was 205 when he died according to verse 32 below. And that was the same time that Abram came into Canaan at which time he was 75 according to 12: 4. To sum up, if Abram was 75 when his father was 205, then Terah was 205 less 75, or 130 when Abram was born. Therefore Abram was not the oldest of Terah's sons.

Verses 27, 28. *Ur of the Chaldees.* The exact location of this place is somewhat uncertain. Stephen says (Acts 7: 2) that it was in Mesopotamia that Abram was dwelling when God appeared to him. This word means "between the rivers" and refers to the region between the two most important rivers there, the Euphrates and Tigris. But this was so extensive that a definite point as to geography would be hard to determine. But the Chaldees was a term that had reference often to a colorful race of people and whose influence was in evidence throughout the greater part of the land of "the East." Hence we should satisfy ourselves with the surety that Abram's native land was east of the great river Euphrates. Note in this paragraph that Haran, father of Lot, died in his native land. This will account for Abram's taking his nephew Lot with him when he left.

Verse 29. *Abram and Nahor.* The two remaining sons of Terah. Haran had died before this. Nahor's seed will figure in the history of the people later.

Verse 30. *Barren.* The leading word Strong uses to define this word is "sterile." This would mean that her inability to have children was solely from lack of fertility and not from any malformation of the reproductive organs. This is in accord with the fact which will be observed later, that after fertility had been provided by miracle, her body was prepared naturally to nourish the unborn child until the usual period for birth.

Verses 31, 32. *To go into the land of Canaan.* Thus the entrance into Canaan was not effected at this time. But on the way, at Haran, they halted evidently because of the age and infirmity of Terah. However, they had left the immediate location of their nativity as commanded by the Lord. But when Terah was dead they resumed the journey.

GENESIS 12

Verse 1. *Had said.* This form of speech shows that what is about to be reported did not take place in this chapter but previously. The student is referred to 11: 31 above and comments thereupon. The halting of Abram and his family at Haran was not on account of slackness in obeying the Lord's command. He has never been accused of any hesitancy in carrying out the commandments of God. Instead, he was always obedient. But the situation as described shows clearly that the pause at Haran was made necessary by the age and infirmity of Abram's father. But the language in chapter 11 does not go into the particulars of the command. This is evidently because the writer was reserving that detail until after the interval made necessary by Terah. But let it be noticed in the present paragraph that not only was Abram commanded to leave his native land, but was to leave his father's house. It might be said that the one fact would include the other. That is true. But God sometimes specifies certain facts that might have been known anyway, evidently to make the seriousness of the situation more impressive. For instance, his specific command in 22: 2 which will be given further notice in the proper place. Another thing that is significant in this place is that God did not tell Abram about the kind of place he was to reach nor where it was. He was to learn that after leaving.

Verse 2. *Great nation.* This is one of the important promises which God made to Abram. Of course it referred to the nation that came to be known as the Jews. Observe further that at the very time when the promise was made that he was to become the head of a great nation he was an old man and childless, also that his wife was barren. But this is a true illustration of faith.

Verse 3. In this verse are no less than three distinct promises. They will be pointed out in italic type with the fulfillment indicated. *Bless them that bless thee.* This was fulfilled in Rahab (Josh. 2 and 6) and the midwives (Ex. 1: 21). *Curse him that curseth thee.* Fulfilled in Pharaoh (Ex. 7 to 14), and Amalek (Ex. 17: 14; Est. 9: 24). *In thee shall all families of the earth be blessed.* This was fulfilled in Christ and the passages are too numerous to cite here. But one that is general is 1 Jn. 2: 2.

Verse 4. *As the Lord had said.* The outstanding point in all of Abram's service to God is that he did what he did because the Lord commanded it. This is the essence of faith and was always the motive in his activities. When a person hesitates at a command until he is able to see what he thinks is the propriety of the command, then even the carrying out of the command could not be justly called an act of faith. Take God at his word and do what is commanded, asking no questions as to the why. Of course the student should here take note of the age of Abram at this time, which is seventy-five.

Verse 5. *Souls that they had gotten in Haran.* This is the place where Abram paused in his journey toward his destination. The fact that enough time had passed in Haran for their family number to increase indicates some considerable stay there. But still we must not attribute it to slackness in obeying God's command. There is nothing in any part of the Bible that criticizes Abram for this. But instead, the language of Stephen in Acts 7: 4, "when his father was dead," is in the form of favorable explanation of the delay at that place. *To go into the land of Canaan.* Similar language to this is in 11: 31. But we have no evidence that Abram knew at this time that the name of the country to which he was journeying was Canaan. The only detail that is recorded on this point was that he was to go to a country "that I will show thee." But it is a common thing to find the inspired writers getting "ahead of the story" and telling the reader something which an inspired man could tell and yet which had not occurred at the time immediately being considered. For instance, the town of Dan is mentioned in 14: 14 and yet that was not its name until Judg. 18: 29. But the writer could see into the future. Another thing, frequently the name given to a place by a writer might be its name at the time of the writing while it did not bear that name at the time that is being written about.

Verse 6. *Sichem* and *Moreh.* These were places in the northernmost part of the country of Palestine and are mentioned here as merely a tracing of the journey of Abram on his way to the place intended by the Lord for him to reach. *Canaanite was then in the land.* The word "Canaan" is from KENAAN defined "humiliated; Kenaan, a son of Ham; also the country inhabited by him"—Strong. And the word "Canaanite" in italics here is from KENAANIY and defined "patrial from KENAAN; a Kenaanite or inhabitant of Kenaan; by implication a pedlar"—Strong. All this agrees with the prediction made by Noah in 9: 25. The various branches of these Canaanites or descendants of Ham through Canaan are named in 10: 15-20. These inferior peoples occupied the main part of that region where Abram made his entrance to the land of his commandment.

Verse 7. Here another promise is added to the ones already given to Abram. We may now group the three outstanding promises made to Abram and afterwards made to his son Isaac and his grandson Jacob. Those three promises are: 1. "I will make of thee a great nation" (12: 2); 2. "Unto thy seed will I give this land" (12: 7); and 3. "In thee shall all families of the earth be blessed" (12: 3). Mention is made also in this verse of an altar. This will be so often in evidence as the student pursues his study of the Bible that it is worth-while to be impressed with its importance. This is because the only form of religion now given from God to human beings is what is known as the Patriarchal. This term means a system based on the Patriarch which means the chief father. The term is not found in the Bible but the idea contained in it is seen clearly by the various references to the chief item of family worship which was the altar on which animals were offered in sacrifice. Useful information along the line of importance of the head of the family in this period may be obtained at 6: 8, 9; 18: 19; Job 1: 5.

Verses 8, 9. Here the town of Bethel is mentioned although it did not get its name as such until the events in 28: 19. But this method of naming places is explained above at verse 5. Note also here again mention of an altar. This was the only visible showing as the established presence of God in the worship of the family.

Verse 10. It is remarkable to observe that about the first thing Abram found when he arrived at the place to which he was directed was a famine. This was not reassuring to a man who had left his native land upon the commandment of God and with the understanding that his was to become a great nation. But such is the working of faith. It does not require faith to accept or perform a duty when the reason for it is apparent. Or where the results are sure of being favorable. But when the appearances seem to be adverse, then the servant of God is called upon to show whether he really has faith. So in the present case. There is no indication, now or at a later time, that Abram thought he was being forsaken by the Lord. Instead, when he was evidently directed to go on down into Egypt by the Lord he did not question as to why but went. It is well to observe here that during famine this country would be a logical place to go. There were no famines in that country except that brought on by miracle. It was not dependent on rainfall for moisture which would have been irregular. But the melting of the snows on the mountains at the head of the Nile River assured an overflow of water which supplied the country for the crops. And because of this unfailing support of crops the country is popularity referred to as "the granary of the world." The famine that came in the days of Joseph was a miraculous one. See Psa. 105: 16. Here it says, "He called for a famine upon the land." This shows this famine to have been brought on by the specific decree of God. And it also harmonizes with the fact that the famine was of an exact number of years and was preceded by a like exact number of years of plenty. And this famine in the days of Abraham does not contradict the statement in Gen. 8: 22. See comments at that place in this work. *Sojourn.* This is from GUWR and defined "a primitive root; properly to turn aside from the road (for a lodging or any other purpose), i. e., sojourn (as a guest)"—Strong. Since the word rendered "sojourn" here means a temporary stay in a place the passage shows that Abram was not preparing to change the plan of God here as to the country which was to become inheritance of his seed. Thus we have the wholesome thought that in spite of the unfavorable condition occasioned by a famine, Abram still persisted in his obedience to the divine commands.

Verse 11. *Fair.* This is from YAPHEH and defined "beautiful (literally or figuratively)"—Strong. *Look.* This is from MAREH and defined as follows: "A view (the act of seeing); also an appearance (the thing seen), whether (real) a *shape* (especially if handsome, comeliness; often plural, the looks), or (mental) a vision"—Strong. This definition is filled with significant information. The Hebrew word under consideration has been translated by "look" in the A. V. six times and five of them are concerning a woman. And in each case the context shows that the form or personal appearance of the woman is in mind. Note the word *shape* as part of the definition. So that the passage means that Abram meant his wife had a beautiful form. A familiar expression would truly be suited to the case, that of sex appeal. And notice, too, that the definition has the idea of "mental vision." This agrees with the thoughts set forth in this work at chapter 3: 16, which see. All in all, the general appearance of Sarai was one that was appealing to the opposite sex. And this would lead to the "mental vision" mentioned in the definition here, and which agrees with the idea of the imagination and its part in causing the male sex to seek intimacy with the female.

Verses 12, 13. In this passage are seen three of the commandments that later were given to God's people. They are those against coveting a neighbor's wife, adultery, and murder. Abram feared the Egyptians would commit two of them in order to avoid the third. That is, they would covet his wife and also murder him so as to have Sarai without comitting adultery. He preferred having them commit a different two of the evils, coveting and adultery so as to preserve his own life. It is difficult to explain all of this. Yet we may remember that Abram is still new in the service of the God of heaven, having been surrounded with idolatry in his former years of life. Also, while the Egyptians would be doing wrong in taking another man's wife, yet they would be in ignorance of the fact and he could have concluded that their sin would not be as great from the fact of their ignorance. Again, if they killed him they could not bring him back even after discovering their mistake. While they could correct the mistake of having taken another man's wife, which thing they actually did. So the whole transaction may be summed up by saying that Abraham acted on the principle "of two evils choose the less." This would not entirely justify him, perhaps, but would somewhat lessen the guilt.

Verse 14. The Egyptians did the very thing Abram predicted they would. For it is the inspired writer of the book who is telling us that they beheld the woman that she was very fair. The same word for "fair" as in verse 11. So that Abram's estimate of his wife's beautiful form was not solely because of his relation to her, but the form and appeal of the woman was so pronounced as to be an evident fact and calculated to arouse the imagination and sensuousness of those who saw her.

Verse 15. *Princes.* This is from SAR and defined "a head person (of any rank or class)"—Strong. *Commended.* This is from HALAK and part of Strong's definition of the word is "to boast; and thus to be (clamorously) foolish; to rave." These princes were important persons in the service of the king and doubtless were supposed to be interested in the things that would make for his pleasure. Hence when they saw a woman whom they considered to be adapted to his bodily pleasure they communicated the fact to him. And the definition of the word "commended" indicates that they were very much impressed themselves by the appearance of Sarai. As a result of their recommendation she was taken into Pharaoh's house. The word *house* is from a word that has a wide variety of meanings. But Strong says its special meaning is "family." Thus we would get the idea that Sarai was taken into Pharaoh's family and he was planning to make her a permanent member. That kings at that time made free to have a plurality of wives need not surprise us. Even God's people at that early date and for some time after, had such. Not that God was pleased with it nor that he "permitted" it as is sometimes said. God never permitted anything that he disapproved. To permit is the same as to sanction. But God has suffered many things in the immature age of the world that he refused to tolerate after the world had stood long enough to be able for stronger teaching. Please see Acts 17: 30. And in this case now before us we see that God did not chastise the king for having more than one wife. But, for taking a woman who was the wife of another man, as will be seen in a paragraph below.

Verse 16. Since up to this time Pharaoh is unaware that Sarai is Abram's wife, and being clear in mind as to the lawfulness of his act, we cannot interpret his conduct here toward Abram as an attempt at pacifying him. Rather, it is his way of showing his appreciation for the new addition to his harem by bestowing these attentions on her brother. With this in mind we see that the second "he" in the verse is Abram.

Verse 17. The plagues referred to here were some kind of physical affliction. And in thus punishing Pharaoh and his house (or family. See at v. 15) God fulfilled one of the promises he had made to Abram recorded in verse 3, that "I will curse him that curseth thee." To curse means either to wish or to bestow an affliction.

Verses 18-20. *I might have taken her to me to wife.* This language indicates that while the woman had been taken into Pharaoh's family with the purpose of making her a part of his collection of wives, yet he had not yet begun such relationship. Of course we may conclude that God prevented him from doing so. This would not be farfetched since we have it in the text that he did that very thing under like circumstances. For this information see 20: 6. And thus the plagues brought upon Pharaoh and his house opened his eyes to the truth of the situation. Upon this he complained to Abraham and sent him away from his midst. He also had charged his men concerning the woman. One thing that claims our admiration of Pharaoh. He regarded the sanctity of marriage more highly than is often shown by people professing great claims to morality now.

GENESIS 13

Verses 1, 2. The riches here mentioned as being the possession of Abram are to be explained by the 16th verse of previous chapter. Not that he was poverty stricken at the time he went down to Egypt, for verse 5 of preceding chapter speaks of "all their substance" which they took with them from Haran. But that which was added to Abram's possessions by Pharaoh contributed to make him a rich man.

Verse 3. Here we again see Bethel mentioned by name although it did not get such name until chapter 28. Hai here is the same as Ai in other places.

Verse 4. Mention again made of the altar which he had built on his way down past this place. The significant thing here is that when he came to the altar he "called on the name of the Lord." This would not merely mean that he prayed to the Lord here for that act of worship was lawful at any place. But use of the statement in direct connection with the altar signifies that calling on the name of the Lord does now and ever afterward also require some specific act of visible worship. As an example of this in the New Testament see Acts 22: 16. During the Patriarchal Dispensation the only material symbol of a meeting place with God was the altar on which sacrifices were made. Later, under the Mosaic religion the tabernacle and temple were the places where the Jews could meet with God formally.

Verses 5, 6. Nothing is said about gifts being bestowed on Lot at the time Pharaoh was entreating Abram. But in verse 5 of 12th chapter, after mentioning Lot whom Abram took to go into the land of Canaan it mentions "their" substance. This indicates that Lot was in possession of such things before entering Egypt. And they increased naturally while in Egypt under the favorable circumstances of Abram. *Bear.* This is from a word that has a literal and figurative meaning. The context here would give it the figurative meaning. That is, the land was not able to support all their animals with food and shelter. For this reason their respective interests began to crowd in upon each other. Since a man possessing as many beasts as Abraham or Lot would not be in direct charge of their care, they naturally had herdmen for that purpose and that brought up the situation that is described in next verse.

Verse 7. *Herdmen.* This word might seem to be confined to one who tends sheep. While that would be its first meaning, yet it also is used in the general sense of one who grazes. This is evidently the range of its meaning here for the word *cattle* in this verse is from MIQNEH and defined "live stock"—Strong. Of course the *strife* between the two groups of herdmen was at first a more formal one. The word is from RIB and defined "a contest (personal or legal)"—Strong. *Canaanite* and *Perizzite.* See comments at 12: 6.

Verse 8. The contest mentioned in previous verse caused Abram to fear that it might grow into a more personal affair as will be seen in the word he used. The word *strife* in this verse is from MERIYBAH and defined "quarrel"—Strong. The highest motive that could be assigned, of a human nature, would be the fact that they were brethren. That is, they were near of kin, which is the general meaning of the original word. In the previous verse the Canaanitish people are mentioned as being in that land then. It might be expected that such people would manifest no great degree of fine temperament, but people in the rank of Abram, the man with the great promises of God on his head, and his near of kin, should certainly be above the petty conduct of quarreling over the material subject of grazing land. This same kind of motive is presented in the New Testament. See 1 Tim. 6: 2.

Verse 9. The reader is especially requested to note that Abram was unselfish enough to let Lot have the choice of pasture land. And he did not say that if he chose the part that would be right to dwell in then he would leave the community and seek pasture in another locality. But he distinguished the "whole land" by just one division, namely, the left or the right. And Abram agreed to take whatever was left. So that, if any criticism could be based on occupying any part of this "whole land" then Abram was as much at fault for agreeing to take it as he would be to actually occupy it. This point will be considered again below.

Verse 10. *Well watered everywhere.* These words clearly state the motive Lot had in the choice he here made of the land. Since the occasion of the controversy was the need for pasturage for cattle this motive was not only a logical one, but a righteous one. Mention of the "garden of the Lord" evidently refers to the garden named in 2: 8 which garden is described as being well watered also since it had the river with its four "heads." Also the reference to Egypt is for the same purpose since that country was perpetually blessed with moisture. *Before the Lord destroyed Sodom and Gomorrah.* At the time this narrative was being written the destruction of the mentioned cities was history. But at the time *of which* the account took place they had not yet been burned. And mention here of the insignificant city of Zoar is due to the fact that the Lord did not destroy that place when the city of Sodom was burned. See 19: 22.

Verse 11. Since the statement was made in verse 6 that the land would not bear for Abram and Lot to dwell together, and since they had come to a conclusion by Lot's having chosen the watered land, it was logical that they "separated themselves the one from the other." Also, this would mean that he would travel in an eastwardly direction. All this was understood and included in the offer that Abram made in verse 9.

Verse 12. This verse has been erroneously interpreted by many to the criticism of Lot. It is a popular phrase to see "tenting toward Sodom" when some one wishes to speak about the evil tendencies of another. Especially if he is considering one's interest in financial or other temporal gain. If the person under consideration has not exactly entered into the practice of that which is wrongfully carnal, yet if it is thought that he is "headed that way" it will be said that he is "tenting toward Sodom." This casts a reflection on Lot that is unjust because untrue. If it be said that Lot was "tenting toward Sodom" right at the time that he made his choice before Abram, then what must we conclude about the latter when we recall that he agreed to take this very side had Lot chosen the other. And here is where the reader is referred to verse 9 and the comments thereon. Critics of Lot in this affair seem not to have realized that all of their remarks apply with equal force against Abram. Yet not one has ever dared to accuse him in connection with it. In the forepart of the verse now considered the statement is made that Abram dwelled in the land of Canaan while Lot in the cities of the plain. If we were to stop here we might imagine some criticism of Abram since the name Canaan did not have a very dignified reputation, while, at the time of this movement of the men we have no account of the condition of those cities. But more than once we have observed that inspired writers will go some years ahead of the events of which they are directly writing and mention a condition then future but known to the inspired writer. And in the present case, the inspired writer foresaw an outcome of Lot's movements that he could not have seen at the time he made this choice being here considered. A proper rendering of the significant words employed will dispel the false accusation made against Lot. *Pitched * * * toward.* These are the words that are misunderstood. They are taken to mean that Lot here and now faced his tent in the direction of Sodom. The implication is that he had a "leaning" toward that wicked city is the reason he thus faced his tent. This is contrary to all the facts in the case and also against the common sense view of it. We have just been told (verse 10) that Lot made his choice in view of the favorable condition for pasturage. Now why inject the idea that he was interested in Sodom? What would the condition of Sodom, even granting that it was at this time as wicked as we know it to have become, have had to do with his interest in his livestock? Besides, when we come to the time of his residence in that city he was considered so righteous a man that God took care to provide for his safety before he destroyed the city. And the New Testament also tells us that he was a righteous man and was grieved over the wickedness of the city. See 2 Pe. 2: 7, 8. But now the correct rendering of these words will be given which will make the whole passage clear. The first one of the words in italic type is from AHAL and is explained by both Young and Strong to mean to remove one's tent. It is from the same word as "removed" in verse 18 below. The second word is from AD and both above mentioned authorities define it as meaning "up to, as far as." Now with the proper rendering of the passage it would read "and removed his tent as far as Sodom." This form of expression shows the writer has gone "ahead of his story" to tell the reader what finally came to pass. But he does not tell us how long it was until Lot got as far as Sodom. Neither are we told what circumstances finally induced him to enter the city. But the statements as to his righteousness at the very last, cited above, disproves the charge that he was prompted by the wrong motives.

Verse 13. This verse is a simple statement of the condition of Sodom at the time of Lot's residence there when the events took place that are about to be recorded. But bear no connection with the fact of Lot's having become a resident of the city as was shown in preceding paragraph.

Verses 14-17. Attention has been called to the fact that the promises so often referred to throughout the Bible generally mean those first made to Abram and then to his next two lineal generations. Here we see God repeating two of the promises, the ones first recorded in 12: 2, 7. Since Abram and his immediate descendants were the ones to whom the promises were specially applicable it was appropriate that God would make this repetition of the promises now after his separation from his nephew. He had just performed the noble part of an unselfish man and thus acted in keeping with the characteristics ever afterward attributed to him. It is thus very well that he be given another assurance that God was to be with him. *For ever.* This expression here made in connection with the promise of holding the land has been the cause of confusion. It is often asked, "Does forever really mean forever?" Of course we would answer yes. But that would not be any approach to the explanation sought. And then in such a case as here it is natural to inquire whether God intended the descendants of Abram to be in the possession of Canaan unendingly or even "into eternity." The word ever is from the Hebrew word OLAM and defined "concealed, i. e., the vanishing point; generally, time out of mind," etc.—Strong. The real meaning of the expression as it was to be understood by Abram was that his seed was to possess that land for a longer time than he would be able to see. That no certain date, as to year or epoch, was to be named to him as the time when they would cease to possess it. With our later knowledge of language we see the idea of "age lasting" or "to the end of the age" as being a practical definition of the term "for ever." The proper meaning of it is "age lasting." This means further that when the term is used with reference to the continuation of a thing it intends to convey the thought that it will last through to the end of the particular age to which it pertains. In other words, it does not mean that the thing or condition spoken of is to be endless unless it is pertaining to an age that is endless. And since the age that is to come after the judgment day, popularly called the age of "eternity," is admitted to be endless by all parties, it follows that if an inspired writer mentions a condition or experience that pertains to the age after the judgment day, then that condition or experience will be endless.

Verse 18. *Removed.* This is from the same word as "pitched" in verse 12. See the comments at that place. *Hebron.* This place is about 25 miles south of Jerusalem and was the dwelling place of Abram for many years. It is significant that he here built an altar unto the Lord. A righteous man like him would not be content to reside in any place without having the Lord represented by the only formal method so far given to him. It should be remembered that Abram is a worshiper of God under the Patriarchal Dispensation and in that system the family altar was the legal representation.

GENESIS 14

Verse 1. The four kings mentioned in this verse were confederates in the present conflict and each had his own jurisdiction. Shinar is the place which afterward was known as the location of the famous Babylonian Empire. Elam is the same as Persia. While Tidal is here mentioned as king of *nations.* This is from the word GOI and means the people generally not under the direct jurisdiction of the other three mentioned.

Verse 2. To avoid any confusion as to the existence of these cities let it be observed that the miraculous destruction of these cities had not yet taken place.

Verse 3. The writer says that the place of junction of the nine kings was the vale of Siddim. But what might be a poser is that he immediately says that this vale is the salt sea. Now we cannot understand why or how a military group of land forces could have a battle at a place that is called a sea. But again we have an instance where the writer identifies the location of an action of time past by calling it by the name it has at the time of his writing. At the time of this battle the vicinity was a vale but afterwards became a place covered with water known here as the salt sea. The same place is known in secular history and geography as the Lake Asphaltites. This is because that substance was a prevailing one in that body of water. And this fact is partially explained from natural grounds since at the time of the battle we are now considering it was full of slime pits (verse 10). The word for "slime" is one which means asphaltites and this substance existed in other localities also. See comments at 11: 3. Thus the apparent difficulty as to facts in this verse is made clear by remembering that at the time the writer is recording the fact the place of the battle had become a lake with asphaltites appearing through it. While at the time of the battle the water had not come yet the source of supply for this slime or asphaltites, the slimepits of verse 10, was there and was the cause of the stranding of the defeated kings by running into it and sinking therein. It is interesting and significant to know that the body of water that has been so noted for years is the site of this first recorded battle. And that the various names, Salt Sea, Dead Sea, Lake Asphaltites, are appropriate since the original condition of that region was one where this substance was already predominant. And the fact that one does not see the definite sites of the cities named in this chapter on the maps is explained by the circumstance that said cities were destroyed by the great burning recorded in Ch. 19. And while the dropping of the fire to destroy these cities was miraculous, yet the condition that remained after the fire should not be questioned even from a logical standpoint. It is well known that such substance as asphalt is inflammable and would continue to burn for a long time. This has been illustrated by a similar occurrence in certain places in our own southland. The soil is so nearly all composed of combustible matter that when a pond of water is desired in some particular spot the fire is started and kept within the desired limits. It will burn until it consumes this material down to the water which is always within a few feet of the surface. After this the water rises to the level of the open space and thus a pool of water is produced. I do not mean that asphalt is the material that is burned in the last named circumstance. The comparison is made only to the fact of there being combustible material over which is the substance afterward appearing in the pool produced. And since so much is made of this famous place it will be well to quote a description of it as given by the Jewish historian. "The nature of Lake Asphaltites is also worth describing. It is, as I have said already, bitter and unfruitful. It is so light or thick that it bears up the heaviest things that are thrown into it; nor is it easy for any one to make things sink therein to the bottom, if he had a mind so to do. Accordingly, when Vespasian went to see it, he commanded that some who could not swim, should have their hands tied behind them, and be thrown into the deep, when it so happened that they all swam as if a wind had forced them upward. Moreover, the change of the color of this lake is wonderful, for it changes its appearance twice every day; and as the rays of the sun fall differently upon it, the light is variously reflected. However, it casts up black clods of bitumen in many parts of it; these swim at the top of it and resemble both in shape and bigness headless bulls; and when the laborers that belong to the lake come to it, and catch hold of it as it hangs together, they draw it into their ships; but when the ship is full, it is not easy to cut off the rest, for it is so tenacious as to make the ship hang upon its clods till they let it loose with the menstrual blood of women, and with urine, to which alone it yields." —Josephus, Wars, 4-8-4.

Verse 4. Mention of Chedorlaomer as being the one they served indicates that he was the leader of the confederacy against the five kings of Palestine. They had come under the dominance of the Elamite king and continued in that servitude for twelve years. But in the next year they fomented a rebellion which induced their overruler to prepare an invasion which took place the fourteenth year, as seen in next paragraph.

Verses 5-9. Mention is made in this paragraph of some not named in beginning of the chapter. But we are to understand them to be inferior allies of the five already named. Then in verse 8 the leading five kings, the ones that had previously been tributaries of Chedorlaomer and his allies, went out in their defence against the invaders. But they were repulsed and fled as following verses will show.

Verse 10. This is treated at length with verse 3, which see.

Verses 11, 12. Mention of Lot's capture here reminds us of the information about him in previous chapter. Some time between events of that chapter and the present one Lot had reached the city of Sodom. Just when we do not know.

Verse 13. We have already seen that Abram had taken up his abode at Hebron which is not far from the site of this battle. Certain friends of his who escaped from the battle and knowing the interest Abram had in Lot, went and told him of what had happened. He is here called a *Hebrew.* The word for this in the Hebrew language is IBRIY and is defined thus: "An Eberite (i. e., Hebrew) or descendant of Eber"—Strong. But since this name becomes so important afterwards in connection with God's great people, it will be well to quote here the information given in the Greek lexicon which is as follows: "A Hebrew, a name first given to Abraham, Gen. 14: 13, afterwards transferred to his posterity descended from Isaac and Jacob; by it in the O. T. the Israelites are both distinguished from and designated by foreigners, as afterward by * * * The name is now generally derived from * * * i. e., of the region beyond the Euphrates, whence * * * equivalent to one who comes from the region beyond the Euphrates, Gen. 14: 13"—Thayer.

Verse 14. *Armed.* This is from RUWQ and defined "to pour out (literally or figuratively), i. e., empty"—Strong. This definition justifies the marginal reading we have here which says "led forth" which is better. The word "servvants" is not in the original as the form of type indicates, but the next word is. *Trained.* This is from CHANIYK and defined "initiated; i. e., practiced"—Strong. This gives us a more general view of the word. It indicates that Abram had a group of men so instructed and under discipline that he could use them for any necessary work, including military. And they were not slaves or servants, that he had bought with his money, but persons who had been "born in his own house." And since his present movement was to recapture persons and things that were related to him it can be truly said the action was one of defense and thus fully justified. *Dan.* Here is another instance where the name of a place as given was that given to it long after the events immediately under consideration. This place was renamed in Judges 18: 29.

Verses 15, 16. *Divided himself.* This means that he distributed his forces so as to be in position to attack his enemy with system and thus showed good generalship. It also teaches us the lesson that even when a man is depending on the favor of God, as Abram evidently did, yet it is expected that he will use his own ability. And that God did lend his aid to this battle is declared by the priest-king personage of whom we are to learn soon. The success of this battle is shown by the fact that he recovered all the goods and also the people. Also that he slew his enemies, which is stated in a general way. Specifications on that item will be given in next verse.

Verse 17. Here it is specified that Chedorlaomer and the kings with him were slain. Also we here learn that the king of Sodom had escaped from the slimepit into which he had fallen in the beginning, and went out to meet Abram on his victorious return. That this meeting of the king of Sodom with Abram was out of gratitude for the service rendered him is evident from a verse later on in this chapter.

Verse 18. *Melchizedek.* This is from MALKIYTSEDEQ and the simple definition that Strong gives of it is "king of right; an early king in Palestine." It might be wondered why the lexicographer gave us so little information concerning this noted person. The most apt answer is that very little was known about him by anybody. And this was not an accident. God knew how to prepare his types for the support of his final arrangements of man's salvation. A priest would some day be presented to the people of God who was to be so different from the kind that will have been in use for many centuries that various items of identification would be needed. There was to be a priest finally who would stand alone in his priesthood. Unlike the priests with whom the people had been acquainted for so long, this last priest was to have his priesthood in his own right independent of all predecessors, and who would not relinquish his office in favor of any other. Thus, all accounts of the previous or subsequent family history of this king were purposely kept out of the records. This will present him to the world as a priest without ancestors or descendants in office as far as the public could see. And so this *apparent* condition of having no descendants would be a type of a man who actually had no descendants. Outside of these considerations, Melchizedek was a normal man, "an early king in Palestine." More information will be found on this subject at Heb. 7 in the New Testament part of this Commentary. But for the present instance, we shall further note that he was a priest with certain functions that are not described, only that bread and wine were brought forth by him. This was not for any fleshly use since in the sequel of this meeting the temporal materials passed the other direction between them. And while the presence and use of an altar which was so evident under the Patriarchal Dispensation would imply that the father was a priest, yet in this case the writer expressly states that he was the priest of the most high God. This is indicative of the special importance this man was to have in God's plan of types. It is also stated that he was a king. This was never true of the priests under the system of religion issuing forth from Sinai. Salem mentioned here was an abbreviated form of Jerusalem and the definition of the word by Strong is "peaceful."

Verse 19. *Blessed him.* According to Heb. 7: 7, Melchizedek was a greater person than Abram. And since the blessing here mentioned could not have been the bestowal of temporal benefits, as seen in preceding paragraph, we must conclude that the blessing here was a spiritual kind. This would be in keeping with the various instances in the Old Testament where God empowered men to bestow miraculous and spiritual benefits on certain deserved ones. This is further proved from the fact that in the verse to come he used the same word for "bless" that he used here and we know he did not bestow any personal benefits on God. So the whole matter rests on the idea of some benediction.

Verse 20. Here is where Melchizedek attributed Abram's victory in his battle to the most high God. Here also we learn that Abram gave to Melchizedek tithes of all. This means that Abram had recovered the goods taken from his people by Chedorlaomer and of these he gave to this priest a tenth. These things could have been of no use to any kind of a person other than a human. One who could consume temporal articles the same as other human beings. But the significant fact here is that Abraham was the giver of these goods while Melchizedek was the recipient. And since the latter was not in a needy condition as is evident, the giving of the goods can be understood only on the basis that Abram recognized a superiority of some kind in Melchizedek. But this very fact of his recognition, even whether he understood what it would mean, came to be one of the vital arguments of Paul in his labors with the Hebrew brethren who were being disturbed by those who would lead them back under the worship of the Aaronic order.

Verse 21. The offer here made by the king of Sodom shows his gratitude for the deliverance which Abram had brought to him. And since this virtue is one of the leading ones required of God it is praiseworthy to see it manifested in this heathen king.

Verses 22-24. *Made Abram rich.* Since Abram has already been said to be very rich it would be unreasonable to suppose the things which he recovered and brought back with him could have exceeded his present possessions. The expression should be understood as meaning that he did not want to be under obligation at all to this heathen king. *Thread, shoelatchet.* The first word refers to the thong or shoe lace and the second means a shoe's tongue. These things of such nominal value are used by Abram to indicate how averse he was to being put under any obligation of financial gratitude. The exception he made for the young men was in justice to them and not in any way to affect his purpose of personal independence. In other words the slogan "to the victor belongs the spoils" was justification for the young men to take their share since they had been faithful in the discharge of duty for their master.

GENESIS 15

Verse 1. It is a frequent thing for God to reaffirm his blessing intended toward Abram. The original promises are often repeated and now in a general way he is given assurance of God's protection.

Verses 2, 3. The renewed assurance of favor just spoken to Abram encouraged him to complain of what he feared was an infringement upon his personal rights. This Eliezer was not his own body offspring but he was born in his household and evidently of some persons near enough to arouse the questioning stated.

Verses 4, 5. Here the Lord wishes to quiet the fears of Abram by repeating the promise first made to him when he was called out from his native home. *Tell, number.* Each of these words is from CAPHAR and defined thus: "A primitive root; properly to score with a mark as a tally or record, i. e., (by implication) to inscribe, and also to enumerate"—Strong. Thus, while the exact number of Abram's descendants would be a fact and known to God, yet they would be so numerous that Abram would not be able to make a specific account or record of them.

Verse 6. The doctrine of "faith alone" is not supported by this verse. Abram has never yet even hesitated about doing what God had told him to do. And since the divine mind could see the sincerity of Abram's mind he could attribute the quality of righteousness to him upon his going as far as he was required to do. It should be borne in mind that as yet no specific date for the accomplishment of the birth promised has been set. Hence no overt act upon the part of Abram and his wife has been required. The time will come when that will be required. When that time comes, then the faith of Abram and his wife will need to be proved by their willingness to cooperate with God to the extent of performing with each the natural act usually needed for reproduction. For this subject compare 18: 9-15; Rom. 4: 18-22 and Heb. 11: 11.

Verse 7. While the Lord here tells Abram what land was intended to be his when he was called out from his home land, yet at that time the patriarch was informed only that he was to journey to a land that was to be shown him afterward. That constituted one important feature of his manifestation of faith.

Verse 8. The principle on which God has always dealth with his created beings is to furnish him evidence. And since Abram has already demonstrated in more than one instance that he has faith in God, the present request is not to be interpreted as any weakening of his faith. Rather, it is an indication of his growing interest in the plans of the Lord.

Verse 9. While nothing is here recorded as to the significance of these creatures nominated by the Lord for the present demonstration, it is interesting to note it. The same were afterward a prominent and frequently required offering of the system of religion in practice under the Mosaic Dispensation. Especially would the reader be asked to observe the degree of worth of these creatures. There are three of them, beginning with the greatest, the large animal, and concluding with the smallest creature, the birds. When these finally become an established part of the altar service of the nation in Palestine, they will be designated for use according to the financial ability of the contributor.

Verse 10. It should be remembered that Abram asked for a sign touching the great promise God had made. Just why these symbols were selected is not stated. But we do know that when the Mosaic system of animal sacrifices was put into effect, much of the same procedure was followed as here regarding the preparation of the creatures. For this information the reader is referred to Lev. 1: 6, 8, 12 and other passages near these. Later in the chapter now being studied the opening provided by the dividing of the parts of the animals afforded a place for the miraculous demonstration of the presence of the Lord to pass. See verse 17.

Verse 11. That it was necessary to guard these animals from the birds shows that use of them was not immediate. But Abram showed no sign of impatience for this but is calmly obedient to the Lord's directions. Furthermore, the protection thus given to these animals against the birds that would have preyed on them is an indication that Abram did not consider it proper that articles being devoted to special use of the Lord should be allowed to become the food of common use.

Verse 12. Simultaneous with the going down of the sun Abram fell into a trance, which is Strong's definition of the words for "deep sleep." At the same time a horror, defined by Strong as a "fright" in the form of darkness enveloped him. With this condition surrounding him, Abram is about to have communicated to him a detailed group of predictions concerning his posterity. These predictions will follow. And with them will be cited their fulfillment as recorded in later portions of the Bible.

Verses 13-15. *Stranger.* This is from GEYR and defined by Strong as "foreigner." This was fulfilled by the fact that the Israelites belonged in Palestine and thus were foreigners in Egypt. *Shall serve them.* This was fulfilled by their service to the Egyptians. See Ex. 1: 13. *Four hundred years.* This was fulfilled by the length of time the Israelites were in Egypt. A contrary theory is sometimes heard concerning the length of this sojourn, claiming the actual sojourn in Egypt to have been only 215 years. In order not to seem to contradict the mathematical statements of the scripture, that the sojourn was 430 years, it is offered for support of the shorter term the idea that the sojourn was to start with Abram's time. But the specific language of holy writ forbids such suggestion. If that had been the meaning God had in mind he would have included Abram in the statement. This he did when speaking of another prediction. For instance, when speaking of the possession of the land of Canaan he said, "To thee will I give it, and to thy seed for ever" (13: 15). This was true for Abram actually lived in the land. But the prediction now being considered does not include Abram in person. Instead it says "thy seed shall be," etc. Again in Ex. 12: 40 this 430 years of sojourn was made of the "children of Israel." But the name Israel was not known in Abram's day and not until the day of Jacob and that was about the time of their entering therein, or at least in the same generation. It will not be amiss here to quote a statement from an eminent historian from the secular field. Since this subject is of the nature of historical background the testimony of a man who has made such subject a special study would be valuable. I shall here quote. "According to the Hebrew text of Ex. 12: 40, 41, a space of nearly four centuries and a half intervened between the entrance of the children of Israel into Egypt and their exodus under the leadership of Moses; and, although the real duration of the period is disputed, the balance of probability is in favor of this long term rather than of a shorter one. The growth of a tribe, numbering even three thousand persons, into a nation of above two millions, abnormal and remarkable if it took place within a period of four hundred and thirty years, would be still more strange and astonishing if the space of time were seriously curtailed. The ten generations between Jacob and Joshua (1 Chron. 7: 22-27), who was a grown man at the time of the Exodus, require a term of four centuries rather than one or two. Egyptian chronology also favors the longer period"—Rawlinson, Moses, His Life and Times, page 6. But aside from all these reasonings, it is too much like presumption to even call in question the exact and positive declaration of the inspired writer. No matter how impossible the statement might seem to our view, the declaration as to the length of the sojourn should be taken just as it is stated. *Will I judge.* The fulfillment of this prediction is seen in the book of Exodus, chapters 7 to 14. Here see the many plagues sent upon the Egyptians, ending with the complete destruction of their king and his chosen military forces. The various plagues imposed upon them included judgments upon their gods. It was their national practice to worship all creatures that had life as well as inanimate things such as the great river Nile. And so in the plagues that came upon the nation in regard to these objects they were humiliated to a great degree. *Great substance.* The fulfillment of this prediction is seen in the matter of getting the valuables in the form of gold and silver and costly raiment. See Ex. 11: 2; 12: 35. Critics have complained about this transaction as being an act of fraud on the part of the Israelites. That since they had no intention of repaying the articles it was dishonest for them to borrow them. But the word "borrow" is properly rendered "to demand" according to Strong and it is so rendered in four places in the Old Testament in other places. The Israelites had been serving the Egyptians for many years without sufficient pay. Now it was no more than right that they demand these things as payment. And since they demanded them the Egyptians had no reason to expect the return of the articles. And thus no injustice has been done. *In peace . . . good old age.* This means he would live to a ripe age and die without violent cause. His death is recorded in chapter 25: 7, 8. The account shows him to have ended his days as predicted.

Verse 16. *Fourth generation.* The reader is asked to consult Ex. 6: 16-20. In that place the line from Levi to Aaron is shown. Levi, Kohath, Amram, Aaron. As is well known, the entrance into Egypt was in the days of

Levi and their coming out was in the days of Aaron, which is the "fourth generation." Moreover, the ages of the first three are stated which add up to 407 years. Add to this the age of Aaron at the time of the Exodus (83, Ex. 7: 7), and we have 490. But this is 60 years more than the 430 which was the length of time the Israelites were to be in Egypt. The reader is to note that in the passage cited about the ages of the first three, it is their entire life that is given without any reference to their age at the time of birth of their first born. Hence the 60 years of the seeming discrepancy will be easily accounted for by spreading them out among the periods elapsing between the births of the fathers to that of their sons. And it is interesting also to note that this circumstance confirms the conclusion treated in preceding paragraph that the sojourn in Egypt was 430, as also is affirmed in the New Testament (Acts 7: 6). *Iniquity of the Amorites is not yet full.* Much light is thrown on the last word by the definition of Young: "The iniquity of the tribe (as the representative of the Canaanites generally) was not yet full (Gen. 15: 16, 21)." There was a particular tribe of people called Amorites. But they were so generally evil that their name was sometimes used to refer to the heathen in general.

Verse 17. The words "went down" here and "going down" in verse 12 are from the same original. But the progress of the events here being reported indicated that at this verse the darkness had deepened. The furnace mentioned here was a portable thing since it is defined as "a fire pot." Thus far no special use had been made of the creatures which God commanded Abram to bring. But the presence of these articles at the latter part of this trance indicated God's acceptance of Abram and his offering. These would indicate the necessary provision for consuming of the sacrifices.

Verse 18. This verse states the ultimate boundaries of the promised land. This will be helpful information in considering other places. For instance, when later the two and half tribes wished to settle on the east side of Jordan it is sometimes asked why God would bless them. They should have been appreciative of God's providence over them and been glad to settle in the land promised. But this passage now under consideration shows that we must make a distinction between the terms "Canaan" and "the promised land." It is true that Canaan was the headquarters of the promised land and the conquest of the territory could not be accomplished until this head land was taken. That is why the army was required to pass over Jordan and fight those then occupying the land. They were intruders since this land had long since been given to the descendants of Abram. But the extent of the promised land is here stated as reaching from the river of Egypt to Euphrates. This "river of Egypt" was a small stream flowing into the Sea in a northwesterly direction, and was the southern boundary of the promised land. The only man ever to possess all this territory was Solomon (1 Ki. 4: 21). But it was because of the disobedience of the people, since all promises of God are based on conditions.

Verses 19, 20. These are heathen peoples then occupying this territory that God had given to Abram's seed. Thus the invasion of God's armies into their midst was a defensive warfare. It was for the purpose of overthrowing the enemies of God and the occupying of the land by the rightful heirs.

GENESIS 16

Verse 1. *Handmaid.* This is from SHIPHCHAH and defined, "A female slave (as a member of the household)."—Strong. These female slaves were much used in ancient times as personal or body servants for women of rank or other privilege. Because of the intimate nature of their services they became much attached to their mistresses and in some figurative way were considered largely a part of their same person. And because of this close relationship a child born of them would be thought of in the light of being the offspring of the mistress. Let it be noted that this handmaid was an Egyptian which will account for the choice she made later of her son's wife.

Verse 2. *Go in.* This expression is one frequently used in the olden times to refer to the relation of a man with a woman in intimate relation. It has the same meaning as the expression "know" when used with reference to this relation. *It may be.* There was no doubt as to whether Abram would be permitted by Hagar to have this relation with her. But the uncertainty would lie in the question of whether the act would result in conception. And this uncertainty was also shared by Hagar as may be seen from the implied surprise she had as indicated in verse 4.

Verse 3. Here is where the term "ten years" should be marked as being one of the informative dates relied on at various times of computation. *Wife.* This occurs in two instances in this verse, once in reference to Sarai and the other to Hagar. And since we know that the relation of these two women to Abram was altogether different from each other we must know that some common definition applies to the word. It is from ISHSHAH in both cases. And the definition is "a woman."—Strong. Hence we could as correctly word it "to be his woman." And with this information in mind we will not be confused by any questions of what was to constitute the relation of "wife" in those days. The simple thought is that in that particular transaction Hagar was to be Abram's woman for this reproductive arrangement. The term "wife" as a social distinction and as is universally used is a designation brought about by the laws and customs of man and no part of the original scheme of God as to the relation of the sexes. Of course, since man has adopted such designation and incorporated it into the laws of nations, then God respects it and requires his people to respect it.

Verse 4. *When she saw.* This is the expression of surprise or uncertainty referred to in verse 2 above. *Despised.* This is from QALAL and means "to make light." The natural thing occurred. Here is a girl who had been only a servant to her mistress and a mistress, too, who had been unable to become a mother. Now she is expectant by the husband of her mistress and hence is led to think of her as being much inferior to her. And not only does she have this feeling of superiority toward her mistress, but she must have manifested it because Sarai knows about it as will be seen next.

Verse 5. *Wrong.* This is not a confession that Sarai had done wrong. It is from CHAMAC and defined "violence * * * unjust gain."—Strong. Thus she charges that the satisfaction which Hagar has obtained through the situation is unjust and she is blaming it on Abram. We recall that in chapter 3: 12 the man blamed his misfortune on the woman. Now the woman does a like thing against man. See comment at that place.

Verse 6. *Dealt hardly.* This is from ANAH and defined "looking down or brow-beating; to depress, literally or figuratively, transitively or intransitively."—Strong. Thus we see that Sarai did not mistreat her physically. That might have caused a loss that even she did not wish to come. But she so overawed her, with a possible threat of personal violence for the purpose of humiliation, that the girl was induced to flee.

Verse 7. *Angel.* This is the second recorded instance of these celestial beings appearing on the earth. The first is in the case of the cherubim placed to guard the highway leading to the garden of Eden. Here it is to a runaway slave. The use of angels in carrying out God's many great plans is to be seen all through the Bible. Frequently these angels are spoken of as being God himself. But that is because they are personal representatives of God. The fact that even Moses was not permitted to see the face of God shows that all instances where it is said that God appeared or said certain things to people means that it was done through the angels. *Wilderness.* The fact that just previous to this word it mentions a fountain of water would prove that a wilderness is not necessarily a place without any moisture or vegetable life as the popular idea is.

Verses 8, 9. Appearances do not always agree with the best interests of a person. The natural impulse was for Hagar to escape unpleasant experience by running from her mistress. But had she gone on, her child would have been born in the wilderness and had no provision for so young a child. But instead, it is better for her to return and retain the protection and provision of the home of her master for the time.

Verses 10, 11. The promise that Hagar's seed was to be very numerous was fulfilled in the production of the Arabian nation which descended from her son. His name in the Hebrew is YISHMAEL and defined "God will hear."—Strong.

Verse 12. *Wild.* This is from PEREH and defined "in the secondary sense of running wild; the onager."—Strong. It is akin to another word which carries the idea of bearing fruit in the wilderness and not under tamed cultivation. And this description agrees with the roaming nature of the Arabs. *Against.* This is from QIRAH and defined "an encountering, accidental, friendly or hostile (also adv. opposite)."—Strong. This shows that the descendants of Hagar's son would not necessarily be always hostile to whomsoever they met, but that on account of being loose in the wilderness, with no certain dwelling place, they would come in contact with various tribes. *Dwell in the presence of all his brethren.* In Gen. 25: 18 the statement is that "he died in the presence of all his brethren." If that was so then he necessarily had dwelt in their presence which fulfills the prediction of the angel.

Verses 13, 14. *Thou God seest me.* How true are these words. And the significance of them here is the fact that apparently this woman was in a forsaken plight with no one to care for her. Yet she acknowledges the presence of God in that her affliction has been recognized and comforting words have been said to her. A good principle for all people to bear in mind is the fact that God sees all that is going on. He will not overlook the slightest creature that needs his attention.

Verses 15, 16. Hagar was in the wilderness away from her master when the angel told her the name to be given to her child when born. Yet in the verse before us we are told that Abram called the son by the name of Ishmael. This concludes that Hagar told her master the conversation of the angel with her. Morever, since there is no recorded indication that he knew from any other source what the Lord wanted to have the son called, he had confidence in the truthfulness of the report which his slave gave him, and also he had the respect for the Lord's will to name his son accordingly. And let it be noted here that another number is recorded. Abram was 86 years old now.

GENESIS 17

Verse 1. Thirteen years have gone by since the close of the previous chapter. God appears to Abram here and states his identity and renews his exhortation for him to continue in his walk of righteousness. The time is drawing near for the more visible signs of the promise made when God first appeared to him.

Verse 2. There were three prominent promises which God had made with Abram and one of them concerned the numerous strength of his descendants. This one is here repeated in this verse and then again a little later on in the chapter.

Verse 3. This posture of the body was one used by the people of the East when they wished to indicate great respect for another. Strong says the word is used in a great variety of senses and that the falling on the face is a statement that means the subjection of the person and not necessarily a literal falling with face on ground.

Verse 4. The significant thought in this verse is that Abram is to be the father of many nations. At this time, however, he has but one son and he was not the one of the original promise. But in chapter 25: the sons from his second marriage are named and they became founders of various nations.

Verse 5. This is the event of changing the name to Abraham. And this change was made so that his name would correspond with one of the predictions given him and that was to become a father of many nations. The name in the Hebrew is the same form as the English and defined, "To be populous; father of a multitude."—Strong. We must not lose sight of the plan that while many nations were to come from his body, yet only one would be recognized as God's peculiar line, and that it is to come from a son not yet born and of whom a reminder of the promise will be given a little later.

Verse 6. *Kings shall come out of thee.* This was fulfilled as seen in the books of Samuel and Kings. The long line of kings that reigned from Saul to the carrying off into Babylonian captivity came from Abraham. It is true that when the nation of the Israelites became dissatisfied with God's existing rule and wanted a king it was displeasing to God. But when he decided to let them have a king it was stipulated that they should set up the king "whom the Lord thy God shall choose" (Deut. 17: 15). This, of course, was in deference to this prediction made to Abraham. And still more interesting is the fact that at the last, when God himself determined to have a king over his spiritual people he decreed that said king was to come into the world through the blood line of Abraham. Hence the significant circumstance that the accounts of both Matthew, in his first chapter, and Luke, in his third chapter, of the genealogy of Christ, show that he came down through Abraham. This was true on the side of both Mary and Joseph, since the fountain head of the two families was a lineal descendant of Abraham. Solomon, the ancestor of Joseph and Nathan the ancestor of Mary were both sons of David and by the same mother (1 Chr. 3: 5).

Verses 7, 8. *Everlasting covenant—everlasting possession.* Critics stumble at these expressions and state that if everlasting means endless then God did not mean what he said here. That according to the other parts of the Bible God never intended that Abraham's descendants should possess that land endlessly. Therefore, everlasting does not mean endless. But no one who understands the meaning of the word will say that "everlasting" always means endless. It depends on the thing spoken about whether it has the force of endless. The fundamental meaning of the word is "age lasting." This definition may properly be given to the word in any place it is used. Then, if the age in which the thing being spoken of is endless the word also means endless. But no one acquainted with the plan of the Bible will say that the age of man on this earth was to be endless. So that, whether we consider this subject from the standpoint of the age of the Jewish nation as a separate people, or the age of those people individually as human beings, such age was not claimed to be endless. And had the Israelite nation always been true to God's laws, then they would never have lost their national existence. Even after the religion of Christ was brought into the world, thus putting an end to all other forms of religion, they still could have retained their national existence and regulation by the law of Moses as a political law. And they could thus have retained their possession of the Canaan land throughout their national age which would have ended with the end of this world. Hence, the promise of an "everlasting possession" meant the possession of it to the end of the age of man on this earth, at the longest.

Verse 9. *Generations.* This here means their posterity. That not only was Abraham to keep this covenant but the generations or posterity to follow were to keep it. That it was not to pass out of use with the death of Abraham.

Verses 10-12. Circumcision was to be a token of the covenant. The word is from OWTH and defined "a signal (literal or figurative), as a flag, beacon, monument, omen, prodigy, evidence, etc."—Strong. The mark of circumcision was decided upon long after Abraham was considered a righteous man (Rom. 4: 11). And to perpetuate the memory of Abraham as a righteous man, God decreed that this fleshly mark should adhere to his descendants throughout this earthly span. This accounts for the ability of Pharaoh's daughter to recognize the child Moses as a Hebrew (Ex. 2: 6). And it should here be noted that the child was to be circumcised at age of eight days. This rite made the child a one hundred per cent member of that covenant, and later of the Jewish citizenship, regardless of the fact that the infant was irresponsible.

Verse 13. The two classes of persons that were subject to circumcision were those born in Abraham's house or the ones bought with his money. Of course it will be understood that this is independent of the requirement for the rite as enforced under the law of Moses. Only during the lifetime of Abraham and his immediate family would original application hold. But there would be infants born in the posterity of Abraham long after his immediate family had passed away and also his money had ceased to be available. The everlasting covenant is again mentioned which is explained at verses 7, 8 above.

Verse 14. It is obvious that an infant could not be held responsible for any neglect of duty. Hence the threat of negligence mentioned in this verse would apply very logically to the parent or parents in charge of the infant. This will account for the near escape from death that Moses made, recorded in Ex. 4: 24. Notwithstanding the importance of Moses as a person and of the mission on which he was now setting, yet the covenant made with Abraham was so precious that God would have destroyed Moses had he not seen to it that his son was circumcised here. More will be said on this case at the place of occurrence.

Verses 15, 16. *Sarai, Sarah.* The first of these words means "dominative" according to Strong, while the second one he defines as "to abound; resources." Thus the reason for the change is plain to be seen. While she would not cease to dominate to some extent, and which will be discovered later, yet the importance of her as the maternal ancestor of nations and kings entitled her to this second name. That nations were to come from her is seen in chapter 25: 23 and also that kings were to come agrees with what is said of Abraham in verse 6.

Verse 17. *Laughed.* This is from TSACHAQ and defined "to laugh outright (in merriment or scorn); by implication to sport."—Strong. Hence the word may mean one of criticism or one of "too-good-to-be-true" significance. This latter is evidently the sense in which the writer uses it of Abraham. He had never doubted the promises of God and had acted promptly at the divine command. Hence we must not conclude that he was scorning the promise here. But it seemed so wonderful for a man one hundred years old with a wife ninety years old to have a child. Not that he considered himself as too old to perform the marriage act for it had been only thirteen years since he had begotten Ishmael. But the wonderful nature of the whole proposition stunned him.

Verse 18. There is no evidence here or elsewhere that Abraham was discounting the validity of God's arrangement to have the promise descend through the son of Sarah. But his father love for his own son beamed forth in this verse. He does not ask God to set aside the plan to wait for the son to be born to Sarah, but only asks that some consideration be given to this his own fleshly son. And the request was not displeasing to God as will be seen soon.

Verse 19. This is a repetition of the promise already mentioned. Not only was Abraham to have another son but he was to be the offspring of the wife who had been all her lifetime a barren woman. And the everlasting covenant as mentioned here has already been explained in verses 7, 8 above.

Verse 20. God's love for faithful Abraham was so strong that he promises to bless this son of his also. The twelve princes that he was to beget are named in Chapter 25: 12-16. And he indeed did become a great nation as here promised. The Arabian people came from him and it is well known that they are a great nation.

Verses 21, 22. *Set time next year.* While miracle was necessary to enable Sarah to conceive, yet God allowed nature to take its usual course in the growing of the unborn child. As this part of Sarah's nature was not defective there was no call to resort to miracle here although God could have caused the child to be born immediately after conception. And so we find various instances where childless women were given power to conceive but then waited the usual period for the birth.

Verses 23, 24. We should observe and admire the promptness of Abraham in carrying out the ordinance of God in this matter. As he is now ninety and nine years of age, and since he is thus 24 years older than he was when first counted faithful and righteous, the argument is that circumsion was not what constituted him the man of faith that he is reputed to be in sacred history. But the ordinance of this fleshly mark was given to him much on the same principle that a soldier is decorated with medals in honor of his services.

Verses 25-27. The statement is made here that Ishmael was thirteen years old when circumcised. The reader has been told also that he was the founder of the nation of Arabians. Some testimony from secular history will be interesting and in order at this point. Following is on the subject. "But as for the Arabians, they circumcise after the 13th year, because Ishmael, the founder of their nation, who was born to Abraham by the concubine, was circumcised at that age," Josephus, Ant. 1-12-2. It might be considered a mere whim for those people governed by the exact age of their founder in attending to the rite of circumcision. But the fact that they do so is another of the corroborating circumstances that point to the truthfulness of the sacred record. And this mark being one of the flesh and yet not inherited, its continuance for the centuries proclaims its origin to have been as divinely declared.

GENESIS 18

Verse 1. Here, as in other places, we must understand that the Lord appeared to Abraham in the person of the angel, but in the form of man. He was dwelling at this time in the place where he went after giving the choice of locations to Lot. As it was in the heat of the day, about noon or not long after, we understand why he was sitting in the door of the tent. This was the most comfortable place to be at this time. The tent would furnish shade and at the same time, being in the door, there would be some ventilation.

Verse 2. Let it be noticed that three persons are here by Abraham. The statement that they were "by" him is relative and not that they were immediately at his side. This is evident from the fact that he "ran to meet them." The act of bowing himself to the ground was just another instance of his courtesy as practiced by people of the east. Abraham did not know they were other than men for he offered them the literal comforts of this material life. And, while they are angels, yet when posing in the form of men they can participate in the ordinary habits of men. In short, nothing should confuse us in the way of miracle when performed by celestial beings for all such are under the power and privilege of God.

Verse 3. Notwithstanding he calls them lord yet his offer of material hospitality shows he thinks them human in their real personality. And offering to serve them in this way furnishes an occasion like that referred to in Heb. 13: 1.

Verse 4. *Wash your feet.* Since this subject will often have occasion to be considered in course of this work it will be well here to insert a quotation from a well authenticated work on the same. "*Washing the hands and feet.* As knives and forks were not used in the East, in Scripture times, in eating, it was necessary that the hand, which was thrust into the common dish, should be scrupulously clean; and again, as sandals were ineffectual against the dust and heat of the climate, washing the feet on entering a house was an act both of respect to the company and of refreshment to the traveler. The former of these usages was transformed by the Pharisees of the New Testament age into a matter of ritual observance, Mark 7: 3, and special rules were laid down as to the time and manner of its performance. Washing the feet did *not rise* to the dignity of a *ritual* observance except in connection with the service of the sanctuary, Ex. 30: 19, 21. It held a high place, hwever, among the rites of *hospitality.* Immediately that a guest presented himself at the tent door, it was usual to offer the necessary materials for washing the feet. Gen. 18: 4; 19: 2; 24: 32; 43: 24; Judg. 19: 21. It was a yet more complimentary act, betokening equally humility and affection, if the host himself performed the office for his guest. 1 Sam. 25: 41; 1 Tim. 5: 10. Such a token of hospitality is still occasionally exhibited in the East." —*Smith's Bible Dictionary,* revised edition, p. 736.

Verse 5. *Comfort ye your hearts.* This is largely figurative. That is, while the refreshments offered were literal, yet by partaking of them after a journey on foot, and having had the previous satisfaction of a bath for the travel-wearied feet, the result would be a comforting of their feelings. *For therefore.* This expression is from a word of various meanings, but its most evident one is as if it said here, "since ye have come, and properly so, to your servant." In other words, Abraham means that as they had for just reason come to him, their servant, he felt inclined to treat them in a manner befitting the occasion. The men gave him their consent to proceed with his acts of hospitality which he does in the following paragraph.

Verses 6-8. The young man was told to "dress" the calf. This is from a word that includes all things necessary to get the article ready for eating. This in the meantime that Sarah was preparing the bread. All this would require some time even though the item of haste is indicated. And thus we are to see that the stay of the men was of some duration. It being in the heat of the day we may see the reason for their eating their meal under the tree.

Verses 9, 10. *According to the time of life.* Read again the remarks on this subject in 17: 21.

Verse 11. This verse means that Sarah had passed the ordinary child-bearing period of life. So that two natural impediments appeared to be against her having any children. She had been barren all her life, to the extent at least that she had not yet been able to conceive. But sometimes a woman appears to be barren for years even though she might experience the usual functioning of the period of life. And it does sometimes occur that a woman will go for years with this kind of experience and then become able to conceive. But even this dim prospect was now denied Sarah since she had passed that age of her life. Therefore, there are now two reasons from a natural viewpoint that make it impossible for her to have children.

Verse 12. *Sarah laughed.* This is from the same word as in 17: 17 at which place the reader should now look for the definition. But since we see below that she denied having laughed we must take the unfavorable part of the definition which is to scorn. The "pleasure" here referred to is evidently that of being a mother; for, contrary to a prevalent sentiment in the world today, being childless was considered a misfortune.

Verses 13, 14. *Is anything too hard for the Lord?* The Bible teaches there are some things God cannot do. But it is not because they are too hard. It is because it is not right. Since it would be right for a barren woman to be given a child, it would be within the power of God to give it to her. For comments on the time of life see 17: 21.

Verse 15. *Afraid.* One meaning of the original word here is "to revere." It is evident that she was awed by the presence of these honored guests and the fact that she had manifested the attitude she did in her laughing. This respect for them is shown in that she did not deny it the second time.

Verse 16. The meeting and its business having come to a close Abraham continues his respects for his guests by accompanying them part way on their journey. As such an act of friendliness is common even in our day we can see that human nature has long been the same as it is today. In fact, human nature has never changed.

Verse 17. Let it be borne in mind that while God sent three angels in form of men to Abraham, yet one angel alone would represent him. And now, since it has been determined to impart to Abraham some information in addition to what was given him at his tent home, the Lord retains one of the "men" for this purpose while the other two go on toward the next mission which will be seen in next chapter.

Verses 18, 19. God is still formulating his purposes regarding the situation and has not yet broken the word to Abraham. But the basis on which he proposes to confide in him concerning the impending transaction is being made known to the inspired writer of this book. *Command his children and his household after him.* Abraham was living under the Patriarchal Dispensation in which the father was also priest and ruler of the religious conduct of the family.

Verses 20, 21. We believe that God knows everything at all times. Yet, he deals with man on a principle of justice. He will not give credit for well-doing until he sees the evidence of it in man's conduct. Neither will he charge man with misconduct without examining the evidence. See comments on this idea at 11: 5, 6. Hence he will send two of these angels on down to Sodom to make the investigation while the third remains to impart the information referred to in verse 17.

Verse 22. *The men* nere refer to the two angels delegated to visit Sodom while *the Lord* refers to the third one remaining to give further information to Abraham.

Verses 23-33. It is not advisable to "read between the lines," especially on matters pertaining to the divine record. But there are some things of which we are sure. Abraham has before this shown concern and love for Lot. This was seen in his unselfish offer as to the choice of pasture land in chapter 13. He showed it further when he followed after the invaders in chapter 14 and recovered Lot and his goods. Now, that the city in which his nephew is residing is to be destroyed he pleads in behalf of his salvation. We have no way of knowing why he ceased to plead at the number ten. However, we may make a few remarks safely. He had been descending in his number of righteous souls by tens. After arriving at the number of ten and the Lord said he would not destroy the city if that many righteous were there, he had reached his limit. The next drop would have come to zero which would have been equivalent to asking the Lord not to destroy the city at all. This he would not do as it would have been a case of putting his own judgment against that of God. Therefore, he merely submits to the will of the Lord and returns to his home. And we may further conclude safely that as God said he would not destroy the city if ten righteous were there, yet did destroy it, not that many righteous were there. But Lot was there with his own family and they were considered righteous since the Lord made provision for their escape from the wicked city. This again being a testimony that Lot should not have been charged with wrong in chapter 13.

GENESIS 19

Verse 1. Note that two angels are here mentioned as coming to Sodom, while in the previous chapter three came to Abraham. Also, in the previous instance they were called "men" and here are called "angels." This is because the angels of God appear in the form of men thus furnishing the opportunity to entertain angels unawares as stated in Heb. 13: 1. *Gate.* This is from SHAHAR and defined "an opening, i. e., door or gate." Thus the word would not be restricted to a movable piece to be closed although it could mean that. But its significance in this case is that these angels were approaching the city at the usual place of entry. Just why Lot was at this time sitting at this place is not made clear. However, it was often the case that men of some standing were allowed to occupy a position at this place. Lot accorded these persons the usual courtesy in practice in the east by bowing with his face toward the ground.

Verse 2. Lot offers hospitality to them. They make as if they will go on. This, no doubt, to bring out further the evidence of his earnestness for we know that it was their mission to this city to bring Lot out of it. Among the items of hospitality we again notice mention of feet washing. For a treatment of this subject see comments at 18: 4. Lot thinks their mission is one that merely calls for them to pass through the city for he states that they may arise early in the morning to resume their journey.

Verse 3. Eating was one of the prominent items of social recognition in olden times. It was not for the purpose of satisfying the needs of the body only, but to betoken the social fellowship. The student is reminded of the advantage to take note, as he goes on through the study of the Bible, that this eating together will often be given prominent place in the courtesies of people coming together. *Baked unleavened bread.* This is significant. The word means "sweet or unsoured through fermentation." Since it was then in the close of the day and Lot thought they were to leave early in the morning he would reasonably conclude he did not have time to wait for leavened bread. The angels (in the form of men) partook of the food Lot offered them.

Verses 4, 5. *Know them.* See the references and comments at chapter 4: 1 on the meaning of this expression. Except that in this case now before us the men wanted to commit immorality with these men, as they thought them to be. In this place we have the subject of sodomy introduced by the scriptures. Today the word "sodomy" means the unnatural act of immorality between men. But the reason such name is applied to that subject is not through any particular meaning of the word. But since the most outstanding instance of this evil was in the city of Sodom, it came to have that name. Had the most prominent city with that evil been some other one and had Lot been in some other city than Sodom, then that evil would have taken a name based on the name of whatever city that had been.

Verses 6, 7. Lot's anxiety for the safety and respect of his invited guests can be seen by his going out to the men and closing the door after him. He calls them by the name of brethren evidently because they were fellow citizens of the city.

Verse 8. *Have not known man.* Again this refers to the intimacy between sexes so that they are virgins at this time. The offer of his daughters to these fiends can be explained only on the principle that "of two evils, choose the less." As it appears now, something terrible is about to happen. If these citizens of Sodom are so moved by carnal desire as to make the demand they just expressed then they will commit an act of violence if not satisfied in some way. As Lot sees the situation there is no alternative but to give them either his daughters or the guests. He feels under a special obligation to protect them because he had invited them to come; yea, had urged them to do so when it appeared they were about to go on. But they were guests of this home and by his invitation. This is what he meant by the words *for therefore came they.* See comments on this form of expression at 18: 5. That is, they have come under his roof very properly and therefore are entitled to proper treatment.

Verse 9. *Stand back.* This was said to Lot. Then *This one fellow came in to sojourn and he will needs be a judge.* These words they said among themselves by way of angry consultation. Their reasoning was that Lot was supposed to be only a sojourner or temporary dweller among them, and yet now he presumes to be a judge over them. This incensed them so that they next address themselves to Lot thus, *now will we deal worse with thee than with them.* Then they tried to attack him. They were disappointed at not being able to satisfy their unnatural lust on these visitors. And disappointed lust produces the worst kind of revenge. Witness the case of the wife of Potiphar in her wickedness against Joseph in 39: 7-20.

Verses 10, 11. Instead of needing protection the angels now become protectors of their host. Being celestial beings they possessed supernatural power. Thus they not only rescued Lot from the hands of the men but smote them with blindness so that they could not find the door to further their wicked design.

Verse 12. Again we see in the form of language used in this verse that God often speaks to man as if he were a man also. This inquiry about the family members of Lot does not imply that he had all of the relations named. Neither does it mean that the angels could not have known the facts. But in order to make the order of the occasion so complete that no item could be overlooked this complete list of possible members is named. We know from what follows that Lot had no sons although they are suggested here. And as to sons-in-law, that will be discussed below.

Verse 13. Since the fire that finally did destroy the city came down from heaven after the angels had gone away we are to take their statement on this point to mean that they had been sent to announce the destruction of the city. See a similar use of such an expression in Ezk. 43: 3 with the marginal reading.

Verse 14. *Married his daughters.* All of the facts pertaining to the family of Lot show that he had just two children, daughters, and they at this time had never "known" men, which means they were never married in the usual sense of that word. But this is a good place to offer some facts on the subject of marriage in its relation to engagement or espousal. In Biblical times an espousal was considered so binding upon the parties involved that the agreement was often referred to as a marriage, and the parties thus engaged were often spoken of as husbands and wives. As a specific instance, consider the case of Joseph and Mary. In Matt. 1: 18 we read that Mary was espoused to Joseph but had not yet come to him. While in this state of virginity she was found with child. Joseph did not understand it and thought her to have been unfaithful to him and was preparing to "put her away." But the angel of the Lord appeared to him and told him to take unto him his "wife." And this expression although they had never had any relations. So that we are to conclude that an espoused person was under such strong moral obligation that the term husband or wife was used freely. A further consideration here is that Joseph was preparing to "put her away" which is a term used in case of married persons. All of which adds up to the conclusion that an engaged person in Bible times was as much bound morally as one actually married. And all this further agrees with the situation in case of Lot and his plea with these sons-in-law. For it would be very unnatural for a man to be so concerned about the men who were living with his daughtes that he would urge them to flee the danger of the city and say nothing to the daughters themselves. But the record tells us that these men regarded the warning of Lot as mockery. This again indicates that they had not yet taken the daughters into intimate relationship, else they would have listened.

Verse 15. *Which are here.* This might mislead some to conclude that Lot might have daughters that were not "here" and thus contradict the statements of preceding paragraph. But the word "here" is from MATSA and one of the words that Strong uses to define it is "acquire." This expression then could properly be made to read "thy two daughters which are acquired." It would refer merely to the fact that Lot had acquired two daughters since starting a family.

Verse 16. *Lingered.* This means to be reluctant, not that he questioned the necessity of leaving. But he had lived in the city for a while and it was but natural to be thus hesitant about leaving. Besides, he could not realize as fully as they, how urgent the case was. As the statement was made that the Lord was merciful to him at this time we would conclude that no grievous fault is to be found with him.

Verse 17. Here is a four-fold commandment in the form of details. There can be no mistaking the order. Not only are they to leave the city, but pass beyond the plain. Also, keep on going till they have reached the mountain and while doing so they are not to give way to curiosity to the extent of looking back.

Verses 18-21. If Abraham was permitted to "argue" with the Lord about the city of Sodom and yet not be entirely rejected, it is no great thing if Lot makes a plea like this. He does not make any request regarding the wicked city nor its punishment. But is concerned about his own comfort and safety outside the city. And since the city he requests privilege of entering is a little one he feels that not much would be left existing even if God were to permit it to survive. Not only was the city a little one but was not far away. So the Lord permits him to have that exception and go to the little city nearer than the mountain.

Verse 22. While God would not promise Abraham to spare the city if less than ten righteous souls were in it, yet neither would he destroy it while four souls were in it. Hence the angel tells Lot that nothing can be done until he leaves.

Verse 23. The two angels came to Sodom in the evening. (Verse 1.) They remained in Lot's house over night. (Verse 15.) Then some time the day following they got Lot started on his way to safety. And it was sunrise when Lot entered Zoar, which means that he had been traveling all the day and night. This indicates the statement of Lot that Zoar was "near to flee unto" is a relative one.

Verse 24. *Brimstone.* This is from COPHRITH and defined "properly, cypress-resin." It is the exudation of a tree similar to the gopher and the material is highly inflammable. And then the fire that was sent down at the same time would ignite this resin and produce a very high tempered combustion. Stating that it was rained down out of heaven means simply that it came down from the sky as a boy would call it when speaking of his kite in the sky. The same word for sky is often translated heaven in the Bible. There was nothing supernatural in the qualities of these materials rained down on the wicked cities. The thing that was supernatural was the fact of producing them in such great quantities and bringing them from the sky. It is therefore a miraculous fire.

Verse 25. Such a devastating fire would leave a country in the condition here described whether brought about miraculously or otherwise. But the significant thing in this case is that no natural resources could have produced the amount of said materials as used here. Hence the Lord sent them from above.

Verse 26. *Pillar.* From NETSIB and defined "something stationary, i. e., a prefect, military post, a statue."—Strong. Since a statue is usually a form of some person, we should conclude that Lot's wife retained her form and size after being cursed as she was here. Salt has been used and referred to in various places and in many kinds of significations. When used in connection with judgments against some person or place or thing it designates desolation. Nothing grows where salt exists. But also, it has the significance of perpetuity, so that in the case of Lot's wife, turning her into a pillar of salt would denote that her folly was to be perpetuated in the memory of the world. Hence we have our Lord telling us to "remember Lot's wife." (Luke 17: 32.) We do not know why she looked back and any attempt to state why must be speculation. What we do know is that she disboyed one of the four commands uttered by the angels and was punished. And we may also observe that the material into which she was turned was the same as that which became a permanent condition of the region previously occupied by the wicked cities.

Verses 27, 28. In this passage we can learn that Abraham had gone with the angels as near the site of the impending destruction as to make the smoke thereof visible. The fire and brimstone came down from heaven but the smoke came up from the earth. So we see that the materials composing the cities, with the houses and people and all that pertained to them, were set on fire and continued to burn until they were completely consumed. Furthermore, as this community was also naturally infested with the material known as slimepits or asphaltitis, a highly inflammable substance, we can see why there would be this rising of the smoke so high. See notes on 14: 3.

Verse 29. Here God's care and love for Abraham can be observed by his sending his nephew Lot out of the destruction.

Verse 30. It is interesting to note that Lot did the very thing that the angels at first told him to do. However, the fright of the coming fire is not present here as it was before. Another thing to be considered is this. Zoar was one of the cities in the region that should have been destroyed, or near it. And doubtless the people of that city were wicked like the ones in Sodom. That being so, they would have made the very existence of Lot in the city a continual uneasiness. He had seen what the men of Sodom wished to do unto the newcomers, and they might do the same to him. So he became fearful and fled the place and became a cave dweller in the mountains.

Verses 31-36. The sincerity of these women in their statement about there being no man in the earth to come in unto them should not be questioned. It would be almost necessary to conclude there were some human beings in the city of Zoar from whence they had fled because it is stated that Lot was afraid to remain there. That could not have been because of the wildness of the country for the same would have been true of the mountain and the cave. Besides, a city would not be called such without people living in it. But such character of men as would have been in that place would not encourage the idea of association with them. Furthermore, their father was with Abraham when he was instructed to separate from all people except the ones pertaining to the promise of becoming a great nation. Hence these daughters would not consider the men of Zoar as proper to be admitted into their family tree. Another thing to be considered is that even if there were men in Zoar, they would not be any relation to the family and hence to have children by them would not be "preserving seed of their father." And so, as the situation appears to them the only way to perpetuate the blood line of their father was to obtain children by him. And the desire to reproduce must be commended in them, since that is often scoffed at today. But it was in keeping with the will of God. We should conclude therefore that the motive these girls had for their act was a pure one and not from lasciviousness. A further observation we may make here is that in order to get their father into this plan they thought they would have to get him under the influence of wine. This is a concession from them to the righteous principles of life which they had previously seen in him. Also, the whole transaction shows that when a man is drunk he does not realize the nature of his conduct. Since God ever afterward manifested a kindly regard for the descendants of this occurrence it would show that he was not too critical of it. However, we need not conclude that any miracle was performed in order to have it turn out as the girls planned. It was their own doing and the time for carrying it out was set by them. They would certainly know something about the time considered most favorable for conception and would choose said time. There is no record of the life of these girls after this so that we cannot charge them with having started a life of loose conduct by this experience. In fact this is the last we will read of the direct personal life of Lot. He here passes out of the picture except when referred to historically.

Verses 37, 38. The Moabites and Ammonites will figure much in the history of later years. They became great nations but very evil. And, while at times certain leniency was shown them for the sake of their common head, Lot, yet as a people they were opposed by the Lord and at times had severe punishment meted out as will be seen.

GENESIS 20

Verse 1. This region mentioned as the place where Abraham journeyed is in the direction toward Egypt. Gerar was a city of the Philistines, so we will learn that he was among that people. They were destined to play a long and important part in the history of God's people. They descended from Ham as will be seen in chapter 10:6-14.

Verse 2. Here Abraham used the same plan he did in Egypt concerning his wife. See comments at 12: 11-15 on this matter. *Took Sarah.* This is a word of wide application and must be interpreted in all given cases by the immediate context. In the one at hand it could mean only that he selected her with a view of finally making her his own. But he had not yet formally "taken" her since we see later that he had not used her as his wife.

Verse 3. *Dead man.* The word is defined as being both literal and figurative. As the person of the king had not been touched we are left with the conclusion that it is used figuratively here. But it also means that if he continues in the plan that he has started then he will become literally a dead man. One of the principles on which God would cause this is expressed in his promise to Abraham to "bless them that bless thee, and curse him that curseth thee." (Chapter 12: 3.) *Man's wife.* These words are respectively from BAHAL, BAWAL. They are defined, also respectively, "a master; hence a husband, or (figuratively) owner (often used with another noun in modifications of this latter sense)" "a primitive root; to be master; hence to marry."—Strong. This is the only place where "wife" is from this Hebrew word. It is a stronger or more specific word than is generally used and translated "wife." Generally the original word would not apply to a married woman any more than to an unmarried one. Thus ownership is the outstanding idea in the original word. But the motive for owning or wanting to own a woman in all cases must be indicated by the context and cannot be determined by the dictionary definition of the word. But the Hebrew word used in this single case at hand is one which carries the idea of intimate relation.

Verse 4. *Slay a righteous nation?* The king could have used the word "righteous" only as regards this present case of this strange woman. He knew he had not knowingly done wrong to this man and his wife and therefore was righteous as to that. And also, since he personally would have been the only guilty one, the mentioning of slaying a nation could have been only on the basis that destroying an important person in it, its king, would be to destroy the nation.

Verse 5. Both Abraham and his wife told the same story to the king. This was in accordance with an agreement they had made when they left their home land. As to why it was thought necessary to use this plan see Chapter 12: 11. Even if Abimelech had a wife or wives already, his claim of innocence here could be allowed on the basis of the accepted practice in those days with regard to marriage. In other words, neither in this case nor the one in chapter 12 was any accusation made against the king on the ground that he already was married. But it was for taking another man's wife.

Verse 6. In preventing the king from intimacy with Sarah God said it was from sinning "against me." Since Abraham was a chosen man of God, any sin against him would be counted as against God. This is the same principle Christ taught concerning treatment of his disciples. (Matt. 25: 40, 45.)

Verse 7. *For he is a prophet.* Mention of Abraham's being a prophet was to show why his prayer for the king would avail and not as a reason why Sarah should be restored. Had she been the wife of any other man it would have been wrong for the king to take her. But the prayer of a prophet would avail more than that of another. This is a principle taught in James 5: 16. And God here threatens that if the man's wife is not restored both he and all his would be destroyed. But this threat had not been made previous to this. Therefore the comments about the "nation" in verse 4 still hold.

Verse 8. Abimelech proceeds to make the necessary adjustment. He first gives instructions to his people since he feels responsible for their actions and safety.

Verses 9, 10, 11. He next complains to Abraham and calls for explanation. In his answer he states that he did not think the people of that place feared God and would therefore slay him. As much as to say that when people commit murder it is because they do not fear God. And yet, while they would not refrain from murder if they had not the fear of God, they would not take a man's wife unless he were out of the way. See comments on this idea in Chapter 12: 12, 13.

Verse 12. Sometimes a smile is made over this "quibble" of Abraham. But there is something more than just an excuse in his explanation. As they had a common father they would be considered nearer than if it were the other way because the family line always descended through the father's side.

Verse 13. This is the mutual understanding between them referred to above. Let it be noted here that Abraham refers to his first experience with God that he was caused to "wander." This word is from TAWAN and defined "a primitive root; to vacillate, i. e., reel or stray (literally or figuratively); also causative of both."—Strong. Now when one vacillates or strays we generally think of him as being a man with no fixed purpose and thus as one to be censured. But in this case it is stated that "God caused" this wandering to be done. And the fact that God caused Abraham to vacillate or stray or go about in an apparent aimless manner it would be evidence of still more faith in God for him to stick to God then than if he could see a fixed objective. And the motive which Abraham presents to his wife for following this arrangement is that it will be a kindness to him. This is a high motive for a wife to feel toward her husband.

Verses 14, 15. The conduct of Abimelech here shows that he was sincere in his expressions of regret over this sad affair. He makes up to Abraham for the injury that he had unwittingly done by a material payment. Also by offer of continued hospitality as a dweller in the land. No resentment or spitework is manifested.

Verse 16. In speaking to Sarah Abimelech uses the same word concerning Abraham that she had used at the first, and calls him her brother. He ignores the truth that he had recently learned, that Abraham was her husband. But, being her brother, she must look to him for protection from the gaze of men and thus be a covering (figurative) for her eyes as a shield from the populace as they would wish to look upon her. And in this ironic language to her she was "reproved."

Verses 17, 18. In this passage we see

that God does at times bring punishment on a king's subjects in reprisal for the wrong act of their sovereign. And here we also see the thing fulfilled that God promised Abimelech, that Abraham was to pray for him and that the prayer would be effective.

GENESIS 21

Verses 1, 2. The word "visit" as used here means to make some practical contact with the person for the purpose of bestowing either a favorable or unfavorable result. And the connection here shows it to have the favorable meaning. Since Sarah was unable naturally to conceive, God would need to visit her to overcome that defect. Then after the conception had taken place the usual process of nature for nourishing the unborn child would be used. For this subject see comments at chapter 17: 21, 22.

Verse 3. Notice how particular the writer is to tell us which one of his sons is being considered. It was the one whom Sarah bare, not the one born of Hagar. And we are reminded that he called this particular son by the name of Isaac. This was to let us know that it was in fulfillment of the announcement made at chapter 17: 19.

Verse 4. True to his wonted obedience to God he circumcised his son. Not only so, but observed the minute detail of having it done on the right day, the eighth. That was considered an important feature of the ordinance. Not all circumcised persons could claim that. The son of Moses could not, but that was through neglect. And the great number of men crossing the Jordan into Canaan could not claim it but that was on account of things they could not control. (Josh. 5: 5, 6.) But Paul could claim it. (Phil. 3: 5.)

Verse 5. For purpose of easily locating it this verse should be marked since it tells us the age of Abraham when his son Isaac was born.

Verse 6. *Laugh.* This is from TSACHAQ and defined "to laugh outright (in merriment or scorn); by implication to sport."—Strong. The context indicates the favorable part of the definition hence it means that Sarah will be merry and that her friends will be merry with her.

Verse 7. There is no evidence that any miracle was performed on Sarah after she had conceived. Therefore her ability to give suck to her child shows further that her general female functions were normal.

Verse 8. The feast was in celebration of the fact that the child had reached the age when he could live on solid food. So a meal of this kind would be appropriate as betokening the glad day when this unexpected child had luanched out successfully on the sea of life. All indications point to the idea that an atmosphere of exultation was prevailing on this occasion, and that Isaac was the occasion for the joy, shared of course by his mother who had been so unfortunate all her life.

Verse 9. *Mocking.* This is from the same word as "laugh" in verse 6 above. And of course the connection shows that the unfavorable part of the definition is to be applied. So that it means that Sarah saw this son of Hagar laughing in scorn. It is not hard to understand why he would be inclined to do this. He is 14 years old and has been the only and thus favored son of his father all these years. Selfishness would now induce him to resent this rival for the affection of the father. But it is as easy to understand the reaction of Sarah on seeing this conduct of Ishmael. She had on the former occasion resented the attitude of Hagar toward her at the time she realized she was to be a mother by Abraham. But that had been somewhat patched up and now it is all stirred up again. That was too much. And in her resentment over the situation she makes the famous statement to follow.

Verse 10. This is the circumstance and the statement cited by Paul in Gal. 4: 30 in his discussion of the subject of the new covenant. There is no indication that Sarah knew anything about what this declaration of hers would mean some day. But it is another one of the many interesting instances recorded in the Bible where God made use of some statement or action of man. Whether he always caused the statement or action to come we do not know. But that would not prevent him from making use of it in his later dealing with his people. At present this seems to be a very natural occurrence of a natural mother in her jealousy for her child. But it proved to be the basis for one of the most unique arguments of the apostle Paul regarding the religion of Christ coming to displace the Sinaite one.

Verse 11. Abraham was a natural and loving father. Ishmael was just as near to him from a fleshly view point as any son could be. Now it is demanded that he cast him out from his home. Had he been left entirely to his own inclination, we could not say what he would have done as to Sarah's demands. But he was not left thus.

Verse 12. Thus we see that his natural impulse will not be the guiding factor in this situation. God tells him to hearken to the voice of Sarah. And a motive that is more important than mere affection is presented and that is the fact that his seed was to pass down through the line of Isaac.

Verse 13. But he is now left out in the cold as far as consolation is concerned over Ishmael. God here repeats what he had already promised, that the son of the bond woman was to become a great nation. And the endearing idea is added that because he is Abraham's seed this promise is made and will be kept.

Verse 14. Still acting under the impulse of a father, Abraham makes provision for the comfort of the child and obeys the command of God to send Hagar out of his home. *Bottle.* This is from CHEMETH and means "a skin bottle (as tied up)." Bottles as known today were not know then and vessels composed of skins of animals and drawn together were as nearly tight as they knew how to make them in ancient times. That this contained a considerable amount of drinking water is indicated by the statement that Abraham put it on her shoulder. He caused her and the lad to leave him and become a wanderer. It is a pathetic scene but will be finally overruled by the Lord for the improvement of the divine plan.

Verse 15. The word "cast" here is defined to have both a literal and figurative meaning. Since this boy was 14 years old we would not make the literal application of the word. But rather, that she caused the child to repose under the shrub. He is doubtless becoming weak from want of water and the shade will provide a little comfort to him during his hours of decline and death as she now is certain will come to pass.

Verse 16. To the mind of the writer this is one of the most touching scenes in history. Let all the background and accompanying facts he woven into the picture. A slave was once asked to admit her master into her intimacy for the purpose of bearing him a child. The joy of finding herself an expectant, and that, too, by her master, was so great that she was unthoughtful enough to incur the mistreatment of her mistress. Her joy was then turned to sadness by being driven from her home. But that sadness was reversed and she was induced to return to that home and accept what might be her lot there. She was also given the promise that her son was to become a great nation. The years rolled on after the birth of the child. Finally there came an unexpected (to her) change in circumstances. Her barren mistress became with child and at the proper time gave birth to a son. Naturally this son of the slave was pushed aside and finally now cast out together with his mother. The wide wilderness is her only home and its uncertain products her only sustenance. Moreover, the child who is her only possession now is dying of thirst and she is helpless. She cannot endure the immediate sight of the pangs to accompany his final hours. She goes away out of sight. But not too far, some beast might disturb him in his agonies and make the closing scene more fearful than only the famishing for water would. So she goes the distance of a bowshot. The distance one could shoot a bow would be far enough that she could not hear his cries, yet near enough to watch. And in this situation she sits down and weeps.

Verse 17. The lad had been crying from anguish and God heard it. He intervenes and calls to Hagar. She is given the consolation that the Lord recognizes where the lad is. Not that God only knows "where" he is in the sense of mere physical location. The Lord knows all locations at all times in that sense. But he fully realizes where he is as regards to his plight, and intends to meet the emergency.

Verse 18. When she is told to lift up the lad and hold him in her hand we are to understand that weakness had overcome him from the want of water. A lad of 14 years would be able to stand and handle himself if in a normal condition. But now she is told to hold him up and in direct connection with posture God repeats the promise he had already made to her that he was to become a great nation. Thus in emergency God often comes with his words of cheer to offset the gloom of the occasion. It is better to permit one to have the experience of suffering or unpleasantness and then accompany it with a sustaining grace than to favor him by entire freedom. So we are told of the experience of

Paul as recorded in 2 Cor. 12: 8, 9. Instead of removing the thorn God gave him the support of his grace.

Verse 19. *Opened.* This is from a word meaning "to be observant." Thus the well was in seeing distance and range all the time but she had not observed it until God called her attention to it. The anguish of mind would be enough for this mother here to overlook all else than what was in line with her son who was dying yonder.

Verse 20. Becoming an archer would fit in appropriately with the wilderness in which he lived with his mother. And this kind of dwelling place was in keeping with the prediction that had been made of him before he was born.

Verse 21. It was very natural for his mother to select an Egyptian for a wife for him since she was of that nation herself. See Chapter 16: 3.

Verses 22-24. Our story now comes back to Abraham who is dwelling in the land of Abimelech, and by his invitation as seen in previous chapter. The prestige that Abraham has with the king of Gerar is such that he wishes to assure himself of his own satisfaction in the future. So he requests some formal stipulation touching their mutual relations. Abraham agrees and joins him with an oath that was to bind each to the welfare and peace of the other.

Verses 25, 26. But it was not long until Abraham thought the agreement between them had been violated. He complained that a well of his had been taken possession of by his servants through violence. But Abimelech explains that he knew nothing about the circumstance. He also makes a mild complaint that Abraham had not informed him about this sooner, implying that he would have made proper adjustment had he known it.

Verses 27-32. A strengthening of the peace ties between them is now sought in a more formal act than had been used before. And to give visible indication that the well belonged to Abraham he devotes things of value, sheep and oxen, to the possession of Abimelech. In other words, Abraham is willing to go "more than half way" in his willingness to make all things right and to show that he is not wanting to obtain something for nothing. And the extra seven lambs set apart to themselves constituted merely an additional formal ceremony to make the covenant binding. The whole action gives us a lesson of unselfishness on the part of Abraham. It teaches that in matters of material interest and where no moral principle is involved, it is better to give the other fellow the benefit of the doubt, even if it makes me the loser. This kind of principle is what Paul taught in 1 Cor. 6: 7.

Verses 33, 34. The text says that Abraham planted a grove. But the margin says "tree." The lexicon gives us for "grove" the word ESHEL which is defined "a tamarisk tree."—Strong. The word has been rendered in the A.V. in various places by both tree and grove. The context would need to be considered in each case. But we know that in the Patriarchal Dispensation the only visible headquarters to represent God in worship was an altar. See chapter 8: 20; 12: 7; 13: 18; 22: 9 and many others. It is necessary to infer that this tree was as a location and shelter for the altar and thus that a single tree is meant in this place. Later on, when God's people came into their promised land and found it infested with idolaters and that they had their groves planted and arranged for the purpose of this heathen worship, God told them to destroy these groves. But the only formal calling on the name of God in those times was in connection with an altar, and that could be built in any convenient place, whether under a tree, on a hill or some other place. Abraham's sojourn was continued in the Philistine land many days. This was in accordance with the invitation which the king of the land gave him. (Chapter 20: 15.)

GENESIS 22

Verse 1. *Tempt.* This is from NACAH and defined "a primitive root; to test; by implication to attempt." — Strong. The word has been rendered elsewhere in the Old Testament by, adventure, essay, prove, try. All this agrees with the way Paul words it as given in Heb. 11: 17. He says he was "tried." James says that God cannot be tempted "with evil." (1: 13.) Then adds "neither tempteth he any man." But the connection shows it means neither tempts he any man with evil. But here is a case where God is going to try Abraham's faith.

Verse 2. The wording of this verse is in keeping with the thought just discussed in the preceding verse. Many things are said here that could not have been said as a matter of information only. Abraham knew he had only one son of promise. He already knew the name of that son. And he did not need to be told that he loved him. Yet all these expressions are made to him. It thus cannot be said that Abraham plunged into obedience at the command of God before he realized the enormity of it. The critic might have said that after receiving the command and even after the instant of starting to obey, on second thought he was sure to reconsider and hesitate. But all these endearing thoughts are placed before him at the same time of the command. So that all the while he was making his preparations he was aware of the fact that the command involved this beloved son of his. That it was his only son as far as the great promise is concerned. That a miracle had been performed in the first place to make this son possible. That although he had a son by his slave, yet God had already stipulated that the promise is to be fulfilled through this only son. Therefore, the only way to account for his unswerving obedience here is in his abiding faith in God and his power to perform any promise he should make. And thus his actions here cannot be laid to any lack of love for his son nor to any underrating of the value of the same. And the strain of going through with the ordeal of slaying his son, even while firmly believing that he would again immediately be restored to him again must be considered as great. But all of the exaggerating speeches that have been made by speculators in describing the awful anguish that this father must have suffered at the thought of having to give up his only son and also be a disappointed and fatherless man the rest of his life—all such is to imply that Abraham did not believe that his son was to be restored to him again. *Land of Moriah*. This would seem to be an indefinite location. But the name is found in only one other place besides this and the lexicon defines the word as being a specific mount. But from the view point of Abraham's location now the particular point at which the offering was to be made would be designated to him later on. And the offering was not to be one that merely would separate him from his son, but it was to be a "burnt" offering. This would require that his son be slain. Not only so, but he must do the slaying himself, all of which makes this test a complete one.

Verse 3. But he is going to stand the test. He does not delay unnecessarily. He arises early in the morning and prepares for the journey. All things needed for the service are taken as they journey.

Verse 4. Somewhere along the journey God told him his destination, for it says he saw the place afar off.

Verse 5. They are now as near the scene of the service as the servants need to be. They are commanded to tarry at that place with the beast. And here is the statement that expresses Abraham's faith in the restoration of his son to him. Not only that he will live again, but it will not be any great length of time, for he expects these servants to be waiting when they return. Notice carefully the wording. He says "I and the lad" when mentioning the ones to go and worship and does not change the subject of his sentence when he says "come again" to you. All this shows he believed that his son would return woth him. This faith as to the restoration of his son was what made him proceed as described at verse 2 above. *Worship*. This is from SHACHAH and defined "a promitive root; to depress, i. e., prostrate (especially reflexively in homage to royalty or God):" — Strong. This definition of the word certainly is appropriate in its various parts. The service will undoubtedly be one of natural depression and yet one of respect to God else it would not be offered.

Verse 6. We do not know how old Isaac was at this time. But we know he was old enough to carry the wood necessary for the amount of fire used in burning a body. As an additional clew we may consider that in previous chapter Ishmael is old enough to be given a wife. It is true that he was 14 years older than Isaac. But at that, he would still have been enough older that it would leave enough years to give Isaac and make him a lad of some years. Furthermore, he is old enough to reason on matters before him as will be seen in next verse. And yet with all this, we have not the slightest intimation that he resisted his father's attempts to make a sacrifice of him. Sometimes a reply to this is attempted by saying he must have resisted since his father had to bind him. But this is an unthoughtful quibble. The strength he would have needed to bind him would have been enough for him to slay him.

Verse 7. Of course Isaac had often seen his father perform the service of the altar and knew there must be the victim. At present all things are at hand except the beast. Thus the question he asked his father in this verse is a logical one.

Verse 8. When the conversation of this verse took place Abraham did not yet know that he was not to slay his son. And we must not explain his answer to Isaac as in the nature of evasion or "stalling" for that would be entirely out of harmony with his wonted frankness and he would also have known that the evasion would soon be known. The statement therefore must be understood, when considered on the basis of elimination, as follows. He expected to slay his son and burn him. Next he expected to see him raised out of the ashes alive and both of them return to the men and to their home. But all this would be possible only through the miraculous intervention of God. And by doing all this which would retain the plan to make a great nation of Abraham through this particular son, at the same time allow the use of that son for the present occasion, it would literally be God who was literally providing himself a living body for a sacrifice. The only feature of the remark that might be considered not literal is in calling Isaac a lamb. And yet, since a lamb was a young of the animal, Isaac could be called a lamb without too much of a strain on the meaning of the word. It has been suggested by some expositors that Abraham was speaking by inspiration and that he really looked forward to the offering of God's son as a sacrifice. But this is a speculation. Nothing of that sort is ever afterward attributed to him. We may be permitted to say that the words of Abraham were fulfilled in the sacrifice of Christ. But that would be our observation without any specific statement of the inspired writing for a basis. All moralizers on the things of the scriptures should be careful not to confuse their own comparisons drawn from circumstances striking their interests with the ones authorized by the scriptures themselves. Neither may we explain this verse by supposing that Abraham was inspired as a prophet and saw beforehand the ram caught in the thicket. For in that case he would have known that his son was not actually to be slain. And that would have prevented an inspired man from saying what we read in Heb. 11: 19.

Verse 9. Why did Abraham bind his son if he was not resisting? Well, we might ask why men are bound when they are about to be executed? The rope or gun or current would produce death just as certainly without the binding. But decency and the feeling calling for as little disorder as possible suggests the binding. After the death stroke would have been delivered the body would involuntarily resist death and put up a struggle that would have interrupted the procedure of the sacrifice. Hence it was the decent thing to do. And of course so far no fire has been applied to the wood. That would be done after the victim was dead.

Verse 10. As far as Abraham was permitted to go was to reach for the knife and take it. Just how much motion toward his son had taken place we do not know.

Verses 11, 12. Here again we see an angel comes to represent the Lord. He is near enough that he can be heard from the sky and intercedes to stay the slaying. The reason given why he will not be required to go farther is that *now I know*, etc. This expression must be understood in the light of God's usual dealing with man. In the physical sense of knowledge God knows everything. But as it regards man's credit with God, he does not know anything until we show him. We must show it by our works. This is the same principle taught in James 2: 18. In fact that writer refers to the very instance we here have under consideration as illustration of his point.

Verse 13. This verse was referred to briefly above. We can see many items in this case that make comparisons; and we may go ahead and make such comparisons. But no inspired writer has referred to this circumstance in that sense and we should be slow to make more out of it than the inspired writers have made.

Verse 14. The name of the place where this service was performed is Moriah. But Abraham gave it a symbolical name and the margin says the word means "the Lord will provide." The lexicon gives about the same definition. If that is the true meaning of the word it can easily be seen why he gave it this name. An unexpected provision has here been made for the situation and this suggests a name with an appropriate meaning. But again let not the reader conclude that Abraham had this in mind when he made the answer he did to his son's inquiry. See again comments at verse 8.

Verse 15. This calling to Abraham the second time out of heaven means as regards the service in this mount, for he had spoken to him many more times than two.

Verses 16-18. Here are two of the original promises repeated to Abraham, that of becoming a numerous nation and of the seed that was to bless the whole world. *Heaven.* This is the second heaven and referred to in chapter 1: 20. You may see 1 Kings 8: 30 for the third. *Possess the gate of his enemies.* This prediction was fulfilled in the book of Joshua. Referring to the "gate" of the enemy is in view of the fact that most important cities were walled and had to be occupied by entering through the gate. And of course that could not be done without military victory.

Verse 19. The original party now returns and Abraham takes up his residence at Beer-sheba. This word means "the well of the oath" and has been rendered noted by some pacts formed in connection with it. See chapter 21: 24-31.

Verses 20-23. Just a little family record that is of interest to us because of two names that will be brought before us more prominently after this. They are Bethuel and Rebekah. In this group we can see the blood kinship of the ones connected with the later history of Abraham's descendants.

Verse 24. Here is the first mention of a concubine. It is sometimes thought that a concubine must be thought of as an immoral mistress. But in those olden times when plurality of wives was tolerated as lawful this view of a concubine cannot be correct. Therefore we must conclude that the principal difference between a concubine and a "wife" is one of temporal or property difference. Their property rights were not equal to those of a wife. In fact, so close to the wife in meaning is the word that they are sometimes spoken of as a man's wives. As an instance, in 2 Sam. 16: 22 we read that Absalom went in to his father's concubines. But in 20: 3 of that book, when David came to punish them it says they were left to live in "widowhood." That term could apply only in the sense of having been a wife.

GENESIS 23

Verses 1, 2. The age of Sarah at death is the principal fact to mark at this passage. It had been 62 years since she left her native land. See 12: 4 and 17: 17.

Verse 3. These sons of Heth were some of the early inhabitants of Canaan and descended from Ham.

Verse 4. This land rightfully belongs to Abraham since it was appropriated to him in the Lord's mind when he told him to leave his native land for a land that he would show him. But God intends that the people of the patriarch shall possess it after a military struggle. And pending that event he will allow these invaders to hold a form of possession in it. And as long as that is the case Abraham will not be satisfied to have permanent use of it without due compensation. Hence he proposes to buy it. And notice the statement that he wishes to bury his dead out of his sight. There is no indication that God intended for human beings to be disposed of after death other than by some form of burial, not by cremation.

Verses 5, 6. The conversation here shows that Abraham had a good standing among these heathen people. They recognized his greatness and willingly offered the use of their burying places for his dead. Even would allow him to take his choice. This recommends him to our consideration as a man of such righteous principles as to produce a good influence among the people.

Verses 7-9. Abraham avails himself of their offer to the extent of making his choice of places he wishes to use. It is the cave of Machpelah. But he still insists that it is to be transferred to him upon a set price. He does not ask any concession from the actual value of the place. In other words, he will not abuse his standing among them by even seeking to obtain the land at some "reduction" of price. Instead, he says he wants it to be made over to him for as much "as it is worth."

Verses 10, 11. The present holder of the property still insists on giving it to him. There is no reason to doubt the sincerity of his motives. But Abraham is taking a practical view of the matter. He knows that time will bring changes in the personnel of the ownership of this land. That future proprietors might not have the same feeling of friendship for him as the present ones have and then a difficulty might arise that would be very embarrassing if not damaging. So the wise thing, even for all concerned, would be to have a clear understanding now and to place that in such a position that it would be fixed. Hence he is going to insist further on his plan.

Verses 12, 13. But while he so insists, he is very courteous and bows himself to the people according to eastern custom. And let it be also observed that he makes his proposition "in the audience of the people." To have witnesses of an important transaction is always best and Abraham here takes care to have this in this case.

Verses 14, 15. Ephron finally names the amount the land is worth and the text says it was "current" money. This word is from ABAR and defined "to cross over; used very widely of any transition * * * specifically, to cover." —Strong. The meaning is that it was legal money and that in common circulation at the time and with merchants. In other words, Ephron does not take any advantage of Abraham's urgent need of the place, or make use of that popular, but vicious basis for setting a price namely, "the law of supply and demand." But honestly states the commercial "worth" of the property, not what he might be able to get for it. And he only does this at Abraham's insistence since he would willingly have given it to him without cost. *What is that betwixt me and thee.* This means that he thinks such a thing as the commercial worth of the land is a small matter to stand between such good friends as they. So therefore he plans for Abraham to obtain his wishes in this case and to be able to bury his dead.

Verse 16. There is no complaint at the price for it is that which the land is worth. And the payment is made in the audience of the people. This means in their hearing and so that not only could they see what was being done but they heard the words of the contract. This is just a continuation of the principle on which Abraham has been dealing throughout this whole procedure.

Verses 17-20. The same form of dealing continues to the end of this action and the writer tells us twice that the property was made "sure" unto Abraham. We do not know of any formal courts of record nor other recording establishments among those ancient people. Hence the items of permanency available were the fact that it was done "in the presence of the children of Heth" and also "before all that went in at the gate of his city." An important fact in this entire transaction is that property was made "sure" unto Abraham. This means that its title passed from one owner to another. And this contradicts a theory often expressed in the political world in regards to ownership of property. It would be out of place in a work such as the present one to mention a matter that is supposed to be a political one did not its advocates claim the Bible as a supporting document for them. They contend that the Bible does not endorse the practice of title or private ownership to property. But the present case disproves their contention for Abraham, the father of the faithful, the beginning head of a great people of God, was careful to obtain title to private ownership and the inspired writer says the land was made "sure" to him.

GENESIS 24

Verse 1. While Abraham is now in the years of old age (stricken in age merely means he had entered into old age) yet the writer tells us he was in the blessing of God. So we see that no intention is present to make us have the impression he is infirm with his age. The fact that later he remarries and begets six sons would show us that his physical forces are not yet denied him. But even at that, he knows that it is time for him to be making some of his plans come to maturity.

Verse 2. The act of putting the hand under the thigh is a custom of that time and is a figurative expression of a willingness to support one in his desires. And the business at hand is so important that he selects the most trustworthy of his servants, one that had already proved himself in that he had been caring for all of the household affairs of his master.

Verses 3, 4. The inhabitants of the land among whom Abraham is dwelling were of a different stock from that of the pure line which God would use in making the great nation he had promised to the patriarch. And while it is the Lord's direction that he is not to live in his native land, yet he is to continue the same line of blood. So it will be necessary to get in contact with his former people. But to do this he must not go there in person nor permit his son to do so. That would be disobeying the spirit of the first command for him to get out of his country and away from his people. The contact must be made by one not personally involved in the command.

This is why he now brings his most trusted servant into the arrangement.

Verse 5. It has been charged against the Bible that it teaches and favors the idea that woman is a mere tool of man. That she is treated without any consideration for her own wishes in the matter of marriage and personal service to man. But we see in this language of the servant that such was not the prevailing impression with him. Had such been the case he would never have thought of mentioning the woman's attitude with regard to the plan. Whether she were willing or not would not have been taken into consideration at all according to this false charge mentioned above. It is true that the woman was made for the man as Paul so teaches (1 Tim. 2: 13), and man is to be the aggressor in their relations with each other. But that does not mean that she is to be treated as a mere possession of man without being due any consideration.

Verse 6. While Isaac was not born in the original land yet he was born of parents from that country. Hence he must not be brought to that country.

Verse 7. Abraham's faith in God has not abated in all these years. He has gone through many experiences and many which were strong tests of his faith. And in them all he has recognized the presence of the Almighty. And now he is still assured that his obedience to the divine plan will bring the angelic assistance needed. Thus he tells the servant that he will be successful in his mission.

Verse 8. Here again Abraham charges his servant not to take his son to that land. Marriage is important and he is eager to have it attended to for his son. Yet it is not important enough to justify setting aside another part of the divine plan. If the woman is unwilling to come with the servant then his duty will have been performed and his oath cleared. But under no circumstances may he take Isaac back to that place. Just why this was the restriction in this case but not in that of Jacob later we do not know. But it is a fact that at the time now being considered the family had not yet been enlarged much from what it was when Abraham left his native land. While in the time of Jacob it had done so. But further than this suggestion we are not certain why God suffered some things at one time that he would not at another.

Verse 9. The servant makes the gesture of good will and places his hand under the thigh of his master and gives the oath.

Verse 10. In making such a long journey as was here contemplated and of such uncertain duration, it was wise to make ample provision for the journey, both ways. Thus the servant is provided with a sufficient train of beasts of burden as well as with goods that might be needed for the mission. It is stated that he went to the city of Nahor in Mesopotamia. This agrees with the statement in Acts 7: 2 and therefore we are to understand that the Ur of the Chaldees, the place named as Abraham's native home, was in this land and not the city of a similar name and shown located in the more southern part of the region.

Verse 11. Mention of the fact that it was the time when women went forth to draw or bail water was to explain how it "happened" that the servant met the woman on his arrival at the place. Of course the believers in divine providence for those times will readily see how that it was not a happen-so as that term is popularly used. But as it would appear outwardly it would seem to be a piece of good fortune.

Verses 12-14. The minuteness of the stipulations expressed by the servant in this prayer is characteristic of providential situations. And this must not be interpreted as a wild guess of the servant as to whether he might properly appeal to God. For his master had told him that God would send his angel before him to direct his way. He has faith in the reliability of his master's instructions. This is another proof of the good influence the patriarch had exerted over his servants or any who had come into contact with him. And the servant does not want to make any mistake. He will not trust his own judgment in the selection of a wife for Isaac. He might put his choice on a well favored woman, from all outward appearances, and yet not get the one that would meet with the approval of God. He thus places his success in this matter on the wisdom of his master's God. And by making so many items in his description or by naming so many "clews" it will be more certain that he will not make any mistake in his acceptance of a woman. It is interesting to note the unselfishness of the servant in this prayer. He is not concerned much as to whether he receives personal satisfaction in the outcome but asks for kindness for his master Abraham. And if the signs which he names are carried out it means to him that the damsel is the one that "thou hast appointed." Thus his belief that the God of his master is to have a hand in the selection of a wife for Isaac.

Verses 15, 16. No time was lost. The damsel of whom we read in chapter 22: 22, 23 came out to where he was. *Fair.* This is from TOBE and defined by the simple word "good." But since the text adds the words "to look upon" we have the idea that she was good to look at, or, using a common expression, she was "goodlooking." No man had "known" her which we already have learned means that she was a virgin.

Verses 17-21. She proceeds to carry out the exact program that the servant had stipulated in his prayer just as if she were a party to the whole transaction, knowingly. Of course we know she was wholly unaware of the signification of what she was now doing. On her part it was purely an act of courtesy and hospitality. But it exhibits the traits of a very sweet tempered girl. This was no small service that she performed here. She drew for all the camels and as we know, there were ten of them. Moreover, a camel takes large drinks of water. And all the while this oriental maiden was doing this kindly service the man stood wondering. He was filled with amazement at what was taking place. The word *wondering* is from SHAAH and defined "to stun, i. e., be astonished."—Strong. Of course it was altogether along lines of common courtesy for her to show some form of assistance. But to see it being carried out down to the very details of his prayer was what stunned him. *Towit.* This means "to know." That is, he was to observe her actions to the end to see if it would finally demonstrate that his master is to have his favor bestowed for which the servant had made this trip.

Verse 22. We would look upon the gift of these jewels about in the same sense as we would think of a "tip" performed for good service, because there had not yet been any conversation between them that would justify the bestowal of these articles as coming from her intended husband.

Verses 23, 24. To confirm the conclusion that the events of the last few moments had already been arrived at he asked her identity. And her answer did so confirm it. Of course that would determine the servant to make her father's house the place for his lodgment so as to carry out to completion his mission. He therefore is emboldened to ask for room with her father.

Verse 25. Her answer was favorable. And she made further offer besides what had been specified in his inquiry, and informed him there would be provender or feed for his camels. Many of the lodging places in the East were a combination of residence for people and stable for beasts and hence this combined offer of hers. This sort of combined lodging place was the kind in which Joseph and Mary found themselves at the time their child was to be born. That explains how it was possible to lay the babe in the manger at the time.

Verse 26. The man worshipped. This is from a word that means he prostrated himself in an attitude that indicated he was worshipping the Lord.

Verse 27. In this verse he gives God the credit for all his good fortune in finding a maid for his master's son. We are here informed that he "said" certain words, so that the damsel must have been a hearer of this prayer of thanksgiving.

Verse 28. Upon hearing the words of the stranger and having seen all the things that had occurred between them, she runs and tells the people of her mother's house. Of course the man is still at the well for he thus far has only the kindly invitation of the damsel. Or rather, the information she imparted to him which might not be construed as an authoritative invitation as she could not thus speak for her father.

Verse 29. But upon the information brought by Rebekah her brother Laban goes out to where the man is at the well. Another item of eastern hospitality.

Verse 30, 31. What a reception here! The brother has already acted upon the word of the sister and prepared to care for the visitor. He only knows what she has told him, and she knows only what she has heard so far. As to the relation all this had to bear to her has not been made known. Hence we know that the motives for all this hospitality are purely unselfish. Even though she heard his praise of the Lord God of his master Abraham, she would not know what that had to do with her. That fact will be made known to her and all the rest of the house later.

Verse 32. *Straw and provender.* There is little difference in the meaning between these words, but the former is somewhat coarser feed for beasts than the latter. Again an occasion of providing water to wash their feet. See the comments on this subject at chapter 18: 4. Mention also is made of these additional men at the time he started out on this journey yet it is not strange that such should be present. There were the ten camels to care for and other needs for assistance that such an important mission might bring about.

Verse 33. A meal was offered to the visitor as befitting the coming of a stranger. Not only because such was doubtless to be relished after such a journey. But it was likewise one of the customs of social recognition of those times. See Chapter 19: 3. But the man considers the subject of his errand of more importance than satisfying his hunger. Not only so, but his journey has been so successful so far and his hopes have been raised so high that something makes him feel that the conclusion of the whole thing should be brought about before relaxing to his own personal enjoyment. Besides, if he has this great matter settled satisfactorily he can enjoy the meal more. Hence he informs his hosts that he would not eat until he had told his errand. They bid him go ahead with his story.

Verses 34-49. Since the passage of these verses is virtually a rehearsal of what we have already read and considered it will not be necessary to make itemized comments on it here. But attention will be called to some of the outstanding parts of it. He begins by saying that he is a servant—Abraham's servant. Then describes the fortunate situation of his master. He also imparts the information that his master had a son born to him after his wife was old and that all his estate had been given to this son. He then describes the scene at the well and brings in the name of Rebekah. It would have been interesting to be present and observe the reaction, as expressed in the countenance of Rebekah, to this speech. Of course the part that is new is that which pertains to the purpose of this man's journey, that it was to obtain a wife for his master's son. And under the nature of the conversation Rebekah knows that she is the prospective heroine of the romance. And viewing it now in the light of her response below, we must know that her feelings through this astonishing speech of the man to her father's house were those of delicacy, surprise and pleasure. As he concludes his speech he puts the proposition up to them and intimates that if their answer is unfavorable he will go on to other parts.

Verse 50. Upon such a recitation the father and brother of the damsel recognize the hand of the Lord as being the guiding one and express an attitude of agreement.

Verse 51. They here give their consent for the match. But it must not be taken as final because later in the conversation the damsel is to be consulted also. This is according to the idea set forth at verse 5, which see.

Verse 52. Again we observe that the servant worships the Lord for the good news. This indicates that he believes the God of his master is the source from whence his success is to come, which is true always.

Verse 53. Once more we see him bestowing gifts. These are not in the form of dowry alone, but it was another custom in olden times to indicate a feeling of friendship and recognition of dignity to make gifts. This will be noted at various places.

Verses 54, 55. After tarrying over night the servant expresses a wish to go on his journey. The family members are reluctant to see them go at once. Natural ties prompt them to plead for the postponement of the departure. They set a time of ten days and wish this to be the minimum of the delay.

Verse 56. The most natural thing in the world is for the servant to be unwilling to delay. He has been so fortunate thus far that the bare possibility of there coming some kind of "hitch" in the program urges him on. So he begs them to "hinder" him not. This word is not from one that means to actually frustrate or oppose his plan. They have been so good to him and everything thus far has been with only one indication, that of favoring his mission, that he does not consider they are trying to oppose him in that sense. But the word is from a Hebrew term that merely means to loiter or lag or procrastinate. He has no doubt as to their ultimate intention of letting him go with the damsel. But he cannot bear the thought of waiting longer and insists on going and being sent away to his master.

Verses 57, 58. These verses indicate that some time in course of the morning Rebekah had retired from the group and hence the occasion of calling her. And also, this is the specific place that shows the error of the charge mentioned before as to the women of olden times having nothing to say as to their husbands. They put their reply to the plea of the servant on the condition of the word of the damsel. Accordingly they call and ask her decision. How beautiful is her answer. "I will go." Could Isaac have heard that answer he surely would have been thrilled. Here is a fair young woman asked to make a journey into a faraway land to meet a man whom she has never seen and with the purpose of becoming his wife. But we must not picture it as an act of wild adventure or a dash for romance on her part. There is not that much uncertainty in the case. She has already seen and heard enough since this servant came under her observation to be convinced that he is no fraud. That he truly represents a great master whose only son seeks her for a wife. It is to be an honor bestowed on her and in the spirit of sweet femininity and respectful cooperation in a divine plan that she is willing to leave father and mother and be joined to her husband. And in this spirit of attitude she makes the simple but complete answer "I will go."

Verses 59, 60. And with a family blessing and with appropriate provisions they send her away with the triumphant missionary, who, unlike the poet's character, was true to his friend, his master's father and son. The wish expressed by the family that Rebekkah become the mother of millions and that they possess the gate of their enemy is characteristic of those people and times. But is also prophetic of actual events to come whether they realized it or not.

Verse 61. Mention is made of Rebekah's damsels. This is from NAHARAH and is defined "a girl (from infancy to adolescence)" — Strong. Doubtless these young girls are to accompany her as her attendants or body servants. Mention is again made of the men. Thus explaining the plural pronoun used at the beginning; also accounting for the plan of taking ten camels for the journey.

Verses 62, 63. It would be unreasonable to conclude Isaac had not been informed of the departure of the servant nor of his mission. And likewise it would be unthinkable to say he had no interest in the affair. Hence we can accept the marginal reading on the word "meditate" which says "to pray." A man usually prays on the subject in which he is the most interested. And it is significant that he went out into the field and that he went there toward evening. What an interesting situation. His father's servant has gone away to obtain for him a wife. He has been gone now long enough to be returning. Out there, all alone with his thoughts and with God, he prays. Will his prayer be answered? Look! He lifts his eyes and yonder comes a caravan of camels. They could be none other than those of his father's servant. Of course that is correct, for Rebekah recognizes Isaac from a previous word from the servant. And if they are that near of course Isaac can also recognize the retinue that belongs to his father. But see, there are additional persons in the group, for there is a beautiful young woman and some young girls. They can be meant for him without question. Yes, he is so certain of all this that he starts walking toward them.

Verse 64, 65. When Rebekah recognizes Isaac from a previous information received from the servant she gets down from the camel. Then she covers her face with a veil which was another custom in the East as a token of modesty and deference.

Verse 66. Nothing here said about Abraham. Isaac is the one who is most directly concerned in the situation at present. So the servant relates to him all that had taken place since leaving on this mission.

Verse 67. Sarah has been dead some years but her tent is now available. Isaac accepts Rebekah for his companion. He is forty years old (chapter 25: 20). He takes her into his mother's tent and "she became his wife." No ceremony, no formality. Just the carrying out of the original law of marriage as God had designated. See chapter 2: 23, 24 and notes at that place. And after she became his wife through the fleshly relation which was God's only ceremony of marriage, it says he loved her. Also that he was comforted after his mother's death. A sublime conclusion to a beautiful story.

GENESIS 25

Verse 1. We do not know exactly how old Abraham was the time he married this woman. However, since Sarah was 127 at death (chapter 23: 1), and he was ten years older (chapter 17: 17), we know he was not a young man. And yet, he was still a vigorous man which was in keeping with the general promises of God concerning him, that he was to come to his life's end in peace. For that would not only mean that he would not be beset with enemies but also that he would not be tortured with the ills of old age that often come to men in declining years.

Verses 2-4. The chief item in this passage is the name of Midian. He will be a prominent figure in the history of God's people as we will see later. But it is well to mark the place where the ancestor of that people is first mentioned. Let it be observed that the Midianites are related by blood to the descendants of Abraham, and yet they will always be considered as aliens from the line and as persistent enemies to the nation. This is in line with the idea that when God decided to have a people of his own he selected one acceptable individual, Abraham, and then restricted those who were to be recognized as that special people to the ones who were not only descendants of Abraham, but the ones coming through a particular son of his who was Isaac. And that would constitute all others, however near to him, as aliens.

Verse 5. On the basis of what is set forth in preceding paragraph, Abraham gave all that he had to Isaac. Of course this means his main estate and not that he cut his other offspring out entirely. He made personal gifts to them as will be seen soon.

Verse 6. This is the circumstance referred to above. And this is a good place to see an example of the difference between a woman who was regarded in the sense of "wife" and one who was a concubine. Morally they were the same in those days, for the concubine was not in the class of women who were classed as harlots and to whom a man would go for that purpose only. In that case he would give her money as payment or hire for her service. While a concubine was a woman whom the man kept or maintained from time to time and thus who did not receive money from her master as a specific wage for her service of intimacy to him. And yet on the other hand, she was not equal to the wife as to property rights as may be seen here in that he gave only "gifts" to the sons of these women while he gave "all that he had" to Isaac. And a further distinction is seen between Isaac and the sons of the second legal wife from this very fact of giving all to Isaac. But that is easily understood when we remember that Isaac was his first son by promise and the one whom God chose to be his heir both as to property and in the fulfillment of the great promises of the far-off future. Attention is called to the statement here that Abraham gave these gifts to the sons "while he yet lived." We may consider this as a sure way of seeing that they get this benefit by not waiting for a will to give it to them after his death.

Verses 7, 8. Here is the place to mark the age of Abraham. *Full of years*. The reader will see the words "of years" are in italics and thus are not in the original. The first word in italics is from SABEA and defined "satiated (in a pleasant or disagreeable sense)."—Strong. Of course the context will require the favorable part of the definition. Therefore the expression merely means that Abraham's life had been full and satisfactory, all of which again coincides with the promise to him. *Was gathered to his people*. This is simply an ancient way of saying that a person had joined his relation who had gone on before. It would sometimes have a specific reference to the place of burial which doubtless may be applied in this case.

Verses 9, 10. Abraham now had many sons, but the writer lets us know which of his sons took charge of the body of their father, Isaac and Ishmael. The last named would be nearer than any of the others after him because he was born through the plan of his father's first legal wife. And it is noteworthy that the burial took place in the grave that Abraham had secured by the contract recorded in Chapter 23: 18-20.

Verse 11. Mention that God blessed Isaac after the death of Abraham must not be construed to mean that he had not been blessed before, for he had. But all the way down the years it will be noted that God kept a tender memory of the patriarch and did many things to his descendants for his sake. And that memory was finally crystallized around the three first fathers, Abraham, Isaac and Jacob.

Verse 12. *Generations*. This is from a word that has as one of its meanings "a family history." The writer is careful here to tell us which of Abraham's many sons he is considering. It is the son of the handmaid. Also he lets us know that she was an Egyptian. We are to understand, therefore, that the nation descending from this son will be aliens as to the main line, and yet near enough not to be considered in the same sense as others.

Verses 13-16. After telling us the names of the sons of Ishmael the writer sums up by saying "twelve princes." This was in fulfillment of the promise the Lord had made to Hagar in chapter 17: 20. To be a prince in those days did not necessarily have any political or official significance. Its central meaning was that of any kind of exaltation. *According to their nations.* The last word in italics is from UMMAH and defined "a collection, i. e., community of persons."—Strong. So the word is different from the one from which the word "nation" usually comes. Here it is more restricted and has the idea that these twelve sons were each outstanding men in their respective communities. And this agrees also with one of the characteristics predicted of their common parent, Ishmael, that he was to be separate from the people in general. So that while the descendants of Ishmael became very numerous yet they were known as people without a fixed habitation and were a roaming people.

Verse 17. Take note of the death of Ishmael and his age at the time. Also the statement that he was gathered to his people. See comments at verses 7, 8.

Verse 18. The most prominent part of this verse is the statement as to the place where Ishmael died. In chapter 16: 12 it was predicted that he was to dwell in the presence of all his brethren. Now if he died in the presence of all his brethren it is evident that he had dwelled there which fulfills the prediction.

Verses 19, 20. Some more family history, this time of Isaac. The age he had reached, forty, when married is worthy of noting. Since we know he was born when his mother was ninety years of age (chapter 17: 17) and as his mother was 127 at death (chapter 23: 1) we can here conclude that his mother had been dead three years when he was married. And he had been occupying his mother's tent after her death as a mourner. But when Rebekah came to be his wife he took her into that same tent and was comforted as is said in chapter 24: 67. Isaac's father-in-law, Laban, is here said to be a Syrian. Sometimes people carelessly think and speak of Abraham as a native Jew, whereas he was a Syrian as we here observe. But we must not confuse this term with the one of which we hear so much in later history of the Bible. This is really a short word for Assyria and referred to the country pertaining to Mesopotamia. While Syria proper embraced a larger territory including first that north of Palestine with Damascus as capital, and later all the country including Palestine. See Rawlinson, *Origin of Nations*, p. 234.

Verse 21. Isaac and Rebekah had been married about twenty years and no children had come to them. He then prayed to God on the matter and his prayer was heard. It is interesting to recall that Sarah, the mother of Isaac, was also barren and required a miracle from the Lord to enable her to conceive. In those days it was generally considered a reproach not to be able to have children and in such circumstances the ones thus unfortunate would appeal to God.

Verse 22. We know not how much knowledge Rebekah had on the experience of being an expectant. The ordinary "quickening" that is present in all cases might have been nothing strange to her mind. But that movement in this case was greater and of a different violence than was to be expected. The original word for "struggle" is defined "to crack, literally or figuratively." Hence we will have the conclusion that a very unusual movement, even for twins, was going on in her body. This caused her to become concerned and decided to enquire of the Lord as to "why am I thus?"

Verse 23. Here one of the famous predictions of the Bible is made, one that will be referred to in later places or dates. *Elder, younger.* The original words for these, both in the Old Testament and the New, have as their fundamental meaning that of more or greater as contrasted with less or smaller. But the dictionary admits the idea of greater or less in years or other terms of age. Thus the context in this present case gives us the idea that it means the one to be born first will serve the other. And this was fulfilled in at least one specific instance recorded in 2 Sam. 8: 14. No reason is here assigned for this choice. And even in the New Testament (Rom. 9: 11) where this circumstance is discussed by Paul the reason for the choice is not given. Only that he gives us to understand that it was not based on their conduct since the decision was made before they could have done either good or evil.

Verse 24. *Days to be delivered.* See note on this expression at Chapter 17: 21.

Verse 25. *Esau.* The original word is defined "rough (i. e., sensibly felt)." The meaning is that he was rough to the touch and this was caused by the hairy condition of his body.

Verse 26. *Jacob.* The original of this is defined "heel-catcher (i. e., supplanter)." Of course we know this circumstance was not usual and neither was it a mere accident. But God had already decreed that Jacob should supplant Esau and this physical signal would be brought about as a beginning of the fulfillment. The age of Isaac when his twin sons were born is here given which should be marked.

Verse 27. *Cunning.* This is from YADAH and defined "to know (properly to ascertain by seeing)." It is a word with a wide variety of meanings but the idea as used here is that Esau understood his business as a hunter. *Plain.* This is from TAM and defined "complete; usually (morally) pious; specifically, gentle, dear."—Strong. As a general thing we think of the word "plain" as meaning the very thing that Esau was here; a man of rugged habits such as those of the field. But here it is Jacob who is said to be a plain man. But the original word explains it. He was content to dwell indoors and do house work such as cooking.

Verse 28. But while Esau did not make a practice of cooking and other domestic work, yet being a hunter he had occasion to do enough of such work to take care of the product of his occupation. The reason given here why Isaac loved Esau is that he ate of his venison. But we are not told the reason for Rebekah's preference. But whatever the cause might have been, this partiality between the parents for the sons will be the occasion of serious trouble.

Verse 29. *Sod pottage.* This expression merely means that he boiled articles in a pot. This may have been soup or other articles adapted for such cooking. Esau came in one day very faint, so much so that he thought he was going to die. He asked Jacob for some of his pottage. It was evidently not the first time he had ever eaten of it for he makes the expression below "*that same red pottage.*" But this time, as Jacob sees the almost helpless condition of his brother he takes advantage of it. This is another instance where the principle of "supply and demand" is resorted to and, as always, is seen to be an unrighteous principle.

Verse 30. Here is where Esau makes the pitiful request for his brother to feed him. The word "pottage" in this verse is not in the original but the word "red" is. Jacob had been in the habit of making various kinds of red soup or other preparations that were acceptable to a hungry man, especially when very weak. Hence he asks for some of the same red food he had served him before. And because he expressed strong preference for that particular diet this time he was given a name with accompanying meaning which was Edom. The definition of this word in the lexicon is "red." Popular notion has it that the elder brother of Jacob was called Edom because he was covered with red hair when born. But the text says he was called that because of his request for this red food at the time he was so faint. And since this red material was the occasion for his act in transferring his birthright, which also was a most important subject of history, it seemed appropriate to have the name Edom, meaning red, to be with him throughout the history. Whether God had all these facts in mind and caused the babe to be born with such colored hair as another significant feature of the whole situation we cannot say without speculation. But we are given the direct statement of the inspired writer that after Esau had called for the red food that "therefore" was his named called Edom.

Verse 31. *Birthright.* Reversing the form of this word we may get the meaning of the word, and that is, the right of birth. And that further means the right a person has by reason of being the firstborn in the family. He would have first right to his father's property. And in those times, it placed him first in the family tree in relation to whatever spiritual advantages that were in store for the family. And therefore it was an important possession. Jacob sees the plight of his brother and decides to take advantage of it.

Verse 32. Jacob did not reckon amiss. Esau figures that it is a situation where he has nothing to lose by selling the birthright. He believes that without food he is going to die soon and he would lose all that he possessed anyway. With this view of the situation in mind he makes the deal and sells his birthright.

Verse 33. Making oaths was an established practice in those times and thus the transaction on hand here was sealed in that way. And with that kind of formality the writer tells us that Edom sold his birthright to Jacob.

Verse 34. *Lentils.* This English word occurs only four times in the A.V. and the original word is not rendered otherwise in any other place. Hence we are left to the English definition for its meaning. It refers to any podded plant or tree whose seeds are suitable for human food. *Despised his birthright.* The first word is from BAZAH and defined "to disesteem." The word is elsewhere rendered disdain, contemn. In other words, it means that he underestimated the birthright. It was a divine possession in that it entitled him not only to the possession of his father's estate, but it would have put him in line to be an ancestor of the promised seed of Abraham. This is why Paul tells us Esau was a profane person. (Heb. 12: 16.) To make a common or temporal use of a sacred thing is to profane it. That is what Esau did, hence Paul refers to him as a profane person.

GENESIS 26

Verse 1. Isaac had been dwelling in Lahairoi which is a place in the desert. (Chapter 24: 62; 25: 11.) But when this famine came upon the land he went over to the land of the Philistines, the place where his father had been once. He might have gone on down into Egypt since that country was always able to nourish in time when dearth struck other countries. But he did not go as we will see next.

Verse 2. Here the Lord tells him not to go down to Egypt. Of course this will mean that the famine is not to become general and that some country other than Egypt will be productive in this instance. So he first tells him he will direct him as to what land he is to dwell in.

Verses 3, 4. In this passage the Lord repeats the promise that had been made before and that had first been made to his father Abraham. He not only repeats to him this promise but assures him that he will be prosperous as to the present state.

Verse 5. The specific reason God is so mindful of Isaac is that his father had been so obedient to the divine laws. And for his sake he would bless his son Isaac.

Verses 6, 7. Gerar was an important Philistine city and it was at this place that Isaac was dwelling. Here the men of the place asked him about his wife. The answer which he gave them indicates they had inquired as to her relation to him, for he told them she was his sister. The lexicon says the original word here has a wide range of meanings. But the context here shows that Isaac used it as having a meaning of near blood relation. And indeed they were blood relation. According to chapter 22: 20-23 they were a degree of cousins. Isaac gave them the answer for the same reason his father had done so with his wife previously. It is said that Rebekah was *fair* to look upon. This is from the same word as that used in reference to Sarah. See the explanation of the word at Chapter 12: 11. Being thus a woman with much sex appeal he feared they would kill him so as to give access to her. They considering murder as less a crime than adultery.

Verse 8. This story was believed for a long time. We do not know how much longer it would have been received had the men not been witness to what they considered as a contradiction of the story. The text says that the king saw Isaac *sporting* with Rebekah. The word is from TSACHAQ and is the same word as rendered "laughed" at chapter 17: 17. Please turn to that place and read the definition and apply the favorable part of the definition since the context shows that Isaac was in a favorable attitude toward Rebekah. The context further indicates that the conduct was such as would be expected only between husband and wife and we must conclude that the proper rules of social conduct had been observed in those times and even among those people, else they would not have reasoned as they did. Also, this conduct of Isaac was in a rather exposed place, for the king saw it as he "looked out at a window." Therefore, if a man would be sporting with a woman in a way becoming only with his wife, and that too in such an exposed way, she must be his wife since he would not have been guilty of such a breach of etiquette with a woman who was his blood relation.

Verse 9. The explanation Isaac gave of his action,. like that of Abraham, is a little hard to understand. It seems that he wanted to save his life at the possible expense of his wife's virtue. See remarks along this line at Chapter 12: 12, 13.

Verses 10, 11. *Lightly.* This is from MEHAT and defined "a little or few (often adverbially or comparatively)." —Strong. This word has been rendered in the A.V. by "little" 51 times and by "few" 24. And since the king spoke of only one of his people as likely to have been involved, and taking the definition as well as the various uses made of it, we should conclude the king meant that one of his men might have taken the liberty to be intimate with the newcomer's sister a few times. But even though it were only a few times, yet the heathen king's sentiments on the subject are such that he would have considered it as guilt upon the nation. How different all this is from the lax conduct and attitude of mankind in modern times.

Verse 11. To make sure about such unfortunate circumstance as described in this paragraph above he gives all his people serious warning and threat concerning it.

Verses 12-14. The prosperous faring of Isaac here fulfilled the promise God made to him in verse 3 above. But the Philistines envied him this success. This is one of the human weaknesses, to envy the good fortune of others. One of the principal definitions of the word in the English dictionary is "Chagrin or discontent at the excellence or good fortune (Of another); resentful, begrudging."—Webster.

Verse 15. The previous passage made mention of Isaac's livestock of which his riches consisted. This would account for the actions of the Philistines in filling up the wells that had been digged by his father's servants. Water being an indispensable article in the keeping of cattle, his riches would wane if this were cut off.

Verse 16. The outward attitude of the king seemed a little more gentle than that of his servants. However, he had some fears of the outcome if Isaac were allowed to remain in their midst hence the request recorded here.

Verses 17-19. Isaac makes a removal but not entirely away, for mention is made of the wells referred to above and in which the Philistines took such an active but unfavorable interest. He not only reopened the wells his father had digged and had been filled by Abimelech's servants, but his servants digged a new well in the valley and found a well there of "springing water." The margin correctly gives us here the word "living." The original word has elsewhere been rendered "runnning water" a number of times. The idea is that while most wells are filled with water seeping from the ground, these others are supplied with a vein of running water and would be preferred.

Verses 20-22. This new fortune of Isaac's was too much for the envious Philistines, so they had a strife over it. But Isaac was very kind to them and moved from place to place until they ceased to strive. The name Isaac gave to this last well was one that corresponded with the circumstances. Since they did not strive for this well it indicated they decided there was room for all of them now, so the name of Rehoboth was given to the place. This is from a Hebrew word that means "avenue or area."

Verses 23, 24. *Beersheba.* This name means "well of the oath" and was made noted by the covenants formed here by Abraham and Isaac. (Chapter 21: 31; verse 33 here.) The Lord now appears to Isaac again and repeats the famous promise and adds the thought that he will bless him for the sake of his father Abraham.

Verse 25. Calling upon the name of the Lord is usually associated with the fact of building an altar. There were no general headquarters as a meeting place for God's people in this Dispensation. The family was the largest unit and its headquarters could be found wherever the family altar was erected.

Verses 26-29. Isaac continues to be prosperous in spite of the opposition of the Philistines. They now conclude that it would be better to have him for a friend than an enemy and their chief men came to him and made a proposition. At first Isaac chided them upon their past treatment of him and now are coming to him for friendship. The motive they gave for their move was a respectful one, seeing that the Lord was with him. If the desire for association with another were always based on such observation as this the world would be happier. They wish now to form a pact of mutual friendship and non-aggression.

Verses 30-33. Isaac is unresentful and makes for the group a feast. This is in keeping with the ancient custom of using the meal as a signal of friendship and social recognition. *Betimes.* This is from a word that means "early." When they arose early in the morning they repeated their oath then departed in peace. *Therefore.* This expression has been used and explained before. See chapter 18: 5. It is an odd form of expression but the gist of it is to say "very properly, or with good reason." Thus in the present instance. At first reading we might get the impression the verse means that the place was so named because these servants just now came and informed Isaac of the water. But we know that this name had been given to it before this as seen in the place referred to. But the sense of the language in the present verse is as if it said "this place is Sheba, from the meaning of the word which is oath. And very properly, therefore, is it so called ever since."

Verses 34, 35. Judith and Bashemath were Hittites and thus were Canaanites. It was not agreeable to Isaac and Rebekah for their son to marry into such blood, hence they were grieved over it. The significance of the mention made of it at this place will be more apparent in the next chapter.

GENESIS 27

Verses 1, 2. Doubtless Isaac had often eaten of the meat which his son took in hunting. He considers himself as so enfeebled with years that death may come without warning. Nevertheless he wishes to have one more enjoyment of this relished dish of his son and so makes the request following.

Verse 3. *Quiver and bow.* These mean the bow and the case for carrying the arrows. *Venison.* This is from a word that means anything taken in the chase and that might be prepared for relished food.

Verse 4. *Savoury meat.* This means a delicacy for food. It refers to the way it was prepared and not specially as to the animal used, for Isaac said "make me," etc. The expression "such as I love" is what shows that he had eaten of this before since Esau was supposed to know this favorite food of his father. The promise to bless his son carried more weight than a mere good wish. Of course a good wish is one of the meanings of the word but when a Patriarch in those times pronounced a blessing it was official and not to be changed. This again is one of the characteristics of the Patriarchal Dispensation.

Verse 5. We remember the partiality that had come between the parents over their two sons. That sentiment will soon bring about some sad experiences. She overhears what her husband had said and Rebekah resolves to defeat the plan and secure the favor for her own beloved son.

Verses 6-8. Calling her favorite to her she relates what she overheard and makes known to him that she has a plan to work out and urges before hand for him to obey her voice. That scheme of hers will be seen in next paragraph.

Verse 9. Rebekah proposes to make "savoury meat" of the flesh of the kids that Jacob is to bring to her. This shows that the form of the dish which Isaac requested refers to the manner of preparation and not to the kind of animal used, as said in verse 4 above. And it also is shown by the language here that Rebekah had previously known what it was that Isaac relished or else she could not have spoken about making the kind "such as he loved."

Verse 10. She only proposes now that he is to take this food to his father and receive the blessing. Nothing said about Isaac's physical condition and nothing about how she proposes to evade that. But the general condition of helplessness must have been very obvious since the language soon to follow indicates Jacob saw the situation.

Verses 11, 12. Jacob here refers to the difference between him and Esau as to their outward condition. And Isaac's blindness is recognized also for Jacob senses the probability that his father will depend on his sense of touch in place of his sight. This very circumstance presents a pathetic picture. Here is an aged father who is blind and must depend on another sense for his guidance. And here are his wife and son plotting to take advantage of his condition to deceive him and obtain a favor he did not intend to bestow. Not realizing the fixed nature of a Patriarchal blessing, Jacob fears that after the deception is discovered the intended blessing will be turned into a curse. Ordinarily this might have been the case.

Verse 13. Rebekah is so persistent that she even agrees to take the curse upon herself if only he will obey her voice and bring the beasts to her. A natural sentiment for us to have in this situation is one of sympathy for Jacob as we see what happens to be an attempt on her part to take advantage of his inexperience and play upon his confidence in his mother. We are apt to think of him as being a youth, perhaps, and not hardened to the ways of the world and that she should be loath to impose on him in this way. But instead of a youth Jacob was at this time a man 77 years old. The basis for this statement is in the comment at chapter 30: 25 which see. Thus there is no excuse for Jacob's actions here on the ground of his "youth."

Verses 14-17. Jacob brought the kids as his mother had directed. She uses the bodies for making the savory dish And as a deception she clothed him with the goodly raiment of Esau. This means the desirable or choice garments. As Isaac was blind, this could not have been for the appearance. But since it was the desirable garments, or, as we would express it, the clothes he had for his "good" ones, he most likely wore them more frequently. Also, this would make them more likely to retain the odor of his body which, as we shall see, was one of the items that helped deceive Isaac. She further planned her deception by placing the fur of the kids on the parts of Jacob's body that would be exposed to the touch. And, provided with this outfit Jacob goes into the presence of his father.

Verses 18, 19. He comes to his father and speaks to him. His father asks him who it was and he deliberately makes false statement both as to his identity and as to what he had done. That is, he had not really taken the game with his quiver and bow as Esau had been requested to do, but had gone to the flock and procured them. But he bids his father sit and eat of the food and bless him.

Verse 20. Something in the situation arouses the suspicions of Isaac and he asks how it came that he had this at hand so quickly. The answer of Jacob is not only false, but it is a very vile use of the providence of God. Of course it is known that God does often bring unexpected and superhuman help to his servants at times and thus it would not be unreasonable to say that such was the case here. But it was a cowardly abuse of the favor of God. Especially is this so in view of the fact that the whole transaction is an envious and lying plot of Jacob through the help of his mother. And to take advantage of Isaac's faith in the Lord to bring into effect this wickedness is one of the most deplorable circumstances on record. It is sometimes claimed that she was only bringing about the very thing that God had predicted, that Jacob was to supplant his brother. But this manner of bringing it to pass was not any part of God's plan. He does not need the crooked actions of man to help him carry out his plans, when those plans do not essentially include some such actions. The setting aside of Esau for the favor of Jacob was predicted it is true, but it was not necessary to resort to this terrible trick to bring it about. And Jacob will have many unpleasant experiences from this as we shall see.

Verse 21. The very thing happened that Jacob predicted and which Rebekah had provided for. The old man being blind it was necessary to depend on another sense, that of touch, and he requests his son to come near enough for this.

Verses 22, 23. It all came out as planned and predicted by the artful woman. Isaac felt of him and said it was the hands of Esau although the voice was that of Jacob. The sense of touch is here seen to be more impressive than that of the ear. So we have the sad picture of an old Patriarch, deprived of his sight and dependent on other senses. But the sense of hearing is still good and discerns the truth. But the sense of touch is misled by the artificial arrangement and the whole scene is one of general misleading and tricks Isaac into doing what he had not intended on doing.

Verse 24. The old man is still somewhat doubtful so he makes one more attempt to assure himself. Perhaps he had not heard distinctly the other time; perhaps something in the situation has been overlooked and that he has not made sufficient inquiry into the matter, so once more he asks, "Art thou my very son Esau?" It is difficult to understand how the son can persist in his awful plot with his envious mother upon such an anxious and endearing speech of his father. But he persists in the lie.

Verse 25. The unseeing Patriarch calls for the food to be brought near him. He is not in condition to appropriate the dish to himself without assistance, thus he asks his son to bring it near to him. But Jacob was not satisfied with the plot for the deception. He had made the statement at the first that his father might find him a deceiver and give him a curse instead of a blessing. He seems still to be uneasy about the matter, for the record states that he brought his father wine. This had not been requested as far as we know. Moreover, the English word "wine" does not always mean the fermented juice although it could be that. But the word used in this case is from YAYIN and defined "from an unused root meaning to effervesce; wine (as fermented); by implication intoxication."—Strong. We do not know that the judgment was affected by this intoxicating drink. But evidently it was the motive of Jacob to insure further his success in deceiving his father. It is the same word for wine in the case of Lot's daughters (chapter 19: 32-35) where we know the purpose was to render the judgment defective. So we are satisfied that Jacob added this article to the arrangement his mother had made and thus his own personal guilt is made still more apparent.

Verses 26, 27. The plot moves on. The aged man wishes a more affectionate embrace and asks him to come nearer and kiss him. In doing so he smelled the odor of his raiment as mentioned at verse 15 above. In recognizing this odor Isaac connects it with the occupation his son Esau had followed, that of being out in the open and roaming the fields for game. He even connects it with the blessing of the Lord.

Verses 28, 29. The deception was complete. And we will remember that it is a Patriarch who is pronouncing the following blessing. Much of it is repetition of predictions already made to his father Abraham and to him, but some added features of the blessing pertain more personally to the relations between him and his brother. Thus far doubtless Isaac thinks all things have turned out as he desired and planned. He knows his days are few and now he has been given the benediction of the final favor of his beloved son. This has brought him to the sacred work of pronouncing the blessing of a father; father not only from ordinary standpoint of flesh and blood offspring, but father in his religious capacity as head of the only unit of religious services under that Dispensation. How happily the aged man of God will now be able to pass his few remaining days or weeks. Alas!

Verses 30, 31. He is aroused from his state of joy by an intruder upon the happy scene. Esau, still unaware of what has taken place comes into the presence of his father with the real article that had been requested. He must have been glad to be now ready to deliver to his father the cherished and requested dish and then to have his blessing pronounced on him. He bids his father eat of the venison.

Verse 32. There should be no reason for him to fail to recognize the voice of Esau under ordinary circumstances. He had been with him recently and was also very familiar with his voice. But the previous deception was carried out so completely that he is thrown into some confusion. He asks who it was speaking to him and was told that it was his son; yes, his firstborn Esau.

Verse 33. *Trembled.* This is from CHARAD and defined "a primitive root; to shudder with terror; hence to fear; also to hasten (with anxiety)."—Strong. We are impressed with the terrible feelings Isaac must have experienced now. As a great flood the whole scene of the past few moments comes rushing upon his mind and he now sees as a reality what he had suspected at times while the plot was being carried out. When he asks "who?" it is not to be taken as meaning an actual inquiry. He knows the true identity of both persons who have been acting out a plot with him as the victim. But under the spell of the shock he involuntarily exclaims "who?" He then announces that another had come before him and given him food. He calls it venison. We know it was the meal prepared from the kids. But we also have learned that the savory meat could be prepared from various animals so that no mistake is made here by Isaac on that point. But thus far nothing is said about whether Isaac doubts the statement of Jacob that the Lord had helped him get the meat. If he has, yet his son has made a deceptive use of it and has secured the blessing. And the stern part of the situation is the fact that when a Patriarch pronounces a blessing on a person, the blessing is sure. Especially when the blessing is itself a righteous one and the person receiving it is the right one. The thing that is not right in this instance is the manner in which the man received it even though it was divinely intended that he should ultimately have that kind of priority. But he will suffer for it even though he is permitted to go on with the possessing of it. The fixed assurance of the blessing here pronounced is indicated by the words of Isaac "yea, and he shall be blessed."

Verse 34. Even in his shaken state of mind Esau does not at first manifest any concern over the fortune of his brother, only concern about himself. He does not ask that the blessing be taken from his brother but that he "also" receives a blessing. The word "cried" is from a word that means "shrieked." The passage would properly be rendered "shieked with a great and bitter shriek."

Verse 35. *Subtilty.* This is from MIRMAH and defined "in the sense of deceiving; fraud."—Strong. The English word "subtilty" does not necessarily require fraud or falsehood. It rather carries the sense of being acutely alert and of the ability to make fine discriminations. It might be possible to use the quality without dishonesty. But according to the lexicon's definition of the Hebrew word here it requires fraud. And since we know the means which Jacob and his mother used to accomplish their purpose we would understand the word here to have the sense of fraud.

Verse 36. *Jacob.* This is from YAAQOB and defined "heel-catcher (i. e., supplanter)." Esau therefore expresses the conclusion that his brother has a name that is true to his practice. We do not know whether he had learned about the circumstances that took place at the time of their birth. If so, he knew that the immediate position of the twins in course of the birth would accord with the name given to his brother. That is, the name "heel-catcher" would be a literal meaning of the word as exemplified by the incidents at the birth. But that it then meant anything prophetic is not clear as nothing is said about it at that time. But now after the events of the present occasion Esau sees a very appropriate reason why he should have the name Jacob, for he had actually supplanted him twice. He accuses Jacob of taking away his birthright and the writer lets the statement go into the record without censure. We might be inclined to say he made a misstatement since he had himself actually made a bargain with his brother that involved exchange of the birthright. And yet again, as the statement stands in the record without any criticism we look for the justness of it. And we will find it. While it is true that Esau sold his birthright in a plain bargain in which he was fully aware of what was being bartered away, yet it is also true that his brother took unmerciful advantage of the plight of his elder brother and under this pressure obtained what he could not have done under normal conditions. It should be observed here that any benefit obtained under pressure is obtained unrighteously. Now, after his remarks concerning the action of Jacob he turns to his father with the view of further inquiry. His father is a Patriarch and perhaps he has not exhausted his store of blessings and even yet will be able to bless him.

Verse 37. Isaac then repeats the gist of the blessing he had just pronounced upon Jacob and speaks as if Esau is still seeking for the one given his brother. After naming the principal items of that blessing he asks what he expected could be done for him after all this.

Verse 38. Esau persists but expresses himself in a manner that indicated he was not expecting to have his brother's blessing revoked. But puts the matter clearly up to his father whether a Patriarch is limited to giving one blessing. Then he repeats the pitiful plea he had made at first. Not that Jacob's blessing is to be recalled. Not that he is to have a blessing even like it. But just to have some blessing. Just "bless me also, O my father" and then emphasizes his request with weeping.

Verses 39, 40. Then Isaac is prevailed upon to give a blessing to Esau. But the reader will observe that it will in no way conflict with the one pronounced upon this brother. It will have some relation to his brother but will not set aside that promised to Jacob. *Fatness.* This is from MASHMAN and defined "fat, i. e., (literally and abstractly) fatness; but usually (figuratively and concretely) a rich dish, a fertile field, a robust man."—Strong. The meaning here is that he will be somewhat at large but will have access to the best of the natural products of the earth. *By thy sword shalt thou live.* Since power in those days was enforced by the sword it would indicate some ruling power was to come to him. And this we find fulfilled in Chapter 36: 31. *Shalt serve thy brother.* This was fulfilled in chapter 8: 14 of 2 Sam. *Shalt break his yoke from off thy neck.* This was fulfilled in 2 Kings 8: 20.

Verse 41. The feeling now existing in Esau's heart against Jacob is very evil. He plans to kill Jacob but does not intend to do so while his father lives. Since he has been his father's favorite son he naturally feels favorably toward him and wishes to spare him the grief that would be brought to him by the violent death of his son. Hence he intends to wait until the death of his father has come and the period of mourning that was customary had passed.

Verse 42. The previous verse says that Esau "said in his heart" that he would slay his brother. But here we see that Rebekah was told the words of Esau. Thus we can see a striking instance of the fruit of the heart. The Bible all along makes much of the thoughts of the heart as being what sooner or later comes out in fruit. Here is a man plotting in his heart to slay his brother. This exactly gives us a case in point that was spoken by Christ in Matt. 15: 20. There the Saviour declares that out of the heart comes murder. While Esau never accomplished his murderous desire and intention it was there in his heart. Finally his heart expressed itself in words and the words were carried to Rebekah. She then calls her favorite son and relates the situation to him. *Comfort.* One meaning Strong gives of this word is "avenge." The thought would be that in planning to take vengeance on his brother he would find comfort.

Verses 43, 44. She advises him to flee from home and go to their homeland and be with her brother. He is to be there until the heat of his brother has subsided. She did not judge amiss when she expected the fury of Esau to pass away for it never was manifested again after this date.

Verse 45. She repeats the statement about the anger of Esau. That it will turn away. When that occurs she promises to send him word and have him return. But she never sent him any such word for, even at the time twenty years later, when Jacob is returning to his former home he is still afraid of him. This indicates that Rebekah never got any information to Jacob. In fact, after this chapter we hear nothing more of the immediate history of Rebekah and she passes from our horizon except as she is referred to by later writers and then only historically. *Why should I be deprived also of you both in one day?* This statement was made in view of the law of capital punishment that God had announced after the flood. (Chapter 9: 6.) The connection there shows that when a person commits murder his life must also be taken in punishment. Now if Esau kills Jacob she will be deprived of him. Then when Esau is executed for his murder she will be deprived of him, and so would be deprived of both her sons.

Verse 46. Rebekah still makes use of her arts. It is probable that she would truthfully say she did not want her son to marry into the inferior blood of the people near them. Esau had done that (chapter 26: 34, 35) and both she and her husband had grieved over it. So how plausibly she expresses her anxiety to Isaac. Of course we will not overlook the fact that her anxiety concerning her son's marriage had not expressed itself until this other affair of her plotting. Nevertheless, it has such a reasonable basis that it makes the desired impression on her husband as we will see in next chapter. But we will here think of her idea of getting the cooperation of her husband in this matter. Were Jacob to leave home suddenly and without the knowledge and consent of his father it might produce a confused situation that would interfere with her scheme and bring Esau into action. Hence she makes as if she is about worried past endurance. *Weary of my life.* In this she makes the extravagant declaration that she would not care to live longer if Jacob married a woman whom she disapproved.

GENESIS 28

Verse 1. The speech of Rebekah recorded in the last verse of preceding chapter had the desired effect on Isaac. Of course his wife had not hinted anything to him about her chief motive in getting Jacob away from home and thus Isaac makes no mention of it. But he calls him and directs him not to take a wife of the daughters of that country. It might seem very strong to us to hear a father restricting his son on the subject of his marriage when the son is 77 years of age. (See note at chapter 30: 25.) But we will also remember that this is the Patriarchal Dispensation and the head of a family had much authority in those times.

Verse 2. He instructs his son to go to the house of Bethuel for a wife. It is interesting to note that he gave the same directions to him about this as did his mother. We have no indication that any conversation had taken place between the parents on this subject. So the conclusion is necessary that an understanding had existed between the members of Abraham's descendants that they were to keep the blood strain true to the original stock; at least until it had become well established. There came a time when the Lord seemed less exacting about this than formerly, but at present it is adhered to pretty much all the time.

Verses 3, 4. This is a repetition of the promise first made to Abraham and has been stated over again and again many times. The occasion for repeating it at this time seems to be one having come through the personal plans of Rebekah and Jacob, but independent of all that, he is the one to whom the Lord had decreed the blessings were to come and thus the statement of the Patriarch is an inspired one.

Verse 5. If one were to read this verse by itself and then close the book he would conclude that Jacob had reached the land sought according to the request of his parents. But a glance at the following verses would show that not to be the case. It is simply one of those instances where a writer has begun the report of an important transaction and touching only the high spots. And while at it jumps ahead and tells the final act. In this case the subject is Jacob's journey to his mother's home land and the writer here tells us in general terms that he accomplished the journey, but does not go into the details. That will follow for he is yet just ready to start on his journey that is to prove so famous and far reaching in its results.

Verses 6-9. We have seen previously that Esau had married into some people that caused a grief to his parents. He learned of their attitude concerning such a matter by overhearing the remarks his father made to Jacob. He then decides to make a move that will be in line with his father's desires. Instead of marrying into the out and out heathen of the stock around them he goes to a near relative, a descendant of their common father, Abraham, and takes a wife from thence. All this shows that he bears no ill feeling toward his father even though he had given his brother the preferred blessing. Now that Jacob is gone he has no immediate occasion for spite work, so he makes this move as a flourish of good will to his father.

Verses 10, 11. Traveling in those days and in that sort of country was not the most convenient nor speedy. The entire area is strange to Jacob. About all he knows is the general direction in which he must travel. The two specific points related to his journey are the starting point and the destination. But even the destination is not as specific as the beginning. He knows that he is at Beer-sheba to start with, but only knows that the land of Haran is the general place of his objective, thus it is stated that he "went toward Haran." He *lighted* on a certain place. This word is from PAGAH and defined "a primitive root; to impinge, by accident or violence, or (fig) by importunity."—Strong. The connection shows the word "accident" is the part of the definition that applies here for Jacob had no motive for selecting this place as far as the particular location was concerned. But the only reason given for his step was that "because the sun was set." Darkness was upon him and traveling would be difficult if not dangerous. Out here all alone and with the wilds around him, he seeks to rest. But we must not have the idea that no settlement of any kind was in this part of the country. In fact, this very location is mentioned in connection with the acts of Abraham on his entrance to this land. However, it is to be considered as not a very inviting place since Abraham built his altar between it and another city. The place had been called Luz previously. But in after times in the Bible it came to be a very noted location, evidently through the important doings that occurred there. At any rate, there was nothing of the modern accommodations for lodging in sight, so Jacob lies down among the stones. As an elevation for the head was desired he used the only object at hand and that was a stone. We know not how much of all this event was caused by the Lord, but we do know that he made use of the occasion for one of the interesting episodes of sacred history.

Verse 12. *And he dreamed.* In Hebrews 1: 1 the writer refers to the variety of means which God used in olden times to make known his will. He words it "at sundry times and in divers manners." This fact will be seen all along the record of the Old Testament. One of those manners was the dream. Not that all dreams are inspired. Natural causes will bring dreams but such dreams have no significance. But when God decides on any given occasion to use a dream method then he causes the person to have the kind of dream that suits the occasion. This is one of those "times" when God wishes to make known his further assurance of blessing on the seed of Abraham. Certainly, it is a very proper time and occasion to give such assurance when we consider what the conditions were surrounding Jacob. Here he is, practically driven from home under threat of death and out in an apparently uncivilized spot. It is true that he helped to bring this condition on himself and also that it is being worked out in the direction of God's plan. Also, it is true, as we have already seen, that he is not a mere youth since he has passed his "three score and ten." But the situation is none the less affecting. *Ladder.* Strong calls this a "stair-case." This sounds more appropriate. We think of an ordinary ladder as an instrument that is generally placed in almost perpendicular position and requiring more or less awkward exertions for moving upon. Of course we realize that nothing is too hard for the Lord nor for his angels, yet we are pleased to have the more graceful impression. *Heaven.* In almost every place where this word is found in the Bible it refers to either the atmospheric area or the place of the planets. It thus must be considered in the present instance. That a material ladder such as a man would see, even in a dream, would be seen to reach to the region where God personally dwells as is sometimes suggested, is a mere fancy. But the familiar expression of a boy is the one the writer prefers as truly illustrating the Biblical term when he says his kite flew up to the sky. The same word he used is also from the word giving us the word "heaven" in the Bible. Whether Jacob's dream permitted him to see up as far as the sky or even as far as the region of the planets we do not know. But the thing that is certain is that it was of great height and indicated an exaltation that was befitting the position of the angels. And to see these celestial beings going up and down on this stair-case as they undoubtedly did very gracefully is in accord with the teaching of the scriptures as to the use which God makes of these servants of his. We are told by Paul (Heb. 1: 14) that angels are ministering spirits sent forth to minister to them who shall be heirs of salvation. And we are expressly told by the Lord (Luke 13: 28) that Jacob will be in the Kingdom of God. Of course this places him among the heirs of salvation and thus a proper subject for this administration of the angels here.

Verses 13, 14. The famous promise is now repeated to him with some particulars added. Abraham had been told that he was to inherit the land of Canaan through his seed. But it is specified to Jacob that the very spot on which he is now lying is to become his possession.

Verse 15. General assurances of protection are not only given him but he is assured that he will finally return to this place again. There came a time when he thought of this specific promise and reminded the Lord of it. And also the Lord did not fail to remember it and at last brought him back to the country.

Verse 16. The dream having served its purpose Jacob awakened. *I knew it not.* This expression must be taken to state his mind previous to his sleep. When he came to this place and decided to retire for the night it was only because night had come upon him and not that any particular evidence of the presence of God was there. But after the experience of the night he concludes that God was in the place. This reminds us of the experience of Hagar (chapter 16: 13) when she unexpectedly realized that God was present in a place so unusual.

Verse 17. *Afraid; dreadful.* Both these words are from YARE and defined as follows. "A primitive root; to fear; morally to revere; causatively, to frighten." Strong. This word is rendered in the A.V. as fear 242 times, terrible 24, dreadful 5. It is the word for "reverend" in Psa. 111: 9. So we see the definition of the word includes the idea of reverence or respect or awe. The thought in the present instance is that Jacob was filled with a feeling of solemnity and reverence or respect for the place because he considered that God was present. And since the stair-case he had seen that was so high had angels on it he would consider the place as the gateway to the abode of those celestial beings.

Verse 18. Jacob had seen his father make use of an altar for the worship of his God. In most instances he would see him offer a burnt sacrifice. But under the circumstances Jacob cannot offer that. Hence he does what he can and pours oil on the stone. This was one of the familiar items in altar and other service to God in the days of ceremonial activities. Oil came from the olive, an article of value and use, and thus was a real sacrifice. It also was a symbol of consecration, hence the propriety of the use Jacob made of it in this case.

Verse 19. *Bethel.* This place was formerly called Luz. But here we see Jacob gives it a name significant of the things occurring in the place. It is a compound word and comes from two Hebrew words. *Beth* means "house" and *El* means "God." Thus the name means "house of God" which Jacob considered a proper name for the place.

Verses 20-22. Abraham was the first man to offer tithes or the tenth (chapter 14: 20) but here Jacob vowed to make it a lifelong practice. And this practice finally became a part of the fixed law of God under Moses. A vow differs from an ordinary promise in that it is a solemn promise to God and not to man. As far as any record shows Jacob kept his promise to the Lord.

GENESIS 29

Verses 1, 2. Reference to the people of the east merely includes the population in general. Having never been in this country before he is somewhat among them as an inquirer at present. Here he found a well with three flocks of sheep lying there near it. Evidently it was a place for the use of various keepers of sheep and protected in the meantime of waterings with a rock covering.

Verse 3. This more particularly brings out the thought expressed in preceding paragraph that the well was for general use. When a service had been obtained from the well it was the practice to replace the stone and then make further disposition of the sheep. If it were a mid-day time of watering they would do so then take the sheep away for further feeding. If in the evening they would water them and then gather them into the folds for keeping.

Verses 4, 5. Upon inquiry Jacob learns the people now present at the well are from the place familiar to his remembrance as having been spoken of by his parents. Upon this he mentions the man in whom he has so much interest and through whom he was to obtain a wife.

Verse 6. His next inquiry is very general and impersonal. He inquires about his health. We do not know how specific he would have become further on in his conversation had they not volunteered the very information that he was wanting. They told him that the man he was asking about was well. Next they informed him that his daughter was coming with the sheep. Now his father had charged him to take a wife of the daughters of Laban. That was so general. He might have more than one daughter. But now he is informed that his "daughter" is coming. Not only so, but his daughter Rachel is coming. Of course Jacob did not know the names of any of Laban's daughters. But he has been trusting in God all the while. And did not his father, who is a Patriarch, assure him that God would bless him? And that did not mean only in material things for he had connected the prospect of blessing with the fact that he was to find a wife among the daughters of Laban. And furthermore, in his dreams at Bethel God had expressly repeated the promise made to his father that his seed was to be numerous. This would have to be through the finding of a wife. Surely, God has sent this daughter of Laban's out here at this particular time. How thrilled he must be at this moment.

Verse 7. Who would want the intrusion of disinterested shepherds at the time he is about to meet the woman for whom he has made this dreadful journey? At such times the space should be reserved exclusively for the ones with more important concern. So he reminds them that it is still midday. That it is not time for the final watering of the sheep preparatory for the evening gathering into the sheepfolds. If that were the case then it would be logical for them to wait for the common work of the last service for the sheep. But since there will still be a final opportunity for this work they might as well not be losing this good grazing time. Give the sheep some drink then go on and see that they get something to eat out in the pasture. If these people will just do this then Jacob can have the ecstasy of meeting his probable and expected sweetheart in the sacred joy of privacy. But his sentiments hid from him the real situation so they will not grant to him this ruse of Cupid.

Verse 8. They inform him that the use of the well must not be made so incidental but that it must be done in a general action and after some one in charge gets the stone rolled from the well's mouth. But he will not have opportunity for further insistence with them, for here she comes.

Verse 9. Yes, right while he was making the speech recorded in the preceding verse, the girl he is longing to meet arrives with the sheep belonging to her father.

Verse 10. All of these other people now fade from the picture. The writer as well as the reader will not have any further need of them and their activities about the sheep entrusted to their care no longer interest us. But Jacob gallantly assists Rachel by removing the stone from the well's mouth and waters the sheep of Laban.

Verse 11. The salutation of the kiss was not necessarily accompanied with any sentiments other than courtesy or civility since that was the established practice in that country. Hence nothing unusual could be made of this "liberty" of his. But we have the New Testament writers charging that the kiss should be holy. This includes the requirement that it not be accompanied with any motives or sentiments that would be unlawful. Thus a man would not be permitted to kiss another man's wife even in those times with the idea of fleshly satisfaction. Not that such pleasure is necessarily immoral. It would depend on the persons. And a man would not have the right to take fleshly pleasure from the salutation of this kiss if it were the case of another man's wife. But in this case of Jacob, he is a free man and she is a free woman. And while the ordinary social practice would permit him to take the liberty of a kiss, yet also the circumstances belonging to the occasion would cause and permit him to deposit this kiss upon Rachel with all the gusto of a lover. We are sure this took place, for the record says he lifted up his voice and wept. It is inconceivable that he was weeping from fear or unpleasantness of any kind. Not only so, it was after he kissed her that he gave this exhibition of his feelings. And that is easily understood. Being a free man and with the conditions as described in preceding paragraph he doubtless gave her a kiss filled with all the emotion and love that the past years of his loneliness had accumulated. So it was the weeping of joy and satisfied thrill.

Verse 12. The first experience of pleasing sensation abated Jacob tells her of his relation to her. Of course the term "brother" means a near relative in Bible times and not always so near as to be objectionable to this love.

Verses 13, 14. This passage informs us that the report of the meeting of Jacob and Rachel had been brought to Laban. But no one had been told of it but Rachel and thus we have the necessary inference that she had told him. And her manner of relating it had not made any unfavorable impression on him for he "ran to meet him." Yes, we know that Rachel was the one who told him for the record says so. But we are also sure as to the manner of her telling as here stated. But the present form of recognition which Laban gives him is one of the relationship. Hospitable welcome was accorded him we know for the record states that he abode with him for a month. This is not in the sense that the month is the length of his stay as we know it was not. So the expression must be taken to mean that nothing but social and kinship hospitality was manifested in this time as far as Laban was concerned. But that does not require us to conclude that nothing further was considered by Jacob. It would be unreasonable to think that all that he saw during this month was the hospitality of his host. Here was the girl who first met him and upon whose lips he had pressed a kiss of love so thrilling that it caused him to weep aloud with the effect of pleasure. This close association in the home of this beautiful girl served to strengthen the sentiment that was already manifested. And if any one should venture the criticism that the scene at the well was only a case of "love at first sight" he would have to recall it for a month of close mingling in the family would have exposed it. Also, we must remember that Laban had another daughter. And if the first scene was only love at first sight, surely the month of association in the family with his other daughter present would have brought to him the realization that he had picked the wrong girl. But such was not the case as we shall see and that his love for Rachel was sure and deep.

Verse 15. The language of this verse tells us that Jacob was not an idle leech on the hospitality of his host but served him usefully during this month. But Laban sees how the situation might be misunderstood. Thus far he evidently had not been giving him anything but "room and board." And no indication that Jacob was dissatisfied. Why should he not be satisfied to work for his keeping if it can be daily in the home of the woman he loves. Hence no indication that he had even asked for additional pay. But Laban sees the justice of giving him something more than room and lodging and makes the proposition to do so. That is, if it might be considered not fair to impose upon a man's hospitality even though he is a relative, neither would it be fair to impose on the other's services even though he is a relative. And with this idea in view Laban asked him what his wages should be.

Verses 16, 17. This is the first mention of Leah. But the full force of the choice of Jacob or of the bargain he proposes would not be as fully appreciated did the reader not know that Laban had another daughter besides Rachel. *Tender.* This is from RAK and defined "Tender (literally or figuratively); by implication, weak."—Strong. Thus the word used to describe Leah has a meaning that might be desirable if applied to a subject where the opposite of ruggedness or coarseness were desired. For instance in Chapter 18: 7 it mentions a calf "tender and good" and the word in the original is the same as here. But the connection shows that the word tender is used as opposed to that which is tough and thus undesirable. But in the case at hand the text does not say that she was tender only, but that she was tender eyed. Then the lexicon definition adds that it implies "weak" which would be very undesirable as regards to a woman's appearance. And especially is this true when the inspired writer immediately adds with a word that indicates an opposite situation and says "but Rachel was beautiful," etc. This means the writer did not consider Leah as beautiful since she had weak eyes. The word *favoured* is from MAREH and defined "a view (the act of seeing); also an appearance (the thing seen) whether (real) a shape (especially if handsome, comeliness; often plural, the looks), or (mental) a vision."—Strong. These qualities are here ascribed to Rachel in addition to the word that said she was beautiful. With all this information at hand we cannot escape the conclusion that Leah was rather uninviting to the eye. Not that she was "hard on the eyes" necessarly, but there was not that in her countenance that appealed to the view of another. While Rachel had a beautiful form and was beautiful in general and had a countenance and gleam in her eye that invited, yea, irresistibly drew another toward her, especially a man, and still more especially a man with a lifetime of unsatisfied love welling up in his whole nature. No wonder then that he offered to serve Laban seven years for the possession of this daughter.

Verse 19. The answer of Laban is just slightly evasive. He did not say specifically that if he worked for him the seven years that "then" he could have the girl. But all the circumstances indicated that and Jacob so interpreted it. Laban merely makes a comparison between the fact of giving her to another man and giving her to this one. The idea of a father giving his daughter in marriage is again here brought up, but that has already been considered and interpreted in view of the customs of that age and place. The only conclusive thing he says to Jacob is "abide with me."

Verse 20. Here a verse of four lines covers a period of seven years. Nothing is said of the particulars of that period of service. Merely that he served the seven years as he had agreed to do. And the interesting and astonishing part of the story is that "they seemed unto him but a few days, for the love he had to her." Viewed from the experience common to men and women we would be inclined to remark that the time would seem as an unending age. Ordinarily that would. But we will bear in mind that Jacob was not separated from her as ordinary lovers are while awaiting the time of their wedding. In such a situation we think of the poetic words "absence makes the heart grow fonder." But the absence is not in this case. His future wife is daily in his sight and doubtless often near his side. If he wishes to follow her as she goes about her own personal tasks he may do so. He is keeping the flocks of Laban, but that does not require all of his time. He will be free much of the time. Rachel can be seen as she moves from place to place on her father's premises. He can observe where she goes and then follow up to the very spot where he has seen her. He can enjoy looking at the footprints that she has made in the earth and muse over the sacred likeness of her feet. The feet of her whom he loves more than his own life and of the woman who will some day be his bosom companion. The sacredness of the betrothal as held by those ancient people assures him that no intruder will endanger his position in her heart and he is permitted continuous and unlimited enjoyment of her charms day after day, restricted only from the intimate relations that are reserved for the final union. No wonder then that the period seemed as only a few days to him.

Verse 21. The period of promised service has ended, his waiting time is over. Nothing now remains to make his happiness complete but the sublime privilege of the intimacy permitted only between husband and wife. This is what he means by the expression that he may "go in unto her." This is the Biblical expression for designating the fleshly relation of the sexes. Nothing now but that relation remains to be done to make their union complete. Thus he asks for the completion of Laban's contract.

Verse 22. Not a word said by Laban as to changing the contract. No questioning of the quality of the service rendered in the seven years and no hint that any misunderstanding had been entertained. No name was mentioned by Jacob for that is well understood. Just "give me my wife." Then Laban gathers all the men together and makes a feast. This is not to be considered as a wedding feast proper as the sequel will show. Besides, and that also will appear in the sequel, the feast customarily made in connection with weddings was given after the wedding and not before. The only meaning that could have been attached to this feast was one of general celebration of the fact that Laban was going to have a wedding in his family. And there was nothing in the happenings of that occasion that designated, officially, who the bride was to be. That is, nothing that was necessarily connected with the union. Had there been, then a breach of morals would have been practiced unless Rachel were given in the ceremonies of the evening. Or, if Leah had been offered in the exercise then Jacob would have protested. So the whole circumstance proves that no marriage ceremony was used in those days. The only "rite" that was necessary to make a man and woman one was the fleshly one and that was in accordance with Chapter 2: 23, 24. Any discussions of the subject of marriage that ignore this basic principle of the institution as set forth in such instances as the one now in hand are a confusion of the subject. Nothing at that time makes a man and woman husband and wife but the fleshly relation. Therefore, until such relation has taken place no union has been formed and no fleshly obligation created. This accounts for the actions of Laban.

Verses 23, 24. The festivities of the evening are over. The guests have departed and the time has come for the actual union. According to another custom, when the moment arrives Laban conducts his daughter to the bed of Jacob, but not the one he had promised. It is night and no one is clearly visible. A woman is put into Jacob's bed and he "goes in unto her" and they become one flesh. Of course we have to conclude that Leah became a party to her father's deception else she would have revealed her identity to Jacob. *Maid; handmaid.* These are both from the same word and defined "a female slave (as a member of the household)." Thus she would have been Laban's slave before but now a personal slave to be at hand for service to his daughter.

Verse 25. Note that not one hint of anything unlawful from a moral standpoint is charged by Jacob. Had there been any law requiring some ceremony to make a marriage proper then that ceremony would have exposed to Jacob the cheat of Laban and he would have protested. Or, had the said ceremony been used for Rachel then he could not have taken Leah to Jacob's bed without violation of the moral law and Jacob would not have been slow in complaining so. But nothing of the kind is said, hence we must conclude that no marriage ceremony was used in Biblical times except the fleshly act. Jacob accuses Laban of having beguiled him. This means to betray or deceive.

Verse 26. Then Laban explains his action. That it is not allowed in that country to give the younger in marriage before the elder. Of course, had he told Jacob this beforehand he did not know what Jacob would have done. Neither do we know.

Verse 27. *Fulfill her week.* This refers to the feast of seven days that was customarily given in honor of a bride in those times. An instance of such a feast is recorded in Judges 14: 10. It there says that Samson made a feast "for so used the young men to do." And the 12th verse of the same chapter tells us the feast was seven days. Now then, what Laban means is for Jacob to honor his bride with the customary week's feast and then he will receive Rachel also. But it is with the proviso that he serve Laban seven more years to pay for her.

Verse 28, 29. It is easy to conceive why Jacob would endure the fraud of his father-in-law, for it is the only way of actually enjoying the woman he loves. Therefore he goes ahead with the feast of seven days. Then Laban gives him Rachel for wife. And so Jacob marries the two sisters a week apart. The one is paid for and the other is yet to be paid for. And the fact that even after he gets his beloved wife and might have escaped with her, yet he has more respect for his contract than did Laban, and so continues his service as agreed. And Rachel also receives a female slave as a marriage gift of her father.

Verse 30. "Went in also unto Rachel" of course means that he had the fleshly relation with her that made her his wife. The expression "loved also Rachel" might leave us with the idea that love for Rachel was as yet an unannounced fact. But the thought is that notwithstanding that Leah had been imposed off on him and he had had fleshly relations with her, yet his greater love for Rachel was unimpaired. Now we are sure that his love was not just "love at first sight."

Verses 31-35. Now begins a contest of very extraordinary character. The wife of Jacob first taken was *hated.* This is from SANEY and defined "To hate (personally)." It is understandable. Whether we approve of his attitude, Jacob had been imposed upon. He had fallen in love with a beautiful woman and worked, according to contract for her seven years. Now when the term of his service had been completed he is cheated and has the unattractive and unloved woman put off onto him. The whole thing is an unfortunate affair and the woman is to be pitied. Therefore the Lord is the one to show the pity. This was done by giving her ability to bear children while her more fortunate sister, as to the affections of her husband, is barren. And as it was in those days considered a great reproach not to be able to have children, this indeed constituted an important factor in the family relations of this house. After the birth of each of the four sons recorded in this paragraph she gives the Lord the praise and expresses anxiety and hope for the affection of her husband. After the birth of the four sons here mentioned Leah ceased bearing children for the time being.

GENESIS 30

Verse 1. The reproach of being childless is felt by Rachel and she expresses it in earnest terms to her husband. "Give me children or else I die" could have but one meaning. She did not suppose that her barren condition was from any voluntary acts of her husband. But it is her way of saying that if she cannot have children she would not wish to live. Her husband is a man of God and surely he can do something to help the situation besides just being her fleshly companion. But she counted too much on the power of her husband.

Verse 2. Jacob became angry. But it was not the anger of malice or evil intent. The original word here has the outstanding idea of great and heated excitement and of a feeling more like provocation than one of malice. His wife had asked too much from him as if he were endowed with the power of God. He evidently realizes her plight but is not able to help it.

Verse 3. The plan of giving a slave into the bosom of one's husband for the purpose of a child is difficult to understand. About the nearest explanation is in the idea that being childless was considered as more unfortunate than it would even be to lose the affection of the husband or than of seeing him become intimate with any other woman. And especially a slave. And yet, perhaps it would be easier to see one's husband being intimate with a slave than with another woman of his equal. In the latter case his affections might be transferred to the woman of standing while in the former only the physical pleasure would be experienced. At any rate Rachel makes the request that Jacob go in unto her maid. Her expression is that she "shall bear upon my knees." This is to be understood as referring to the manner of conducting childbirth in those days. Instead of using a bed, a stool so arranged for the purpose was used. This posture of the mother assisted the delivery and was used at that time. It will be well here to quote from an authority on this subject since this is an unusual matter. "Obstetrics. The suffering of child-birth is the penalty for the sin of Eve (Gen. 3: 16). Midwives in the Near East from the earliest time, have conducted deliveries upon the obstetric chair (Ex. 1: 16), and continue to do so today. The obstetric chair is mentioned by ancient Greek writers. Rachel offers the use of her knees in lieu of an obstetric chair, as a symbol that the child borne by her maid is her own."—*Standard Bible Dictionary,* Funk & Wagnalls, Disease and Medicine, No. 8. If Rachel's maid takes a position on her knees instead of the chair and gives birth to the child, it will be as near to having the child come "from between her own knees" as could be done under the circumstances.

Verses 4, 5. Jacob complied with the request of his wife. But the record says that the maid bare Jacob a son. It was true in spite of all the planning of Rachel, she could not claim the child except as a thing of possession. And that is not the main reason the statement is made. In those times the blood line in any important family was always accounted on the father's side and often not any record was kept of even his own daughters. And after this when the twelve sons of Jacob are referred to there will be no distinction made between his sons through his wives and those of his wives' maids. Of course, after he had formed the intimacy brought about by begetting sons through them, all other men were to regard them in the same light as his wives, under the tolerance in use at that period of the world's history.

Verses 6-8. The words of Rachel indicate that it was considered in the light of contest with her sister that she wished to have children. Unlike the case of Leah who connected her good fortune of motherhood with the prospects of winning her husband's affections, she only connects it with God. She already had the affections of her husband and so that was not one of the motives for her present contest.

Verses 9-13. The period of child bearing for Leah seemed to have taken a pause. And the doings of Rachel with her maids rouses the spirit of rivalry in her and she uses the same plans adopted by her sister. She gives her maid into the bosom of her husband in two instances and two additional sons are born.

Verse 14. *Mandrakes.* This is from DUWDAY and defined "a boiler or basket; also the mandrake (as aphrodisiac):"—Strong. The second word in parenthesis is defined by Webster as "exciting to sexual desire." This fruit is the same as the common May apple in America. The belief was held by people that eating of this fruit had effect on the reproductive functions. And in a situation where love and reproduction are running a contest this article would be considered desirable. With this notion being in existence we can see the significance in Rachel's request that Leah divide these pieces of fruit with her.

Verse 15. Leah thinks she sees the motive of the request. In protest she tells Rachel that she has the affections of their husband already. This reply shows she understand's Rachel's purpose of the mandrakes is to assist her in her contest for the supremacy. But after such a complaint Rachel counters with an offer to submit the company of their common husband to Leah that night. Rachel can afford to make this apparent sacrifice since she will now have the mandrakes and can soon instigate a like experience with him and possibly have better success finally. *Therefore.* This word has been explained previously but will be again here. It has the idea of something that is appropriate or just or right. It is as if Rachel said "it will be proper for you to have his company tonight." Since Leah seems to think that Rachel wants the mandrakes for the sole purpose of outsmarting her sister, she is willing to give her the present priority to see whether, even with the use of the mandrakes, she can have success. As to the agreement about who has to accompany with the common husband on any particular occasion, doubtless that was a conversation that occurred often. It is plain that a man with more than one wife could not accompany with each of them at the same time. Therefore it would be a frequent question "which of us this time?" And in the present instance Rachel unselfishly gives way to her sister.

Verse 16. *Hired.* This is from CAKAR and defined "the idea of temporary purchase; to hire."—Strong. Especially note the word of temporary purchase. All this agrees with the remarks in the preceding paragraph. The question of which was to have the pleasure of the husband's conjugal company on any given night would necessarily come up in the family life. The husband would not always be the sole judge. The attitude of the wives would naturally often figure in it. And in the present instance Leah informs Jacob that a bargain has been made between her and her sister and that he is to give her his company that night in the intimate relation. With this situation placed before him Jacob complies with the invitation or request of his wife that night.

Verse 17. *God hearkened unto Leah.* Under the circumstances we know what was the prayer of Leah. Her ability to live in the relation of wife to Jacob had already been demonstrated, so that was not the subject of her prayer. And she knew she was not permanently unable to conceive since she already had four sons. But for some reason she had not been successful for a period. Her prayer therefore had to be one for a counteracting of whatever was causing the stoppage in her conception.

Verses 18-21. In this whole passage we see the same accounting for her success we saw at the start. That God had been her helper and also that it might have the effect of bringing the affections of her husband more in her favor. And in reasoning as she did as to her child bearing being a cause for the respect and attentions of her husband, it is in keeping with the general state of things in those times. Children were universally desired and not to be able to have them was considered a reproach. Thus in this passage, as in most other places, the success in the way of children is treasured and interpreted as a favor from God, but also as a means of strengthening the ties between herself and her husband. It should always be that way. The unnatural customs of society and other causes have interfered with the laws of God and nature and many means have been resorted to in order to thwart the very first commandment that God gave to the first pair. We see that Leah uses the circumstances in the way just remarked, that they indicate favor of God. If people are unable to have children it is a misfortune. If they are able to and refuse it is a sin.

Verses 22-24. *Hearkened to her*. This is the same thought as in verse 17. It shows that Rachel also had prayed for a child and when the child was given she says that God had taken away her reproach. Her attitude toward children was the righteous one as shown in preceding paragraph. And we can see a finer motive in her case than in that of Leah. In the case of Leah she seemed to be concerned principally with procuring the love of her husband by way of her children. Rachel does not need that assistance. She knows she already has his preferential love. Hence her desire for children is motivated by one based on the fixed laws of nature, that which requires and inclines living beings toward reproducing their kind. The name Joseph is from a Hebrew word that means "let him add" according to Strong and "he shall add" according to Webster. Whether Rachel had received any divine information of a future son which led her to name her firstborn as she did, we do not know. However, the name was predictive of that fact although she did not live to enjoy the second son.

Verse 25. Beginning with the 23rd verse of previous chapter and ending with the one of this paragraph we have covered seven years of the family life of Jacob. This will appear more clearly later. By consulting chapter 31: 41 with the present verse we will learn that Joseph was born at the end of the fourteen years of Jacob's service for his two wives. When Jacob came to Egypt he was 130 years old. (Chapter 47: 9.) The famine had then been going two years. (Chapter 45: 6.) These had been preceded with seven years of plenty. (Chapter 41: 29.) Just before the years of plenty started Joseph was 30 years old. (Chapter 41: 46.) Now then, Joseph was 30 when he stood before Pharaoh and predicted the years, seven of them passed with plenty at which time Joseph would be 37. Then two years of the famine had passed when his father came, and that would make him 39. So, if Joseph was 39 when his father was 130, it follows that Jacob was 130 less 39, namely, 91, when Joseph was born. And Joseph was born 7 years after his father was married so that Jacob was 91 less 7, namely, 84, when married. And he was married seven years after leaving home so that he was 84 less 7, namely, 77 when he left home and had the vision of the staircase.

Verse 26. Jacob's term of service for his wives has been faithfully kept and he asks to be released from further service to go to his own home.

Verses 27, 28. Here Laban not only makes no complaint against the quality of service Jacob has rendered but admits that the presence of Jacob has meant blessing for him. This reminds us of the promise of God to Abraham that he would bless others if they blessed him. And no hint is made that Jacob owed anything further on his debt. That is all settled now. But if he will continue with him he will receive wages.

Verses 29, 30. Jacob lays the foundation for the proposition he will make later. He is not going to claim any certain price in money. So now he reminds Laban that his livestock had increased much since his coming to him, but had nothing of his own to show for it or to appropriate specifically to his own family.

Verses 31, 32. Laban sees the point and again asks Jacob to name his price. But again he will not name any specific amount. Instead, he makes a very unusual proposition. It involves the matter of "scientific breeding." Jacob proposes to accept for his pay all of certain animals with defects. We will observe that the defects of the contract are external and have no necessary connection with the general physical state of the creature. Of course this makes it easy to distinguish which is which among the cattle afterward.

Verses 33. So settled and satisfactory would this condition be with Jacob that he agrees beforehand that if any animal should be found among his group that did not have any of these defects on it then it was to be considered as theft on his part.

Verses 34-36. Laban agrees with the proposition. It is sometimes charged that Jacob took advantage of Laban but this is not the case. That is, he did not take any unjust advantage, only he took advantage of the favor of God. Later we have the statement that God gave to Jacob the cattle of Laban. Also, Jacob was very patient with Laban and tried to please his changing whims as many as ten times. We know from usual observation that while certain "prenatal" influences may account for certain results, yet not all the things that happened in the experience of Jacob could have been accomplished merely through manipulation of breeding. Therefore we must conclude that God wished Jacob to have the cattle that he did acquire. And if God so willed it we dare not say it was wrong. In this paragraph Laban was the one who separated the defective animals from the flocks. The statement is made that he gave them into the "hand of his sons." Some quibbling has been done here as to whose sons are meant. But that should not be difficult to solve. The oldest son Jacob had at this time was not more than six or seven. They could not be entrusted with the handling of the herds of animals. And whether we suggest that he called upon his sons to do this as a measure against fraud on part of Jacob, that would be farfetched also. He has already admitted that God had blessed him on account of Jacob and thus could not believe that any injustice would be done by him. But this was no more than a fair way to start out the term of the new contract for his own forces to lend some assistance. And the three days journey distance between the two groups would only be a businesslike precaution against unfair mingling of the groups of animals.

Verse 37. *Pilled.* This word means "peeled." Jacob took poles of green growths. This was because he wanted to take advantage of the sap that would be flowing between the bark and the body of the rods or poles. This would enable him to first cut the bark in places and then peel off the part between the cuts, leaving a stripped condition similar to the stripes of a barber's pole. This arrangement was for the effect on the impression of the animals while mating.

Verses 38-40. These rods with the impressive stripes were kept near the place where the animals came to drink. They were conveniently arranged so that when desired they could be placed in sight or removed, according to the wish of the owner.

Verses 41-43. Jacob would be acquainted with the breeding season of his various charges. He would watch, and if the time for any particular animal had come that was the fertile period, if it happened to be one of the stronger individuals he would place the striped rods in their sight. While if the weaker ones were about to breed he would leave the rods out of sight. The result was that when a sheep or goat was born of the stronger kind it would have some marks on it and thus would be Jacob's. This scheme would not have been so universally successful had God not helped. We will see finally that God took quite an important part in the whole manipulation of the scheme and thus we are not to accuse Jacob of taking undue advantage.

GENESIS 31

Verses 1, 2. In spite of the fairness of Jacob's contract the monster of envy began to work. The sons of Laban noticed Jacob's success and told their father. The statement is made that Jacob beheld the countenance of Laban that it was changed. It thus indicates that he was so well acquainted with the fairness of the whole contract that he could not make any specific charge of fraud. All that he could do was to act in a sullen manner. But the same God who had caused the proposition of Jacob to be a success will take further interest in him and direct his activities.

Verse 3. Upon the situation arising from the complaint of Laban's sons and of his own attitude toward Jacob, God bids him return to the land of his fathers with the promise he would be with him.

Verses 4-13. Upon this Jacob calls his wives to him in the field for consultation. He reports to them the changed attitude of their father, further reminding them of his faithful service to their father. He details much of the carrying out of the plan agreed upon between them at the start of this last contract. He states to them that their father was changeable and inclined to be dissatisfied even though matters were going according to the contract. When he thought that a little minor change in the manipulation of the scheme might be to his advantage he asked it and Jacob always agreed to the change. Then if Laban decided that change was not so good and wanted to change back Jacob agreed to that also. In the 12th verse in this paragraph is where we see God as taking direct part in the scheme of the breeding. Also that the reason for this direct intervention of God was the unfair treatment that Laban had been giving to Jacob. He tells his wives that in all the unfair treatment of their father towards him, God suffered no harm to come to him. He then makes mention of the God of Bethel as having spoken to him and now bids Jacob to return to the land of his people.

Verses 14-16. How blessed it would be if all wives would take the attitude that Rachel and Leah took, and thus prefer their husband to their father. This is as it should be. When God first gave the law of marriage he decreed that a man should leave his father and mother, etc. Of course this does not mean that one must necessarily desert his parents. But in all cases where the interests of the parents conflict with the just interests of the married child, then the latter must prevail.

Verses 17, 18. Jacob prepared to leave and take with him his own possessions only.

Verse 19. Laban was away from home at the time that Jacob left. Since he was told by the Lord to leave and also since he is not breaking any contract, it is only a wise thing for him to take his leave in the absence of Laban so as to avoid the unpleasant hindrance that might occur were he present. Mention is made that Rachel had stolen her father's images. These were small portable objects of worship. It should be observed that all of the people of that country were idolaters. (Josh. 24: 2, 15.) Rachel had not yet been in any other land nor under any other system of worship but that of her father's people. And Josephus tells us (Ant. 18-9-5) that the people of this country worshipped such gods that were images of the gods of the land. Also, that when they traveled they carried them with them in their journey. We might suppose they carried them as a sort of amulet. At any rate, Rachel wanted the benefit of these articles, and evidently had none of her own. This is a silent tribute to the purity of Jacob's religious life through these years he has been in this country.

Verse 20. Again we have the word Syrian. See comment at Chapter 25: 20 on this. Jacob would steal away as here stated for the reasons shown in verse 19 above.

Verses 21-23. The river that Jacob is here said to have crossed is the Euphrates since that is the stream between the country of Laban and the vast spread of land that he must pass over before reaching his home land. It was told Laban of the departure of Jacob, but he did not hear of it till Jacob had been gone three days. He had to travel seven days before he overtook him. That means that in seven days he had traveled fast enough to gain the three days that Jacob already had made and the other distance besides. He overtook him at mount Gilead.

Verse 24. Before coming in contact with Jacob God appeared to Laban and gave him charge concerning his treatment of Jacob, that he was to let him alone as far as interfering with his business.

Verses 25-29. After overtaking him and getting their encampment arranged Laban addresses himself to Jacob. He pretends that his grievance consists in having his daughters taken from his presence without the privilege of telling them good-bye. That he might have sent them away in connection with rites of mirth. But it is doubtful if that would have been done. He further claims the power to injure Jacob but reports that the God of his (Jacob's) father had appeared and warned him not to hurt him.

Verse 30. Then admitting that Jacob was induced to leave because of homesickness, yet why should he steal his gods in his departure. This shows that Laban had missed them and he concludes that Jacob had taken them. The fact that Rachel wanted to take these images along shows they had none of their own. And the fact that they had none of their own is evidence that

Jacob and his family had not been practing that form of religious service while in the land of Laban. It should be a matter of knowledge to Laban that Jacob was not in the habit of using these articles. But he is anxious to have some basis for making a complaint and this is what he falls upon.

Verses 31, 32. Jacob first answers the question of why he left as he did. That it was because he was fearful lest his wives be taken from him by force. Next he answers about the charge of theft. Being innocent of the facts in the case he is very positive and makes a strong, if not rash statement. That if the gods are found in the possession of any of his people, such guilty person should die.

Verse 33. Laban then begins his search for the gods. Mention is made of the tents of the different members of his family indicating that the husbands and wives had their separate tents. This would account for the various expressions found along through the ancient literature about the husbands visiting certain of their wives. And the speech of Leah in chapter 30: 16 may be understood in this light.

Verses 34, 35. *Furniture.* This is a camel's saddle. They were made in the form of an enlarged and soft pad and very suitable for sitting upon for comfort. Also, being fluffy and of some size they would furnish an opportunity for secreting small articles about in the same manner that one could use a modern pillow. Somewhere in this article Rachel had hid the images of her father. *Searched.* This is from MASHASH and defined "to feel of; by implication to grope."—Strong. This indicates the effective manner Laban took in trying to find his images. Of course as they were small things he would not expect to see them in plain view, especially as he suspected them to have been stolen. Thus he feels of all the places where he thinks they might be. No wonder then that Rachel does not want to expose the saddle on which she is sitting. Since he had felt of all the other things in the tent, if she should rise up before him, as was the rule then for younger persons to do when an older one entered, he would at once see the article and feel of it too. Thus she must devise some reason as apology for not rising. *Custom of women.* The first word is from DEREK and one part of the definition is "a course of life or mode of action." She means to say that the course of life for women is upon her. Of course Rachel is still in the child-bearing age of her life and thus is subject to the functioning coming upon them periodically. Some women are very much indisposed at such a time and find it inconvenient if not detrimental to exert themselves at that time, especially to assume a standing posture. Hence the plausibility of her excuse. He looked in the other things but found not the images.

Verses 36, 37. The deception was effective completely. At this Jacob becomes very positive and chides Laban. He specifies certain things that now have been proven to be false. Triumphantly and defiantly he bids Laban set forth all the stolen articles as accusing witnesses and then leave the verdict to the judgment of the brethren.

Verse 38. He makes reference to his score of years of service. He affirms that he had not used any of his stock. Also he had taken such good care of the mothers that they had not cast their young. Cast here means to miscarry.

Verse 39. If one of Laban's animals was damaged by wild beasts he took it for his own and replaced it to his flock with a good one of his. Or if one of the beasts were stolen, Jacob made it good even though it was not his fault.

Verse 40. This verse recounts the hours of sleeplessness and other wearisome experiences he had for the sake of his master's interests.

Verse 41. This verse should be marked as useful in determining certain other inquiries of dates and periods. See the note at chapter 30: 25.

Verse 42. The verse in general means that God had been his protector. The term "fear of Isaac" could mean only the fear or reverence for God that his father Isaac had. He believes that even God would not have been with him had he not been true to the faith of his fathers.

Verses 43-45. Of course Laban has never learned the truth about his gods. He is at the end of his resources for further complaints, except to become a whiner. Since he is not going to be able to win in his expectations against Jacob he now wants him for a future friend. He then proposes a pact of friendship. It was a custom to set some kind of visible mark of any important agreement and in this case Jacob sets up a stone for a pillar.

Verse 46. This pillar was reinforced

with a pile of stones. It was of some considerable size for they were able to eat on it. And here is another instance where the eating is mentioned in connection with an important occasion. Let this custom be noted along the journey of study through the Bible.

Verses 47, 48. Both the words that Laban and Jacob gave to the monument they had here set up mean the same. Thus it was merely a matter of each choosing a word of the available vocabulary that answered the purpose. The meaning is "a heap as witness."

Verse 49. The meaning of Mizpah is given in the text and is justified by the critical meaning of the original word which is "an observatory." And indeed the Lord is the most gracious watchtower or observatory for all who will rely on him. As a watchman on the top of an observatory can see the enemies and dangers unseen to the ones below and thus can warn of the same, thus the Lord, from his eminence of infinity can see and will warn us of dangers we cannot see if we will listen to his instructions.

Verses 50-53. The agreement is again gone over and Laban adds a few words that constitute the covenant one of non-aggression. If the specific terms of the pact are violated then the whole covenant is void. Laban refers to the God of Abraham and of Nahor. This is significant. Abraham is the grandfather of Jacob and Nahor is the grandfather of Laban. (Chapter 22: 20-23.) He hereby acknowledges God as common to both.

Verses 54, 55. Jacob prepared beasts for food and again they did *eat* and tarried together in friendly association all night. When the morning was come they had a friendly parting and Laban returned to his own home. Laban now disappears from our story and will be heard of only historically by later writers.

GENESIS 32

Verses 1, 2. Again we have the mention of angels. See note on this subject at chapter 16: 7. The angels of God play an important part in the providence for man.

Verses 3-5. Jacob has never forgotten the circumstances that drove him away from home over twenty years ago. He knows the dwelling place of his brother. As a mark of respect and also precaution he sends messengers before him to Esau. He wants him informed as to where his brother has been spending the years of their absence. He has not been roving over strange ground or among objectionable people. Neither is he an object of charity that he might be thought as seeking help from him. He possesses livestock and servants and humbly wishes to tell his lord this and bids for friendship.

Verse 6. The messengers return with the announcement that Esau is coming his way with four hundred men. Nothing is said about the class of men nor of any other circumstances of the retinue. The simple fact that Esau is coming with that much force is related to Jacob.

Verses 7, 8. With nothing but the guilty remembrance of his past treatment of his brother as accuser Jacob becomes frightened. He concludes that Esau is coming on a hostile mission. Thus he is beginning to reap additional punishment for his actions. As a matter of strategy he divides his people and property into two groups with the plan of letting one escape while the other is being attacked.

Verses 9-12. Jacob now makes an earnest plea to God. He reminds him of his past promises. Also makes a humble acknowledgment of his own unworthiness. But withal, he prays to be delivered from the hand of his brother.

Verse 13. *Present.* One meaning in the definition of this word is "a tribute." It will be seen all along in the history of ancient people that an outstanding custom of recognizing royalty or other dignity was to make a present. It did not necessarily indicate that the recipient was in need. The queen of Sheba gave Solomon presents, but surely not to help him financially. The wise men presented gifts to the babe, but not as a "shower" to cover his needs. It was in recognition of his importance. And so, as an overture to Esau to obtain his friendship Jacob resorts to the custom.

Verses 14-18. The instructions are delivered to the servants so that Esau will understand the purpose of the articles in the present. And as a further gesture of humility and to acknowledge Esau as his equal if not superior in the present situation, they are to inform him that Jacob is following in the rear. We are bound to observe the altered condition of Jacob with his brother from what it was before he left home.

Verses 19, 20. Several different servants were instructed to address Esau, one after the other, on the pleading mission of Jacob. This will give Esau an impression as to the eagerness of his brother to recognize his greatness and to gain for him his favor. It is further understood that unless the favor of Esau is secured he will not presume to see his face.

Verses 21-23. The "present" is sent in the forepart of the march. That is very appropriate. Unless the favor of Esau is obtained there is no use for the rest of the group to go on. But the time is too near night to complete the journey. After a brief rest he cares for the families and his goods and passes over the brook Jabbok. However, he personally remains on the other side and spends the night in a very unusual manner and in a way that becomes significant in history as we shall see.

Verse 24. Being left alone as to his company he had a wrestling contest that lasted throughout the night. The record here says he wrestled with a "man" but the prophet Hosea (chapter 12: 4) says it was an angel. All of which is understood by the fact that the angels come to human beings in the form of men. Otherwise they could not be seen and heard with the natural organs nor be able to partake of temporal food as they sometimes do. For another case of this kind see that of Abraham and Lot. When they came to Abraham (chapter 18: 2) they are called men and when to Lot (Chapter 19: 1) called angels. An angel is a messenger and thus a messenger from heaven is an angel.

Verse 25. As long as the angel conducted his wrestling match as a man only he was losing. He then invoked his supernatural powers and produced an impediment in Jacob. He touched his thigh and caused it to get out of joint and then he was able to put Jacob on the defensive. However we may think of the motive of all this circumstance, we should observe that lesson shown. As long as we depend on the ability of man only we will fail. But if we rely on the help of God we will accomplish what is right.

Verses 26, 27. The angel requests to be released as it is day. But Jacob will not consent unless the angel blessed him. Upon this the angel asked Jacob his name and it was told him.

Verse 28. This is where the additional name was bestowed, that of Israel. The meaning of the name in Hebrew is "he will rule as God." This name is here given to him in token of the success he just had over the angel of God. And it should be noted now that the term Israelites originated at this time and place and became one of the familiar names of the descendants of Abraham.

Verse 29. Then Jacob asked the angel his name but was chided for doing so. It was a natural curiosity for Jacob to wish for this information. But we can get the lesson here that heavenly messengers have more authority and rights than mere human beings. There was a practical object in view in discussing the name of Jacob. But nothing except curiosity would have been satisfied had Jacob's question been answered. But while the angel would not tell his name yet he blessed Jacob. This was something that would really benefit him while the knowing of the angel's name would not.

Verse 30. Since no man can see the personal face of God and live (Ex. 33: 20) we must conclude that Jacob considered the face of the angel with such great awe that he thought of him as of God. There would be no final authority in the statement he made further than to accept the statement as a true record of the writer in telling us of the impressions of Jacob at this time.

Verses 31, 32. *Penuel* This is the same as "Peniel" in previous verse. It is so named by Jacob because of his impression of the face of God. And the statement in the present passage merely meant that, as Jacob started to leave this place where he had the unusual experience and where the angel had touched his thigh, he halted upon his thigh. That is, he limped. Therefore, true to their inclination for superstition, the children of Israel will not eat that part of their food animals that corresponds to this of Jacob's thigh.

GENESIS 33

Verse 1. Jacob now gets a look at the forces of Esau and seems to be still more unfavorably impressed than he was when he first heard about it. He now makes a further arrangement of the ones in his own company. He makes a special distribution of the children and places them in the personal care of his four women.

Verse 2. It is interesting to observe that he placed them in the relation as to danger so as to favor them in the order of his preferences. Hence we see that the handmaids were placed first, as being in the most dangerous place, Leah comes next, while Rachel and her only child come last.

Verse 3. But we must admire the gallantry of Jacob in that he preceded all of them on this expedition, which he considered to be dangerous. He not only observes the usual custom of courteous salutation by bowing but does it seven times. That is, as soon as he is in immediate sight of Esau he begins his bowing. Then repeats it at intervals until he is in the presence of his brother. Doubtless all the remembrance of those events of long ago are crowding into his mind. He has never learned of any change, if any, that has come in Esau's feelings toward him. This is what makes us know that his mother never carried out the promise to send him word if any such change did come.

Verse 4. But the whole situation is opposite what Jacob expected. His brother ran to meet him and they engaged in an intimate embrace. *Fell on his neck.* This is a common expression found in the scriptures meaning a very close and affectionate contact of two people as a symbol of some common interest.

Verses 5-7. Esau next observed the people coming up in the same order that Jacob had arranged. As they approached they all bow themselves in token of respect as was the custom in use at that time and in that country. Jacob gives God the credit for all his blessings in the form of children and that they are graciously given him. But we should observe the expressions of humility and subjection used by Jacob. In speaking of himself in relation to Esau he calls himself a servant. We are not to understand this as at variance with the prediction made previously that "the elder shall serve the younger." That prediction never was repealed and applied to the permanent position in the world of the two peoples. But the instance at hand here is that which pertains to the men personally only and is a reflection back to the past deception which Jacob had practiced.

Verse 8. Upon inquiry Jacob informed Esau of the purpose of the drove of cattle present. That it was to find grace or favor in his sight. This not only was to assure him that he was wishing to make the ususal gesture of friendly recognition in the form of a "present" but that he also acknowledged his indebtedness to his brother. That if Esau should grant to Jacob his good will it would be a favor that might not have been justly expected. In short, it was a sort of apology for the past injustices done him.

Verses 9-11. Esau protested such a large present but Jacob insisted. He said for "therefore" have I seen thy face, etc. We have already learned the meaning of this word, that it is the sense of "properly or appropriately." So that it is very proper that Esau accept the present as a symbol of common friendship since that friendship has just now been demonstrated. The friendship is finally sealed and formally acknowledged, for the record says he took the present.

Verse 12. Esau then proposed a joint journey and that he would lead the way.

Verses 13, 14. The proposal of Esau is favorable to Jacob but he suggests that the mass of his group could not travel as fast as such a journey might cause. He will not ask Esau to be delayed in his journey to his own home community by the encumbrance of the large gathering connected with him. He then very respectfully suggested that Esau go on to his home and he would follow after with the women and children.

Verse 15. Esau accepts Jacob's suggestion about the order of their traveling. And as an indication of the friendship that has just been formed proposes to leave some of his folks with Jacob to make the journey with him. *What needeth it?* This is a somewhat awkward expression as the A. V. translators have given it to us. The second word in the expression is not in the original at all. The first one is from MEH and defined "properly interrogatively. What? (including how? why? when?)" — Strong. This shows the statement of Jacob merely meant he did not consider that necessary. And yet, he is glad to accept the suggestion because he wishes to find grace in the sight of Esau.

Verses 16, 17. The word Succoth as used here is descriptive and means a place where booths were made. The paragraph means that Jacob carried out his agreement to follow his brother to his own home community. And yet he did not want to impose all his own cattle as an encumbrance on him so he built places for their sheltering. But he did not intend this as a permanent dwelling place as the word "booth" has the meaning of a temporary shelter. After the friendly journey of the two brothers had been carried out as agreed then Jacob sought other territory.

Verses 18, 19. The area mentioned in the paragraph is farther north and is in the land of Palestine proper. Here is where Jacob purchased some ground on which to pitch his tent. This would indicate a more extended stay than would the building of booths as mentioned in preceding paragraphs.

Verse 20. *El-elohe-Israel.* The lexicon justifies the marginal definition as found here for this word. El is Hebrew for God. This word then signifies God. But not only that. There might be other so-called gods. So it is distinctly specified in this place that it is a certain God; yea, the God of Israel. Since this was the name lately acquired by Jacob through his unusual experience with the angel it is easy to see why he would wish to give such a name to this newly erected altar. The nations which had come under the observation of Jacob worshipped so many kinds of strange gods that he would logically be impressed with the superiority of the God that he worshipped over all these other Gods. Hence this expressive name.

GENESIS 34

Verse 1. Jacob is now dwelling in the community mentioned in close of preceding chapter and surrounded with people of foreign blood. His only daughter goes out on a sort of social adventure to mingle with the other girls of the country. This brought her into contact with society.

Verse 2. She was not mingling with what we might consider the "slummy" parts of the country for the man here brought into the story was a prince or at least his father was one. The simple statement is made that this young man lay with Dinah. Of course he was out of his bounds even under the unceremonial atmosphere of the marriage institution of those times for he was of a different nation than she. And there is nothing in the account that indicates violence for had that been the case she would have revolted against him. But no evidence that she did. And further indication of such conclusion will be seen in the next paragraph.

Verse 3. The writer expressly states that Shechem loved the damsel. This meant more than the mere fleshly pleasure involved for that was often experienced where there was no sentimental love. For instance, the case of Amnon and Tamar. (2 Sam. 13: 15) In the case here we are told that his soul, not merely his flesh, clave unto Dinah. Not only so, but he made love to her. It says he spake kindly to her. The word "kindly" is from LEB and defined "the heart" by Strong. This justifies the marginal reading here that he spake "to her heart." Altogether different from the conduct of a man who merely commits criminal assault.

Verse 4. As further evidence that the attachment which Shechem has formed for Dinah is pure and not base passion, he desires to make her his own legally and thus give her all the protection that an honorable marriage would bring. He requests his father to bring about such an arrangement.

Verse 5. Jacob heard of the affair and kept still till his sons returned from the field where they had been tending the cattle.

Verses 6, 7. In compliance with his son's wish Hamor contacts Jacob on the matter. In the meantime the sons of Jacob have returned from the field and were grieved. It is noteworthy that what is outstanding is that the folly had been wrought in Israel. The moral question involved is not all there is, but it is the additional fact that it has been done in Israel. This is God's people and these other people are aliens. We will not forget that the subject of marriage in original times was largely one of the fleshly relation. The mere fact that a man had become intimate with a woman might not constitute a breach of etiquet. It would depend upon the circumstances and the persons involved.

Verses 8-10. Hamor makes an earnest plea for mutual friendship. Not only in the matter of marriages between their respective sons and daughters, but also of property. He invites them to trade with them and secure land and possessions with them.

Verses 11, 12. Then the would-be husband adds his plea to that of his father. It was customary to give a dowry on behalf of the woman to become one's wife. Shechem is willing to go the limit in this also if only he can have the woman for wife. We can have no reasons to doubt the sincerity of his statements whether we approve of it or not.

Verses 13-17. The rite of circumcision had been the distinctive mark of the people of God from the days of Abraham. Now it is proposed that the Shechemites may be recognized if they will adopt circumcision. But they were not sincere when they made the offer as the inspired writer states. Besides, circumcision was to be observed with those either born in Abraham's house or bought with his money. These Shechemites did not come under either of these qualifications and the sons of Jacob surely knew it.

Verses 18, 19. The proposition was agreeable to the young man and his father and no delay was had in making the arrangements.

Verses 20-24. Hamor and his son took the proposition to the people of the city and insisted on their complying with it. The matter was agreed on and the men were all circumcised. Again we can have no doubt as to the sincerity of these people.

Verse 25. Surgery was not as scientific then as now and the work of circumcision was naturally a greater shock to the physical system than now. Besides, in the ordinary observance of that rite it was performed on infants eight days old and thus attended with less shock than with mature men. As a consequence there would follow naturally a period of enforced inactivity. Besides, note the record states they waited till the third day. That would doubtless be when the incapacity would be at its height and the men would be the less able to resist. Besides, since they had been sincere in all of the transaction they had no occasion to be armed nor suspicious. And under these conditions, two of the sons of Jacob, Simeon and Levi, armed their servants and came upon the city and slew all these circumcised men. It says they came upon the city "boldly." This is from a word that means "with safety." Since the Shechemites had no hint of anything fraudulent about the situation they were not prepared. So that the sons of Jacob were not only guilty of murder, but that after taking advantage of their victims, and still further, doing it on the pretense of a divine institution.

Verses 26-29. The sons of Jacob did not stop at the wholesale murder but took all their property that was in the house and in the field. They also took their wives and children captive and made general havoc of the place. All this because they said that Shechem had defiled their sister. Now the crime of criminal assault was punishable with death and was so instituted when God gave the national law through Moses. But this was not a case of that kind. Had that been so they would not have even pretended to accept the situation on condition of their adopting the rite of circumcision. But the only argument they made at the start was that it would be against their national policy to grant their request unless they adopt circumcision. But now, when they have them in their vengeance they lay it all to the so-called misdeed of defilement.

Verses 30, 31. Jacob protests their action. *Make me to stink.* This means they would make him to be abhorred of the surrounding people. At the present he seems to be interested in the immediate effect the tragedy might have on him more than on the great wrong that was done. But later, when he was speaking as an inspired Patriarch, he will lay more serious charge against them. (Chapter 49:5-7.) The only reply his sons made to their father's protests was that Shechem dealt with their sister as with a harlot. But this was insincere for they made no such complaint against the young man in the beginning. They only made an objection of national policy.

GENESIS 35

Verse 1. Bethel has become an established location geographically but not from the standpoint of any permanent buildings there. So Jacob is told to go up there and make an altar. That had been done before more than once. But these altars in the Patriarchal Dispensation were not always fixed objects, but had to be provided on occasion and for immediate use. He is reminded that God had appeared to him here at the time he was fleeing from the face of Esau.

Verses 2, 3. Jacob had dwelt for a score of years in the country of his wives' people where they were accustomed to idol worship. And they had brought some of them along with them. Now he commands his people to put them away and be clean. All this was preparatory to their going up to Bethel where they will meet with the living God. Yes, the God that heard Jacob there in the day of his distress.

Verses 4, 5. His people obeyed him and he disposed of all the objects they had among them that had been used for worship. After that they journeyed toward Bethel. The surrounding people did not pursue them because the terror of God was upon them. Since the pursuit if attempted would have been unfriendly but was prevented by the terror of God, we would be left with that phase of the term fear or terror that is unfavorable. That is, something caused them to be afraid of the punishment of God should they attempt to interfere with the actions of his people.

Verses 6, 7. The original name of Luz is mentioned here again which was what it had before the time of Jacob's dream. And after building the altar he added a syllable to the name in honor of the special providence that had been his at this place. The simple word Bethel means house of God. But Jacob wishes to combine it with the idea that not only does God have a house but that the God of that house was present there.

Verse 8. We have long ago lost trace of Rebekah. But her nurse was still living at the time we now have reached. In some way she seems to have got into the company of Jacob and his people. At this place she died and was buried near Bethel.

Verses 9, 10. This passage does not contain any new thoughts. But it was a common thing for God to repeat his promises and other important statements.

Verses 11, 12. The famous promise is here repeated. *Loins.* This is from the Hebrew word CHALATS and defined "(in the sence of *strength*); only in the dual; the loins (as the seat of vigor)" — Strong. This gives us a clearer view of this term that is frequently used in the scriptures regarding the offspring of men. Since it is known that a child is the product of a man's whole nature we would pause and wonder when it so often speaks as if it were from the loins especially. But the strength of a man is contributed to bring about his offspring. And since the loins of a man are the place of most bodily strength physically it is very properly used as a figure in this place.

Verses 14, 15. A drink offering simply means that he used an article otherwise used for drink. This would indicate the sacrifice or giving up of something that could have been used personally. And olive oil being the only kind of oil they had in those days it likewise indicated a sacrifice of an article of value. Also, oil came to be used in consecration ceremonies. In this place Jacob is consecrating the altar to God. Jacob called the place Bethel. This does not mean that the present was the occasion that the place received that name for we know that was not the case. But the word means "house of God." And just as Christians repeatedly speak of the assembly as God's assembly without implying they are then giving it the name, only recognizing it again, so Jacob recognizes this place as the house of God.

Verses 16-20. The sad event of the death of Rachel occurred at this time. Jacob had taken up his journey southward and had reached a place near Ephrath which is another name for Bethlehem. At this place the time came for Rachel to be delivered of her second child. But the ordeal was too much for her physical strength. We are not told whether her strength had been run down by the perils of journeying, only that she had hard labor and died at the time. However, she lived long enough to know that it was another boy. She could have recalled that when Joseph was born she named him so from the belief that she was to have another son. At least she was conscious long enough and near enough to the delivery that the midwife could assure her that the child was to be born successfully and that it was a son. She named him even, before she died, and the name was in token of her sorrow. While that was appropriate from her view point, yet she was to be gone soon and he would remain. Hence his father gave him another name, one more in keeping with the success of the future. Jacob marked the place of her grave which is a Biblical example for gravestones. Before leaving this paragraph it is well to notice the expression "soul was in departing." Materialists of various kinds deny that anything lives after the death of the body. That all there is of a human being dies at one time and thus nothing leaves. But here is the plain statement of an inspired writer that her soul departed. This upsets the doctrine of materialism.

Verses 21, 22. Bilhah was previously the handmaid of his wife Rachel.

But after the union he formed with her at Rachel's request she had the position of concubine to him. As already explained, in those days of plural marriages, a concubine was as legally a wife as the other, but had inferior property rights. And thus when Reuben was intimate with her he thereby defiled his father's bed.

Verses 23-26. This paragraph is a tabulation of Jacob's twelve sons, showing by which wife or concubine each was born to him.

Verse 27. By this we learn that Isaac had been dwelling in the original location used by his father, in Mamre or Hebron. Jacob thus gets back from his absence from his father, an absence of a quarter of a century. We are glad to know that he got to see his father again although he never saw his mother after his flight from home.

Verses 28, 29. The age of Isaac should be marked here for convenient and useful reference. In relating his death the writer uses the expression "give up the ghost" which is the same in thought as used with reference to the death of Rachel in 18th verse. If materialism is true then a man at death does not give up anything. He would retain everything that had ever been a part of him. But the statement that he did give up something disproves materialism. And what a satisfying thought comes to us from the fact that the sons of Issac, Esau and Jacob buried him. All past enmities are over with them and they unitedly render their loving services at the last scenes of their father. Furthermore, by consulting chapter 49: 31 we learn that they buried him in the burial place that had been provided for that purpose by their grandfather, Abraham. It was in the cave of Machpelah. This became the last resting place for the bodies of the great Patriarchs, Abraham, Isaac, and Jacob.

GENESIS 36

Verse 1. *Generations*. It will be remembered this word means "family history." The chapter will give the history of Esau's family as it concerns the marriages and various ones born to the family tree.

Verse 2. This verse relates names of the Canaanitish women Esau married, the thing that had grieved his parents. He then made a different selection as follows.

Verse 3. This is the woman he married after seeing that the daughters of Canaan displeased his father and mother (chapter 28: 8, 9).

Verses 4-8. Here is another instance that shows the rather friendly feeling Esau had for Jacob in that he was willing to give way to him in the matter of land for their cattle. In this connection it is stated that he dwelled in Mt. Seir or Edom.

Verses 9-14. This paragraph is somewhat repetitious of some former statements of the family history of Esau. Particular attention is called to the name of Amalek in verse 12. He will figure prominently in a later history of God's people.

Verses 15-19. *Dukes*. This is from ALLUPH and defined "familiar; a friend, also gentle * * * and so a chieftain."—Strong. We can appreciate the value of Esau's rank among the people of the earth when we recall his past indignities.

Verses 20-30. *Sons of Seir the Horite*. This is to be understood as meaning the sons or inhabitants of Mt. Seir related to the Horites. These were people who had possession of this place prior to Esau's taking it. Read chapter 14: 6; also Deut. 2: 12, 22. Since the valor of Esau in supplanting these original inhabitants of Seir would be an important item, the history of these people is also recorded here. That is, it was to show that they were no weak or insignificant people. *Mules*. This is from YEM and defined "a warm spring."—Strong. I do not know why we have the strange translation as it is in the A. V. This original word is not used in any other place in the Bible. And also, there is a true word for "mule" used a number of times, and thus it is not clear what led the translators to give us such an odd rendering here.

Verses 31-43. We are not specially interested in the family history of Esau any further than to observe that he did not dwindle out as an unimportant person. Verse at the beginning of this paragraph states that Edom had kings before Israel. This would be no detriment to reputation of Israel from the viewpoint of God since it was not his desire that his people have kings. But from the standpoint of worldly importance it is a significant fact that Esau or Edom, the man who was pushed from his possessions by fraud, was blessed much in the way as described here.

GENESIS 37

Verse 1. *Stranger.* This means that he was a temporary resident. Not that he expected to move out in a short time, but that Isaac was lately a native of another country and at the time of our story was a newcomer. But Jacob has now been in this land at least for 17 years so that he could be rightfully called a dweller. Hence the text says he "dwelt" in the land where his father was a newcomer.

Verse 2. Again we read of the generations of a man which means here his family history. This is the verse that gives us the age of Joseph at one time of his life and it should be noted carefully. Joseph is here said to be feeding his father's flocks and doing this "with" his brethren. However, he was specially grouped with the sons of Bilhah and Zilpah. These were younger than the sons of Leah. Yet the others were out in the work also as we will hear from them in the story. *Evil report.* This is from RAH and DIBBAH and together as used here means that the brothers were living a dishonest life in some way and thus acting slanderously. But in spite of their attempts at stealth, Joseph detected their evil life and reported it to their father. We do not endorse the spirit of the ordinary "tattle-tale" but the circumstances here are to be considered. The good name of the father of these men is about to be disgraced through the misconduct of the sons and it is proper that Joseph inform him of it. He did not spread the report generally as a gossip would, but brought the report to his father, the man who was most vitally concerned and thus who had a perfect right to know what was going on. Joseph thus did the right thing in reporting this matter.

Verse 3. There is no reason for speculating on the cause why Jacob favored Joseph since the text plainly tells us it was because he was the son of his old age. He was born when his father was 91. See note at chapter 30: 25. What other reasons that may be assigned to this would be guess work. *Colors.* The margin here gives us "pieces" and the lexicon justifies it. However, the definition in the lexicon also suggests the idea of many widths and that the writer is conveying to us that the father made him this coat with ample provision as to size. He is yet a lad of not more than 17 when he gave him the coat. Since he is not yet fully matured he will wish him not to "outgrow" the coat, hence makes it generous in size. And this would not be objectionable from the standpoint of appearance since the definition indicates the coat was in the nature of a tunic and thus would be expected to be loose.

Verse 4. This is the old story of envy and shows the violence of that feeling which is born of regret at another's good fortune. They at first get their revenge on Joseph and later will get it on the aged father.

Verses 5-8. There is nothing in this story that says anything about what Joseph thought of the dreams. Whether he thought they meant any prominence of him over his brethren we do not know. He merely told them his dream. But they correctly interpreted it as the sequel will show. But it was very illogical and thus cruel for them to blame him for the dream. Had he pretended to be a prophet and ventured upon a prediction of his preeminence over them they might have laid it to his personal ambition and would have had some ground for feeling against him. But he simply told them his dream.

Verses 9-11. This dream is more extensive than the first one in that it included others besides his brethren. He does not offer any solution of the dream but tells it to his father and brethren. His father made the application this time and interpreted it to apply to the subjection of the whole family to him or before him. We know that the personal mother of Joseph was not living at this time (chapter 35: 18). But since the Lord selected the family set-up as the scene of the present dream he would name one complete. The trend of the dream is that the entire family will some day be brought to dependence upon him. The difference in the attitude of the father and the brethren toward the dream is to be noted. The brethren envied him while the father observed it. That means that he kept it in mind and did not try to pass it off as of nothing.

Verses 12-14. When his father wished him to go look after the welfare of the brethren he was ready. Evidently by this time something had caused Joseph to remain at home instead of working with the brethren in caring for the sheep as he did at the first. The fact that he reported their conduct to his father would make his presence objectionable to them and that suggests the only plausible explanation we can have at present. But it is interesting to notice that he is free from resentment or even fear of them. When requested to go in the interests of his brethren he said, "here I am."

Verses 15-17. Joseph got astray and was found by a man as he was wandering. Upon inquiry he told the man for whom he was seeking and was put on their trail from the remark the man had overheard them make. He found the brethren at Dothan.

Verses 18-20. Instead of being filled with appreciation and love for their brother upon seeing him coming to them, it was opposite. They knew that he could not have been coming for any purpose but one of good to them. Yet their old envy is so strong that they decide this is the time for them to "get even." But while their hatred is wicked enough to plot murder against him, it is cowardly enough to want to evade the guilt. Hence they plan a deception. At first they word their story as a deliberate lie to their father but we will see how the wording was changed in form although not in meaning.

Verses 21, 22. It is plain that not all of the brothers were directly included in the plot, or at least not to the same extent. For it says that when Reuben "heard" it. He then plots an escape for Joseph by suggesting casting him into the pit and not slay him outright. Then the writer tells us his purpose was to deliver Joseph free again.

Verses 23, 24. The suggestion of Reuben was accepted for they took Joseph and after robbing him of his coat that had been the gift of his father, they cast him into a pit. There was no water in the pit. Just what they intended further we do not know. But it was necessary for the writer to tell us the pit was dry that we could understand how Joseph would be available alive when they get ready for another disposition of him.

Verse 25. While their further actions were pending the brothers sit down to have a meal. While they were eating they saw a group of traders on their way to Egypt to sell their wares. Egypt was a market for the products of the east and always had money because their country was always productive.

Verse 26, 27. Judah makes a plea that sounds very sympathetic for Joseph. Why slay their brother and be guilty of his blood? But I fear his motive is not wholly one based on his love for the brother. He asks "what profit" will it be. This would be part of the motive, that of profit. If they sell him they will get him away from the father, get revenge on him and his father, too, and will be the gainers financially from the deal. To this they agreed.

Verse 28. This verse, as well as others in this chapter refers to the Midianites and Ishmaelites interchangeably. This does not mean that they were the same people for they were not. The Midianites descended from a son of Abraham through his last marriage while the Ishmaelites descended from Abraham through his son by Hagar. But the two peoples were more or less wild in their habitations and traveled as a common group. We cannot even conclude that one was mentioned incidentally as traveling with the group that bought Joseph for both of them are mentioned as having had him. Hence the first explanation made here is the correct one.

Verses 29, 30. Reuben was the one who suggested placing Joseph in the pit and it was for the purpose of delivering him to his father. We therefore know he would not have consented to having him sold. But the statement in this paragraph explains that he was away when the deal was made and as far as we know never learned the full truth. They calmly let him grieve over the matter, at least for the present.

Verses 31, 32. In those days there was no knowledge of chemistry that enabled one to discover whether blood were human or not. Hence they can use the blood of a kid for their purpose. Notice how different their actual statement to their father from what they said they would tell him. In the proper meaning of "finding" a thing they lied to their father about the coat for they did not find it. But they let the old man come to his own conclusion about the situation.

Verses 33, 34. It had the desired effect. Jacob recognized the coat. He concluded that Joseph had been torn with wild beasts. This circumstance proves that a lie if believed has the same effect on a man's mind that the story would, were it true. And if that is true of an unfavorable lie the same would hold in that of a favorable one. So that if a person were to claim a certain impression of good from a story, the fact of that good impression would be no evidence of the truth of the story.

Verse 35. It says *all* his sons rose to comfort Jacob. This gives us one of the blackest instances of hypocrisy we have on record. This must include the brothers who caused all this sorrow. They know they have sold the brother into slavery and yet allow the aged father to mourn his son as if dead. They pretend to want to comfort him which can be nothing but pretense. Had they not wanted to acknowledge their guilt at this time, it would have been bad enough to have been silent and let the father suffer alone. But instead of that they pretend they know of the death of the brother and wish to console the father from day to day.

Verse 36. By some inattention to the text people often entertain the wrong idea of Joseph's master. Note here it is not Pharaoh but an officer of his. But we will notice that it is an important officer for he had charge of Pharaoh's guard forces.

GENESIS 38

Verse 1. This chapter is a break into the history of the more direct story of Joseph. But the facts recorded therein will have a direct bearing on the history as a whole. This verse merely records a little episode in the life of Judah that would not seem to be very important at first.

Verse 2. While here in the community of Hirah Judah saw a woman of the Canaanites who attracted him and he "went in unto her" which is one of the Biblical expressions meaning the intimacy between the sexes. We have previously observed that God was very particular to have the blood strain kept in line with the original stock for a period. Just why he relaxed on this regulation we are not told. But we do know that a number of instances will be found in the record where strangers were admitted into the line and became connected with the ancestry of Christ. But with all this variation we should not forget that the line on the male side was not thus changed. So that when we get to Christ we have two lines of blood on the male side that come down to him.

Verses 3-5. In this paragraph take notice of the three sons born to Judah and the order of their birth. This will account for the transactions soon to follow.

Verses 6, 7. The usual custom for the father to select a wife for the son is here observed and the firstborn son is thus provided for. We are not informed what the wickedness was of which Er was guilty. But it must have been serious for the Lord punished him with death. On this circumstance we likewise observe that God is taking a hand in this situation or else he would not have been active to the extent of slaying the man. This idea will be still more evident in the events soon to follow.

Verse 8. Here Judah gives a command that later became one of the ordinances of the law of Moses. If a man dies without offspring his brother or nearest relative is to take the widow and beget children by her. But the seed thus begotten was to be placed in the records under the name of the dead brother.

Verses 9, 10. Quack doctors and medicine venders have exposed their ignorance of the very words of this passage in their desire to find some scripture for their fake merchandise. Reference to the perversion of nature artificially that is supposed to be a common practice among men and even women (but called masturbation in women) lately, is usually termed "onanism." This implies that God punished Onan because of his perversion of nature here. But the very wording of the text contradicts such a conclusion. Had Onan consummated the act in a perfectly natural manner, but had done anything else that would have prevented the result of conception he would have been punished just the same. The sin for which he was punished was "birth control." This is a vice that is practiced commonly today by many people who have never once suspected that they are committing a grave sin. The intimate relation of the sexes is God's plan for replenishing the earth with human kind. As an inducement for man to cooperate with Him in this result he has made that relationship a pleasureable one. But when human beings proceed with the pleasureable feature of the relationship and yet use means to prevent conception, that constitutes cheating God out of his part of the transaction while securing the human part.

Verse 11. Judah's remaining son was not of marriageable age; he tells Tamar to remain a widow until he is grown. She obeys his directions and waits faithfully.

Verse 12. Judah now lost his wife by death. After the period of mourning was over he decides to look after his property interests and see how the men were getting along in the business of sheepshearing. He invites his friend to go with him. This takes him away from the immediate vicinity of his home and indicated he had forgotten about his promise to Tamar. She had been waiting patiently all these years.

Verses 13, 14. The fact that Tamar had continued wearing widow's garments up to this time proves she had been true to the directions of Judah. For had she planned on taking in a stranger she would have been compelled to lay aside her garments of widowhood else no man would have received her. This is proved by the events about to happen. *Veil* and *wrapped* are from the same and merely mean that she put a covering over herself. This alone would not identify herself as a harlot as such posture was often used by very modest women. But she does not want to be recognized by the man whom she plans to decoy. The thing that led him to take her to be a harlot was the place where she was sitting. The text says an "open place." The margin says "the door of eyes" and the lexicon justifies that renderin.g It means that she selected a very prominent place, a place where many people were passing and sat down there. A woman with no legitimate reason for remaining in such a public place would be suspected, at least, of being a public woman. Not that it was a specific advertisement of such character, but would be open to such conclusion. Another consideration of this covering that might lead to the conclusion she wished to cause, would be that a woman who desires to lead that kind of life might not want her acquaintances to recognize her and so she would hide her identity by putting a veil over her face.

Verse 15. It had the desired effect. Judah noticed her and took her for a harlot.

Verse 16. Judah proposes intimacy with her but she gives him the information that she must obtain some profit from the transaction and asks for a bid. A professional harlot would probably not have asked any such question as she would already have her "price" and would promptly tell him so But this is not to be a simple matter of intimacy for money on her side. Hence she asks the question. And the fact that she did so would indicate that she would require something worthwhile. But Judah did not come away from home with anything like this experience in mind and was not prepared to pay her any great price.

Verse 17. He proposed to send her a kid from the flock. But of course that, too, was not present, so she would have nothing but his word for it. Hence she asks for a pledge that would bind him to it.

Verse 18. He told her to name the pledge. Of course she is going to name something whose personal ownership could not be questioned afterward. So she asks for his body ornaments and walking cane. He delivered them to her and went in unto her.

Verse 19. Having accomplished her purpose she returned to her home and resumed the garments of her widowhood. Of course, since Judah is away temporarily looking after his sheep he has had no opportunity of missing her from her accustomed place even if he were in the habit of seeing her there. The inspired writer tells us that she conceived in this first act of intimacy. That does not mean that she knew it then, of course. But she is going to bide her time until nature tells the story. Should the required period of time pass with no signs of pregnancy she can still have recourse to the pledge in her possession and confront him with it.

Verses 20-23. Judah will be true to his pledge to a harlot but was indifferent about his promise to his daughter-in-law. He sent his pledge by the hand of his friend who was unable to find the woman after inquiry. Judah's concern in the matter is not the most refined. He fears he will be held in contempt by the people of the community if it is reported that he did not fulfill his pledge to a woman, even though she is a harlot. But nothing could be done about it.

Verse 24. It was true, as often said, that "time will tell." At the usual time the evidence was visible that Tamar was an expectant. And since she is not a married woman it means that she has been playing the harlot. And as the penalty for that evil was death, Judah gave commandment that it be done in this case.

Verse 25. Tamar has the articles of the pledge still in her possession. Of course he would expect to conclude that the woman to whom he gave those articles still had them, but who was she? She presents the evidence to him.

Verse 26. Not only does Judah acknowledge the justice of her claim but also the justice of her actions. He says she has been more righteous than he. But the record further states that he knew her again no more which means that he did not wish to take advantage of the woman whom he had neglected.

Verses 27-30. The point of interest to us in this passage is that of the birth of one of the men in the line of Christ's pedigree. There is nothing especially irregular in this whole circumstance as far as affecting the legitimacy of the line of blood of Christ. It is clearly in keeping with the status of the marriage relation that was suffered through those years. Tamar was a pure woman in her general life and also Judah did the right thing by her after learning her identity. He knew her no more.

GENESIS 39

Verse 1. The inspired writer now takes up the story broken off at the last verse of chapter 37. The importance of the purchaser of Joseph should be noted. Not only was he an officer of Pharaoh's. But he was connected with the guard. Not only was he connected with the guard but he was captain of this service. Foreign men were sometimes employed by kings for important services, but this particular one was of the same blood as his master, so that his general importance should be recognized.

Verse 2. The Lord was with Joseph and again we see God's remembrance of Abraham in that he is looking after his seed. Joseph not only obtains a service of importance, but one of great confidence since he was taken into the house of his master. This brought a slave into very intimate association with his family and other items of trust.

Verses 3, 4. This confidence of the master in his slave was increased. This was caused by his observation that prosperity had come to his house since his purchase and he attributed it to his God. And if that be the case it would be folly to overlook or mistreat this wonderful slave. Therefore he makes him ruler over all that he has.

Verse 5. The Lord blessed the Egyptian's house for Joseph's sake. This again is according to the promise made to Abraham (chapter 12: 3).

Verse 6. Since the food he ate was necessarily brought into contact with him he knew that he had it. Otherwise he would not have known about its presence in the house because he had left all his possessions completely in Joseph's care. This is merely an expression of the writer to impress us with the position which Joseph had. *Goodly, favoured.* These words are from originals that mean he was beautiful both in his countenance and form of body. This is to account for the events following.

Verse 7. The appeal which Joseph's appearance made to the lustful eyes and desires of this woman led her into making this proposal to him.

Verses 8, 9. Joseph does not pretend any physical indifference on this subject. His first protest is made on the thought of betrayal of confidence. He reminds her of the complete dependance his master has shown on him. That he has kept nothing from him that would be right for him to have. But let us observe his significant conclusion of this matter by saying that in yielding to her suggestion he would be sinning against God. Hence we have the wonderful principle portrayed before us here that to betray righteous confidence and use it as a means of obtaining carnal pleasure would constitute a sin against God as well as man.

Verse 10. This wicked woman was not content to let the matter rest after Joseph had refused but continued her solicitations. Josephus says she begged and pleaded with tears in her eyes but to no avail over him. It is worth our while to contemplate the situation. It is often claimed today that certain temptations are so great that even God would not expect one to resist. Men will contend that when the surroundings are of a certain combination it is impossible to resist. But how could a situation ever arise with more "irresistible" features than this one before Joseph? Here he is, away from all his people with no reason to think he will ever see them again. The woman who is soliciting him is his mistress and thus in position to shield him from all others afterward since she would wish to continue this practice. Thus there would be perfect protection against discovery. And she being a married woman would free him from the fear of the consequences of their act. He is in the house daily by reason of the kind of service that his master assigned to him so that his presence cannot be cause for gossip. Everything in the case was favorable for the yielding to the temptation. If there is such a thing as an "irresistible" temptation, this is one. Yet Joseph makes complete refusal. Not only does he refuse to comply with her request, but refuses to be with her. He is taking no chances.

Verse 11. *Business.* This is from a word that means a higher type of employment than mere servile work. It refers to the more responsible matter of looking after the interests of his master. And this harmonizes with the complete confidence that his master is said to have placed in him. That accounts for the fact that at the time now spoken of there were none of the men there. They were out and engaged in the servile duties of common slaves while Joseph was about the more personal affairs of his master's house. There they are, all of the men gone and Joseph there alone with her!

Verse 12. This wicked woman imagined she could compel him to gratify her since she was his mistress. That she had the right to command him and that it was his duty to obey her. But even all this did not move him to yielding. He protested that he was to be excused from obedience in such matters. Men wore loose garments in those times and in that country. Her attempted contact with him was by this garment. But also the nature of this garment gave him opportunity for escape. He did not try to recover his garment but got out of the house as soon as possible.

Verses 13-15. With the garment in her possession she has a visible evidence of his supposed guilt. Her reference to "he" of course means her husband. But she is low enough to play upon the idea of Joseph's being a foreigner and a slave to give a show of plausibility to her story. And, of course, the fact that the slave has fled without taking his outer garment is apparent proof that he had discarded it at the time of his attempted attack. This is a practical demonstration of the fact that even when appearances seem conclusive we should be careful before coming to decisions. In spite of the appearances we might be deceived.

Verses 16-18. This wicked woman depends on the same "evidence" to convince her husband. There is no question that disappointed lust is a cause of the most vicious plots of vengeance. This woman has been thus disappointed and now plans to take her spite out on Joseph. With this end in view she makes the same speech she had made to the men and confirmed it by showing the garment in her hand.

Verses 19, 20. The husband did what was the most natural thing. He accepted the speech and evidence of his wife and concluded that this Hebrew slave in whom he had placed so much confidence had deceived him. The secular record of this incident says that the husband praised his wife as being more virtuous than he had previously thought her to be. Thus, this woman with the disappointed lust gnawing at her nerves causes one of the most virtuous of young men to be classed as a would-be ravisher and worthy of punishment. Not only will he be imprisoned, but to make sure that he is in safe keeping he will be put into the prison used by Pharaoh for his prisoners.

Verses 21-23. True to his promise to Abraham and his seed, God remembers Joseph and causes him to be shown favor by the keeper of the prison. He is placed in charge of the prison including the other prisoners. And, as in the case of his former master, he never violated that confidence.

GENESIS 40

Verse 1-4. When these two servants of Pharaoh offended the king he decided to have them imprisoned. But they were placed with other prisoners where they could be put under the guard of some one else besides being inside a prison. This happened to be the place where Joseph was. But instead of being placed under Joseph in the sense of rank they were placed under the service of Joseph. Of course, since Joseph is a prisoner of Pharaoh's employ, he is logically inferior, even as a prisoner to the prisoners of the king. Hence, he is charged with serving them. That means of course, he is to see after their needs. They were to continue "a season" in this situation. This is from a word that means the arrangement was intended to be temporary. This will accord with the events that are soon to be reported. Whether all this was brought about by the decrees of God we know not. But we do know that the imprisonment of the two servants mentioned was not permanent.

Verse 5. *According to the interpre-*

tation. This expression occurs a number of times in the Bible. It is more significant than is usually realized. The ordinary dream may be caused by various conditions and would have no meaning as to the future. But when God wishes to use a dream as one method of revealing something to man, and this is one of the methods he used in olden times, (Heb. 1: 1) he would cause the person to have a dream that would harmonize with the thing already decided upon. That is, it God decrees that a certain thing or things shall happen, he will then cause the party to have a dream to suit the coming events. Therefore, the facts already decided upon by the Lord that are to come to pass would be the explanation of the dream. From this standpoint we would see that the thing for which the dream stands was arranged in the divine mind first, and the dream came afterward. That is why we have the expression in various places that the dream was according to the interpretation. It was according to the thing already determined upon and God is the one who so determined it.

Verses 6-13. The subject matter of this passage is so obvious that detailed comments on particular verses is unnecessary. God had determined that each of these two prisoners was to be taken out of the prison in three days. But one was to be taken out to be executed while the other to be restored to his former service to the king. No one knows why one was executed and the other restored to service. But since God knew all about it, he caused these men to have a dream to fit the facts, which, however, required an inspired interpreter to explain it. And Joseph is the one to do this service. God is still with Joseph and is preparing the groundwork for his future greatness in this country.

Verse 14. This simple, reasonable, logical, plea of Joseph cannot but create in our minds the greatest sympathy and interest. What better opportunity could anyone have for showing his gratitude for favors than by mentioning him to the king. He would need only to state the facts without any special pleading. Just "make mention" of his fellow prisoner to Pharaoh and the facts would do the rest. We are seriously impressed with the solemnity of the occasion.

Verse 15. He does not mean his accusation to be against the people who purchased him, for that was considered a legitimate business at that time. But his brothers had no personal possession of him that gave them the right to make merchandise of him.

Verses 16-19. The facts of this paragraph are noticed in the one near above and will not need further comments here. However, it should be noticed that the baker asked Joseph for interpretation of his dream when he saw that the other was good. Had that of the butler been unfavorable the indication is that he would have refrained from seeking word from Joseph. This shows another trait of human nature. Men profess to be wanting information but many times they mean to want it provided it is information that will be agreeable to them.

Verses 20-22. Pharaoh made the occasion of his birthday the one for the carrying out of the things already pictured in the dreams and interpreted by Joseph. He thus celebrates the occasion by executing the baker and restoring his butler to the personal service of bringing the wine to his lord upon requirement.

Verse 23. This is a very sad verse. Ingratitude is classed among the worst of weaknesses. After the favor had been done him by his fellow prisoner he forgot his own duty. Not that Joseph had caused his release from prison, but having correctly explained his dream, gratitude should have prompted him to return the kindness as he was requested. And there was no excuse on the ground of the length of time for it all had happened within three days. And we are sure those three days were days of wondering. There was no specific evidence that the interpretations were true. Time alone can tell. For this reason we know the subject was constantly in his mind. But the third day has come, the day he is to be released. Will it come to pass? Yes, the day has come. An officer comes to the prison and leads him forth to the outside and to freedom and leaves his friend, Joseph, in the prison. He is taken into Pharaoh's house to be restored to his former service and to join in the happy festivities of the occasion of the king's birthday. But poor Joseph is forgotten. What a test upon his trust. But no evidence now nor afterward that he faltered in that trust.

GENESIS 41

Verse 1. Two years have passed since the events of the previous chapter. It is again time for God to take a hand in the historic movements and again decides to make use of the dream. Don't lose sight of Heb. 1: 1. The things that are to come to pass in the next 14 years have already been decided upon by the Lord. He is in charge of the universe and manages it according to the counsels of his own will. But he does not propose in this instance to reveal in direct language the predictions. He chooses to do it by the dream method. And of course, he will cause the king to have dreams which, when explained, will coincide with the facts already determined upon. That will make the dream to be "according to the interpretation."

Verses 2-4. The first dream pertained to kine. Since the sequel will show that the thing determined upon was related to the productions of the land, it would be fitting to use objects that would be affected by the products of the same. Hence the use of kine in this dream. The simple narrative is that seven fat fleshed kine came up first out of the river. It is significant that they came up "out of the river" because the land of Egypt depended on this as the source of their fertility. See comments on this at Chapter 12: 10. It is also significant that the other seven kine that were so poor also came up out of the river. This object of their worship and the source of their nourishment. That seven poor kine could come up out of it could mean nothing but that even their chief source of life and one of their gods would be prevented from giving them its accustomed support. *So Pharaoh awoke.* Why not let him have both dreams while asleep? God wants him to be assured that he had two distinct dreams. If he should have them while in the one period of sleep their emphasis might not be as great. So he awoke.

Verses 5-7. Again the objects for the dream are such as depended on the fertility of the land for life and that fertility depended on moisture. But this moisture, while coming primarily from the river, yet it must be spread out over the land. And so in selecting the grain for this dream it would properly be merely stated that there "came up." *One stalk.* This is from a word meaning stem or reed and means the same that we would in speaking of a straw of wheat. Of course also we understand the word "ear" here is the same as we call the head of grain since the small grain was in the Bible called corn. It is the rule of nature that each stem or straw will have just one head or ear. But here are seven on the same stalk. But this is not the end of the unusual growth. Not only were seven ears made to shoot out from this one stem, but below or after them were seven other ears made to shoot out. But the second set of seven ears were blasted and thin. Not only so, but, as in the case of the kine, the seven impoverished objects consumed the other seven in their group. At the present we are not told what effect, if any, the eating of the seven good objects had for the others. The thing that is likely to be overlooked in this second dream is that the fourteen ears were all on one stalk. That would be as true to nature as could be done without a separate miracle. If there were two stalks of wheat growing separately it would be conceivable that one could have a good ear on it while the other a thin one. But even if such a rare thing should happen that seven ears would show up on each of these two stalks, yet their being on two separate stalks would make them independent of each other. Then if the shriveling of the seven good ones is to come as result of contact with the others an additional miracle would have to be performed to have such contact take place. God did not see fit to burden his narrative with this additional miracle. But if all of the ears are on one stalk so that they have a common source of nourishment, then it could be understandable how the seven blasted ears drew on the sap already having been supplied to the seven good ones and thus cause the seven good ones to become shriveled also. Therefore, from all these considerations we must not be confused and overlook the wonderful circumstance here, that the Lord caused fourteen ears of small grain to grow out of one stalk or stem.

Verse 8. *Magicians.* This is from CHARTOM and defined "a horoscopist." —Strong. These were men who claimed to understand the future that pertained to a human's personal interests by a system of circles. And since the interpretation of such circles might be a matter of uncertainty the king also called for his wise men. This is from a word signifying chiefly men of unusual intelligence and not necessarily supernatural ability. But with the use of these magicians to draw the lines and circles and then the wise men to help interpret them, he hoped to obtain the desired information. But we are informed that none of them could interpret the dreams to the king.

Verses 9-13. Of course the chief butler has been near his lord ever since he was restored to his service two years ago. And when all this commotion took place about the dreams of Pharaoh he naturally was aware of it and it stirred up his memory of a certain time when he too was confused over a dream. The A.V. gives us the word "faults" for the expression of the butler. But the original word is CHET and defined by Strong as "a crime or its penalty." This indicates that the butler was guilty of serious neglect of duty. And indeed, ingratitude is a most serious sin. The only redeeming feature about it is that the butler forgot about it and thus we do not have to think about his failure of duty through contempt or cold indifference. And thus, since he has the subject brought to his mind he acknowledges his "faults" and then tells the king the story. We notice the familiar expression "acording to the interpretation."

Verse 14. Upon hearing the story of the butler they called for Joseph. The record says they brought him hastily. But not so much so that Joseph did not make the preparation that would make him presentable to the king. It sometimes happens that people make as if they are "just as good" as men in authority and show their attitude toward them by a disrespectful and contemptuous conduct. But Joseph wishes to show his respect to a man in high position. He shaves and changes his raiment. This is a principle that is taught in the New Testament. (1 Peter 2: 17.) This is not all of the fine temperament we here see in Joseph. He has been unjustly imprisoned and has been languishing under a false charge of violent immorality. No one seemed to care about him enough to investigate to see if the accusation against him were true. Now then, when some great authority wishes a favor he calls on him. But there is not the slightest indication of resentment nor revenge. He comes willingly and presents himself before the king.

Verse 15. Pharaoh states the reason of his being called and that he has heard of his ability to interpret a dream.

Verse 16. Here again the humility of Joseph is manifested. How good it would be if all servants of God would give him the glory for whatever good they might be the means of accomplishing. But too often men love the praise of men and thus are constrained to take the credit of their feats to themselves. But Joseph expressly says it is not in him. Then declares that God shall give Pharaoh an answer of peace. The use of this last word would not necessarily mean that the interpretation of the dreams will show coming events to be nothing but desirable ones. But, the answer is going to be so complete and wise that the king will be at perfect peace as to the meaning.

Verses 17-24. The things related in this paragraph are practically the same as in the first part of the chapter except that it mentions the fact that when the poor kine devoured the fat ones it left them still ill favored. But the story is the same so it will not be necessary to say more on it here.

Verse 25. This verse brings out the same thought expressed above, that an inspired dream is always preceded by the determination of God to have a certain thing come to pass, then causes the person involved to have a dream to correspond with the events to come. Here Joseph tells Pharaoh that God has shown him what he is about to do.

Verses 26-31. The seven years of plenty and then the same number of years of famine would be a miraculous occurrence. In the first place it was impossible for Egypt to have a natural famine since the Nile River supplied it with moisture and was never an entire failure. Thus a famine would have to be brought on by divine decree. This is what is taught in Psa. 105: 16-23. Also, the fact that an exact number of years of extreme plenty was foretold and to be followed with the same number of years of famine would be so arbitrary as to prove it to be a miracle. But it is God's method of bringing the descendents of Abraham into Egypt and thus fulfill the predictions he made in Chapter 15: 13, 14.

Verse 32. *Doubled, twice.* This might confuse technical persons who think it means the thing happened four times. But the first word is from SHANAH and defined "to fold, i. e., duplicate." The second is from PAHAMAH and defined "a stroke."—Strong. The whole sentence therefore means as if it said the dream was given to Pharaoh in a duplicated stroke. And the purpose for so doing is explained as being because the thing is "established" by the Lord. The margin says "prepared" and the lexicon agrees with that rendering. Also, it agrees with the comments offered previously that an inspired dream is made to fit a determination of God already decided upon.

Verses 33-36. This passage deals merely with the general advice for Pharaoh to take advantage of the seven plenteous years to lay up provisions for the famine to come. He makes no mention of himself as being the proper one for this work. He does not seek any personal honor. He is merely carrying out the instructions that God had enabled him to give and that are to have such far-reaching results.

Verses 37-41. The best part of Pharaoh's speech is that wherein he gives God the credit for the wisdom of Joseph. We are not to conclude that this heathen king knew anything definitely about the God of Abraham. But in his first speech to the king Joseph told him that God would give him an answer of peace. Now this remark of his means only that the God to whom he ascribed the answer of peace was the one truly who had given him this wisdom.

Verses 42, 43. This conduct of the king toward Joseph must be considered in the light of royal and authoritative demonstration and not in the sense of pride. And since Joseph has been voluntarily humble up to now it is proper and just to him and all the rest that his true position of authority be signalized by these decorations from the king. Else there would be no certainty as to the attitude of other men in the country.

Verse 44. Here the specific decree is made and announced that nothing can be done in that land by any of the people except that it must be done through Joseph. That all other persons in the land will be subject to him.

Verse 45. Pharaoh attached to Joseph a name that corresponded with his work of interpreting the dreams. Then further added honor to him by giving him to wife the daughter of an important person, a prince in the city of On. Then Joseph took up his duties as food administrator of Egypt.

Verse 46. This verse should be noted as giving the age of Joseph at another important period of his life.

Verse 47. *Handfuls.* This might give us the impression that the crop was not large whereas the connection we know is that the production was great. But we will remember that the means of harvesting grain in those days was not the same as now, and a handful of the grain would not be found in any one spot until after it had been cut down and thrust into a pile by the hand sickle. But in this case it will be growing in such rank amounts that a person could thrust his hand down at any one spot and grasp a handful. This would require a very heavy crop.

Verses 48-49. This paragraph will tell us briefly that Joseph did his duty as assigned to him by Pharaoh and laid up the surplus grain through the years of plenty.

Verses 50-53. The birth of the two sons of Joseph took place some time in the seven years of the plenty. His remark that God had made him forget all his toil and his father's house should not be misunderstood. One does not naturally forget his home and family. But with Joseph it is a special situation. He has no idea that he will ever get to see his father again. With this in mind he wishes to forget all about the grief he has had in connection with it. The word "toil" here is from a word that means worry. Not that he has had so much manual labor but has had much worry. The interest he will have in this new source of happiness will help him forget his worry.

Verses 53, 54. True to the determination of God and the predictions interpreted by Joseph, the years of plenty passed and the years of famine came. It was so general that no land was exempt except Egypt. That is, the famine was even in Egypt, but the condition of want was not there because Joseph had prepared for it in the years before.

Verse 55. Very naturally when the people were in want they looked to Pharaoh. But true to his statement to Joseph he would not dispense food to them. He sent them to the man who had been appointed to handle this matter. We might think of Joseph as a material mediator between the people and the king. And when a mediator is appointed it is not permitted for any one to obtain a favor except through the mediator.

Verses 56, 57. Here it is Joseph who opens the storehouses of food for the people. Not only for the ones in Egypt but those of other lands, for it states that all countries came to Egypt to buy bread.

GENESIS 42

Verses 1, 2. An interesting use of the word "saw" may be found here. After telling us that Jacob saw there was corn in Egypt it says he told his sons he "heard" there was corn there. This is a proper use of the word for we can see with our mental eyes as well as with our fleshly ones. Such use of the word "see" will be found often.

Verses 3, 4. Ten brethren are mentioned here. The reason is obvious. Joseph is gone and Jacob fears to let Benjamin leave home. He is the youngest besides being the only full brother of Joseph. It is but natural for the old man to keep him at home.

Verses 5, 6. The expression that Joseph was governor over Egypt must be understood to mean his jurisdiction over the food administration. The act of bowing down before Joseph by his brethren meant only the usual custom of respectful attitude expected in the East when persons came up with those considered as of dignity. Verily, a man who has charge of the sustenance of life and to whom they have come for food is worthy of this salutation. Hence their homage before him.

Verses 6-8. There are obvious reasons why Joseph knew his brethren while they did not know him. He has now become a man of 39 years whereas he was a lad of 17 the last time they saw him. Also, they believed him dead and were not looking for him. And even had they thought of him as being yet alive, they had sold him to slave traders and would not expect to find him in this position of dignity. And it is easy for him to recognize them. Here are ten men in one group. The family similarity would be significant. Also, since there are the ten together, not all of them would have outgrown his recollection of their features. If one or two or three had materially changed, not all of them would. Another thing, Joseph knew that all lands were compelled to come to Egypt for food and he would expect that his brethren would be among them. He made himself "strange" unto them. This is from a word that means he acted as if he did not know them. Or rather, he assumed an attitude of indifference toward them as far as personal interest in them were concerned. *Spake roughly.* This means he spake in severe language to them. We will bear in mind that God is with Joseph and is bringing some just punishments upon these brethren for their past wickedness. Therefore we will not censure him for his conduct here. It is just, because being prompted of God.

Verses 9-13. While much punishment will be meted out to these brothers before this affair is finally solved, yet it is with satisfaction that from now on they will always state the truth as far as they understand it. Joseph remembered his dreams when he saw these brethren bowing down to him. And he metes out further punishment to them in the form of severe accusation. It was of the gravest concern to be guilty of being a spy. This accusation he made against them. But this was not only for the present punishment it would mean to them, but it will lay the basis for other demands he will make on them and that will eventually bring the family to Egypt. *One is not.* This could mean merely that one brother is not with his father or that one is not alive. But they said it in the sense of his being dead (Chapter 44: 20.)

Verses 14-16. Joseph repeated his charge that they are spies. But proposed a test of their sincerity. He will detain them in prison while one brother goes home and brings their youngest brother down to Egypt.

Verse 17. As if he intended to carry out the threat he placed them all in prison for three days. This is a temporary guard house.

Verses 18-20. At the end of the three days he made as if he had changed his mind. He told them he feared God and now instead of sending just one for the other brother, he will keep just one as a hostage and the rest can go to take food back and also to bring the brother. They agreed to this test as being unable to avoid it.

Verses 21, 22. Pending the arrangements agreed to above they have conversation among themselves. Reference to the anguish of their brother many years ago, they now admit they were guilty. This has no indication of present recognition of Joseph. It is merely their conclusion of the reason God is permitting this distress to come upon them. In other words, they regard it as a "judgment" sent upon them for their sin. And Reuben truthfully but severely reminds them of his protest at the time and of their unwillingness to listen to him.

Verse 23. Having spoken to them all this while in the language that was foreign to them they naturally supposed he did not understand the Hebrew language. This caused them to speak freely in his hearing as thinking he would not understand the conversation.

Verse 24. The censure is necessary for the brothers have been guilty. Yet Joseph is a humane being and his sympathy is moved so that he turned from them that he might not be discovered when he gave way to weeping. Then recovering himself he carries out the agreement and binds Simeon before their eyes and prepares for their return journey.

Verses 25, 26. Unknown to the brothers the sacks were filled with corn and also the purchase money placed in the sacks.

Verses 27, 28. On the way home one brother had occasion to feed his beast and in so doing discovered his purchase money. This startled them. It could be the basis for a dangerous accusation. Just why none of the other sacks were opened we are not told. Their surprise and fear could have completely confused them and caused them to hasten on homeward to their father.

Verses 29-34. Arriving home they told their father a true story of what had happened to them in Egypt. No one in the family has any idea of the identity of the man who had sold the corn to them and who had been so severe in his speech to them.

Verse 35. The report the brethren gave to their father must have produced a condition of much unrest in his mind. But when they opened their sacks all of them had the money therein. Of course this increased the fear they already had suffered. Did the man of Egypt intend to charge them with theft in order to prove his claim that they were spies? The presence of this money would certainly be a strong suggestion of their guilt. Hence we can appreciate the state of their minds at this time.

Verse 36. The complaint of the old Patriarch is pitiful. Two of his sons are now away from his sight and still they have told him that Benjamin must go if they are to obtain any more food. He says that all the conditions are against him.

Verses 37, 38. Reuben in vain tries to calm his father to the consent of Benjamin being permitted to go with them for more food. But the old father says "no." He says that his brother is dead. This is what he has now believed for 22 years upon the deceptive presentation his sons made with the bloody coat. He fears that a sorrowful death would be caused were he to consent for Benjamin to go and possibly never return. Thus we have a further confirmation of the thought offered at chapter 37: 33, 34. Through all these years Jacob has been certain that his son Joseph was dead and that by violence. It will now require more evidence to convince him to the contrary than it did to produce the deception in the beginning.

GENESIS 43

Verses 1, 2. Having consumed all the food they had brought from Egypt the sons of Jacob were asked to return for more. *Sore.* This means the famine was severe.

Verses 3-5. Judah replied to his father's request by repeating what they had already told him. That they need not go down there without Benjamin for the man will not receive them without him. So it is put up to Jacob to decide this question.

Verse 6. Jacob complained because they had told the man about another brother. Apparently it would seem unnecessary for them to tell such a matter to a stranger when they were only on a mission of business and wanting to buy food.

Verse 7. Upon this they truthfully explained how it came about. That the man had asked them directly about the family and had even specified certain details of the family including their other brother. And then they asked the very reasonable question, if they had any reason to suspect that he would require the brother to come.

Verses 8-10. Judah again becomes the spokesman and binds himself personally to be responsible for the return of Benjamin. He closes his earnest speech by stating that they had now been lingering so long discussing the matter that had they gone on at the first mention of the subject they would have been back by now.

Verses 11-14. Jacob now saw that he must consent or they would perish. He very sadly gives instructions about their journey. Among these is the one of taking to the man a "present." We have already seen the significance of this. Of course we will observe the articles they were to take for this purpose were staples of the land and such as would not be affected by a famine. Also to make sure that no accusation of fraud could be lodged against them they were to take double money and also the money that had been found in their sacks. The man might claim it was an oversight and they should not leave themselves open to dishonesty by retaining it. He concludes his speech with a despairing resignation on the possibility of losing his son Benjamin.

Verse 15. With these instructions and provisions the brethren returned to Egypt and were admitted to the presence of Joseph.

Verse 16. Seeing Benjamin Joseph arranges to be in more intimate association than they just now are having. For this purpose he makes command of "eating" together.

Verses 17, 18. Instead of being made happy over this mark of attention they were filled with unrest. They suspected the man of Egypt was seeking an opportunity for close contact so that he might lodge the accusation of fraud against them. When people are under the influence of penitence they put a construction on various appearances that would never be thought of otherwise.

Verses 19-22. With this self-imposed accusation in their minds they approach the door of the steward's house and explain how it all came about that they had the money. And truthfully stated that they did not know who had put the money in the sacks.

Verse 23. The steward assures them that peace is theirs. Then he told them that their God was giving them treasure in their sacks and that through Him the money had reached the hands of its rightful owner again. At this he brought Simeon out to them. He was the brother who had been held as hostage when they were in Egypt before.

Verse 24. They were brought into Joseph's house. Also they were provided with water to wash their feet. See Gen. 18: 4 and note on this subject of feet washing.

Verses 25, 26. The "present" is mentioned again. People who are victims of famine and coming to another country for food would not be thought of as bringing a present on the ordinary ground of making a gift. This action can be understood only in light of the custom which has often been referred to in this work. (See chapter 32: 13.) We also observe that they bowed themselves before Joseph. This was not only another custom of those times but it was significant of the dreams Joseph had years before and which were referred to so contemptuously by the brothers.

Verses 27, 28. Joseph made as if he were interested impersonally in their family condition. But all this was to keep them at a distance until he was ready to bring the matter to a head. All the while they manifested the attitude of extreme respect toward him. They referred to their father as his servant.

Verses 29, 30. He beheld Benjamin. He is not only his brother, he is his full brother, his mother's son. Of course a full brother would be one's mother's son, but the inspired writer makes the subject more impressive by this detail in the narrative. The show of indifference was overcome by Joseph's affection for his full brother and he is forced to give way to weeping. But not being ready to make the climax of his act he seeks the privacy of his personal room and there weeps.

Verse 31. Weeping affects the countenance; then as now. It is interesting to observe the fact that nature is always the same. The effect of weeping on the face is so pronounced that it is visible. Joseph wants still to be unsuspected in his drama and so we are told he washed his face and gave orders to set the food ready.

Verse 32. A separate service was prepared for Joseph and his brethren Also for the Egyptians who were to eat with them. This was because of a rule in force in Egypt which will be given explanation later.

Verse 33. How did this stranger know anything about which of the brothers was the oldest? Yet they notice he arranges them at dinner according to their birth. The mystery deepens all the while and the men marveled.

Verse 34. *Messes.* In some places this word would not necessarily mean food or other articles belonging to the table. But in the present connection it has to have such meaning. Its general meaning is an article or token of favor. Here the favor would logically consist in things of food and drink. And the preference Joseph had for Benjamin was again manifested in that he made his tribute to him five times as much as any of the others. This could be only on the basis of his personal feeling for we would know that he gave all of them a sufficient amount for their hunger. And we are told that they drank and were merry with him. This word "merry" would apply to the effect of much food or drink either. Since all of them had enough to make them be satiated we must conclude the five times to Benjamin was to show his feelings.

GENESIS 44

Verses 1, 2. The former procedure was repeated regarding the money in the sacks. But in addition the steward was told to put the personal cup of Joseph in the sack of the youngest. The plot is deepening and Joseph is making successful plans for bringing his brothers into complete humility before him. And all this is proper in view of the fact that God is using the situation to punish the brothers for their wickedness.

Verses 3-5. In the early morning the men were started on their homeward journey. But they had only reached the edge of the city until a new sadness came upon them. The steward was told to pursue them and chide them for taking away his drinking cup. That they had rewarded evil for good. Not only had taken valuables not belonging to them but had taken a very important item. That it was an article by which his lord "divineth." This is from a Hebrew word that means to perform some form of magic including the ability to detect mysteries. It would therefore be considered foolish to say the least to steal such an article from a man of prominence.

Verses 6-9. The steward did as he was told. Overtaking the men he made all these charges against them. Of course they denied all and very honestly so. Again they recounted their past dealings with him and protested their innocence and were so sure as to the matter of the cup that they were led to make a very rash proposal. They agreed that the particular man in whose sack the cup should be found was to die for his act. Also that the rest of them would become servants to the lord of the place.

Verse 10. The man accepted their proposal with the exception that the one in whose sack the cup was found was to be his servant and the rest be cleared.

Verses 11-13. So confident were they of their innocence that they "speedily" took down all their sacks and opened them. Of course the mere opening of the sacks would not expose the cup because the steward had been the one who placed it there and would know how to find it in with the corn. It says *he* searched. That would be according to any situation in which some one was suspected of having goods in his possession that were stolen. And to make the suspense all the greater he began with the sack of the oldest. Having done so they would naturally not expect to have him look in the sack of Benjamin until the last. Each time a sack would be opened and the cup not found would strengthen their feeling of innocence and confidence. Of course the feeling of innocence was complete at the first since they were truly innocent. But also the feeling of confidence that nothing wrong would be discovered became stronger as the sacks were opened one by one and nothing appeared. But at last, the sack of the youngest is reached. Only one more chance for them to have trouble about this. Surely there will not be any now. If any one of them would have taken the cup it would not be the youngest. But it was!! They are in consternation. They "rent their clothes." This was another strange custom of ancient times when one was in unusual distress or anxiety. They had already committed themselves on this subject and now their difficulty is looking grave. Of course all they can do is to return to the city to see what can be done about it.

Verse 14. Since this whole action was by Joseph's direction of course he is looking for the men to return, hence they find him still at his house. They come before him and fall before him on the ground. The usual salutation of respect in those times was to bow before another even to the extent of almost touching the head to the ground. But in very exceptional cases the person fell prostrate on the ground before the other. That was what was done in this case. They not only must know that Joseph is a dignitary but they have gravely offended him, although unintentionally.

Verse 15. Joseph made use of the occasion to deepen his drama. He chided them for the misdeed they had done. Then reminds them of its foolishness even from the standpoint of policy for he asked them if they did not know that such a man as he could certainly "divine"? Of course this means, as seen above, that a man of his standing could detect actions which would escape others.

Verse 16. The men were stunned.

But Judah feels the sting of it especially for he was the one who induced his father to let Benjamin come with them. He confessed they had no way of answering the situation. Then unintentionally admitted what had actually happened, that God had "found out" the iniquity of them. Had Joseph been some other he could not have understood the force of that statement. This "iniquity" did not refer to the affair of the cup for they had not committed any wrong about it and Judah knew that. Therefore we must conclude he had reference to their past treatment of Joseph which he now classes as iniquity. And unknowingly makes the admission in the hearing of the very person who had been the victim of their wickedness. How heavy must be the feeling of guilt when it is brought to one's mind in so helpless a situation. A part of the admission Judah makes before Joseph is that they are now committed to bondage under the man whom they have just now offended.

Verse 17. This is the limit of the stroke. Not only is their "guilt" to be punished but it is to fall on the very one whom they wanted most to shield. Not only would such a thing cause all of them sorrow but it would be too much for the heart of the old father and would result in his death from shock. But Judah was the one who made special guarantee that Benjamin would be brought back and now it is up to him to make intercession.

Verses 18-34. All these are grouped in this one paragraph because I did not wish to interrupt one of the most touching, pleading speeches on record. I will call attention to various parts of it but wish the reader to keep the speech as a whole in mind. Every word of it is pure truth as far as Judah understands it. He carefully sums up the events that began with their first appearance in Egypt for food down to the present moment, and even goes on to the events that will assuredly happen soon if this sentence just pronounced by Joseph is carried into effect. Since the material facts mentioned in this speech are well known and have been repeated in the pages preceding the present it is not necessary to name them here item by item. But the loving unselfishness of Judah is remarkable. He is not praying for the least consideration for him. Not one word of self-pity as far as it would affect him personally. The only distress that he suggests for himself would be due to his own sympathy for his aged father and on whose account he had bound himself to return the brother. And his proposition at last will be for the sake of his father. He cannot bear to see his father's shock at not seeing his beloved son present when they return. He concludes his speech with the offer to remain in bondage to Joseph if he will let Benjamin go home.

GENESIS 45

Verse 1. The speech with which the preceding chapter closed brought this tense and most interesting drama to a climax. Stout-hearted indeed would be the man who could carry the performance further after hearing such a speech. Joseph knows that every word is true as far as Judah understands it. Not only so, but his own personal sympathy for his aged father, and who was not responsible for his life of slavery, prompts him to yield. The punishment of the brothers is now complete as far as he is concerned. But the scene of the next act will be too sacred for outside intrusion. Complete privacy is desired and thus all men are ordered out of the group.

Verses 2, 3. Nothing makes it necessary now for him to restrain himself. He gave way to audible weeping that was so loud that the people of Pharaoh's house heard it. What could have been the feelings of the brethren when he said "I am Joseph." He then asked about the only member of his father's immediate family whom he has not seen—his father. Is he yet alive? They are so stunned with the weight of the revelation that they cannot answer his question. The margin says they were terrified at his presence and the lexicon agrees with that rendering. To be in the immediate presence of the brother whom they had so wickedly mistreated years ago and that for money as well as to get revenge for their envy, was enough to make them stand astonished with fright.

Verses 4, 5. Joseph awakened them from their shock by inviting them to come near to him. They obey. He then bade them not be grieved over their past action. The last sentence of verse 5 should not be read too carelessly. It merely states that God sent Joseph before them. It makes no claim that God had anything to do with the wicked act of the brethren that sent him away from home. But after the thing was done God took charge of the victim to see that he would be conducted to the right place to be of service afterward in bringing about other divine plans.

Verses 6-8. This passage should be noted as the one which gives another important bit of chronology. It is now two years after the famine started. And again notice the word "hither" in 8th verse. This word is what shows God's part in this whole experience of Joseph as to his coming to Egypt. Had that not been done the Ishmaelites might have resold him before they reached Egypt.

Verses 9-15. Hurried instructions are given for their return to their home to get the father. He said for them to tell the father that he was lord over Egypt. That would not be on the basis of pride for Joseph has already proved that he has none of that. But his father might feel hesitant about making such a complete move unless he were assured that Joseph is really in position to take care of him. He then had a personal greeting of affection with Benjamin with tears of joy, followed with a like demonstration with the other brethren. By this time they are sufficiently recovered to talk.

Verses 16-23. In this paragraph we can see the complete cooperation of Pharaoh in the matter of Joseph's family at home. He directs that full provision be made for the conveyance of the members of the family together with their personal belongings, down to the land of Egypt. *Regard not your stuff.* All the context leaves the conclusion here to mean that since there is plenty in the land of Egypt they do not need to be concerned whether they can take all their stuff with them. With these instructions and provisions out of the possessions of Egypt Joseph loads his brethren for the trip.

Verse 24. Joseph is very eager to see his father. All preliminaries have been gone through with. The punishment of the brothers has been ended and mutual good will manifested. All things are ready for the coming of his father to live in that land. No unnecessary delay should be caused. They should make their journey homeward and then back with all possible speed. It is with this in view that he exhorts them not to "fall out by the way." It might be possible we would miss the meaning of this language did we not have the original and its definition in the lexicon. The word "fall" here is from RAGAZ. This is defined "to be angry" by Young, and "a primitive root; to quiver (with any violent emotion, especially anger or fear."—Strong. We do not know whether Joseph feared they might get into quarrels over their provisions or on the subject of their respective guilt in what had happened, or what. The book does not inform us. But we do know he meant for them not to get into such condition. That would of necessity retard their journey and he wants to see his father as soon as possible.

Verses 25, 26. The brothers arrived home and reported all to the father. The first effect of the report was so unexpected the record says his heart fainted. That means he was stunned. *Believed them not.* This must be understood in the light of a common saying "too good to be true" because he finally responded to the arrangement.

Verses 27, 28. The property in the hands of the sons that bore evidence of having come from Egypt was finally convincing. Jacob said it was enough and he would go to see his son Joseph before he died.

GENESIS 46

Verse 1. It will be observed that the names Israel and Jacob are used freely as being the same. They are the same as to the person meant hence may be used interchangeably without confusion.

Verses 2-4. This passage is of peculiar importance. It is the final repetition of the promise made first to Abraham, then to Isaac, then to Jacob. Now it comes to the last named in the final statement. One of the items of the promises made to Abraham was that his seed should be a stranger in a land not theirs and serve them four hundred and thirty years. Jacob is now on his way to that land and God has appeared to him at his animal sacrifices and assures him that he will be with him. This is the man and the time in chronology where God "confirmed" his covenant to Abraham. We are not merely presuming this. In Psa. 105: 9, 10 we are expressly told that the covenant was confirmed in Jacob, and this must be considered when Gal. 3: 17 is used in an effort to shorten the term the scriptures say was to be the sojourn in Egypt. See comment on this at chapter 15: 13-15.

Verses 5-7. Not much new information in this paragraph yet we do not wish to lose the trend of the story.

Notice it says not only that they took all their goods but all their seed or people.

Verses 8-25. The subject of this long paragraph is the naming of the people who made up the family of Jacob. But we should be careful not to take some statements too literally when it says that certain souls were born to Jacob. It might mean those born to his near kin and not of his own body begotten. That indefinite method of naming one's descendants in those days was common. Jacob personally had just thirteen children. The others spoken of as having come out of his loins are his near relation.

Verses 26, 27. In this one short passage we are given two different accounts of the number. But one distinction that is brought to our attention is that some of them were born in Egypt and also Joseph and his wife were already there when Jacob came. Such considerations as these will account for the apparent discrepancies in the different accounts of the number. *Loins.* This is from YAREK and defined "From an unused root meaning, to be soft; the thigh (from its fleshy softness); by euphemism, the generative parts."—Strong. The word "euphemism" is a word that means that a less offensive expression to the ear or mind has been used in the place of the literal one. Thus, the word "loins" here is used by the translators in the place of "generative parts."

Verse 28. The text does not tell us why Judah was selected to go on and direct the way. But he had made such strong assurances to his father at the time of their second journey that possibly that is the reason. Joseph had already told them they would dwell in the land of Goshen (chapter 45: 10) hence it is mentioned here.

Verses 29-31. Joseph has his first meeting with his father in the land of Goshen. The meeting was mutually cordial and deeply affectionate. Jacob expressed satisfaction at the reunion and is willing to die. Then Joseph informed them he would inform Pharaoh of their arrival and make plans for introduction.

Verses 32-34. Upon the presentation of Joseph's brethren to Pharaoh he tells them, he will state their possessions. Next it is expected that Pharaoh will enquire as to their occupation. When that is done, they are instructed to reply that it is keeping cattle, which includes the work of shepherd. The reason for this is that "every shepherd is an ambomination unto the Egyptians." A quotation from history will help to explain this attitude toward shepherds or at least toward the occupation in general. "Soon after the bright period of the twelfth dynasty, Egypt again suffered a great eclipse. Nomadic tribes from Asia pressed across the eastern frontier of Egypt and gradually took possession of the inviting pasture lands of the delta, and established there the empire of the Shepherd Kings. These Asiatic intruders were violent and barbarous, and destroyed or mutilated the monuments of the country."—MYERS, A. H., p. 26. This dark period on the history of the Egyptians had led them into a national policy of averseness to the vocation of shepherds in general. And yet, knowing that individual groups might be innocent, they wished to be friendly to these now near them since they are relatives of the man who has done so much for them. Thus they assign them to a separate place in Egypt, this as a "face saving" deal, and yet in the best of the land which shows it was not from any motive of injury to them.

GENESIS 47

Verses 1, 2. Joseph informed Pharaoh of the presence in Goshen of his people with their possessions. Then he presented five of his brethren to the king. This is a mark of respect for the dignity of the king. To ask him to become a sight-seeing man only upon the general mixture of men and women and slaves as well as women of varying ranks would not be worthy of the king of Egypt. Hence Joseph's respect for his king in making a special selection of his men for purposes of introduction.

Verses 3, 4. True to Joseph's predictions Pharaoh asked them about their occupation. Their reply was according to the instructions Joseph had given them. And in requesting the king that they might dwell in the land of Goshen they relieved him of the embarrassing necessity of assigning them to that place. So the entire matter was understood at once.

Verses 5, 6. Pharaoh authorizes Joseph to assign the best of the land to his people, the land of Goshen. Also, he proposes to employ any of the men who are given to activity to have work with Pharaoh's cattle.

Verse 7. All things are now ready

for the personal presentation of Jacob to the king of Egypt. When this was done Jacob blessed Pharaoh. This was possible and right since Jacob is a Patriarch and Pharaoh is a friendly king and their national host.

Verses 8-10. When people in the Bible were asked their age they did not evade it or make some untruthful answer as many do in our time. When any one is ashamed of his age it is a suggestion of inferiority complex. And this is another mile stone in our record of chronology about the important persons of scripture. Jacob states that his life has not been as pleasant as that of his fathers. He could not but have been including his years of sorrow over the loss of his son Joseph, now restored to him.

Verses 11, 12. It is here stated the brethren of Joseph were placed in the land of Rameses while another places them in Goshen. There is no contradiction. Goshen is the name of the area in general while Rameses is the name of a more central part of the land.

Verses 13, 14. The severe famine continued. Men had money as yet and had to spend it for the corn which Joseph had stored up. He then places the money in Pharaoh's houses and it becomes his capital.

Verses 15-17. But the money finally was spent and still they needed food. Then Joseph exchanged food for their livestock and it became Pharaoh's.

Verses 18-20. The next item of exchange was their land. But not that only. They sold themselves into servitude to Pharaoh. *Give us seed.* It would seem strange in a time of dearth for people to cry for seed. But this is one of the places in the scripture where an item of future application is included with others taking place at the time. See the 12th chapter of Exodus for this idea with reference to the days of unleavened bread. This provision of seed is a case where the writer gets ahead of his story and mentions a feature of the arrangement that can not apply till the present condition of the land has changed.

Verse 21. Since the land is not useable under the dearth it would not be any use to them any way. But also now the land has become Pharaoh's and the people would not have the right to occupy it. Thus the arrangement for cities.

Verse 22. *Priests.* These were not necessarily men of the strictest meaning of that word. It includes any acting official of a community. And because of their importance and need they were exempt from the general subjugation under poverty. They were to be supported out of the king's provisions.

Verse 23. Mention is again made of the seed provided to the people. But it could not mean for immediate use because nothing was growing at that time. But it was simply a statement of the dealings to be used in the future.

Verse 24. The tax of one fifth would be exacted when the time came again when the people could raise grain.

Verses 25, 26. The people gladly agreed to the covenant of taxation. It was only fair that Joseph should exact this from them since he had saved their lives. Now when the days of the famine are over they should show their appreciation by this payment.

Verse 26. The language of this verse verifies the remarks above about the seed. It says Joseph "made it a law" and the writer further states it was a law "unto this day." This shows that the language along in these verses had to do with the general conditions after the famine was passed.

Verses 27, 28. The statement is here made of the prosperity of the children of Israel in Egypt. Not only in wealth but in population. The writer also gives us an advanced announcement of the age of Jacob. The figures stated here agree with what has been said. He stated his age on arrival as 130 and now the length of his residence in Egypt being 17 would make his entire life as 147.

Verses 29-31. Jacob is concerned about his burying place. He resorts to the old custom of placing the hand under the thigh when some important promise or instructions are to be given. With this binding signal he pledges Joseph to bury him in the land where a burying place had been already provided. This service Joseph promised. Upon the promise of Joseph we are told that Israel bowed himself upon the bed's head. This was a gesture of calm and respectful satisfaction.

GENESIS 48

Verses 1, 2. Jacob is now sick with age and soon to die. Upon hearing it Joseph takes his two sons to visit him. Being informed of his son's coming he exerted himself enough to sit up on the bed.

Verses 3, 4. He referred to his meet ing with God at Luz which is Bethel and states the parts of the promise given to him there. It included possession of the land.

Verses 5, 6. Jacob appropriates to himself the two sons of Joseph. He claims them, but explains they are to be his "as Reuben and Simeon." As he then tells him that all children that might be born to him afterward should be his, we are to understand that the two sons of Joseph are to be counted as among the original sons of Jacob. That means they will finally become the heads of full tribes each. Jacob is a Patriarch and speaks by inspiration even if he did not personally know the significance of his speech. But God knew that an extra tribe would some day be necessary and now is preparing for it.

Verse 7. The sad account of the death and burial is next given to Joseph and he is told the location. It is near Bethlehem. That is the death of Rachel.

Verses 8-11. He asked who the persons present were. This shows the things he said about them before were words of inspiration, for he had not as yet seen the boys to realize it. Bringing them near their grandfather he embraced them. Then makes the happy observation that he had not expected to see Joseph's face but lo he has been permitted to see his seed.

Verses 12, 13. Joseph expects his father to bestow the Patriarchal blessing on his sons. That was customarily done accompanied with the placing of hands on the head. In order to have this matter correctly ordered, as he thought it should be, he led the lads toward his father in such a manner that the eldest, Manasseh, would be near the right hand of his father, etc.

Verse 14. But Jacob had a different plan and future for them. Crossing his hands it brought his right hand to be on the head of Ephraim, etc.

Verses 15, 18. Joseph thought his father was making a mistake and tries to adjust his hands. The rule was to prefer the older son of a family. Joseph has no knowledge of why there should be any change in the rule applied to his sons.

Verse 19. Jacob soon informs him he knows what he is doing. That Manasseh will indeed become a great people but that his brother will become greater. If the reader will consult Num. 1: 33, 35 he will see that this was actually fulfilled.

Verses 20, 21. General predictions of favorable estimate to be placed on the two boys are then made to Joseph and also predicts his near death.

Verse 22. This verse is a specific prediction of a double inheritance that Joseph will some day obtain through having two sons who are to become great peoples. This is fulfilled in Deut. 21: 17; Josh. 17: 17; 24: 32; 1 Chr. 5:1.

GENESIS 49

Verses 1, 2. It should be borne in mind that Patriarchs under that Dispensation were men of God and that predictions were often made by them. When this was done their sayings were as true as those of any other inspired prophets. Thus in this chapter we will have his forecast concerning his twelve sons. However, not all of the statements are predictions. Some are historic references. Also, the historic reason why certain ones of his sons were not permitted to be in the blood line will be shown. And some of the predictions will be nothing more to us than a reference to some incidents in the lives of the people of which we now have no detailed account.

Verses 3, 4. Normally Reuben should be first in the line. But because of his sin in defiling his father's bed, we will not see him in the line. See the record of his sin in chapter 35: 22.

Verses 5-7. The complaint against Simeon and Levi is about the time they betrayed the Shechemites into circumcision then murdered all their males. This is recorded in chapter 34: 26.

Verse 8. Judah will receive more important predictions than any of the sons. The prediction that his hand would be in the neck of his enemies is a figurative way of saying that he would be victorious over his enemies. Since the sword was a common instrument for warfare and was used to behead or otherwise maim the enemy fatally, this expression came to be a common one in olden times.

Verse 9. Some more figurative language referring to Judah's success over his foes.

Verse 10. This is one of the most outstanding passages of scripture in the Bible. It pertains really to Christ, who was the descendant of Judah. The various parts of this famous prediction will be considered now. *Scepter.* This is reference to a rod or stick or gavel that a man of power and authority would wield. To see one being produced by a man indicated his official position of importance. *Depart from.* This means it shall not come out of or be produced by. That Judah will not wield or produce the scepter of law giving and authority until, etc. As illustration of this thought see Num. 24: 17; Isa. 11: 1; Micah 4: 2. *Judah.* He was to be the one from whom the scepter is finally to come. See Heb. 7: 14. *Shiloh.* This is from SHIYLOH and defined "Tranquil; Shiloh, an epithet of the Messiah."—Strong. *Gathering of the people.* As fulfillment of this see Mark 12: 37; John 12: 32. The thought of the verse as a whole is this. The son of Jacob called Judah will produce a tribe. But that tribe will not produce the law of government for God's people for a while. The tribe of Levi will have that and will be administered through the law of Moses. That will not be changed till this person comes who is here called Shiloh which means rest. And of course it means that the tribe of Levi will continue to be the tribe to produce the authority of law until Shiloh, the Messiah, of the tribe of Judah comes. And when he comes, then the people will gather unto him. The verse is a beautiful prediction of the coming of Christ to become a law giver and ruler and that people will then gather to him and not Moses.

Verses 11, 12. These are more predictions about Christ of the tribe of Judah. Wine when used figuratively refers to blood, either as used in sacrifice or as shed in vengeance. Christ will do both. He will shed his blood for the sins of the world; also he will pour out wine as blood, and blood as wine, in his wrath against those who rebel against him. See Isa. 63: 3; John 19: 34; 2 Thess. 1: 8.

Verses 13-14. Not much can be said further about these verses. We observe however, that the dwelling place of Zebulun is as here stated. See Josh. 19: 10, 11.

Verse 16. In Judges 13: 12 and 15: 20 we see that one of the judges was from the tribe of Dan.

Verses 17, 18. *Serpent by the way.* This is like the saying "snake in the grass." Please consult Judges 18: 27. There read of this unexpected attack the men of Dan made upon these quiet, harmless people, then think of an adder by the way, "snake in the grass."

Verses 19-21. Another passage I do not understand. Hence will not guess.

Verse 22. In the other chapter Jacob had predicted that Joseph would become two peoples through his two sons. Here the same thing is predicted in the picture of a fruitful bough by a well whose branches are so thrifty that they hang over the wall.

Verse 23. This verse is a reference to the mistreatment the brethren gave Joseph. It is compared to people with their bow and arrow and shooting at him.

Verse 24. But he withstood those who attacked him and was able still to wield his own bow. This is accounted for by the fact that the hands of the mighty God of Jacob sustained him. And while in this verse makes another prediction that pertains to Christ. Having mentioned the name of God he says from "thence" is the shepherd, the stone of Israel. Of course this is the Christ. See Psa. 80: 1; Isa. 28: 16; 1 Peter 2: 4.

Verses 25, 26. More references to the blessings received from God. He here states to Joseph or about Joseph that the blessings of his father (Jacob) had prevailed above the blessings of his progenitors. This might seem to contradict chapter 47: 9. But not. He personally had suffered more than his forefathers but in general blessings he had exceeded the others. And now he predicts that these blessings shall be on the head of him who was "separate from his brethren" which we recognize to be a pathetic reference to his bondage in Egypt.

Verse 27. Very little is said about Benjamin, but what he does say means that he will be successful against his enemies and be able to take much prey.

Verses 28-32. After going through with this picture, past and future, of his twelve sons, Jacob refers again to his approaching death. He further gives directions about his burial place. The cave that Abraham had purchased for that purpose is to be his, and he names over the ones who have been buried there.

Verse 33. Evidently he had mustered all his remaining strength to make the speech set down in this chapter. As soon as it was finished he relaxed, yielded up the ghost.

GENESIS 50

Verses 1-3. Embalming at this time required 40 days and the period of mourning by the Egyptians was 70 days. This must be understood as a formal ceremony.

Verses 4-6. When the proper time had come Joseph asked for and was granted leave of Pharaoh to go and bury his father according to his dying request.

Verses 7-9. The respect entertained in Egypt for Joseph is indicated by the fact that many of them accompanied him on the burying mission and made mourning for him.

Verses 10, 11. The exercises must have been impressive for it produced remarks from the Canaanites who witnessed them.

Verses 12, 13. The record states that Jacob's sons did for him as requested and buried him in the cave previously selected as his burial place.

Verse 14. There will be no AWOL charged against Joseph and his brethren. When the burial of their father was completed they returned to Egypt, the place of their sojourn.

Verses 15-18. This passage shows that Jacob had spoken to his sons about the affair of Joseph and predicted the possibility of his taking vengeance on them after his death. They now confess this to him and plead for forgiveness. This caused Joseph to weep. Doubtless it was for sympathy toward them in their distressed frame of mind.

Verses 19-21. But Joseph assures them again that no evil will be done them. And again he makes the statement which we should not overlook. that God meant the affair to turn out for good even though they had thought to do him evil. Then he comforted them and spake kindly to them. He also promised to nourish them in the land of their sojourn.

Verse 22. This is another of the chronological passages and marks the age of Joseph. However, his death is a few verses below.

Verse 23. The joy of seeing one's grandchildren can be appreciated only by those who have experienced it. This joy came to Joseph regarding both his sons.

Verses 24, 25. The death of Joseph is now approaching as he is aware. He states the fact to his brethren and predicts that God will finally visit them in this land and take them out of it as promised to Abraham. And so confident is he that such happy event will occur that he makes them take an oath that when that time comes they will take his remains with them.

Verse 26. After this Joseph died at the age of 110 years. They embalmed him and put his body in a coffin in Egypt. Here he will remain until Moses leads the Children of Israel out from Egyptian bondage.

EXODUS 1

Verses 1-4. *Children of Israel.* In this place this term is to be understood as referring to the sons of Jacob directly and not to his descendants generally as is often done. And it will be observed that just eleven of the sons are named here since Joseph was already in Egypt and thus did not come "with" his father. This idea will be mentioned in a verse below. The name "Israel" is explained in Gen. 42: 28.

Verse 5. *Loins.* For an explanation of this word as here used see notes of Gen. 35:11 and 46: 26. *Seventy souls.* On this account of the number that came into Egypt see again the notes at Gen. 46: 26, 27.

Verse 6. This verse should be thought of as belonging in thought and date at the conclusion of the book of Genesis, since the death of Joseph is recorded at that place. Only, the additional fact is recorded here of the death of *all that generation.* Here the last word is from DOWR and defined by Strong "properly, a revolution of time, i. e. an age or generation; also a dwelling." The meaning is that all the people were dead who lived in the time of Joseph. This would give us the idea that no one was living who had been acquainted with Joseph and what he meant to the nation. Of course we must now bear in mind that several hundred years will pass before the events next to be recorded.

Verse 7. This verse shows the fulfillment of God's promises as recorded in Gen. 12: 2; 13: 16; 22: 17.

Verse 8. *Knew not Joseph.* The first of these words is from YADA and defined "A primitive root; to know (properly, to ascertain by seeing); used in a great variety of senses, figuratively, euphemically, and inferentially, (including observation, care, *recognition;* and causation, designation, punishment,)" — Strong. The word is rendered "acknowledge" 5 times, "regard" once, "familiar friend" once. In the place now being considered it means that the people, and especially the man who was king of Egypt now did not have a friendly attitude toward the history of Joseph and did not recognize nor acknowledge the true worth of what he had been to Egypt.

Verses 9, 10. The motive of the king of Egypt is very evident here. Seeing the increase in numbers of the children of Israel he figured that in the event of war they would take advantage of the situation and escape. Of course we are to understand that they had been serving the Egyptians for some time which was also in fulfillment of the prediction of God to Abraham in Gen. 15: 13. But the severity of that service became worse upon the change of attitude as described in this paragraph. This is what the king meant by his decision to "deal wisely" with them. That "wisdom" will be described in the following paragraphs.

Verse 11. There was an enforced labor put upon the Israelites which was in the nature of a labor tax. Not as one would work for another willingly in order to obtain some desired wage, but a labor performed as under the watchful eye and constraint of a hard foreman. And this agrees with the thought of the cities mentioned in this verse. The common text says "treasure" cities. This is from a word that means a magazine or store house or city. So that as a store place is for goods not needed at the present, we can see that the Israelites were not only required to produce things wanted for immediate use by their masters, but as a matter of hoarding. And the extreme rigor of their productive and enforced labor is seen in the fact that store *cities* were needed to care for the surplus of their labor.

Verse 12. Again we see one of the promises or predictions fulfilled. In Gen. 15: 14 as well as in the initial promise in Gen. 12: 3 we see that if God's people were ever mistreated they would be especially cared for by their divine Master.

Verse 13. *Rigor.* This is from PEREK and defined "to break apart; fracture, i. e. severity." — Strong.

Verse 14. The class of service mentioned in this verse would not be anything to complain of were all other considerations reasonable. But the statement tells us they were made to accomplish this in bitterness and with rigor and this last named word is the same as explained in preceding paragraph.

Verse 15. *Hebrew.* These midwives were not Hebrew women but Egyptian women according to Josephus. But they are here called Hebrew midwives because they had the special assignment of that work for the Hebrew women. This is apparent also from their names which are not Hebrew in form. Also, in verse 22 it says *his* people when charging those on duty at the time of birth of the children. Furthermore, it is not likely that Pharaoh would entrust the business to the Hebrew women since he was much interested in having the babies destroyed in whom they would have a personal interest.

Verse 16. *Stools.* This refers to the birth stools that were used in those days at time of childbirth. The writer has been told by a medical man that if women used this kind of arrangement at such times many of them would be more fortunate than they are with the modern method. For the historic information on this subject see note at Genesis 30: 3. It is to be noted here that the sons were the ones commanded to be destroyed at birth. The reason for this is not hard to see. The girls would be more persons for servitude and thus a help to the Egyptians. But the boys might grow up to become soldiers in case of war in the land, and they might join with the enemy.

Verse 17. It is said here that the midwives feared God. The meaning of the word as used here is to reverence. Thus it means respectful fear, or regard for God.

Verses 18, 19. The language of the preceding paragraph indicates that the midwives did not state the truth in this paragraph for it plainly states that they saved the boys alive and it was because they feared God. The question that naturally arises here is why God would favor these women after their words of falsehood. But we will bear in mind that God has always dealt with people on the basis of their knowledge of right and wrong. These women had never been instructed in all the fine points of truth and falsehood as had God's people. And, since in this case their story was on behalf of what they believed to be a good cause and against the interests of a wicked king, they were given some consideration. They were favored on the general basis of good motive and in spite of their falsehood, not because of it. It is similar to the case of Rahab in Joshua 2. She is said to be justified by her works and not on account of her falsehood. It was in spite of it. Of course no such principles are favored by the Lord today. A complete revelation of divine truth has been made and mankind has been given full instruction on the principles of truth and its responsibility. So that, while in the past God overlooked some irregularities in conduct, he now requires all to adhere to the right. (Acts 17: 30, 31)

Verse 20. *Therefore.* This word might lead to the impression that God dealt well with the midwives just because they had told a falsehood. This is not the case as was shown in preceding paragraph. But the word is from one of a variety of meanings and shades of uses. The most evident sense of its use here is as if the text read that "for good reasons God dealt well" etc. And not the least of those reasons is the fact that the people multiplied and thus was fulfilled the promise in Gen. 12: 2; 22: 17.

Verse 21. Because the midwives feared God. Not because they falsified, but in spite of it, he built them houses. These women being a special class of servants could appreciate having houses of their own posession similar to the arrangements often made for nurses near a hospital. And the fact that God was the one who provided them with these houses indicates that previously they had not been thus supplied.

Verse 22. The Egyptians worshiped many things both living and inanimate. And one of their chief gods was the river Nile. (Ezk. 29: 3, 9). Thus to cast the infants into the river would be like making a sacrifice to their god.

EXODUS 2

Verse 1. Levi was one of the sons of Jacob and became the head of one of the twelve tribes of Israel. This tribe had now become numerous although not numbered as were the other tribes. But sufficiently numerous that one "of the house of Levi" could marry a daughter of Levi without forming a marriage supposed to be restricted.

Verse 2. *Goodly.* This is from TOWB and Young defines it as "good of form." Stephen says he was "fair" (Acts 7: 20) and Paul says he was "proper" (Heb. 11: 23). These last mentioned two words are from ASTEIOS and defined by Thayer "elegant of body, comely, fair." The conclusion is that when this child was born he was seen to be one of unusual beauty as to his body and for this reason the mother hid him with the purpose of preserving him alive. We are not told why this fact was the reason for her hiding the child. We would suppose that a mother would desire to preserve her offspring regardless of appearances. Yet we do have the inspired statement on the matter which shows that his appearance had some connection with the matter. Josephus gives us further information as to this child. (2-19-3). The father of Moses had gone to God in prayer concerning the danger his people were in and had received assurances that deliverance would be provided. That, as Abraham had been blessed with a son who meant so much to him, so, through the child soon to be born to Amram and wife, great deliverance would be experienced by their people. It is reasonable then, to understand why the favorable appearance of the child Moses would suggest the idea that God would use him to fulfill the promise made to Amram in his prayer.

Verse 3. A child three months old could not be so easily concealed so it became necessary to do something about it. And in a sort of subterfuge manner the mother prepared to cast him into the river. The bulrush is a name for several varieties of growth in wet areas and is also known as papyrus. It is very porous and thus light as to weight. This would make it ideal for a vessel expected to float on water. But, as it was porous it would be necessary to counteract its absorbent qualities. This is why she daubed it with slime and pitch. Thus, with the material from papyrus for the body of the ark for lightness of weight, and the slime coating to keep out the water, she had a successful vessel for the safety of her child. Furthermore, by placing the ark in the flags or reeds, which naturally grew near the shore, the vessel would not be on the channel of the river and thus would not be in so much danger of drifting away.

Verse 4. The sister was near enough to wit (or know) what would take place, yet stood "afar off" so as not to be observed and suspected of any personal interest.

Verse 5. Nothing surprising in the act of this woman coming down to the river to bathe for it was a sacred thing to the Egyptians and their use of it would be of a respectful motive. But this presence of hers brought about the event of her discovering an object among the flags or reeds and of course would direct her maids to bring it to her for further inspection.

Verse 6. A child of three months would be old enough to realize the presence of other people and would naturally expect some service. And also would use the only manner within his ability for making it known, so the babe wept. She had compassion on him. What person with even a fraction of humanity in her sentiment could do otherwise? Here is a babe, all alone in a bed consigned to the elements and doubtless needing some ministration. And it expresses itself in its babyish language, and weeps. The daughter of Pharaoh has had many opportunities for seeing the Hebrews in all their various relations of life, even though they had originally been segregated in the special land of Goshen. However, a child of three months would not possess any natural features that would certainly reveal his race. Yet she recognizes him as one of the Hebrew children. This furnishes us with an illustration of what Paul said in Rom. 4: 11 where he speaks of circumcision as being a "sign." Since the descendants of Abraham still followed the ordinance received through him it furnished the sign or clue by which the child was recognized as a Hebrew.

Verse 7. Of course the suggestion of the sister was connected with the remark of the woman. But if the girl had been "afar off" enough at the first not to be seen and suspected, she could not have been near enough to have heard the conversation reported in previous verse. The necessary inference is that the activities of the maids and the mistress in bringing out the ark from the reeds justified the "curiosity" of this casual passer-by in coming up to the group. And hearing the remark of the woman that the child was one of the Hebrews, what more logical thing could be suggested than that a Hebrew nurse would be the proper kind to procure. Of course it was to be taken for granted that a woman of the social rank of a king's daughter would not think of personally nursing the foundling. So this innocent suggestion of the babe's sister was very properly made and accepted.

Verse 8. And according to the ideas set forth in preceding paragraph the expected thing occurred. The girl went to bring her mother since she would be "a nurse of the Hebrew women" as was stated in the suggestion of the sister.

Verse 9. Hired nurses were not uncommon and thus we see nothing on the surface in this transaction that is surprising. But under the surface we see the hand of God and the beginning of another epoch in the great plans of the far away future.

Verse 10. *Grew.* If a child lived normally for one day longer we would know that he "grew" as we generally use that word. Therefore we must understand it to have a more extended meaning here. It is from GADAL and defined "A primitive root; properly to twist, i. e., to be (causatively make) large (in various senses, as in body, mind, estate or honor, also in pride)." — Strong. In connection with this definition of the lexicon it will be well to consider the expression in Heb. 11: 24, "come to years" and the one in Acts 7: 23, "full forty years." Likewise the one in verse 11 of the chapter now under consideration, "When Moses was grown." All this shows the word "grew" to carry the idea of advancement toward maturity. And it was after he had grown far enough that he did not need the services of a nurse that his mother brought him to Pharaoh's daughter. But, not that he was yet fully matured. He was still not old enough to form conclusions of his own for it says here that he became her son. While Heb. 11: 24 states that when he arrived at that age he refused to acknowledge that relationship. The name given to him is from MOSHEH and defined "drawing out (of the water), i. e. rescued." — Strong.

Verse 11. It is clear from this verse that Moses was interested in the welfare of his people the Hebrews. Not only so, but that he thought he should do something about it although God had not specifically instructed him yet to go about that. But that he had had previous reasons for thinking along this line is evident from what is stated in Acts 7: 25 which please see. As to why Moses supposed this of his brethren is explained by the vision his father had when in prayer to God and which was cited above as from Josephus Book 2, chapter 9, section 3. It will be well to quote part of this section here since it throws much light on the whole subject. "A man whose name was Amram, one of the nobler sort of the Hebrews, was afraid for his whole nation, lest it should fail, by the want of young men to be brought up hereafter, and was very uneasy at it, his wife being then with child, and he knew not what to do. Hereupon he betook himself to prayer to God. * * * Accordingly God had mercy on him, and was moved by his supplication. He stood by him in his sleep, and exhorted him not to despair of his future favors. * * * Know therfore that I shall provide for you all in common what is for your good, and particularly for thyself what shall make thee famous; for that child, out of dread of whose nativity the Egyptians have doomed the Israelite children to destruction, shall be this child of thine, and shall be concealed from those who watch to destroy him; and when he is brought up in a surprising way, he shall deliver the Hebrews from the distress they are under from the Egyptians." Josephus was a qualified historian living in the first century of this era and had access to much material for his writings. And since his report here explains some statements of the Bible without conflicting with it we would have no good reason for doubting his authority in this matter under consideration. And it would be reasonable that Amram had imparted to his son the vision he had while in prayer and that was the basis of the interest he had in the situation. And while he supposed also that the thing was more generally known, as per statement in Acts 7: 23, yet he had miscalculated the extent of the knowledge of God's plans.

Verse 12. While Moses had reason to expect to be called into the service that his father had learned of in the vision, yet he was too eager to start the work and so took upon himself the initiative of it. He evidently realized that he was acting largely on his own authority from the conduct described in this verse. This shows why he looked both ways before he acted. A man does not do that when about to perform some deed which he feels fully authorized to do. His feeling of guilt was also indicated by the action of hiding the man in the sand.

Verse 13. The thought here to be observed is that the one who objected to the presence of Moses was the one in the wrong. This is significant. It is a common thing to have people object to doing anything about settling a trouble if the objectors are the ones in the wrong. While those who are not conscious of fault in a matter are more ready to have the case investigated and the wrong brought to judgment.

Verse 14. Another common sentiment is here exhibited. If a peacemaker offers to act in a difficulty so as to settle it according to justice, the ones in the wrong often resent it and accuse the would-be arbitrator of being a tyrant. And in his resentment against Moses in this case the wrong doer chided him with the circumstance of the previous day. This seemed to be a surprise to Moses and revealed to him that his deed was known.

Verse 15. The previous verse says Moses feared, and this verse tells of the threat from Pharaoh. Upon this Moses became alarmed and fled from the country. It is sometimes said that a contradiction is here found of the statement in Heb. 11: 27 which says Moses forsook Egypt, not fearing the wrath of the king. But the instance Paul refers to is forty years later than the one here. Then is when God told him to take the lead and flee Egypt with the children of Israel. At that time he did not fear the king in the sense that he did not regard or respect him. But at the time we are now considering he feared in the sense of being afraid.

Verse 16. *Priest.* This is rendered in the A. V. as follows: chief ruler 2, priest 725, prince 1, principal officer 1. It is defined "KOHEN. Literally, one officiating, a priest; also (by courtesy) an acting priest (although a layman):" — Strong. "Priest, prince, minister." — Young. It should be remembered that the Patriarchal Dispensation of religion is now in force and the fathers of a family had the right to act as a priest and offer sacrifices. This will be dealt with more at length later. As to the use these daughters sought to make of this well, see the comments on Gen. 29: 1-10. By right these girls had access to use of this well as their due.

Verse 17. Unlike the case of Jacob in passage referred to in preceding paragraph, Moses had no previous interests in the situation that we are informed of. But being a man inclined to defend the ones imposed on (as per verses 12, 13 above) he came to the rescue of these daughters of the priest.

Verse 18. Evidently the services of Moses both in driving the shepherds away and also helping with the watering of the flock accounted for their unusual or unexpected return so soon. This is indicated by the mention of both services in the next verse when the daughters are answering their father's inquiry.

Verse 19. *An Egyptian.* Moses was brought up at the court of Pharaoh and of course was trained in the customs and general manners of the Egyptians. In Acts 7: 22 Stephen says he was "learned in all the wisdom of the Egyptians." So it is not to be thought strange that these girls considered him an Egyptian.

Verse 20. Their father chided them for not inviting the man to come with them. He then bids them call him so that he might eat bread. It is significant that an outstanding social custom in old times was to eat with another. It will be well for the student of the Bible to take notice of this custom as he goes on through the study of the Bible for it will be useful information when he comes to the New Testament.

Verses 21, 22. Again the practice of the father in giving his daughter in marriage is here seen. But the statement that Moses was "content to dwell with the man" would indicate that some conversation had been previously had. Also in this paragraph we have an instance of the conciseness of the Bible way of recording events. For in this short space we have the marriage and subsequent parentage of Moses and Zipporah.

Verses 23-25. The hardships of the children of Israel are growing worse and worse and the attention of God is again called to their condition. Moreover, mention is made of the covenant made with the fathers, Abraham, Isaac and Jacob. This was made prominently first in Gen. 15: 13. We will therefore soon be introduced to the preparations for fulfilling that covenant.

EXODUS 3

Verse 1. *Jethro.* This is the most familiar name of Moses' father-in-law. The others are Reuel and Raguel. *Midian.* This was the name of a son of Abraham who became the ancestor of the people called Midianites. As here used it means the land on the Arabian pensinula and largely desert. However it had grazing territory and Moses kept the flock of his father-in-law and had the sheep in this area often. *Horeb.* This is sometimes referred to as the "mount of God." Several important things took place at and on this mount which made this term appropriate. Another name is Sinai and the two are used interchangeably much of the time. But in making the distinction the topmost point is Sinai. See chapter 19: 20.

Verse 2. *Angel.* On the presence and use of these beings see the comments on Gen. 16: 7. This bush burned but was not consumed. This is typical of Israel's afflictions in Egypt which were not able to consume them. See Deut. 4: 20.

Verses 3-5. *Holy ground.* This could not refer to the essential quality of the earth for it was the same place where Moses had been taking the sheep for pasture. Besides, inanimate substance is not spoken of as being holy in itself. But in the present instance it is holy because of the person who is present and the purpose of the appearance of the angel at this time. Any place is sacred or holy where and when holy proceeding takes place.

Verse 6. Mention is made of the father of Moses in connection with God. Then special mention is made of Abraham, Isaac and Jacob. This is found in many places in the Old Testament and thus the expression "fathers" is to be understood generally to refer to these three men. The logical explanation of it is in the fact that Abraham was the one to whom the promise of Christ was first made. Also the one first to receive the promise of a great nation. Then, Jacob was the one in whose day the fulfillment of the national promise was confirmed. (Psa. 105: 9, 10). In this way these three men comprehended a prominent epoch of the history of the blood line. Thus again, let the idea be firmly impressed on the mind that reference to the "fathers" generally means these men. *Afraid.* This is from YARE and defined "a primitive root; to fear; morally to revere; causatively, to frighten." — Strong. This word, like a corresponding word in the New Testament, has two shades of meaning. The connection then must determine which is to be used. In this case Moses would not be frightened since he has been told that he is on holy ground and hence not in any danger of harm. Therefore we conclude that he was filled with awe because of the majesty of God and felt unworthy to approach.

Verses 7, 8. *Cry.* This is from TSAAQAH and defined "a shriek." The Israelites were literally caused to shriek because of the physical hardships imposed on them by the taskmasters. This was according to the divine predictions but God has tolerated it long enough and now proposes to go about their deliverance. *Flowing.* This is from the word ZUB and used frequently in figurative sense. Its predominant meaning is that of a condition where the thing mentioned is very plentiful or even in super-abundance. The reason for such condition was that the land was especially good for pasturing on the plains and foot hills and also for fruit (and other blossoms) on the hillsides. The peoples mentioned in close of 8th verse were among the most prominent heathen ones then occupying the country.

Verses 9, 10. This is the first time that God told Moses to go to deliver the children of Israel from their bondage. Forty years prior to this he took it upon himself to interfere with the situation but got into trouble. Now when God calls upon him to go he hesitates and proposes various excuses or objections as we shall see.

Verse 11. If the reader wishes to tabulate the excuses or objections of Moses he may mark this as the first. *Who am I?* There is some logic in this objection considering the experience before. At that time the Israelite asked him who had made him a judge and ruler over him. (See 2: 14). Now the question embraces the subject of his authority, also that of the assurance of his success. That query will be answered in the following verse.

Verse 12. God first makes the positive promise that he will be with him. But he also makes a test in the form of a prophesy. *Ye shall serve God upon this mountain.* This prediction was fulfilled as seen in the latter chapters of this book. As one specific reference of its fulfillment see chapter 24: 13. A similar form of evidence was given by Jesus in Luke 21: 13. There Jesus made a prediction of something to happen to his disciples and then makes the statement cited. That means that when the thing predicted came to pass then it would constitute a testimony. Anyone might make a prediction. But not until said prediction came to pass would it prove the authority or standing of the one making it.

Verses 13, 14. *AM.* This is from HAYAH and defined "a primitive root; to exit, i. e. be or become, come to pass (always emphatic, and not a mere copula or auxiliary);" Strong. The meaning is that God is self-existent and not created. That he thus has always been and always will be. And certainly such a Being would have the right and power to take their case into his hands.

Verse 15. Here God repeats the thought expressed before about the fathers. Thus, not only does the eternal, self-existent One address himself to them, but he is the one so closely related to them in that he is the God of our own lineal ancestors, Abraham, Isaac and Jacob. *(For) ever.* The second word is from OLAM and defined "properly, concealed, i. e. the vanishing point; generally, time out of mind (past or future), i. e. (practically) eternity; frequently adverbially. (Especially with prepositional prefix,) always." — Strong.

Verses 16-18. *Elders.* This is from ZAQEN and is defined by Strong simply as "to be old." Young defines it as "Old, age, bearded." It has been rendered in the A. V. as follows: aged 3 times, ancient 10, ancient man 1, elder 115, eldest 1, old 24, old man 19; as used in the text at hand it refers to the seniors of the nation and not to old men in the sense of officials. This class would be called forth in this case in respect for their age and experience. *Wilderness.* This is from MIDBAR and defined "a pasture (i. e. open field, whither cattle are driven); by implication a desert." — Strong. The word is rendered desert 13 times, south 1, wilderness 253. The leading thought is that of a place not inhabited and not so much of a place that is barren or unproductive. For a contrasting term against the wilderness of the wandering see chapter 16: 35. Moses demanded they be permitted to go three days journey from Egypt before attempting to sacrifice to God. This distance would afford better assurance of non-interference from the enemy.

Verse 19. *Not by a mighty hand.* The marginal reading has this "but by strong hand." This is evidently the correct rendering. We know God does not mean to declare that the king will never let them go for he finally did. But he did not until the mighty hand of God overpowered him.

Verse 20. This verse describes the

mighty hand of God referred to in preceding verse and that is to finally compel Pharaoh to release the people. The use of the word 'wonders" expresses the leading principle in the word "miracle" as used generally in the Bible. Without any specific context the word "miracle" means any kind of wonder.

Verse 21. *Not go empty.* This will be fulfillment of the promise in Gen. 15: 14 that they were to "come out with great substance."

Verse 22. *Borrow.* This word has been a target for the criticism of enemies of the Bible for years past. The charge of dishonesty is made in that borrowing without any intention of repaying is dishonesty. In the ordinary sense of the word and with the usual transactions of man that would be true. But we will make a closer study of the word. It is from SHAEL and defined "a primitive root; to inquire; by implication to request; by extension to demand." — Strong. The word is rendered in the A. V. as follows: ask 87 times, beg 1, be lent 1, borrow 6, demand 4, desire 9, and others of similar strength. Thus the word is a different one from the one commonly used when a mere temporary favor is expected. The Israelites had served the Egyptians for several centuries without proper pay and it was just that they demand these articles at this time. And since their dispositon would have been to reject the just plea of the servants God influenced them to turn the articles over. Spoil. This is from NATSAL and means to "snatch away." Of course since the Israelites were entitled to these articles of value and demand the same, that amounted to the act of snatching them.

EXODUS 4

Verse 1. *They will not believe me.* This is the second excuse or objection that Moses made. And it is also a logical one. He could not forget how he was rejected by one of his fellowmen 40 years before when he offered his services. Now it was natural for him to doubt his reception by them. God seems to have agreed with his view of this subject as will be seen by what follows.

Verses 2-4. This rod was a walking staff and cut from the branches of a bush or tree. It had not life in it until it was cast upon the ground and God turned it into a serpent. When Moses took it by the tail and it returned into a rod demonstrated not only that God could do such a wonder but that he would do it through the agency of Moses.

Verse 5. Mention is again made of the "fathers" and their names given. See comments at 3: 6. Here the idea is set forth that Moses is to give indication that he is not acting on his own power but on that of another. And that other is no less than the God of the fathers, hence they should believe him.

Verses 6-9. The placing of the hand into the bosom twice constituted one "sign" even as the two transactions with the rod constituted one. This is evident from the expression "two signs" in 9th verse. Then the pouring of water on the ground to be turned into blood will be considered a complete sign even without the return of the blood into water. And the reader should not confuse this turning of water into blood as one of the plagues as yet. This instance is to be for the benefit of the Israelites and not before the Egyptians, hence not one of the plagues.

Verse 10. Here is the third excuse of Moses. The marginal wording is that he is not "a man of words." When the Israelites had asked him a question as in 2: 14 there is no report of any reply. Possibly he now felt the need of being able to use speech in his contact with them. This would be especially important since he is to call upon them to follow him out of that country and in resistance against their ruler.

Verses 11, 12. The logic of the Lord's reply to Moses here is a fundamental shot not only at the complaint expressed, but is one that no unbeliever could answer. It is evident that man exists, and yet, man knows that neither he nor any other creature like him could have brought him into existence. Therefore, whoever or whatever power it was that made the man can certainly manage him. Just as the man who makes a machine should certainly know how to use it or how to repair it if needed. And this general assurance from God should have been sufficient for Moses but apparently it was not as will be seen in the following paragraph.

Verse 13. This is the fourth excuse of Moses but is general in its form, though God knows what is in his mind as next verse shows. ***Wilt send.***

In the margin this is rendered "shouldst." This is evidently correct although there is no word given in the lexicon for the first word. But the speech of the Lord in following verse agrees with the margin here.

Verses 14-17. This is a very significant passage and should be carefully noted. It teaches that both Moses and Aaron were to be inspired of the Lord in their teaching and acting. Observe especially the words in 15th verse where God says he will be with *thy* mouth and *his* mouth. In view of all this we should consider any opposition to these men as rebellion against God and as questioning the truth of their words.

Verse 18. The foregoing speech seems to have convinced Moses for he now makes preparations to take up the great task. But he first speaks to his father-in-law on the subject. This shows a fine spirit in Moses. He has been obligated to him in a temporal and social way and it is fair to consult him before breaking away. Of course, had there been any opposition it would have been his duty to obey the Lord regardless, and no doubt he would. But it was proper to contact Jethro and it was favorable for he not only told him to go, but go in peace.

Verse 19. There is nothing new in this command from God for Moses to go to Egypt. But he is given the additional assurance of safety in that those who would have harmed him forty years ago are now dead.

Verse 20. This verse might give the impression that Moses' wife and children went with him to Egypt. But while he started with them and doubtless took them part of the way, yet he sent them back to his father-in-law before he entirely left the country. This is stated in chapter 18: 2.

Verses 21, 22. Here God announces to Moses that the heart of Pharaoh will be hardened. This will be considered at length later. Here the Lord speaks of Israel as his firstborn. Since this was not the first being God ever had we know it does not apply in that sense. But we do know that Israel was the first distinct people the Lord had. Besides, Strong gives as one definition of the word that of "chief" which is easy to understand as applying to this people at this time. And because of the high estimate which God placed upon this people he proposes to take care of them.

Verse 23. Here the threat that God makes will be finally carried out literally. Such will be appropriate. If Israel is God's firstborn in so important a sense, it would be fitting that the fleshly firstborn of Egypt should be sacrificed to procure the deliverance of this great people from their bondage.

Verses 24-26. This interesting circumstance has much significance. It shows, for one thing, that no man is "the indispensable man." That even as important a man as Moses will be sacrificed if the dignity of God's ordinance demands it. In Gen. 17: 14 the ordinance of circumcision is given to Abraham and so exacting is it to be that if it is neglected "that soul shall be cut off from his people." Now if an infant is the one concerning whom the neglect is committed the punishment must be administered to the adult responsible. Evidently in this case Moses has permitted his busy situation to lead him into neglect of this ordinance. Also, it is very probable that, having a foreigner for a wife, she would not be as prompt in attending to this as she should be. Hence the matter has been neglected and God will bring the one responsible, Moses, to just punishment. As angels are among the instruments which the Lord used in carrying out his plans, he would send one for the present mission. But when the matter was brought before the attention of Moses he proceeds at once to attend to it. And the mother would be the logical one to perform the act which she does. But the matter was displeasing to Zipporah as indicated by her remark to Moses. She had no personal regard for the rite of circumcision. To her it was merely a bloody performance and since her husband caused her to perform the deed she makes the accusation. But after this interruption of the story the writer resumes the former trend.

Verses 27, 28. *Wilderness.* This word is defined at 3: 18. Mount of God. See comments on this at chapter 3: 1. Also chapter 18: 5 and 1 Ki. 19: 8 where it is so called. Upon the meeting of the brothers at this mount Moses gave to Aaron the information he had received from God and the following record shows the conversation to be agreeable.

Verse 29. Note that the brothers act together here even as they do usually in the performance of the services for the nation. The many-sided types of Christ that these brothers constituted will be evident from time to time as the Old Testament is studied. Moses was lawgiver as was Christ. Aaron was priest as was Christ. The initial mention of this here is only for purpose of suggestion. It will become more pronounced later on. *Elders.* This word is explained at 3: 16 which see. It was proper to go to these men first as being leaders in example and influence.

Verses 30, 31. Here Aaron spake the words that the Lord had spoken to Moses. This was according to verse 15. *Did the signs * * * people believed.* This is what these signs were for. Not only so, but God has never asked people to believe the words of other people claiming to be sent without furnishing them evidence. And here we are informed that belief was produced by the performing of them. This is similar to the evidence furnished mankind as to the identity of Jesus. See John 20: 30, 31. The reception which the people accord Moses and Aaron here was good. Had their conduct afterwards been according to it they would have been happier many times.

EXODUS 5

Verse 1. Having first obtained favorable reception at hands of the Israelites they are now ready to contact Pharaoh, which they do. They do not make their demand on their own behalf nor merely on the behalf of the people. But it is made in the majestic name of "Lord God of Israel." The wilderness here mentioned is the same as explained previously. *Hold a feast.* Ususally this would give one the idea of some kind of sumptuous meal or banquet. But the word from which these three words are derived does not require that such meaning be included. They are from CHAGAG and defined "properly to move in a circle, i. e. (specifically) to march in a sacred procession, to observe a festival; by implication to be giddy." — Strong. The word has been rendered in the A. V. as follows: celebrate, one time, dance 1, hold a feast 1, keep 8, keep a feast 1, keep a solmn feast 1, keep holyday 1, reel to and fro 1. The thought in this verse is that they wished to go out on a solemn march of three days duration and to render due services to God enroute.

Verse 2. The various answers of Pharaoh will be noted as they appear in the narrative. This is the first one and is a flat rejection of the plea of Moses and Aaron. In this speech he makes one statement that is true and another that is rash. It was true that he did not know the Lord as yet but is destined to learn of him before the case is settled. And the boast that he would not let Israel go will be counteracted.

Verse 3. *Desert.* This is from the same word as "wilderness" and explained at 3: 18.

Verses 4, 5. Here the king accuses Moses and Aaron of hindering the work of the people. This is a true charge but not to the dishonor of the people. Since their God had met with them (verse 3) and promised deliverance they would naturally be encouraged to pause in their labors. But it irritated the king and he referred to the fact that the people had become numerous. This meant that stoppage of work was all the more a loss to the king.

Verse 6. *Taskmasters.* This is from NAGAS and defined "a primitive root; to drive (an animal, a workman, a debtor, an army); by implication to tax, harass, tyranize." — Strong. *Officers.* This is from SHATAR and defined by Strong "active part of an otherwise unused root probably meaning to write; properly a scribe, i. e. (by analogy or implication) an official superintendent or magistrate." So here is the set-up. These last named men gave the official instructions and commands for the tasks and it was the duty of the taskmasters to see that they were done. And all of them were urged on by the threats of Pharaoh. See further comments at verses 10, 14, 19.

Verses 7, 8. Pharaoh had hitherto furnished the straw for the brick, but now they are required to furnish it themselves. Straw is used in brick making in countries where rainfall is very light. The brick or adobes are not burnt and the straw is put in as a binder and to resist erosion from what small amount of rain that did come. *Tale.* This is from a word that means "a fixed quantity." So that the stipulated number of bricks they had been required to make had to be kept up now the same as when the straw was furnished them.

Verse 9. *Vain* is from SHEQER and defined "an untruth; by implication a sham (often adverbially):"—Strong. The pronoun "them" means the taskmasters or officers placed over the people. The people are accused (though falsely) of making false complaints about their hardships. See verse 8 where they are accused of being idle. So in the verse at hand it means that the men over the people are to push the work onto the people and pay no attention to their pretended claim of hardhship.

Verse 10. *Taskmasters of the people * * * officers.* See comments at verse 6, also at verses 19-21. All of these passages considered together show us that these taskmasters and officers were to work jointly to overwork the people. The taskmasters were Egyptian and the officers were Israelites. See the citation from the lexicon in verse 6 as to the comparative status of these two classes of overseers. The officers being men of the children of Israel, and being somewhat cultured men, would be thought of as being capable of more influential appeal to their own people. Then the taskmasters from the Egyptian people would be naturally prejudiced in favor of their own king and against the Israelites. And together, urged on by the threats of Pharaoh, they would harass the people.

Verses 11, 12. The king of Egypt could not have been ignorant of the fact that the grain had been gathered in and that nothing but the stubble was available to the people in the field. Notwithstanding, they are ordered to find it and still come up with the usual day's work. All of this in fulfillment of the prediction in Gen. 15 that they were to be evilly entreated.

Verse 13. Here the taskmasters are mentioned as the ones who were directly at the people to see that the demands of the officers and Pharaoh were carried out.

Verse 14. The language of this verse makes it plain that the officers were men of Israel while the taskmasters were Egyptian as shown at verses 6, 10.

Verses 15, 16. Here the officers think to appeal to Pharaoh in defense and show cause for objection to their treatment. They specify a just cause of their inability to produce the usual amount of bricks by the added task of finding their own straw. On this ground they venture the complaint that their failure is on account of his own people and not their own.

Verses 17, 18. But this did not benefit them any. Instead, the king again makes the false accusation that they are idle. He accuses them of false motives of wishing to sacrifice to the Lord.

Verse 19. This verse is very clear that the officers mentioned before were men of Israel who were expected to form the demands to be made upon the laborers. *In evil case.* The last word is not in the original. The word evil is here in an expression that might aptly be expressed by the colloquialism "in bad."

Verse 20. The word "they" here refers to the officers in the previous verse. This fact, together with the conversation related in following verse confirms the conclusions expressed at verses 6, 10, 14, 19.

Verse 21. This is one of the murmurings that the children of Israel made against Moses and Aaron and which will be repeated several times. This murmuring is mentioned by Paul in 1 Cor. 10: 10. *Savour.* This is from REYACH and defined by Strong "odor (as if blown)" Young defines it "smell, savour, fragrance." It is rendered in the A. V. by savour 45 times, scent 2, smell 11. *Abhorred.* This is from BAASH and defined "a primitive root; to smell bad; figuratively, to be offensive morally."—Strong. So the whole expression could be rendered literally "hast made us smell bad (figuratively) to the Egyptians." This charge was not correct in strict sense. This bad smell was already there before the work of Moses and Aaron had begun. This bad odor was caused by the successful growth of the nation and the growing fear that the people might bring trouble on the Egyptians in case of war. And they were here trying to lay this unpleasant odor on their so-called idleness.

Verses 22, 23. Here Moses acts as mediator for the people. *Evil entreated.* The second word is not in the original but has been supplied by the King James translators. And we should not think of the word "evil" as always having a moral significance. It has been translated a number of times by the word "afflict." It is from RAA and the definition in the lexicon will justify this mentioned rendering. And the situation with the people would agree with such rendering for they were certainly being afflicted. And it could be said that the Lord was the one who had thus afflicted them since it was his prediction and arrangement that it should be. And we notice here that Moses seems to be in a critical mood towards the Lord in the case. But our feeling of questioning will be less when we remember that Moses is to be a type of Christ in more than one sense. And a mediator is one of those senses. Of course a mediator must take the role of one who is interested in the wishes and comfort of the one or ones for whom he is mediator and must make his plea and complaint accordingly. This would call for a statement from Moses of the grievances of the people, and one of the main grievances just now is the fact that they have not yet been delivered.

EXODUS 6

Verse 1. *With a strong hand.* See comments on this thought at 3: 19. Of course the "strong hand" that will force Pharaoh to release the people is that of the Lord.

Verses 2, 3. In this paragraph we have four words in the A. V. applying to the Supreme Being which are *Lord, God, Almighty, Jehovah.* The first and fourth are from the same original which is YEHOVAH and defined by Strong "the self-existent or Eternal; Jehovah, Jewish national name of God." Let the reader specially note the last four words of this definition which will be mentioned again presently. The second word is from ELOHIYM and its outstanding meaning is a Being worthy of worship. The third word is from SHADAD and defined "a primitive root; properly to be burly, i. e. (figuratively) powerful (passively impregnable); by implication to ravage." This definition is from Strong. With these critical definitions before us the passage as a whole is as follows. God imparts to Moses, the present lawgiver for God, this great meaning. That the entire proceeding is from the Being that has always been and who is of unquestioned authority. But the position of the fathers, Abraham, Isaac and Jacob in the grand scheme of the ages was such that they could not need nor fully appreciate this meaning. Instead, they were made acquainted with God as an object of divine worship and also a great powerful Being. But since the name Jehovah was to become specialized as the name of a national God, such name would mean little or nothing to these fathers since they had no nation-formation.

Verse 4. *Established.* The word for this is QUWM and the simple definition that Strong gives in his lexicon for the word is "to rise." That is, to make or cause to come into existence. We generally think of the word "established" as meaning that the thing spoken of has been fulfilled, which we know is not the case here. However, the covenant was made with these fathers and God is telling Moses that the present mission on which he is sending him is to bring about the fulfillment of the covenant.

Verse 5. God has taken notice of the suffering of his people and also remembers his covenant. Therefore he is now about bringing the covenant into existence as fact.

Verse 6. As inducement for the children of Israel to listen to Moses they are to be told that God is going soon to bring them out from under their burdens imposed by the Egyptians. And that he will do so by the use of great judgments.

Verses 7, 8. *People.* This is from AM and defined "a people (as a congregated unit); specifically a tribe (as those of Israel); hence (collectively) troops or attendants; figuratively a flock."—Strong. This is significant. Since they are soon to become a people in this collective sense and thus form a nation, the new name Jehovah will be appropriate as noted at verses 2, 3. In the present paragraph the name Lord is used twice which is the same in the original as Jehovah and means a national God.

Verse 9. The awful condition of depression among the Israelites must have been extensive since it seemed to dull them against the subject of their own interest. They failed to heed the words of Moses on account of this condition. A similar situation is recorded in Luke 22: 45 where we have the apostles sleeping instead of watching. And the inspired writer tells us they were "sleeping for sorrow." So it was with the children of Israel. Their bondage was so cruel that it depressed them into ignoring the words of Moses. While they are not entirely to be excused for this attitude, yet it is not to be condemned as severely as if it came from pure indifference.

Verse 10. The form of expression seen in this verse occurs hundreds of times in the Old Testament and hence must be considered as very significant. It gives us the thought that Moses was directly connected with God in the legislation for the children of Israel. No one doubts God's ability to speak directly to each of the people had he so wished. And, if such a thing were necessary in order to make the instructions to be binding, he certainly would have done so. All of this shows that when we read of a commandment uttered or written by Moses it is the same as if God had spoken it by his own mouth to the people. There are many people in the religious world who might be classed with the Judaizers of the days of the apostles. They teach that we should "keep the Sabbath" today. But these people do not even pretend to observe all the other requirements of the Old Testament. When confronted with this inconsistency they reply with the charge that Moses was not of such authority as to require that of us. That a distinction is to be made between the law of God and the law of Moses. That the law of Moses has indeed been nailed to the cross but that the law of God is perpetual and thus that the Sabbath commandment is still binding. If these false teachers were exposed on this point their whole fabric would be practically exposed. If the authority of Moses is the same as that of God in regard to the legislation found in the Old Testament, then this whole institution is shown to be wrong. And the fact of the multitude of instances in which the verse here considered is repeated proves beyond any doubt that no distinction can be made between God and Moses. And the Lord must have been looking forward to such false teaching when he caused this expression to be recorded in his Book so frequently. The conclusion then is that if Christians are bound to "keep the Sabbath" on the ground that God commanded it, then we are also commanded to keep all other items of the Jewish law since God also gave them to the people through the instrumentality of Moses.

Verse 11. It is to be noted that while Moses first appealed to the children of Israel in order to convert them to the idea of leaving, yet he did not attempt to lead them out by stealth. He did not wish to have them leave the country in the appearance of "escaped convicts" but to leave by the knowledge and consent of the king. So the king is to be approached and given opportunity for co-operation.

Verse 12. This verse does not contradict 4: 30, 31 because at that time the people really did believe. But at present Moses is thinking of what is stated in verse 9 above. If the children of Israel would not be impressed by the words of Moses, when they were supposed to be already the ones to be benefited by him, then he did not think that Pharaoh would hear him. Especially when he is of "uncircumcised lips." When circumcision is used figuratively, which it certainly is here, then it has the meaning of being unfit or unconsecrated. See Lev. 19: 23 where the word is used in connection with trees and where we know it can have only a figurative meaning. Moses is still thinking of his unfitness from the standpoint of speaking ability. It was the same idea he expressed in 4: 10.

Verse 13. God does not take the complaint of Moses here seriously for he makes no reply to it. Instead, he repeats his orders by speaking to both brothers and "gave them charge unto the children of Israel." Here we see again the comments at verse 10. Also note here that the charge was unto Pharaoh. Now there is one who will question the complete authority of the demand upon Pharaoh to let Israel go, and that his refusal to do so was actual rebellion against God. And yet this demand was made through the same Moses as were the commandments of the laws of the Old Testament. This is thus another proof that the attempts to discredit the authority of Moses as distinct from that of God is an act of rebellion against God.

Verses 14, 15. *Heads of their fathers' houses.* Frequently this means the twelve sons of Jacob while in this case we have only the first two sons of Jacob. This is evidently in preparation for the history of the third son whose family line will take up the rest of this chapter. At present we are not told why the first two are passed by with brief mention of their names and those of their offspring. That will come out in a later part of the book.

Verse 16. Since Levi and his three sons will figure very prominently in the work of the nation of Israel all through their history it will be well for the reader to take note of the mention of the four names as they are in this verse.

Verses 17-20. The families of the three sons are outlined in this paragraph. But only the names to be connected with the work of the nation need be noted. And these are here restricted to the line of Levi through his son Kohath. This is because the priesthood will be confined to this particular family, also the legislative department. That brings in the names of the brothers, Moses and Aaron.

Verses 21-27. The family members of Moses are recorded in an earlier chapter of this book and hence not given here. But the various members of the family of Aaron are what take up the present paragraph. Mention will be made of the four sons of Aaron given in 23rd verse because they will become familiar in after years.

Verses 28-30. Again Moses is reminded that it is the Lord who is speaking to him. We have learned this name means the same as Jehovah and that it means the self-existent One. He is again told to relay to Pharaoh all that is given to him. And once more Moses complains of his unfitness for the work. See verse 12 for comments on the idea of "uncircumcised lips."

EXODUS 7

Verse 1. *God.* This is from ELOHIYM and one part of the definition of Strong will explain the use of the word here. "Occasionally applied by way of deference to magistrates; and sometimes as a superlative." That is , Moses is to be superior to Pharaoh. *Prophet.* This is from NABIY and defined "a prophet or (generally) inspired man."—Strong. This definition is confirmed by the text in chapter 4: 15. The verse means that Aaron will give inspired instructions and Moses will enforce them against Pharaoh as being in authority over him for the present crisis.

Verse 2. Here again note that when Moses speaks it is by the command of God and has the same force as if spoken directly by the Lord to the king.

Verse 3. *Harden.* The outstanding principle in this word is to "make obstinate." It is used frequently in connection with God's dealings with Pharaoh and occasionally with others. There is no doubt that God actually hardened the heart of the king for the statements are too direct to admit of denial. But the question of *how* he did it is still an open one. Some might think that God acted upon Pharaoh arbitrarily and that he had nothing to do with it himself. That is the theory that is unfounded. It states in some places that Pharaoh hardened his heart which shows that he had a part in it and was thus responsible. When God removed the plagues then it was said that the heart of Pharaoh was hardened. So a short but true statement would be to say that God hardened the heart of Pharaoh by giving him the occasion and Pharaoh hardened his heart by grasping the occasion. It could be aptly, though roughly, illustrated by an old adage that if you "give an animal enough rope he will hang himself." The owner hanged the animal by giving him plenty of rope and he hanged himself by using the rope. And it was perfectly just for God to treat Pharaoh thus since he was brought to the seat of Egypt's power for the very purpose of carrying out the divine plan. (See 9: 16). Pharaoh was already a wicked man before this experience with God started (1: 8) and thus his moral character was not made any different by this use to which God put him.

Verse 4. *That I may lay, etc.* The explanations in foregoing paragraph will be applicable here. But the direct construction in this would be as if it said "Pharaoh shall not harken, and that will make occasion for God to lay his hand upon Egypt." And the fact that the king will continue to be obstinate will give God occasion to accomplish his deliverance of his people with great judgment.

Verse 5. The Egyptians are to be made to know that God is the Lord. That is, that he is the self-existent One which would make him superior to all gods they had ever known. And certainly they would have this great fact demonstrated by the signs that are to be brought about among them.

Verse 6. Again we see the authority of Moses and Aaron in that what they did was according to what the Lord commanded them.

Verse 7. This verse should be marked and noted as of specific information as it relates to other portions of their life's work.

Verses 8, 9. *Miracle.* There are three different words in the original for this word in the A. V. of the Old Testament but their meaning is practically the same. And the fundamental meaning is, a wonder, omen, sign or something out of the ordinary and not produced by established and simple causes. It was to be expected that Pharaoh would call for something in this line, hence God had qualified the brothers to perform such deeds. It was also to convince the Israelites of their authority. (4: 9, 30, 31). And thus they are prepared to demonstrate for Pharaoh.

Verse 10. It is the inspired writer who tells us the rod became a serpent. So it must not be said that Pharaoh merely thought the rod became a serpent but that it actually did.

Verses 11, 12. The actions of Pharaoh here show that he did not think his eyes were deceiving him. He is certain that something miraculous has happened. However, he wants to believe that it arose from a power like that possessed by his own servants. *Wise men, sorcerers, magicians.* The meaning of these three words is practically the same and evidently should be considered in the same light. However, if there is any real difference and if all three kinds responded when Pharaoh called, yet only the last named performed as will be seen in this and the following instances. The names of these men are given in 2 Tim. 3: 8. The word is from CHARTOM and defined "a horoscopist (as drawing magical lines or circles:"—Strong. Doubtless the general practice of these men was that of deception. But in this case they actually accomplished what is attributed to them. But the explanation is in the fact that God sometimes either makes direct use of an evil character for his special purpose or suffers others so to use them for the present. This is seen in the cases of the serpent talking in the garden, the beast of Balaam talking to him and the woman of Endor bringing up the spirit of Samuel. But while God is suffering this miraculous work to be done, it is to be charged up to the motive of the wicked men and to be regarded as their work. The work of God never fails while this will as will be seen later on. And even with the success which the magicians appeared to possess, the superiority of Aaron over them is evident when their rods were swallowed up by his.

Verse 13. See comments at verse 3 on the matter of hardening Pharaoh's heart.

Verses 14, 15. *Against he come.* The last two words are not in the original but supplied in the A. V. as being implied by the word for "against." That word is from QARA and defined by Strong "to encounter, whether accidently or in a hostile manner." And since the forepart of the verse stated that Pharaoh would come to that place the translators added the words to the other. So the verse means to say that Pharaoh is coming out to the river which was one of their chief gods. And Moses was to be there to encounter and oppose him. And the rod in his hand was the instrument he was to use in this opposition.

Verses 16-18. Pharaoh is to be given another chance but is told what the consequences will be if he still refuses to let the people go. And let it be noticed that it is the water of the river mentioned here that is to be plagued. However, the following paragraph extends this to include all the water in open containers such as ponds and pools and all the streams.

Verses 19, 20. This paragraph records the plague of blood which is to be counted as number one of the plagues. It will be well for the reader to keep account of them and he may mark them as numbered in his Bible if he so desires. The previous works by Moses and Aaron are not to be considered among the plagues but only as miracles to convince Pharaoh. The water being turned to blood as mentioned in 4: 9 was never resorted to that we have any specific mention. If it was it was not a plague on the Egyptians but a miracle to convince the Israelites.

Verse 21. All the land of Egypt as having the blood must be understood to mean the main part of the land and not that part near the Israelites. There was a severance between the two parts as may be seen at chapter 8: 22. Of course this severance is not mentioned at the first three plagues because it would not be the nature of the articles used in them to spread of their own accord as it would with flies. But the Lord made severance in them in that he did not bring them upon the land of Goshen.

Verses 22-25. How could the magicians find water on which to perform when Moses had fouled all the water in Egypt? The answer is in the 24th verse. That is why special mention was made of this in verses 16-18. So by digging into the ground they could find water for drinking purposes as well as for this act of their magic. But even with all this demonstration, since his men could apparently keep up with Moses, Pharaoh hardened his heart which means that he continued to be obstinate. As long as there seems to be the least chance he is going to hold out. And he persists in this stubborn conduct for at least seven days. That is, God gave him seven days to ponder over the situation and change his mind.

EXODUS 8

Verses 1, 2. The text does not say whether the Lord had removed the plague of blood from the rivers but the implication is that he did. The present paragraph has the threat of frogs and they are to come from the river. In the plague of blood it is stated that all the fish in the river died. While the frogs are not fish yet they live in water and certainly would have died when the fish did. And it will not admit of the theory that they were created as a special creature outside of the water. Besides, the following verses state that they are to be brought forth from the river, also are said to return to the river when the plague is removed.

Verses 3, 4. It is in accordance with God's dealing of justice to warn Pharaoh and give him another chance before bringing on the next plague.

Verses 5, 6. In this paragraph the actual fact of the frogs is stated. Therefore, those who are marking their books will make this number two.

Verse 7. Here note that it is the magicians who oppose Moses. Nothing said about the other actors of Pharaoh. See comments at 7: 11, 12. *Enchantments.* This English word occurs here and in 7: 11, 22. It is from different words in the original but both have practically the same meaning which is that it was some kind of secret performance that was supposed to produce the desired effect without exposing to the spectators the means used. And, while this was usually a case of deception and one in which the onlooker was misled into thinking the feat was real, yet in the present instances the feat was real because the Lord has seen fit to use the magicians for the purpose. Again, let the reader see the comments at 7:11, 12.

Verse 8. This is answer number two of Pharaoh. Note that it is a complete compliance with the demands of Moses and had he been sincere it would have solved the situation for the present.

Verse 9. The word "glory" is from PAAR and means to boast; either to boast one's self or to boast over another or "at his expense." Moses evidently has little or no confidence in Pharaoh's promise since he had broken the one before. And he as good as tells him so in a later instance. (8: 29). In that place he warns Pharaoh not to deal deceitfully "any more" which is a reflection on his past conduct. In the event of the present paragraph he makes the same charge in a more direct speech. In view of the meaning of the word "glory" and under the circumstances of Pharaoh's lack of sincerity we could well paraphase the verse thus: "I do not believe you are in earnest in this promise, but if you are I will be willing for you to boast yourself over me and taunt me with the idea that you were right and I was wrong." If I were to use a familiar expression I would say that Moses is so sure that Pharaoh will not do as he promises that he is willing to agree that the king "has the laugh on him" in case he does actually perform his promise. However, he asks the king to name the time the bargain is to be carried out.

Verses 10, 11. One object of clearing the land of the plague was that the king should be made to know there was none like the Lord God. This would be demonstrated by the removal of the frogs. For, even if it should be suggested that the plague came accidently or naturally, yet the removal of them at a pre-set date would be proof of the power of God. Especially if they are so completely removed that not any of them would be present in the river from whence they had come. Another thought here; the fact that the frogs were to return to and remain in the river proves the river had been cleansed of the former plague as discussed in verses 1, 2. To be exact, the frogs then not in the river were to be disposed of in the land. But still, the statement that there were to be some in the river leaves our conclusion here correct.

Verses 12-14. In this paragraph which is plain without comment as to the facts, it is well to note that Moses again appeals to God which is just another instance of his work as a mediator between him and the people.

Verse 15. True to his character and also true to form for his past conduct, the king breaks his promise when the plague is removed. *He hardened his heart.* For comments on this see chapter 7: 3. Also Pharaoh failed to make any answer this time.

Verses 16, 17. This is to be marked as plague number three. The word "lice" is from KEN and defined by

Strong "from 3661 (a word meaning to set out or plant) in the sense of fastening; a gnat (from infixing its sting)." Young's first definition is also "gnat." I am sure this is the correct rendering. What we think of as lice do not have wings and thus make their appearence upon man or beast by bodily contact. It is true that God could bring them onto a body through the air unnaturally. But it is not necessary to suppose a miracle that the conditions described in the text do not require. The fact that the magicians tried to bring these insects indicates that they were in existence independent of the bodies of men and animals. Otherwise, had they succeeded in this plague there would have been no evidence of it since the lice were already on the men's bodies. But a gnat which is an insect with wings could be produced in the dust independent of all bodies, then fly to the bodies the Lord wished to be attacked. And then with their sting would produce great discomfort.

Verse 18. The magicians could procure dust that had not yet been infected upon which to perform their magic. This would have demonstrated their magical power to the same extent as the previous instances even though they might not have been able to add to the discomfort of the ones already tormented. See previous paragraph also on this.

Verse 19. Much of the meaning in this verse is around the word "this." It is from HIY and defined "a primitive word, the third personal pronoun singular, he (she or it); only expressed when emphatic or without a verb."—Strong. So the magicians account for their failure to bring the lice by using the expression "this is the finger of God." Since they used a word that is in the third person they must have reference to the being who has caused their failure and the success of Moses. And doing so they say that this (this failure of ours) is caused through the power of God. That is the same as acknowledging that they have been operating by some other power. Of course that would have to be a power coming from a being opposite of God which is the devil. See comments at 7: 11, 12. Again Pharaoh makes no answer or proposition.

Verses 20, 21. *Swarms of flies.* The last two words are not in the original but the James' translators supplied them because of the idea of swarming. The first word is from AROB and defined by Strong "a mosquito (from its swarming)" Young defines the word "a beetle, dog fly." This is plague number four.

Verse 22. A severance is to be made between the part of the country where the children of Israel lived and the place of the Egyptians. This was not stated by Moses at the former three plagues since the nature of those plagues would not suggest the necessity of miraculous management of the pests. A mosquito, created independent of any other element, as were the gnats, would be free to travel where it willed unless prevented by miracle.

Verse 23. Any person might make a general prediction of presence of flies or other pests and trust to the future law of averages to bring its fulfillment. But the Lord specifies the day and also that it is tomorrow. This would preclude the idea that already signs of approaching swarms were visible and that the prediction of them here would be somewhat on the order of weather "forecasts."

Verse 24. Pharaoh's house was not the only victim of these swarms. They attacked his servants also. This would disable these servants for assisting Pharaoh now.

Verse 25. Here is answer number three of Pharaoh. But it is a compromise. He represents himself as thinking that privilege to sacrifice to God was all that the children of Israel were interested in. It is easy to see why he might be willing for them to perform relgious services as long as they were in his land. He would still have perfect possession of them. In this he was like Satan. He has no objections to the religious professions of mankind as long as they do not enter the church of the Lord. In fact, the more religious a man is while in the world the more advantage he is to the cause of sin. This is because others will look to this self-righteous person as a good example of life without the Church and conclude it is just as good. Of course when such conclusion is formed the devil has won a victory. All the so-called good one does as a religious act, and outside of the Lord's Church which is his vineyard, will be without any reward from God.

Verse 26. Of course Moses rejects this proposition. He does not state all of the reasons he would have for rejecting it. But he does bring before him one that would be unanswerable from the standpoint of the Egyptians. He states it would be offering a sacrifice that would be an abomination to the Egyptians and then they would stone them. This was because of the idolatrous practice and ideas of the people of Egypt. They worshiped almost all kinds of animals as well as other things in nature. One of their most venerated gods was the sacred bull which they called Apis. And of course the Israelites would sacrifice that kind of animal in their services. Now if the Egyptians should see the beast which they worshiped thus abused as they would consider it, they would be induced to resent it to the extent of stoning the Israelites. Hence the reasoning that Moses makes with Pharaoh.

Verse 27. As stated before, the three days journey from Egypt would take them to a safe distance, and thus make less danger of interference.

Verse 28. This is Pharaoh's answer number four. He ventures another compromise in connection with the proposal that they are not to go very far away. But Moses has already told him how "far" they will go if they are let out so it was not necessary to make any special response to that part of the answer. And the same reason why the king did not want them to go far away was one reason why Moses would insist that they go three days journey. Pharaoh here again reminds us of Satan. If a man is bound to go into the religious life the devil will not object so much provided the man does not go very far into such life. While one cannot really leave the devil's territory at all without completely doing so outwardly at least, yet in effect he can just barely make the move. He can go through the outward form only but in heart still be interested in the things he once practiced in the world. Paul said he forgot the things that were behind and reached forth for the things ahead. (Phil. 3: 13).

Verse 29. This is where Moses accuses Pharaoh of having dealt deceitfully in the previous instances. See comments on this at verse 9.

Verses 30, 31. In keeping with his office as mediator Moses entreats the Lord and also agreeable with his usual practice the Lord hears him and removes the plague from the Egyptians.

Verse 32. In this place it states that Pharaoh hardened his heart. This is to be considered in connection with the various places where it says that God hardened the heart of Pharaoh. See comments at 7: 3.

EXODUS 9

Verse 1. Attention is called to the fact that in the various demands upon Pharaoh to let the children of Israel go he is reminded that they are the Lord's people and he wants them to go free so as to serve him. This short declaration includes much fundamental thought. Since they are God's people he has right to demand their deliverance. Also, if they are to serve their master they must leave the territory of the usurper. They must come out. This is the same principle shown in the call of the Lord recorded in 2 Cor. 6: 17 and Rev. 18: 4. No one can serve the Lord acceptably while in the territory of the enemy of the Lord.

Verses 2, 3. Be sure to note that the cattle "which is in the field" is to be the extent of this plague which is to be number five. This will leave cattle still living for other plagues if necessary. This murrain is translated "pestilence" 47 times in the A. V. and is not definitely defined in the lexicon. It means some kind of disease put upon the animals that was fatal.

Verse 4. Since the Israelites were forced to work for Pharaoh it would be logical that some of their cattle or beasts of burden would be mixed up with those of Pharaoh. This would make it necessary for the Lord to make a distinction between them.

Verses 5, 6. Again the Lord sets the day when the plague is to come which shows the miraculous nature of it. The statement here that all the cattle of Egypt died is explained by the stipulation in verse two, which see.

Verse 7. As an instance of wishful thinking doubtless, Pharaoh investigates and finds that the cattle of the Israelites escaped the plague. But he is not yet brought to repentance so he hardens his heart again. We will not forget that God hardened the heart of Pharaoh by giving him the opportunity and then he used that opportunity.

Verses 8-10. This is plague number six. *Boil; blains.* The first of these words is from a word that means an ulcer while the second one is from a word that means an eruption. The meaning of the verse is that ashes were made to cause ulcers on the bodies of the men and beasts and that these ulcers became running sores. Just why the Lord directed that ashes should be used in the bringing of this plague is not told. We are sure it was not as a material cause for the plague nor that the Lord needed any help from nature for the effect desired. He brought other plagues without the use of any visible means. But sometimes God sees fit to combine material and visible means with the miraculous. As instances of this fact see chapter 15: 25 and 2 Ki. 6: 6.

Verse 11. *Stand.* This is from AMAD and is rendered in the A. V. by abide 4 times, be present 1, continue 6, endure 8, withstand 2. *Before Moses.* This is from PANIM and rendered in A. V. as follows: Anger 3 times, countenance 30, face 356, looks 2, sight 40. The thought of the verse is that the magicians could not endure or withstand the countenance or sight of Moses because of the boils. This would be from a realization that their miserable condition was on them through the influence of Moses whom they had tried to withstand. And since this suffering of theirs was the worst that yet had been thrust on them their state of mind is a mixture of shame and despair, with an added feeling of guilt.

Verse 12. The Lord hardened Pharaoh's heart as explained in 7: 3.

Verses 13, 14. Much of this passage has already been commented upon. But again the reader's attention is called to the purpose the Lord here states for bringing all these plagues upon Pharaoh. It is to prove to him that there is no one in all the earth like the God of the Hebrews. *Upon thine heart.* While many of the plagues affected the body of Pharaoh, yet his heart or mind would also be afflicted to see his own power so much overcome by this very God whom he was despising.

Verse 15. This threat to cut him off from the earth was literally fulfilled. He was destroyed at the same time his armies were destroyed as will be seen later.

Verse 16. That God forsees conditions and then prepares to use characters that are evil for his service is here set forth and at other places in the Bible. See comments on 7: 11, 12 for this subject. A chief motive for using Pharaoh is here stated in that God's name was to be declared throughout all the earth. Had this same kind of miracles been performed upon some private or insignificant person the affair would not have been reported widely. But since it was upon the king of one of the most noted of nations, this conquest of the king would be the astonishment of the world.

Verse 17, 18. As he was accustomed to do, before God brings the next plague upon the land he warns the king and sets the time when the plague will come. Doubtless there were sometimes occurrences of hail that would be considered great, especially for that kind of country where rain, and other precipitation, was scant. Thus, in order that the impending one may be considered as miraculous it is stated that it is to be greater than any that had ever before been experienced in that land.

Verse 19. God furthermore gives the people a chance to escape the next plague if they have sufficient faith in the announcement of Moses. The plague about to come now is to affect both man and beast that is exposed.

Verses 20, 21. This paragraph indicates that the citizens of Egypt possessed servants. These citizens were given opportunity for preserving their servants and cattle. Some of them reacted favorably on the warning of the Lord while others did not.

Verse 22. This verse adds the items of the herbs to the previous warning. But as they could not have provided any shelter for the growing vegetation it was not necessary to mention them in the warning. But since they were warned about the cattle that gave them an opportunity to prepare for another crop by saving their cattle.

Verses 23, 24. This is plague number seven. *Hail; fire.* These words have no strained meaning but are defined in the lexicon simply by the word here used as their translations. Not only so, they are not translated otherwise in other places in the Bible. Thus we should take them here as literal. There is nothing miraculous in the nature of these elements. The thing that is miraculous is their great amount and that it was unusual for such to come in Egypt. Of course the fire was in the form of our lightning and most of us have seen displays of electricity in connection with other storms so that the condition here is explainable. And the physical effect on the trees and other vegetation as seen in next paragraph also indicates hail or frozen moisture.

Verse 25. Here the exception was made according to the warning instruction given in verse 19, so that only the cattle in the field were killed. And the hail broke all the trees of the field which indicates it was made of material with weight.

Verse 26. Here we see the usual severance between the community occupied by the children of Israel and that of the Egyptians. This distinction was made besides that between the cattle and men in the field and those in the house.

Verse 27. *This time.* The first word is not in the original but the second one is from PAAM and rendered in the A. V. by such words as time, once, anvil, rank. A glance back over the other instances of the plagues will discover that not one of them brought an admission from Pharaoh. So that the verse means as if the king said "I will admit that I have sinned and that thy people are righteous." And if anyone had said "you have been sinning all the time," he could have replied in the negative, or at least have retorted that he had not admitted it and it would be up to them to prove it if the case were put to a test.

Verse 28. This is Pharaoh's answer number five. In it he admits that he has had enough. And makes no reservations in his promise. But Moses has no confidence in his sincerity. After his answer number two Moses intimates his lack of confidence. See comments at 8: 9. And after answer number three Moses accuses the king of breaking his promise at previous instances and prays him not to do it again. See comments at 8: 29. But this time he will expressly tell him that he expects the king to break his promise as we will see in the next paragraph.

Verses 29, 30. We should note that in promising the removal of the plague now on the Egyptians Moses connects it with appealing to the Lord. And this was to prove to Pharaoh that he was working through the Lord and not on his own power, not that he expected to break the stubbornness of the king as the verse 30 indicates.

Verses 31, 32. This paragraph explains why some plants were destroyed and others not. Some were farther along in their season than others. The flax was "bolled" which here means that it was in bloom and thus its destruction would be complete.

Verses 33-35. All happened as Moses said it would. The plague was removed at the plea of Moses, the mediator. This is another instance where the writer says that Pharaoh hardened his heart. It was because he saw that the plague was removed. In so doing he availed himself of the occasion for hardening his heart that God furnished him by removing the plague. See comments at 7: 3 on this subject. And when the king hardened his heart it was according to the prediction of the Lord.

EXODUS 10

Verse 1, 2. In this paragraph God says he hardened the heart of Pharaoh which is mentioned and explained in closing paragraph of preceding chapter. In all of these great demonstrations taking place the main purpose of God is to make known to Pharaoh the superiority of Israel's Lord, and for the information of following generations.

Verse 3. The two brothers again demanded release of the people of God. In his speech to the king the question is asked why he refuses to humble himself. This is a significant word here. It tells us the motive for Pharaoh's stubbornness which is pride. It is natural for man to resist any opposition to his pride. Only when he is ready to do right will his pride be thrust down by the influence of righteous humility.

Verses 4, 5. In 9: 31, 32 we are told why certain vegetation plants were destroyed, that they were grown enough for such destruction, while others had not yet come up. Now enough time had passed for the other crops to have come and they are to be ruined by the locusts. It says they shall also eat every tree. But we must understand this to mean the foliage and buds of the trees, not the body. This is indicated by the reference to the fruit of the trees in verse 15 below.

Verse 6. This verse is self-explanatory as to its meaning. But the reader should note how terrible is the next plague to be. And since all the previous plagues had been brought just as threatened, the Egyptians had no reason to doubt this one. And the servants did not doubt it as will be seen in the following paragraph.

Verse 7. *Snare.* Usually this means

something fixed to take a victim but which is hidden from him. But it is not so used in this case for the victim has been told each time about what to expect. So it is to be understood as used of a trap deliberately set to take the victim and yet warning first being given of the presence of the trap and what will make it "spring." Thus the Lord cannot be justly accused of taking an undue advantage. So the servants, who do not have so much pride of position as the king, are willing to admit their defeat and urge their king to yield to the demand of Moses and Aaron.

Verses 8-11. Here we have Pharaoh's answer number six. But it is divided and requires the first and fourth verses to give the entire answer. This is because he coupled his first agreement for their release with a question that implied a proviso. Then when Moses answered his question as to who were to go, the king recalled his unconditional agreement. Moses told him that their entire population was to go, also their flocks and herds. Verse 10 should really also be part of the sixth answer since he still makes it appear that he is willing for the people to go. But just before the verse is completed he suddenly reverses himself and denies their request for release. Much of this verse needs some critical explaining in order to the appreciation of it. The first instance of "let" is not in the original. The word "so" is from an original which has for its principal meaning the word "just." Next, the reader should read chapter 5: 3 where Moses replies to the first answer of Pharaoh, that if they did not go and sacrifice to God he might fall upon them with pestilence. Thus with all these explanations I shall paraphrase the verse 10 of present paragraph as follows: "The Lord should deal justly with you and not fall upon you with pestilence as you feared in your first request. He will not have reason to do that for I am going to let you go to sacrifice to Him as you requested." He then suddenly changes his mind. He says "look" or "take notice" for evil or the pestilence you predicted is before you; is about to come upon you. "Not so" or "no, I will not let all of you go but only the men." And then as if to impress them with the finality of his decision he drove them from his presence.

Verses 12-15. This paragraph gives the eighth plague, that of locusts. These insects are a form of grasshopper and the original word is sometimes so rendered. In verse 12 is the statement that locusts were to eat "all that the hail hath left" and the 15th verse states the fruit of the trees. These statements indicate that the bodies of the trees were not eaten by the locusts.

Verses 16-20. There is no proposition of promise in the speech of Pharaoh. But there is a pitiful plea for mercy. He again admits sin against the Lord and Moses and Aaron. It is true he implies that he will not sin again which could be construed to mean that he will let them go after this. But he does not say so and there is no indication that Moses has any more confidence in his plea for forgiveness than he had before. And the only thing that even indicates that he was forgiven as to his sin is the fact that the plague of locusts was removed. But, as before, this relief from the plague only gave him another occasion to harden his heart which was another act of God by giving him this opportunity.

Verses 21-23. The plague of darkness was the ninth one. The word "felt" is from MASHASH and Strong defines it "a primitive root; to feel of; by implication to grope." It is rendered in the A. V. as follows: By feel (verb) 2 times, grope 4, search 2. The thought is not that the darkness itself could be felt by the sense of touch. But it was so dark that moving would have to be done by relying on the act of feeling one's way or groping. That is why the people never rose from their place for three days. Rather than feeling their way around by the slow and unpleasant means of groping, they just remained in their places. This c o n d i t i o n continued for three days. In this place the word for days is from an original that is defined in the lexicon as the period from sunset to sunset. That is, three periods of 24 hours each this dense darkness continued with the Egyptians.

Verse 24. This is Pharaoh's answer number seven. This time he removes the proviso concerning the children made in the preceding answer but requires them to leave their flocks and herds with him. It is easy to perceive his motive in this. With all their assets behind concerning the cattle they would naturally be so connected with their interest in them to be tempted to return to Egypt. This is another instance where Pharaoh is like Satan. If one does not break loose from his love of the material things in the world he is not likely to be sufficiently interested in the Lord's work. But Paul gives us the proper attitude on such matters in Philip 3: 13. And Moses will give the king to understand that no part-way release will be accepted.

Verses 25, 26. The foolishness of the last proposition is seen in observing that the specific purpose that Moses had already given for their wish to go away from the land of Egypt was that they might sacrifice to God. And since the formal system of sacrificial worship had not yet been given to the nation they would not know entirely which of the cattle would be required. Therefore they must take all with them, not a hoof to be left behind.

Verses 27-29. Again the heart of Pharaoh is hardened and he spurns the demands of Moses and Aaron. He orders them to leave his presence and declared that if they come into the presence of his face again they will die. Moses "takes him up" on this threat and tells him that he will see his face no more. This statement of Moses has been thought to have proved false and that Moses did see his face afterward. They base this on statements in 11: 10 and 12: 31. But the first is only a summing up of the work Moses and Aaron had been doing since appearing to Pharaoh the first time and down to the time they were forbidden, under threat of death, to come before his face again. And since they are not to come before him again it means that no further miracle will be performed before him and thus it is an appropriate time to give a summary of the ones that were done before him. The second passage proves nothing to the point since there are many instances of calling a person without doing so face to face.

EXODUS 11

Verse 1. Note the difference in the statement of the Lord to Moses from the ones before. This time there is not to be an appeal first to Pharaoh before bringing this plague which is to be the last before releasing the people. And also, contrary to the other instances where God predicted that the king would not let them go, this time he will not only let the people go but will do so without any delay or any reservations. On this point see Chapter 12: 31-33.

Verse 2. *Borrow.* See Ch. 3: 22.

Verse 3. Since we have learned that one meaning of the word for "borrow" is to demand, it would be reasonable that something should be done to make the demands avail. So the children of Israel were not to take the jewels by force but obtain them by demand; and to assist in the success of this demand, the Lord caused the people and the servants of Pharaoh to think kindly of Moses.

Verses 4-6. *And Moses said.* But we must remember that he was to say this to the Israelites, not to Pharaoh. See verse 2 above. *Firstborn* This is a term that is almost if not entirely used with reference to children of a family not yet in homes of their own. And the word "house" is from a word that means both house in the sense of a home building or a household in the sense of the people who make up a family. So that this last plague was to bring one death to every household or family.

Verses 7, 8. Students of the Bible can observe that in many instances the events recorded are not chronological. Thus it is in this paragraph. Chapter 12: 33 tells that the people of Egypt joined in the urgent demand that the Israelites be allowed to go. At this place it will be well to quote from Josephus in regard to the activities of the Egyptians on the night of the slaying of the firstborn. "For the destruction of the firstborn came upon the Egyptians that night, so that many of the Egyptians who lived near the king's palace, persuaded Pharaoh to let the Hebrews go. Accordingly he called for Moses, and bid them be gone." Josephus, Ant. 2-14-6. Since we have seen that Moses never saw the face of Pharaoh after last verse of previous chapter, and in view of citations above, the most obvious conclusion here is that the conversations recorded and implied took place after the tenth plague was brought. The use of the third personal pronoun should be understood by the observation that the king was not to be addressed face to face, but that did not hinder addressing him through his servants as was evidently done on the night of the plague of death of firstborn.

Verses 9, 10. For explanation of this paragraph see comments in latter half of paragraph on Chapter 10: 27-29.

EXODUS 12

Verses 1, 2. For a reason we are not here informed about, the Lord wished a change in the order of the months of the year for his people. This of course applies to the lunar months since the appearance of the new moon was to regulate the time of beginning of the new year. In this way the numerical position of the days of the week would always correspond with that of the month. This will account for the expression "on the morrow after the sabbath" in Lev. 23: 11 which will be explained further in that place.

Verses 3, 4. The lamb was selected on the tenth day although it was not to be used until the 14th day. This would give opportunity for more exact examination of the animal which was required to be without blemish. The number of lambs to be selected was based on the requirements for food for each family. Here we see that the word "house" and "household" mean the same, since both are used in same connection in this place. If it was thought that a lamb would be too much to be consumed by one man's family then he and his neighbor were to form one household and occupy the same building that night. This was done on the basis of economy.

Verse 5. It should not be overlooked that the animal must be a perfect one. But even if a man used his best judgment in selecting one from a flock, such short judgment would not be as reliable as the individual notice of it through the three or four days after being separated from the flock. And attention is called that the passover might be either a sheep or a goat.

Verse 6. *Whole assembly.* As each family was to observe this ordinance, this statement is to show that one ordinance and its regulation was to be for each family alike and that no discrimination was to be made. *In the evening.* The marginal here renders it "between the two evenings." This would mean the same as our 3 P. M. since the entire afternoon was considered in general as the evening and "between" would thus mean the midst of that period. On the meaning of "evening" in some places consult Webster's Collegiate Dictionary, article "evening."

Verse 7. What we call the jambs and lintel of doors were the places where this blood was to be applied. It was to be done to each house (building) where people were eating the lamb. No blood was put on the threshold which indicates that it was not to be trodden upon. As this blood was a type of Christ it was fit that it should not be trodden upon. Neither should the blood of Christ be trodden upon. Heb. 6: 6; 10: 29).

Verses 8, 9. While they were instructed to eat this passover with unleavened bread, that did not prohibit them having or eating leavened bread otherwise. The restriction not to have any leaven in their homes was given later which will be explained in this chapter below. They were not to eat of the beast prepared in any manner except roasting. This would more aptly represent a burnt sacrifice and hence a proper type of Christ; whose sacrifice, while not literally burnt with fire, was the most complete one possible. *Bitter herbs.* Since this is a type of the sacrifice of Christ it was appropriate to use these bitter things at this time. (See Isa. 53: 10, 11; Luke 22: 44). *Purtenance.* This is from QEREB and defined by Strong "properly the nearest part, i. e. the center, whether literal, figurative, or adverbial especially with prep." Since the head and legs are mentioned just before the word now being considered, and since also this word means the center, the conclusion is that all the eatable part of the beast was to be prepared for eating.

Verse 10. No part of the lamb was to be preserved till the morning. This means that it was not to be preserved for eating purposes. This is evident from the next statement, that what did remain was to be destroyed. It was not to be used for food in the ordinary sense since it had been previously used in a religious way. And as this is a type of the body of Christ which is represented by the Lord's supper we should take a lesson. It should condemn the practice of some congregations of handing the remains of the bread after the service to children to make common food. It should be reverently destroyed, either by burning or burying. Of course this would also apply to the fruit of the vine although it is seldom that anyone has made a common use of that article after the service of the Lord's supper.

Verse 11. God knew that they would not have any spare time after the death of all the first born had been discovered, therefore he directs them to be prepared for travel. They were to eat it in haste. This is not to be especially the speed with which they partook of the food but to the general idea of the situation now surrounding them. That it was to be a time of much unrest and stir and therefore they should not delay.

Verse 12. *Gods.* This is from ELOHIYM and defined "gods in the ordinary sense; but specifically used (in the plural thus, especially with the article) of the supreme God; occasionally applied by way of deference to magistrates; and sometimes as a superlative."—Strong. The marginal reading in the A. V. gives "princes." This is doubtless correct since one word in the definition of the lexicon is "magistrates" and the word is rendered "judges" three times in the A. V. The significance of the statement is in the fact that the rulers or judges or magistrates of Egypt, who had been foremost in advising the people against Moses and Aaron were now to feel the sting of humility in that the God whom they had so wickedly opposed is about to punish them.

Verse 13. Here is the origin of the word "Passover." Seeing the blood on the posts and lintel of the doors the destroying angel was to pass over that house. If we join these two words into one we have the famous word used with reference to this feast of the Jews in the Old Testament and to the sacrifice of Christ in the New.

Verse 14. *A memorial.* A thing by which to keep in memory, formally, the great deliverance from their bondage. *For ever.* This term means "agelasting" according to Young and this definition agrees with the lexicons on the subject. Hence, whenever it is said that a thing is to be "forever" it means that it will last as long as the age does in which, or concerning which, the thing is said. That is true of any age regardless of the actual duration of that age. Thus a thing is predicted as being "for ever" that pertains to the age after the final judgment, it means that thing will last as long as that age, which we know is to be endless. While if it is a thing that pertains to an age that is to end at a certain date then that thing will last just that long. In the present verse the term is used of a thing that pertained to the Jews, which means it was to last through the Jewish age, as long as the Jews had a nation.

Verse 15. These seven days constitute what is known generally in the Bible as the feast of unleavened bread, or as the days of unleavened bread. But it finally came to include the day of the passover, making eight days of unleavened bread. In the beginning, we know that the Israelites did not keep the seven days deliberately, for they were thrust out in haste and had no opportunity for observing this feast in the manner as soon to be described. But it is well to explain now that some things given as law in this chapter had to do with the future conduct of the people and were not expected to be done this night. But since the Lord is giving for the first time the directions regarding this ordinance for the initial observance, while he is at it, he includes some things that could not be done now, but will become a fixed program for future generations.

Verses 16, 17. *Convocation.* This is from MIQRA and defined "something called out, i. e. a public meeting (the act, the persons, or the place); also a rehearsal." This definition is from Strong and agrees with the context here, except that by adding the word "holy" and further by specifying what may and what may not be done on such days, we have the conclusion that these convocations were sabbath days in which no manual work was to be done. See the words "no manner of work" etc., in the verse. And with this specific description of the day as used by the Lord concerning the day, we should consider the word to mean a sabbath day in all places, whether the word "work" is used or not. See remarks on meaning of term "for ever" at verse 14 above. Also see verse 15 on the matter of time when this ordinance was expected to be observed.

Verse 18. In this verse the passover day and the seven days to follow are combined to be considered as one unit as mentioned in verse 15 above. And this use of the term is found in the New Testament. (Mt. 26: 5, 17; Mk. 14: 1, 2; Lk. 22: 1).

Verses 19, 20. See comments at verse 15 above. Also see verses 34, 39 below, chapter 13: 7-9 and Deut. 16: 3.

Verses 21, 22. See 3: 16 on meaning of "elders." The blood was to be dashed or struck, as with a brush, by the hyssop, which was an aromatic plant and evidently with a bushy top. This would be indicated by the fact that when those standing by the cross wished to administer to Jesus they put vinegar on hyssop and put it to the mouth for his use. This blood was to be put on the parts surrounding the doors of the houses in which the Israelites were that night. This would suggest that one would have to go through blood to enter the house which was the place of their safety from the angel of death. Therefore they were not to leave the house until the morning. Of course when the morning had come the danger would be past. Likewise, when the morning of the eternal age comes all danger from sin will be past.

Verse 23. It must not be overlooked that none but the Israelites were given the right to use the passover for the Egyptians have been condemned to the plague about to come and nothing can stop it now. But even the Israelites would not escape this plague unless they observed this ordinance. So that on the fatal night as the Lord is passing through the land he will take a general view of the same. And should there be one of the families that had neglected the ordinance, it too would feel the sting of death.

Verses 24-28. In this paragraph may be seen the significance of the ordinance and why it was to be observed "for ever." In years to come the rising generations would be interested in seeing it observed and would call for explanation. In this way the event of their release from bondage would be kept in memory.

Verses 29, 30. This records plague number ten. On meaning of word "house" see comments at chapter 11: 4-6. Also on the statements of verse 30 see remarks at 11: 7, 8.

Verse 31, 32. This is answer of Pharaoh, number eight. Notice that it is one of "Unconditional surrender" as to terms of release. But he had the audacity to ask a favor for himself in the form of a blessing. This could come from no other motive than pure selfishness. And that spirit would account for all his mistreatment of the children of Israel in the past.

Verse 33. On this see comments at 11: 7, 8. Also this verse should be placed just before verse 30 in this chapter.

Verse 34. See verse 39 blow.

Verses 35, 36. For meaning of the word "borrow" see comments at chapter 3: 22.

Verse 37. Rameses is a portion, either of the land of Goshen, or, was another name for it. And according to Num. 33: 3 the children of Israel did not leave there until the fifteenth which was the day after they ate the passover. But this is easy to understand when we recall that it was at midnight that the death of the first born was discovered. After that, occurred the call for Moses and the order for their departure. But even though they are said to have left in haste and that they were prepared for travel before eating, yet it would require some time for about 3,000,000 people (on the basis of five to each man of war) to get started. And let us note that they traveled on foot.

Verse 38. *Mixed multitude.* The first word is from two words of slightly varying definitions. One is EREB and Strong defines it "the web (or transverse threads of cloth); also a mixture, (or mongrel race)." The other is ARAB and is defined "a primitive root; to braid, i. e. intermix; technically, to traffic (as if by barter); also to give or be security (as a kind of exchange)." Let the reader be sure to study well these definitions for they will account for much of the trouble this mixed multitude caused the Israelites. Of course they should not have been permitted to go along with the people of God, but many times today there will be persons who attach themselves to the people of God and pretend to be His people. And their motive often is the same as that of these mixed races. Their motive is for personal gain at the expense, or through the means of, the true servants of the Lord. Much of the trouble in the church today is traceable to the unconverted "members" harbored therein.

Verse 39. *Leavened.* This is from CHAMETS and defined "a primitive root; to be pungent; i. e. in taste (sour, i. e. literally, fermented, or figuratively harsh), in color (dazzling)"—Strong. Thus we have the explanation. The people had never yet been given any instructions or orders concerning leavened bread, hence they had never ceased to put the yeast or any leavening agent in their bread mixture. But it takes some time for the yeast to "work" and until that is done the bread dough is sweet and thus unleavened. Thus, unleavened bread would not necessarily mean that no leaven had been put into the mixture. But on the occasion now being considered the children of Israel were thrust out of the land in such haste that they did not have time for the bread mixture to work, or "raise," as the expression is used. For further comments on this subject see chapter 13: 7-9.

Verses 40, 41. Here the length of the time Israel was in Egypt is plainly said to have been 430 years. The word "sojourning" is from MOSHAB and Strong defines it "a seat; figuratively a site; abstractly, a ssesion; by extension an abode (the place or the time)." While the word "sojourn" is understood to mean a short or temporary stay in a place, yet it does require that such stay be in the nature of a residence and not merely a visit or call on a place as was the case with Abraham. So that we are not authorized to include the visit of Abraham to Egypt in this 430 years. But for more comments on this subject see the ones at Gen. 15: 13-15.

Verse 42. This idea of being observed means more than a mere remembrance as an act of the mind, but means that some formal or outward conduct in the way of an ordinance was to be attended to. See comments on 1 Cor. 11: 24, 25.

Verses 43-45. Circumcision was the distinguishing mark of the people of God in this relationship. And while baptism did not come "in the room of circumcision," as is taught by certain people today, yet it is what introduces one from the world to the church of the Lord. And since the Lord's supper is intended for such people only, it follows that people not of the true Church have no right to this ordinance, even as uncircumcised persons were not permitted to eat of the passover.

Verse 46. That was the age of types and in many instances a material or secular thing was to be considered in the same light as spiritual things in this age. The material house was to contain the units of the families in Egypt and the passover of each unit was single and for all the ones in the building. That is why they must eat in one house. Also, they were forbidden to carry it forth out of the house. And since we are to consider this house, as used here, as a type of the church, we should take the lesson that the Lord's supper is not to be taken "abroad" from its proper place of observance. This would disallow the practice of some of taking the "emblems" around over the community or "abroad" into the private situation in some private home. The Lord's supper was not intended to be peddled round and used privately just because some member of the church is sick and not able to leave his bed. If he is actually unable to go to the regular place of assembling, then he is not required to "commune." A further thought in this verse is that they were not to break a bone of the lamb. This was not because those bones were to be considered as sacred in the sense of preserving them. We know that was not the idea since they were to burn them in the morning. But the Lord knew that on the cross the bones of Jesus would not be broken, as was the common practice after crucifixion, but instead, his side was pierced, leaving his bones unbroken. This is mentioned in John 19: 36.

Verse 47. All the congregation were to keep the passover. That would mean that it was not an individual matter but one to be observed as a united institution. This is another idea confirming the statements in preceding paragraph.

Verses 48, 49. While circumcision did not come to be replaced by baptism as is sometimes taught, yet it was the sign chosen by the Lord to designate his people from those who were not. So that the teaching here is that none but the Lord's people had the right to the passover. Likewise, today, none but the Lord's people, (not only does this mean that they have been baptized, but also continue faithful, or in the favor of the Lord) have the right to the Lord's supper.

Verse 50. Here is the significant statement that the children of Israel did as the Lord had commanded—them? No. It was for them, of course. But it states that it was as the Lord had commanded Moses and Aaron. Thus, here is another instance where we see that God directed his people through these men and that whatever they commanded of the children of Israel was the same as if directly commanded them without the mediation of these men. And thus again we see the false basis of the sabbatarians who try to distinguish between the law of Moses and the law of God. Their purpose in this idea is to avoid the inconsistency in their practice wherein they do not even attempt to carry out all the requirements of the "law of Moses." In doing this they are self-condemned and are in rebellion against God.

Verse 51. *Selfsame.* This is from ETSEM and is used in many varieties of senses. But it is rendered in the A.V. in two places by "very." The thought would show that in the present verse, also in the other places in this chapter, it is as if it said, "in this very day," etc. That is, the statement means that the thing spoken of is to take place on the specific day and not just in the days near the event. That it is specific. And the direct application in the present instance is that the coming out of Egyptian bondage was to take place immediately in connection with the observance of the passover.

EXODUS 13

Verses 1, 2. *Sanctify.* This is from QADASH and defined "a primitive root; to be (causatively make, pronounce or observe as) clean (ceremonially or morally)"—Strong. Be sure to observe every word in this definition so as to make the proper application to the various instances; not only here but in all others in the Bible, especially in the Old Testament. The word has been rendered in the A.V. as follows: Be hallowed 3 times, be holy 5, be sanctified 10, consecrate 2, hallow 14, prepare 6, proclaim 1, sanctify 51, appoint 1, dedicate, and many others. Thus, as there are so many shades of meaning in the word, it requires in each case that care must be taken not to apply it in a wrong manner. In the present case, since we know that many of the firstborn would be mere infants at the time the command was given it could not mean to make clean morally, since infants are already clean. So we must apply the words "pronounce or observe clean." Not only so, but while these firstborn were clean already morally, they were to be observed clean ceremonially also, since the Lord had a special use for them in the future. And so we should take the commandment here to mean that God directed them to consider and pronounce all the firstborn as consecrated to Him. The closing words of the verse are "is mine," which corresponds with the comments here offered. And in Num. 3: 12 we can find the intended exchange mentioned which is being planned in this present demand for the firstborn. And it was just that such demand be made, for their deliverance from Egyptian bondage was procured by the death of the firstborn of that nation. Thus, while not informing the Israelites as to the purpose in mind, God now directs that the firstborn of all their tribes should be "ear marked" for his use.

Verses 3, 4. *Strength of hand.* This must be understood as meaning the Lord's hand. It took that to force the hand of Pharaoh. See comments at 3: 19. It is interesting to note that the command to put all leaven from their diet is "sandwiched" between two references to their coming out from their bondage. This will be considered more at length below.

Verse 5. The people mentioned here are among the leading groups that were then living in the land of Canaan and thus should be considered as usurpers since that land had been given to them through the promise made to Abraham. *Flowing with milk and honey.* The first word is from a word that means "abounding" or, that they exist in great measure. See comments at Chapter 3: 7, 8.

Verses 6-10. This is a passage of scripture that has been overlooked by many religious people for ages. Just because they read of the seven days of unleavened bread in the 12th chapter they conclude that the feast was observed on the night of the passover. But a little study of the subject will show that such could not have been. Turn back and read the comments at chapter 12: 15, 39. There the reader will learn that nothing had been explained as to why the Lord willed that they keep the feast of unleavened bread in their future years. The fact that they had the yeast or leaven in their bread mixture that night but had to get out in haste before it could work or rise, shows that it was not understood to be observed that night. But it was to be observed afterward as a memorial. This is made clear by the words "this is done *because*," etc. God wanted them always to have a set observance to commemorate their being forced to leave Egypt *in haste.* Their leaving was not an affliction for that was what they wished to do. But to be compelled to leave without the simple courtesy of "well wishing" from their hosts and that, too, in such haste that they could not even wait till their bread mixture had become ready for baking, this was something God wished to be observed yearly. The sign on the hand and memorial between the eyes were figurative. As proof of this statement observe that the pronoun "it" has for antecedent the observance of the seven day feast. And the object of these figurative badges is that they will be induced to have the Lord's law in the mouth. And the object of having this law in their mouth is that they would "show thy son," etc. The children would not understand the meaning of the putting all leaven from the homes each year at this time. Thus the Lord directed that they explain to their sons that when they left Egypt they had to get out so hurriedly that he arranged that they would do the thing purposely each year.

Verses 11, 12. *Openeth the matrix.* The last word is from RECHEM and means the womb. Since the command of consecrating to the Lord all that openeth the matrix here is the same as the one to consecrate all the firstborn, of course that calls for explanation of use of the word "openeth." This is from the fact that the womb is forced to open for the expulsion of the child and that this organ is, or has been, closed more firmly all the time before the birth of the first child, than it will ever be afterward. And, like a door that has been previously closed tight, so the womb has been thus closed until forced open by birth of the first child. It is true that every birth will, more or less. have to cause this opening. But the connection will make it plain that it means the son that opens the organ for the first time is the one that is meant for this particular occasion.

Verse 13. To redeem means to ransom. If an ass is born and the owner of its mother wishes to keep it, he must obtain privilege by giving to the Lord's service a lamb. If he wishes not to give up the possession of the lamb then he must kill the ass just born. The ransom for their firstborn of the children is to be given although they are still to be consecrated or "ear marked" for the Lord. The meaning of such a peculiar ordinance will become more apparent in later parts of the law of Moses.

Verses 14-16. These verses are in large part a repetition of what has already appeared in this chapter. It would be natural for the rising generation to wonder at seeing this feast of unleavened bread each year and they would ask about it. Then they are to be told of the enslavement of their forefathers and of the miraculous deliverance from it. Also, that at the time of their release the firstborn of the Egyptians were killed to bring about the consent of Pharaoh for their release. In view of this it is no more than fair that they give the firstborn of their children in token of appreciation. And it is to be noted that the children are not to be killed as were the firstborn of the Egyptions but only to be devoted to the Lord's service.

Verses 17, 18. God always considers the strength or ability of his people in his dealing with them. Since they are now in the beginning of their experiences as a separate people they have many things to learn and endure, before they will have become strong. Hence they are led by a laborious, but less unpleasant route than in the direction that would have made a severe test on them, one they should not be expected to withstand. See the same thought in John 16: 12 and Heb. 5: 13. 14. *Harnessed.* This is from CHAMUSH and defined "Staunch, i. e. able-bodied soldiers." — Strong. It is the word for "armed" in Josh. 1: 14; 4: 12. The thought is that they went out prepared for war if they should be called upon for defense. We may see how well they were prepared for war in case it became necessary by consulting Num. 1: 45, 46.

Verse 19. This refers to the request that Joseph had made near his death and at which time they promised with an oath to comply with the request. And in making such a request he showed that he had faith in the promise of God, that they were to come out from bondage, as had been promised Abram. And this faith of Joseph is mentioned among the other instances of faith. See Heb. 11: 22.

Verses 20-22. In all the dealings of God with man he has had various means of letting them know what he wanted them to do or where to go. In this case it was the cloud. Not a rain cloud, for it was a pillar of fire by night. It is one of the many means used to "speak" to the people, as referred to in Heb. 1: 1.

EXODUS 14

Verses 1, 2. The cities mentioned in this passage are near the Red Sea at the place where the children of Israel will soon cross.

Verses 3, 4. The map of this section shows a wilderness country where the children of Israel were to be just before crossing the sea. And Pharaoh will conclude that as the people are between the sea and the wilderness he will have them, as in a cage. Of course he had seen many miracles as great as would now be required to make a way of escape for the people, but he seems to be very forgetful. But the explanation of it is that stated at chapter 7: 3, which the reader should see. Attention is called to the statement that Pharaoh *and* all his host will be in this punishment from God. This is mentioned because sometimes a man is said to do a thing, when it means he did it through his agents, or servants. But since it mentions his servants and himself it indicates that he personally is included in the overthrow.

Verse 5. It came about just as God said. Pharaoh and his servants turned against the people which shows their hearts were hardened. *Serving us.* These words indicate the main reason the Egyptians wished to retain the people. It was pure selfishness.

Verse 6. *People with him.* Again a statement that shows Pharaoh was personally in the movement. This is stated also in Psa. 136: 15.

Verse 7. We would think that "all the chariots of Egypt" would include the chosen ones. Then why mention them separately? It is true that all chariots would include these. But the statement would not have told the reader that Pharaoh had any of this kind of chariots, chosen or selected, had they not been named in this way. And all the chariots had captains over them. Sometimes this word means a group of men on horseback. But when referring to the vehicle they usually were drawn by horses. And again, sometimes these war chariots would carry more than one man. So these captains would be the men who had command of whatever forces were used in connection with them.

Verses 8, 9. This passage indicates that about all the main military strength of Pharaoh went with him, whether footmen or horsemen, or whatever form their services. They were prepared to travel faster than the children of Israel with all this equipment. Besides, the Israelites were not aware that they were just now being hotly pursued.

Verse 10. But while they had been told that the Egyptians would come after them, yet when they actually saw them so near with all that military array they forgot all the demonstrations of power God had used before for their help and now they are affrighted.

Verses 11, 12. This is another one of the murmurings of Israel against God. In spite of their many instances of favor and deliverance by miracle, they frequently complained and seemed to forget all the great favors they had received. This is what Paul referred to in 1 Cor. 10: 10. Sometimes Christians get discouraged soon after they start in the new life when they see the discomfort brought upon them because of the enemy of souls. Of course the present instance of murmuring is before they have become entirely free from their enemies and thus before a type of Christians. But my remarks here are made as a general reflection on the many complaints they made.

Verse 13. *Stand still.* These words are often cited by preachers when asked by a sinner what he must do to be saved. He will then be told that he cannot do anything for his salvation, but that he must stand still. But even if he should be fair enough to quote the entire sentence here, that he must stand still and see the salvation of the Lord, it is still a deceptive use of the words. The Israelites had not yet been shown what to do, therefore it was proper for Moses to make the statement. And likewise, if a sinner were to ask what to do to be saved but had never been taught anything about the first principles of salvation, it would be proper to tell him to do nothing until he had been told what the salvation of the Lord required. That need not take more than a few minutes. And thus Moses stated this to the Israelites and we will soon see the plan of their salvation pointed out. The last statement of the verse might appear to contradict the last part of verse 30. But this is another strong proof that the outward part of man is the less important part. That when the inner part is gone, which is the case when a person is dead, he is considered as gone. See this use of the idea in Acts 9: 39. Dorcas' body was right there in front of their faces, yet Peter was being told of the things she did while she was "with them." So, while the Israelites will see the dead bodies of the Egyptians, the inner man will have gone and thus in reality they will not be seen after the present day.

Verse 14. Note that it is constantly being kept before the children of Israel that in all their experiences under Moses it is the Lord who is doing the work. This should be further rebuke to the sabbatarians who try to distinguish between authority of

Moses and God so as to bolster their erroneous doctrine.

Verse 15. Even now the entire plan of their escape is not visible but they are told to "go forward." At least they are here given definite instructions about their required activity. Had they not obeyed this command they would not have received the benefit of the further means God was about to use. Their faith in God and Moses caused them to go forward whether they knew just what was coming next or not. But their ignorance of what was to be the next move of the Lord did not prevent them from being benefited by it when it was shown them.

Verse 16. *Dry ground.* This form of expression is used in various places and is from various original words. But they are all practically the same in meaning. The thought is that of a place where it is earth and not water, not that the place is necessarily without moisture. If such state of dryness is meant the connection must show it.

Verses 17, 18. Note again that in declaring the impending destruction upon the Egyptians, God says that His honor is to be demonstrated. This is the outstanding idea all through his dealings with the enemy. And all through the transactions of man's stay on this earth, he has been blessed in proportion as he recognized and conducted himself in view of the honor due the Lord.

Verse 19. God is present everywhere in spirit, yet in his dealngs with mankind he uses the services of various agencies, especially angels. (Heb. 1: 14). In the present case the cloud is the visible instrument used since the Israelites would have to see it in order to be benefited by it. Yet the angel of God is the immediate supervisor. And, while the cloud had previously been in front to guide them, now they need its help to shield them from the enemy they know, by the fact that only one route is possible for them and it is made visible by the light of the cloud behind them. At the same time, being a miraculous cloud, it is like a lamp with an opaque reflector on one side. It would throw the light forward and around the ones in front of it but be a shade to darken the way of the ones in the rear.

Verse. 20. The same cloud that assisted the people of God was a hindrance to the enemies of God. It kept them far apart. Thus it is today. The plan of salvation as revealed in the Gospel is so unlike anything in the world that it makes a wide gulf between the true servants of God and the enemy. And when we observe a nearness between the people of the world and those professing to be the people of God, we know that there is more profession than practice with the latter. There should be so much difference between the world and the people of Christ that no one would mistake the one for the other.

Verses 21, 22. *Dry land and dry ground.* These two expressions occur in this paragraph and are from the same original word. We would not ordinarily speak of a narrow strip of exposed earth as "land" because that would convey the idea of an extent greater than this. But it means a place where the water has been removed and left the earth visible. See also the comments at verse 16 above. The "wall" spoken of here will be explained at chapter 15: 8.

Verses 23-25. *Morning watch.* In the ancient times a vigilance committee was a very common means of protection. The night was divided into four watches beginning at six o'clock (as we count it) in the evening and going to six in the morning. Thus the four watches began respectively at 6, 9, 12, 3. The one beginning at 3 would be the morning watch. It was still dark at this time when the Lord looked through the cloud, for it is here referred to as the pilar of fire and that was its condition at this time. The Lord troubled the Egyptians by taking off their chariot wheels. Thus it is worded in the A. V. But the word "off" is not in the original. And the word "took" is from SUWR and Strong defines it "to turn off (literally or figuratively)." So the expression means that the Lord did something to make the wheels turn with difficulty. It states that the chariots were driven heavily. But had the wheels been literally taken from the axles they could not have driven them at all. There being no natural reason for this condition of their chariots the Egyptians concluded it was the Lord causing it. Not only that, but it was in favor of the Israelites.

Verses 26, 27. God could have operated directly to bring the sea back but he did not see fit to do so. And by his using Moses, He gave another instance of the authority of Moses in the work. Mention of appearance of morning here agrees with statement in preceding paragraph of the morning watch. The Egyptians were overthrown in the midst of the sea.

Verse 28. Sometimes a statement of general form concerning a group of individuals or things may have a general meaning only. But the last statement of this verse makes a definite assertion that not one of them remained. This would give us the information that Pharaoh was destroyed in this overthrow since we know he was there in person.

Verses 29, 30. As to the "dry land" see comments at verses 16, 21, 22 above. Since the Egyptians could be seen by the Israelites, dead, on the seashore we know that the journey through the sea was about over when the destruction came.

Verse 31. *Feared.* This is used in the sense of reverence for it immediately states that they believed the Lord. Also it says that they believed Moses. This is all in the same connection and in the same sense. This is another point against the theory of the sabbatarians who try to distinguish between authority of God and Moses.

EXODUS 15

Verse 1. The term "children of Israel" would have included Moses. But he is mentioned separately in this place. And it should be observed that the song was sung by Moses and them. Since Moses is an inspired man we are to conclude that the song recorded here was by inspiration and that the statements herein are to be accepted as being the teaching of God.

Verse 2. The word "song" is from a word that means "praise." As used here it is as if it said, "The Lord is the object of my praise." *Prepare him an habitation.* It means "I will make him be welcome with me as if it were his home."

Verse 3. *Man.* This is not used in the sense of man as human. But it is from a word meaning "an individual" with the added idea of "male." So it has the sense of "an individual of war." And there were unnumbered individuals who conducted war and liked it, yet not all were successful. But God is an individual who wins in his war against his enemies. And it is right that he should for he never makes war against any but evil characters.

Verses 4-7. These verses do not contain much additional information, yet it is good to note the expressions of strong praise to God; and especially when contrasted with the complaints they have made against God and still will make.

Verse 8. *Blast, nostrils.* God has the abstract power to produce a wind of any desired volume or strength. But in using the figure of his nostrils, which pertains to his person, we should get an impression of the power and effectiveness of him who is the creator of all things. *Congealed.* This is from QAPHA and defined "a primitive root; to shrink, i. e. thicken (as unracked wine, curdled milk, clouded sky, frozen water)."—Strong. So whether the word be rendered as frozen or some other of its meanings would depend upon the matter spoken of. If it were used in regard to milk, the word would mean curdled. While if about water, the word would mean frozen. Since it is here used in regard to water it means frozen. Now there is not one who will have any doubt of God's power to hold liquid (water) in suspense if he desired. In this instance he did not choose to do so.

Verse 9. From all appearances the Egyptians had the same opportunity of going into the bed of the sea as the Israelites. But it shows how short-sighted they were. A little reflection would have reminded them that the same Power that could open up the water, could surely reverse the condition to their destruction. But it is just another case of hardening their hearts.

Verse 10. The word "wind" is from the same original as "blast" in verse 8 above. See comments at that place.

Verse 11. *Gods.* This is from a word that means any being considered mighty, including objects of worship such as the idolatrous deities. And how true are the implied admissions of the true God here. Had they always acted in accordance with such idea they would not have committed the idolatry recorded in chapter 32. *Fearful in praises.* That is, worthy to be feared and praised.

Verse 12. The last word in this verse refers to the Egyptians.

Verse 13. Here we note the idea that the people were led forth after being redeemed. This is logical and historically correct The redemption had been effected the night of the 14th while the people were still in Egypt. Likewise, our redemption was accomplished for us while we were still in sin. And the Israelites would have had no benefit of the redemption made for them had they not been led forth, or had they not followed when told to go forth. And we would have no benefit from the redemption provided by Christ had we not followed up with our duty.

Verses 14-17. These verses name some of the peoples then occupying the country which God intends to turn over to his people. The present mighty circumstance of the deliverance of the Israelites by the miracle at the Red sea will be reported ahead of them and will produce panic. As an outstanding instance of this condition see the report of Rahab and her statements on this in Josh. 2: 9-11.

Verses 18, 19. What a wonderful tribute to the Lord! And how much happier the people would have been had they conducted themselves accordingly.

Verse 20. *Prophetess.* This is from a word that has indefinite meanings, including a woman who is inspired, as also one who is merely a poet. The context here could mean the latter since the wording of her speech was recent history and did not require inspiration to say it. But of course the recording of it in the Book was by inspiration, since Moses is the one who did the recording.

Verses 22-24. Almost immediately after their deliverance the people murmur again against Moses. All of this shows how human they were and how much they conducted themselves as people do today. When matters do not go as wanted the common practice is to complain without any logical reason for it. But all such murmurings are condemned and indicate a lack of faith. (See Heb. 3: 19 and 1 Cor. 10: 10.)

Verse 25. Moses cried unto the Lord. This was another action of his as mediator between God and man. Casting the tree into the waters was God's plan in this case to accomplish his purpose. Using this material object in sweetening the waters did not in the least lessen the miraculus nature of the deed. It would require as much supernatural power to sweeten them in this way as by direct edict for anyone would know that the tree possessed no such quality. The statute and ordinance mentioned here follows.

Verse 26. On condition that the Israelites obey the Lord in all things and do that which is right in *his* sight, they will not be punished with the same afflictions as the Egyptians. But if not obedient they will be so punished.

Verse 27. *Elim.* This is described by Strong as a place in the desert, and such fact explains why the passage mentions the existence here of twelve wells of water. And the effect of these wells is to produce or nourish 70 palm trees. This would make an excellent place to spend some time. Thus the record tells us they encamped here.

EXODUS 16

Verse 1. The reader should not confuse this wilderness of Sin with that of Zin. The former is near the sea and not far from the start of their journey. The latter is up near the place where they will end their wanderings. Note the date now is the same day of the month on which they left Egypt, and one month later.

Verses 2, 3. Here is another of their murmurings referred to in 1 Cor. 10: 10 and which Paul condemns. When we reach Num. 21: 5 a complete list of these murmurings will be cited so that if the reader wishes to make a chain of the references he can do so. In the present instance the complaint shows the usual trait of mankind. They recall the fleshly pleasures they had while in the land of bondage. Today it often occurs that after people have come into the church they will repine for the "good things" they had while still in the world and will wish they had never started into the life of Christianity. God was displeased then and he still is at such murmurings.

Verses 4, 5. *Certain rate.* This means a day's ration. *That I may prove,* etc. The point here is that on the complaint made it is implied that if they were furnished the necessities of life they would be content and obedient. God proposed to give them this necessity to test their sincerity. The reason for the double amount on the sixth day will be considered later.

Verses 6-8. Reference to the evening applies to the quails which will be promised soon. But the most necessary observation for us to make in this paragraph is about the one against whom they were murmuring. Not really against Moses and Aaron but against the Lord. It should never be forgotten that when a complaint is made against God's constituted leaders, it is against Him.

Verses 9, 10. The people were so inclined to disbelieve that some visible evidence was necessary. So the Lord caused a cloud of glory to appear in the direction of the wilderness, the territory where they had been journeying. This should have taught them the lesson that in that awful region the Lord was with them.

Verses 11, 12. No reason is given for bringing the flesh in the evening and bread in the morning. But the lesson of the whole thing is that it was not necessary to remain in Egypt to eat bread and meat. They will be fully supplied with these things out here, and that without the labor they had to do for them while in bondage.

Verses 13, 14. Here we are told what the flesh was, but at present nothing is said to identify the article accompanying the frost, except that it was small and granular.

Verse 15. *It is manna.* The words in this expression are constructed in reverse to the original meaning. They should read "what is it?" They had just asked the question of each other, and then the writer tells us why they asked the question, was because they did not know what it was. It would be very foolish to make a positive statement about it, and then immediately tell what it was, as the authorized version puts it. And this rendering is confirmed by the fact that Moses answers their question in the close of the verse. The word "manna" is from the Hebrew word MAN and defined "literally, a whatness (so to speak), i. e. manna (so called from the question about it):"—Strong.

Verses 16-18. Just enough to supply their needs was expected to be gathered. The stipulated amount was an omer for each person which was about one-half or three-fourths of a gallon, according to various authorities. There were some 600,000 families in the nation and of course they would not all be provided with exact measure vessels out there in the wilderness. Thus the Lord would expect them to use their best judgment and be conscientious in their gathering. If they did this it would be seen that no one would have any lack. This literal fact is cited by Paul in 2 Cor. 8: 15 as an illustration of the moral equality recognized by the Lord of the financial responsibility of Christians.

Verse 19. This verse was a warning against unnecessary hoarding. It was unnecessary since they had been promised a new supply each morning.

Verse 20. The spirit of hoarding seems to be universally prevalent with the children of men. There was not the least excuse for this case since they had been gathering the manna every morning. This brought forth a feeling of wrath in Moses.

Verse 21. This verse teaches the lesson of promptness. In order to obtain the food thus provided they must get up at a reasonable time. No chance for delay.

Verse 22, 23. On the sixth day there was a double amount of the manna gathered because there would be none falling on the seventh, which is here called the holy sabbath. Much has been made of this passage by the sabbatarians. They use this to show their theory of observing the day as a holy day, that, it was not a part of the law sent out from Sinai, exclusively. That the sabbath had been in force before Sinai since this instance here recorded occurred before reaching the mount. But some things set forth in the scriptures are overlooked on this point. See Jer. 34: 13 which reads "Thus saith the Lord of Israel; I made a covenant with your fathers in the day that I brought them forth out of the land of Egypt, out of the house of bondmen, saying." And then follows the covenant or law about the required treatment of servants regarding the seventh year. And yet this statute was not given till they reached Sinai. Therefore, the words, "in the day" etc., are indefinite and refer to that day in general, in which Sinai was the point of interest. This indicates to us that since they were about to reach the holy mount where the national law was to be given, and since the sabbath law was there for the first time to be given to man, it was appropriate to give this much of the coming law to them now, inasmuch as their murmurings about food had called for this part of the law a few weeks ahead of the central date. Also let the reader see this same use of the expression "the day" in Heb. 8: 9. Furthermore, let us consult the language in Neh. 9: 14. This reads thus: "And madest known unto them thy holy sabbath, and commandest them precepts, statutes, and laws, by the hand of Moses thy servant." The connection here shows the writer is telling about the Israelites and their deliverance from Egypt and gathering at Sinai. Now it is plain to any sincere student, that if, at this time, God made known to the people his holy sabbath, then it had not been a stipulated ordinance before, as the sabbatarians teach. Another idea here seen is that God made these laws known through Moses. This is another exposure of the false teaching of the sabbatarians who try to distinguish between the authority of Moses and God.

Verses 24-26. Not much additional to be said here. But it should be observed that when the extra manna was kept over on this occasion no harm came to it because it was according to the direction of the Lord.

Verses 27-30. The greedy disposition of man is here manifested. There was not a single reason for looking for this food on this day since they had been sufficiently supplied, but the rebellious spirit of the people acted. In reproaching the people for their disobedience God does it through Moses. Another instance showing the position of authority that he had between God and the congregation.

Verse 31. Coriander seed is in the class of mints with a pleasant taste and fragrance. It is also inclined to allay disturbances in the digestive organs. Besides all this, the manna was sweet to the taste as if made with honey. Thus the bread food here provided for the people was very desirable and should have caused them to be more appreciative than they were.

Verse 32. In the centuries before the last Era the people were given many and various institutions and ordinances, for the purpose of keeping them reminded of God and their dependence on him. This specimen of the manna would not always be in view of the people since it was kept in the most holy place and no one but the High Priest went in there. But it was there in case the use of it became necessary. Its preservation through the 40 years would be by the same miraculous power that preserved it each week over the sabbath.

Verse 33. Here we see that Moses had superiority over Aaron in some things. And thus again we have a refutation of the theory that attempts to belittle his authority. The original word for "pot" does not occur in any other place in the scriptures. It is defined by Strong "a vase (probably a vial tapering at the top)." As to the amount of manna stored up here, see comments at 16th verse.

Verse 34. *Before.* This is from PANIM and has been rendered by a great many words in the A. V., but the most outstanding one is "presence." This passage therefore means that the pot of manna was placed in the presence of "the testimony." And according to statements too numerous to name here, "the testimony" means the tables of the covenant. Another interesting thought here is that the tables of the covenant had not yet been given. So we have another example of the unchronological nature of the Biblical narratives. And we see also in this verse another indication that this whole period reaching from the Red Sea to Sinai is placed as one "day."

Verses 35, 36. The children of Israel are as yet only a few weeks out of Egypt. Yet the fact of eating manna 40 years is mentioned. The writers often go ahead in their recording and drop in a statement that will throw light on the subject that is under consideration. Attention is called to the words "land inhabited" here. This is said in the same sense as the word "wilderness" in chapter 3: 18. It shows that a wilderness does not aways mean a dry or infertile waste. An area that is not settled with people in a fixed residence is often spoken of as a wilderness.

EXODUS 17

Verse 1. For comments on the wilderness of Sin see first verse of previous chapter. It was in that district they had the experience of food shortage, as they thought, and complained to the Lord about it. That need was fully supplied. Now they have reached another difficulty. There is no water to drink. We will see how much of a lesson they had learned from the former circumstance.

Verses 2, 3. Another of the murmurings. (See chapter 16: 2, 3 and remarks). The place they have reached now is in the same desert mentioned before. The absence of drinking water here does not affect the comments as to a desert in the least. In the most cultivated spots there might be particular sites where no well or other provision of the kind had been made. But such fact should not have discouraged them. And especially since all their needs had been abundantly supplied before this. But such is human nature. Also in this instance the people complain against Moses as if he were to blame. But they were immediately told that all such complaints are against the Lord and that in so doing they were guilty of tempting him.

Verse 4. Although Moses was not responsible for their seeming misfortune yet they are so angered against him as to threaten his life. It is often so today. The men who are God's constituted rulers and leaders in the Church are blamed for unpleasant experiences when they insist on carrying out the requirements of God. This is seen especially in cases of corrective discipline. But it must not be forgotten that all opposition to scriptural church government is rebellion against God.

Verse 5. For explanation of "elders" see Chapter 3: 16-18 and comments. No officials had as yet been designated among the children of Israel.

Verse 6. Horeb and Sinai are used interchangeably in much of the scriptures. But when a distinction is made, the topmost peak is called Sinai. This is indicated by the language in chapter 19: 20. It is appropriate to have the event here recorded to happen at this place. They are destined to spend about a year at this place in which time the people will be nationalized by receiving the law that is to guide them in their religious and civil life. And here their need for water will be obtained by smiting a rock. At Jerusalem, the Rock of Ages will be smitten to give to mankind the water of life.

Verse 7. *Tempted.* This word comes from a variety of original words in both the Old and New Testaments and is used in many different senses. It is therefore necessary to be attentive in order not to come to wrong conclusions. The most common impression created at mentiion of the word is that of luring to sin. But since it is impossible for God to sin we cannot use this meaning of the word with reference to him. The original word in the passage under consideration is from NACAH and defined by Strong "a primitive root; to test." It has been rendered in A. V. by adventure, assay, prove, tempt, try." In referring to this and kindred instances, Paul says these people tempted the Lord. (1 Cor. 10: 9). In that place the Greek word is EKPEIRAZO and Strong defines it "to test thoroughly." With all these considerations in view the thought of tempting the Lord is to put him "on the spot" so to speak. Try out his various attributes; his power, patience, mercy, etc. God is not unwilling to prove his power and other qualities when honest inquirers need the proof. But when it comes from those who have already had abundance of such evidence then their making the test is considered in the light of a challenge and is displeasing to him.

Verse 8. *Amalek.* See Gen. 36: 12 for the origin of this people. It will be found to be from Esau the elder brother of Jacob. The younger had been preferred to the elder and the latter's descendents had become enemies to God and His people. The Amalekites became a prominent group and had to be dealt with very severely before being finally destroyed. Notice this fight was in the same community where the miracle was performed for the water. It was near Horeb the birthplace of the nation formally.

Verse 9. *Joshua.* This is the first mention of this righteous man, but he will be in favorable evidence many times after this. He was a leader under Moses, obeying his commands and carrying out his orders. In ordinary times he was a leader of men under the direction of the lawgiver and in times of war he was the commander of the armed forces. At present he is told to choose men to go against Amalek with the promise that Moses will oversee the movements.

Verse 10. As Moses went to the hilltop to oversee the battle against Amalek he took Aaron and Hur with him as aides.

Verse 11. Here is another instance where it appears that some literal or visible means had to be resorted to in order to accomplish the effect the Lord desired. However, we know such was not actually necessary. In that early age of God's dealings with man it was more necessary to connect the divine power with some visible evidence of it. Now then, if it is observed that Israel is successful in proportion with ability of Moses to hold his hands up, a condition that any one would know had no physical effect on the battle, then the conclusion would be plain that God was in the situation.

Verse 12. Many familiar sayings are based on some specific occurrence. Here we see the physical fact of holding up a man's hands resulted in success. Aaron and Hur were not in the battle at all, neither did they have any moral or miraculous effect on Moses. But by holding up the hands of the man who did have such qualifications they became supporters of him. Thus we have the expression of "holding up the hands" of some one who is engaged in a good cause. We may not be personally able to accomplish the work some other is doing but by assisting him and supporting him in his work we become partners with him and will receive credit from the Lord for it.

Verse 13. *Discomfited.* This is from a word that means to overthrow completely.

Verse 14. While the army of Amalek was completely overthrown in this battle yet the Lord wishes to have the entire people destroyed and here declares it. And as a means of keeping the edict alive in the minds of generations he orders it to be written in a book and also rehearsed in the ears of Joshua, the military leader. This complete extermination of the Amalekites was accomplished as recorded in Esther 9: 24.

Verses 15, 16. So far the Patriarchal dispensation of religion prevails and that was centered round an altar. So it is according to form for Moses to erect one here. The people have just had a successful battle with a bitter enemy and it is fitting that a religious service be offered to God to whom they attribute their victory. And the special name given to this altar signifies the truths involved, that Amalek is to be regarded as a perpetual enemy of God's people and to be fought against from one generation to another until he is completely destroyed.

EXODUS 18

Verses 1, 2. In chapter 4 the wife of Moses was with him as he was journeying in the direction of Egypt. At that time occurred the event of Moses' close escape from death over the circumcision of his son. After that was settled Moses sent his wife back to her father's land as indicated in this paragraph now being considered. The father has heard of the success of his son-in-law over the Egyptians and decides to see him and offer congratulations.

Verses 3, 4. In ancient times most if not all proper names had some significance or special meaning. Here we may see the reason why the sons of Moses were given the names mentioned. The explanation in the margin is useful for this information.

Verse 5. This "mount of God" has already been explained to mean Horeb. This was a familiar spot to Jethro since it had been connected with his business of sheep and their care. (See chapter 3: 1).

Verses 6, 7. This paragraph pictures a friendly meeting between the members of this family. The conduct of each indicates that perfect harmony existed between Moses and his father-in-law. *Obeisance.* This is from a word that means to bow down as a friendly gesture and indicating good will.

Verse 8. Since Jethro has shown so much interest in Moses and his work as to come to meet him here, bringing his loved ones to him, it was befitting that he relate to his father-in-law his great success under God, against the enemy, the Egyptians.

Verses 9, 10. The reaction was entirely favorable and Jethro gives credit where credit is due by praising God for the good fortune coming to his son-in-law.

Verse 11. The conclusion formed by Jethro as to God's superiority was just what was intended. The personal benefits that came to certain individuals or the punishment inflicted upon others did not constitute the primary motive that God had in mind. But in those times of almost universal idolatry it was needful to impress upon men that only one God was true and that he was creator and ruler of all.

Verse 12. The question that is natural to ask here is, what made it right for Jethro to offer a sacrifice to God when he was not one of God's people. But this last statement is too strong. True he was not one of the special group of God's people that was being formed with the lineal descendants of Abraham. But it must be remembered that God has had some form of religion among men from the beginning and that was the Patriarchal Dispensation. It is true that most men had departed from that law and were worshipping idols. (Josh. 24: 2). And at the time we have reached in our study, about all of the line of Patriarchs had become transgressors. This is about the same date that Job lived and he was practically the only one of the Patriarchs who had remained true to that Dispensation. (Job 1: 8). And because the transgressions against the Patriarchal laws had become so many God determined to strenghten the (desired) effect of the promise to Abraham by adding the law. (Gal. 3: 19). This is what is about to be done and it will be less than two months until that event will be in the making. Thus, as Jethro has been under the immediate influence of his son-in-law he has been reclaimed to his duties and privileges under the Patriarchal Dispensation so that he here offers a sacrifice to God. But not being an Israelite he will not be expected to join in the national movement but will continue his life as a servant of God under the Patriarchal Dispensation. This is indicated by the last verse of this chapter. But having been reclaimed as here stated he would be interested in the same God that Moses served and would thus be perfectly in line when suggesting the idea soon to be set forth in this chapter.

Verse 13. Since Moses has been placed between the people and God they look to him for advice and instruction on all their matters of interest. This very naturally made him a very busy man and it kept him constantly engaged.

Verse 14. Of course there are yet some things that Jethro had not learned about the position and work of his son-in-law and he inquires what it is all about.

Verses 15, 16. In explaining it to his father-in-law Moses makes it plain that while he answers the inquiries of the people and decides their disputes, yet he does not do so on his own opinion alone. But he makes them "know the statutes of God."

Verses 17-22. These verses are grouped in one paragraph because they belong to one subject. It is that of sharing the burdens of the matters of judgment with others who are capable of assisting. Jethro is viewing the matter from the standpoint of the physical endurance of Moses and not in any way considering his authority. But he thinks of the many petty matters that would not involve questions of right and wrong and that could be solved by the common sense of good men. So his advice is to let such men take part of the burden off the shoulders of his son-in-law.

Verse 23. This verse shows the great reverence that Jethro had come to have for God. All of the advice he had given to Moses was to be subject to the approval and command of God. What a wonderful attitude to take. And how consistent it is with his newly reclaimed position with God under the Patriarchal Dispensation.

He does not even show a disposition to dictate to his son-in-law. Instead, he puts his advice on two "ifs." If thou shalt do this thing. That is, if Moses himself sees fit to take the advice of his father-in-law. He does not presume to imply that Moses does not personally know what is best, so, if he sees fit himself. But also another "if." That is, if God command thee so. If all suggestions and advice that men feel disposed to make to others on religious quetsions were placed on such conditions, how different the religious world would be.

Verse 24. Since the advice of Jethro was expressly based on the provision that God approve it we must conclude that God did so, else Moses would not have hearkened to the voice of his father-in-law in all these things.

Verse 25. Moses chose able men to work under him. But even they were not given the entire burden of the secondary judgment. The mention of thousands, hundreds, etc., indicated that the work was spread out among various degrees of judging talent.

Verse 26. *All seasons.* This means that in the daily and ordinary times these under-judges attended to the questions arising among the people.

Verse 27. See comments at verse 12 above.

EXODUS 19

Verses 1-2. The date mentioned in this paragraph is to be reckoned from the time the children of Israel left Egypt and not what originally would have been the third month of their year. For we see in chapter 12: 2 that what had been another month in their calendar was now to be the first. Thus we observe the children of Israel arrived at Sinai about two months after leaving Egypt. They came to the desert of Sinai which means the uninhabited area in which the famous mount was located and from which mount they are destined to receive great revelations.

Verse 3. *Moses went up unto God.* This and such like expressions will be seen along in this part of the narrative and should not be misunderstood. Moses actually went up to the top of the mount only two times. (Deut. 9: 9, 18, 25). Thus we are to understand the many expressions about his coming up or going down, or going to the people, or going up to the Lord, etc., as relative and intending only to refer to the near approach to God only far enough to converse with Him out of the hearing of the people.

Verse 4. *Eagles' wings.* Of course this is used figuratively here. An eagle is bold and fleet. Also it is able to soar far above all obstacles. Thus it is a fitting figure of God's success in carrying his people above and beyond all their enemies.

Verse 5. This proviso of obedience is always either specified or implied in the promises of God made to his people. And their failure to comply with the condition will explain why they so often failed of grace of God. *Peculiar treasure.* This is from words that mean a "special possession" and thus separate and apart from God's other things of ownership. All the earth belongs to God for that matter, but this people are offered the distinction of being his favorite, as a people.

Verse 6. *Kingdom of priests.* God had priests under the Patriarchal Dispensation all the while, but that system of religion was not an organized one nor one forming a kingdom. Now the nation of Israel is soon to be formed into a kingdom with priests to administer its religious activities. It is well to note here that in all of God's dealings with man there have been just two organized or systematic forms of religion. They are the Jewish, or Mosaic, and the Christian. That is why so much of the reasoning of Paul and other inspired writers seems to overlook the Patriarchal Dispensation.

Verses 7, 8. Here is another instance of Moses as "go-between" for the people and God. He takes the words of God to the people and then in turn takes theirs to God. But we are soon to see that an exception will be made at times.

Verse 9. Here is an exception mentioned above. It will not do for the people to see God directly, yet it is desired that they actually hear his voice as he speaks to Moses so as to have evidence that Moses is their authorized mediator. Hence the cloud. But we will see before the conclusion of this interesting subject that the people did not wish to hear the voice directly and hence some other plan was used by the Lord.

Verses 10, 11. They are about to be in a very important meeting, that with their God. *In the sight.* We have seen that no man is to see God directly; that is, to see his person. But it means they are to actually see the conditions that are to demonstrate God's power and spiritual presence.

Verses 12, 13. That the people might be impressed with the importance of this mount, they are forbidden under threat of death to touch it. This is the circumstance that Paul referred to in Heb. 12: 18-21.

Verse 14. Here the word "sanctified" means they washed their clothes and made themselves "presentable."

Verse 15. *Come not at your wives.* They are about to be engaged in a transaction of momentous importance and that will not be repeated. It is no time to be concerned with the ordinary pleasures of home life with their wives in the marriage privileges. Just dismiss all such subjects for the time and give your undivided attention to God.

Verses 16-18. The demonstrations recorded here were in sight of the people and also in their hearing. This is what was meant by "sight" in verse 11 above.

Verse 19. Please bear in mind the book of Exodus, as well as some others, is not always chronological. This verse belongs just before the first verse of following chapter, for the ten commandments were first spoken orally in the hearing of the people. For information on this point see chapter 20: 18, 19; Deut. 4: 10, 11; 10: 4. Then when the people were frightened at the sound of the voice of God and did not want to hear it again, they were told they would not hear it. But the commandments were then written on the tables of stone by the finger of God and delivered to Moses to be kept as a testimony against them. Now, having explained the connection of the verse of this paragraph we come back to the activities still going on before Moses goes to the summit of the mount to receive the law.

Verse 20. The principal purpose of looking at this verse again is to note that the top of the mount is named "Sinai," as was indicated previously. The statement here that the Lord called Moses up to the top of this mount is again indefinite as to the time of his going up there. It seems that the people were so moved by curiosity and eagerness to see what was going on that they endangered themselves. Thus, while this verse reads as if Moses went at once to the top of the mount, yet God is still concerned about the conduct and safety of the people and still has Moses going back and forth between the people and the partial ascent up the mount. This is seen as follows.

Verses 21-24. In this paragraph we see the back and forth movements referred to in preceding paragraph. Even Moses is somewhat uneasy it seems and speaks of the danger the people are in and of the restrictions God has made. But the Lord urges him to go on down once more and charge the people so that they will be at a safe distance and ready to listen to the voice of the Lord.

Verse 25. The speaking to the people mentioned in this verse is what has been mentioned in the several places in this chapter. After a sufficient amount of warning and instruction has been given the people, God is going to speak with audible voice and give them the ten commandments. That will come in next chapter and will be followed by the expressions of fear from the people which have already been spoken of in this chapter. Please reread comments on this chapter again before going further.

EXODUS 20

Verse 1. *Spake.* That is, he spake them orally as already explained. The tables of stone have not yet been delivered to Moses for he has not yet been at the top of the mount. As you read this chapter please be mindful that it is the voice of God now speaking to the people orally. *These words.* The number and order of the ten commandments are related by Josephus and it will be well to quote him here as confirming the account we have in our version of the Bible. "The first commandment teaches us, that there is but one God, and that we ought to worship him only; the second commands us not to make the image of any living creature to worship it; the third, that we must not swear by God in a false matter; the fourth, that we must keep the 7th day, by resting from all sorts of work; the fifth, that we must honor our parents; the sixth, that we must abstain from murder; the seventh, that we must not commit adultery; the eighth, that we must no be guilty of theft; the ninth, that we must not bear false witness; the tenth, that we must not admit of the desire of any thing that is another's." Josephus, *Antiquities* 3-5-5.

Verse 2. God intends that his people should never forget with whom they are dealing and that it is not an idolatrous being who gave them their freedom.

Verse 3. This is commandment number one. It is a general statement pertaining to idolatry. There were three forms or classes of idolatry among the people which may be designated as artificial; (man-made such as those of gold or silver or wood); invisible or imaginary (such as Baal, or Ashtoreth, or Tammuz); and natural, (such as animals or trees or rivers or planets, "host of heaven"). These three are referred to in the book of Ezekiel chapter 8. (See the comments at that place). And the first commandment of the Decalogue refers to all the forms of idolatry in general.

Verses 4-6. This is a specification of one of the three forms of idolatry referred to in preceding paragraph. Since man wished to worship the things of nature he also fell to making likenesses of them out of wood or stone or gold, and he is commanded in this place not to do so. *Iniquity.* This is from AVON and has also been rendered in the A.V. by "punishment" 6 times, and "punishment of iniquity" 4 times. It can thus be seen that the word sometimes means the results or consequences, likewise the penalty of sin, as well as the sin itself. The word as used in this paragraph means the results. *Visiting.* This is from PAQAD and defined by Strong "to visit (with friendly or hostile intent); by analogy to oversee, muster, charge, care for, miss, deposit." It has been rendered in the A.V. by such words as appoint, bestow, call to remembrance, remember, reckon, and many others. This passage was given a wrong interpretation by ancient people and is also misunderstood in our day. The principle of individual responsibility as manifested in God's dealings with man on moral questions would forbid such interpretation. Since the human family lived under the Patriarchal Dispensation so long, in which the father was priest and chief; it was consistent to pass the results, or fruits, of the haters of God on down to following generations. This could be done without allowing it to affect the spiritual status of any of the children.

Verse 7. This is the third commandment. To take the name of the Lord in vain means to make a useless application of the holy name. The word "vain" is from SHAV and defined by Strong as "uselessness." To use the name of God in a way that is authorized would be effective and beneficial and that would be right. But to use the name in an unauthorized manner would bring no good result and thus would be in vain.

Verses 8-11. This is the fourth commandment and the one about which sabbatarians have been so inconsistent. The command to keep the day holy is explained by the following statements, that no labor was to be done on that day. But the people who pretend to observe this commandment are guilty of violating it themselves. This command not only forbids them to work themselves, but also they must not work their beasts. Yet these same pretenders can be seen driving their horses to their place of meeting on Saturdays, on the plea that they are keeping the sabbath under the fourth commandment. At the same time they are breaking the said commandment by working their beasts. This shows that their claim of keeping the "holy sabbath" is insincere. It puts them in the same class with the Pharisees of the time of the apostles who made such a fuss about circumcision, as pretending to keep the law. *Six days* and *seventh day*. These expressions are used in the same connection and thus with the same force as to the length of each period. Now there is no one who claims the seventh day to have ever been any different in duration from what it is now. Therefore, the six days mentioned in direct connection with the seventh must be understood to have been six periods of the same duration as the seventh. The seventh was a regular day, as we now use the term. And another thought is offered to us here. In the beginning of Genesis the simple statement is made that God created the heaven and the earth in the beginning. And as far as that statement goes we could not say at what date or time that took place. If that were the only place where anything could be found on the subject then it might be difficult to confute the claim of "scientists" that millions of years passed between the creation of "the heaven and the earth" and the formations related in the next verses. But in the paragraph now under consideration we have the writer using practically the same language, that the Lord "made heaven and earth," but he says he did this "in six days." Thus we must conclude the inspired writer meant to tell us that God created and formed and ordered the universe in six days, which are here seen to mean regular days.

Verse 12. This is the 5th commandment and the first one of the ten that has a special man-ward bearing. The first four had a special God-ward bearing. The word "honor" is from KABED and defined "in a good sense (numerous, rich, honorable): causatively, to make weighty."—Strong. We can see in this definition that it meant the child must hold the parent in high esteem and as being weighty or important. Also that he was to impart money or material value to him. This explains the use of the commandment that Jesus made in Mark 7: 10-12.

Verse 13. This is the sixth commandment and one that advocates of non-resistance try to twist into a support of their error. No one will accuse God of contradicting himself. It is true here that it says not to kill. But in Gen. 9: 6 the killer is to be killed and that too, by man. Thus we must see that the killing forbidden here is that of an unauthorized individual. And when he does so, then he must be punished by having his life taken from him by man. See the comments at Genesis 9: 6 on capital punishment.

Verse 14. In Biblical times a man became one flesh with a woman by the sexual act, and it has been so considered ever since by the Lord. When that takes place then neither of them may become sexually intimate with another without the guilt of adultery.

Verse 15. This is the eighth commandment. Its meaning is not different from that in any age of the world. To take from another unlawfully, what he possesses, is to make one guilty of theft or stealing. The mere taking of it against his consent would not constitute the crime, but doing it unlawfully.

Verse 16. This is the ninth commandment. In this place the command relates to lying against another. But in the general teaching of the Bible; all lying, whether it be against another or only on a general occasion is forbidden. (See Rev. 21: 8).

Verse 17. This is the tenth commandment. The simple definition of the word "covet" is "to desire." But the connection shows it means to have an unlawful desire. For instance, no man would have a lawful right to another man's wife, hence he must not desire her. This would not mean he should not admire her and think about her in a favorable frame of mind, but he must not desire to have her as his own.

Verses 18-20. This circumstance has already been commented upon. (See chapter 19: 19). The audible voice of God so frightened the people that they requested not to hear it again. Moses assures them that no harm is to come to them from this experience but that it was an instance of testing them. They agree that Moses may speak to them and they will hear, but they do not wish to hear the voice of God. And they are then informed that the whole matter is for the purpose of testing them.

Verse 21. While the audible voice heard by the children of Israel was frightening to them, we need not conclude that God, in bodily person, was there. Even when Moses was finally called to the top of the mount to receive the law God was represented by the angels. (Acts 7: 38, 53, Gal. 3: 19, Heb. 2: 2). Even an angel was often in such august form, that man was unfit or unable to be in the immediate presence. (See Chap. 3: 2-5). Thus, a thick darkness was brought here for the protection of Moses.

Verses 22, 23. In a general sense all that God does or says is from heaven since that is his dwelling place. But in a particular manner here he talked to the people from heaven. This was not said because Moses was inspired from Heaven to speak to the people, for that was always the case. But it means that the Lord sent his angel as his personal representative and talked with audible voice to the people. And this would be for the purpose of impressing them as to the importance of the great God of all. In direct connection with this impression the warning is repeated that they must not make "with me" gods of silver and gold. This term carries the idea that idolaters virtually put their idols in the same class with the true God, and that is something which will not be tolerated on account of the divine jealousy. (See verse 5).

Verses 24, 25. Let us not forget that the Bible is a closely-written narrative. Events that seem to be near in time may be separated by days or weeks. At the time of which we now are reading, we know that it will be at least 80 days before Moses will come to them with the law and the description of the tabernacle and its instruments of service. Until that time they are practically still under the Patriarchal Dispensation. In that arrangement the family altar was the central place of worship and the instrument would be made by them as occasion suggested. And the significant statement is made about the various altars that are places where "I record my name." God has had some place that represented his presence in all ages and whatever and wherever that was, his people must respect it in order to have the blessing of the Lord. Just why the instructions are given here as to the kind of material they might use and what they might do in forming the altar, we are not told. It was the divine direction and we are certain that unless such directions were observed, the favor of God would not be extended to the people. They must therefore observe these restrictions and commandments for the time being. Before they will receive the fixed and permanent order of national service there are many days to pass as observed above.

Verse 26. The word "steps" is from a word that means "an elevation." A sort of ramp, as we would call it. They must not construct their altar in such a manner that to reach it they would need to make an ascent above the crowd looking on. And the purpose of this restriction was that they would not expose their nakedness by climbing to a place above the heads of the ones below. Men in those days wore loose flowing skirts, with no close-fitting undergarment. Thus the position that would be taken while going up over an elevation might expose their bodies, which would be displeasing to God. This instruction is in keeping with the general teaching which God gave to man after the sin in the garden. (See Gen. 3: 21). Ever since then it has been the will of God that men and women keep their bodies clothed in a modest way so that their shameful parts will not be exposed to others. This is especially required of both men and women when in the presence of the opposite sex. All commandments in the New Testament touching the subject of modesty are based on this principle. It has been the law of the Lord that men and women should make such use, and take such liberties with their bodies, as will contribute to modesty, and not coarseness in mind and manner of life.

EXODUS 21

Verse 1. The principal meaning of this verse rests largely on the definition of the word "judgments." It is from MISHPAT and defined "A verdict (favorable or unfavorable) pronounced judicially, especially a sentence or formal decree (human or divine law, individual or collective) including the act, the place, the suit, the crime, and the penalty; abstractly, justice, right or privilege (statutory or customary), or even a style."—Strong. It will be well for the reader to become very familiar with this definition for it will help to understand the various expressions to be found in the law of Moses as given to the children of Israel. And again, here is an instance of the importance of Moses, as lawgiver. The attempts of the sabbatarians to distinguish between the authority of God and that of Moses in the Old Testament writings are shown to be misleading. It is here stated that Moses was to set these laws before the people, which means that when he delivered a command or edict it was the same as if delivered by the Lord in person. Again, let it be remembered that the children of Israel did not have any other law to guide them either in their religious or their civil life. Hence, the system was a combination of the two. That is, while many of the laws were in the nature of directions for their treatment of each other in temporal or civil life only, others were to be observed as a religious obligation. This was in the same sense that Christians are to perform their duties to the government and fellow citizens, as a temporal or civil duty, yet, at the same time, not forgetting that God requires them to be done; and, hence, a Christian will perform these requirements with a conscientious or "religious" frame of mind.

Verses 2, 3. We do not know just why God permitted the practice of buying and using servants, especially from their own nation. However, that was the formative age of the world and people had not been very well trained in the responsibilities of independent life. They had been servants in Egypt for 400 years and naturally were somewhat accustomed to that life. But since all things are liable to abuse, God placed many restrictions and regulations around the subject. Thus in this passage we see a limitation of length of service. And when the time came to be discharged from the service then whatever was his social status when he came in that was to continue.

Verse 4. Since the privilege given to the servant of taking a wife and producing children was given by the master it would be very reasonable for the master to make a claim of an interest in the enterprise. On that basis he could rightfully claim jurisdiction of the family of the servant that had been formed after entering the service and hence the law of equity would direct that when the servant went out of the employ of his master he should leave behind him that which had come to him from his master.

Verse 5. A very natural thought here would be that a man who really became attached to his family would be heart-broken in leaving them behind. Therefore, in justice to his sentiments as well as to the right of his master, a provision was made that both could be satisfied, and this provision will follow.

Verse 6. *Judges.* This is from the same word as "gods" in chapter 12: 12. See that place for the definition of the word. Even the possible attempt at shamming a love for his family, that he did not actually have, was to be forestalled. If the servant claimed that he wished to continue his servitude because of his love then a test was made. He was to have his ear pierced with an instrument as the ceremony that was to continue his relationship with his master. It is plain to understand that if his claim to love for his family were only a pretense used as means of continuing a life free from responsibility, then he would not be willing to undergo this pain; also the humiliation of having this mutilation placed on his body.

Verse 7. A difference was to be made in the treatment of female servants. The reason will be indicated in following verse.

Verse 8. *Betrothed.* This is from YAAD and defined "To fix upon (by agreement or appointment); by implication to meet (at a stated time), to summon (to trial), to direct (in a certain quarter or position), to engage (for marriage)"—Strong. This word is thus seen to be one of general meaning. It may mean to betroth in the ordinary sense of that word, but not necessarily. In the present verse it must take the more general meaning, that of fixing upon or appointing by agreement. And of course the agreement was with the father or owner of the damsel. *Redeemed.* It might occur after having used the female servant a while that he would become dissatisfied with her. In that case he was privileged to dispose of her independent of her feelings. He might not be allowed to sell her to strangers. And if she were willing to leave his service, she could do so by buying herself, so to speak, thus avoiding the humiliation of being sold to others. This was done in consideration for her personal rights. And 'f she did not value her freedom enough to furnish her own redemption price, then she must face the unpleasantness of continuing in a service with a master whom she knew to be dissatisfied with her.

Verse 9. In this verse the word defined above would take the last meaning since it pertains to the owner's son. And when that was done then the maid would take on the relationship of a daughter (in-law) and must be treated as a daughter. She would then be out of the class of an ordinary servant. See verse 7 above.

Verses 10, 11. The fact that he has disposed of his servant by giving her to his son in marriage commits him to that use of the female servants taken in. So that, if, after giving the first servant to his son in marriage he decides to take another maid to himself, it is to be understood that he has taken her in the sense of the last part of the definition of the word for "betrothed" as seen in verse 8. In this case he is to deal with the maid as with a wife; namely, furnish her with food and raiment and the things needed by a wife. And if he becomes dissatisfied with this woman then he must let her go free. He shall not be permitted to sell her to a stranger nor may he require her to pay a ransom for her freedom.

Verse 12. This verse considers the case of a deliberate act resulting in the death of the victim. In that case the death penalty must be inflicted. See Genesis 9: 6 and comments on this subject.

Verse 13. This verse considers a case where death was not inflicted deliberately. The expression that God delivered the victim into the hand of the slayer means that in the ordinary accidents coming through the providence of God, a man might come in contact with another in a very surprising and suspicious manner, which would provoke the one to attack the other fatally. This would not be considered murder and the slayer would not incur the death penalty. Yet the avenger of blood (again see Gen. 9: 6 and the verse before it) would be disposed to inflict such penalty. And thus in view of justice to all concerned an arrangement was made, referred to in latter part of the verse. Here note the references. (Num. 35: 11; Deut. 4: 41; Josh. 20: 2.)

Verse 14. *Presumptuously.* This is from a word that means "insolently" and thus means that the slayer not only intended to attack the other but was insolent about it. Of course that would mean that the slaying would be deliberate and constitute murder as in verse 12. *Guile.* This is from a word that means "trickery." So that not only did the slayer make the attack with insolence in his mind but used trickery in order to get access to the victim. Such a man is a vicious murderer and must be dealt the death penalty. Even if he flees to the altar, thinking that such a sacred place would provide him protection against the executioner, yet he must be taken therefrom and killed. See 1 Kings 2: 28-34 for an instance of this.

Verse 15. The relationship of parents to child is so sacred that if a parent is given the insult of a mere attack, even if it does not result in death, then the guilty one was to be put to death. The word "smite" usually conveys the idea of killing. But in this case it does not call for that meaning. The word is from NAKAH and defined "to strike (lightly or severely, literally or figuratively)." Of course we have already learned that smiting to the extent of causing death was to be punished with death. And that would be true regardless of whether the victim were a parent. Therefore, we are to understand the word here to come from this other original which takes the milder definition in general, and yet as calling for the death penalty when a parent is the victim.

Verse 16. The crime mentioned in this verse is otherwise called kidnapping. In our day this is a serious crime and in Biblical times was punishable with death. This is an indication that civil government might inflict the death penalty for crimes other than murder. This will be seen in other passages later on.

Verse 17. *Curseth.* This is from QALAL and defined by Strong "to be (causitively make) light." Thus another instance showing the great regard that was to be had for parents. Here the offence is merely that of making light of them. So grave was an insult to a parent that the death penalty was inflicted for it. Were there some such laws in the governments of today there might not be so much disrespect to parents.

Verses 18, 19. This passage describes a case where the parties are mutually taking part in the conflict. Yet since the damage is charged up to only one of them, we must conclude that one man attacked the other and the latter man was striving in self defence. But even so, should the fight not result in death, then the one making the attack was to be quit (acquitted) of any criminal charge. But he was to be held liable as in a damage case and make the victim whole for his loss.

Verses 20, 21. The act of smiting one's servant was considered as within the right of the owner. Yet he was supposed to use discretion and not go too far. And if a master allowed his anger to carry him past discretion to the extent of causing the death of his servant, then he was to be punished in some manner short of the death penalty. If the servant does not die on the spot but lives a day or two, that would indicate that the punishment inflicted on the servant was not entirely out of reason since the victim did not die instantly. And his living a couple of days indicated that he had not been treated with the severest kind of punishment, even though it was very severe. And these two days that he lived and yet was not able to be of service to his master would be considered as that much loss of service time to the master. So, the Lord considered that since the slave was the master's money (property) anyway, just let that loss of the two days' service be sufficient punishment for the master. This may seem as a strange kind of law, but we must always remember that God's ways are not man's ways and that He has reasons for his requirements which we cannot always understand.

Verse 22. Here again the connection shows that the striving was brought on by one man as against another. Also, the man being the victim is the husband of the woman with child since he is to be consulted about the amount of damage done. But note that he alone was not to determine the extent of damage. His natural inclination would render him somewhat biased since the woman injured was his wife. This sets forth a good principle of dealing between man and man. All parties to any dispute should have something to say in the settlement.

Verses 23-25. If anything serious results from the circumstance then the man bringing on the strife resulting in the damage shall be punished. The punishment must be in accordance with the damage and it was to be in kind. But we must bear in mind that when the aggressor was thus punished it would be by the proper person at that time in charge of penalties. So then when the punishment was inflicted it would be a judicial one and not considered as a personal action. This is what Jesus referred to in Matt. 5: 38 and which has been so greatly misinterpreted. The case in the Old Testament applied to said punishment inflicted by the proper official or person otherwise designated lawfully to do so. But the thing Jesus meant should not be done, was for a person who had been damaged to "take the law into his own hands" and return evil for evil, according to his personal feelings.

Verses 26, 27. It will be remembered that in times of slavery or servitude a master was permitted to punish his servants. And because of this the possibility arose of a man's becoming too severe in his punishment without necessarily intending to be. And as a precautionary measure he was told that if he went too far or was too severe with his punishment and damaged the body of the servant, then he would be required to set his servant free and would receive no pay for him. This knowledge would serve as an influence to keep him within reasonable bounds in his discipline of the servant.

Verses 28, 29. This passage furnishes us with an example of the law in Gen. 9: 5. That is, if a beast killed a person then it was to be slain because it had caused the death of a being made in the image of God, and in which body was the blood of life. And as far as the act of the beast was concerned, the owner was "quit" which means that he was acquitted of any charge of murder. Yet, it might be that he, too, would have to pay with his own life. But that was in case he knew his animal was dangerous and yet had not kept him away from the public. In that case he must be slain under the law of capital punishment stated in Gen. 9: 6. This is a just law and ought to be used today to the same extent as then.

Verses 30, 31. This passage reveals the only exception that could be made about inflicting the death penalty on the owner of the ox. He could pay the required fine and thus save his life. Doubtless the principle on which God permitted this exception to be made was that the owner was not deliberately guilty of the man's death. It was in the nature of what is now called second degree murder, or manslaughter. But even at that, the crime was considered great and called for severe punishment.

Verse 32. The mere fact of pushing or goring with the horns would not always mean that the victim was killed. That is why in verse 28 the stipulation is made that the ox had pushed or gored a man "that he die." In the verse now under consideration the simple fact is that the beast had gored a man's servant and not to the extent of killing him. Then it was to be considered as a damage case and the owner of the ox must pay.

Verses 33, 34. Here is a plain instance of laws required to be obeyed in the interest of public safety. We frequently see occasions today where such a law is needed and where it is in operation. In public works when an improvement is under construction and where the condition of safety is not possible as to the completion of the work, then a barricade or other device for public protection is put up. Of course this is specially true where the construction is being done on public property. But I understand that even if a man were doing improvements on his own property and where the spot is such that the public might have access to it (whether rightfully or otherwise), the owner is required to make the place safe. All such laws are based on the principle that we are "our brother's keeper" and that we cannot be isolationists.

Verse 35. This verse is considering only the case where two beasts get together through no fault of either owner and one ox kills the other. It is to be considered as a misfortune to be shared jointly by the two owners. This is evidently just.

Verse 36. This verse is different from the foregonig. This is a case where one ox was known by his owner to be a vicious one and yet he has not kept him in. If the other beast is killed then the owner of the vicious beast must bear all the loss by repaying the other man in full.

EXODUS 22

Verse 1. I do not know why the numerical difference here in the restoration of the stolen animals. In each case the number required to be repaid was doubtless for the purpose of making a strong preventive against such theft.

Verses 2-4. Theft is a detestable crime. And if a man finds one in the act the degree of provocation is considered to be so great that the injured party is authorized to take the life of the thief. And if he does so then nobody is to be held responsible for the death of the thief. But should a man discover that a theft had been committed and finally the thief be found, then the provocation is not supposed to be as great or urgent. Hence he would not be given the permission to kill the thief. And if he did, then he would be liable for the killing. One reason for this is that if the thief were killed that would prevent opportunity for recovery of damage from him. But if the property that was stolen is gone then the thief must be sold into slavery as pay for the loss to the other man. And in case the stolen article or animal is still in the possession of the thief, then he is to restore double.

Verse 5. This verse does not differ in principle from others already considered. It is just another instance of right dealing between man and man. It is evidently a righteous principle for the injured party to be reimbursed by the other.

Verse 6. This speaks of fire "breaking out," which would sound as if the fire were accidental; but the words "he that kindled" indicate this ordinance concerns a case where the fire was not an accident (as to starting it), while the extent of the damage might be. Be it so, the one kindling the fire should be more thoughtful about starting fires, and if he is made to pay for the damage, he will be more careful.

Verses 7, 8. It is taken for granted that a man had confidence in the honesty as well as responsibility of the one into whose hands he placed his property. Then if the property is stolen from the house of the custodian it may be possible to recover in double amount from the thief when he is found. If the thief cannot be found then the charge or at least the suspicion that the custodian had proved faithless might suggest itself. In such event the case must be brought to the attention of the judges. The nature of the action that would be taken will be indicated in verses below.

Verse 9. When a dispute such as here named, and also in preceding verse, comes up, then the judges are to hear "both" parties and their decision is to be final. To "condemn" here means to find guilty or responsible. The guilty man must pay double.

Verses 10, 11. The proviso that determines this case is that no man saw what had happened to the property delivered for keeping. When that is the situation then it becomes a matter of veracity. This was backed up by each making an oath and that would settle the case and both were to be content.

Verse 12. "Stolen from him" is the expression that decides the responsibility in this case. That would indicate that the custodian was present at the time of the theft and should have protected it. He might make the claim that he was not able to prevent the theft. Then he should not have accepted the responsibility of guarding the property. This law would have a tendency of causing men to be careful about taking into their care and keeping a charge that they were not sure of being able to keep.

Verse 13. In this case the beast was not known to be stolen, or if so the thief is not known. But after being separated from his owner the beast gets torn in pieces so that it is worthless. In such case, the custodian is not to be held. This is somewhat like the provision sometimes made by common carriers, regarding the property of patrons placed in their care for transportation. They will provide that they will not be responsible for loss that it caused by "an act of God" meaning, such as a storm, or some other occurrence, over which no man could have any control.

Verses 14, 15. The act of borrowing and lending is a commercial or financial transaction and to be entered into on the basis of mutual responsibility. However, if the property is damaged in the absence of the owner then the borrower is required to make it good. But if the damage comes to it while in the presence of the owner then he is expected to have sufficient interest in his own property to protect it. And if he does not, then he must bear the loss.

Verses 16, 17. This passage considers a maid who is not betrothed. In such case the man is to protect her reputation by making her his wife. That would be the honorable thing to do. And since she is not already engaged she is free and there would be nothing in the way of perfecting the arrangement. The proviso that the maid be one who is not betrothed is significant. In Biblical times an engagement was as biding morally as an actual marriage. In fact, it was considered so much that way that in many cases the engaged parties were spoken of as being married or as being husbands and wives. On this subject see comments at Gen. 19: 14. If the father is unwilling to give his daughter to the man for his wife (which was a possibility that the man should have thought of when making his advances to the maid), then he is required to settle the usual financial obligations toward an espoused maid. Such a law might have a tendency to restrain him when about to make his advances toward the maid.

Verse 18. *Witch.* This is from KASHAPH and defined "to whisper a spell, i. e., to enchant or practice magic."—Strong. The influence of such a character would be evil only because no one would wish to patronize such who was satisfied with the revealed Word of God. Any attempt to obtain information that called for resort to such characters as here described would be displeasing to God.

Verse 19. This kind of immorality is called bestiality today and is highly abominable in the sight of God. A specific reason for condemning the practice is given in Lev. 18: 23, where it says that it is confusion. Of course it would mean that it is confusion in the kingdom of nature to attempt to mix human and brute blood in this intimate manner.

Verse 20. In chapter 20: 5 they were told that God is jealous and because of that, no tolerance would be shown for those who provoked his jealousy. God is the great One who has made all things and given man his very being. Therefore no other being has any right to the attentions of the creatures of God.

Verse 21. The reader will see this kind of reminder to the children of Israel in many places as he passes on through the Old Testament. Consideration for the unfortunate condition of others was intended by this frequent reminder.

Verses 22-24. It is sometimes known that men will take advantage of those not in position to resist the imposition. Such conduct is always condemned in the sight of God. Jesus had the same principle in mind when he pronounced a woe on the scribes and Pharisees for devouring widows' houses. (Matt. 23: 14.)

Verse 25. The sense of this verse is couched in the word "usury." It is from NESHEK and defined by Strong "interest on a debt." Thus the word does not allow the frequent twist of its application by saying that it means undue interest. The motive for such a definition is to justify the practice of taking interest from every person to whom money is loaned. But the word does not make any distinction as to the amount of interest charged at all. The distinction that the verse makes is between the kind of persons in volved. Notice it says "poor" people. If a brother wants to borrow money because he is poor, which would mean that he wants the money to obtain necessities of life, then it was wrong to charge interest on the money. That would not be like lending money as a business proposition, where the borrower wanted to use the money as an investment. In such a case there would not be any wrong in the interest.

Verses 26, 27. Here is a proposition somewhat different and yet belonging in the same class as the one previous. It is well known that a poor man is not always honest. He might ask for money on the claim that he is needing it for the comforts of life. If he is being fair about it he will be willing to demonstrate his sincerity by offering to make some sacrifice himself. And it would be taking some chance to give up the possession of some of the things used for bodily comfort even though for only a few hours. If he is not willing to trust his friend a few hours he should go elsewhere for his favor. On the other hand, the fact that the borrower was willing to trust his raiment into the hands of his friend for a while should be all the guarantee the lender needed. Thus the law on the basis of "give and take."

Verse 28. The word "gods" is from ELOHEEM and means "magistrates" or "judges." They were forbidden to treat them with disrespect. It is the same kind of direction given in the New Testament in Acts 23: 5. Christians are commanded to honor the rulers.

Verse 29. The law requiring that the first of their products be given to God had already been made for them and this verse comes under that rule. *Liquors.* Strong defines the original word here, as "juices." It is well known that all people in Bible times as now, made much use of the juice of grapes. And so, along with the other products they must give the first of the juice to the Lord. And it should be understood that such article would be for the use of the tribe engaged exclusively in the service of the tabernacle and for their personal needs.

Verse 30. We also have learned that it is the first of the animals that was to be given to God. This verse is based on that law. And the Lord was very considerate in the enforcement of this law. The milk of the mother would not be used anyway for several days and thus the owner would not be deprived of any benefit he would have had from the animal. So the young was permitted to remain with the mother a few days.

Verse 31. They have already been forbidden to eat blood. If an animal allowed for food is being prepared for food purposes then they must see that the blood was shed first. And of necessity they would have to learn how to bleed the beast so as to get the fluid to flow out of the body. But this might not have been done in the case of an animal torn by another beast. So much doubt would exist as to whether the blood had been permitted to flow out that such a piece of flesh was considered unclean.

EXODUS 23

Verse 1. It is wrong to start a rumor. It would be in the nature of a lie and thus violate Ex. 20: 16. Not all rumors are false, of course, but to "raise a false report" would be such, and that would do much harm; possibly more harm than the simple act of lying to a man direct. It could be that he alone would be harmed by it, but a rumor based on falsehood would harm the people in general. Also, this verse forbids becoming a witness in a case where a wicked person would use the witness in support of his cause.

Verse 2. A popular practice is to follow the crowd whether right or wrong. In matters resting purely on human judgment it would be right to consider the crowd for Solomon says that "in a multitude of counselors there is safety." (Prov. 11: 14.) But the doctrine that "might makes right" has always been a vicious one and often the only excuse offered for the part taken in disputes. The fact that in matters pertaining to right or wrong the majority has always been on the wrong side should be considered.

Verse 3. *Cause.* This is from RIB and defined by Strong: "A contest (personal or legal)." It is the same word in preceding verse and in verse 6 below. The thought is that a poor man has a dispute with some other person, and we should not favor the poor man in the dispute just because he is poor. A poor man is not always right and we should not be prejudiced in his favor on account of his poverty.

Verses 4, 5. Many of the laws pertaining to man with man, were made in view of the traits of the flesh. The impulsive thing would be to refuse to help a beast in distress or in danger of being lost in order to "spite" the owner who is an enemy. But the Lord never has sanctioned such attitude. We should remember that every one of us was an enemy of Christ yet he was willing to die for us. And here is another thing to be considered in connection with the present verses. If we show kindness to our enemy by saving his property, that act of kindness may be the very thing that will break down the enmity and make him a friend instead of an enemy. See Rom. 12: 20, 21.

Verse 6. This is explained in verse 3 above, except it is in reverse. In that other case the inclination would be to favor a man in a wrong cause because he is poor. In the present verse the idea is not to hold a man in contempt or ignore him because he is poor. There have been many instances where the claims of poor men were just and yet they could not interest others because of their lowly state. This attitude of the more fortunate against the poor constituted one of the common evils in the history of the nation of Israel. (2 Sam. 12: 1, 3, 4. Isa. 3: 14; 10: 2 and many others.)

Verse 7. This is largely a repetition of some verses already considered. If God will not justify the wicked as is stated here, then if a man sides in with the wicked by injuring those whom the wicked are oppressing that will cause him to be classed with the wicked and displease God.

Verse 8. *Gift.* This is from SHACHAD and defined by Strong "a donation (venal or redemptive)." The words in the definition mean a gift that is purely a money gift as a personal favor, or, something offered to "hush" the mouth of the judge. In other words, it means a bribe. And it is the judge who is here forbidden to accept this gift. The reason given is that it would pervert his honest judgment and turn him into a "policy" man. It is natural for a man to feel kindly toward another who has bestowed some material favor on him and this might corrupt his judgment when called upon to decide a case.

Verse 9. Being forbidden to oppress a stranger would not mean that strangers should be tolerated in all their doings. A stranger means a newcomer or one dwelling temporarily with them. Such should be treated with kindness for the Israelites were themselves strangers in a land not theirs. They were greatly oppressed in that land and should therefore realize what it is to be oppressed.

Verses 10, 11. This introduces what was afterward known as the Sabbatical Year. It became the occasion of grievous wrongdoing by the nation and finally caused them to be carried off into captivity. The law is evidently based on the same principle as that of "rotation" which all good agriculturists know to be a good thing for the soil. In the long run, if land is given a rest every seven years it will produce better than if "run" constantly. But the greed of mankind is so great that it was thought to be a loss to let the land rest. And there are always certain ones in a nation who are too poor to own land, and in these years of rest the natural products which would be there, regardless of cultivation, would furnish food for the poor.

Verse 12. See chapter 20: 7-11 for extensive comments on this. Especially note what is said about the rest for the beasts as well as the people.

Verse 13. To be circumspect means to "watch your step." Look where you are going and guard against evil influences or surroundings. Idolatry was so prevalent that the bare mention of gods might provoke an interest in them. Therefore they were to exclude their names from the conversations.

Verses 14-16. The three yearly feasts or national assemblies are referred to by various names. I shall here quote the names as given at present passage and follow with corresponding name in parentheses. 1. unleavened bread (passover); 2. harvest of first-fruits (pentecost); 3. feast of ingathering (day of atonement). The reasons for the variations in the names will appear more clearly as we proceed in the study of the book.

Verse 17. The three times of assembling here are the same as in preceding paragraph. But the specification is added here that the males were the ones who were required to assemble. Of course no restrictions were made against any who wished to make the journey to Jerusalem to be at the feasts and generally a promiscuous multitude went. In the case of the family of Jesus it says his parents went every year to Jerusalem to the passover. This was one of the required feasts and we see that Mary went. Also, in Acts 2 we know that various classes were at Jerusalem. That was on Pentecost which was another of the three required gatherings. But since it would be frequently impossible for married women to travel the Lord graciously exempted them from the obligation.

Verse 18. Leaven was one of the things that were never to be burned on the altar. There were certain other restrictions as to what not to burn and what not to eat, and they will finally be pointed out in one statement. Also the "fat" mentioned here was to be regarded as belonging to the Lord exclusively. But this means that part of the animal that was exclusively so, and not what is sometimes called "fat meat." There is no such thing as fat meat in the sense that the word is used in the scriptures. This also will be noticed again.

Verse 19. The first half of this verse has been explained. The word "seethe" means to boil. To boil a kid in his mother's milk would indicate that it is a newly born kid or one not yet weaned. And a consideration on the basis of "being kind to animals" would suggest that the mother be left the company of her young for a while yet.

Verse 20. The word angel has a varied meaning. It could refer to celestial beings and in the absence of a context should be so considered. We know the scriptures teach that angels are ministering spirits for the assistance of heirs of salvation. In the days of special providence God made use of them, in a visible manner, frequently. But the word also is defined as a prophet or teacher or guide. And while God used these angels as occasion called, yet the most constant guide and teacher was Moses. And they were to obey his voice. More of this in next paragraph.

Verse 21. The word "pardon" is from a word that means to accept or tolerate. We know that God does pardon in the sense of forgiving, when the guilty person makes the required amends. But he will not accept the sinful conduct of his people.

Verse 22. The main thought in this verse for us is that of association. If I claim to be a friend of God I dare not be a friend of God's enemies. That would make me also an enemy of God. This is the principle set forth in this passage. The example given by the Lord is that he considers the enemies of his people as being his also, and he will treat them as such. Sometimes today professed disciples of Christ will claim they do not endorse the unscriptural practices and teaching of certain people. Yet they will show friendliness toward them or take pleasure in them. To do so makes them equally guilty with them.

Verse 23. The tribes mentioned here were products of the inferior descendants of Noah. They are here regarded as intruders since this land had been given to Abram and his posterity many years before. Therefore, it will be necessary to cut them off. In this they will be assisted by the power of God.

Verse 24. This is treated in chapter 20: 4-6. It is the same as here, except that not only must they not make any of these images, but they must destroy the ones made by other people. This harmonizes with the teaching found in the New Testament. For instance, in Eph. 5: 11 we are not only not to have fellowship with works of darkness, but also we are commanded to reprove them. Many preachers and others will profess not to believe in, or advocate, unscriptural things, yet will not oppose them. We are only halfway loyal if we refrain from advocating humanisms but do not also oppose them.

Verse 25. This verse mentions some of the temporal blessings that were to be placed on them on condition that they obey God. That was an age of providential rewards and punishments and they were based on condition of obedience.

Verse 26. To cast the young means that they miscarry. God would prevent this and would also see that their animals would be able to conceive. The promise that the number of their days would be fulfilled had a general application but especially here it means that the number of days of gestation would be fulfilled so that none of their cattle would miscarry.

Verse 27. One notable instance of this fear that preceded the Israelites is that of Rahab. (Josh. 2: 9.)

Verse 28. The hornet as mentioned here is defined by Strong as stinging wasps. The hornet as we know them today is not as much inclined to migration as the wasp. So they would be a very effective instrument in God's hands for the purpose he had in driving out the enemy. This does not mean that the Lord had to depend on material, or any other visible, means to accomplish his purpose. But he saw fit to use them here.

Verses 29, 30. These wild beasts have been kept under control through the years. Now if the heathen tribes were expelled completely at once the wild beasts would have a chance of multiplying before the Israelites had time to get settled. For this reason God designed to accomplish the desired result gradually.

Verse 31. The full extent of this verse has been overlooked by a vast majority of Bible students. It is the almost universal thought that the "promised land" and Canaan are one and the same. Were that the case then the two and half tribes who requested to be settled east of the Jordan would have been subject to censure for their request. Canaan was restricted to the land west of Jordan and the tribes mentioned here would have been outside of the promised land. Yet no criticism was ever made of them for wanting to settle there after their real desire was understood. But the verse now under consideration describes the bounds of the "promised land" and they take in all the territory from the Red Sea; sea of the Philistines, (meaning the Mediterranean because the Philistines bordered on that sea); the desert (Arabian Desert); and the "river," meaning the Euphrates. It is true that the nation never but once occupied or ruled over this territory because of disobedience. But Solomon did do so. (1 Kings 4: 21.) Now a question that has been presented in connection with this subject is: Why do we say that Moses never was permitted to enter the promised land if he was already in that land when he died. All that is necessary to have this clear is to observe that all lands or countries have a central site upon which, and around which, the whole territory is concerned. In great wars the objective is always to reach to the heart of the land of the enemy before feeling free in the possession of the place. Now Moses never was permitted to enter that part of this territory. He was permitted only to see it from afar. This excluded him from being in the center of the territory toward which he had been leading the people. So that, if we will always remember that while Canaan was in the bounds of the promised land, and the most central and desirable part, yet we must always make a distinction between the terms "Canaan" and "the promised land."

Verses 32, 33. Again we have a prohibition against association with improper persons. The reason for this is based on a fundamental fact of influence. In 1 Cor. 15: 33 Paul says that evil communications (companionships) corrupt good manners (morals). That is why Christians are so constantly warned about the kind of associates they have.

EXODUS 24

Verses 1, 2. *Come up.* For an explanation of this expression let the reader be sure to consult chapter 19: 3 and comments. Otherwise he is apt to become confused as to the number of times Moses went up on the top of the mount. *Elders.* This word is explained at length at chapter 3: 16, which see.

Verse 3. The "judgments" mentioned here are the same explained at chapter 21: 1. Let us observe that in the assurance which the people made to Moses what they would do, they considered the words which Moses gave to them as words "which the Lord hath said." This was true and they did not attempt to make a distinction between the authority of God and that of Moses, as the sabbatarians today are doing.

Verse 4. *Moses wrote.* Since we know that God did the writing on the tables of stone we will know that in this place it refers to what Moses wrote. And this thought is confirmed by the mention of a "book" in verse 7, which will be considered later. But let it be observed that Moses wrote words of the Lord. Now the author of this statement is the inspired writer of this book. Therefore, those who deny that the law of Moses was the law of God are rejecting part of God's law.

Verse 5. In the close of preceding verse and in this, mention is made of an altar and of sacrifices. This will not confuse us if we bear in mind that the institution of the Mosaic worship has not yet been installed. They are still under the Patriarchal Dispensation and thus an altar under a hill or any other place would be in order.

Verse 6. Mention is made of blood. It should be remembered that since the days of Abel, God has required that blood be used in connection with the services rendered to him. Doubtless this was partly for the purpose of educating the world as to the value and necessity of bloodshed in any system of religion used for spiritual benefits. As to why half of the blood was first put in basons will appear in verse 8.

Verse 7. Here the book is mentioned in which Moses had done the writing. This then could not have been the tables of stone for Moses did not write on them. Yet the book that is mentioned here is called "the covenant." The sabbatarians try to make it appear that the "covenant" is what was written on the tables. This is in order to avoid their inconsistency of not obeying all of the law which they pretend to be "keeping." Another thing that should be observed here is that the book of Exodus is not always in chronological order. Sometimes the narrative will jump ahead of the immediate connection and include an event or report of something related to the present line of thought but taking place at another time. This will explain the statement of the promise the people here made to Moses that they would obey all that was commanded them in the book. And yet, right at the time all these conversations were going on, Moses has not even been to the top of the mount, where he actually received the tables, or the book. But the matters being related are statements that are historical as to what happened, but not so as to date. Not until we reach the end of this chapter is Moses at the peak of the mount, which is the place where all the instructions were given. As further proof that such is the case, let the reader see chapter 32: 1 where he will see that all that has been recorded previously was before Moses came down from the mount the first time, and had been there forty days and nights.

Verse 8. This explains why he divided the blood in verse 6. And by consulting Heb. 9: 19 we will see that not only did Moses sprinkle blood on the people at this time, but also on the book.

Verses 9, 10. See chapter 3: 16 for explanation of "elders." Since no one can see God directly and live (ch. 33: 20), we must conclude that the angel of God is meant. We have information that all the communications at this place were between Moses and the angel of God. This is shown in Acts 7: 53; Gal. 3: 19.

Verse 11. *Nobles*. This is from ATSIYL and defined "(in secondary sense of separation): an extremity, also a noble."—Strong. These seem to be outstanding men but not necessarily the older men. The verse means that on this class God did not lay his hand at this time, in the way of calling them up at the same time and manner he called Moses and Aaron in verse nine.

Verse 12. We know what is meant by the tables of stone. Also in this particular place the "law" mentioned had to be the same for it says "I have written," which was true of the words written on the tables but not true as to the book, for we have already read that Moses did that writing. And so we have an additional proof that the ten commandments were relayed to the people through Moses and hence, whatever distinction we are to make in the authority of Moses and God as to the book or "ceremonial law," we should also make as to the decalogue.

Verse 13. *Minister*. This is from a word that means an attendant. We see Joshua in that relation to Moses in various places. He was always "in waiting" on Moses and was always faithful.

Verse 14. In this verse we can see that Joshua was allowed to be nearer to him than the elders or even than Aaron. The people were told to bring their inquiries to Aaron and Hur in his absence.

Verses 15-17. Here Moses goes farther up toward the peak of the mount. Then the glory of God in the form of a cloud settled on the mount. This condition continued for six days before Moses was addressed. Evidently this near approach to the Lord was as a means of preparing Moses for the closer and more intimate approach which is soon to follow. On the 7th day the Lord called to Moses out of the midst of the cloud and he could have a sight of him, (or the angel of God). And this glory was so great that it could be seen in a general way by the Israelites.

Verse 18. This verse brings us to the time when Moses finally went to the top or extremity of the mount where he remained for forty days and forty nights, and where he actually received the instructions we have been reading about for several chapters, and also the ones to be found in following chapters, as far as chapter 31. Hence, let the reader bear in mind that all the things we will be reading about in the chapters to come, down to the end of chapter 31, were said to Moses while in the mount the first time.

EXODUS 25

Verse 1. The language of this verse is repeated so frequently that the force of it ought to be recognized. If the Lord spake to Moses and then commanded him to tell it to the people it indicates that whatever Moses commanded was equivalent to its having been spoken by the Lord to the people. Hence again, the sabbatarians are in contempt of God when they discount the authority of Moses.

Verse 2. A stipulation in the giving of these materials was that it must be done with a willing mind. God does not appreciate gifts or services offered to him that are forced or given grudgingly. The same principle is taught in 2 Cor. 9: 7.

Verses 3-7. All of these materials except the wood were brought with them from Egypt. See chapter 12: 35, 36. This wood which is the only kind used in the building of the tabernacle and its furniture is named in the Hebrew text SHITTIYM. It is translated by Strong as "acacia." And in the Oxford Cyclopedic Concordance it is described as follows: "acacia wood, a very hard wood, used for the tabernacle and its fittings. It is one of the trees from which gum arabic is obtained." From here on when this wood is to be mentioned it will be called acacia.

Verse 8. *Sanctuary*. This is from a word that Strong defines "a consecrated thing or place." Now we know that God is everywhere and none can get out of his sight. Yet in a special sense, he has always had some specified thing or place where he would meet with his people in a certain relationship. In the Patriarchal Dispensation it was at the family altar on which the animal sacrifices were offered. Now in the more public institution of the Mosaic Dispensation he wishes a building to be used for the purpose. And that means that in order to meet with God in the congregational services it is necessary to come to the building made for that purpose. In the Christian Dispensation that place is the church. (Eph. 3: 21.)

Verse 9. Had Moses not made the tabernacle according to the divine pattern, or seen to it that the workmen made it that way, he would have been condemned. But since no criticism was ever made against him on this score we must conclude that it was so made. And so again we have an instance of the authority of Moses.

Verses 10, 11. This ark was made of acacia wood and plated with gold. It was to be "pure" gold. The fundamental and universal meaning of this word is "unmixed." This would apply whether the word is used regarding moral or physical character. In this present case it would have the force of meaning gold without alloy. A cubit in the Old Testament times was about one and a half feet and will be so considered in this work. The "crown" mentioned is an ornamental moulding of gold around the ark.

Verses 12-15. The rings were of gold and placed at the four corners of the ark. But they must be so placed that their openings would serve the sides and not the ends of the ark. This was to let the staves be used as handle bars. These staves or handle bars were made of wood and plated with gold. They were used by slipping them through the rings at the corners of the ark. The purpose of all this is here stated to be that the ark might be borne with them. These staves were to be in the rings at all times. This provision for moving the ark explains the mistake that was made in 2 Sam. 6. The ark was being moved on a cart instead of being carried. Also, the reason Uzzah was slain was that he touched the ark at all, not because he was not a priest, as is popularly thought. Even a priest had no right to touch the ark, neither did they need to, since these staves, which were supposed to be placed in the rings constantly, were there for the purpose of carrying the ark.

Verse 16. The words "testimony," "testament," "witnesses," "covenant"; have a generally similar meaning. The tables and also the book which Moses wrote were referred to usually as the testimony. And the ark was the repository of this testimony and hence is referred to in many places as the ark of the testimony.

Verse 17. *Mercy seat.* The second of these words is not in the original. The first one is from KAPPORETH and defined by Strong "a lid (used only of the cover of the sacred Ark)." Strong further says the word is derived from KAPHAR which he defines "a primitive root: to cover (specifically with bitumen); figuratively to expiate or condone, to placate or cancel." Thus we see the mercy seat literally means a covering, and served that purpose over the Ark. But since it was to be the place where God would meet the High Priest in the atonement service for the congregation, it came to be thought of as a figurative covering in the sense of cancelling the sins of the nation or covering them. So we have the interesting fact of the mercy seat serving two purposes. A literal lid or covering for the Ark, and a figurative covering for the sins of the nation.

Verses 18, 19. These cherubims are said by Strong to be imaginary figures of uncertain derivation. The Schaff-Herzog Encyclopedia describes them as being creatures somewhat like angels yet a distinct class of beings. They take on many of the glories of God and are reprensentative of the divine presence. The figures considered at present were placed on the lid of the ark, one on each end.

Verse 20. As to the posture of these cherubims whether standing or kneeling, we have no information. All the pictures I have seen of them represent them as kneeling, but that is purely speculation. Other features of their posture are stated in the text. They were spreading their wings in a protective or shielding manner. They were facing each other and had their faces inclined downward toward the mercy seat as if in an inquiring attitude. This reminds us of the statement in 1 Peter 1: 12.

Verse 21. We will notice that the testimony was placed *in* the ark.

Verse 22. See comments at verse 8 as to the meeting place with God.

Verses 23-25. The table was made of acacia wood and overlaid with gold. Some of the details of the ornamentation are a little indefinite. But it is evident that this table was to have ornamentations that were not necessary for practical use. These borders and crowns were ornamental mouldings set off with a margin or apparent binding, and it was a hand breadth.

Verses 26, 27. These rings were for the same purpose as those in the corners of the ark. They furnished a place to receive the staves to be used when moving the table. The rings were fastened over against (near) the ornamental moulding.

Verse 28. These staves were made of acacia wood and plated with gold and used for the purpose of carrying the table.

Verse 29. The need for these vessels is not apparent here since nothing was done with these loaves during the seven days following their placement on the table. After they had been left on the table a week, in solemn religious memorial, they were taken from the table and put in a proper place of storage for the literal use as food for the priests. (Lev. 24: 5-9; 1 Sam. 21: 6). It is reasonable to conclude that in using this bread as food to be eaten in the holy place, they would have need of some vessels and utensils. And what better or more appropriate place to keep them than on the table where the bread had been kept? It would be furthermore unreasonable to suppose that the bread would be eaten alone, and not with the accompanying articles of diet which would call for such things as mentioned here.

Verse 31. Another rendering for candlestick is "lampstand." This is more accurate since in those days they did not have candles as we think of them. The only artificial means of lights was by the burning of olive oil. And this would call for a stand and some kind of containers to hold the oil. Of course since all the things about the tabernacle were to be made "for the glory and for beauty" which was typical of the spiritual building of the New Testament (the church, Eph. 5: 27), there was much more detail required that was not necessary for the practical use. These knops and flowers were ornamental figures hammered into the candlestick. Also some ornamental bowls were made in likeness of the practical ones at the top of each stem and used to contain the oil. The knops had a bodily existence as a whole and were beaten into ornamental form. The word for them indicates they were in appearance a circular band not only for ornamental purpose, but also as a sort of reinforcement and as a base on which another part of the instrument rested. The word candlestick is used in two senses. One is to take in the entire article of furniture, and another is in reference to the central shaft from which the six branches extended.

Verse 32. These are the branches referred to above. They were to come out of the "sides" of the main shaft. This means that they were to come out in a uniform direction so that all the six branches would be parallel somewhat in the form of a candelabrum, and on the top of these six branches as well as on the main shaft, there were bowls for containing the oil for the light.

Verse 33. The items mentioned in this verse refer to the ornamental forms beaten into the several branches.

Verse 34. This refers to the main shaft of the candlestick. Since it was to have four bowls, the three were for ornamental purposes and the one was for practical use at the top of the shaft.

Verse 35. Gold is heavy and soft, especially gold without alloy. So as a reinforcement for the branches coming out of the main shaft, then turning and going upward to support the oil bowl, there were other knops ornamented with flowers in the main shaft just under the place where two branches came out. That would call for three of these reinforcements and explains the peculiar repetition of the "knop under two branches of the same" in this verse.

Verse 36. *Of the same.* This means they must be alike and that they must be made of pure gold; and also, that they must be beaten, not cast nor carved.

Verse 37. *Against it.* This means the light was to shine over to the opposite side of the room of the tabernacle. We have already seen that the instrument was made in the form of a candelabrum and by placing it so as to face the opposite it would give full benefit to the area facing it.

Verse 38. *Snuffdishes.* This is from MACHTAH and defined "a pan for live coals." Olive oil, like other combustible material in liquid form, would not readily burn in a way satisfactory for continuous light. Therefore some form of wicking would be used. By the coming of morning this wick would have become charred and need to be snuffed or pinched off. And this would be while it was still hot. Hence the tongs or snuffers for pinching off the charred parts, and the dishes for catching them.

Verse 39. *Talent of pure gold.* This is given in Oxford Cyclopedic Concordance as 6150 pounds, worth $29,940. And by consulting chapter 37: 22, 24 we learn it was to be made of one piece which was hammered out into the required form.

Verse 40. God has always told his people what he wants done and how to do it. It is therefore without excuse for a mistake to be made in performing the Lord's work.

EXODUS 26

Verse 1. It should be understood that these "curtains" consist of separate strips of this fine goods to be fastened together as described in following verses. The first group of these strips contained ten, and were to form one great sheet as a covering for the tabernacle.

Verse 2. The size of these strips was 4x28 cubits, and they were to be uniform.

Verse 3. Of these ten strips there were to be made two separate groups and they were to be coupled or joined together in some way, doubtless with a needle. There would then be two large pieces, each 20x28 cubits. Now they must be fastened together so that only one grand piece, or curtain, or covering would be formed. This was done by forming loops in the long edges, that is the side 28 cubits long.

Verses 4-6. The edges or selvage of these groups of five were to be formed into loops so as to make a place to join the two groups. After this was done there were to be fifty taches, or clasps of gold made, and used to connect these loops that had been formed from the selvage. And by closing these clasps through the loops that would join the two groups of strips into one grand sheet or curtain, 28x40 cubits. The row of gold clasps would be through the center of the whole piece. That is, the fifty clasps would be distributed along the 28 cubit sides of the groups of five strips. In other words, there would be 20 cubits on each side of the row of clasps. Since this is the first curtain it would be the first one to be spread over the tabernacle.

Verses 7-11. A second curtain was made similar to the first one, yet with some variations. There were eleven strips instead of ten. Five were joined in one group and six in another. The two groups were to be joined into one grand curtain with brass clasps instead of gold. Another difference was that the strips were 30 cubits long instead of 28. Now if this second grand curtain were spread over the top of the first one and in a way to correspond by matching them from the end where the five strips were joined together, then there would be an extra curtain or strip in the front. This was to be doubled in the forefront of the tabernacle. This word "forefront" shows that the two curtains or coverings thus formed are to be matched from the rear of the tabernacle. That would leave one curtain or strip, four cubits hanging over and down in front. That would be a benefit in stormy weather. But when not needed for such purpose it would be folded or doubled back over the top out of the way.

Verse 12. In this verse the word "curtain" is used with reference to the one group of five strips. This group we have seen would be 20 cubits. But it says here that half of it was to hang over the back of the tabernacle. That means that ten cubits would hang down over the back of the tabernacle. And that would also show that the tabernacle was ten cubits high, which corresponds with the length of the boards standing up as stated in verse 15 below.

Verse 13. This verse indicates that the first strips or curtains lacked a cubit on each side of covering the tabernacle, or of coming to the ground. Since we already know that this grand curtain was 28 cubits that direction we can understand that it was 30 cubits from the ground on one side to the ground on the other. Also, since we know the tabernacle was ten cubits high, from the length of the boards, we can find the width by subtracting 20 from 30. The words here, "remaineth in length," mean that the first grand curtain lacked a cubit on each side of covering the tabernacle. But the second one, being thirty cubits instead of 28 would completely cover the building.

Verse 14. We are not given the details for making these additional curtains. We do not know the size nor manner of fastening. But being made of skins they would naturally be stronger and specially adapted for protection over the more delicate ones underneath.

Verse 15. These boards made of the acacia wood formed the solid or framework part of the tabernacle. They were to be standing up, which means they were the sides of the building and gave it the size and formed the structure of the institution.

Verse 16. Here is where we learn the height of the tabernacle since these boards formed the framework. Also we should observe the width of each board since that is the way we will learn the length of the building.

Verse 17. A tenon is a pin, or projection, formed at the end of a piece and made to fit into a mortise, to form a joint or connection. There were two of these made in the end of these boards. They were to set in "order" one against the other. This word is from SHALAB and defined by Strong "to space off; intensively (evenly), to make equidistant." By making the two tenons of each board equally distant from each other that would insure uniformity and the rigidity of the general framework. And thus the foot of the boards would be kept aligned. The top will be held in line by long bars to be described below.

Verse 18. This gives the number of boards in one side and since we have seen they are 1½ cubits wide, that makes the length of the tabernacle thirty cubits.

Verse 19. These blocks of silver were to form the foundation of the tabernacle. Each block or socket had two mortises to receive the two tenons described in verse 17. Since there were twenty boards on the side, it would require forty of the sockets, or blocks.

Verses 20, 21. This is identical with the description of the south side, verses 18, 19.

Verses 22-25. I do not know why the word for the west end is in the plural. But at this place there were six of the regular sized boards which would enclose nine cubits of the end leaving one cubit to be divided between the two corners. While they are here called boards we would think of them more in the nature of corner posts. Taking them as a group there would be eight of the boards and each must have the two tenons and two sockets. No details are given as to the form of the rings used. In some manner the corners of the sides and end were hooped together by the use of the rings.

Verses 26-29. Even the use of the tenons and mortises together with the rings at the corners was not sufficient to hold the work together as the Lord wished it. Thus the bars of the acacia wood were required. There were five of them altogether. Four were used by slipping them through rings of gold arranged somewhat in the manner of eyelets up and down on the sides of the boards. These rings were placed on the boards in equal spacing. In that way they formed a row of rings from one end of the tabernacle to the other and would serve as a general bracing for the framework. But still this was not sufficient. It must be made not only firm but rigid. For this purpose the fifth bar was used. This was called the "middle" bar. This word is from TAVEK and Strong defines it: "from an unused root meaning to sever a bisection; i. e. (by implication) the center." There was a mortise cut through the middle of each board in a way that would form one continuous opening through the boards of the side. The fifth bar then would be made in such a size and shape that it would fit into this continuous opening and act as a key to the whole formation and thus lock it and make it firm.

Verses 31, 32. This vail became a famous article, as part of the holy building in the literal temple later, and in the tabernacle here. It was to form the partition between the two rooms of the tabernacle known as the Holy and Most Holy places. The vail was suspended on four pillars of acacia wood overlaid with gold. And the pillars were to rest on four sockets or blocks of silver. Now we can sum up the number of silver blocks or sockets used in the tabernacle. There were forty on each side, sixteen at the end and four under the vail, one hundred in all.

Verse 33. We have learned that the tabernacle as a whole was thirty cubits long, that it was divided into two rooms, and that the partition was this vail. But thus far we have not ascertained just where this vail was placed so as to tell us the sizes of these rooms. The present verse will give us this information. As already learned in verses 1-6, the gold taches of the first covering were used to join the two group of five strips and that twenty cubits of the grand curtain would be on each side of the taches. Also, the grand curtain was placed over the tabernacle in such a way that the whole of it started from the ground at the rear and reached up and to the "square" or end of the top in front. That would bring the row of clasps or taches at a place twenty cubits from the front and ten cubits from the top of the rear. Now the present verse says the vail was to be hung up under the taches. Therefore, the holy place or first room of the tabernacle was twenty cubits long and the second room or Most Holy place was ten cubits. And in a further summing up on this point, the first room was twenty by ten by ten cubits; the second room was ten cubits each way.

Verse 34. The mercy seat was described in chapter 25: 17. It was to form a cover for the ark as well as a place for the High Priest to meet with God to obtain mercy for the congregation.

Verse 35. Two of the articles of furniture for the first room or holy place are located here. The table on the north and the candlestick on the south.

Verses 36, 37. Thus far we have the tabernacle described as to its sides, top, west end, and partition between the two rooms. But the east end is still open and that is to be described now. There was to be a vail of the same material and workmanship as the one used for the partition, but this one was suspended on five pillars of acacia wood overlaid with gold. The foundation was of sockets of brass instead of silver.

EXODUS 27

Verse 1. The altar here was made of the same wood but overlaid with brass. Since it is to be used to hold fire for the sacrifices it would be necessary to make it of hardier metal than gold. It was five cubits square and three cubits high.

Verse 2. Flesh does not burn as readily as other material so it would assist in the procedure to have these horns at the corners to help hold the carcass up from crowding down in a dense heap. The horns were to be "of the same," which means they were to be alike and to be made of brass.

Verse 3. These articles mentioned would be necessary where wood is being burned daily, and also, the flesh-hooks would be needed in handling the bodies of the animals. All these things were to be made of brass.

Verse 4. Imagine a large box with the top and bottom out. It is three cubits high and five cubits square. It is to be used as an altar. That requires a place on which to lay the animal and also a place to receive the ashes. This was arranged by making a brazen net just the size of the altar and suspended down inside the altar on four rings to connect with the inside walls of the box. Thus the animal would be on the grate and underneath would be the ash pit.

Verse 5. *Compass, midst.* The correct definition of these words will lead us to the meaning of the verse. The first one is from KARKOB and defined by Strong, "a rim or top margin." The second word is from CHETSIY and defined, "the half or middle." So the verse means that this grate was allowed to go down under the top rim as far as to the middle of the altar.

Verse 6-8. Staves made of acacia wood and overlaid with brass were run through rings at the corner on the same principle as those on the table and ark. This arrangement provided a means of carrying the altar when it was necessary to journey.

Verses 9-11. The tabernacle proper has been described, now we will see the description of an enclosure for the building. This enclosure is called the court. This word is defined by Strong: "as a yard as enclosed by a fence." There were no boards used in it as was the case in the tabernacle. It is composed of pillars and curtains. The north and south sides were the same and here described. There were twenty pillars made of acacia wood and overlaid with brass. On these pillars was suspended a curtain made of fine twined linen. Twined means it was woven from threads that were twisted, which indicates a hard, firm fabric. The curtain to be suspended on each side was one hundred cubits long. The curtain was attached to the pillar with hooks on the pillars and with the fillets (fasteners) in the curtain.

Verse 12. The description of the yard enclosure for the west end was the same as for the sides except that it was fifty cubits instead of one hundred.

Verses 13-15. The east end of the enclosure was the same in extent as that of the west but was divided as to the curtains in order to provide a gate or opening for entrance. That calls for fifteen cubits on each side of the entrance, with their corresponding pillars and curtains.

Verses 16, 17. The gate of the court was made of fine twined linen and of the pieces of blue and purple and scarlet. It would require four pillars with their sockets.

Verse 18. Here we have in explicit language the dimensions of the court. It was one hundred by fifty by five cubits. A much larger place than the tabernacle proper. But there was more need for room here since the people in general were allowed to enter it while none but the priests could enter the tabernacle.

Verse 19. No mention has been previously made of these pins and no description is given here except that they were to be made of brass. Some items of a plan are so evidently necessary that specific mention is not necessary. Elsewhere in the Bible mention is made of cords. (Chapter 35: 18.) Of course, these cords and pins were used as further supports for the structure and would be used as needed.

Verse 20. Pure olive oil would mean unmixed or unadulterated oil. The word "beaten" is just another word of the same practical meaning as pure. This light is said here to burn "always." This is from a word that means "constantly," in the sense of the general practice. It does not mean that the light burned 24 hours of the day for the specific statement of it elsewhere (chapter 30: 7, 8; Lev. 24: 2, 3), shows that not to be the case. The expression is used in the same sense as Christians are commanded to pray always.

Verse 21. This verse corroborates the thoughts offered on preceding one. To order it means to put it in order; get it in readiness for use. And here also is an interesting statement as to what it meant by "before" the vail or testimony where the ark is located. It is in the first room or holy place since we know that is where the candlestick was located. Thus when anything is said to be before the vail we are to understand that to mean in the first room, or holy place.

EXODUS 28

Verse 1. Here is a place for the reader to have a clear knowledge as to the position of Aaron and his family in the system then in force. They were to be separate from all the rest of the congregation for the priesthood. No one who was not a member of Aaron's family had a right to that office or work. See 1 Chr. 23: 13 for even more specific statements on this subject. Throughout the entire existence of the nation of Israel no one could lawfully serve as priest but a lineal descendant of Aaron.

Verse 2. The priesthood of Aaron and his sons was a type of the priesthood of Christ and his disciples. (Heb. 3: 1; 1 Peter 2: 9.) Since we know that Christ and his followers were to have spritual garments of spiritual glory and beauty, so the priests under the Jewish system had them. The words "glory" and "beauty" are defined by Strong as "splendor" and "ornament."

Verse 3. These "wise hearted" persons were not necessarily inspired in a miraculous way as we generally think of that word. It refers to the talents that God gives to people through the providence of nature. It is well also to note that God requires the people to do something. No one will doubt God's ability to compose the tabernacle, all the things pertaining to it, and the garments for the priests, by miracle. But it has always been the rule for him to require his creatures to cooperate with him. Had it been impossible for them to make these things, of course the Lord would have done so if he wished them to be used. But it was not impossible.

Verses 4, 5. The six articles of priestly garments are mentioned in this paragraph. Their several descriptions will follow in this chapter. They were composed of gold as the only metal; and of blue, scarlet and fine twined linen.

Verses 6, 7. The ephod was made of a piece large enough to be folded and reach from the waist to the shoulders. Since it was doubled it would have the "two shoulder pieces joined at the two edges." That is, since there are two shoulders and also since there were two thicknesses, there would be two loose ends or edges at the shoulders. So they were directed to join them.

Verse 8. The curious girdle is called "skilfully woven band," but since the word has nothing in the original, I will pass this on as it is. But as there would be a tendency to be unsteady and loose at the waist, this girdle would serve as a thing to hold the ephod.

Verses 9-12. The onyx being a semiprecious stone and beautiful, would provide a very suitable surface on which to do this carving. The names here mean the sons of Jacob and wherever the starting place was, Reuben would be first engraved and then the others in the order of their birth. Six of the names would be carved on each stone and these stones were placed at the shoulders of the ephod. The engraving was like a signet. That is, the engraving was in the manner of that carved on a signature ring. These stones were put in "ouches," which means settings.

Verses 13, 14. These chains were wreathen or braided and had a gold setting at the ends and served as a fastener to the garment.

Verse 15. It is called the breastplate of judgment because one of the means that God has of delivering his judgments or decrees was connected with it and will be explained in verse 30 below.

Verse 16. This piece was square after being doubled and the size in length and breadth of a span. This means the spread of the fingers.

Verse 17-20. These were ornamental gems of a texture to be carved as were the ones for the shoulder pieces. The names of the twelve sons of Israel were engraved on these stones and they were fastened with gold settings. All this was to symbolize the idea that Aaron would be carrying the nation with him when he was about the service of the tabernacle. It was a material type of the function of Jesus who cares for us.

Verse 21. This was referred to above, the expression "children of Israel" again meaning the twelve sons of Jacob who represented the entire nation of Israel.

Verses 22-25. These chains were wreathen, which means they were braided or made by small wires of gold, twined and woven into a sort of tape. At the ends were gold rings, and the rings were fastened at the shoulder so that the combination of rings and chains would furnish a support for the piece. With the twelve stones attached it would have some weight and these chains were for their support.

Verses 26-29. This breastplate was doubled, making it necessary to provide for its support underneath. Hence these chains and rings mentioned in this paragraph.

Verse 30. *Urim and Thummim.* Not much is known about these curious objects. The Schaff-Herzog Encyclopedia has this to say of them: "Mentioned first in Ex. 28: 30, in connection with the 'breastplate' of the high priest, and in a manner to imply that they were sensible objects, at least two in number, which were put into the 'breastplate,' which was, indeed, a sort of bag. This is all we know about them. They were used as a sort of divine oracle, probably with certain traditional ceremonies: sometimes no answer could be obtained from them (1 Sam 28: 6)." While we do not know just how these objects worked, we do know that they were one of the various means God used to communicate his word to his people. It should be borne in mind that these things were of no use unless in the hands of the rightful person. (Ezr. 2: 63.) In thinking about this strange means of divine communication it is well to refer to Heb. 1: 1. In the days of preparation for the final and complete revelation of God's will through Christ and his apostles he used various literal and material means to make known his will. If the reader wishes to know all that the Bible says about these objects he may read the following passages: Ex. 28: 30; Lev. 8: 8; Num. 27: 21; Deut. 33: 8; 1 Sam. 28:6; Ezr. 2: 63. Since this breastplate was folded or doubled the inside furnished a place for these.

Verses 31, 32. This was a loose garment to be worn over the other pieces of the priest's wardrobe. A habergeon was a kind of stout coat of mail or protective garment. And it would be reinforced at the neck where the opening for the head was made by a twisted binding. The comparison here is only to this kind of binding that was made in both the priest's robe and the coat of mail used by others. Not a comparison between the garments themselves.

Verses 33, 34. These pomegranates were ornamental creations made of the fine materials like those used elsewhere in the service. They were fastened on the hem of the robe for ornament, also to form a protection for the bells fastened there. As they would alternate round the hem of the garment the sound of the bells would be clear.

Verse 35. Of course we will not suppose the sound of the bells was to prevent death. But as long as the bells could be heard the watchful people on the outside would know that all was well, and that no irregularity had been committed by the priest to cause him to be smitten by the Lord while in the place.

Verses 36-38. The mitre was a head piece and this plate was made of gold on which was engraved "HOLINESS TO THE LORD." This kind of expression always means that holiness is to be attributed to the Lord. The plate was mounted on a lace of blue. It was then attached to the mitre. For Aaron to bear the iniquity of the congregation means that he was to be responsible for their conduct as a people. That is why he performed the services in the tabernacle. It was to atone for the sins of the congregation as a whole, not for the individual's sins. As for those, each man had his individual duty to perform.

Verse 39. This coat was a garment somewhat in the style of a cape and worn by the high priest in connection with the other articles of clothing.

Verse 40. We observe a great difference between the garments for the sons of Aaron from the ones described before. That is appropriate since they represent the common priests today (Christians), while the priesthood of Christ was typified by Aaron. The "bonnets" were a form of cap. And all these things were for glory and for beauty. These qualities were literal but represented the spiritual glory and beauty of Christians.

Verses 41-43. These verses include all the garments for Aaron and his sons to be worn according to directions.

EXODUS 29

Verses 1-3. All official or professional services for God must be prepared by some forms of consecration. That is true of both the Old Testament and the New Testament systems.

Verse 4. Since the tabernacle was the place where God met his people it would be the proper place to bring these men for consecration just as the church is the place where men must come today to be inducted into the service of Christ. Those men were to be washed with water just as water of consecration is used in the system of Christ.

Verses 5, 6. These men were not allowed to enter into active service to God until they had put on the holy garments. Likewise, men are not permitted to enter the active service to Christ today until they have put off their garments of sin and put on Christ.

Verse 7. The oil used in Bible times was olive oil. It was used for various purposes. Among them was the practice of pouring it over the head of the person to be consecrated or to be acknowledged as to his service. As olive oil was the means of light in those days the pouring of it on the heads of men in a ceremonial manner would signify that light from above was bestowed on them. It came to be considered as a symbol of mental and spiritual bestowal on people, in the Christian Dispensation. (1 John 2: 20, 27.)

Verses 8, 9. After putting on the garments of the priests the significant statement is made that the priesthood was to be theirs perpetually.

Verses 10-12. It required the shedding of blood for the consecrating of these priests. So in the system of Christ. But the difference is that sacrifices were provided by others for the O.T. priests, while Christ had to furnish his own sacrifice for his consecration, and that was himself. The bulk of the blood was poured out at the bottom of the altar. And the blood of Christ was poured out at the foot of the cross.

Verse 13. We do not know just why the Lord wished these partitions of the animal since all was to be consumed with fire. But it was the divine command and was to be done or be rejected. When mention is made of "fat" in connection with the service it does not mean what the common speech of mankind calls by such name. It means the part that is like the suet in cattle. God always claimed that for himself, and the people were not permitted to eat it nor to make any other personal use thereof. The caul is the diaphragm, a sort of membrane that is between the liver and the upper part of the body. All the parts of the animal designated in the verse were to be burned on the altar.

Verse 14. The significant idea in this verse is that the body of the animal was to be taken on the outside of the camp and burned. This was a type of the fact that Jesus did not die in the city but was taken to the outside. (Heb. 13: 11-13.)

Verses 15-18. While we are not permitted to speculate as to why these details were required yet we may and should observe that God has always had his own plans for having things done and that man was always happy when he respected those plans. One object in requiring the performance of services that did not have any apparent reason, yet which brought a blessing on the ones faithful, was to teach people in that educational age of the world that we should have faith enough in God to do what he commands whether it looks reasonable or not.

Verses 19, 20. In putting the blood on the persons of the men to be consecrated to the Lord we note the significant portions to which it was applied. The ear, hand and foot. That would suggest that consecrating the ear would mean hearing the truth. The hand means doing the right things. The foot means going in righteous paths.

Verse 21. We see that much use was made of blood in those times. It was to get the world ready to appreciate the blood of Christ that was shed for the salvation of men and that represents the great cost of our redemption.

Verses 22-25. The parts of the animal mentioned in this passage were first waved before the Lord. That is, they were placed in the hands of the men and they would give a swinging motion from side to side before the Lord. This may seem to be a useless performance, but is just another instance where the faith of the performer is tested. After this waving was done, then the shoulder that had been waved was taken out and all the rest was burned on the altar.

Verses 26-28. The strange actions described in these verses have been already commented on to some extent. But let it be always borne in mind that it is the typical and educational age. God is teaching his people by object lessons. He is preparing the world for the perfect system some day to be brought in where his people shall "walk by faith." In those days God had people perform acts that could not have had any possible physical effect and yet which brought the blessing of the Lord. Then when the time came vhen he would command other appar-ently useless acts of obedience, where he blessings would not be visible as hey were back there, yet they would perform them by faith, being sure that he promised spiritual blessing would come even though invisible. The breast was waved or swung from side to side, and the shoulder was lifted up and down.

Verses 29, 30. This passage reveals to us that not only did the priesthood descend from Aaron to his son, but also his garments. Here is one contrast between Aaron and Christ. Aaron had a son while Christ did not. Again, Aaron died and would leave a vacancy to be filled by another. But Christ never died and thus does not need a successor.

Verses 31-33. The men to be consecrated to the priest's office ate of the food that was connected with the ceremony of consecration. But while Jesus ate of the old passover on the night of his betrayal, yet he did not eat of that which was to represent his own bodily sacrifice. This will be brought out in the study of Luke 22.

Verse 34. The remains of the flesh of consecration should not be eaten as food in the common manner but must be burned. Likewise, when the Lord's supper is observed and some of the bread is left it should not be given to children to be made ordinary food, but should be reverently destroyed.

Verses 35-37. Much repetition is seen in this period of the consecration occasion but the matter in hand is a serious one and nothing was left out that would impress them with the dignity of the office and work they were about to assume.

Verses 38-42. I have included all these verses in this paragraph because taken as a whole they describe one of the very prominent institutions of the Mosaic system. The title that might be aptly applied to the paragraph is "the daily sacrifice." It is also called the "continual" offering. Read carefully the items of description that are given here. There were two lambs offered each day. One in the forenoon and one in the afternoon. These were doubled on the sabbath day. It should be further remembered that this daily sacrifice was a national ordinance and the animals furnished out of the money of the public treasury. As corroboration of this I shall quote from Josephus the historian of that people. "The law requires, that out of the public expenses a lamb of the first year be killed every day, at the beginning and at the ending of the day; but on the seventh day, which is called the Sabbath, they kill two, and sacrifice them in the same manner." Josephus 3-10-1.

Verses 43, 44. Again the outstanding idea is that God had a specified place where he would meet with the people. The tabernacle and the altar in connection therewith were the places or things where he would meet them. And this fact is what sanctified them. The church is the place today where God is to be met in a spiritual way.

Verses 45, 46. The good situation of the children of Israel was never to be lost from sight. They had been in bondage so long in Egypt that God wished them never to forget it. And as a signal indication of the great fact in their history the various animal sacrifices were ordered and were kept by the congregation. This was all the more necessary in view of the prevalence of idolatry being practiced by the heathen nations among whom the children of Israel were constantly to be thrown. The power of example is so great that some kind of preventive was necessary.

EXODUS 30

Verses 1-3. Unlike the other altar, this one was overlaid with gold. Also it was for the purpose of burning incense and not anything produced by animals. It was made of acacia wood and was a cubit square and two cubits high. The horns would be for ornamental purposes only, since no flesh or other solid matter was ever burned on it. The crown or top moulding would also be for ornament.

Verse 4. Since this article of furniture would not be as heavy as some of the others, there were but two rings made and they would be fastened at the corners diagonally opposite each other. These gold rings were fastened under the crown or moulding.

Verse 5. Staves of acacia wood were made and overlaid with gold and these were used as handle bars slipped through the rings to carry the altar.

Verse 6. It was to be placed "before" the vail. This was seen in chapter 27: 20, 21 to be in the same room as the candlestick, which was the holy place, or first room.

Verse 7. As the lamps had been burning all night they would be needing dressing or having the charred wicking snuffed. So when Aaron went in there in the morning for that purpose he was to burn incense on this golden altar.

Verse 8. In this place we see that the lamps were not burning 24 hours of the day, but were burned from evening until morning. And when Aaron went in to light the lamps at evening he was to burn incense on the golden altar. "Perpetual incense" means that the practice of burning it as here described was to be observed continually.

Verse 9. This verse prohibits the burning of anything on this altar but incense. Not only so, but they must not burn any strange incense. That means incense obtained from outside of the congregation and the lawful source. (See verses 34, 35.)

Verse 10. On the tenth day of the seventh month the high priest always went into the most holy place with blood that had been taken from the sacrifice for sin offering. As he passed by this golden altar he put some of the blood on the horns of it. But it was not burned and hence did not contradict verse 9.

Verses 11, 12. This taking of the number of the people would be considered in the light of a poll tax. That is, the "ransom" required was to be seen in that light. And the Lord threatened that a plague would be placed upon them if they neglected it. In the case of David (2 Sam. 24: 15), we necessarily will conclude that the king failed to take this money since a plague was sent on him and the people, and no other act of wrong doing is charged up against him in this instance.

Verse 13-15. The amount required was so small that it is not to be reckoned on the basis of financial ability. It is a type of the fact that mankind today in sin need to have a ransom for their souls. That ransom comes through the blood of Christ. And all classes, rich and poor, learned and unlearned, need the ransom that Christ gives.

Verse 16. This money was to be used in the public benefit and not for the personal use of anyone. Part of it would be used to provide the lambs for the daily sacrifice since those animals were to be furnished out of the public treasury. (Ch. 29: 38-42).

Verse 18. A laver is the same as a lavatory and both have the idea of "lave," which means to wash. It was made of fine brass and located between the altar and the tabernacle of the congregation.

Verse 19. The use of this basin was the washing of the hands and feet of Aaron and his sons before going into the tabernacle. They should wash their feet so as not to take any uncleanness with them by their feet. They should wash their hands so as not to defile any of the holy things in the service they were to perform.

Verses 20, 21. All of their service at this place must be preceded with a washing in this laver. If they neglected this duty they would be punished with death. God was very strict in the administering of his law even under that Dispensation.

Verses 22-25. Again a number of verses will be found grouped here because they compose the official formula for anointing oil. There were five ingredients and olive oil was the "vehicle" to hold in solution the items for aromatic purposes. In after times when we read of some instance where the "holy anointing oil" was used it will mean this article.

Verses 26-31. In the setting up of the tabernacle service the articles of service as well as the men intended for the priesthood were anointed with this oil.

Verse 32. This oil was for the service of the tabernacle only and no man was permitted to make a personal use of it. Neither could he make any like it for his own personal use.

Verse 33. It was not permitted to put any of the oil on a stranger. That means one from the outside of the congregation, not merely one whom they did not know.

Verses 34, 35. This is the formula for the official incense. All of these ingredients belonged in the class of spices and will be found described in any good Bible dictionary.

Verse 36. After this collection of ingredients had been compounded it was to be kept for use of the service. Then some of it was to be crushed into a powder and put before the testimony. This means it was to be burned on the golden altar which was also just east of the ark in which were the tables of the testimony.

Verses 37, 38. Like the anointing oil, this incense was never to be used in private application. Whoever did use it thus would be cut off from the people. It would be the same as profanity for that word means the making of a common use of something sacred.

EXODUS 31

Verses 1-6. A very significant fact was that God inspired these master workmen for the work of the tabernacle building. Also that men who were already endowed with a natural talent were given added ability in this work. This should be a suggestion to us that if we find instances where the description of the tabernacle seems to be obscure, there is no need to be alarmed and think there is something wrong with the direction or with our understanding of it. For instance, where we have the indistinct statement in chapter 26: 24, that the boards were fastened together at top and bottom with one ring, these men being inspired would know just how this was to be done. And we have a wonderful type here. As it required inspiration to understand how to form this building, so it required inspiration to form the church among men. But a difficulty may appear here. If it required inspiration to form this type, why must we not conclude that when men wish to start a church in a new locality they would have to be inspired? Not so. After the tabernacle had been first made, any ordinary man could see how to assemble it when necessary. And so with the church. After the apostles had formed the divine institution according to inspiration, then ordinary man can reproduce it by following the divine pattern laid down in the scriptures.

Verses 7-11. The mention of these items would be just another example of the preciseness with which the Lord gave his will to the people. There would be no reason for misunderstanding the duties of these inspired men nor the work for which they had been inspired. If they should be interested in some other work apparently similar, yet of their own personal business, they would have no more knowledge of it than they always had. And so with the apostles. Outside of their direct work of writing and speaking the Gospel they had only human or ordinary information. That is why we read in various places of things concerning which they said they did not know.

Verse 13. In this verse it is noted that sabbaths, plural, is used. This is a general statement and applies to any and all of the holy days; for the Israelites had a great many of them. And one was as binding as another even though there might be some items of observation required in one not required in another. The word sabbath in the Old Testament is defined by Strong: "Intermission; to repose, i. e., desist from exertion." Thus it does not necessarily carry with it the idea of relaxation from labor in the sense of resting from being weary or tired. See comments at Gen. 2: 2. Any day on which the people were required to desist from their ordinary temporal activities was a sabbath, and thus a holy day. Some of these days came on regular dates or at uniform intervals; especially was this true of the weekly sabbath which, on account of its very frequent and regular occurrence, was called "the" sabbath.

Verse 14. Much helpful information is found in this verse. The term "the sabbath," of course, here refers to the weekly one as stated in preceding paragraph. And the strictness of its requirement is also given. Another bit of information is in the use of two statements about the fate of those violating the law. One is "put to death," and the other is "be cut off from among the people." Such use of the terms tells us what is meant by being cut off from the people, an expression used very often.

Verse 15. No one has ever claimed that the sabbath day is anything more than one of the regular days of the week as to length. And here again the day is mentioned in connection with the six days of creation. Some have a fanciful idea of the length of these days as if they were equivalent to thousands of years. But their mention in the manner as seen here shows they were days of the same length as the sabbath day.

Verse 16. The children of Israel were to keep the sabbath perpetually, and that law or custom was never taken from them.

Verse 17. Notice it is stated that the sabbath was between the Lord and the children of Israel. This agrees with Chapter 9, verse 14, of Nehemiah. There it is stated that God made known to the Israelites his holy sabbath. This would prove that while the Lord observed the seventh day yet he never required anyone else to do so until the Israelites came into being and then it was given to them. Neither has it ever been given to any other people, as the sabbatarians erroneously teach.

Verse 18. We have been studying so long on the description of the tabernacle and its service that we probably have forgotten that Moses has as yet not gone to the people with the commission from God. All this time he has still been in the mount and receiving the will of the Lord. Of course, the reason these stones were given to him is for something that had occurred before he ever came up to this place. (See chapter 20: 1.) He is about to end his first stay in the top of the mountain and be sent down to see after the congregation that has gone astray. See following chapter.

EXODUS 32

Verse 1. The impatience of the people is somewhat natural. And their long stay in Egypt had ingrained into their minds the habit of idolatry. But as Aaron was left among them they call upon him to grant their petition. Of course they might have told the truth when they said they did not know what had become of Moses. That is, we do not have any information as to what knowledge they had received as to this affair. But as they previously had the assistance of Aaron they should have borne in mind that God had not deserted them.

Verses 2, 3. These articles of jewelry had been procured in Egypt on the night they left that country. And as they had called for these "gods" to go before them it was consistent that they be required to furnish the material.

Verse 4. There were three ways of getting metal into the desired form. They were by casting, chiseling, and hammering. In this case the first two were used. Let the reader observe the inspired statement that he, Aaron, was the one who did this forming of the idol and that it did not just automatically come that way. Making the calf as the particular kind of idol thought of here, is explained by their long experience in Egypt. That nation worshipped about everything, but the sacred bull Apis was their principal idol. Hence the choice of the Israelites here.

Verse 5. *When Aaron saw it.* This does not mean "it", the calf, for he was the one who made it and thus had already had full vision of the image. But the previous verse tells us the people called the image their god. And when Aaron saw or noticed it, then he joined in with their idolatrous conduct and furthered their iniquity by making an altar and announcing a feast to come tomorrow.

Verse 6. This whole performance is to be understood to be a sort of religious one for it says they offered burnt offerings. *Play.* This is from TSACHAQ and Strong defines it "to laugh outright (in merriment or scorn); by implication, to sport." By reference to verse 19 we will see what kind of play or sport they were indulging. This is the identical circumstance Paul had reference to in 1 Cor. 10: 7, where he is discussing idolatry. So we are to understand that dancing belongs to the class of idolatry. It is proper thus to class such iniquity. Idolatry is the worship or adoration of any thing or person but God. And dancing is the worship of the goddess of lust. If that element were removed from the practice of dancing it would cease to be practiced. This proves that people practice dancing because of the gratification to their lusts that they get from it.

Verse 7. Moses now is told to go down to the people. This will end his first stay of forty days and nights in the top of the mount.

Verse 8. The point to be noted here is that they are said to be worshiping "it," which is the calf. The church of Rome uses many images in their services, and bows down to them. But they deny that they worship the image; that they are worshiping what the image represents. God has never had himself represented or visualized by a dumb idol. Therefore the worship before an image is counted as worshiping "it." So the church of Rome is guilty of literal idolatry in all of their churches and also in their private lives. Most of them carry so-called images of the virgin Mary as well as other Biblical characters. And even if God was pleased to have these persons worshiped (which he is not), he would not permit the worship of any image.

Verse 9. To be stiffnecked as used in the scriptures means to be stubborn or obstinate or contrary. Inclined to have one's own way and to be disrespectful toward authority. This was charged against the Israelites in many instances.

Verse 10. Two proposals are in this verse. One is to destroy that nation and the other is to put a great honor on Moses. The purpose of this statement to Moses is discussed in following paragraph.

Verses 11-13. In many respects Moses was to be like Christ and one of the great items was that of intercessor. The idea of someone to come between man and God in the case of threatened danger needed to be established. This would prepare the world to appreciate the need and benefit of a perfect mediator. And this great principle must not be forgotten all the way through this history. At times it would seem almost as if Moses were being arrogant with God. That he argues with him and seems to be contending. But God wishes this to be the case in order to portray the office and rights of a mediator. Thus we should always keep this principle in mind in the various instances where Moses makes a plea to God. And of course God knows all things. He did not need to be informed of what the Egyptians would say if the Israelites failed. Nor did he need to be told anything. But it is his pleasure to have his creatures manifest great earnestness and to have them realize the outcome, were the ways of man not stopped. So the passage of this paragraph should be titled "Moses as mediator."

Verse 14. This verse will be understood in light of preceding paragraph. God was pleased to heed the plea of his servant Moses and change his decision. It states the Lord repented of the evil he had thought of doing. Again I shall state the short but complete principle common to all applications of the word "repent." The idea of change must always be present. But as to what or who is changed depends on the connection. Therefore, when man repents he *changes* his will. When God repents he wills a *change*. In this case God wills that the decree to destroy the people be *changed* so that the people will not be destroyed. And it was because of the mediation of Moses.

Verse 15. Tradition represents that the four commandments that were specially God-ward were on one of the stones while the other six were on the other stone. We do not know how much truth there is in that. But what the text does tell us is that both stones were used on each side.

Verse 16. It must always be remembered that God did the writing on these stones in both instances of making the tables. The part that Moses had will be seen later. And the writing is also shown here to have been done in the manner of an engraver and not a writing on a smooth surface as might be thought.

Verse 17. Just any kind of noise would not always mean the same thing. It was evidently a very strong noise here and led Joshua to come to a conclusion that it was the noise of war. It will be remembered that Joshua had been part way up on the side of the mountain all these days that Moses was in the top of the mount. He has been "standing by" and has been faithful. Now as Moses comes on down toward the congregation he joins Joshua, and together they proceed. When they got within hearing of the camp Joshua made this statement to Moses.

Verse 18. Moses does some reasoning. War will bring noise all right. And the ones on the losing side would make one kind of noise or sound while the sound of the victorious ones would be another kind. And Moses said that what they were hearing was not like either. Of course, we must not conclude that this "voice" or "noise" was merely something audible without any significance. The words "voice" and "noise" in this verse are both from QOL and Strong defines it: "To call aloud: a voice or sound." The word has been rendered in the A. V. by noise 48 times, sound 39, and voice 383. What was heard was the sound of voices indicating the state of mind of the persons. Moses said he heard the noise of them that sing. This is from a word that indicates the use of the voice as expressive of the situation in which they considered themselves. They said they had been without their leader. That a state of depression had come upon them and they were treating the whole circumstance with a ceremony. of religious activities.

Verse 19. Notice that Moses saw the calf and the dancing simultaneously. Which agrees with the idea that the dancing was on behalf of the calf and thus a part of their idolatrous performance. There is nothing to justify a conclusion that Moses meant to break the tables when he cast them down. His anger was righteous indignation. He was required to furnish the blank stones that were to replace them, but he is in no place criticized for the act.

Verse 20. By burning it, the gold would become charred or crystallized, and in a condition to be pulverized. That would make it suitable for being held in solution so as to compel the people to drink of it. They were thus punished by making them take a bitter dose compounded from their own iniquity. Evil often works its own rebuke in moral instances and here it is accomplished literally.

Verse 21. Moses had already learned that Aaron had brought about this instrument of their sin and calls for an explanation.

Verses 22, 23. The human nature of Aaron is manifested here in that he passes the sin on to another and thus blames it on the people. Many times today the leaders will try to justify their misleading by referring to the demands of the people. But such a flourish is illogical to say the least. The very fact of being a leader should carry with it the idea that wrong doing suggested by the people should be held in check by the leader. And the inclination of the people in the wrong direction is all the more reason for firmness for the right on the part of the leader. This is what Paul taught Timothy in one epistle (2 Tim. 4: 3). Had the people really been so ignorant as to think they could be benefited by a dumb idol, yet no small pretense even could be made for Aaron. He had been with Moses when they made the intrusion into the country to demand the release of the Israelites. He had seen all the mighty evidences of God over all other gods. But this circumstance is a manifestation of the influence that can be had by the populace over a man wishing to please the people.

Verse 24. How foolish and unreasonable is the statement here. Not only so, but it is a plain falsehood. Verse 4 says that Aaron first cast this piece, then shaped it up with an engraver's tool. But he wishes to imply that all he had to do was toss this gold into a fire and the image crept out, making it appear that a miracle had brought it forth and therefore it was partly the work of God. This was not the first nor the last time that men in error have tried to lay their mistakes on Providence.

Verse 25. Aaron knew he had done wrong and finally felt chastised himself. So he indicates his attitude by making them naked unto their shame. The word "naked" is from PARA and defined by Strong "to loosen; by implication, to expose, dismiss." In olden times it was customary to wear extra outer garments when in ordinary habits and then to have close fitting garments near the body. All this would tend to keep them covered and completely unexposed. But here it indicates that Aaron required them to get their garments in a condition of "undress" which would be considered shameful in the eyes of their enemies. That would suggest that they were in no condition to meet any foe that might be brought against them.

Verse 26. The events of this short verse will have far-reaching results and meanings. We have no information in any place of why the tribe of Levi responded to the call of Moses. And not only did Levites respond but *all* of them did. That includes the entire tribe. And it is noteworthy that when the call was made they did not know what was to be required of them. Also, since Aaron was of the tribe of Levi and since it says that "all" the sons of Levi responded we must conclude that he was now repentant and willing to make amends. Neither do we know how many, if any, of the tribe in general had been implicated in the demand for the calf. But the fact that Moses now called for all who would to indicate their willingness to be on the Lord's side to "come unto me" shows that the matter was to be settled by some test.

Verse 27. In this verse the words brother, and companion, and neighbor are used figuratively and mean the person nearest to the man with the sword. They were not told to ascertain first whether the person about to be attacked was guilty in the matter of the calf. The fact that such person had not responded when the call was made to be on the Lord's side made him guilty and subject to punishment. That principle holds good today. If a man refuses to take his stand outwardly in favor of a righteous cause he is considered as being on the wrong side. (See Matt. 12: 30.)

Verse 28. It will be interesting to make a comparison here. The congregation is at the place where they are to become a nation. The first occasion of their use of a sword resulted in the slaying of three thousand foes of righteousness. At Jerusalem, the place where the spiritual nation of Christ started, the first occasion of the sword of the Spirit resulted in the conquering of three thousand foes (Acts 2: 41).

Verse 29. This is rather a lapping back over the previous verse. The word "consecrate" is from a word that means "open-handed" as opposed to a closed hand. And thus the whole passage and its connection means that when Moses told them to go against the man next to each he used this language. As if he had said "open your hand for action against your brother," etc.

Verses 30-32. This is another passage that must be explained in the light of the office of Moses as mediator. See remarks at verses 11-13. He is allowed to form his language in the frame of mind of a person who is deeply convinced of wrong doing and who is very anxious to be set right. The peculiar language in verse 32 is to be understood as a final plea for forgiveness and so earnest is he that he would as soon be entirely erased from all of God's group of servants as to live with the guilt of the nation still held against them. But again, please remember that such language is in perfect keeping with the supposed character and frame of mind of a conscientious mediator.

Verse 33. Moses is given to understand that he will not be rejected just because the people he represents are in the wrong. The man who is to be blotted out is the guilty one. And then he is told in next verse to go on with his work.

Verse 34. God repeats the assurance he had previously made of caring for the nation and allowing them to be brought into the land promised. And the whole connection indicates that the people were forgiven for the time, but that in the future when God saw fit to chastise them for sin he would do so. That is, the promise was to bring the nation as a whole into the desired termination, yet when sin reared its head the foregoing promise would not protect them from the vengeance of God.

Verse 35. This verse does not refer to anything additional in the way of punishment. It is in the nature of a summing up of what has just happened. And it is significant to note that "they" made the calf and also that "Aaron" made it. All this shows that whoever has something to do with any transaction, whether to ask for it or to perform it or to endorse it, all are held guilty as having had fellowship therewith. Again we have a principle set forth that is also taught in the New Testament. (Rom. 1: 32.)

EXODUS 33

Verses 1, 2. These are general directions and a repetition of what has already been given. But the actual movement will not take place yet until Moses has been back to the top of the mount for another forty-day stay. Also until after the tabernacle has actually been made. We are to understand this as a signification to Moses that God had not changed his plan for the conduct of the nation.

Verse 3. "Flowing" means abounding with milk and honey. God will not go up with them in person, nor at all, unless they preserve themselves by penitent conduct. Otherwise they will be consumed in the way.

Verses 4-6. These words show the warning the people were given against their sins. Of course we know the three thousand that were slain did not comprehend all that were guilty. In fact, every member of the tribes, except those of Levi, were guilty. But enough had been slain to indicate to the rest how God feels about sin. And now the survivors are given this verbal chastisement and they are brought low by it.

Verses 7-10. So many times in order to avoid confusion we have to recall that the book of Exodus (as well as others) is not always chronological. So it is in this passage. After the tabernacle was finally constructed and assembled it was handled just in the manner described in this paragraph. But we will not forget that all of the things will take place first that require him to go back to the top, get the stones written on, come down, actually make the tabernacle, etc. Then the things described in this paragraph will take place.

Verse 11. "Face to face" means that Moses conversed with God directly, without the aid of a middle person. And the action of Joshua here is still in the future and to be understood in the light of explanation in verses 7-10 above.

Verse 12, 13. Just as Moses is permitted at times to converse with the Lord as mediator and thus seem to argue with him, so he is also conversing with him from the standpoint of an anxious disciple. God wishes his children to be thus minded. Here is an appropriate place to compare the form of prayer Jesus submitted to his disciples and that is recorded in Matt. 6: 9-14. God would never forsake nor mislead his children, yet he wishes his children to be concerned about it and expects them to pray to him over it. The great responsibility that Moses feels over the work of leading the great people is cause for his concern at this time. The word "way" in verse 13 is from the same word as "way" in Isa. 28: 8, and means "a course of life or mode of action." So the plea of Moses in this place is that God would show him how to conduct himself in leading the people. Just as the disciples were to ask for guidance in their daily walk.

Verse 14. As assurance, God told Moses that his presence would go with him and give him rest.

Verse 15. Moses' dependence on God is so complete that he does not feel disposed to go on without it. That is the way we are supposed to feel toward our Lord. And our prayers should reflect that feeling.

Verse 16. They are soon to be among various heathen people and Moses wishes them to be regarded as a separate kind from all the nations that will be around them. If the presence of God is not in evidence then it would not be known but that they were only another nation like the rest. Even so today God wishes his people to be separate, and so different from the world that the identity is plain. And in order to assist us in leading that kind of life the example was set by Jesus. (1 Peter 2: 21.)

Verse 17. The reason the Lord gives here for his assurance to Moses is interesting and fundamental. It is because Moses had procured the grace or favor of Him. Unless we conduct ourselves in a manner that pleases God we need not expect him to be with us.

Verses 18-23. This remarkable passage should be carefully marked in your Bibles because of its many and far-reaching meanings. The word "glory" means "splendor." The Lord knows that Moses is wishing for more intimacy with him than he has yet enjoyed. It would include a glance at even the face of the Creator of all things. While the splendor of God's person as a whole would be without human description, his face would be unbearable by a man in the flesh. No man can see that and live. An interesting circumstance to be considered in connection here is that of Saul on the road to Damascus. In order to be an apostle it was necessary to have seen Jesus after his resurrection. To do this it was necessary for him to show himself to Saul visibly. Ordinarily it would have resulted in his death. But a miracle was performed to make it possible for him to see and yet live. With all that, it came this near to being fatal, that it made him blind for three days and required another miracle to restore his sight. Now Moses would have been killed had he been granted the privilege he asked for. But by being hid in the cleft of the rock he was saved from physical death. This is the basis of one of the most familiar songs. There is a death coming that is more terrible than a physical one. But the great Rock has been cleft and from that side has come the means of shielding mankind from that endless death. Hence we sing "Rock of Ages cleft for me, Let me hide myself in Thee."

EXODUS 34

Verses 1-3. The first tables were given to Moses with the writing already and all this was done in the mount. But Moses broke them at the foot of the mount. And the stones to replace them must be furnished by Moses this time. But it should be carefully observed that God did the writing in this, as in the first instance. The exclusiveness of this occasion is the same as at the first. No one was to be with Moses. And this time he is to come up as far as at the first which is to the "top of the mount."

Verse 4. This verse gives us certain evidence that Sinai is that part of the great mount called "the top." Horeb, therefore, should be considered as the place in general.

Verses 5, 6. We must not overlook the fact that in all these connections where it says the Lord came down and appeared to Moses it means the angel of God. We have already seen (chapter 33: 18-23) that no man can see God personally and live. In all this experience of receiving the law it was through the agency of the angel acting for God.

Verse 7. Of course we will remember that God forgives when man complies with the terms of forgiveness that are laid down for him. And the visiting of the iniquity is the same as explained at chapter 20: 4-6.

Verses 8. 9. This is another occasion of Moses acting as mediator. And in it he recognizes the necessity of the Lord's presence for their safe conduct.

Verse 10. *Terrible.* This word is from YARE and one of its meanings is that of a thing to be feared or reverenced or respected. The great works that God proposes to do are such that the people of the earth will be overawed by them.

Verse 11. The people mentioned here are of the inferior ones who have been occupying the land that has already been given to God's people. Therefore the aggression that seems to be taking place by the intrusion of the Israelites, is to be considered in the sense of a defensive action.

Verse 12. There was to be no fellowship with the idolatrous people among whom they will journey toward the promised land. It would be a snare to trap them and hold them in the bondage of a false mode of life.

Verses 13, 14. Many instances will be seen where God refers to the trees in connection with idolatry of the nations around the children of Israel. They had made such a fixed practice of seeking the trees as a place for their temples and altars that the very sight of a tree would suggest an idol. Hence God wished his people to avoid the presence of these groves of the heathen. Reference to this subject is made under various expressions such as groves, trees, oaks, etc.

Verse 15. It may help us to see the need for such special precaution against the practice of idolatry by recalling that the nation of Israel spent 400 years in Egypt and were saturated with the idea of that false religion. Therefore God wishes to have them fear him and no other god.

Verse 16. *Whoring.* This is from ZANAH and defined "to commit adultery (usually of the female, and less often of simple fornication, rarely of involuntary ravishment); figuratively to commit idolatry (the Jewish people being regarded as the spouse of Jehovah)"—Strong. This is a principle taught throughout the Bible. The divine plan as to intimate association is one man for one woman, and the intimacy of a man or woman with another who is not the rightful partner is considered adultery or fornication. Since God is the only one with whom we have right to be intimate religiously, it means that if we are thus intimate with any other being or thing religiously, we are guilty of spiritual adultery. And in the verse now under consideration we see the danger of God's people marrying into those who are not his people. It always has and always will cause serious trouble.

Verse 17. Molten means melted or cast. Such as the golden calf which was first cast and then formed with the graver's tool (chapter 32: 4).

Verse 18. This feast was brought about by the fact that they were compelled to leave Egypt in such haste that their bread did not have time to ferment or become leavened (see chapter 12: 34).

Verse 19. The matrix is another name for womb. To "open" the womb would refer to the birth of the first born since that would be the first time the womb was opened. And as to why these first born ones were claimed, see comments at chapter 13: 1, 2.

Verse 20. Since the ass would be desired for service and yet belong to the Lord, the Israelite was permitted to retain it after paying for it with a lamb. But if he was not disposed to spare the price of the lamb then the ass colt must be killed and not used by its owner. The first born of the people would not be slain even though retained as a member of the family. But the redemption money must be given to the Lord. And none were to appear before the Lord empty. That is, when they came up to the place of national service they must bring some offering.

Verse 21. While certain emergencies allowed of working on the sabbath day, yet other occasions, even as important as raising and caring for the crop, were not to be allowed to interfere with the observance of the day.

Verse 22. "Feast of weeks" is the Old Testament name for what the N. T. calls Pentecost. This is because Pentecost is a Greek word, and the O. T. was written in Hebrew. It is called feast of weeks because it came a certain number of weeks (seven) after the feast of the passover. The last part of this verse refers to the third of the three annual feasts of the Jews, which centered around the day of atonement. This last named came on the tenth day of the seventh month (Lev. 23: 27).

Verse 23. The three feasts just mentioned are meant here. And we note that it was the males who were required to be present at these feasts.

Verse 24. The Israelites were required to go to the place of national worship three times in the year. Of course, this part of the law was made with the understanding that after settling down in the promised land they would have their personal title to land. It would require some time to make the journey to and from the place of meeting. And the Lord assured them that no one would be allowed to even desire to take possession of their land while they were gone.

Verse 25. Leaven was never to be offered on the altar of animal sacrifices. The surplus of the passover must not be preserved till morning. There could be no lawful reason for preserving it because no common use was allowed to be made of it. Therefore, what was not needed for the service should be destroyed.

Verse 26. The same law as already seen is meant here by giving the Lord the first of everything. And the principle of being humane would suggest that a kid would not be seethed or boiled in its mother's milk. The kid would necessarily be young, and in consideration for the mother, it should not be taken away for a while yet.

Verse 27. *Write thou these words.* Language could not be more direct and positive than this. The "ceremonial law" has been the immediate subject under consideration. And now Moses is commanded to write them and God says that according to those words He had made a covenant with thee (Moses), and with Israel. The error of the sabbatarians of distinguishing between the authority of Moses and God is again seen to be glaring. In fact, there is so much said in the scriptures against that false doctrine that we cannot regard the advocates of it as anything other than rebels against God.

Verse 28. The use of the pronoun "he" is a little indistinct here. But by reading Deut. 10: 4 it will be clearly seen that the pronoun in "he wrote" means the Lord who did the writing. This agrees also with other places on the subject.

Verse 29. This brilliancy on the face of Moses is what is referred to by Paul in 2 Cor. 3: 7 where he shows us that this shining represented the law that had been given him while in the mount. That law, even though intended for that people only and destined to be done away, was so important that its brilliance was reflected on the face of Moses unknown to him at the time.

Verse 30. That brilliance was so great that Aaron and the children of Israel were afraid to come near.

Verses 31, 32. Moses invites them to come near and, of course, assures them that no harm would come to them. But since it was unpleasant to them to face the brilliance of his face he will do something about it.

Verses 33-35. This vail is used here literally to shield the faces of the people from the brightness of that light which was a reflection of the law. But it is made a subject of illustration by Paul in his great argument in third chapter of 2 Corinthians, and no advocate of sabbatarianism can honestly face this argument and remain as he was.

EXODUS 35

Verse 1. Let us bear in mind at this part of our study that Moses has now come down from the mount after his second stay of forty days and nights. And he is about to deliver directly to the people the instructions he has received while in the mount. Again let it be noted that the statement is made that the following will be words which the Lord (not merely Moses) commanded them to do. About all of what is to follow in this book will be repetition of what we have already studied. For this reason it may be that not so much detail will be used in comments. And if the reader wishes a more extensive explanation than he finds in this part of the book it is suggested that he turn back to the chapters from 25 to 31 and read the comments.

Verse 2. Death was the penalty for working on the sabbath day. That law was never changed while it was in force.

Verse 3. This is merely a specification of what the Lord meant by working. If they needed fire for cooking they must arrange it the day before.

Verses 4-10. In bringing these articles to the work for the tabernacle we see the proviso for them was that they must give with a willing heart. That is the demand made of God's people under the Christian Dispensation (2 Cor. 9: 7).

Verse 11. The tent means the structure as a whole, which was so conspicuous as to be visible at a distance, while the covering refers specifically to the curtains.

Verse 12. The word "covering" is from a Hebrew word meaning to screen or shield. It has been translated by the words covering, curtain, hanging. It refers to the vail that formed the partition between the Holy and Most Holy rooms in the tabernacle. It is spoken of as a covering or vail because it hid the ark from the view.

Verses 13-19. These paragraphs are a repetition of the names given previously for this part of the work of the people for the tabernacle.

Verses 20, 21. After being instructed what to do, the people of the congregation departed from Moses and proceeded to carry out his instructions. They came with their offerings. Their hearts were in the work and were stirred up to put forward the work of the tabernacle and the service connected with it.

Verse 22. Then as now, the Lord expected the women to have something to do in the work of the Lord. While the nature of their work would differ from that of the men, yet they had a work to do.

Verses 23, 24. *With whom was found.* This expression is used twice in this paragraph and is very significant. It is in agreement with all of God's dealings with man. In 2 Cor. 8: 12 it is stated that our contribution to the Lord is based on what we *have.* And not only may we emphasize the word "have" but as appropriately the word *we.* That would mean then that we are to be judged by what *we* have, and not by the ability of some one else.

Verses 25, 26. The more delicate handwork was performed by the women. Being wise-hearted would not mean their intelligence in general, but their knowledge of the particular kind of work that was needed. And these women did this work with a willing heart because it was stirred up in interest for the work of the Lord.

Verses 27, 28. These rulers were some of the outstanding men in the congregation and not men of authority as the word usually signifies. But the articles mentioned as being brought by them were personal assets and of special value. So that it would be expected that these outstanding men would have such things in their possession.

Verse 29. In a more general and indefinite sense the people of the congregation are said to have contributed willingly to the work of the Lord.

Verses 30-35. The children of Israel are given the assurance that their work will be done right because the Lord has called two men to the special work. He has also inspired them to oversee the work. Not only to do this, but to teach others who will be helping with the work. It is the same as we have in the New Testament system. Christians need have no uneasiness as to the righteousness of the work they are asked to do because the Lord "called by name" certain men and gave them special power from on high to oversee the work. They were given the ability, through the Holy Spirit, to teach other men what to do.

EXODUS 36

Verse 1. The men went to work. In one verse the two men to oversee the work are named and also mention is made of others to work with them. So that the actual work of making the tabernacle is now under way.

Verses 2-4. The offerings of the materials were brought to Moses. Then he in turn called for the two master workmen and their fellow-workmen and turned over to them these materials. When any man needed more material he came to Moses for it. This is what is meant when it says in verse 4 that they "came every man," etc. Of course, we must not conclude that the materials were literally or bodily handled first by Moses from the hands of the people and then by him to the workmen. That would be unnecessary. But all materials were under the jurisdiction of Moses and as each man needed material Moses dispensed it to him.

Verses 5-7. As Moses was directing the workmen to appropriate the materials being brought he was informed finally that the supply coming from the people was more than the demand. They had even brought more than was needed. Then Moses gave announcement that they should cease collecting the materials. The liberality of the people in this case is wonderful and sets an example worthy of emulation.

Verses 8-13. For explanation of these verses see chapter 26: 1-6.

Verses 14-18. See chapter 26: 7-11.

Verse 19. These coverings of the skins would be rougher and stronger and would make a special protection for the finer curtains underneath.

Verses 20-30. These boards comprised the body or framework of the tabernacle. By them we may ascertain the height and length of the structure. For further information on this paragraph see chapter 26: 15-25.

Verses 31-34. These bars or rods were for the purpose of stabilizing the sides and west end of the tabernacle. See chapter 26: 26-30.

Verses 35, 36. This vail is what is referred to as the covering of the ark because it covered in the sense of screening the sacred vessel from the view of the first room. It was made of the finest materials and not only served as the vail already described, but formed the partition between the two rooms of the tabernacle.

Verses 37, 38. While the west end of the tabernacle was made of the same kind of boards as the sides, the east end was yet open. For the closing up of that part of the institution a hanging of fine material was made and suspended on five pillars of the acacia wood, and rested on a foundation of brass.

EXODUS 37

Verses 1-5. This ark was the most exclusive of all the articles of furniture because in it was the law on the stones and also other precious articles. Also because it was kept in the most holy place where no one but the High Priest dared to enter, and he only on one day of the year. Another thing that made this ark so special was that on it was the mercy seat with the cherubims where God communed with the High Priest on behalf of the congregation. So sacred was this piece of furniture that no hand was allowed to touch it. To avoid any necessity to touch it the provision was made that it should be borne with the staves run through the rings at the corners.

Verses 6-9. There was no wood in this article. It was made of pure gold which means that it was gold without alloy. It was called the mercy seat because the word is derived from the idea of covering literally when used in connection with a literal thing that needed a covering such as the ark. And of covering in the sense of forgiving when used in connection with sins that needed to be covered or forgiven. And this was done before this mercy seat on the tenth day of the seventh month each year when the High Priest appeared here on behalf of the congregation.

Verses 10-16. See chapter 25: 23-30 for the previous explanation of this paragraph.

Verses 17-24. This is the other of the two articles that had no wood in them. And this is the account that tells us the amount of gold to be used in the article. For a detailed description of this subject see chapter 25: 31-40.

Verses 25-28. This altar was for the purpose of burning incense only and never to have anything else burned on it. Neither may they burn incense of private production but must use that prescribed by the Lord and under the administration of the priests.

Verse 29. While the work or compounding of the anointing oil and the incense was according to the apothecary or standard formula, yet it was under the exclusive use of the persons authorized to administer it.

EXODUS 38

Verses 1-7. This was made of the acacia wood and overlaid with brass. It was put at the entrance, or door hanging of the court, or yard of the tabernacle. To this place all burnt sacrifices must be brought except certain ones whose bodies were to be burned at a place outside of the camp. This matter is discussed in another place.

Verse 8. A laver is a vessel for the purpose of washing as the word "lave" means to wash. It was made of the "looking-glasses" of the women. The margin says "brasen glasses." It means the plates of fine brass so polished that they could be used as mirrors. They would naturally be of the finest grain in order to take on the required polish. This vessel was placed near the door of the tabernacle and yet in the court, and the priests were required to wash their hands and feet therein each time they entered the tabernacle. If they neglected to do this they would be punished with death.

Verses 9-20. This is a description of the outside enclosure around the tabernacle. It served about the same purpose as a yard fence around a residence. Its description is explained in chapter 27: 9-17.

Verse 21. A general summing up of the great work of the tabernacle. It is called the tabernacle of testimony because in it was deposited the law of God.

Verses 22, 23. *Bezaleel—made—Lord —commanded—Moses.* I have arranged these words in this manner in order to call attention to the position of Moses. In the first place, the instructions came from the Lord. Then he commanded Moses. Not that Moses was to do the work, Bezaleel did the work. But this setup again shows the authority of Moses in the whole matter and concludes that the authority he had was the same as that of God as far as its being binding on the people.

Verse 24. According to Oxford Cyclopedic Concordance the gold was worth over $868,260 in present day estimation of value.

Verse 25. By the same estimate the silver was worth $194,000. Thus the gold and silver used in making the tabernacle was over a million dollars' worth. We do not know what would be the value of all the brass and fabrics and other materials used in making the holy building. But we will bear in mind that all this was for a purpose. It was in the typical and educational age and was to symbolize the spiritual institution that was finally to be set up among men, the church. That building was to be costly, yea the value of the blood of Christ (Eph. 5: 25).

Verse 26. A shekel was worth 65c and the poll tax taken from the people was half a shekel or one bekah. The amount of this poll is stated here but official numbering of the people is not given until we reach the book of Numbers. (1: 46.)

Verses 27-31. These verses record the various uses made of this precious metal and the brass, and refer to the articles described in the previous chapters.

EXODUS 39

Verses 1-5. The fabrics and various kinds of needle work are here distributed in the account as to their uses. Mention of blue, and purple, and scarlet means that materials already of those colors were used. The pieces or garments were not first made and then colored but the pieces had the color to begin with, hence the colors were "fast." This idea holds good in other parts of the Bible. When a thing is said to be made of many colors it means of many pieces already colored. (Gen. 37: 3; Judg. 5: 30; 2 Sam. 13: 18.) Here we see how they got the gold into the garments and other pieces. They did not have the art of spinning metal as we have it. But that metal is very malleable. They would beat it into thin plates and then cut it into wires or threads so that it could be worked into the fabrics designated.

Verses 6, 7. A signet is an engraving showing some signature. Thus these onyx stones were carved with the names of the sons of Israel who were the heads of the twelve tribes. Then these stones thus carved were put in ouches (settings) and arranged to be placed on the shoulder-pieces of the garment called the ephod.

Verse 8. *Cunning.* This is from CHASAB and defined "to plait or interpenetrate, i. e. (literally) to weave or fabricate."—Strong. This means that the piece was made of the mentioned materials by weaving them together in a beautiful manner.

Verse 9. It was square after being doubled. It was doubled in a way that would make it into a sort of bag.

Verses 10-13. On the outside surface of this piece were attached twelve stones on each of which was carved a name of one of the sons of Israel, or Jacob.

Verse 14. This was used for the same purpose as the ones on the shoulder piece in verse 7. It was a symbolic method of bearing the interests of the congregation by the priest when he was engaged in the service of the tabernacle.

Verses 15-21. For more detailed description of these pieces see chapter 28.

Verses 22, 23. A habergeon is a part of armor and the opening for the neck was reinforced with a band. This robe was also strengthened at that place with a binding.

Verses 24-26. These pomegranates were made of the fine fabrics and used as ornaments and also would alternate with the golden bells. That would leave each bell free to sound clearly while the priest was officiating.

Verses 27-29. These coats were in the form of a cape, and thus a loose fitting garment. Both Aaron and his sons had these to use in their service. The bonnets were like caps and so rendered in some translations. And all of these articles were made by hand and done with the fine needlecraft of that age.

Verses 30, 31. A plate of gold was furnished and on it was engraved a signature of honor toward the Lord. This plate was attached to a lace of blue and it was then put on the mitre to be worn on the head.

Verse 32. The thought to be noted here is that the children of Israel had no way of knowing what the Lord wanted them to do except as they learned it from Moses. So we are to be impressed with the position of authority which he held and should never say anything that would lessen that authority. To do so would be to disrespect God.

Verses 33-43. *Brought.* Of course, they did not move all that building bodily to the presence of Moses. It means they brought the work to the attention of Moses. And this was for the purpose of having it inspected. Moses was their lawgiver. He was their leader. To him they had been listening for instructions and from him they received all their directions. If the work passes his inspection it means that it pleases God since he is the authorized spokesman between them and God. And when Moses had seen the work as thus made he gave it his blessing. It was done according to the word of the Lord.

EXODUS 40

Verses 1-16. All of the parts of the tabernacle institution now having been made and ready for service, the time has come to rear it up. Like the previous instances, the assembling of the parts is not mentioned in a chronological order as would be necessary in the physical transaction. The work would really be done according to the particular stage in the process of erection. A summing up of the order of the whole structure will be given near the close of this chapter.

Verse 17. This verse gives us the date the tabernacle was reared up. Since they left Egypt the 15th day of the first month and the tabernacle was reared up the first day of the first month in the second year, it has been about a year since they left the land of their bondage. But they were two months reaching Sinai. Thus, about ten months were consumed in the work of receiving the law and the building of the tabernacle.

Verses 18, 19. This paragraph briefly states the rearing up of the tabernacle proper. It is logically stated as a building would be set up.

Verses 20, 21. The testimony here means the tables of the covenant. They were to be kept there and were so kept as long as the service was intact. They finally were taken away. That is, the whole article was finally separated from the building as will be seen in the later history of the nation. It might be suggested that Moses must have had occasion to touch the ark since some things were done before the staves were placed in the rings. But it must be borne in mind that the service has not yet been started and everything is in the preparatory state. Besides, Moses was even higher in authority than Aaron and had special authority here.

Verse 22. In this connection the "tent" has special reference to the first room of the tabernacle and is called the Holy Place, for it was without the vail.

Verse 23. This was the unleavened bread that had been ordered to be placed on the table and was to be renewed each sabbath.

Verses 24, 25. Here also the candlestick was put in the "tent" of the congregation. We know from other passages (chapter 26: 35) that the candlestick was in the same room as the table which all know was in the first room. So the conclusion is that the "tent" here is that first room.

Verses 26, 27. The golden altar was in the "tent" which we have already seen means here the first room of the tabernacle. Hence the altar of incense was not in the Most Holy place as some have thought.

Verses 28-33. Here will be the proper place to give a general description of the order or arrangement of the whole institution which will be done briefly. First, the foundation was composed of the silver and brass sockets which were placed in the ground at the proper place. Then the boards were stood up and the bars run through the places provided for them. Next the coverings or vails were spread over the framework. Now put up the four pillars and suspend the vail on them, twenty cubits from the east end and this will form the Most

Holy place. Next, set up the five pillars at the east end to form the enclosure for the first room or Holy Place. Now the tabernacle proper has been set up and is ready for the furniture. Then the ark with the mercyseat and cherubims will be brought into the Most Holy place, just inside the vail. Next bring in the table of shewbread and set it on the north side of the first room or Holy Place. Then bring in the golden candlestick and set it on the south side of this same room and so arrange it that the candelabrum will face the table, and then light the lamps. Now we are ready for the golden altar. It is brought into this same room or Holy Place and set near the vail that separates this room from the second or Most Holy place. Incense is now burned on this altar. With the tabernacle proper thus composed and set up it is in order to set up the court or outside enclosure. After doing so, bring in the altar of burnt sacrifices and set it just on the inside of the gate or closing curtain. One more article of furniture is to be brought. That is the laver which is placed between the altar of burnt sacrifices and the entrance to the tabernacle. This completes the entire structure and it is now ready for the Lord's personal or direct inspection.

Verse 34. Of course no one must see the actual face of the Lord, but some visible evidence will be given of his approval. Hence the cloud covered the tabernacle and the glory of the Lord filled it. All this signified that the divine approval was extended.

Verse 35. This verse might be thought to contradict the statement in chapter 33: 9. That place says he entered the tabernacle while the present one says he was not able to enter. But the explanation is in the various senses of the word "enter." One meaning of the word is "to abide," and is so rendered in Num. 31: 23. The two passages mean that while Moses went into the tabernacle, yet he could not remain in it because of the glory of the Lord. Not that it would have been impossible physically for him to do so, but it was too great a glory for him to abide therein.

Verses 36-38. This cloud was the only visible indication that the Lord wished the congregation to move. It was a cloud by day and appearance of fire by night. This was always in sight of the people so that they could observe its movements whether by day or by night. No advance notice was given them of the intended move. Hence it was necessary for them to be always on the alert and to keep their attention on the cloud. If they did not, the cloud might move and the congregation as a whole leave the present location and the careless ones be left behind. The whole lesson is the same as one given by Jesus to his disciples and that lesson is couched in the word "watch."

LEVITICUS 1

General remarks. The third book of the Bible is so named from Levi, one of the tribes of the Israelites. When Moses called for the ones on the Lord's side to come to him after the affair of the golden calf the tribe of Levi responded. Now it was fitting that this tribe should be honored with the work and service of the congregation, and have charge of the law. And since this book is made up of the special directions for the religious activities of the congregation it is fitting that the book should have the name. Furthermore, while in this general statement, I will say that the first five chapters give us what should be regarded as the five major sacrifices of the law. They will be described in their respective chapter in these five.

Verses 1, 2 Once more we have the significant statement that the Lord gave Moses commandment to speak to the congregation and hence is authority over them.

Verse 3. This verse tells us the major sacrifice described in this chapter. It is the *burnt* sacrifice and should be scored for purpose of easy citation. One animal accepted in this sacrifice was of the herd or the cattle as we use that term. The Lord is specific in his requirements. It must be a male and without blemish. Also he must offer it willingly. Moreover he must bring it to the door of the tabernacle. Of course, that means to the door of the court, since the term "tabernacle" is often used as a general name for the whole institution.

Verses 4, 5. The one making the sacrifice must lay his hand on the head of the animal thereby signifying that it is offered to the Lord. Then he is the one who must kill the animal. After that is done then the priests shall take charge and use the blood as directed.

Verse 6. The one making the offering must flay (skin) the animal and cut it into pieces.

Verses 7-9. The priests shall then take charge again and after washing, the parts of the animal must be burned on the altar by the door of the court.

Verse 10. If a man was not able to bring the larger animal, then he could bring a smaller. It could be either a sheep or goat, but must be without blemish.

Verses 11-13. No reason is given why the animal must be killed on the north side of the altar. But the lesson is evident that when God says for a certain thing to be done it is best for man to obey. In this paragraph the reader should observe the part performed by the one bringing the sacrifice and that of the priest. The former killed the animal, cut it into pieces, and washed the parts, and the priest did the rest.

Verses 14, 15. God has never required anything of man that was beyond his ability. One person might be able to bring the largest animal and if so he must do it. If able only to bring the smaller animal that will do. But some might not be able even to bring the sheep or goat. In that case the fowls might be resorted to. But the ones designated are what he must bring, either turtledoves or pigeons. Also he must bring them to the place of sacrifices. For some reason in this case the priest did the killing by wringing off the head. The blood must be expelled from the body and poured down at the side of the altar.

Verse 16. The crop means the craw. It, with the feathers, was taken away and cast by the east side of the altar near the ashes. This indicates that it was not to be burned on the altar but taken just as it is and disposed of with the ashes.

Verse 17. The bird is cut into two pieces but the parts must not be separated. Then the whole of it thus remaining must be burnt on the altar. "Offering made by fire" denotes that not all offerings were burned, which will be found later on in this work. The word "savour" is from REYACH and means "odor" here, and in the many places in the Bible where the word is used. The meaning is, when used favorably, that it is pleasing.

LEVITICUS 2

Verse 1. This chapter describes the only one of the major sacrifices that was wholly vegetable. The word "meat" here means meal or product of the grain. A variety of forms of this product was accepted but directions given for the form decided upon by the one bringing it. In the present verse it is fine flour. It is prepared by pouring oil (olive) on it and putting frankincense on it.

Verse 2. The giver must bring the flour to the priests and first take out a handful of it for burning. The priest shall burn this handful on the altar as a memorial. This means it was a reminder that the man was a sinner and must do something about it.

Verse 3. After the handful had been taken out and burned on the altar the priests were to use the bulk of the flour for their food. (See 1 Cor. 9: 13.)

Verse 4. The word "oblation" is a general name for something offered. The giver might choose to bring a bakemeat and if so then it must consist of unleavened cakes. They must be made of fine flour and mixed with oil. Or, if he uses wafers they must be anointed with olive oil.

Verses 5, 6. The margin here gives us "plate" instead of pan. The idea is that it was cooked on top of the stove or whatever instrument was used for cooking. It also must be unleavened for they have already been told never to burn leaven. The cakes here prepared must be cut into pieces and have oil poured on them.

Verses 7-9. This selection was cooked in a frying pan. By allowing such a variety of means for preparing these meat offerings the Lord was gracious to his people. They might not all be equipped alike and if a man did not have a certain utensil he could use another. In all cases it must be of fine flour and the article must be brought to the priest. The priest shall take out a small portion to be used as a memorial and burned on the altar.

Verse 10. Here again the major portion of the oblation was used by the priest for food, as cited by Paul in 1 Cor. 9: 13.

Verse 11. Here we are told the two things that must never be burned on the altar. They are leaven and honey. No reason is given for this restriction.

Verse 12. Fruits containing honey and certain prepared foods containing leaven could be used as oblations (offerings) to the Lord in other manner but never burned.

Verse 13. Another restriction that should never be forgotten is that the meat or vegetable offerings were always to be seasoned with salt. When used figuratively, one idea conveyed by salt is that of perpetuity. This service of the Lord was to be considered as permanent while that nation endured.

Verse 14. A devout Israelite might wish to make an offering to God in the very beginning of the crop season and before the crops were fully ripe. In that case he was to dry the ears so that they could be beaten out. But he must select full ears. Of course the word "ears" means what we would call heads of wheat or other small grain.

Verses 15, 16. As in the other cases, a small portion must be taken out of the lot and oil and frankincense put on it. This part was called the memorial which means it was used to keep in memory the fact that something had to be done to remind them that they were sinners. The priest burned this part on the altar.

LEVITICUS 3

Verse 1. This chapter describes the peace offering and might be selected from the herd, which means the larger animals. In this case they were allowed to use either male or female but it must be without blemish. Such restriction was always made. They must not offer to the Lord something of inferior quality.

Verse 2. The one bringing it was to kill the animal at the door of the tabernacle which means the entrance to the court. After it was killed the priest must sprinkle the blood upon the altar.

Verses 3-5. The word "fat" as used in connection with the sacrifices of the Lord is from a Hebrew word meaning the richest part and applies to such parts as the suet and like matter. The Lord always claimed that part of the animals and the people were not permitted to eat that portion. Also certain portions of the animal here were to be burned upon the altar. Again we notice that the expression "made by fire" is used which reminds us that some offerings made by the children of Israel were not so handled. And this sacrifice was to be a "sweet savour" (pleasant odor), unto the Lord.

Verse 6. As in the case of the first sacrifice described in first chapter, the person was not required to sacrifice what he was not able. If he cannot furnish a cow or bullock he could select one from the flock and it could be either male or female. It must be without blemish.

Verse 7. It was required that he offer it "before the Lord." This means he could not just build a fire in his own dwelling and offer it. He must take it to the place where the Lord had prepared to meet the people which was at the altar, a part of the furniture of the tabernacle.

Verse 8. The one bringing the sacrifice must lay his hand upon the head. Of course the animal must be killed. But there might be some means of bringing about its death by attacking some vital part other than the head. This expression means that the head was to be severed from the body. This would accomplish two things. It would kill the animal and also would cause the blood to be shed which was a very important thing. All through the Bible the value of blood is kept before the reader. God was looking forward to when his own Son was to shed his blood for the sin of mankind and it was necessary to build up the impression as to the importance of blood. And for this reason no one was allowed to eat blood.

Verses 9-11. These choice parts of the animal were taken from it to be burned upon the altar. The caul mentioned is the membrane across the central part of the body that is just above the liver. Note the use of the word "food" in this place. The idea is that they were required to offer the Lord something that would have been useful to them. So the case is today and always. If we are not willing to offer to the Lord something that is of real value to us then we are not making any real sacrifice.

Verses 12-16. We will learn later on that the goat was among the clean animals of which people were permitted to eat and thus could be offered as a sacrifice when not able to furnish a greater beast. This animal was to be prepared after the same manner as the other ones and the blood sprinkled around and about the altar. And the one bringing the animal must do the killing while the priest did the handling.

Verse 17. Here the two things they were never to eat are mentioned which were fat and blood. It will be well here to state five things that are of special interest. Two things that must never be burned are leaven and honey. Two things that must never be eaten art fat and blood. And one thing that must never be lacking in the meat or vegetable offerings is salt.

LEVITICUS 4

Verses 1-3. This chapter describes the sacrifice that is the most extensive of all the sacrifices in that it is needed in more special cases and would be called for on more frequent occasions than the others. The chapter will describe sacrifices for four classes and will be noted as we come to them, but might be stated now in the beginning of the chapter. They are the priest, the whole congregation, the ruler, and the private individual. Just why the Lord was particular to consider these classes separately we do not know. But the last two words of the paragraph now being considered give the title of this chapter which is "sin offering." And the class needing the use of sin offerings now described is that of the priests. Yes, even the priest had to do his duty and offer for sin. Here is one of the contrasts between the priests of that Dispensation and our priest. The contrast is because our priest, though living in the flesh and subject to temptation, never sinned and therefore never had to offer a sacrifice for his own sin. The priest was required to bring a young bullock. This means the male of the cattle, and it must be without blemish.

Verse 4. As in all other cases he must bring his offering to the door of the tabernacle and do the killing of the animal.

Verse 5. Observe the expression "that is anointed." All of the sons of Aaron were eligible for the priesthood but all would not be needed at any given time. And when the services of a priest were needed it must be from one acting which is the meaning of the expression stated here. Of course if a priest had committed sin he would have to lay aside his robes of official service and submit his case to one who was in active service. But another contrast is noted here. Instead of sprinkling the blood around about the altar it must be taken to the tabernacle. This does not mean the tabernacle in general because the animal had already been brought to that place as seen in verse 4. This is the tabernacle proper and will be explained in next verse.

Verse 6. Here we see this blood was sprinkled or dashed seven times "before the vail." This was in the first room or Holy Place. We do not know why this exception was made as to where the blood was to be sprinkled, but we do realize that a difference existed in the case of a priest.

Verse 7. While in the Holy Place to sprinkle the blood before the Lord the priest officiating must also put some of the blood on the horns of the altar of incense. And we have another evidence that this altar was in the first room and not the second.

Verses 8-10. Certain parts of this animal were taken from it and burned upon the altar of burnt offerings as in other cases.

Verses 11, 12. This paragraph gives us much information. The major portion of the sacrifice was taken to a place outside the camp and burned on a fire of wood. This was an exception to the general rule which required that all burnt sacrifices must be done on the altar. Of course we will not overlook the fact that this animal had first been brought to that place and part of it burned on the altar. But the most of it was burned as here stated. At this place I will ask the reader to read Heb. 13: 11 for there is a most impressive comparison. More will be said on that subject when we reach the passage itself in this work. But it is well to have the subject brought to our attention now. Another helpful piece of information in this paragraph is in the words "where the ashes are poured out." Occasionally a person expresses concern about the condition that would come around the altar with so many animals burned there and so much wood that would have to be burned. In the first place we should not be concerned about the Lord's arrangement but should remember that he knows his business. And even if he does not see fit to tell us all the particulars yet we are certain that all will be cared for. In this instance we do have some information. The ashes of the altar were taken out to this place on the outside of the camp and deposited. This would warrant the conclusion that the accumulation of filth from the blood sprinkled around the altar also would be disposed of as the need appeared.

Verse 13. Another of the special provisions for sin offerings was for the "whole congregation." Of course this would have to refer to some kind of public action since the sins of the individual members of the congregation are taken care of in another sacrifice later in the chapter. The words "and are guilty" here are explained in the next verse which see.

Verse 14. This shows the writer is considering a sin that the congregation as a whole has made but was ignorant at the time of the action. Such action was not charged against them until they learned of the mistake. When that was done, then a young bullock must be brought. This would be provided out of the congregational fund and it must be brought to the tabernacle just as other sacrifices were.

Verse 15. The elders were leading men as to experience and judgment and not any officials. See comments at Ex. 3: 16. They were here to represent the congregation in the bringing and killing of the sacrifice.

Verse 16. Again the priest "that is anointed" is stipulated. See explanation at verse 5. And in this case some of the blood must be brought into the tabernacle as it was in the case of the offering for the priest.

Verses 17, 18. This blood must be sprinkled or dashed seven times (seven in figurative language indicating completeness) before the vail in the Holy Place. Also some blood was to be put on the horns of the incense altar but the bulk of the blood must be poured out at the bottom of the altar of sacrifices. It reminds us that the blood of Christ was poured out at the foot of the cross.

Verses 19, 20. The additional thought in this paragraph is the declaration "it shall be forgiven them." A popular teaching in the world is that under the Jewish Dispensation the sins were not actually forgiven, but were "rolled forward." This is not a scriptural teaching. It is rather a direct contradiction of positive statements of the scriptures. Special attention will be given to this subject at the study of the book of Hebrews. But it should be observed that in many instances in the Old Testament the statement is made that after the performance of the duty required in the animal sacrifices their sin was forgiven.

Verse 21. As in the previous case, the body of this animal was taken to the place outside of the camp and burned.

Verse 22. This sacrifice is for a ruler. This word is from NASI and defined by Strong "an exalted one, i. e., a king or sheik; also a rising mist." The word has been rendered in the A.V. by captain, chief, cloud, governor, prince, ruler, vapor. So these were men of outstanding recognition and finally had some place of authority under the jurisdiction of the official priests. If such a person does a wrong even through ignorance, he is guilty.

Verse 23. However, his guilt will not be held against him until he has obtained knowledge of the fact. Then he must bring an unblemished kid of the goats.

Verses 24-26. The one bringing the goat must kill it; then the priest shall put some of the blood on the horns of the brasen altar, then pour all the remaining blood at the foot. The fat or tallow must be burned on the altar. Nothing said here as to what must be done with the rest of the animal.

Verse 27. This sacrifice was for the private individual of the congregation. He might commit a sin through ignorance "and be guilty." This expression is explained in verse 14.

Verses 28-31. This person may bring a kid of the goats, a female without blemish. He must kill it and the priest will handle it as in other cases. The choice parts were burned on the altar. And again the statement that the sins were forgiven.

Verses 32-35. The individual was permitted to bring a lamb, a female without blemish. The preparation and handling of this animal was the same as for the goat. And when it was done then the sin of the individual was forgiven, not rolled forward.

LEVITICUS 5

Verse 1. This chapter deals with the fifth of the five major sacrifices and is named in the 6th verse which is trespass offering. The word "swearing" is from ALAH and defined "a primitive root; probably to adjure, i. e. (usually in a bad sense) imprecate."—Strong. The word means to curse and is here used of a person who pronounces some evil wish against another without a just cause. That would be wrong and might be overheard by another who would not know the truth about the case. He might not have seen or known about the circumstance that provoked the expression of cursing and hence could not judge of its justness or lack of it. Yet it is doubtful and the one thus overhearing it should expose the threat of the one making the curse. The public good might be endangered by the threat or curse of the one pronouncing it and the protection of mankind would call for the exposing this threat. If the one overhearing it does not make it known then he is guilty of a sin against the Lord.

Verses 2, 3. Later in the law certain restrictions will be given on the subject of uncleanness, here provided for with the sacrifice under consideration. And let it be noted again that when the person learns of the facts, then he is guilty.

Verse 4. A man might swear to do a certain thing. It might be a determination to bring on some other person or thing a good or evil. The words "good" and "evil" here are not used in a strictly moral sense, for in that sense it would never be a sin a do the good. "Evil" means some unpleasant or unfavorable condition. There could be cases where such condition would be justified and thus not a sin. Or a pleasant and favorable condition might be brought to a person which would not be justified. In that case an unworthy person would be encouraged and hence something "good" would be a sin, and the man doing this swearing would be guilty "in one of these" which means he would be guilty in either the case of the "good" or the "evil."

Verses 5, 6. This person must confess his wrong. That alone would not suffice. He must bring a "trespass offering." This is the name of the major sacrifice we are considering in this chapter. It may be of the sheep or goats but must be a female and the priest will use it on behalf of the guilty person.

Verse 7. If not able to bring an animal then he may bring two doves or pigeons. While the occasion of this action is the sin of trespass, yet it must be atoned for by invoking the provisions of the first and fourth major sacrifices. We are not told why this peculiar requirement. It is enough to know the Lord required it and of course it is always best to do as God instructs.

Verses 8-10. The priest must officiate again and kill these birds in the order and manner here described. "Manner" is from a word that means "decree or divine law." It refers to the established law concerning the five major sacrifices. As said before, the first five chapters of this book describe respectively as to chapters, the five major sacrifices of the Mosaic system. Afterwards when any one of the five is called for and no specifications are given, then the persons concerned must go to these five chapters and find the one, or ones, required to determine the formula for that particular sacrifice. Here again please note that the sin atoned for was forgiven.

Verses 11-13. Here is a case where a man is too poor to bring any living creature, not even the birds. So his condition may be attended to, by bringing the second of the major sacrifices as listed in this part of this book. It is in the class of meat offerings but is offered for sin. An ephah was a little more than a bushel so the man was to bring a little less than a gallon of fine flour. I do not know why he was to put no oil or incense on it. But such was the stipulation. And the bulk of the flour shall be used by the priest for food. (1 Cor. 9: 13.)

Verses 14, 15. Certain things were appropriated to the Lord. A man might not know about it in some instances. That is, he would not know that the articles had already been "earmarked" for the Lord and would make personal use of them. Then he must bring a ram to the priest for an offering. This would be the penal part of his atonement. The priest is the one who must estimate or decide whether the ram is worth as many shekels as it should be worth.

Verse 16. But the penal requirement is not all. That would not restore the things taken from the possessions of the Lord. So he must also make amends by restoring the thing taken and as a further item of penal nature he must add a fifth. With this the priest will make atonement for him and he *shall be forgiven.*

Verses 17-19. There is nothing new in this paragraph but the repetition will serve to emphasize the importance of the service and also give us another reminder that when a man did what he was told to at that day he was forgiven.

LEVITICUS 6

Verses 1, 2. The five major sacrifices have been described in detail in the preceding chapters of this book. After this we will see many special applications of them. And in some cases the particular instances in which one of the sacrifices will be required will be shown. All this may test our patience but ought to impress us with the mind of God and show us how exact he is about our service. While we have seen that the various conditions of man are considered, whether poor or rich and whether sin of ignorance or otherwise, yet in each case the directions were to be observed. In the present paragraph the sin of lying is cited. Especially lying concerning the personal property of another delivered into hand for safe keeping. He might claim it had been taken away by another when it was not the truth. If a man accepts the property of some one else to keep that commits him to the safety of that article.

Verse 3. The popular saw "finders keepers and losers weepers," is not justified by the law of God; neither is it by the laws of man. If a person finds a thing of value he should make an honest effort to find the owner and restore it. Not to do so is considered dishonest and is unlawful now as then. If the owner suspects that the person considered has found the lost article or knows something about it, then he must not lie about it.

Verses 4, 5. If guilty as above stated, he must make it right commercially by restoring the lost or other article to its owner. Also add a fifth to it for interest, or as a sort of punitive requirement.

Verse 6. Making a thing good financialy does not always settle the whole case. It is even so now. If I steal a man's property and am apprehended I must return the stolen goods. But in addition I must suffer the penalty under the law. So under the law of Moses this man must bring an unblemished lamb for a trespass offering. "With thy estimation" means that the priest must be the judge of the quality of the animal.

Verse 7. The priest is the one to handle the case as in others. When it is done then the man's sin was forgiven.

Verses 8, 9. Here the explanation is given that the term "burnt offering" is derived from the continual burning on the altar. This subject will be considered more in verses below.

Verse 10. While officiating with the sacrifices the ashes might become too much accumulated for the proper burning of the fire on the altar. In that case he could continue in his priestly clothing even though doing the necessary and incidental work of clearing out the ashpit. But he must remain near and dispose of the ashes temporarily, by putting them beside the altar.

Verse 11. Afterward these ashes must be disposed of in the permanent way by being taken to a place outside of the camp. Before doing this he must put off his priestly garments and put on others. This circumstance is the origin of the familiar comparison that Jesus put off his robes of glory before coming to earth. The comparison is quite interesting but we should not be too dogmatic about it for many contrasts also could be cited. In all of our comparisons, and there are many proper ones, we should be careful not to drift off into speculation.

Verses 12, 13. This passage must be considered in the light of Num. 4: 13, 14. Please see that place now. The reader will learn that when moving, the delicate fabric of a vail was put over the altar and the heavy things of the altar service were placed on top of the same. This would force us to the conclusion that no fire was on the instrument at such time. Thus we must understand the paragraph here being considered as applying only when in service, not when in transportation.

Verse 14, 15. A repetition of the law already given on this subject. A small part of the flour was taken out of the supply and burned on the altar and it would be a sweet savor or pleasant odor to the Lord.

Verse 16. It is interesting to note that "holy place" and "court" are used in the same connection. This is because while certain distinctions are made as to which is the Holy Place and which not, yet in the sense of quality, or as an adjective, all of the things of the Lord are holy.

Verses 17, 18. This food was for the exclusive use of the ones officiating in the sacrifice. No one else had a right to it. That is the meaning of the last three words. It means that no one may touch it except those who are holy or who are consecrated.

Verses 19-23. As already seen, the priests had to offer sacrifices as well as did others. But not all of them were for sin. They were also for the purpose of consecration or inducting into active service. Whenever a new priest was needed to be put into service then this offering of consecration must be made. And an interesting contrast here is that no part of the offering was to be eaten. It must be wholly burnt. The reason for the difference is that the major portion of the other meat offerings was for food for the priest. But this offering is already for the benefit of the priest so therefore it should be put altogether on the altar.

Verses 24, 25. There was only one altar for burnt sacrifices. That is the main point in this paragraph. This altar was before the Lord. That is, it represented the presence of the Lord in that Dispensation and hence that was the place where the offering should be made. Such restriction will appear more significant as we pass along.

Verse 26. This holy place is explained in verse 16 above.

Verse 27. It was not the touching of the flesh that made him holy. The meaning is that none was permitted to touch it unless he was holy or consecrated. This was because the whole procedure was of a holy nature. This is indicated by the close of the verse since the blood of the sacrifice had been sprinkled on certain things and then spoken of as being holy.

Verse 28. In order that this vessel may not be used again it was to be broken, if an earthen one. But since a brasen one could not be broken it must be cleansed by being scoured and rinsed. These are some of the peculiar regulations that were a part of the law of the Lord. No reason is assigned why this was required. Only, the lesson of obedience is found in the instructions.

Verse 29. There were certain directions given as to who should participate in the activities, such as who must go to the tabernacle community every year; and now, as to who may eat of this sacrifice. No particular reason is given.

Verse 30. We should bear in mind that the terms "sin offering" and "holy place" are used a little freely and the connection must be always considered. We do not believe the Bible contradicts itself. But in one place it will direct that the flesh of a sin offering be eaten in the holy place, the court. Perhaps in another it will say that it must not be eaten at all. But the explanation in the present verse is that the flesh of an animal whose blood is brought into the tabernacle for sin is not to be eaten. Not all the animals were so used so far as their blood was concerned. And the ones that were must be considered in this verse.

LEVITICUS 7

Verses 1-6. This paragraph does not offer anything new but is another instance of the repetitions that will be found frequently in the book. And the slight variation that may be found in the different accounts would serve as an explanation of the subjects as a whole. It is similar to the fact of there being four accounts given of the Gospel. They all agree in thought even though different in wording. But this very difference serves as an explanation one of another.

Verse 7. This provision for the priest was referred to by Paul in 1 Cor. 9: 13.

Verse 8. The skin could be treated and then used either as clothing or in some mechanical purpose. Thus we see that the necessary "food and clothing" came to the priests through their service of the Lord.

Verses 9, 10. This means of course that all except the small portion that was taken out to be burned was to be theirs for food. The word "much" is not in the original directly. But it means that the right of one of the sons of Aaron to this food was as much (or great) as that of another.

Verses 11, 12. We are about to read of a little variation from the services that have been considered. That is, there is a combination of sacrifice on the altar with a sort of religious feast. The altar feature is considered in this paragraph and conforms to the previous regulations. The variation will come next.

Verses 13-15. This is the variation mentioned in preceding paragraph. We see that leavened bread was permitted and might lead us to confusion unless attentive. We have been impressed with the thought that no leaven was ever to be burned. But it is plain here that the service now being considered in this paragraph is wholly in the class of a feast in connection with the sacrificial activity named in preceding one. The word "eaten" in verse 15 is the key to the situation.

Verses 16, 17. Usually the requirement was made that no remainder of an offering could be eaten the second day. But an exception is made here for no reason that is stated. Simply that the Lord said so and that makes it a law to be obeyed in faith.

Verse 18. So particular was the Lord about the restrictions just given that if they were neglected and the eating was done on the third day it would not bring any credit to the performer. Not only so but it would bring a curse on him. The same principle is true now. If a person performs some religious service that is not in harmony with the law of the Lord, it not only will not be any benefit to him but it will bring the displeasure of God upon him.

Verse 19. Suppose that a sacrifice has been attended to. Then the parts reserved for the priest, the breast and shoulder, should come in contact with something that was regarded as unclean. Then that flesh is rendered unfit for food and must not be used as food. It must be destroyed by fire.

Verse 20. Uncleanness in the Old Testament did not always mean a condition of literal or actual filth. A thing might be considered unclean ceremonially that was not so in its natural sense. This is evident from the fact that many things considered unclean in that day are said by Paul to be "good" and not to be refused. (1 Tim. 4: 4.) And when a person ate of the things of the Lord while he was unclean he was to be cut off from the people.

Verse 21. This verse explains what is meant by being unclean in the preceding one. It means a person that had come in contact with some unclean thing. And if the fact of touching an unclean thing made a person unclean in that day, much more would it be so regarded by the Lord in our day. Paul teaches this in 2 Cor. 6: 17.

Verses 22, 23. The law against eating fat is again repeated. The fat means the choice part of the animal, such as the suet of the beef, or the tallow of the sheep.

Verse 24. The fat of the animals was the Lord's and was to be burned on the altar if used at all in the service. But a distinction was made against the fat of an animal that was found having been torn by some beast. Such fat must not be used in the sacrifices. But they could make a personal use of it with the restriction that they must not eat of it.

Verse 25. So strict was the Lord about persons eating this fat that belonged to the sacrifices that whosoever did so was to be cut off. See Ex. 31: 14 for explanation of the meaning of this expression.

Verses 26, 27. Eating of blood was as objectionable to God as the eating of fat and the person guilty was to be "cut off."

Verses 28, 29. The words to be emphasized here are, "unto the Lord," which meant the sacrifice must not be transacted in their private homes but must be taken to the place where the Lord was to meet with them.

Verse 30. He could not delegate to another his duty. He must bring the offering to the place and not expect the Lord to send his priest after it.

Verses 31-34. The parts to be for the use of the priests are again named. Note the expression "for ever" in connection with the statute. It means "agelasting." As long as that age or Dispensation continued that statute was to be in force.

Verses 35, 36. The information in this paragraph is to the effect that the regulations under consideration had their beginning at the time that Aaron and his sons were introduced into the priesthood service of the Lord.

Verse 37. The five major sacrifices described in the first five chapters of this book are named in one connection here and it would be well for those marking their Bibles to underscore the names and make reference to the chapters referred to.

Verse 38. In one verse we have the expressions "commanded Moses" and "commanded the children of Israel" used in the same connection. Which means of course that one expression is as strong as the other. That means that the sabbatarians who try to distinguish between the authority of God and that of Moses are in grave error. Since they do this in order to cover up their gross inconsistencies it makes their perversity all the more condemnable.

LEVITICUS 8

Verses 1-3. This is the same service described in Ex. 29. Let us take notice that the congregation was to assemble and be present at the consecration service. It is much like the requirements of certain activities in the New Testament. They must be considered in the presence of the church. This great principle of God's government of his people will be discussed in detail in the proper connection.

Verses 4-6. The first thing that was done for the consecration was to wash them. And the first thing that is done to consecrate a person for the service of God in the Christian Dispensation is to wash him in water. (Heb. 10: 22.)

Verse 7. After being washed the garments were placed on them. The garments for the spiritual priests today consist of living for Christ. (Rom. 13: 14.)

Verse 8. These objects must be put into their proper place as a means of communication with the Lord. (Ex. 28: 30.)

Verse 9. This is the piece on which were the words, "Holiness to the Lord."

Verse 10. See Ex. 30: 26-29 for description of this oil and observe the restrictions as to its use.

Verse 11. To sprinkle or dash seven times is a figurative indication of complete consecration to God. The term "seven" is so used in the scriptures.

Verse 12. The frequency and importance of pouring oil on the head as seen in the Old Testament ceremonies of various kinds must not be overlooked, because it established the basis for the figurative use of the term. Thus we have the statement in Heb. 1: 9, that God had anointed the Son with the oil of gladness.

Verses 13-16. See Ex. chapter 29 for detailed directions for this consecration.

Verse 17. Again we have the interesting circumstance of taking this animal's body to the outside of the camp to be burned. (Heb. 13: 11.)

Verses 18-21. Perhaps the reader has noticed that it was Moses who was officiating in this service at the altar. That was because the priesthood has not yet been established but is in the act of being established. This makes it necessary for Moses to act since he is the lawgiver and in this respect is greater than Aaron.

Verses 22-24. The application of blood to the ear, suggested the hearing of the right things; to the hand, meant the doing of right things; and to the feet, of walking in the right paths.

Verses 25-27. Since Aaron and his sons were the ones to be consecrated, these articles were placed in their hands to be put through a formal presentation before God.

Verses 28, 29. After the formal actions of the prospective priests then Moses put the pieces on the altar and burned them in a sacrifice.

Verse 30. Not only must the bodies of the priests be consecrated as described above, but also the garments they are to wear in the service. So the robes of righteousness which Christians must wear, which means their mode of religious life, also had the consecration of the blood of Christ who is our sacrifice.

Verse 31. An exception is here made of the manner of preparing the flesh for the service. It was to be boiled instead of roasted. No reason is given for this.

Verses 32-36. Moses is the spokesman in this paragraph and he is directing the actions of Aaron and his sons. Just why these seven days were required as the period for remaining at the tabernacle is not stated. But it is a common idea set forth in the several situations coming up in the Old Testament that seven is considered, and is suggestive of, the idea of completeness. Also in this paragraph is another statement of the commandment of the Lord "by the hand of Moses."

LEVITICUS 9

Verses 1, 2. The eighth day here means the day after the period of seven of the consecration set forth in the previous chapter. The priests have been placed in their office now so they are the ones who are to make the offering. In the act of consecration Moses did the offering for them.

Verses 3-7. Not only must the men to be priests be consecrated but the people also must be consecrated. That is commanded here and the priests just having been put into office are the ones to act in consecrating the people.

Verse 8, 9. The articles of furniture for the service must be consecrated with blood. So the blood was sprinkled on the horns of the altar and then all the blood was poured out at the bottom of the altar. At this place we will again recall that the blood of Christ was poured out at the foot of the cross.

Verses 10, 11. After taking certain portions from the animal to be burned on the altar the body was taken outside of the camp to be burned. (Heb. 13: 11.)

Verses 12-14. Since the transactions are still concerned with the consecrations of the service we are to understand that "he" refers to Moses. That is, Aaron and his sons cooperated with Moses in this whole procedure just as God and Christ cooperated in all the transactions of the system of salvation.

Verses 15, 16. I shall merely repeat here the remark that the word "manner" refers to the ordinance established in the beginning of the book as pertaining to the law of the sacrifices. See explanation at chapter 5: 10.

Verse 17. The meat offering was the vegetable offering consisting of meal or fine flour. A handful was taken out to be burned on the altar and the rest of it was to be eaten by the priest.

Verse 18. This bullock was for the people. After it had been slain the priests presented the blood and Moses sprinkled it on the altar. We compare the fact that Christ presented his blood to be used in consecration of the system of religion to be maintained under the last Dispensation.

Verses 19-23. The parts to be burned on the altar are again mentioned. Then we are told that Moses and Aaron went into the tabernacle and when they came out they blessed the people. They could not have done so had the people not been there in waiting. This is a similar thought as expressed in Heb. 9: 28.

Verse 24. We know from various sources that the art of fire-making had been known by humanity long before this. It was not necessary therefore that the fire be miraculously started here, just to give them fire, but this would be the Lord's manner of demonstrating his approval of the situation. It was not the last time that God expressed his mind with fire. 1 Kings 18: 38.) All this again reminds us of Heb. 1:1.

LEVITICUS 10

Verse 1. *Strange fire.* This means fire obtained from the outside or from some source other than the one expected of the Lord. An indication of the source from which the fire was to be obtained is in chapter 16: 12. The Lord had consecrated this by starting the fire miraculously and there is where they should have obtained it. The R.V. words the last part of the verse "had not commanded them." That explains the verse to mean that the Lord had not commanded them to get this fire which they used, and therefore it would be wrong to use it. The principle is taught that God does not have to say "don't do it" to make a thing wrong. If he has not said "do it" with reference to subjects on which he is legislating, then to do a thing makes it wrong. In other words, we must respect the silence of God as well as his spoken word.

Verse 2. Here is another instance where God demonstrates his will by the use of fire. But this time it is to condemn and not to bless. It was very appropriate to use this means for punishment in this instance. These men had gone on the outside to get the fire they intended to use, so God brings fire from the outside (miraculous source) to punish them. It says they were devoured. Yet verse 5 shows they still existed which proves that devouring or destroying does not always mean annihilation.

Verse 3. Since God was never, and never could be sinful, the statement of being sanctified does not always mean the act of cleansing from sin. It also means to recognize as sinless. As such he would be possessed of absolute authority and should be obeyed strictly and reverently. This is what these men had not done. After Moses made this speech we are told that "Aaron held his peace." He was the father of these men and the natural inclination would be to defend them or at least try to apologize for them. This speech of Moses quelled any such action if he had intention of defending them.

Verses 4, 5. Something must now be done with the bodies and Moses called certain men to perform the task. Since these men were not members of Aaron's immediate family they did not belong to the priesthood. The service now to be rendered was not of a priestly nature, hence, some one outside of the sacred class should do it. Sometimes it is necessary for the church to have certain work done that is not a part of the religious activities. In such cases it is proper to employ those not Christians to do the work, such as building or improving the church house, etc., etc. They did not interfere with their clothing arrangement for that would have been outside their task. They were told only to carry the men outside the camp. Whatever was finally done with the bodies, the garments were not buried with them for Ex. 29: 29, 30 shows that when it was necessary for one man to replace another in the priesthood the garments were to come to him for service also.

Verses 6, 7. The situation is so grave and the greatness of the sin is so depressing that Moses puts a ban on all demonstrations from the remaining sons of Aaron.

Verses 8-10. While all the sons of Aaron were eligible for the priestly service, not all of them were in active service at one time, but just as many as would be needed for the work. So now these two remaining sons came into active service which would require them to go into the tabernacle to officiate in the service of that place as their brothers had done before them. Nothing has been said as yet about the cause for the rash actions of the first two sons. Therefore we would necessarily conclude that the precaution here against going into the service while under the effect of intoxication implies that such was the state of the sons who were slain. And we incidentally get a thought as to the effects of liquor. When men are under its influence, it renders them irresponsible and dangerous. The use of alcoholic liquor as a beverage is condemned all through the Bible and the declaration is made that no drunkard will enter the kingdom of heaven. One specification here as a reason to put the use of it away, is that they be able to recognize the difference between the holy and unholy things.

Verse 11. Here we see that one of the duties of a priest was to teach the people. This is taught in other places. (Deut. 17: 9; Mal. 2: 7.) Moses will not always be with them and yet the people will need the services of teachers. The Lord designed that the priests should do this work. In order to be able to do so, and be informed in the law, they must keep their minds clear from the befogging of drink.

Verses 12, 13. Since there are some new priests in office or active service, Moses repeats to them a part of the functions and privileges of their office. This included the use of making food out of the part of the meat or flour offering that was left after the small portion had been burned on the altar.

Verses 14, 15. Among the things to be repeated to them was the instruction about the wave breast and heave shoulder. This was a very unusual procedure and one that did not exhibit any logical reason. As such it might be the more easily forgotten and neglected. Therefore, it is expressed to them here. The breast was put on the hands of the person officiating and waved or given a sort of swinging motion, back and forth, before the Lord. The shoulder was placed on the hands and given a heaving, or up and down, motion, then appropriated to the personal use of the priest for food.

Verses 16-20. The goat of the sin offering should have been used in a different way from what it was here. Part of it was to be eaten in the court, part was to be burnt, and the blood was to be brought into the Holy Place. But when Moses made inquiry he found that the whole animal had been burnt and no use made of the blood in the holy place. He complained to Aaron about it. The 19th verse is a little indefinite, if taken alone. It will be clear when we bear in mind the circumstance that has just happened to the other brothers of the present acting priests. That affair had evidently intimidated all of them, and they feared to enter the Holy Place. It was thus an action from fear or fright, and not one of deliberate disobedience. When Moses heard this explanation he was content.

LEVITICUS 11

Verses 1, 2. Before going further into the study of this chapter it is well to make some general observations. The Old Testament period was one of education and preparation for the more informal and spiritual service to come in the New. Mankind had not been instructed fully about the finer principles later to be taught and in which they were to be guided by the spirit of the Christian Dispensation and not the letter of the Jewish Dispensation. Among the primary or object lessons was that of distinction between certain animals for food or sacrifice. The ones that are here to be classed as unclean are not to be regarded as such literally or physically, or even from a sanitary standpoint. Paul declares in 1 Tim. 4: 4, that every creature of God is good and nothing to be refused. And he was talking about eating them too. He is not presuming to give directions as to what a man might or might not prefer to eat. He meant there was nothing any more, that was ceremonially unclean as was the case of old. And so we are to consider the restrictions of this chapter in the light of divine authority. Or, they were to observe these distinctions because the Lord said to, and not because they could see something unclean in any of the creatures mentioned.

Verse 3. Two characteristics were required of the larger animals in order to be classed among the clean. They must have cloven feet and must chew the cud.

Verses 4-8. There could be no reason to misunderstand what the Lord meant by his instructions in verse 3 because he names some specific animals that did not come within the description. That is, these animals mentioned had one of the characteristics but not the other. That made them objectionable to the Lord. Naturally, then, any animal that had neither of these points (such as the horse) would not be permitted for food.

Verses 9-12. Among the kinds of fish to be rejected were those not having both fins and scales. This would exclue the catfish which all people know today to be one of the most desirable and delicate kinds of food. But it is unclean, according to verse 12 at hand. The lessons of obedience prompted by faith is the object to be taught.

Verses 13-19. Instead of stating some characteristic by which to classify the fowls to be eaten and those to be rejected, they are named. The word "kind" is frequently found in this chapter. It means a variety of the various things mentioned. For instance, every variety of the eagle was rejected.

Verse 20. *Fowls that creep.* The Revised here says "winged creeping things." It does not mean what would be termed insects, but some sort of living creatures that usually moved by use of their feet, yet had wings so that they could mount the air.

Verses 21-24. Some specification of the kind of living things referred to in preceding paragraph is given here so as to avoid confusion. This indicates that the general classification was to have some exceptions.

Verse 25. *Until the even.* This statement or expression shows that many of the laws and restrictions imposed on the Israelites were ceremonial and not physical. For it would be easily understood that a physical condition of uncleanness would not just continue till evening and then be gone; especially after having been put through some form of purification as was done here. But again we have the lesson of divine requirement based on authority, and not on the logical understanding of man.

Verses 26-28. This would have excluded the bear and yet today many people think the bear to be very acceptable food. And according to Paul in 1 Tim. 4: 4 it is good. But under that Dispensation it was a religious requirement to show divine authority.

Verses 29-31. A few more specifications. Here it is not only forbidden to eat certain animals but the touching of them rendered the person unclean. That would mean that such a person would not be fit to engage in any of the services until made clean again by the manner of purification to be described elsewhere.

Verse 32. If a vessel of service comes in contact with one of the unclean things, such as dead animals, that vessel is considered unclean and must be put into water.

Verse 33. Should one of the unclean things fall into the earthen vessel used for service, that vessel must be broken. This is to be considered as an exception of the preceding verse. For some reason this vessel was considered so unfit that it was to be broken and not cleansed by putting into water.

Verses 34, 35. Even meat that is ordinarily considered clean and fit for food, if it comes in contact with the water that had been used to cleanse a vessel, is to be considered unclean. Even the cooking utensils, important though they may be, when coming in contact with this unclean material are unclean and must be destroyed.

Verse 36. Water is here presented with the thought that it has great cleansing properties. If there is plenty of water (much water) into which some article of use happens to fall, then it is considered as cleansed. However, if a person comes in contact with that thing that is about to fall into the water he is unclean.

Verses 37, 38. If a part of a dead carcase comes in contact with seed intended to be sown, that seed is still clean, provided it is left dry. But if water had been put on the seed previous to its contact with the unclean carcase, it was rendered unclean. No reason is given for this. We know that water is considered as a cleansing agent. But when it is used in a way that would cause it to be a dissolvent then the thing so affected by it would be more susceptible to the uncleanness of the carcase.

Verses 39, 40. Even the beasts considered were rendered unclean by dying of themselves. All persons touching them were unclean. The law had already been given against eating blood. An animal dying of itself would not have been bled properly and hence must be considered unclean. Of course, it will be necessary for someone to dispose of the carcase, yet the one who was called on to perform that service must wash his clothes. That still left him unclean until the evening. That would mean that even though he went through the cleansing ceremony of washing his clothes, he would not be permitted to come in contact with any of the holy things till even.

Verses 41, 42. Just a slight variation in the specifications. This paragraph includes the snake among the rejected articles of food. It is used today by many people, and if they wish to eat it there is no law against it, now. But there was then.

Verse 43. Here is some strong language. It shows them that if they eat of or touch these unclean things then not only would they be rendered unclean, but they would be considered abominable in the sight of God. That would mean, of course, that none of their services rendered, while in that condition, would be accepted. To accept them would be the same as accepting uncleanness, which God will not do.

Verses 44, 45. The fundamental reason is here given why they should do as told. It is from the Lord their God. The things they were commanded to observe did not have any logical basis therefore they would be led to observe them through reverence for the one making the demand. Also, a reference is made to their former bondage and the one now demanding their obedience is the very same one who delivered them. Therefore, gratitude as well as absolute reverence should prompt them to obey.

Verses 46, 47. The principle of action in this whole subject is expressed in the words "make a difference." In all of God's dealings with man he has been particular to have him observe that principle. It has always been objectionable to the Lord for man to be careless about such distinctions. As a final summing up of this whole chapter, let it be remembered that what God wished to do was to teach the children of Israel, and through them the whole world, that He is supreme. His creature, man, must learn the lesson of obedience from the motive of reverence and not merely on the ground of logic. As a means of getting this important lesson across, the Lord has laid down such arbitrary regulations as these, about clean and unclean animals and things.

LEVITICUS 12

Verses 1-5. Here is another and a noted instance where the requirements were not based on any actual condition of uncleanness. The birth of a child was according to the law of God, and a woman was to be honored who had gone through that experience; yet this ceremonial condition of uncleanness and its treatment was placed in that law to teach the lesson of obedience. We can see that no physical condition was in the mind of the Lord since the period of uncleanness was doubled in the case of a female babe. The period of preliminary uncleanness or separation in the case of a male child was only half as long as the other. This was in order to comply with another provision that had been made with Abram and his seed. It was stipulated that when a boy baby was eight days old he must be circumcised. (Gen. 17: 12). Therefore, the period was regulated so as to harmonize with that covenant. With the female babe such ordinance had no relation, therefore the woman was required to consider herself unclean for double the time, as with the other.

Verses 6, 7. There is no charge of sin or wrongdoing from a moral or actual standpoint against a woman who has borne a child. As already stated, such were in high praise in the estimate of God. Yet she must observe some of the formalities of the divine law. Again we note that the period of days and weeks which she had to observe while waiting for her condition of blood to pass, did not settle the matter. She must then go through some of the religious exercises in connection with the altar. She is told to bring a lamb and a bird for an offering. She must bring it to the priest and he shall officiate in the service at the altar. All this was in order to settle finally the whole affair and put her in a state of compliance with the law.

Verse 8. As in other cases of the animal sacrifices, God did not make any demand on the woman that was beyond her financial state. Thus, if she were not able to bring a lamb, she could bring two turtles (turtledoves) or two young pigeons. Note that she would be accepted in this lesser offering only if she were not able to bring the other. In Luke 2: 24 we read of the case of Mary, that she brought the birds. Since there was no criticism of her devotion at that time we must conclude that her offering was acceptable. And that makes us conclude also that the parents of Jesus were poor.

LEVITICUS 13

General remarks. It would be difficult and unnecessary to consume the space required to comment on this chapter, verse by verse, since there is so much repetition. The importance of noting every detail of this horrible disease was more significant in the light of the plan of making the children of Israel a nation among nations and composed of strong men who could cope with the heathen nations surrounding them. Hence, they were given all these various symptoms for detection. According to the Schaff-Herzog Cyclopedia the leprosy of Biblical times was unlike that of modern times. This work of reference sums up the description of the disease as recorded in our present chapter with so much brevity, and yet, clearness, that I can do no better than quote from it the paragraph on the subject, as follows: "Lepra Mosaica, leprosy of Lev. 13 and 14. Its most marked symptoms were 'a rising, a scab, or a bright spot,' 'in the skin of the flesh' (Lev. 13: 2), with a hair turned white in the rising, scab, or bright spot, these being deeper than the scarf-skin (13: 3), and spreading of the scab, etc. (13: 7, 8.) As a more advanced case we have 'quick raw flesh in the rising' (13: 10). In verse 18 we find that the disease may take its origin in a boil, with the same symptoms. In verse 29 we have the disease appearing in the beard, or hair of the head,—a great calamity to the Jew, who was so proud of his beard; and here it comes in the form of a scall, with thin yellow hairs in the patches. These are all the symptoms we have; and they are probably given merely as initial symptoms, so that the priest should recognize the onslaught of different diseases in their earliest stages. The 'rising' may correspond to the tubercles of Lepra tuberculosa, or the bullae anaesthetica of the most recent authora. The scall of the head may be the Morphoea alopeciata, or Foxmange, placed by Kaposi (Hautkrankheiten, Wien, 1880), as a subdivision of the second form of leprosy,—the Lepra maculosa. In verses 12-17 we read, that, if the patient is white all over, he is clean, no doubt because the disease had then run its course. In this case it is probably a general Psoriasis."—Article, LEPROSY.

Regardless of the actual condition of disease with those afflicted or suspected to be afflicted with this disease, many formal requirements are to be noted, such as the term of "seven days" in verses 4, 5, 26, 33, 50. All this indicates that even in this terrible affliction the rule of formality or ceremony, based on the authority of God was to be observed. To the detail of leprosy in a house or garment or other thing of an inanimate nature, attention will be given in the next chapter.

Another interesting item in the regulations of this disease and those afflicted with it is given in verses 45, 46. After it had been concluded that a person had the disease he must have his dwelling in a segregated district and not try to mingle closely with the public. If it became necessary to go abroad he must protect the public by covering his mouth and also by announcing to those in hearing that he was unclean. This will explain the state of mind of those afflicted when they saw the Saviour. We read in the New Testament (Matt. 8: 2; Luke 17: 12), how the lepers came toward Jesus with pleading and humble attitude and seeking relief from their humiliation. The lepers were placed by the law in perpetual quarantine.

LEVITICUS 14

Verses 1, 2. Leprosy has been pronounced an incurable disease. However that may be, it might run its course or it might be cured miraculously. And if that took place, then the patient was still not ready to be admitted to society. There must also be a ceremonial cleansing. Now we have no scripture statement that leprosy is a type of sin and thus are not warranted in making a positive statement to that effect. But we certainly would be permitted to note some of the outstanding comparisons. Because, while a sinner may get rid of his actual life of sin by repentance or reformotion of life, that alone does not make him whole before God nor qualify him for the fellowship with the society of the Lord's people religiously. We shall now notice the ceremonial program for the cleansing of the leper after being freed from the actual disease.

Verse 3. When it was thought that the leper had been cleared of the actual disease, he was to be brought to the priest who was the official person to handle all the ceremonies pertaining to the altar service. When the priest made the examination and found the patient healed physically then he must proceed with the ceremonies.

Verses 4-7. It would be unwise to speculate about the significance of all the details of this peculiar ceremony. There have been already too many instances of the requirements of the law that were so illogical that we know we cannot press them too far, without seeming to get out of the cases what the Lord did not put in them. But there can be no doubt that in a general sense this whole procedure typifies the plan of spiritual cleansing of man from the stain of sin, even after he has become free of its practice. Some living creature had to die in each case and some blood had to be shed. Also some fortunate creature was to be turned loose while another had to be slain. And there had to be a dipping of one in the blood of the other. This may well be taken as a good comparison, then, between Christ and the case now being considered here. Christ had to die for the cleansing of man from his sin, while the man to be cleansed is to be permitted to live. By making this great sacrifice for the world, Jesus, the sinless one, made it possible and right for a sinner to become whole and cleansed from his sin and prepared for the fellowship of God's people.

Verses 8, 9. Even after the man had been physically and ceremonially cleansed, he had some further precautions to take. After a man has repented and is then made free from the guilt of his sins by the blood of Christ, still he must make sure that he will not return to his former practice of sin and thus become stained again.

Verse 10. For a detailed description of how such creatures were to be prepared and used in the altar service see the first five chapters of this book and the comments.

Verses 11-13. It must never be overlooked that in the performance of the sacrifices of the Jewish law it required the services of the priests. They were the lawful representatives of that system. And the spiritual priests (Christians, 1 Peter 2: 9) are the ones who are to execute the divine law today since the law of Christ was given.

Verse 14. We here have another statement of the peculiar application of the blood. On the ear, to signify the hearing of the truth. On the hand, to signify the doing of right things. On the foot, to signify walking in right paths.

Verses 15, 16. Incidentally, we have in this paragraph a clear setting forth of the distinctive meanings of the three words, "pour" and "dip" and "sprinkle." The New Testament requires sinners to be baptized in water for the remission of sins. Certain ones contend that either one of the words which I have here placed in quotations may be used as a definition of the word for baptism, that there is practically no difference. But here in one connection the three words are used and the original in each case will be given, that the reader can see for himself that the three words do not have even a similar meaning, since they come from different words. The Hebrew words for the three words under consideration are, respectively, YATSAQ, TABAL, NAZAH.

Verse 17. Oil is here applied to the same parts that had been consecrated with the blood. Oil was a symbol of light and so the person cleansed also needs further instruction.

Verse 18. Similar to preceding verse except that it is done in the form of more honor since it is poured over the head, thus indicating the blessing of God. See that shade of meaning of the ceremony in Heb. 1: 9.

Verses 19, 20. The former patient could not attend to the ceremonial purification for himself. He must contact the priest in active service at that time who shall handle the sacrifice according to the law.

Verses 21, 22. Same provision here made for the man too poor to bring a larger offering. According to his ability he must bring. The same principle is taught in the New Testament. (2 Cor. 8: 12.)

Verses 23-30. This paragraph does not differ from various passages already considered. But attention will be called to the fact that not only must the sacrifice be submitted to the priest, but that must be done at the door of the tabernacle. It was the place designated by the Lord for the official performances of sacrificial service, so the priest could not leave the tabernacle and go to the man's private home to do that service for him.

Verses 31, 32. We cannot be too observant of the provision made according to the ability of the peop.e of God. Many institutions of man make an arbitrary stipulation as to what will procure their benefits and the poor as well as the rich are exacted. But God does not deal thus. We should not overlook the other feature of this subject either. If God will make allowance for a man's poverty or other lack, he also will make the stronger demands of the man with more ability. That also is a principle that holds good under the Christian Dispensation. (Luke 12: 48.)

Verses 33, 34. *I put plague of leprosy.* This is the expression referred to in previous chapter. This shows that while leprosy was a disease of the flesh and had its symptoms as related to the tissues of man, yet God caused inanimate objects, such as houses and garments to be infected with it. In this connection we will bear in mind that the preparatory or educational age of the world is still going. The people, like children or young people in literary schools, need to be gradually brought into the understanding of the higher and more logical principles of life by first becoming accustomed to training under the "object lesson" method. The Old Testament period may be justly considered as the object lesson period. This will explain many situations otherwise difficult of understanding.

Verse 35. The private individual was not permitted to decide the case. Neither did he have right to be indifferent about it. If there should be any indication that something was wrong, he must make it known.

Verse 36. Nothing could be clearer than the thought that most of the regulations practiced at the time of which we are writing, were formal and not actual or physical. Here is the case in point. If the condition of leprosy had to do only with the literal sense of the word, then the things in the house would have been just as much tainted whether the priest saw them before, or after, he had entered the house. But as the case was considered, only the things that were in the house after he came in would be considered unclean if he found the house to be so. Again we have the matter presented as already expressed in this study, that many of the regulations were arbitrary and for the purpose of educating mankind in the principle of obedience and respect.

Verses 37, 38. This is one of the instances where the seven days were observed. That was often done in Bible times. The condition of the house was allowed to progress under the Lord's will, and the whole thing done to teach the lesson of obedience.

Verses 39-42. Since this whole situation is under the management of God, through the priest, we would think that miraculous power could have cleansed the house of the plague at once. This is true. But there is more than the specific value of the house at stake. God is teaching the lesson of obedience as stated above. Besides this, the lesson is seen here, that an effort should be made to save anything that is threatened. That is a principle taught all through the Scriptures. The admonitions found in many places about trying to "restore" and bring doubtful ones to repentance are in harmony with the procedure recorded here.

Verses 43, 44. The word "fretting" is from a word that means "painful." The thing that is being examined is a dumb object. But the effect the disease would have on one who would be affected thereby would be painful. And thus it must be considered for the sake of those who would occupy, or even come into the house, occasionally.

Verse 45. After the house has been officially pronounced unclean and definitely infected with the disease, and after all efforts have been used to remedy it that were available and they failed, then the last resort for the safety of others is to destroy the house completely.

Verses 46, 47. After the house has been pronounced diseased, then all who had been in the house while it was being considered are unclean, but not to the extent of having the disease. He must wash his clothes and be considered unclean "until the even." That is, he must consider himself as unfit to engage in anything that would require him to touch any holy thing, and this state of his condition was to be observed all that day. As to whether he would ever have any more trouble over the plague would depend on further developments. If, after the present precautions against infection, he should develop in himself any suspicious symptoms, then he would be required to undergo the experiences described in chapter 13.

Verse 48. If the priest finds the conditions as described in this verse then he shall pronounce the house clean. It will not be considered as having the disease of leprosy at the time of final examination although it was so infested before.

Verses 49-57. When the plague of leprosy in a house has been removed by the treatment given it by the priest, then the ceremonial cleansing must be administered as in the case of a man so afflicted. The reader will here consult chapter 14: 4-7, and apply the thoughts there offered to the case now at hand.

LEVITICUS 15

Verses 1-13. The system given to the children of Israel through Moses was all the government they had, either for their religious or civil life.

It had to take care of all their needs as a nation and as individuals. This explains in part why the requirements are found in so many instances that might seem to be unnnecessary, were we to be thinking only of religious activities. So we have all these sanitary regulations. It is considered needful by all that we have some restrictions to be enforced by law for the protection of the public. We are "our brother's keeper" in more than one sense. Even though a man were so careless or negligent about his own welfare as to take no precautions about his physical condition, others might be affected by it and thus he is not permitted to do as he pleases. The public safety is at stake and all means possible must be used for its sake. Of course, while the actual interests of health in general are being taken care of, the lesson of respect for law is also given.

Verses 14, 15. Similar ceremony must be observed for the legal cleansing as was used in the cases of leprosy. Some exceptions as to detail but the same principle.

Verses 16, 17. This refers to the action of nature in relieving a man of normal strength, of the pressure from the reproductive impulse. If he is not married or for some other reason his life germ is not expended by cohabitation, but is discharged by the involuntary urge of his physical impulse, that would bring him under the condition described in this paragraph.

Verse 18. The relation of the sexes is an experience necessary for the reproduction of the race and is therefore not unclean, actually. But the same idea of precaution is needed in this case as in others. Extreme carelessness in this lawful action could result in disease. Cleanliness is thus required.

Verses 19-23. The same precaution of isolation for the sake of others is required in this case. No benefit could come to a woman thus afflicted by coming in contact with another, hence it would be no injustice to her to put her off from society until such time as would be necessary to make proper treatment and disposition of her case.

Verse 24. The woman might be a married one. The "flowers" refer to the discharge of a woman at certain periods through the child-bearing portion of her life. If her husband should be so unreasonable as to have relations with her at such time, then he is to be considered unclean as here described.

Verses 25-28. The ordinary time for the condition of discharge above mentioned must always be considered as a time of uncleanness. If she should run over that regular length of time, all the extra days must be included in the time of uncleanness.

Verses 29, 30. The ceremonial cleansing is again regarded as necessary as before.

Verse 31. Many of the instances of uncleanness that have been treated previously in this study had no direct connection with the tabernacle. The women never came into it to officiate, nor did all of the men. Yet the writer says these requirements were made that the tabernacle be not defiled. The tabernacle was a type of the church in many respects and is required to be kept clean. (2 Cor. 6: 16, 17.) Thus, we see again that many of the requirements of that ancient system were typical and not literal.

Verses 32, 33. This is a summing up of previous requirements. The word "sick" in verses 33 is from DAVEH and defined by Strong "sick (especially in menstruation)."

LEVITICUS 16

Verse 1. In stating that the Lord spake to Moses "after the death," etc., it is not for the purpose of giving us the date of the conversation. We would necessarily know it was not before. But the expression has the effect of "in view of." The terrible visitation which God thought necessary to make at that time was to be a lesson to all others on the sanctity of the tabernacle and nothing should be attempted that would violate that sanctity.

Verse 2. Aaron, the High Priest, was the only person at that time who had the right to enter the Most Holy place of the tabernacle. And even he did not have the privilege of entering that place at just any time he might choose. Hence the warning given here. The words "at all times" mean that he must not come at any time the desire might enter his mind. To do so would bring death. Incidentally, we also have a lesson in this verse as to the authority of Moses. In a matter so important as to involve life and death he was even above Aaron the High Priest. Thus we are again to be made aware of the error of those who try to lessen the authority of the Mosaic law.

Verse 3. In a technical sense we

speak of the first room in the tabernacle as the Holy Place and the second room as the Most Holy. But in a descriptive sense, both rooms were considered holy. That was true even of the court. The connection here makes it plain that the second room is the place now being considered. And it will be helpful for the reader to know that the chapter now before us is the one that gives the procedure of the famous day of atonement which was the third one of the three yearly feasts of the Jews, and one on which all the males must go to the tabernacle community.

Verse 4. The garments here mentioned are described in their making in Ex. 28, and were prepared for the use of the High Priest when he was officiating as such.

Verse 5. In verse 3 mention was made of a young bullock that was to be offered by Aaron when he came into the holy place. We are not to conclude that he took the body of the animal there. It was only the blood. (Heb. 13: 11.) And the blood of this particular animal was for himself. (Heb. 5: 3.) In the verse now being considered the smaller animals were taken of the congregation and for it. The reference is made to two kinds of offerings, "sin" and "burnt." The reader again should consult the first and fourth chapters of this book for details on these offerings.

Verse 6. This is explained in preceding paragraph.

Verse 7. The door of the tabernacle here means the entrance to the court that was surrounding the tabernacle proper. The use of these goats was for the benefit of the congregation and will be understood soon.

Verse 8. The one "for the Lord" here means the one that is soon to be offered to the Lord on the altar of burnt sacrifices. The other is to become the scapegoat. The meaning and significance of this word will be fully discussed in verses 20-22 below.

Verse 9. This is the action referred to in preceding verse. This animal was killed and offered on the brasen altar at the entrance to the court.

Verse 10. This goat was presented alive and was never killed as will be shown in a later paragraph in this chapter. The decision as to which goat was to be used for this was made by casting lots. That was an action resorted to in ancient times as a means of deciding questions. There were various methods used at different times, but in all cases where God wished to use it as a means of making known his will he would always see that the outcome would not be "just luck" but come out as he willed in the case. (Prov. 16: 33.) In using this means of declaring his will at times we have indication of significance of Heb. 1: 1.

Verse 11. This same action is meant in verses 3 and 6. But the reader must not be impatient with the repetition. He should bear in mind that we are studying the great day of atonement on which the spiritual status of the whole nation of the Israelites was being adjusted. The day which typifies so much that is said in the New Testament. The day whose activities have so much relation to the service of Christ. So the words "bring the bullock" means he brought the animal and killed it in order to obtain the blood to be taken into the Most Holy place in the tabernacle. The disposition of the body of the bullock will be explained later on in the chapter.

Verse 12. *Censer.* This is from MACHTAH and Strong defines it: "a pan for live coals." The same Hebrew word has been translated in the A.V., by the words firepan and snuffdish. It is plain therefore that it was a portable instrument and not a piece of furniture located there permanently. He must take this instrument with him to the altar that is at the court entrance. There he will find live coals because that fire was always burning while the institution was in service. There he obtained the fire which he brought into the Most Holy place here described as ""within the vail." He also had a handful of the sweet incense that had been prescribed and prepared for this purpose (Ex. 34: 35), to burn on this censer in the Holy Place.

Verse 13. The cloud or visible fumes of the incense acted as a covering for the mercy seat "that he die not," or, that he may obtain the blessing of Heaven.

Verse 14. The particular manner of applying the blood of the bullock is here described. He was to sprinkle or dash the blood over and toward the mercy seat. At this place the promise was made that God would meet with the priest. And at this place it would be proper to offer this blood which was to be to appease the Lord. This dashing of the blood was done seven times which signifies a complete sacrifice.

Verse 15. After the procedure of the foregoing verse the priest must go out and kill the goat that had fallen to the Lord. Then he must bring of its blood into the place where he had taken the blood of the bullock. At this point a question may have come up in the mind of the reader. We can see that the priest on this day enters the Most Holy place more than once. And does this agree with the language in Heb. 9: 7 where it says he entered this place "once a year"? There will be no difficulty if we let the language be used as meaning the same as we would use it. For instance, we might say that Americans celebrate the Declaration of Independence once a year and no one would question or misunderstand it. Then it might be asked, "How do they celebrate it?" and the explanation would be "by burning fireworks and making speeches." But the fact that they burnt these fireworks and made speeches several times on that day would not affect the statement that they celebrate the event "once a year."

Verse 16. *Because of their transgressions.* This refers to the people, but the expression is sandwiched between two others pertaining to the tabernacle. This shows that some general sense is meant and this will be fully discussed at verses 20-22.

Verse 17. The High Priest is in one part of the tabernacle at this time. Therefore, we must conclude that the word in this verse is restricted to the first room or Holy Place. It must not be occupied while the High Priest is officiating in the Most Holy place. We are not told why this restriction was given to them. Verses 18, 19. All of the parts of the institution were to be cleansed by the use of the blood. This is what is meant by Paul in Heb. 9: 22. That verse is erroneously cited often as referring to the blood of Christ. It refers to the literal blood of the animals slain under the Jewish Dispensation.

Verses 20-22. The tabernacle and its furniture have now been purified and atoned for, by the blood of the sacrifices. This typifies the cleansing and purifying of the church which is the spiritual tabernacle with the people of Christ under the Christian Dispensation. (Eph. 5: 25, 26.) Next will come the service for the congregation in the use of the live goat, called the scapegoat. This word is from AZAZEL and Strong defines it "goat of departure; the scapegoat." The meaning is clear when we remember that this goat was used to let the sins of the nation escape from them into the wilderness. The figurative use of this goat was that the sins of the nation were placed on the head of the animal to let him bear the burden instead of the guilty. It is the basis of the expression often used among people of "making one the goat." Doubtless this is thought to be nothing but slang. But it is used in cases similar to the one where the term originated. A case where the real responsible person in a given matter of supposed wrong doing is either not known or is wished to be unknown, and then some other unfortunate fellow will be named in order to distract attention from the real guilty one. That is when the saying of "making one the goat," is used.

When the priest laid his hands on the head of this goat and confessed all the sins of the nation, those sins were figuratively placed there and then the goat was lead away in token of the vanishing of the sins. This action is what John had in mind when he spoke of Jesus as the Lamb of God that taketh ("beareth" in the margin) away the sin of the world. It should not be thought that the individual sins of the Jews were all atoned for by this great service of the scapegoat. If, after the service had been attended to by the High Priest, it remained that some individual Jew owed the Lord a sacrifice for his individual conduct and he did not attend to it, this service of the High Priest would avail him nothing. Likewise, even though Jesus died for the sins of the whole world, if individuals fail to attend to their own duties of service to God, the sacrifice of Christ will do them no good. The activities of the High Priest in the Jewish system were for the benefit of the congregation as a whole.

Verses 23-25. One of the particulars not already mentioned in this chapter was that before the priest engaged in the offering of the sacrifice for sin, he must put off his special clothing long enough to wash himself. So it was with Christ. Before he proceeded with his great work of making a service for man, he laid aside his heavenly garments of glory (Phil. 2: 7), and came to earth. Then he also washed himself. (Matt. 3: 13-15.) He explained to John the purpose, that it was to fulfill all righteousness. Jesus carried out his personal duties through his earthly services and then completed the great matter by offering himself as a complete sacrifice for sin.

Verse 26. Nothing new especially here, but we should remember that the goat that was taken by this man into the wilderness was never brought back and thus never used again, although not slain. Neither was it the plan of God that Jesus should be made to become a sacrifice for sin a second time.

Verse 27. The transaction of this verse and the like has been referred to a number of times in this work. But it contains such a significant and beautiful thought that I shall offer a few additional remarks on it. The language in Heb. 13: 11 is in reference to this circumstance. The rule was that animals offered to God in sacrifice must be burned on the brasen altar inside the court gate. But this was one of the few exceptions. And the feature of it that Paul brings out is that the blood of this animal was brought into the tabernacle for sin, but that the body was taken outside of the camp to be burned. This typified the fact that Jesus was not permitted to die in the city. The place of crucifixion was on the outside which indicated some humiliation was intended to be imposed upon him. The Romans had various methods of executing the persons whom they found guilty of murder, or any crime calling for the death penalty. Crucifixion was one of the methods and was the one resorted to when the "convict" was supposed to be the most vile and disgraceful of all. Such a person was not worthy to die inside the city but must be taken to the outside and killed. While this was the motive for the action of the Romans in the case of Jesus, the hand of God was in it and brought it about that way, for the purpose of its humiliation. Not only did the secular government consider this form of execution as one of shame, but so it was considered by the law of Moses. (Deut. 21: 22, 23.) Paul cites this scripture in his argument to the Galatian brethren. (Gal. 3: 13.) He has the same circumstance in mind in his admonition in Heb. 13: 11, where he says for us to go forth with Christ in his exile to the outside and thus bear his reproach with him.

Verse 28. This is just another mention of the ceremonial formality that has been mentioned a number of times.

Verses 29, 30. While this chapter as a whole is on the subject of the great day of atonement, this passage is the climax of the subject and would be the appropriate place to mark the passage if the reader is doing such marking. This feast always came on the tenth day of the seventh month regardless of all other dates or occasions. Of course it was a holy day and no manual work allowed to be done in it. The priest on that day entered the Most Holy place in the tabernacle and performed the service that was to atone for the sins of the people as a whole and it was not repeated until that same time the following year.

Verse 31. To "afflict" their souls means that they were to be in a state of great humiliation in view of their being sinners, and requiring some visible transaction, to make themselves at one with God.

Verse 32. The priesthood had been given exclusively to Aaron and his family. When it became necessary for another to fill the place of the one having served previously, he must be consecrated unto that office. The consecration ceremonies would be attended to before the death of the acting priest but he would not take full charge of the work until the death of the present one.

Verses 33, 34. This indicates that on this great day in each year not only was the congregation atoned for, but also the tabernacle. This is plain when we remember that the tabernacle was a type of the church and the church is composed of human beings who need the services of an atoning Saviour.

LEVITICUS 17

Verses 1, 2. Aaron was an inspired man and God guided him as such. Yet in this instance we note that God placed Moses between him and Aaron in giving the commandment which again proves the great authority of Moses in the law to the people.

Verses 3-5. God has always had some specified place or thing at which he will meet with his people religiously. In the Patriarchal Dispensation it was the family altar of burnt sacrifices. In the Jewish Dispensation it was the tabernacle. This does not mean that no services of any kind were permitted elsewhere. But those exercises pertaining to the tabernacle service must be performed at that place and if any one attempted to substitute his own home or other privately chosen place his act would be considered as one guilty of blood.

That means it was a guilt that called for the death penalty. While on this subject it will be proper to state that in the third and last Dispensation the place that corresponds with the ones formerly considered is the assembly of the Christians. And it likewise requires that certain services must be done in such a gathering. (Acts 20: 7; Heb. 10: 25.)

Verse 6. The blood must be sprinkled on the altar; hence, the reason for the order set forth in preceding paragraph. The fat or suet must be burned on the altar. That part of all the beasts used in sacrifice belonged to God.

Verse 7. *Sacrifices unto devils*. Sometimes a fact is attributed to the actions of men that might not have been their intention. These people of old did not know much if anything about demons as we think of them. But the word used here, while directly it means something rough such as the goats or other rough animals offered in sacrifice, yet the inspired writer concludes that such sacrifices must be counted as offered to some being other than the true God. Paul comments on this subject (1 Cor. 10: 20), and says that the heathen sacrificed to devils or demons. The word for "demons" is defined by Thayer as: "a deity inferior to God." Every act of religion is given to the credit of some being supposed to be greater than the one doing the act. Since the act of sacrificing to some being other than the true God would have to be to some imaginary one, the inspired writers conclude that the demons or fallen angels must get the credit.

Verses 8, 9. This is explained in verses 3-5 above.

Verse 10. The law against eating blood was never repealed. It is still the law of God in the Christian Dispensation. (Acts 15: 29.)

Verses 11, 12. A reason is given for the ordinance of the preceding verse. The life of all flesh is in the blood, and therefore, it is considered too exclusive to be used for food for the body. All through the dealings of God with man the importance of blood is held out. From the first sacrifice commanded, as far as we have the account, a creature having blood was used. All of which was getting the world ready to appreciate the one and great sacrifice to take the place of all others, the Son of God.

Verses 13, 14. The sacredness of the blood is still the subject of the writer. When a man is hunting and takes a living creature, that is among the ones permitted to be eaten, he must shed its blood. Also, he must show the respect to it that we do to the body of a man. Respect it by covering it with the earth. The penalty for a man who ate blood was that he be cut off or slain.

Verses 15, 16. The beast that had died in the manner here described was not considered as perfect, and the one making use of it was thus unclean. Not physically but in a ceremonial sense. Therefore, he must go through the formality mentioned for cleansing.

LEVITICUS 18

Verses 1, 2. The underlying reason the children of Israel were to observe the instructions about to be given was that they came from the Lord their God. Not necessarily because they could see the logical connection, but because they were divine commands.

Verse 3. They had spent many years in a heathen country and are about to come into another such country. The power of example is so great that constant warnings had to be given them against imitating the examples of iniquity.

Verse 4. *Judgments, ordinances*. There is little practical difference between these words yet some distinction exists when used together as they are here. The former especially refers to decisions or verdicts that might be expressed by the Lord when the occasion arose. The latter had special reference to laws established as a fixed practice.

Verse 5. A statute is the same as an ordinance and used in the scriptures with the same effect. But this place has special application to the fixed requirements of the outward services of the law. If a man would do those services he was considered as living in them or by them. This is again in view of the thought of their living in the object-lesson period of the world.

Verse 6. Here the special subject of the chapter is introduced. No physical reason is given why close kin were not to marry. The theory that such marriage would result unfavorably in the offspring has long been a popular one. Later authorities have discounted it. In fact, there are numerous instances on record where immediate relatives have ignorantly lived in the intimate relation and produced children with no ill effects. Aside from the positive law of God that would make it wrong for these people, the social confusion of such intermarriages would be an objection to them.

Verses 7-16. I have grouped all these verses in one paragraph because the comments to be offered will apply to all. The reader may go through the verses and note the following relations specified: Mother, father's wife, sister, son's daughter, daughter's daughter, father's wife's daughter, father's sister, mother's sister, father's brother's wife, daughter-in-law, brother's wife. The only expression used in connection with this relation is "uncover the nakedness." This is in perfect keeping with the Biblical basis of marriage. The only "ceremony" required or used as far as the Lord was concerned was the fleshly act that made them one. When a man and woman have the fleshly relation they are by that act made into one in God's sight, and that constitutes the basis of marriage as far as the Lord is concerned. (See Gen. 2: 24.)

Verse 17. This verse agrees with one comment in preceding paragraph, that social and not physical reasons were the motive for this law against the marriage of near kin. There could not be any possible effect physically of producing offspring from two different women even though they were of the same family blood. But there could be very evil results socially.

Verse 18. The physical results of offspring from two sisters would be the same whether both women were living or not. But the danger of jealousy would be greater if both were living at the time of the marriage to the same man. This was manifested in the case of Jacob, and the two sisters, in Gen. 30.

Verse 19. Decency and cleanliness would be sufficient motive for this law even if God had said nothing about it. (See chapter 15: 24.)

Verse 20. This is the same law given in Ex. 20: 14, 17. The word "carnally" could mean anything wrong and thus something prompted by the desires of the flesh. In this case it refers to the act of fleshly union with a woman belonging to another man.

Verse 21. The word "fire" is not in the original. The thought of the sentence is in the word "pass" which means to be devoted to or given to. Molech was the chief imaginary deity of the Ammonites, a heathen nation near the children of Israel. The verse therefore means they must not permit their children to worship this heathen god.

Verse 22. This verse refers to what is known as sodomy and was the outstanding sin of the cities destroyed in the time of Lot. This vile iniquity has been practiced for centuries and indicates a depraved state of the passions. It is accomplished by various methods, but the fundamental principle in the subject implies that one man uses the body of another in some way that will gratify his sexual nature. This is considered by Paul in Rom. 1: 27.

Verses 23. This vile sin is called bestiality in modern language. The sin was punished with death under the law of Moses.

Verses 24, 25. Besides being vile and vicious in their very nature, these practices were common among the nations surrounding the children of Israel and the Lord wishes his people to be a separate people in their manner of life, as well as in their state of national life.

Verses 26, 27. Not only were the children of Israel required to abstain from these evil practices, but the sojourners who might be among them must likewise not be allowed to do them. And if people of the world are pleased to be present with Christians, they must be made to understand that they cannot be suffered to conduct themselves in any way that would do violence to the proper conduct of said people. They cannot be compelled to take active part in the religious activities of the Lord's people, but they can and should be required to respect their conduct and not to obstruct it.

Verse 28. The threat that is indicated here was actually carried out in later history of the nation. Because of idolatry, in imitation of the practices of the heathen about them, the nation of the Israelites was made to go away into captivity.

Verse 29. Even before the nation as a whole was thrust out of the land, the individuals who were guilty of the evils named were cut off or slain.

Verse 30. The great motive for the commands and the obedience thereto is that they came from the Lord their God.

LEVITICUS 19

Verses 1, 2. God is a holy being and his creatures should have him for example of their life. Not to the same extent, which would be impossible, but to the extent agreeable with the nature of man. The leading thought, as applied to the people, was that they were to be separate from other nations and consider themselves exclusively as belonging to God.

Verse 3. "To fear" here means "to respect" and is the same idea as in Ex. 20: 12. It should be noted here that the word "sabbath" is in the plural. That is because the seventh day of the week was not the only sabbath. Every holy day was a sabbath and there were various days of that kind in their system. All of them were to be observed by abstaining from manual labor.

Verse 4. Molten gods would be the objects made by man by casting the metal in the form of some imaginary deity. Idols in general would be things on earth or in the sky that they might worship. All of such was practiced by the heathen people around them and that was forbidden. The first and second commandments of the tables of the law forbade all such practices.

Verses 5-8. This is the same stipulation given in chapter 7: 11-18. It is not stated why it was so objectionable to God for them to eat of this offering on the third day unless it was in order to encourage promptness. We should note that one of the requirements here is that it be offered of their free will. A further suggestion may be found in the eighth verse. If the person tries to prolong the offering to the third day he has "profaned" the hallowed thing. That word means to "make a personal or temporal use of a sacred thing." If a man started out to render a religious service to the Lord and then tried to stretch it out to an unauthorized time it would be interpreted as indication that he was getting a fleshly satisfaction out of it.

Verses 9, 10. Consideration for those not as fortunate as ourselves is taught in this paragraph. There will always be individuals among us that are needy (Deut. 15: 11; Matt. 26: 11), and it is a duty to assist them. For this reason the remnants of their crops must be left for them.

Verse 11. We can see three degrees of "crookedness" in this verse. One is to steal outright. Another to manipulate a transaction in a deceptive manner so as to cheat the other fellow out of his property; the other is to lie deliberately about the whole deal and thus try to get the financial advantage of him.

Verse 12. It should be noted that false swearing is here condemned. Some people try to offset the teaching of Christ on this subject (Matt. 5: 33-37), by saying he was only condemning false swearing. But that is not the case. He was condemning something that was allowed in the Old Testament. False swearing was not allowed even then as this verse shows. Also, they must not profane the name of God. This is the same as taking the name of God in vain or to no good purpose and is condemned in commandment 3.

Verse 13. According to this verse "pay day" came daily. This indicates that the laborer needed what he was working for so much that he could not wait till some future date for his pay. This further indicates that what could be considered "fair and living wage" does not necessarily require so much money that a man would be able to lay up great amounts of it for hoarding purposes.

Verse 14. The word "curse" here is from a word that means to make light of, which would be a grievous sin. Also to hinder a blind man and take advantage of his misfortune would certainly bring the wrath of God on the guilty. God is the maker of all mankind and reverence for Him as well as consideration for the unfortunate should prompt us to be a helper and not a hindrance to them.

Verse 15. The word "judgment" means to render a decision in a dispute. In such a situation we should not allow ourselves to be influenced, either by our sympathy for a poor man, if in the wrong, nor in favor of another man in the wrong because of his popularity or other greatness. We should always be impartial in rendering a decision.

Verse 16. The scriptures never require one to hide the truth nor shield a man in wrong. But this verse means one who makes a public use of a scandal or rumor. That kind of a person would be inclined to give testimony against a neighbor falsely that would result in having him condemned to die by the executioner.

Verse 17. Solomon says that "open rebuke is better than secret love." (Prov. 27: 5.) It is no real favor to a brother to withhold a rebuke that is due him. He will never be led to repent by our knowledge of his sin unless we let him know about it. It may be that if we come out and frankly show him his fault he will be led to reformation.

Verse 18. The principles commanded in this verse are also taught in the New Testament. (Rom. 12: 19; Matt. 19: 19), but we should always distinguish between individual action and official or judicial action. The Corinthians exercised vengeance (2 Cor. 7: 11), but they were acting as a church and not as individuals. The present verse is against a man taking personal vengeance in the way of retaliation.

Verse 19. Here we have another law that is not based on any moral principle that we know of. There is no objection to this kind of thing elsewhere when the product of such breeding is in evidence. For some reason not made clear to us now the Lord wished all things to be kept in a pure strain.

Verse 20. The reader is urged not to forget the basis of the marriage relation as it existed in the beginning. All formal ceremonies on the subject have been started by man and the violation of the "moral law" really refers to the neglect of observance of these ceremonies. This fundamental principle will help to understand many circumstances relative to this perplexing subject. Also, the Lord was not as strict on the subject in those times as he is now. In the present verse there was no violence used against the maid and thus she was a party to the action. Since she was not a free woman she cannot be held as responsible as otherwise and hence her services to the man to whom she was promised must not be entirely taken away. There must be some punishment and that was scourging. The R.V. gives the pronoun in the plural which is correct since both the man and woman are involved.

Verses 21, 22. In addition to the personal punishment put on them for their sin, the guilty man (since he was the one doing the seducing), must bring an offering to the Lord. Of course, he must bring it to the door of the tabernacle where the priest has charge and there the offering will be appropriate according to the law. When this is done the sin of the man "shall be forgiven him."

Verses 23-25. At present the children of Israel are wandering in the wilderness. Many of the laws being given them had special application in accord with that condition. It was expected that finally they would be settled in their own country and then certain other regulations would apply. This passage states one of that kind. They will start groves of fruit trees. The fruit of the first three years is considered as unsuitable for food, as it would be somewhat immature. The fruit of the fourth year, while suitable for human consumption, must not be used by the person raising it. It must be used to praise the Lord. Of course, that could mean only that it must be turned over to the Levites who were the official people for the Lord's institution. And this agrees with the law given at other places that the first of everything was the Lord's.

Verse 26. The law against eating blood has been noted a number of times. The word "enchantment" means a human prediction supposed to be based on some unusual faculty possessed by the prophet. The word "times" is not in the original but the thought of the expression is in the word "observe" which is to cover or speak indefinitely. This would be done to confuse the patron and make him think that the prophet knew something that he did not. The whole subject refers to people who are not satisfied with the things God wished man to know, but presume to find out further information. Such activities have always been condemned and violate Deut. 29: 29 and many other passages.

Verse 27. Of course we understand the head here means the hair of the head even as we would understand the beard to be the hairy growth of the face. And the verse has in mind some of the heathen practices of making some particular condition in these parts of the hairy growth in honor of some of the heathen deities. To cut the hair of the head so as to leave the man with short hair, was not forbidden here. We will see as we go on through the book that it was the practice for men to have their hair short, except when under the Nazarite vow. (Num. 6: 5.) This passage means they must not make these peculiar alterations in their hair or beard.

Verse 28. The preceding paragraph forbade the misuse of the hair. This verse goes further and condemns the mutilation of the body. Some heathen practiced the gashing of the body either as an act of penitence toward their god or in token of some feeling of depression over the loss of loved ones. The law against printing marks on the flesh would have ruled out the horrible practice of tattooing. The same principle is taught in the New Testament. (1 Cor. 6: 19.) When people mutilate their bodies either by tattooing or by printing other marks on them such as "make-up," which makes them look unnatural, they violate this principle taught in both Old and New Testaments.

Verse 29. The margin gives us the word "profane" in the place of prostitute. That is in agreement with the lexicon. The word "profane" means to make a lower or common use of a sacred thing and could well be applied to cases other than those of the subject of morality. In this verse, though, it refers to the latter topic. The human body is a sacred possession and should be used in a way that will please God. If it is used for base passion or greed only, then, that is a lowering of the body and constitutes profanity. And a man who would take advantage of his parental authority over his daughter would be a great sinner. Not only so as to his own conduct, but he would be setting an example that would result in widespread immorality in the land.

Verse 30. Explained at Ex. 31:13, 14.

Verse 31. In a general way this verse is explained in verse 26 above. The word "familiar" is not in the original but supplied by the translators. The thought of the expression is in the meaning of the original word for "spirits," which is given by the lexicon as a "ventriloquist or necromancer." It means a person pretending to have some special knowledge not possessed by people in general and through this deception tries to get the confidence of his dupe. The word "wizards" is from YIDDONIY and Strong defines it: "properly, a knowing one; specifically a conjurer; (by implication) a ghost." The meaning is much the same as the word just explained. And the principle involved is that of a person who makes believe that he possesses some faculty of looking into the region considered unknown to the masses. The whole business implies that such person is that much more of a supernatural being than his fellows.

Verse 32. Perhaps this command was and is ignored more grievously than many of the other commands. Respect for older persons is thought by many young people to be a kind of lowering of their own dignity. It results in disobedience to parents and other persons in authority. All through the Bible the Lord has taught children and young folks to regard with respect those who are older, and to conduct themselves accordingly. Great sorrow may come to them if they neglect this.

Verses 33, 34. Another reminder of their pilgrimage in the land of Egypt in which they were strangers (temporary dwellers), and were so badly treated. Knowing by experience how such treatment makes one feel, they should be led to consider others.

Verses 35-37. A general summing up of the various regulations previously given as to their obligations to each other as citizens of the commonwealth. If all men would consider the happiness of others and not be centered in self alone the world would be a better place in which to live.

LEVITICUS 20

Verses 1, 2. This is the same law as in chapter 18: 21, which see. The particular mode of execution is here stated and the people of the land are the executioners. This is just. When a man leads his children to serve this heathen deity, it tends to break down the purity of the nation as a whole and would threaten the merging of it with the one that is destined to be finally destroyed by the Lord. It is therefore of national interest to keep out all forms of idolatry.

Verses 3-5. Aside from information already considered, this passage gives us a very clear definition of the expression "cut off," so often used in the Old Testament. In verses 3 and 5 are the words "cut him off." And in verse 4, the the words "kill him." This gives us an insight to the strength of the expression so often found. There is a further thought in this passage. If the people fail to do their duty, and fail to execute the law of death on such a person, that will not shield him from the wrath of God. In such a case, God will take personal charge of the case and execute him. The same principle is taught in the New Testament regarding the action of discipline to be finally inflicted on an unworthy character. See Paul's statements regarding the one at Corinth who was worthy of drastic action and rejection. (1 Cor. 5: 3.) Paul, as the inspired representative of the Lord had already decided against that guilty man. Even if the church had neglected its duty that would not have been any benefit to the guilty person. He would have been rejected of the Lord, anyway.

But, the church would have been guilty before God.

Verse 6. Already explained in chapter 19: 31.

Verses 7, 8. The word "sanctify" means to be separate and set apart for some holy and special use. God required the people to be separate as a nation and not mingle with the other nations in their sinful practices.

Verse 9. "To curse" in the sense of the word here means "to make light of." It is condemned in the light of chapter 19: 32. See comments at that place.

Verse 10. It will be noted that both guilty parties were to be killed. In the case of the Pharisees in John 8: 3-5, the woman only was brought. This could not have been explained by saying they did not know the guilty man for they claimed to have taken her in "the very act." This showed their hypocrisy and their attempt to mislead Jesus into contradicting the law through his supposed sympathy for womankind.

Verses 11, 12. This is considered in chapter 18: 8, 10.

Verse 13. This is the sin called sodomy and considered in chapter 18: 22. Both men were to be killed. This sort of iniquity is what Paul means in 1 Cor. 6: 9, at which place more detailed explanation will be found.

Verse 14. Explained in chapter 18: 17.

Verses 15, 16. See chapter 18: 23 for other comments on this horrible evil.

Verse 17. This is just a more detailed form of the law given in chapter 18: 9, and was regarded as abominable in the sight of God.

Verse 18. This refers to the indecency of cohabiting at the time the woman is going through the period experienced by those in the childbearing age. Such practice was to be punished severely.

Verses 19-21. A repetition of the law in chapter 18: 12, 13.

Verse 22. They were not just to keep part of the law, but must keep all of the Lord's judgments and statutes. The threat that the land would "spue" them out was an indefinite prediction of what happened when they were driven from their land and taken into the captivity by the Babylonians, and other heathen.

Verse 23. Sometimes people who profess to belong to the Lord will try to justify their conduct by saying that other people do so and so. But even here in the Old Testament times we see that God's people were expected to be different from all others. If they do not intend to do so, they should make no profession of being another kind of people.

Verse 24. This land was not "their land" by rightful possession but by usurpation, for it had been given to God's people in the days of Abraham. (Gen. 12: 7). At present it was being held in usurpation by the heathen, and God proposes to let the rightful heirs come to their own, on condition that they conduct themselves as they should and not be as evil and abominable as the present occupants. Many things forbidden of the children of Israel might not have been objectionable to God were it not that the heathen made a prominent practice of them. God wished to remove all things that might identify his people as being like the heathen.

Verses 25, 26. In harmony with the thoughts expressed in preceding paragraph they must make the distinctions already set down, and thus make themselves different from the wicked nations around them.

Verse 27. See chapter 19: 31 for explanation of this verse.

LEVITICUS 21

Verses 1-3. The word for "defiled" here is from an original that means "to be foul, especially in a ceremonial or moral sense, contaminated," according to Strong. It thus refers to the fact of coming in contact with a dead person. This was forbidden as far as one's distant relation. Those near of kin, such as are named in this passage, of course must be taken care of and in such case it was permitted with certain execeptions, to be mentioned in next verse.

Verse 4. A "chief" man was prohibited from such activities as referred to in preceding verse. This would have special application to men with position of public service. Such a man should let others care for the dead so that he would be "clean" and free to perform the service that required a "clean" officiant.

Verse 5. This is explained in chapter 19: 27, 28.

Verse 6. This verse indicates that the "chief" men in verse 4, has special application to the common priests because they were the ones who did this officiating. If a man had come in contact with a dead person, that would disqualify him for the work of the altar. Hence he must remain holy which here means he must not be ceremonially unfit.

Verse 7. These priests, unlike those of the Church of Rome, were permitted to marry. They must marry a moral woman and one not divorced.

Verse 8. Here is a good definition of the word "sanctify." The priest was to be kept away from the service of caring for the dead so that he will at all times be prepared (ceremonially), to wait on the altar. This presents a condition of separation from the common duties of social life.

Verse 9. So serious was the crime of harlotry considered, and so important was the office of the priesthood, that if the daughter of the priest became thus guilty, she must be put to death by fire.

Verses 10-15. This passage deals with the restrictions laid on the High Priest, which are more stringent than the ones for the common priest. Of course, he must not marry an impure woman nor any other who is not in proper condition. He is restricted beyond that. A woman could be a pure woman morally, even though having been married, but while a married woman is a pure woman; yet she is not a virgin. The High Priest must marry a virgin. Just here some reader may think the type does not harmonize since our High Priest, Christ, never married. There are at least two thoughts to be taken into consideration here. In the first place. it is a mistake to think that all types were to be identical with the antitype. We know that is not the case. An instance or two will be cited. Moses was a type of Christ and yet he was put to death for his sin. Canaan was a type of Heaven yet it contained sinners and other evils while Heaven will have nothing vile in it. So we must bear in mind that a type, like a parable, is intended to apply only at certain points and the rest of the story or description is given to complete the connection. There is another thought that may have been overlooked by those making the objection on this subject. It is true that Christ did not marry in the flesh, but he will be married finally, spiritually. Like the High Priest of the law, he will marry only a virgin. (2 Cor. 11: 2; Eph. 5: 25-27). So the type and antitype agree perfectly here.

Verses 16-21. Again the reader is reminded that we are studying the typical and educational age of the world. Actual or physical objects must be used to teach the people because they are not yet ready for the higher and spiritual lessons. Thus, as spiritual unfitness is to be rejected when the perfect Dispensation comes, so the idea is impressed on the people during the preparatory age by making the restrictions apply to physical things ceremonially. Most of the items in this passage are understood, but the word "stones" in verse 20 may offer an inquiry. At the time the A. V. was produced, certain words were used by the English speaking people in a serious and respectful sense but may have since been debased to a state of "slang" or other objectionable form. Such is the case with this word. The original word shows it to have reference to the reproductive organs of a man. Such a man would not be able to reproduce after his kind. As a type, it refers to a man in the profession of spiritual priesthood today who has become impotent by sin. Such a person of course could not bring forth any spiritual fruit for Christ, therefore, such person is not permitted to participate in the spiritual service of the church.

Verses 22, 23. Here is another instance where the type varies from the antitype. The person in the latter is not authorized to even partake of the spiritual activities of the church, while the former is permitted to eat of the bread that has been set by, for the support of the priesthood although not allowed to officiate in the services. That was because such men had no other means of living since they had no land of their own and were not mingled with the outside in general.

Verse 24. Once more we see the great superiority of Moses. God did not tell this law directly to Aaron although he was an inspired man. But he told it to Moses, and he in turn told it to Aaron and his sons.

LEVITICUS 22

Verses 1-3. All of the statements in this paragraph must be considered, to avoid confusion. We would naturally think that the priests were the very ones to have charge of the holy things of the people. That is true unless they have become defiled in some manner. If that has taken place with any of them then they are disqualified for the usual service because their "uncleanness" is upon them. If they presume to officiate while in that condition they are to be cut off.

Verses 4-6. Some items of this ceremonial uncleanness are specified because the people had to be reminded from time to time just what God meant by his restrictions. These items have already been explained previously in this work.

Verse 7. "When the sun is down" here has the same meaning as "at even" in other places where this ceremonial uncleanness is the subject. And again we must note that it is not actual or physical uncleanness that is being considered. No arbitrary time, such as the sundown, would make the person clean. But some rule had to be established while they were being trained in the practice of obedience. So this rule was given.

Verse 8. This was considered in chapter 7: 24.

Verse 9. In this verse the word "die," is used in the same connection and about the same persons as "cut off" in verse 3.

Verse 10. A stranger is one from the outside, and thus, not a member of the priesthood. Such a person must not eat of the holy things. Likewise, one who is not of the Christian priesthood (meaning a disciple of Christ), is not authorized to partake of the things belonging to the service of Christ.

Verse 11. If a man is bought by the money of the priest, then such person was permitted to partake. Or if a child is born to the priest he also is permitted to partake. Likewise, a person who is bought with the money (price, or blood) of Christ is permitted to partake of the divine service and claim its benefits as his own.

Verses 12, 13. The outstanding thought in this paragraph is that the services and benefits of the priesthood were not for those on the outside. If a priest's daughter married one outside that disqualified her. It is true today, that if a disciple of Christ joins himself to any institution outside of the church, that disqualifies him from further participation in the Lord's services. If the priest's daughter becomes separated from the objectionable person and is returned to her father's house, then she may again partake. Likewise, when a disciple who has erred and gone from the Lord's fellowship, shall return to the fold, then he may again have fellowship with the service as before.

Verse 14. To eat "unwittingly" means to do so without knowing the facts at the time. After learning the truth, then he must make it right as stated.

Verses 15, 16. This means that such persons must not be permitted to go on in the divine service until the trespass has been made right.

Verses 17-19. Again, the importance of the Lord's service and its required purity is the reason why there is so much repetition. Even in the Christian Dispensation a large amount of the teaching was done by repetition, for this purpose. (2 Pe. 3: 1).

Verse 20-22. The perfect animal was always required when offered in the specified services of the Lord. This was always demanded.

Verse 23. Distinction is made here between "freewill offerings" and a "vow." Here is another view of the ceremonial or formal nature of that law. As has been stated so often, many of the requirements were ceremonial and not physical or logical. That is why certain services would permit of things not perfect. I shall suggest by way of illustration that in the N. T. system we learn that certain qualifications had to be present in a man before he could serve as a bishop of the church. Yet, there are some of them that would not be required of unofficial men before they might partake of the services of the Lord as a Christian. (See 1 Tim. 3).

Verses 24, 25. We have previously seen (chapter 7: 24;, 17: 15; 22: 8) that they were not permitted these mangled beasts to be eaten. Now they were also not permitted to offer them to the Lord. Surely, if an object is not fit for private use it is not fit for the service of the Lord. Today people will sometimes be more exacting about the things they want for their own use than they are in what they offer to Christ. They will allow conditions and explanations to be applied against the demands of Christ that they would not even consider if their personal interests were concerned. Such persons should take a lesson from the teaching here. It is required of Christians to take such lessons. (Rom. 15: 4).

Verses 26-28. This paragraph is on the same principle set forth in Ex. 23: 19. It is one that encourages the spirit of being humane. Kindness to animals is plainly taught in the Old Testament. (Prov. 12: 10).

Verses 29, 30. Certain offerings that were not directly required might be offered voluntarily. If offered, then the Lord gave certain regulations. In this case the offering must be used in the day first offered. It might not be contributed so as to make it stretch out over an extended period. See comments on this subject at chapter 19: 5-8.

Verses 31-33. Two great facts were kept constantly before the minds of the children of Israel: That it was the Lord who was commanding them, and that it was the very One who had delivered them from bondage of Egypt. Gratitude should have urged them to be obedient to his holy laws.

LEVITICUS 23

Verses 1, 2. This is the chapter that gives us the most detailed description of the three yearly feasts of the Jewish law and we shall study it with great care. In the present paragraph these feasts are called "holy convocations." The second of these words is from MIQRA and defined "something called out, i. e. a public meeting (the act, the person, or the place); also a rehearsal."—Strong. And since every one of these occasions on which a gathering of the people, or certain ones of the people, was required was also a day of rest from manual labor, the name came to be synonymous of sabbath. In view of this we shall so consider the convocations about to be mentioned.

Verse 3. As further proof of the idea in the preceding paragraph, in this one we have the expression "seventh day" used in the same connection with the word "convocation." Of course we should bear in mind that thus far the subject matter has specifically to do with the weekly sabbath which came and was to be observed regardless of all other holy days. The strictness of its requirements will serve as an insight into the mind of the Lord as concerning the other holy days and occasions. The expression "of the Lord" is not to be taken as indicating that the other sabbaths did not come from the Lord. But the weekly sabbath is referred to in this way because it is the one which God himself actually observed at the instance of the week of creation. God used six days for his creative work and at the end of the six days his work was ended. The day following the days of creation was therefore observed by the rest or pause of God on that day. Since he was the one who established such a day at that time it is referred to in after chapters in the Bible as "my rest" (Heb. 3 and 4).

Verse 4. Here the feasts of the Lord are called holy convocations. This brings in the special feature of the word. It not only means any holy day but includes the idea of some sort of assembling. That would be necessary in order to carry out the activities of these feasts as we will see. They were to come at stated times as here mentioned since they were to be "proclaimed in their seasons."

Verse 5. We cannot give much attention to the teaching that the passover was one of the sabbath days of the Old Testament system. Here it is mentioned immediately after that of the "holy convocation" of the previous verse, which is an introduction to these holy days. Therefore, whether here or in the New Testament times, let us never lose sight of the truth that the passover is always to be reckoned among the sabbath days. Since it came only once a year while the weekly sabbath came over fifty times a year that would make it a sabbath day of unusual significance. This is what John meant by the expression "high day" in John 19: 31.

Verse 6, 7. The occasion for this feast of unleavened bread, also called the seven day feast, was the fact that they had been rushed out of Egypt the night of the slaying of the firstborn so that their bread did not have time to "rise" or ferment or become leavened. As a reminder of this eventful night God required them to celebrate it at that season each year. That is, they were to eat bread that was unleavened for the period of seven days in addition to the one of the passover. While each of these seven days was a part of the "feast of unleavened bread," the first and the seventh were the only ones that are called convocations. (See Num. 28: 18, 25.) Throughout these seven days they must not even have leaven in their homes. Therefore, each year there would be a period of eight days in all in which there would be no leaven found in their houses. So the distinctive meaning of the two feasts that same together in this way was; the one was in memory of their deliverance through the death of the firstborn of Egypt and the other was in memory of their hasty exit from the land. Also, because of the relation between the two feasts, and the fact that they came together, the two came to be referred to often as one and the same feast. Hence, if a writer wishes to make general reference to that particular season he may do so either by calling it the feast of the passover or the feast of unleavened bread. This conclusion is very essential to the understanding of the various places where reference is made to this time of the year, and the reader is urged to make note of it.

Verse 8. Here we see that the seventh as well as the first of this period of seven days was a holy day. Lest the reader might be confused I shall state again that while the first and seventh are the ones that were spoken of as holy days, yet all seven had to be observed on the point of having, or using unleavened bread. That kind of bread only was used through the whole period.

Verses 9, 10. The first of the "three yearly feasts" has just been studied, now we come to the second one. At this time it was supposed that some of their crops were far enough along that a small part could be gathered to use in religious observance before the Lord. Hence, they were required to take a sheaf as the firstfruits. It has already been seen that God claims the first of everything and thus it was appropriate that the first handful of the grain that was produced should be given to the One who had made any harvest possible.

Verse 11. There is nothing new in the formality of waving this first sheaf as we have previously seen done with regard to the breast of certain animals. Now we see the same action used in the presentation of this first sheaf of the grain. It was to be presented to the Lord in the manner of waving it. The time when it was to be waved is the all-important thing as far as it pertains to the matters of the New Testament events. It is known by all students of the scriptures that the first Gospel discourse and setting up of the church came on Pentecost. (Acts 2). But back here where we are now studying we do not find that word. That is because the word is from the Greek, and the Old Testament was written in Hebrew. The description of it as it is given in the observance agrees with the Greek name for it, as we will see before leaving this chapter. The reference to the second feast that was made in the preceding paragraph is not to be taken to mean that we are yet actually in the second feast. The basis on which its date came is here being laid while still at the first one. Since this first feast came in their first month which corresponds to our March and April, we can see why the first products of their grain would be ready to pluck as was stated at verse 10 above. So we read that this first sheaf was to be waved "on the morrow after the sabbath." The term "the sabbath" might cause us some confusion since they had so many days that were called sabbath days. But when the expression is used and the context does not require some special application we must take it to refer to the weekly sabbath, the day on which God rested from his creative work; the day which came every week regardless of any and all other days. Also, in the instance now under consideration, the last regular or weekly sabbath that they have had was the one that followed the passover which was the seventh day of the week. This was also the first of the seven day feast of unleavened bread which we have already seen was a sabbath or holy day. (verse 7, 8). And the verse we are now considering says this first sheaf was to be waved on the morrow after this sabbath. Therefore, the first sheaf was waved on the first day of the week which is now called Sunday in the legal calendar.

Verses 12-14. This paragraph is a continuation of the details of this day on which they were to offer the sheaf of the first fruits which was on the day we call Sunday. They are cautioned not to make a personal use of this beginning of their crop production until they had given the Lord his part first. And the term "green ears" indicates that the crops were just barely far enough along to be used, yet they could be used for the purposes of the season.

Verses 15, 16. Now we come to the actual study of the second feast referred to at verses 9, 10. After the sabbath has passed, the one just before the waving the first sheaf—after that day is gone, then they are to begin counting for another great day. They start counting down the calendar of the days of the week and each time they come to one of the regular sabbaths, they are to make note of it. They continue this until they have come to seven of these weekly sabbaths. Of course the one just following the passover must not be counted in this seven because that one had already gone when they were told to begin to count for the seven. Thus, if they counted until they had counted seven of the weekly sabbaths that would make 49 days since the day they waved the first sheaf, which was our Sunday. Now the count has brought us up to a weekly sabbath. But the instruction was not to stop there. After they had counted until they had come to seven of these sabbaths, then one more day must be taken in, the "morrow after the seventh sabbath." Of course we know that would also be another first day of the week, which is what we call Sunday, or Lord's day. That would make fifty days after the day of waving the first sheaf (including that day of course) in the Old Testament times, or fifty days after the resurrection day in the New Testament times. And of course that would fall on the day we call Sunday. On that day they were to bring a "new meat offering" unto the Lord.

Verses 17-21. This paragraph gives the details of the activities of this 50th day described in preceding paragraph. The reader should note the expression "firstfruits unto the Lord" in 17th verse. It corresponds to the three thousand converts to Christ in Acts 2, which were also the firstfruits of the Christian Dispensation. And the last verse of this paragraph again required that this day must be a holy day. This is the feast that is called Pentecost in the New Testament because the Greek word from which it comes is PENTEKOSTE and defined by both Strong and Thayer as "fiftieth." It gets that meaning from the fact that it came fifty days after the passover week as we saw in preceding paragraph. And also this all agrees with the facts in the New Testament events. It was on the day of Pentecost that the Holy Spirit came upon the apostles and started them in the great work of setting up the church and for the first time bringing in the fruits of the Christian Dispensation. When we are asked to show on which day of the week the church was set up, we answer that it was on the first day of the week, commonly called Sunday. That is correct, but unless we go to secular history to prove it we cannot do so at all without the information in this chapter we are now studying. That is the reason I am devoting so much detail to the study of it. Before leaving this part of the chapter, that deals with the first two of the three yearly feasts, I shall make a brief summing up statement, based on what has already been presented. The first month of the year came in on what we call Saturday. That would be their first day, or beginning of the month. (See Num. 28: 11; 1 Sam. 20: 5, 24, 27.) The passover was on the 14th day of the month which would be on Friday. The next day (Saturday) would be the beginning of their seven day feast of unleavened bread. Counting after this Saturday that began the seven day feast they would go till they had counted off seven of the weekly sabbaths, which would make 49 days, stopping on a Saturday. Then on the morrow after this 49th day they would have the feast, which is called Pentecost, in the New Testament.

Verse 22. This verse is a repetition of general regulations already explained and has no special connection with the feasts of this chapter.

Verses 23-25. The Jews had exercises required at various times in connection with the major feasts. One of them is here described as coming in the seventh month. This is the month in which the third of the great annual feasts came. But before the time of the actual date for that third feast they had the activities described in this paragraph. Of course we remember that the first of each month, brought in a holy day. And this one is given special mention because it begins the month in which the third of the great festivals will come.

Verses 26, 27. This paragraph gives the third yearly feast of the Jewish Dispensation which consisted of only one day of services. It is called the day of atonement. On that day the High Priest officiated for the sake of the nation as a whole. The individual sins or obligations of the children of Israel were not atoned for on this day unless they also performed their own personal obligations. See comments at Chapter 16: 20-22. To "afflict" their souls meant they must become humble and serious minded on this day, and refrain from all manual labor. It was the day on which the fact that man is a sinner, was publicly indicated in the great sacrifice offered to God. And it is or was the most prominent type of the complete sacrifice of Jesus for the world.

Verse 28. Here it is said that the atonement was made "before the

Lord." That means that the High Priest went within the vail and stood before the ark over which the presence of God was promised, to commune with the national representative of the people.

Verses 29-31. No work was allowed to be done on this day since it was a sabbath. The penalty for violation was death and in that way the guilty one was to be cut off from the people.

Verse 32. Much indefiniteness is apparent as to the exact hour in which the sabbath of any particular date was to begin. If this evening to evening should be interpreted literally, then the conclusion here would be that they were to begin their perod of rest near sundown of the ninth day. That would still leave the whole period of daylight of the tenth day for the services of the day of atonement.

Verses 33-36. This is called the feast of tabernacles. The reason for this name will be considered later on in this chapter. This feast is specified as being a feast of seven days, beginning on the 15th day of the 7th month. Mention is made of the 8th day in connection with the feast, because the beginning date and the closing one are both counted. That is, from the 15th day till the same hour on the 16th day would be one day. So that, in order to have seven days' extent for this feast, the period would have to extend into the 22nd day of the month. Then, counting both the 15th and 22nd days of the month would make the 22nd the 8th day. Both the beginning and closing days of this feast were holy convocations or sabbath days.

Verse 37-39. Nothing much new in this paragraph but a general summing up of the subject already discussed in the chapter. The most significant feature of the passage is in the word "beside" in 38th verse. It sometimes is easy for man to think that if he is very attentive to one line of services to God, he may be excused from some of the others. But this teaches that such is not the case. The special or extra services that one might offer to the Lord will be blessed, all right, if they are in harmony with the revealed law of God. But no amount of zeal or activity in one direction will take the place of the things specifically required elsewhere.

Verses 40-44. In this passage we have the more detailed description of the Feast of Tabernacles and the purpose of its observance. The R. V. as well as the lexicon renders the word here called "boughs" by the word "fruit." The branches of the palm trees were selected because of their tendency to cover, and the boughs of the thick trees together with willows of the brook, also for their use as a hiding place. With these crude materials they made booths or temporary shelters. Something on the order of the Indian teepee. Then for seven days they forsook their permanent dwellings and dwelt under these places. The purpose is stated in verse 43 to be a reminder of their experience while going through the wilderness after leaving Egypt. Since they were on the march all of the time with no certain length of time to remain in one place, they did not have opportunity of building more solid homes. Now that they will be able to "build houses and dwell in them" after they reach the promised land, he does not wish them to forget it. An account of how and where they observed this feast is given in Neh. 8: 14-18. The lesson to us is that while we are going through this world we should bear in mind that we here do not have any permanent residence. (Heb. 13: 14).

LEVITICUS 24

Verses 1-3. In the second verse is the word "continually" and in the third verse is the expression "evening unto morning." This shows that the use of these bowls on the candlestick was for the night time only, yet the practice was to be continual, that it was not to be neglected.

Verse 4. "Pure" condlestick means that the metal used was not to contain any alloy.

Verses 5-8. In most places in the Bible these cakes are referred to as the twelve loaves of unleavened bread on the table of shewbread. The original ordinance is shown in Ex. 25: 30. They were placed on the table in two groups, or rows. This bread was renewed every sabbath. While on the table no actual use was made of them. But after being there for the week they were removed, and then used as food for the priest.

Verse 9. The tribe of Levi as a whole was supported by the tithes of the other tribes. Num. 18: 21. The priests who were serving at the altar had a special provision of being given certain parts of the materials brought to the place for service (Heb. 9: 13).

And this bread that had been on the table for a week then became the exclusive food for them. (1 Sam. 21: 4, 5).

Verses 10-14. This is an incident inserted historically to show us how the laws of God were to work in actual practice. This woman had married an Egyptian and thus her son was not respectful toward God. He was heard to speak blasphemously. While the law had expressly provided that the children of Israel must not curse the name of God, yet they were somewhat undecided what to do with a guilty person of this relationship. They bring him to Moses to learn what to do. If Moses had been a man who spoke and wrote on his own authority, as the sabbatarians falsely claim, then he certainly would have gone ahead in this case and acted on his own authority also. But he put the man under guard until he could consult the Lord. He was then instructed that the man must be killed. The witnesses were to lay their hands on the head of the guilty one. This was to designate the man to be executed and to indicate their approval of the penalty.

Verses 15, 16. Since this kind of subject was now brought to the public attention the Lord goes on and repeats some of the law that had already been given on the matter of blaspheming. When a man was thus guilty, the congregation must execute him and not expect the Lord to do it miraculously.

Verse 17. The law of capital punishment for murder which was given to man many centuries before (Gen. 9: 6), is here repeated.

Verses 18-20. It should be constantly borne in mind that the Mosaic system was both civil and religious. All of the laws as to conduct between man and man were given in this plan. Thus a part of them are here repeated. And when the action of "eye for eye" is taken, it must be regarded as a lawful action and not a personal one of vengeance.

Verses 21, 22. In matters that had a strictly religious benefit the stranger was not included. In those of a civil nature the same law that applied to the children of Israel was to apply to the stranger. That was right and is so today. If a person of another nation is visiting in our country he is expected to obey our laws.

Verse 23. In putting this man to death, they were obeying the Lord by obeying what Moses commanded them to do.

LEVITICUS 25

Verses 1, 2. It is well that we "keep our bearings, "and remember that the people are still at the place where they have been for some time, at Mt. Sinai. God expects to bring them finally to the land promised to them and to the fathers. It will be necessary for their happiness in temporal as well as spiritual matters that they make the proper use of the land. Even uninspired men know that it is a good thing for the soil to rotate it. The same end was to be accomplished with the children of Israel by giving the whole land one complete rest every seven years.

Verse 3, 4. This noted ordinance will figure much in the experiences of the national life of the Jewish nation. The seventh year is spoken of as the sabbatical year. The violation of it gave them serious trouble as we will see.

Verses 5-7. Not only were they not to till their soil, but they must not make any use of nor gather the voluntary products. This sabbath of the land was declared to be "meat" for them. The meaning was that by giving the land this rest it would be a benefit in the long run and result in more food for them than they would have if they tilled the soil continually without any rest.

Verses 8-10. In addition to the seventh year which was always to be a year of rest for the land, after seven of these sabbatical years had passed there was another year of rest. This year was to be observed just as the seventh year in regard to the tilling of the soil. It had more purposes and restrictions than the regular seventh years. This fiftieth year was also to be regarded as a year of jubilee. This word is from an original that has the first meaning from its strong sound. It was used to announce to the nation that the year of the great rest was at hand and for everyone to conduct himself accordingly. And because this great year was announced by the blowing of his jubilee kind of trumpet, the period announced by it came to be called the "year of jubilee." It is interesting to note that this great year started on the tenth day of the seventh month, which was the day of atonement, a very fitting time to start the great year of rest with all its benefits and advantages. Among the radical effects this year was to have, was that of causing the land to revert to its original owner, if it had been transferred for some reason. This subject will be treated more fully later in the chapter.

Verses 11, 12. The land in this year must be treated the same as in the seventh years. Verse 12 is to be understood in the light of 6th verse. By letting the land have this extra rest it will bring them still more increase afterwards so that they will have the advantage of "eating the increase" as a result.

Verse 13. In this year of jubilee the land was all to go back to its first owner if for some reason it had been transferred temporarily. The object God had in view by this law is stated in Ezk. 46: 18, "that my people be not scattered every man from his possession." God wished to keep the nation together and not be scattered all over the earth. And as an inducement for them to remain near, if some man was unfortunate and had to use his land as security for a money favor, it would be regarded as a loan only and would have to be returned to him at the year of jubilee. With this prospect in view he would linger near and wait for the return of his possession.

Verses 14-17. To "oppress" one another, here means that they might take advantage of a man's financial straits and exact more from him as a price than is right. But instead they must take only what the land would be worth for the number of years till the year of jubilee. In reality the transaction amounted to a rental of the land for the number of years yet to come before the year of return. So that if it were to be still ten years only until this great year, then the price of the land at the time of the transfer would be whatever that much land was supposed to produce in ten years.

Verse 18. That they might dwell in the land in safety is here again given as the purpose of this provision in the sale of their possessions.

Verse 19. This is virtually the same thought as expressed in verse 6.

Verses 20, 21. The Lord knew that it would cause some anxiety among the people as to their food supply, so this assurance is given. In the sixth year the land will be made to produce the amount of three years. That would take in the necessitise of the sixth year, also the requirements of the seventh, and then in the eighth they would have a supply to use while making another crop.

Verse 22. All of this production would not ordinarily be required, but it is the graciousness of the Lord to be abundant in his blessings. Hence even unto the eighth there was still some of the old fruit on hands.

Verses 23-24. In the New Testament the Lord generally speaks to his people on the principle involved while in the Old he uses specific instances. So, in the former he will tell us that we are not our own (1 Cor. 6: 19, 20), which means that all that we are and have belongs to God. In the latter case he specifies how they must handle the title to their land since it belongs to the Lord. On this basis they must sell their land in the nature of a loan and not a permanent sale or transfer.

Verse 25. Here is a variation from the use of the fiftieth as to the redemption of the land sold under misfortune. If a man gets into close circumstances and has to sell his land, then he has the consolation that at least it will come back to him in the year of jubilee. In the mean time, if any of his kinsmen should be able to redeem the land and return it to its original owner they may do so. An instance of this is seen in the case of the husband of Naomi. Ruth 2: 20; 4: 4, 6). Of course we understand the term "brother" as used in such connections always means any near of kin.

Verse 26. A man's circumstances might change before the year of jubilee so that he is able to redeem the land himself. If so he is permitted to do so.

Verse 27. If the situation becomes as intimated in preceding verse then the man must compute the worth of the land for the number of years yet lacking to the year of jubilee. That amount is what is meant here by the word "overplus." One rendering of that word is "remaining." So it means that when he takes his land back it must be on condition that he restores this overplus or remaining amount of the rental that would have still been his had the borrower or renter kept the land till jubilee.

Verse 28. This sounds somewhat like a repetition of the previous statement. To some extent it is, but it also has the idea that a man might think he is able to redeen the land

and make it known that he is ready to "take up the note" so to speak, and would tell the other man so. Then when the computation is made it is found that he is not as able along this line as he thought. If so, then he must wait till jubilee.

Verses 29-31. Almost all laws have some exceptions, especially those that have to do with the dealing with man and man. So there must be some stipulations on the matter of redeeming a property. For instance, a man might think he was so close run that he had to sell a residence in a walled or defended city. In that case he is required to redeem it within a year if at all. If the year pass by and he has not come to redeem it, then the sale becomes permanent and will not be released in the jubilee. This exception is made on the principle that land or fields that are for farming and production of life's necessities is to be regarded in a different light from a property that is only used as a dwelling. This is indicated by the word "fields" in 31st verse. That is, the unwalled towns are to be regarded as in the same class as the country open to the public, or open for cultivation of the soil.

Verse 32. Here is an exception to the other exception. It is made in favor of the Levites. From the importance of their position in the nation this consideration is made for their property.

Verse 33. If a Levite is compelled to sell a house in one of these defended cities he is not required to redeem it within a year (if at all), as the others did. He has the entire period in which he may redeem it, if able. And if he never becomes able to redeem it financiallly, then it will become his in the fiftieth year.

Verse 34. Still another exception. The fields or surrounding land of the suburbs belonging to the Levites must never be sold away from them. It is their perpetual possession. All of these special favors given to the Levites will seem fair when it is remembered that their special duty was to take care of the tabernacle service for the congregation. Also, in appreciation of their faihtfulness in going over to the Lord's side, alone, of all the tribes in the matter of the idolatry at Sinai.

Verse 35. This verse is of more general application than the others since it takes in even the sojourner. It is right to be merciful to the poor whether they be members of the Lord's society or not. This same principle of helping those on the outside is taught in the New Testament. (Gal. 6: 10). Also this verse has more specific reference to the transactions of money. If the unfortunate man falls into close circumstances and needs money then it should be loaned to him. This is the meaning of the words "decay" and "relieve" in this verse.

Verses 36-38. In a case like the one referred to in preceding verse the lender of money is not allowed to take usury. This is from NESHEK and Strong defines it as "interest on a debt." Some teach that usury means only excessive interest. But it does not mean that as used by the Lord. It should be noted that the case being considered is one where a man is compelled to borrow money because of poverty. It does not pertain to a case where a man borrows money for speculative or investment purposes. In that kind of situation it would be just as proper to take interest from a brother as from any other man. That would be just because the money was not borrowed because of the misfortune or poverty of the party.

Verses 39-41. In the old times the relation of servant was permitted between the Lord's people. "Strange," did I hear you say? Well, it must be still borne in mind that God was taking them through the educational period in which he was getting them accustomed to some items of obligation that were to be placed on a higher spiritual basis later on. God wanted man to be able to appreciate what it means to be free and one of the best ways to do this was to have him experience bondage and freedom, literally. Even though such relationship was permitted, a distinction was to be made. It was between a bondservant and a hired servant. The one indicated the condition of forced servitude and the other a voluntary one. A brother who was too poor to get along and who had no property for security could offer his personal services as security. In that case it must be in the nature of a voluntary service. So, even in the matter of servantage the type is complete. Because even Christians are said to be servants. Like the type, they become voluntary servants to God, whereas they were involuntary servants to Satan. I do not mean that a man serves Satan unless he wishes to. But the thought is that unless he is willing to be a servant of God then he is left with no other alternative but to serve Satan. (Rom. 6: 16-18). In the case of the poor brother under the law of Moses, if he never becomes able to redeem himself before the year of jubilee, then at that time he was to become a free man. All this agrees beautifully with the arrangement of the great feast of atonement. By comparing chapter 23: 27 and verse 9 in this chapter we see the year of jubilee, the year of the release of the servants, was the same as the year and date on which the nation was made free from the guilt of the past sins. Likewise, when Jesus officiated as our High Priest and entered Heaven with his own blood, that laid the plan for the release of those who had been in the service of sin. (Heb. 9: 24; Rom. 6: 17, 18.)

Verses 42, 43. God claims these servants. He had purchased them from bondage in Egypt by the sacrifice of the first born of the Egyptians. He has also purchased man from the bondage of sin by the slaying of his first born or "only begotten Son." In view of this, Christians are enjoined to treat their brothers as brothers, and not as some inferior creatures even though they may be less able and less talented.

Verses 44-46. Since the relation of master and slave was permitted for reasons shown in verses 39-41, the lesson is carried on out that a distinction was to be made between the Lord's people and those on the outside. Christians are likewise told to make a distinction as shown above and cited in Gal. 6: 10. Lest the reader might get too rough an impression as to the meaning of the word "heathen," I shall state that the original word has been rendered in the A. V. by the words "gentile, heathen, nation and people." The underlying meaning is a person from the outside of God's nation.

Verses 47-49. A man's brother or near kinsman might fall into straitened circumstances and be compelled to borrow money of one of the strangers or "outsiders." If so, then a more fortunate brother was permitted and encouraged to redeem the other. If his own circumstances should change and be able to redeem himself, then he may do so. And this stranger, though not a professed adherent of the law, must be made to understand that since he is living in the territory ruled by the Lord, he must be subject to it. Our civil law holds the same principle, and if an alien is not willing to abide by our laws then he is expected to leave the country.

Verses 50-54. The exchange or release of personal servants was regulated on the same basis as the land. The whole subject was related to the year of jubilee. Hence, if a man had taken money from a more fortunate brother in exchange for his bodily services, he was to continue that service till the year of jubilee unless he had become able before that time to redeem himself. If he does not become that strong financially, he will have to continue his servitude till the fiftieth year. The master is warned not to take advantage of it and rule with rigor, or harshness.

LEVITICUS 26

Verse 1. Having lived for centuries in a country where the people worshiped all the host of heaven and every living creature on the earth, they had been so filled with the impression of idolatry that God did not intend they should lose sight of the evil thereof. Hence the warning against such iniquity is often repeated. Not only is the subject of idolatry in general condemned. Man is so inclined to take advantage of the slightest loophole that it was necessary to specify many variations of the sin of idolatry. Hence, the technical specifications of this verse. God is the maker of these very materials from which man had made images for worship. The lesson is that the Maker of the materials should be worshiped and not the materials.

Verse 2. The word sabbath is in the plural. This is because there were many days of holy observance besides the seventh day of the week. (See chapter 23.)

Verses 3, 4. A heavy proviso in the form of "if" and connected with their obedience was placed under all the promises of God. Their failure to comply with this proviso explains their falling short of enjoying all the blessings of God.

Verse 5. This is a descriptive picture of the greatness of their prosperity if they obeyed the Lord. The crops would be so great that by the time they had the grain cared for, it would be time to gather the grapes. By the time that crop was cared for, it would be time to sow for the next crop. All the while they would have bread without any rationing necessary.

Verse 6. This was a promise of protection from the evil nations that would be about them through the years of the occupational period, especially. The promise was made on the same condition as the others.

Verses 7, 8. It was the will of God that his people should expel the heathen nations from their land and as assurance of their success it was said that even a few of them would be able to chase great numbers of the enemy. Of course this would not be on account of their superior military might for they did not have that. God would assist them on condition that they obey his law.

Verse 9. In warfare it is common for an army, even though successful, to be greatly reduced in numbers and have to call for "reinforcements." In this case God would see that they not only would make successful headway against the hostile army, but their own forces would increase all the while.

Verse 10. At times when the future production might have been uncertain (in their estimation), they laid up a surplus for future use. This teaches that the immediate prospects of plenty will be so bright that they will bring out that stuff that had been stored up and consume it. That is the same action that man makes now. Frequently when an abundant crop of fruit or other food is on hand, the cupboards will be opened and the old things stored up will be brought out and used.

Verses 11-13. The tabernacle was to be the visible evidence of God's presence. Its existence accompanied with the blessing of the Lord would be a constant incentive for them to continue as a righteous people and to depend on the divine government for their prosperity in both religion and national life. All this was related with the one great fact at the beginning of their service as a people. They had been delivered out of the bondage to the Egyptians. There they not only were forced to serve the kings over them, but were led into such service as disrespected their own God.

Verses 14-16. The negative as well as the positive side of God's law must be kept before the mind. The pleasant result of obedience as well as the unpleasant result of obedience. And the nature of the unpleasant results was specified for them so that there could be no misunderstanding as to what God meant. "Terror" here means a condition of panic. "Consumption" here is from a word that means "emaciation." "Ague" is defined in the lexicon as "inflammation." All these awful conditions were to be brought upon them if they disobeyed the law of God.

Verse 17. In all their military operations the success was dependent on the help of God. If they disobeyed him then he would turn against them and they would be the victims of the army against which they were fighting. It would even become so terrifying in their defeat that they would make a disorderly retreat when no army was pursuing them.

Verse 18. The further punishment of "seven times" is to be understood as a figure meaning completeness. Their further punishment then would be complete.

Verse 19. These are more figurative expressions. Making the heaven or sky as iron indicates that it would be hardened so as not to give any rain, and the earth as brass would mean that no growth of crops would be possible for it could not be tilled.

Verse 20. This verse is literal. They would strive to produce desired results, would work hard but all in vain. And the trees that ordinarily produced fruit for them without their labor would be made barren by the Lord.

Verse 21. If these punishments still fail to bring them to repentance then they would be put to still stronger tests indicated by the figure seven again.

Verse 22. This verse specifies the kind of plagues that would be used against them if they continued to rebel. Visible punishment for sin was necessary in the period of their national training.

Verse 23. The word "reformed" is from YACAR and Strong defines it "to chastise, literally (with blows) or figuratively (with words); hence to instruct." This agrees with the statements that have frequently been made in this work; that God was taking the people through a kind of training or educational period even as a child is taken through such. At such a time or stage of existence it is necessary to use means that will impress the student by the unpleasantness it causes him since he seems not to be able yet to realize the meaning of the training through his higher reasoning.

Verse 24. To walk contrary unto them, of course, meant that God would oppose their conduct with more complete punishments. This does not mean completeness in the sense that the entire amount of items would be poured on them at once. It could not mean that because the same expression is repeated a number of times. It means that the punishment selected by the Lord each time would be complete of its kind. The great number of times and things stated in this chapter as brought against the people by the Lord proves that he is gracious and always gave the people opportunity from time to time to profit by their experience and straighten up before further evil was put on them. This is the same principle expressed in the N. T. (2 Pe. 3: 9).

Verse 25. This was the sword of the enemy. It would be the means God would use to bring about the punishment selected for that occasion. "Avenge the quarrel" is from words meaning "execute the vengeance." The covenant mentioned here means the law that had been given to them at Sinai and that required them to worship the true God and not do after the heathen nations round them. So complete would God intend the punishment to be, that it would not avail them any to flee from the enemy into the city. They might escape the actual contact of the enemy's sword thereby, but they would not escape the hand of God. He would follow them there and bring a pestilence upon them.

Verse 26. *Staff of your bread.* This is the same thought as commonly heard, that bread is the staff of life. This means that God would reduce their bread supply until it would have to be rationed to them. So scarce would be their supply of flour that the women of ten families would have room in one oven to bake all the bread they had for their families. Since their supply of the necessities of life as to bread became so low, naturally we would expect their provisions in general to be short. So why waste the fuel to heat up ten ovens when one would hold all the bread they had to bake? The amount of bread on hand would not satisfy their hunger.

Verses 27, 28. This passage is a further warning of a general nature, to let them understand that if necessary God would bring more punishment upon them.

Verse 29. This awful thing doubtless took place on more than one occasion, but a notable one is recorded in 2 Kings 6: 29.

Verse 30. The high places means the places of elevation which were often selected or even prepared for the purpose of idolatrous worship. The conclusion is apparent in most instances that their attachment to the idolatrous people and their ways accounted for their departure from the true God. Hence, the punishments inflicted on them from time to time were in connection with that national vice.

Verses 31, 32. This has general reference to their misfortune of falling into the hands of their enemy nations so that their own worship would be rendered impossible.

Verse 33. This is more along the same line as preceding paragraph except that it goes further. The other pictured their downfall in their own country. This verse shows that they would also be taken out of their land and be scattered among the lands of the heathen nations whose gods they had been serving.

Verses 34, 35. The seventh year of rest for the land was violated by the nation, and this is referred to in the threat here predicted. A more detailed explanation of this revolution will be given in its proper place. It is well to note here that God is able to overrule the disobedience of man. When the land had been violated by running it to death by constant cultivation, they would be taken from it to give it a chance to catch up with its rest. This was fulfilled by the great captivity.

Verses 36, 37. General panic would be a fitting description of the condition here described. When a man is guilty of wrong against God it gives him a feeling of fear so that each unusual sound startles him. He thinks it is some omen of punishment about the judgment of the Lord whom he has disobeyed. So complete will be this panic that their actions will be those of persons unsettled in conduct and cause them to attack each other as if attacking their enemies.

Verses 38, 39. The great reduction of the nation while in the land of captivity is here predicted. The fulfillment of this is seen in Ezra 2: 64. There the number at the end of their captivity was fifty-two thousand, while it was about three million in the days of their national strength.

Verses 40-42. The love and graciousness of God is here shown. If the people should prove favorable toward the punishment and acknowledge their own sins and repent, then God promised to bless them. And he would do this in respect to the covenant made with their fathers, Abraham, Isaac and Jacob.

Verse 43. This verse must not be looked at as a sort of "rubbing it in" after they had indicated their desire to return to God. Even if they must continue in the country for the sake of the land that had been wronged, it must have time to catch up with its years of rest. All this would be on the same principle recognized by all government. Even though a man makes a literal restoration of a thing of value he has unjustly taken, he must pay the penalty of the law personally.

Verses 44, 45. So, while they must continue in the land of their captors for the sake of the land and for the sake of their personal punishment, yet if they then see their mistake and repent, then God will see to it that they will not utterly be consumed but will survive the trial and be allowed to return to their own country.

Verse 46. This verse informs us that the tables of stone given Moses while at the top of the mount were not the only law given for the children of Israel. These various laws were given to them by the very same agency as were the two tables. That was "by the hand of Moses."

LEVITICUS 27

Verses 1, 2. The word "singular" means a vow that is great or unusual or distinct. In that Dispensation a man was allowed to devote his children or servants to the service of God if he wished. But it might occur sometimes that circumstances of a just nature would cause him to wish to redeem such person to his own use again. In that case he must pay the redemption estimated. And of course the estimation must be made by Moses and not by the individual making the vow.

Verses 3-8. This paragraph gives the various ages and kinds of persons who had been offered in the vow, and then wished to be redeemed.

Verse 9. In the preceding paragraph we see that a vow of devotion as to sons or daughters or servants might be redeemed with money. But this paragraph is to show that animals devoted in a vow must not be redeemed. They must be considered as holy or belonging to God and thus must be sacrificed and not redeemed.

Verse 10. In spite of the restriction of preceding verse, a man might think to change his vow by substituting something for the thing he had vowed. It was not to be accepted. Not only so, but if he attempted such a thing he would be a greater loser than he would have been had he let the first vow stand. For if he tries to give one thing in the place of the other, then both articles will be taken from him. A lesson should be drawn from this for us. God will never accept one act of obedience in the place of the other. If circumstances make it impossible to perform some particular duty, we are exempted, but we are not permitted to do something else in its place. Neither may we put the performance of some other divine command in the place of the one we cannot perform.

Verses 11-13. All beasts offered in sacrifice must be clean, but there were services with beasts other than sacrifice. Such might be offered in the vow that had been made. If it is desired to redeem such a beast, the man must make an additional payment of one fifth of its regular value. The expression, "shekel of the sanctuary," seen in so many places means that it must be money of legal tender according to the requirements of the sanctuary.

Verses 14, 15. A vow could be made concerning a house as well as a person. In such case it could be redeemed. If so he must do as he did in redeeming the unclean beast. He must increase the payment by one fifth of its regular value.

Verse 16. Much the same regulations applied when a man had offered part of his land in vow. He might redeem it under these restrictions.

Verses 17, 18. The expressions "from the year of jubilee" and "after the jubilee" are the forms used here to mean the nearness to the fiftieth year. If it is nearer the one past than the one coming, then it is said to be "after" it, and so on. Since this year of jubilee was the great leveler of everything, it had to be figured in all considerations of land value.

Verses 19, 20. If the field is to be redeemed, then the fifth part must be added. He will have one opportunity to redeem the field. If he does not use that opportunity, then it must be allowed to stand according to the vow.

If he has sold a piece of land, then he cannot vow that property but will have to wait till the year of jubilee to repossess it. That is, if he had merely sold it and had not tried to vow it to the Lord. If such a thing had taken place, then he would never repossess it as will be seen in next paragraph.

Verse 21. This field that he wished to vow to God even though he had sold it, will finally become the Lord's in the jubilee, and will be turned over to the priest.

Verses 22-24. A man might have just bought a piece of ground from another. That seller would be thinking of the jubilee at which time he expected to receive it again and would have right to thus expect it. So if this buyer wishes to vow it to God he may do so. But that vow will give such land to the Lord only until the jubilee, then it will become the property again of the original owner.

Verse 25. The standard of value according to the sanctuary is here given as twenty gerahs. This was a small coin of varying value. Hence, whatever was the accepted value of it at any time for use of the sanctuary was to be required for vows.

Verse 26. The special possession of the first born of beasts could not be redeemed at all. All such must be turned over to the sanctuary use.

Verses 27, 28. This paragraph is merely a detail of what has been already offered in this chapter. A thing devoted to God must be considered as something holy.

Verse 29. This has reference to enemies that are devoted or promised for destruction. If the children of Israel make any such vow, then they cannot change their minds and try to substitute something in its place. A noted example of this kind of transaction is recorded in Num. 21: 2, 3. It will be interesting and helpful for the reader to turn to that place and read the account of the vow of the people of God and their faithful performance of the vow.

Verse 30. The tithe or tenth of all their products belongs to God. This was for the support of the tribe of Levi in general. They had no opportunity for producing anything since they were constantly "standing by" for the special service about the tabernacle. Thus they must be supported by the tithes of the other people.

Verse 31. If some particular beast or crop is thought to be needed at home, then he could retain it by giving an extra fifth of its value in money.

Verse 32. "Passeth under the rod" means that the young were thus counted off to see how many had been produced that season. One out of every ten must be given to the Lord.

Verse 33. He must not try to show partiality and see if number nine is a specially good animal and number eleven not so good, etc. He must be fair and give the Lord each tenth beast. If he tries to redeem it with some other article then he would lose both the same as in verse 10.

Verse 34. A grand summing up of the law. The Lord commanded it. He commanded it to Moses. And he commanded it to Moses for the children of Israel. Again the great authority of Moses in connection with the so-called ceremonial law is plainly stated. And this law was given to Moses at Mount Sinai, the very same place and the very same occasion as were used in giving the tables of the ten commandments.

NUMBERS 1

Verse 1. By comparing Ex. 40: 17 here, it will be seen that it has been just one month since the tabernacle was reared up. And by further comparison with Lev. 1:1 it will be learned that the time of this month was used in connection with occupation of the formal place of meeting between God and his people and must be recognized as the proper place for them to attend with their sacrifices.

Verse 2. A census is now commanded to be taken. It was not to include the entire population, but just those of military age; the males only to be taken into this numbering.

Verses 3, 4. In addition to being of the age of twenty they must also be able to go to war. They must be able-bodied. These restrictions brought the group to contain only those who would pass a physical examination and be of the necessary age. Thus it was not for the purpose of determining the amount of the population as is generally done by nations today. The future of the nation was to be beset with conflicts with the enemy, so their military strength was the important thing with them.

Verses 5-16. Aaron was commanded to work with Moses in this numbering. They were to select a man to represent the tribes and each one was to be a head or chief person. The personal heads of the tribes were the sons of Jacob. They had all been dead for some time and thus it was necessary to appoint a man for each tribe now, in order to keep the tribal distinction intact. The paragraph now being considered is a list of these men.

Verses 17-19. Having assembled the congregation as commanded, these representative men declared the "pedigrees." This word means the record of births of the several families. It corresponds with the documents called "birth certificates." This enumeration was by their "polls." This is a word for "heads" and the statement means they did not merely give an aggregate sum of the people, but it was an individual list.

Verses 20, 21. All the specifications required for the ones to be numbered are mentioned in connection with each tribe. It will not be necessary to write them in this place at each listing of the tribes. The language is identical and corresponds with the stipulations of the verses in the beginning of the chapter. A paragraph will be assigned for each tribe, expressing in figures the number of each tribe. The present one is for Reuben and the number is 46,500.

Verses 22, 23. The number of the tribe of Simeon is 59,300.

Verses 24, 25. Gad has 45,650.

Verses 26, 27. The tribe of Judah has 74,600. It will be interesting to note that the tribe of Judah had the greatest number of military men. This is the tribe that brought the Saviour of the world to the earth. And this great person produced also a great host of soldiers; soldiers of the cross.

Verses 28, 29. The tribe of Issachar has 54,400.

Verses 30, 31. Zebulun has 57,400.

Verses 32, 33. The tribe of Ephraim numbered 40,500 military men.

Verses 34, 35. Manasseh has 32,200 attributed to his tribe. It will be interesting here also to make an observation. In Gen. 48: 19 Jacob made the prediction that Ephraim, though the younger of the two brothers, was to become stronger than the other. And at this enumeration we see that such was the case.

Verses 36, 37. Benjamin was the only brother of Joseph. The two sons of Joseph were taken to become each a head of a tribe. This was done by Jacob in the land of Egypt when the two sons were brought to him for his blessing. (Gen. 48: 5.) At the present we see that the entire numerical strength of Joseph is more than that of Benjamin, which is 35,400, leaving us the conclusion that the brother of Joseph headed the smallest tribe of the nation if the original sons of Jacob are considered. This suggests the statement in Psa. 68: 27 about "little Benjamin." The word "little" is from TSAOWR and defined by Strong "little (in number) few." This also harmonizes with the statement of Saul in 1 Sam. 9: 21 that he was of the smallest of the tribes of Israel. No great concern would be had as to the veracity of Saul when we have in mind his later life. At the time of the statement he was in good repute and we are pleased to find his remark true to the facts, which is the case when Joseph is compared as one tribe.

Verses 38, 39. The tribe of Dan numbered 62,700.

Verses 40, 41. Asher had 41,500.

Verses 42-44. The tribe of Naphtali numbered 53,400. The foregoing is a list of the various tribes given under the heads of the men selected to represent them. These men are here called "princes" which corresponds with the term "renowned" used before.

Verses 45, 46. This is the sum of all the twelve tribes as recognized in the list given above. It is 603,550.

Verses 47-49. The tribe of Levi was not numbered with the rest. They will have a separate enumeration. All this is logical when we remember that the list was to enroll the military men and the Levites were not to be called into that service for reasons soon to be indicated.

Verse 50. Here the general statement is made that the Levites were to have the work of the tabernacle. This would prevent them from entering the military service.

Verse 51. This makes a more specific statement of the duties of the tribe. The children of Israel were to be directed as to their journeys and the time thereof by the cloud that hovered over the tabernacle. No warning was given them as to when the cloud would move. At the instant of its moving the people must move. Thus it was necessary that one tribe be released from all duties except those of taking down and setting up of the tabernacle. In this verse the word "stranger" would apply to those not of the designated tribe. The word literally means "one from the outside." In the present connection therefore, the word would have to mean one outside the Levites.

Verse 52. The command for order in their encampment is given here in general. The particular form of that order will be given in the next chapter. At the present we understand the congregation would be encamped at some distance from the tabernacle as directed later on.

Verses 53, 54. This paragraph relates to the duties of the Levites as a tribe. They had the entire charge which included the special services of the tabernacle when at rest and in service, as well as the physical work of handling it when being moved. The more particular assignments for the work will be given in another place. (Ch. 3.)

NUMBERS 2

Verses 1, 2. A more detailed set of instructions will now be given for their order of encampment. The point is obvious that God requires system and orderly conduct in the activities of his people. (Col. 2: 5.) The word "far" here is not one that refers to distance. It is from NEGED and defined "a front, i. e. part opposite; specifically a counterpart, or mate; usually over against or before."—Strong. So it did not mean that the children of Israel were to be at a great distance from the tabernacle, but that they must be arranged in such a manner as to be in view of the building.

Verses 3-9. A division into four camps was made and these camps were to be located in the four directions from the tabernacle. That made each camp consist of three of the tribes. Each camp was named by the tribe considered as head of the same. Each had a man designated as captain over the group. The camp that was to be on the east of the tabernacle, consisted of Judah, Issachar and Zebulun and Judah was the tribe giving name to this camp. The several numbers of the tribes are given which are the same as those given in first chapter. Also the sum of the three tribes forming the camps is given. That will be the figures put down in this place for each camp. The number of the camp of Judah is given as 186,400. The statement is made that when the congregation is to start out on a journey the camp of Judah must take the lead.

Verses 10-16. The statement common to the four camps need not be repeated each time. The camp consisted of Reuben, Simeon and Gad and Reuben gave it the name. The sum of the three tribes is 151,450. It is directed that when the march is indicated, this camp must go second. This will make one half of the congregation. Therefore it will be orderly for the tabernacle to be placed in the midst of the congregation. Hence, after the second camp starts on the march, the Levites, having charge of the tabernacle, must arise and follow the camp of Reuben.

Verses 17-24. The first verse of this paragraph is commented upon in preceding paragraph. After the Levites with the tabernacle have entered the procession, then the third camp must proceed. But at present their place of encampment is what is being described. The camp consisted of Manasseh, Benjamin and Ephraim and Ephraim gave it the name. The sum of the three tribes is 108,100. This camp was situated on the west.

Verses 25-31. The fourth camp as listed here was on the north. The three tribes comprised in this camp were Dan, Asher and Naphtali and Dan gave the name to the camp. In the march this camp was to go last. This whole arrangement was so directed that no confusion need result when the alarm of war or of march was sounded. All would know their places in the procession and proceed in an orderly way.

Verses 32-34. This paragraph is a repetition of preceding plan and summing up. In verse 33 mention is again made that the Levites were not numbered with the other tribes. Their enumeration will be given separately and also their special work for the Lord.

NUMBERS 3

Verse 1. The word "generations" is from a word that means "family history." Hence it does not always refer to the particular descendants of a family, but to any account that may be considered of the family or of a man. It would be a proper form of expression to say that "this is the family history" etc., of Aaron and Moses.

Verses 2, 3. This paragraph goes back to the first of the history and names all the sons of Aaron because, as stated in preceding verse, it is a family history. And these sons were all eligible for the place of common priests and had been consecrated for that particular part of the tabernacle service.

Verse 4. *They had no children.* This statement is made to explain why Eleazar and Ithamar took the place of their brothers in the administration of the priest's office. Had they left sons old enough to serve, then they would have succeeded to the office and work of their father.

Verses 5-10. Aaron was, himself, of the tribe of Levi. While his personal family had exclusive charge of the priest's office, the tribe as a whole was to be used in the service of the Lord for the congregation. Whatever was needed to carry on the congregational activities the tribe of Levi must supply it. For this reason the whole tribe was exempt from obligation to engage in productive occupations. In place of such occupation for a livelihood, the other tribes were to turn over a tenth of their entire income for this special tribe. When such support was given, it is referred to as having been given to the Lord. The "stranger" mentioned in 10th verse would here mean one on the outside of the camp of Levi.

Verses 11-13. The reader will refer to Ex. 13: 2 where the Lord laid claim to all the first born of the children of Israel and from that time forward they were considered as special possession of his. The basis on which this claim was made was the fact that their release from bondage had been finally obtained through the death of the first born of the Egyptians. Now it is fair that in return for this great favor the first born of the nation be appropriated to God. The difference is that they were not to be slain. They were to be devoted to the Lord's service. Now it is desired to make a change in the whole setup. Instead of claiming the first born of all the tribes, God wishes the service and possession of one entire tribe. And for this he will exchange his possession of the first born for that of the tribe of Levi.

Verses 14-16. In taking the enumeration of the tribe of Levi we note another change of the basis. It is to be, of all the males from a month old. As soon as a boy baby was that old his prospect of living would have been well established and he was then recorded in the register of the tribe. When his age became such as would be accepted for the service of the tribe he would be used.

Verses 17-22. The entire tribe of Levi would be classified under the sub-heads of the three sons whose names were Gershon, Kohath and Merari. Also the sons of these several branches of Levi formed still further classification as to the family record and their particular work about the tabernacle would lie under the assignment that had been made to their father. The entire number of the males from Gershon that were a month old and upward was 7,500. This gives the sum of all the males in the tribe of Levi at this time who were eligible for the general work about the tabernacle. The particular portion of the service would be further restricted to whether they were from Levi through his son Kohath, or from one of the others as will be seen below.

Verses 23, 24. We see that orderliness is still observed. The members of the Gershonite families were to pitch "behind" the tabernacle. In the same connection it calls the place "westward" which indicates that the building was always pitched in the eastward direction. The word "behind" has also a more specific significance than that of direction. It means that it was near the tabernacle as compared with the entire camp of Ephraim which was also located on the west. (Chapter 2: 13.) This unit was to be immediately near, to be ready for their particular part of the service when called.

Verses 25, 26. This paragraph states the special work of the families of the Gershonites. It pertained to the building and its parts. When it was time to march this group took down the building and when the place for setting up the tabernacle was pointed out, they were to do that work.

Verses 27, 28. The important branch of the Kohathites had 8,600 in number. Their charge is stated in general term here as that of the sanctuary. It will be given more detailed description in next paragraph.

Verses 29-32. Kohath was to pitch on the near south of the tabernacle. This group had charge of the furniture of the tabernacle; and also the curtains which included the fabrics used to cover the articles; and also the enclosures in the various parts.

Verses 33-35. The Merari unit pitched on the near north of the tabernacle. This group numbered 6,200.

Verses 36, 37. This group had charge of the heavy part of the tabernacle or the framework. This is understood to mean the boards and foundation, also the pillars of the tabernacle proper and also the ones sustaining the curtains of the court. The word "charge" used in connection with these three groups pitched near the tabernacle means that they were to watch over and care for and handle the various parts of the whole structure as described. Each man, or group of men, was to know his place and do his particular work when needed. Thus we see that system was observed in God's plan.

Verses 38, 39. In this paragraph we see "before" and "east" used in the same connection, which is a further indication that the institution was always pitched in the easterly direction. Moses, Aaron and his sons had this position in the general encampment. It should be regarded as the superior position since it was at the entrance to the sacred building. The word "stranger" in this specific place means anyone not of Moses or the immediate family of Aaron. The number of this unit was included in that of the whole tribe and the number was 22,000. It will be well now to take a look at the whole encampment as set forth in this and preceding chapter. The congregation of the twelve tribes was divided into four camps situated some distance, (but in full view) from the tabernacle. Nearer to the building were the three groups of the three sons of Levi located on the south, west and north sides with their own work assigned as to the various parts of the whole building and service. Then on the east, which was the front, were Moses and Aaron with his sons, having the immediate services of the worship of the institution.

Verses 40-43. This paragraph is a repetition and summing up of information that has already been given. The reader may think a discrepancy occurs in the number given in verse 43 compared with that given in verse 39 above. But he should note that only in the odd numbers is there a difference. The number in verse 39 considers the even thousands only, which is a practice common to all kinds of literature, while the number in verse 43 is more definite as to the amount.

Verses 44, 45. Much of this paragraph is repetition, but it should be noted that mention is made here of taking the cattle of the Levites as well as the people. That is because they were to cease their secular activities and thus would have no occasion for personal possession of these. They would be considered as consecrated to God.

Verse 46. When the exchange was made between the tribe of Levi on one hand and the first born of all the tribes on the other, there was an excess of the first born.

Verses 47, 48. From each man or other male that was over, or more than, the entire tribe of Levi the Lord exacted a poll tax of five shekels. Since they will not be required to engage in the special work of the sanctuary the Lord takes this mehthod of equalizing the obligation to him.

Verses 49-51. This money was turned over to Aaron and his sons to be used in the work or service of the sanctuary. That is, this money was placed in the general treasury of the congregation. It would be used for such instances as purchasing lambs for the daily sacrifice (Ex. 29: 38-42), and other public necessities.

NUMBERS 4

Verses 1, 2. To keep our minds clear on the line of service it will be stated again that the priesthood must come, not only through Levi, but through his son, Kohath. Not only through Kohath, but from the particular family descending from Kohath, that came through Aaron. There was other service besides that of the priesthood that was restricted to the sons of Kohath. Hence, in the present paragraph the listing of them is required.

Verses 3, 4. The age limit as now set for the general service of the Kohathites is from thirty to fifty years. Certain exceptions were made at times as will be seen.

Verses 5, 6. The directions now about to be given pertain to the time of moving from one camp to another. The sons of Kohath must first come forward because the holy articles have to be prepared first. The work began with the ark. The "covering vail" refers to the one screening the ark from the other room of the tabernacle. When it is taken down it was to be used as a covering immediately on the ark. It must be further protected with a covering of skins of animals. *Shall put in the staves thereof.* This might confuse the reader since Ex. 25: 15 required that these staves were never to be taken from the ark. The meaning is that thy were always to be kept in direct nearness to it for use when needed. As to whether they were fully in the position of lifting the ark would be immaterial. Just as a detachable handle for some implement. It would always be kept together with the tool for ready use, although not necessarily inserted in the place for its operation.

Verses 7, 8. Preparation of the table was next. The question would be natural as to what use could be made of these vessels since nothing was kept on this table but bread. We should remember that after the week's occupation of the table by this bread, it then became the food of the priests. They ate it as food the same as anyone else would eat bread. At such a time they could eat it in connection with other articles of food as their taste suggested. In that matter they would have need of these implements. Therefore, this table would be a fitting place to keep them.

Verses 9, 10. The order to cover all these holy pieces of furniture would agree with the thought that they were so exclusive that the public gaze should be shut out.

Verses 11, 12. The same thought of protection is here observed as for the other pieces of the furniture for the tabernacle.

Verses 13, 14. The altar of burnt offering is meant here since the golden altar has already been cared for. Besides, the golden altar did not have occasion to be strewn with ashes. The brasen altar has been in daily use since encamping before and the residue of ashes from the service would still be on the grate of brass. This must be cleared away and then the covering be spread as here required. Also the instruments must be placed on the piece after being covered. From this it can be seen that when they were commanded never to let the fire on the altar go out (Lev. 6: 12, 13), it meant to apply when in service, not when in transit.

Verse 15. Aaron and his sons were "sons of Kohath," but the expression as used in this verse means the descendants of Kohath in general. Not all of the Kohathites were of the particular family of Aaron, who alone had the priesthood. A distinction must be made in the mention of the sons of Kohath in general and the particular ones coming through Aaron. These were the ones to prepare the holy articles for travel and the others were to come to carry them. They must not touch them, and that will be unnecessary since the staves are there for bearing them.

Verse 16. *Office of Eleazar.* This is significant. It shows that this specific service was not to this particular man only, but to the men who will succeed him from time to time.

Verses 17-19. The word "tribe" is not used here in the same sense that is properly applied to the word when referring to the twelve tribes. It is from a word that means "branch" and is used of the particular branch of the Levites coming through Kohath. They were to be regarded with respect and guarded from danger. They had to do special service over other Levites and yet they must wait till the sons of Aaron have prepared the things for their service.

Verse 20. Idle curiosity is condemned and if these sons of Kohath give way to it they will be punished with death. They must wait until the covering has been done before going near the things to be carried.

Verses 21-26. This is the same instruction given in chapter 3: 25, 26, but the additional item is given here about the age limit. It is from thirty to fifty.

Verses 27, 28. Once more we see a distinction between the sons of Aaron and other descendants of Levi. This distinction must be kept in mind throughout the system.

Verses 29-33. The age limit is the same here as with the ones of the preceding paragraph. The service is the same as described in previous chapters.

Verses 34, 35. The numbering of this group was under the oversight of Moses and Aaron, assisted by the chief men of the Kohathites. These "chief" men were not officials but were men deputized by Moses for the work.

Verses 36, 37. The simple statement of the number of these special families is the subject of this paragraph.

Verses 38-41. The number of the various groups is repeated and the general statement of "entering into the service" is detailed at the original mention of the duty.

Verses 42-45. Same comments as on the preceding paragraphs.

Verses 46-49. The total number of these special Levites is the subject of this paragraph which has been described in the foregoing chapter.

NUMBERS 5

Verses 1-4. Remembering that the nation of the Israelites was expected to be for future relationship with a final Dispensation, it can be realized that the citizens must be kept within a clear blood. Hence certain restrictions would have to be made that would not have been necessary if only personal salvation were considered.

Verses 5-7. This paragraph is concerning a case where a man has done some financial or other material trespass against another but was ignorant of it at the time. When made aware of the fact, he would be "guilty." When such knowledge came to him he was to make it right by restoring the thing trespassed against, and add a fifth.

Verse 8. The very wording of this verse indicates that the trespasser might not learn of his wrong until after the one suffering the wrong had died or otherwise got out of touch with the guilty one. In that case he could make it right by returning it to a kinsman. It might be that no kinsman would be known. In such a situation he would make it right by giving the return of the trespass to the Lord. It would be a suggestion for this time of ours. A Christian discovers that he had trespassed against some man in the past but whose existence might be unknown. It would be right for the guilty person to consider such property as being the Lord's and he could give it to the church and thus make it right.

Verses 9, 10. This does not mean that the wrong of trespass had been against the priest personally. The priest was to live by the things that were devoted to the service of the tabernacle. (1 Cor. 9: 13.)

Verses 11-13. The subject introduced in this paragraph is of a case where a man's wife is actually guilty of adultery. Since the act would not be witnessed in many cases, that would make an opportunity for denial. Hence some means must be used to decide doubtful cases for determining whether a woman be guilty when suspected. This provision will be described below.

Verse 14. Since the "spirit of jealousy" might come into a man's mind regardless of the guilt or innocence of the wife, it was necessary to use the plan here at hand.

Verses 15, 16. Let it be noted that the ceremony was performed by the priest who was the official representative of the Lord in the government of the people. Also since the ceremony is to be "before the Lord" it would be at the tabernacle since that institution was the place where the Lord had recorded his name.

Verse 17. Water in its natural state is all the same and posseses no moral characteristics. It is considered holy when no contact had been made with it, of some unclean object. It must be water therefore that is clean. Into such water the priest was to put some dust from the floor of the tabernacle. Since nothing unclean was ever allowed to be brought into the tabernacle the dust therein would also be clean. So, the entire formula would be from materials that were clean. Hence, if any unfavorable result appears it cannot be laid to the physical effect of the formula. Such result would have to be explained by the miraculous intervention of God. That must furthermore be understood in the light of Heb. 1: 1. Attempts have been made in modern times to compare this performance with the use of the "lie detector" that is used in some cases by officials trying to discover guilt. The comparison is made as an attempt to discredit the miraculous nature of the Biblical case and is therefore one of the ruses of the unbelievers of divine revelation. There is no comparison. In the case of the lie detector there is no physical result; it is purely confined to the mental or nervous system of the person being tested. In the case we are considering there would be an apparent physical result as we shall see.

Verses 18-23. The woman is expected to submit to the test. Her refusal would be an admission of guilt. The drinking of this water could not possibly injure her by any law of nature. Therefore, she should not hesitate to drink it if innocent. In order that her cooperation in the performance could not be doubted she was required to answer the statement of the priest by saying "amen, amen." After drinking the water if guilty, her body would react accordingly. Vital portions of her body would became diseased and repulsive but not necessarily fatal at once. Instead, she would continue to exist, but as a person to be aborred among her people. Also, the case was to be recorded by the priest in a book so as to clear the good reputation of the nation at large.

Verses 24-27. This paragraph describes the carrying out of the ceremony already mentioned, which had been agreed to by the woman.

Verse 28. If not guilty the woman was to be freed. The statement is also added that she would be able to conceive. This indicates that the condition of her curse had she been guilty was to be deplored, especially because it would have prevented her from such privilege. In those days such disability was regretted very much.

Verses 29-31. Some criticism has been suggested that the man should make some amends for the false accusation against his wife. The guilt of adultery was such an abhorred one, that it should be exposed at every suspicion thereof. If a woman is not guilty it will not injure her in the least to be tested. The same principle holds good, generally. A guilty person is often unwilling to be examined and the very refusal to be tested is indication of guilt. An innocent person is glad to be tested if any doubt has been raised concerning his conduct.

NUMBERS 6

Verses 1, 2. We are about to learn of a special vow that was performed among the Israelites. The Lord did not command the making of vows as a regular practice. But if a person wished to make one then God did regulate it. The one now under consideration was a very spcial one and had close restrictions. It was called a Nazarite vow. The word is derived from the Hebrew word NAZAR which means "separate." Since a person making this vow agreed to separate himself from the rest, in a special sense of conduct and observance, the vow received its name as stated.

Verse 3. Some things are specified from which the person must separate himself. They were to include all of the products of the grape in whatever condition they were.

Verse 4. This restriction against the product of the vine held good during the period of days he had stipulated as the period of his vow. This period might be long or short, according to the will of the one making the vow.

Verse 5. Since this vow required the man to let his hair grow uncut during the period of his vow we have the conclusion that men had their hair short as a rule. Having it long would be favored only when under this special vow. Paul used this vow on one occasion. (Acts 18: 18.)

Verse 6. The prevailing meaning of this vow is that of separation. Therefore the person must keep separate from dead bodies during the term of the vow.

Verses 7, 8. The foregoing restrictions would not even permit the exception of the body of near kin.

Verses 9-12. A man under the Nazarite vow might be conscientiously trying to observe the obligations belonging to it, but a sudden death might occur near him and bring him into contact with the dead body. In such a case the whole status of the vow would be changed. And the person must go through certain ceremonials in order to be in favor with the Lord. This is another instance to show us that many of the ceremonies of that system were typical and not literal or of a physical nature. After the accident had interfered with the progress of the vow the whole time already passed under the vow was lost and it had to be started over.

Verses 13-17. Almost all activities performed under the Mosaic system were connected with animal and other sacrifices. The literal and logical transactions were required always, of course, and no amount of gifts could be substituted for the personal obligations in force. Such obligations though observed to the letter did not suffice to the Lord. So in the case now at hand, after the person had continued faithful to the termination of his vow, he was still required to carry out these religious items. He must be brought to the door of the tabernacle and make the offerings named. Four of the five major sacrifices described in beginning chapters of Leviticus are listed here, and the reader may consult those chapters for the particulars of how they were to be performed. All this was required before the person was free or "purified."

Verses 18-20. This act of shaving the head at the end of the time for the vow is what Paul did as recorded in Acts 18: 18. No one knows just what was the occasion of his vow or how long it continued. Having made the vow he was bound to abide by the regulations placed under the law.

Verse 21. See comments in paragraph verses 13-17 above. This present passage is a restatement of those obligations. That is, he must faithfully carry out the personal acts of behaviour during the term of his vow, besides the things he provides for the

Lord's institution here referred to by the words "that his hand shall get."

Verses 22-27. This is the benediction to be used at various times for the consolation of the nation of the Israelites. We note that the Lord did not speak directly to Aaron in this case. He spake to Moses, and he, in turn, was to speak to Aaron. Another indication of the authority and position of Moses.

NUMBERS 7

Verses 1, 2. The rearing up of the tabernacle is recorded in Ex. 40: 17, 18. At that time Moses completed the formalities directly pertaining to his duty and office as lawgiver. But in addition to those ceremonies there were others who volunteered certain sacrifices and offerings and this chapter will be the account of their performances. The men here called "princes" are the same as the ones called "ruler" in Lev. 4: 22. But in that case the directions were for a ruler when he had committed an offense and was called upon to atone for it with an offering. For that reason we will not see all of the items listed, that are shown in the present chapter. That is because in this, the whole performance is a voluntary one and intended for a more complete ceremony.

Verses 3-8. The sum of the things which these princes brought is given in this paragraph. Moses was directed to accept them and turn them over to the Levites. The stipulation is made that they were to be used by the men of the Levites "according to their services." In other words, the instruction to turn these things over to the Levites is a general one since all persons who had anything at all to do with the service were Levites. Certain ones of the tribe had special duties which will be given more description below.

Verse 9. These sons of Kohath were of the tribe of Levi but were the special ones referred to above. None of these articles listed were turned over to them since the kind of service they were to perform did not call for such. Their sole work was to carry the articles of furniture, "bear upon their shoulders," and otherwise handle these articles. That would not call for the use of the sacrifices.

Verses 10, 11. The importance of being orderly is again manifested. These princes were to take turns in their several ceremonies and take a day for each.

Verses 12-17. A detailed list of what each prince offered on his day is here given. In connection with the naming of the article the particular one of the five major sacrifices to which each was to be applied is pointed out. It will be interesting to make note in each case that the law was carried out. Thus, in verse 15 after naming the articles offered it is stated that they were offered for a "burnt offering." And by reference to Lev. 1: 3, 10 the reader will see that the law of sacrifices was observed. In verse 16 the "sin offering" is named and reference to Lev. 4: 22, 23 will show that the directions for that ceremony were observed. And in verse 17 the "peace offerings" are cited which refers us to Lev. 3: 1, 6, 12.

Verses 18-83. The long list of verses in this paragraph will not require much space with comments. The offering of each of the princes was exactly the same and it will be sufficient to go through the passage and mark the number of the day and the name of the prince as follows: Verse 12, first day, Nahshon. Verse 18, second day, Nethaneel. Verse 24, third day, Eliab. Verse 30, fourth day, Elizur. Verse 36, fifth day, Shelumiel. Verse 42, sixth day, Eliasaph. Verse 48, seventh day, Elishama. Verse 54, eighth day, Gamaliel. Verse 60, ninth day, Abidan. Verse 66, tenth day, Ahiezer. Verse 72, eleventh day, Pagiel. Verse 78, twelfth day, Ahira.

Verses 84-88. This paragraph is another summing up of all the articles offered in this ceremony. The whole passage might be bracketed and labeled "altar dedication."

Verse 89. The first occurrence of the pronoun "him" means God. This was the place ordained by the Lord where he would meet and commune with the High Priest. (See Ex. 25: 22.) We realize that Moses was not a priest at all in the regular sense of that word. Here again is an indication of his great position. He was even over Aaron, since he was the lawgiver of the whole system under God. The exact spot at which the meeting was to take place is named. It is between the cherubims, which were on the mercy seat, over the ark.

NUMBERS 8

Verses 1-2. The seven lamps mentioned here are the bowls on the top of the seven branches of the candlestick. "Over against" is explained at Ex. 25: 31, 32, 37.

Verses 3, 4. "As the Lord commanded Moses" is another showing of the superior position he had over Aaron. The candlestick had been described to Moses while he was in the mount and now it has been made according to the directions. It was formed into the desired shape by hammering. And when it was ready for service, olive oil was poured into the bowls, and then, Aaron the priest lighted them.

Verses 5-13. The tribe of Levi as a whole was given over to the exclusive service of God. The particular classification of their several duties has been already described. They were to be consecrated in connection with use of the "water of purifying." This water is described in chapter 19: 9, 17. It will be understood of course that not each individual of the tribe was acted upon as described. Since the formality was one for the tribe as a whole, some particular representatives were pointed out for the occasion and the devotional program would be effected upon them. This form of the ceremony is evident in 13th verse. There the Levites were to be set before Aaron and his sons, yet we know that they were Levites also. Therefore, the other directions applied to the tribe as a whole and as such would have representatives.

Verses 14-18. The exchange of the first born of all the tribes for the entire tribe of Levi is the subject of this paragraph. The death of the first born of the Egyptians was the final and deciding act that procured the release of the Israelites from their bondage. Thus it was fair that God claim as his all the first born among the children of Israel. When a special tribe was needed for the divine service, the tribe of Levi was selected and the exchange made. The reason for making that selection of the particular tribe of Levi is that when Moses called for all who would, come over to the Lord's side, this tribe responded. A helpful view of the word "sanctified" is set forth in this paragraph. In verse 14 it is said that the Levites were "separated" from the other people. In verse 17 and in direct connection with that same subject, it is said that they were "sanctified." This shows that the word does not have some mysterious meaning as sometimes taught, but means the simple fact of being devoted to a particular position and service.

Verse 19. The word "gift" is not in the original and is added as a detail. It means simply "I have given the Levites to Aaron and his sons." The verse goes on to show that the transfer was not made for the personal service of this family. Instead, it was that they might do the service of the children of Israel. By setting one entire tribe apart for the special service of the tabernacle there would be left no reason for others to come near the sacred institution beyond their proper bounds. To do so would have meant their death.

Verses 20-22. The Levites were purified according to verse seven and then washed their clothes. It was after this ceremony that they began their service of the tabernacle. Previous to that, it would have been unlawful for them to act.

Verses 23, 24. The beginning age limit of service for the Levites seems to have been changed from time to time. The first limit was from thirty years. (Chapt. 4: 3). It is now from twenty-five. Later (1 Chr. 23: 3, 24, 27) it was changed to twenty. The men in charge at these changes were men of authority, therefore we conclude the Lord authorized the changes for reasons which he did not make known to us.

Verse 25. The age of retirement was fifty years. It should be understood that the common priests are the ones meant here. The High Priests served until death, according to chapter 35: 25.

Verse 26. This verse teaches that even after these Levites had passed the age of official service they were still expected to do what they could about the work. And the same principle applies to the Lord's servants under the Christian Dispensation. If a man becomes too old or otherwise disabled for the usual or full activity in the work, there is no time when he is exempt from doing what he can.

NUMBERS 9

Verses 1, 2. It has now been fourteen days since the tabernacle was reared up (Ex. 40: 17), and the first occasion to keep the passover in the proper time and manner. The command now is to observe the feast.

Verses 3-5. The warning is here to keep the feast according to all the rites pertaining thereto. The reader may see Ex. 14, for details of this feast.

Verse 6. In chapter 5: 2 and 19: 11, 16 the instruction is found to the effect that contact with a dead person renders one unclean. An unclean man would not be permitted to participate in the feast of the passover. No provision had been as yet made for this kind of situation, thus they bring the case to Moses and Aaron.

Verse 7. This verse indicates they did know that such a person was prevented from partaking of the passover in the "appointed season," but did not know what to do about it.

Verse 8. Let it be remembered that the system of the Mosaic Dispensation is now in the making and that all of the law pertaining to it has not yet been given. It will be necessary therefore to extend its provisions as the call for them appears. This is why Moses told them to "stand still" or wait until he had consulted the Lord. Now if Moses had been acting on his own authority, as the sabbatarians so disrespectfully allege, then he would have proceeded here to tell them what to do. Especially would he have done so since it pertained to one of the "ceremonial" ordinances and not to anything even mentioned in the decalogue. But he did not. He held up the case until he had opportunity for consulting God.

Verses 9-12. In this emergency the Lord directed that another date should be taken for the feast which was one month later than the regular one. This circumstance has been misused by certain ones who wish to take the privilege of substituting some of their own plans for that of the Lord. The fundamental principle involved is that it was the Lord who made the change and not man. Unless there is a provision in the law of God for our alternating something for the thing we are supposed to do, then we have no right to make any change. If circumstances over which we have no control prevent us from doing what the Lord commands, in any given case, then we must not do anything. We will be exempt from the activity.

Verses 13, 14. When the second date has been taken for the observance of the feast, all the other restrictions must be observed that would have been required at the regular time.

Verses 15-23. The original word for "cloud" here is the same as for the ordinary rain cloud. Yet the connection shows that it was not that kind of a cloud. It would mean whatever kind of covering and appearance the Lord saw fit to use. It was to make known to the children of Israel the will of God concerning their journeying. Another instance to remind us of Heb. 1: 1. This cloud was the signal for their moving or locating. The length of time they would remain at any given place was not made known except as this cloud moved or remained over the tabernacle. Hence, it was necessary for them to be always attentive to this cloud and not wander off to some distance too far to see the cloud. Should some man be forgetful and fail to be observant of this cloud the congregation might move off and leave him behind. There was no excuse for any man to be left behind for this cloud was always over the tabernacle. This would make it visible to all the congregation. No regular time of encampment was settled upon. It might be as short as two days or as long as a year. (Verse 22). Hence the need for their always being on the alert. They must be always watchful lest they be surprised and left. The same kind of warning is given to Christians. (Matt. 24: 42; 1 Thess. 5: 1-6).

NUMBERS 10

Verses 1, 2. Some three million people would not hear the voice of a man if called upon to make any movement. Yet it would be necessary for the order to be heard by all at the same time. Otherwise, their movements would be disorderly. We have already noted that order was one of the things the Lord required. So these silver trumpets were made for the purpose of the general call.

Verse 3. This is a general call and the people must respond to it by assembling at the door of the tabernacle. That would give opportunity for any special instructions, to be observed at the time.

Verse 4. There were two trumpets made but not always used. The "code" must be understood and that is referred to in this verse. If but one blast, or the blast of but one trumpet sounded, it was a signal for the heads of the people to assemble before Moses. There might be some special instructions for that class of men.

Verses 5, 6. Some manner of using these trumpets indicated whether the sound meant an alarm or merely a call to attention. And if it were an alarm to march, then the order of march is stated. Logically, if the east side starts and the south follows, then the same order would require the west and north to follow, respectively.

Verse 7. This is considered in preceding paragraph. This distinction in the meaning of the various codes is an illustration of Paul's statements in 1 Cor. 14: 7, 8.

Verse 8. The official persons to use the trumpets were the priests. Otherwise, if just any person had right to blow them they might be carelessly used at different times and the congregation be thrown into confusion.

Verse 9. The significant word in this passage is "oppresseth." It shows that the war they were going to make was one of defense. And indeed that is the only motive for war that God ever endorsed. The general wars of the Israelites in taking the land of Canaan were wars of defense. That land had already been given to the seed of Abraham, and these heathen nations then occupying it were intruders. So that it was necessary for the rightful owners thereof to fight for their defense and that they could take possession of what was already their own.

Verse 10. Times of war were not the only occasions for using these trumpets. The males were all required to appear at the tabernacle at stated seasons. All the rest of the congregation should join in rejoicing for the goodness of God, and at hearing these trumpets sounding with the proper code, they would be thus reminded.

Verse 11. The subject of this verse is "removal from Sinai." A very significant occasion. It has been less than a month since the tabernacle was covered with the cloud, at which time their official life as a systematic nation began. Now their first order to move is given. It is made known by the removal of the cloud as shown in preceding chapter.

Verses 12, 13. Now the children of Israel start on their famous wandering through the wilderness, to be strewn with so many and varied experiences. The first stop as shown in this paragraph is called Paran. This is the same location as Kadesh-barnea which was the place they reached on the border of the land of promise. (13: 3; 32: 8.) What places they may have halted in the meantime are not mentioned here. It is asserted that they here took their journeys by the commandment of the Lord. Further, that this commandment of the Lord was by the hand of Moses.

Verses 14-16. This order of march was according to the arrangement set forth in chapter 2: 3-7.

Verse 17. By consulting chapter 3: 25 the reader will see that the Gershonites were to have the handling of the tabernacle, assisted by Merari. (Verse 36). So the activities here described are according to the law.

Verses 18-20. Chapter 2: 10 shows this camp also to be following the schedule set by the original directions. All things in proper order.

Verse 21. Of course there should be the proper place to set the articles of the tabernacle service. Hence, it was in order for the ones bearing the institution to precede the ones carrying these articles. As soon as the ones in charge of the tabernacle had been indicated to stop, by the resting of the cloud, they would set up the tabernacle. Then the Kohathites bearing the holy articles would come up and place them in the proper order as directed by the original commandment.

Verses 22-24. See chapter 2:18-24 for the original description of this action.

Verses 25-28. The original outline of this paragraph is in chapter 2: 25-31.

The word "rereward" means "rear guard" and applied to this camp because it came last in the order of march.

Verse 29. One form of the name for Moses' father-in-law was Raguel. His son was Hobab, and in gratitude for the services of his father, also in view of the family relation between them, Moses invites him to share their prospective advantages.

Verses 30-32. Hobab declined at first to accept the invitation of Moses. Then he was entreated to accompany them as a guide in the wilderness. No statement is here made as to whether he changed his mind. The language in Judg. 1: 16 and 4: 11 indicates that he did. The family relations are mentioned as being with the Israelites and they would hardly be expected to journey with the congregation had Hobab persisted in his determination to return to his own people.

Verses 33, 34. *Mount of the Lord.* By reference to Ex. 3: 1 it will be seen that Horeb is meant by this term. The ark was the most important article of the tabernacle system. It contained the tables of the covenant, also a pot of the manna. It was fitting that it should be in the lead when the congregation was on the move. This will be the case when they cross the Jordan. (Josh. 3: 3). In addition to the lead provided for them by the ark, the cloud hovered over them to indicate God's presence.

Verses 35, 36. This is the form of benediction Moses pronounced at the movements of the congregation when being lead by the ark. *Return.* This does not mean that the Lord had left them. The beginning two letters do not signify anything special. The remark means that as the Lord had been with them all the while they were encamped before, and then in the march, now also let his presence be assured as they encamped.

NUMBERS 11

Verse 1. This is another one of the murmurings already referred to, which will form one of the links in the chain announced to be outlined at Ch. 21: 5. The punishment was not total, but sufficient to indicate the mind of the Lord.

Verse 2. The people had previously learned of the authority of Moses as their mediator and hence they now cry to him. Since he was the recognized intercessor between God and his people he is granted his plea here. The fire was quenched.

Verse 3. Proper nouns usually had special meaning in Biblical times. The word "Taberah" is defined in the lexicon as "burning." It was therefore applied to the place at hand because the Lord used the instrument of fire to punish the complainers.

Verses 4, 5. Another of the murmurings and one of the outstanding ones. The subject of their complaint this time was that of food. Often when people become dissatisfied with their present condition they can look with much favor on conditions which they even loathed before. Here their memory goes back to the knicknacks of the land of their bondage. Sometimes today when Christians become weary with the obligations of their new life they begin to think with longing of the "happy" times they had while in the world. They even may forsake the church and go back into the world. The children of Israel would have done the like had they been able. Not being situated so they could, they did so in their desires, figuratively. (Acts 7: 39). It is significant in this passage that the trouble was caused by the influence of the "mixed multitude." This term is defined by Strong "a promiscuous assemblage." The same people are defined by him at Ex. 12: 38, as "mongrel race." It frequently happens today taht people get into the membership of the church who are not really converted in heart. Then when some occasion of trial presents itself this group will start trouble. Which gives us a strong motive for carefully watching the conduct of all professors of religion.

Verse 6. Before the manna was given they acted as if their main need was bread. That if they only had that article of food they would be satisfied. Now that nothing in that line is needed they see a deficiency in it. All of which proves that when men clamor for a thing that is not really indispensable they are apt to tire of it soon and want something else.

Verse 7. Description of the manna as to its taste and outward appearance is here given. In Ex. 16: 31 we are told it tasted as honey. The coriander seed was a seasoning, and the bdellium pertained to the color. It was either a pearl or gum of the color of amber.

Verse 8. This manna was of such firm texture that it could be handled in about the same manner as one would handle wheat. This would account for the fact that it could be upon the ground and be gathered up and stored as it was. In this verse the taste, as of fresh oil, is added to other descriptions of it. Olive oil was the only kind of oil they had in those days. It is probable that after grinding it there would be the added taste as result of its being bruised in grinding, thereby exuding this taste, as of oil.

Verse 9. There is no special significance in the mention of dew in connection with the manna except to identify the time of the night when the manna fell. Also it may be observed that, since the dew fell at the same time as the manna, and the manna was there after the dew left, it shows that it was of a firmer texture than actual bread would be, or else the moisture would have affected it.

Verse 10. This verse harks back to the complaint mentioned a few verses earlier in the chapter and commented upon, especially verses 4, 5.

Verses 11-15. Once more our explanation of the passage before us lies in the fact that Moses was the mediator between God and the people. As such he was a type of the great Mediator for the Christian Dispensation. Because of this he was permitted to express himself at times in a manner that might have been condemned, if only his personal interests were considered. Jesus made pitiful pleas to his Father also, regarding the bitterness of his lot. (Luke 22: 42, 43. Matt. 27: 46.) But in both cases the unpleasantness of the situation did not cause any rebellion against God.

Verse 16. The elders here were not officials but were so called in view of their age and experience. And even they were to have officers over them. These were to be rather as go-betweens to relay the instructions of Moses to the elders.

Verse 17. These men were to work under Moses much the same as the apostles were to work under Christ.

Verse 18. This command meant for them to prepare themselves to receive the blessing of God about to be brought to them. And they are reminded of their recent murmuring against the Lord.

Verses 19, 20. In years gone by there was a practice in certain states to offer a reward of many hundreds of dollars for any person who could eat a whole quail each day for a month and retain it in the body, until digested. No one ever won the reward. Instead, those attempting it had the very experience described in this chapter, also described in this passage. It appears that man is so dull of learning his lessons that he must be made to have some physical punishment to get him to learn.

Verses 21, 22. It is difficult to understand this statement of Moses. After having seen all the wonders the Lord did in Egypt and the Sea, he now asks how the feat of feeding this people can be done. The most plausible explanation is in the fact that Moses was a natural man and subject to slips of the memory.

Verse 23. The question the Lord asked of Moses is significant. The Bible in some places shows us that there are some things God cannot do. In no case is it because the thing considered is too hard. It is because it is not right. So, were it wrong to feed these thousands of people by miracle then God could not have done it. It was not wrong. Since the Lord's hand was not short, not weak, there was no reason to doubt the fulfillment of the promise to the congregation.

Verses 24, 25. No doubt this group of seventy elders was practically the ones we read about in Ex. 18. The difference between the conditions of the two instances is that in the latter the Lord took direct part in the arrangement and inspired these men to act. In the former there is nothing said about that. The only fact indicated then was that God endorsed the arrangement and blessed it in that way.

Verses 26, 27. The word "prophesied" is from NABA and defined "to prophesy, i.e. speak (or sing) by inspiration (in prediction or simple discourse):"—Strong. These men were to help in the teaching of the people about their daily conduct and thus in the spirit they could do so. That caused them to become distinct from the other men, and was the occasion of the demonstration of surprise manifested by these around them. And it caused one man to run to Moses with the report.

Verse 28. There was nothing wrong with the motive prompting Joshua to make this suggestion. He was the servant of Moses and was concerned for the authority of his master. He was not speaking on his own behalf but was not approving of any rival against the man whom he regarded as the sole human authority.

Verses 29, 30. The unselfishness of Moses is exhibited here and verifies the statement in verse 3 of next chapter. This is one of the finest characteristics a man can have and in this case, especially, it is appreciated since Moses is a type of Christ.

Verse 31. God's power to accomplish any result he wishes and by no visible means will not be questioned. Yet he often used such means in connection with his works. They usually were the kind that would furnish no logical explanation of the result obtained. That would have tendency to strengthen the faith of the observer in the power of the Lord. The nature of the sea was not that of great swarms of quail as most of them knew. Yet here came those great numbers at the instigation of God. The conclusion then would be plain that the divine power was the explanation. The convenience of securing the birds is seen in that they were brought right down to the camp, and the plentifulness of them, is indicated in the fact that they reached in each direction from the camp as far as a day's journey. Also by the further fact that they came down to within two cubits (three feet) of the ground.

Verse 32. The convenience of the situation is further indicated by the fact that all the people had to do to obtain the quail was to stand up and pick them right out of the air and then spread them on the ground round the camp.

Verses 33-35. God sometimes suffers the people to have their wishes granted, but under protest. This he did later when they clamored for a king. God directed that a king should be granted them but under protest. (1 Sam. 8: 8, 9). And so in the present instance God is wroth at the complaining mood of the people. The desire for flesh would not be in itself a wrong. But under the present circumstances, with all the items of plenty that had been showered on the people, their clamor for the food was prompted by a spirit of unrest and lack of appreciation for the Lord's goodness.

NUMBERS 12

Verse 1. There is nothing more said about this circumstance in the scripture, but it is reported in secular history. While he was under the Egyptian connection and thus before he had fled Egyptian threat from Pharaoh, the country got into a war with the Ethiopians nearby. Moses was given an important military commission and made the attack. A certain city was an objective. In the meantime the daughter of the king fell so deeply in love with Moses that she made the offer of marriage. He agreed to it, on condition that she obtain the surrender of the mentoned city, which she did. The marriage was then carried out. As to what became of the relationship I do not have information. But the fact must have been well-known and authenticated since Miriam and Aaron accused him of it, and it is not denied. In fact, the statement is here made in the divine narrative that he had married an Ethiopian woman. The reader is given some citations which he may read and then form his own conclusions as to how much of the details to accept. Josephus, Antipuities 2-10-1. Moses, His Life and Times by George Rawlinson, pages 48, 49. This complaint was not the real motive for their opposition to Moses as will be seen in next verse.

Verse 2. Had Moses been guilty of usurping authority as they charged, it would have been just as wrong, regardless of his marriage entanglements. If they knew about the circumstances now, they knew them before. Yet there is no account of their accusation against him before. That shows that their real motive was jealousy of Moses and they were using the marriage subject as a pretext.

Verse 3. Moses, as the inspired writer of this history, is saying that Moses as the leader and law giver of the people was a very meek man. This idea must be kept in mind in order not to think of him as being guilty of self-praise. As we read that Moses the mediator of the Old Testament religion was meek, we think of the one who is mediator of the New as being also meek. (Matt. 11: 29.)

Verses 4, 5. The tabernacle was the place for the official transactions pertaining to the congregation. So now these three persons are summoned to meet at that place. When they did so, the Lord came down at the place in the form of a cloud. After that was done the Lord called out of the cloud for Aaron and Miriam to come apart and near the cloud, where God was represented.

Verse 6. The ordinary prophets among them would always have evidence of their call to authority by having some special vision or dream. Yet these two had to know that no such experience had been given to them.

Verses 7-9. The great difference as to the superiority of Moses was indicated in that God did not leave him to depend on visions and dreams. Instead, the Lord spoke to him directly and in such close range that the similitude of his form could be seen in the personage sent to represent him. This whole situation was well known to the brother and sister and hence their false accusation was malicious. After making this statement to them the Lord departed from the place in anger.

Verse 10. The foregoing verse states that God departed from the place. Of course that would mean also that the cloud would depart. When it was cleared away, the plague imposed as visible protest was that of leprosy. That was a very distressing and humiliating affliction, but not necessarily fatal. Hence it was here used as one form of punishment for those acquiring the wrath of God. We are not told why only Miriam was afflicted, and not Aaron although he was equally guilty. But God evidently had a specific reason which he has not seen fit to reveal to us.

Verses 11, 12. Aaron makes his plea to Moses, on behalf of the sister, not directly to God. In his plea he admits sin and places himself in the guilt. There is no evidence that Miriam made any acknowledgment of sin. It is reasonable to think of this fact as the explanation of the question mentioned in verse ten.

Verse 13. Moses as mediator would properly pray for his sister. The thing that was objectionable in the prayer was the word "now." In his eagerness for the comfort of the afflicted one he becomes impetuous and asks for a favor that would have made confusion concerning the awful character of the disease of leprosy and tended to miniimize the gravity of the plague when the law had already shown it to be a most terrible affliction. (See Lev. 13.) While Moses was a type of Christ as mediator, yet he was a man and was subject to the mistakes of man. Jesus was man also but never submitted to the influences of the flesh. Yet he did imply the possibility of his prayers being at variance with the will of his Father. (Matt. 26: 39.)

Verse 14. To spit in the face would actually be only an affront or violation of courtesy. Its physical effect would be nothing. Yet it would have been considered of such importance under the strict formalities of that law as to render the victim unclean. So much the more in a case of the loathsome disease of leprosy. Therefore, the command was given that Miriam be quarantined seven days.

Verses 15, 16. Here is a case where the whole congregation was held up in its march to wait on Miriam's recovery. While no direct mention is made of the recovery, yet that is necessary inference since she was allowed to be brought into the camp.

NUMBERS 13

Verses 1, 2. Not all of the facts of transactions are given in each case. In the present one we consult Deut. 1: 21-23, and learn that this movement of spies was suggested by the people. It would not have been put into effect had not the Lord approved of it. Therefore the present passage ignores the request of the people and speaks as if the Lord initiated it. That was fitting since it is really the act of the Lord which required his endorsement.

Verse 3. Paran is another name for Kadesh-barnea. See chapter 32: 8 and 10: 12. This place was at the border line between the land of the wandering and that of Canaan. Before entering upon the conquest of that country it was decided first to send out this reconnaissance group.

Verses 4-16. This paragraph gives the names of the men sent out on this tour of survey, which were the heads of the children of Israel spoken of in previous verse. The two who deserve special mention are Caleb in verse 6, and Oshea in verse 8. Verse 16 says Moses called him Jehoshua which is still another form of Joshua. Each tribe was represented in this commission.

Verses 17, 18. A general order for inspection of the land and country folk is given in this paragraph. More detailed inspection will be indicated in next paragraph

Verses 19, 20. The fortifications of the cities must be noted. "Fat or lean" means whether the land is rich and strong or thin and poor. Also the wood would be a very important asset in a country intended for residence, but which must be possessed from its intruders by war. As concrete evidence of the productiveness of the country they were to bring of the fruit back with them.

Verses 21: 22. This paragraph is a geographical statement of the areas which they examined. It included some of the most noted parts of the country. Special mention might be made of Hebron which was the home of Abraham after his return from Egypt.

Verses 23, 24. We should be careful not to enlarge too much on the size of this bunch of grapes just because two of them carried it. Yet we know it was of great dimensions from the fact that it gave the name of Eschol (meaning cluster) to a valley. This indicates unusual proportions and importance. They brought also some of the figs and pomegranates in obedience to the order to bring of the fruit.

Verse 25. Originally there was no apparent significance in the exact term of their search. But it became afterward a token of a fact that was significant as will be seen in next chapter.

Verse 26. In this verse are mentioned Paran and Kadesh in connection which is further information on the related meanings of the words. Upon the return the spies showed to the people the fruit they had taken from the country.

Verse 27. There is no dissenting voice heard in the report of the twelve men as to the productiveness of the land: That it flowed, abounded, with milk and honey.

Verses 28, 29. There still is no disagreement expressed as to the facts of the conditions they found. All are agreed that the country had fortified cities, that strong people lived here, people of whom they had heard much. That the people took up the land in general, for some of them dwelled by the sea and others in the mountains. While the outward statement of the facts was not varied, yet the attitude of these men in most cases must have been unfavorable from the statements in next paragraph.

Verses 30, 31. Here is where the difference came in. All agreed that the land was strong. That it had fortified cities. That many heathen peoples occupied the land. Most of them formed a conclusion on the situation that differed from that of Caleb. The former said they would not be able to take the land while the latter said they could. This is the difference that must always be considered when discussing this great crisis in the experiences of the children of Israel.

Verse 32. The words "evil report" are from one word and mean "slander." The word "eateth" is from AKAL and Strong defines it "A primitive root; to eat (literally or figuratively)." We get the thought these spies wished to make the impression that in some way the land they had just visited would devour its weaker inhabitants. It would be evident that no land would literally eat up the people, so the figurative meaning of the word must be the one attributed to it here. Yet that was a slander.

Verse 33. Anak was one of the men of the heathen variety and one of the giants. This word is understood to refer not alone to their stature but also to the coarse nature of their bodies and temperament. (Gen. 6: 4). Their comparison between themselves and the grasshoppers ignored the factor of God in the case. A grasshopper and God would make a majority in real strength, but they overlooked that fact.

NUMBERS 14

Verses 1-4. This passage states another of the murmurings of the people and one which embraced such rash statements that it had far-reaching results. Another thing we should note here is the power of example. The people allowed themselves to be influenced by the conclusions of the unfaithful spies instead of listening only to their report as to the facts and then forming their conclusions from what they had seen already of the power of God. They had seen abundance of proof that God is powerful and able to overcome all opposition. Instead of using their better mind they gave way to unbelief and made two very rash wishes. Those were that they had died in Egypt; and, that they might die in the wilderness. The statement in the end of verse 4 agrees with the one made by Stephen in Acts 7: 39.

Verse 5. This prone attitude of Moses and Aaron was their expression of grief at the rebellion of the people.

Verses 6-8. Joshua is associated with Caleb in the good attitude toward the situation. They will later be seen to be blessed highly of God for their service. They reasoned that if the Lord takes delight in them, he will lead them into the good land in spite of all the apparent obstacles. That statement implies that if they do not find themselves successful in the attempt it will be because God is not delighted in them. This would mean, further, that such lack of delight would be on account of their misconduct. In the very start of the whole project of the children of Israel, the promises of God had been on condition that they be obedient to the Lord's voice.

Verse 9. The language here implies that their rebellion against the Lord was prompted by their fear of the nations of the land. Today, it often occurs that professed Christians shun to acknowledge their relation to God because of the people of the world. They are ashamed to own their Lord. Joshua advises the nation that the people of the land will be bread for them. That is, their property and accumulations will be taken by them and thereby furnish them with sustenance. One cause of this change was that they had become panic stricken themselves and not able for defense.

Verse 10. The trait of persecutors in all ages has been to use violence against teachers whose teaching is opposed to the evil doing of those to whom they speak. The foolish notion appears to be that by destroying the teaching they can also destroy the truth of their teaching. In this case it is thus. The people had made up their minds that they did not want to go against the heathen in the land of promise and now they are angered at the voice of the commander who would encourage them in the work.

Verses 11, 12. We should never forget that God is one of justice and vengeance as well as one of love and mercy. When sin rears its head, the justice of God is called forth and threatens the severe treatment for the sinner. So it is here. On the basis of merit this nation ought to be desroyed and the new start made for a nation. Now such action is suggested by the Lord. The reader will not forget that Moses is the mediator of the Old Testament and as such is a type of Christ. By making the speech here set down it opens the way for the performance of his duty and privilege as the one to plead in behalf of the people.

Verses 13-19. The general title of this passage which I have grouped into one paragraph is, "Intercession of Moses on behalf of the children of Israel." It should be understood that an intercession logically requires argument, and no argument is of any account that does not cite facts. Hence Moses reminds the Lord of the Egyptians from whom the nation had been released by the mighty hand of God not very long ago. They will have something to glory about if, at last, the plan of God fails. They will naturally be prompt to tell other nations of the circumstances and all will rejoice together. They will account for the tragedy by saying the Lord had started something he was not able to finish. That would lead to the further conclusion that the God of the Israelites was not superior to any of the other gods of the age. As contradiction to such conclusion Moses pleads that the power of God be here made manifest. He also reminds God that he had declared himself to be a God of longsuffering and mercy. Not that he would clear or justify the guilty who would not reform. Nay, he would punish such very severely as would be right. On the other hand, he would forgive when the guilty one repented. Thus the mediator here, although acknowledging the iniquity of the people, begs the Lord to pardon the people. A truly effective speech and one that is proper in a person placed between two other parties as intercessor.

Verse 20. What a gracious, direct, significant reply! The Lord grants the plea of Moses and the wonderful basis is given, "according to thy word." That means that pardon will be granted, but not on the basis of the personal worth of the ones for whom the pardon was asked. It is on the strength of the plea of the mediator. So it is now. God has promised to forgive "for Christ's sake." Now, as then, the office of mediator will avail nothing to those who ignore the wishes and demands of the mediator.

Verse 21. The dignity of the Lord must be maintained. So while he will pardon his children when proper appeal is made, yet he will demonstrate his power in some way that will leave his greatness still undiminished before the world.

Verses 22, 23. The people as a whole will receive the benefit of the intercession of Moses. But the particular men who have caused the present condition of rebellion must pay the penalty for their great sin. They must be removed from the scene of action before the entrance into the promised land. And in doing so they will be receiving what they rashly asked for in their rebellion.

Verse 24. God makes an exception to the threat of general destruction of the men who had brought on the uprising. He excepts Caleb (and later Joshua) because he had "followed me fully." This is a very significant expression. Many people will follow the Lord in part but only those who follow him fully may have the divine reward.

Verse 25. The children of Israel are still in the region of Kadesh-barnea, the place from which the twelve spies had been sent. They will not be permitted to pass on into the promised land because of the great sin here. They will not be allowed even to go in that direction. Instead they are directed to go into the wilderness by way of the Red Sea. The reader might be confused here. The Red Sea is always thought of as being restricted to the immediate locality of the famous crossing after leaving Egypt. A look at the map of the country will show that the body of the Red Sea is actually far south of the territory of the movements of these people. That body of water divides into two arms, one going northeast and the other northwest. The last named one is where they crossed miraculously, while the other is the one meant in the present verse. While these two arms have separate names in our modern geographies, the Bible considers the whole water unit as one named Red Sea.

Verses 26-29. God repeats the threat already made. Notice that it is against the men who had been numbered from twenty years and upward. We do not know how many others will have died in the ordinary course of life when they get to the end of the wandering. We do know that many innocent persons now living will also be living and be permitted to enter the land of Canaan.

Verse 30. In this place the Lord names together the two men who are to escape the general overthrow of the men of war. They had wholly followed the Lord.

Verse 31. This is considered in verses 26-29 above.

Verses 32, 33. In order that these guilty men may have their rash wish fulfilled, and yet not all die of direct miracle, they must wander in the wilderness 40 years.

Verse 34. The arbitrary basis is here given on which the length of the wandering is to be determined. They had used forty days for the time of search, now they must wander a year for each day. Of course we should remember the forty years will include the two years they have already been out of Egypt. *Breach of Promise.* We do not like to think of God as being one who will break a promise. In the first place, we should not forget that all of the promises of God are on condition of obedience; and when the obedience is not present, then the promise is lawfully left omitted. In the present instance the word "promise" is not in the original. The whole term is from a word that means "alienation." The thought is that by seeing all these men of war being left strewn along the way of the wilderness, they will have a demonstration of the alienation that comes between God and man when disobedience occurs.

Verse 35. Explained at verses 32, 33 above.

Verses 36, 37. The group of men from twenty years and upward fell to complaining at the slander of the ten spies. They are the ones who must wander in the wilderness until they die. The ten spies who caused this uprising will not get to pass out in that way. Instead, they were punished at once by some plague before the Lord.

Verses 38, 39. The word "mourned" here is not the same as the murmuring noted in other places. It has the ordinary meaning; that they bewailed and lamented the death of these ten spies when Moses told them about the tragedy.

Verse 40. They see the mistake they had made in doubting their success under the hand of God against the heathen. Now they think they can undo their mistake by making the attack. It is too late.

Verses 41, 42. Moses told them not to go now because God will not be with them. To make an attempt that the Lord does not wish to be made, would be just as fruitless as they had claimed it was going to be, when God really wished them to go. They are warned that it will result in a fall before their enemies.

Verse 43. The significant accounting for their failure is on the fact that, as they had turned away from the Lord, he will turn away from them.

Verses 44, 45. *Presumed.* This is from APHAL and defined by Strong "to swell; figuratively, be elated." How foolish to be so self-important now. They did not feel big enough to go against their enemies while God was with them. Now when he has cast them off they feel big enough to do what they are told not to do and what they are told they cannot do. It is often so today. God has given us a perfect plan of salvation. Men sometimes say that the plan of God will not work. That it will not succeed in saving the world. Therefore they presume to be able to form institutions and plans of their own which they arrogantly claim will do the work more successfully than will the divine plan. All such will fail just as did the attempts fail here.

NUMBERS 15

Verses 1, 2. God never lets the people lose sight of the promise to bring them into the land which is to be their permanent national home. The significant idea is often expressed that the land has already been given to them and it will be left to them to take possession of it by doing their part of the occupation.

Verses 3-12. This paragraph repeats the same instructions that had been written in the law as to offerings. See the first five chapters of Leviticus for detailed description of this service. The same will be repeated frequently because it is the common tendency with man to forget.

Verse 13. The privileges and provisions of the law were for those who belonged to the country possessed by the nation. They would not have any special significance to any others as long as they did not compose a part of the nation.

Verses 14-16. The word "stranger" means one from the outside. If such should come into the country and wish to sojourn there, he must do as the people of the land. The difficulty that might occur to the mind of the reader is that such provision seems to justify sinners in participating in the activities of the Lord's people. It must be borne in mind that the system given through Moses was a combination of civil and religious government. As a civil government it was the privilege and duty of all who dwelled in the land to be subject to its laws. The same is true in our day. If a person from another country comes among us, we require him to comply with the same law that citizens obey. Since that system combined both religion and civil government in one system, it made it unavoidable that aliens would participate in both, if at all.

Verses 17-21. The principal thought in this passage is the same as previously noted, that the "first" of anything is to be the Lord's. The priority of God in all the relations of activity must never be overlooked. Such is proper from many considerations. God is, and was, and always will be. He had no beginning, was thus in existence before all other beings and things. All things that exist are the result of the mighty hand of the self-existing One and therefore he has right to the first.

Verses 22, 23. The reader is again asked to note the authority of Moses as set forth here. The Lord commanded the activities referred to but he gave this command by the hand of Moses. Again we see the arrogance of those who depreciate the authority of the law-giver of that Dispensation.

Verse 24. The mistakes that were made through ignorance were not imputed against the actor until knowledge of it came to the front. God is so particular that the nation as a whole be kept clear, that if knowledge comes to the leaders of the nation that some individual in it has done wrong, then the congregational treasury must be drawn on for a sacrifice in atonement. The word "manner" means the ordinance about the particular sacrifice. That ordinance will be found in some one or more of the chapters in beginning of the book of Leviticus which has been frequently referred to.

Verses 25, 26. The thought here in addition to the ones already stated above is that the procedure of the sacrifices is under the jurisdiction of the priest. He was the authorized official to have such charge.

Verses 27-29. *Shall have one law.* That is, the law as to atoning for the sin of ignorance is the same whether in the case of a stranger or one born in the country.

Verse 30. Likewise, one and the same fate is to come to the stranger as to the one born in the country, when the sin is one of presumption. This means a sin committed in defiance of law, and with the attitude of doing a thing regardless of law. In that case the same law also applies to both the stranger and the one born in the land. He is to be cut off. See Lev. 20: 3 for explanation of such punishment.

Verse 31. The word "despised" means to hold in contempt. In some ways this attitude is more objectionable than one in which the law is admitted to be dignified. To disregard the law of God with the spirit of belittling it is very grievous in the sight of God and the offender is worthy of death.

Verses 32-34. The fourth commandment (Ex. 20: 8-11) plainly forbade any manual labor on the sabbath day. The act of gathering sticks is certainly a manual act. Now, notwithstanding the positive commandment the man had violated, yet they did not know what should be done with the man. If the decalogue, written on the tables of stone was intended to contain the complete law of God, why was it they did not know what to do with this man? The answer is clear. There is no complete law where no penalty is given. So that proves that the writing on the tables did not constitute the whole law of God. Neither was it claimed to be. Therefore, we again have evidence of the arrogance of the sabbatarians who reject the law of God as written by the hand of Moses, but pretend to accept the law of God as written by his own fingers on the tables of stone. So this man was put in ward or temporary imprisonment to await the order from the Lord.

Verses 35, 36. God gave his penal decree in the case. He made it known through the same Moses who had done the writing in the book of the law. The penalty for violating the commandment which God had written on the stones was made known through the man who had written the laws that were in the book of the law. The guilty man was stoned.

Verses 37-41. If a certain arrangement is brought about in connection with prescribed significance, then the very appearance of that arrangement should serve to call to mind that thing signified. Even more so, if there is no logical connection between the thing observed and the idea to be commemorated. These fringes or tassels were on the edge of the garments. As additional ornamentations there was a twining or woven piece of the blue material, put on top of the row of tassels. These articles by themselves had no literary significance. The embellishment was commanded at the same time that importance of the law was emphasized in their hearing. Sometimes a person will exhibit some peculiar article which does not show any meaning to the observer. The owner will then state that he obtained the article at a time of great interest and that the very sight of it reminds him of the circumstance. Thus it is in this case. When the children of Israel would see these ornamental attachments to their clothing they would recall that they were instituted at the time that God warned them of disregarding his divine laws. Later, in the time of the New Testament, the Pharisees had been making a literal application of these things and were putting material strips of a surface admitting being written upon. Jesus taught that when it was done in that way, it should be considered as mere profession.

NUMBERS 16

Verse 1. This verse is to identify the tribes from which the men came who were chiefly concerned in this famous rebellion against the government of God. The word "men" is not in the original. The word "took" is there. Of course since it is a transitive verb it requires that they took something. The context which is in the next verse shows that the children of Israel were what they took. So that the wording as we have it in the A.V. is correct. The fact of conspiracy is what made their sin the more grievous.

Verse 2. The men with whom the conspiracy was formed are here mentioned as being chief ones. They were princes or men of some prominence in the congregation. Often it occurs that when men are given a little latitude of importance they want more and will even trample upon established law in their quest for more recognition.

Verse 3. It is the age-old situation. Men in private position will envy those in public and official position and accuse them of usurpation. The claim was made here that the people of the congregation were holy as well as these rulers. Even if all of their claim were true, that would not be a logical basis for their complaint. It was never assumed that Moses and Aaron were chosen as the leaders of the congregation only on the ground of their holiness. It is always necessary for the order and unity of any great system that some authority must be vested in a definite place. So it was in the system of the Lord at that time. It was not a presumption of these men that they are in charge of the work. They had not taken this upon themselves on their own choice. (Heb. 3: 5; 5: 4.)

Verse 4. This attack upon Moses was humiliating to him and caused him to fall prone as he did at Kadesh-barnea. (Chapter 14: 5.)

Verse 5. This Moses who was said to be the meekest man on the earth is still seen to be such. Notwithstanding the wickedness of these rebels he is willing to submit the controversy to a test. Referring to chapter 26:9, 10 we will learn that the "company" mentioned here comprise the three men named in verse one and also the two hundred and fifty princes. Moses makes the challenge for this whole group to be put to the test as to whom he has chosen to be near him in the position of authority.

Verses 6, 7. Since Korah and his company are Levites it would be fitting in the test for them to provide themselves with the censers since the use of incense was that which especially belonged to the religious department of the service. In connection with the challenge to the test Moses returns the accusation they made by saying they had taken too much for granted as to their authority.

Verses 8, 9. All priests were Levites, but not all Levites were priests. Only the particular ones descending through Aaron had the right to the priesthood. While only such could be priests, yet the entire tribe of Levi had been sanctified to be near the Lord in the system and had special dignity over the other tribes. Moses here asks them if they are not satisfied with the honor already put upon them. He implies that they are not, but are now wanting still further honor by having the priesthood.

Verses 10, 11. They are told that the Lord had brought them near him as it is, and yet, now they want to usurp the special work that belongs properly to the sons of Aaron. He further accuses them of being against the Lord in that they are opposing Aaron who was chosen of the Lord for the special work.

Verse 12. These men were from a different tribe and did not have any separate place at all as the Levites had. Yet they were in the conspiracy and thus Moses invites them to be present to witness the test. They refuse to come up to it.

Verses 13, 14. Here they tauntingly describe their former land of residence as one that flowed with milk and honey. Just their way of saying it would have been better to have remained in Egypt instead of being brought out into the wilderness to famish and die. They further accuse Moses of having done so in order to get the advantage over them, to rule over them. Moreover, they complain that the promise made to them of being given a land that also abounded in milk and honey had not been carried out. That the scheme was one for the purpose of demoting these men opposing Aaron.

Verse 15. Moses was mediator. The office of such was for the purpose of pleading on behalf of the people to secure the favor of God. Also, we see here that the same office might intercede to cut off the favor and blessing. When the persons for whom a mediator is to plead favorably, make themselves unworthy then that same mediator will be their judge and ask for their rejection. This will be the case with Christ in the cases where his professed servants are unfaithful. (Mark 8: 38.)

Verse 16. The company of Korah here refers to the 250 princes who were to take the censers for the test. They were to be "before the Lord" which means they were to come near the tabernacle since that was the place where the Lord acknowledged his presence.

Verses 17, 18. Korah did as he was commanded and they all came to the door of the tabernacle, the proper place for them to be for the present purpose.

Verse 19. The spirit of rebellion persists in Korah and he incites the whole congregation to an action that is unfavorable by assembling here also.

Verses 20, 21. God then directs Moses and Aaron to separate themselves from the multitude that now is in a state of mob protest and let them be destroyed.

Verse 22. Here again is the work of a mediator. Since Aaron is the lawful High Priest for the congregation, he is joined with Moses in this instance also as mediator and pleads for the life of the men of the congregation.

Verses 23, 24. This command had the general meaning that they were to disassemble themselves from these conspirators and thus not be classed with them in their rebellion.

Verses 25, 26. This passage more definitely carries the idea mentioned in the preceding one. The residences of these wicked men were to be considered as improper places for righteous persons to be gathering so they are commanded to depart. If they remain they will be classed with them and will partake of their destruction also.

Verse 27. The multitude obeyed the command to depart. When they did so, it attracted the attention of the leaders in the rebellion who then came out and stood at the door of their tents together with the immediate members of their families.

Verse 28. The fundamental difference between official action and mere personal one is here made. Moses expresses it in the words "not done them of mine own mind."

Verses 29, 30. An impostor might offer to be put to some indefinite test. He might mention some general thing that could be construed in various ways because of having no certain meaning. Moses shows his sincerity, also his confidence in the righteousness of his position, by naming some definite demonstration. Not only so, but one that would be so unusual and seemingly impossible, that only the Lord could cause it to happen. If he did cause it to happen it could be construed only as a divine demonstration in favor of the one calling for the test.

Verses 31-33. At the conclusion of the speech of Moses the demonstration came. The earth opened up and swallowed the company. It must be understood that it was the men directly in the conspiracy who were destroyed, for they were guilty. Reference to chapter 26: 11 shows that the children of Korah were not included in this destruction.

Verse 34. The sight must have been terrible, also the cries of the people were piercing, for the children of Israel, although they had removed some distance from the tents of the families, (verse 27), were so impressed that they fled in alarm.

Verse 35. The foregoing tragedy slew the group immediately connected with the families of the conspirators. It remained then for the special group of princes with the censers to be removed. This was done by a fire from the Lord. The possession of the censers did not protect them since they had been given to have them here as a test.

Verses 36-38. While the men are slain, yet the censers are still intact in the midst of the fire. Eleazar is then commanded to gather them from the fire for they are "hallowed." The instruments had been in the hands of wicked men as a test against them. Therefore, they would be considered as a matter of demonstration of God's holiness. As such they must be preserved; and thus they will be a sign for the future generations of the children of Israel.

Verses 39, 40. These censers were formed into plates and fastened to the altar where they could be seen. That would be a visible and constant warning to others not to usurp the place of God's chosen servants.

Verse 41. One of the commonest things is for righteous men to be charged with the supposed evil effects of their righteous deeds. The people who had professed themselves to be of the Lord had just been killed. And the killing was done through the offices of Moses and Aaron. Yet the whole procedure was so miraculous that common honesty should have told them that no mere human power could have brought about such effect. They were so blinded with prejudice for the conspirators that they gave way to another of their wonted murmurings.

Verses 42, 43. God is always ready to vindicate his righteous servants, in his own way, of course. So while the people were in the act of opposition against Moses and Aaron the Lord is preparing a demonstration. Their attention is directed to the tabernacle and behold, the cloud showing the divine glory and favor is seen. At this, Moses and Aaron came before the tabernacle.

Verses 44, 45. This is another threat of the Lord, springing out of his attribute of justice, to destroy the people. This caused the lawful officers to fall prostrate.

Verse 46. The threat of the Lord made another occasion for the mediator to act and the man who is High Priest is directed to make atonement against the plague which has already started.

Verse 47. In this verse is another instance of the authority of Moses. He was even superior to Aaron who was High Priest. It is certainly arrogance to belittle Moses as being of so little authority that his law is to be ignored while at the same time professing to keep the law of the Old Testament.

Verse 48. This is the origin of the expression "between the living and the dead," that has been a poetical one with public speakers for generations. In this case it meant the ones actually dead, and those not yet affected by the plague. Right while the plague was having its devastating effect on the complainers, the priest was offering his services to counteract its further progress. Likewise, Jesus the High Priest of the Christian profession came into the world of sin and offered his services to counteract the deadly effects of sin.

Verses 49, 50. The number slain by the plague must not be confused with the ones who died at the opening of the earth and the fire from the Lord. These last died of the plague that was brought as a punishment for their murmuring and their slanderous accusations against Moses and Aaron. It was one of the circumstances Paul warns about in 1 Cor. 10: 10. When people are discontented with their lot they sometimes allow themselves to give way to extravagant speech and say things they would recall afterward if they could. It is always dangerous to object to the arrangement of God for the performance of his systems among men.

NUMBERS 17

Verses 1-3. The demonstrations recorded in the preceding chapter were a negative proof of the righteous work of Aaron. Now a further and positive proof is to be effected. In ancient times a rod, taken from a tree or other natural growth, was used for many purposes. One of them was as a token of power and authority; such as a scepter in the hands of a king, or a gavel in the hands of a judge. Thus in the present test the men to represent the nation were to provide themselves each with a rod. There were twelve tribes in the general assembly and then an extra tribe, Levi, for the special office of the service. There was to be a man chosen from among the princes of the twelve tribes, and the thirteenth rod was to have the name of Aaron written on it, to represent the tribe of Levi.

Verse 4. These rods were to be laid up in the Most Holy place, the place where the ark was kept and where God met with the High Priest.

Verse 5. Here again is a specific test proposed. A rod cut from a bush or tree would not have any power to grow over night, especially while detached from all other objects. So the Lord proposed this test.

Verses 6, 7. The test was agreed to. Each of the princes came with a rod and gave it to Moses, who placed them in the position directed by the Lord.

Verse 8. A slight swelling of a bud that might have been the starting for a limb or twig could have been taken as a natural thing, even though the rod was cut off. The demonstration did not stop there. The rod for Aaron produced buds, bloom and fruit. This was accomplished over night.

Verse 9. The test is to be shown to be fair. Bringing out just the rod of Aaron could still leave the question whether all of the rods had the same condition. Thus Moses brought out all of the rods, which they saw and took to themselves again. No chance to claim anything for their own rods. It had turned out just as Moses had proposed before the test was made. The decision is now complete and final.

Verses 10, 11. The Lord told Moses to replace the rod of Aaron in the Most Holy place to be kept as a testimony against the rebellious ones. There are now in the ark the three articles mentioned by Paul in Heb. 9: 4.

Verses 12, 13. This language should be considered more as a bewailing than as one of murmuring. The people are so overawed by the events just closing that they give out such expressions of despair. The question of authority is completely settled.

NUMBERS 18

Verse 1. *Bear the iniquity.* This means they shall be held responsible for what is done about the sanctuary. Not that the people would be exempt from all personal guilt but that these persons, being in authority, would be held first.

Verse 2. Here is another instance of noting the distinction between the tribe of Levi as a whole, and the ones pertaining to Aaron and his sons in particular. All were to work together in the ministry but the priests were to do that which was directly connected with the tabernacle exercises.

Verse 3. The service of the tribe as a whole was referred to as the service of the tabernacle. The actual distinction was indicated by mentioning the vessels. So strict was the Lord on that subject that death would be the penalty for offense.

Verse 4. When the congregation was to march, the Levites were to take down the tabernacle. When the march was ended at any certain place then they were to set it up. Thus the tribe furnished the labor necessary to care for the building. A stranger meant one outside of this tribe.

Verse 5. The charge of the sanctuary always meant the service of the holy rooms of the tabernacle including the offering of sacrifices, burning of incense, lighting the lamps, application of the blood of the sacrifices, etc.

Verses 6, 7. We should not be impatient at the frequent repetition of these various instructions. The importanance of them cannot be overestimated. It is interesting to note the basis on which the exhortation is made here to the family of Aaron. The relation of the tribe to them in the general service of the Lord is represented as a gift. It is the same with the work of God today. While we know we are commanded to serve the Lord, yet we should consider it a great privilege or favor to serve him.

Verses 8, 9. The tribe of Levi as a whole was supported out of the tithes of the other twelve tribes. This included all their increase whether of the land or the beasts. The family of

Aaron was engaged exclusively about the service of the vessels of the place. Their part of the several sacrifices was determined not on a per cent, but on a specification of certain parts. For instance, when a beast was to be burned on the altar, the breast and shoulder were taken away first to be food for the priests. And this ordinance was to hold good "for ever" which means to the end of that age.

Verse 10. The "most holy" place here must not be construed to mean the second room of the tabernacle. It is used only as an adjective and pertains to the character of the parts of the tabernacle as distingushed from other buildings.

Verses 11-13. This is a summing up of the statements preceding. The outstanding idea is that the family of Aaron was to have the first and best of all products.

Verse 14. *Devoted.* This is from CHEREM and defined: "physically (as shutting in) a net (either literally or figuratively); usually a doomed object; abstractly, extermination." — Strong. In the A.V. the word has been rendered accursed, accursed thing, curse, dedicated thing, devoted, devoted thing, things which should have been utterly destroyed, etc. Thus the particular application of the definition in any given place must be determined by the connection. If it is used with reference to the favorable relation to God the word would have the idea of being devoted to him. If with reference to some object or person not in favor with God, then the word would mean destruction. In the verse of this paragraph, therefore, the word means the things intended by the Lord to be consumed in the services of the tabernacle and its related items.

Verse 15. *Openeth the matrix.* This refers to the first born, the one that first opened the womb of either man or beast. God claimed all such. Since it was not permitted for the first born of man to be either slain or kept apart from the rest of their families, they must be compensated for with some money. Likewise, the unclean beasts would produce their young. They were also the Lord's as to ownership. Since there was no use for them in the divine service, the owner was to redeem or "pay" for them and then they could be used in his secular occupation.

Verse 16. The "shekel of the sanctuary" means the standard of amount, and quality of money, accepted as legal tender in the service of the sanctuary.

Verse 17. The beasts named here were all clean and the kind accepted at the altar. If they produced their young the owner could not redeem them with money. Instead, they must be given to the service of the sacrifices. That is, the first born of such.

Verse 18. Certain parts of these clean animals were to be the personal food for the priests, such as the breast and shoulder.

Verse 19. *Covenant of salt.* Salt has the quality of preserving things. When used figuratively as it is here, it means that the covenant was to be perpetual. It has the same idea as the words "for ever" in that the thing spoken of was to be perpetuated throughout that age or Dispensation.

Verse 20. Since Aaron and family were to be constantly occupied with the service at the tabernacle and the vessels thereof, they would have no business with general land possessions as an estate. Their business would be to care for the Lord's part.

Verse 21. The oft mentioned "tithes" must not be confused with the particular parts of the altar services, such as the breast and shoulder, or the bulk of the grain of the meat (meal) offerings. The latter was a special provision for the priests and to be used by them as food for the body. The tribe of Levi as a whole was to get support from the congregation by receiving a tenth of everything produced by all the other twelve tribes. This gave the one tribe some advantage financially. For if each tribe was to surrender one tenth of all its income that would leave it only nine tenths for its own support. Since twelve tribes contributed this proportion that would make twelve tenths for the benefit of the Levites. However, this advantage might not be as great as at first thought, for the actual number of each tribe would affect it.

Verses 22-24. There is nothing additional in this paragraph. The warning cannot be repeated too often about the tribes "outside" that of Levi venturing near the tabernacle. It would mean severe punishment from the Lord.

Verses 25, 26. The Levites, although engaged constantly and exclusively in the work of the tabernacle, were not exempted from the duty of tithing. Out of the tithe which they received from the other tribes they were to give also a tenth to the Lord. Paul in 1 Cor. 9: 14 says those who preach the Gospel shall live of it and prefaced his statement by reference to the service under the tabernacle system. No one thinks this exempts the preachers from the duty of making contributions to the work of the Lord.

Verse 27. This verse means that when the Levites contributed their tenth to the Lord, it was considered the same as if they had produced the materials from their own property even though it had actually been given to them.

Verse 28. In this verse we see that giving to the Lord was the same as giving to the priest. That was because the priest was engaged exclusively in the service of God.

Verse 29. They must give the "best" of the things. This would include the fat or choicest part of the beasts, whether from the standpoint of its use in sacrifice or as an article of food for the priest.

Verse 30. The thought here is the same as in verse 27 above.

Verse 31. This means that in every place or occasion they had of eating this, it was on the basis of its being their reward for their service of the tabernacle.

Verse 32. Although the priest had the right to this part of the sacrifices as his food, yet he must not use it if in a state of uncleanness. In other words, the particular privilege of partaking of this certain portion of the sacrifices did not excuse him from the obligation of being clean under the requirements of the law.

NUMBERS 19

Verses 1, 2. This chapter gives the formula for the water of purification used under the Mosaic system, and referred to in the other parts of the Bible. The carcass of a red heifer without blemish was to be selected for this ordinance. It must be one that had never been used in physical service.

Verse 3. This animal was turned over to the priest and it was taken out and slain "without the camp." Jesus was slain outside the gate. (Heb. 13: 11).

Verse 4. Some of the blood of this animal was sprinkled "directly before the tabernacle." Jesus offered his blood as a cleanser before God. (Heb. 9: 12).

Verses 5-8. The entire animal was burned together with certain articles such as cedar wood and material of a scarlet color (corresponding with blood) and the entire lot was to be burned into ashes. The person performing this service was placed under strict orders as to his state of cleanliness. That is, he must observe all the rules previously set down in the law pertaining to such formalities.

Verse 9. When the materials above mentioned had been reduced to ashes, a man who was clean was to gather them and put them in a clean place, but on the outside of the camp; to be used in connection with the water of purification. The formula and uses thereof will appear in other verses of this chapter.

Verse 10. To "be unclean" is to be understood as a formality under that system that was made up so much of formalities. The whole restriction was for the purpose of impressing the people with the importance of the ordinance.

Verses 11, 12. Touching a dead body was considered as causing uncleanness. The period of this formal uncleanness was seven days. Such periods would not terminate the seventh day, unless certain ceremonies were observed. Those required that he begin the third day after contamination by using this water of purification. If he does so, then on the seventh day after contact he would be considered clean. If he had not begun his ceremony of cleansing by using the water the third day, he would not be clean on the seventh day. He would have to start all over again.

Verse 13. There is nothing necessarily sinful in touching a dead body. Therefore, if a man does so he may make it right by using the water of purification. Should he neglect to attend to the formality and yet presume to act in the tabernacle service he would be condemned to die.

Verse 14. This plainly indicates that the various regulations under the law as to uncleanness in connection with dead bodies were ceremonial and not actual. We know that merely coming into a tent where a man had died would not defile one. This was a law of education for the world as well as one for the immediate activities of that nation. The human family must learn the lesson of divine authority. When God declares a thing to be such and such, we are to respect it and act accordingly.

Verses 15, 16. This paragraph is only repetition of the various arbitrary formalities under the law, that have already been considered.

Verse 17. This verse completes the formula of the water of purification referred to above and in other places in the scriptures. Running water means "living" water. Not necessarily running as to motion, but water that was clean and fresh, as against being stagnant and stale. Such kind of water was selected and the ashes of the foregoing burning were to be mixed with this fresh water. This solution was the formula for the water of purification. It was in view of this mixture that Paul uses the term "pure water," in Heb. 10: 22. He does not have any reference to the sanitary state of the water at time of baptism. It was water simply, not water mixed with certain materials such as the ashes in the water of purification under the Mosaic system.

Verse 18. Hyssop was a variety of cedar and noted for its aromatic scent. It could be used as a brush to dash the fluids used on any occasion. In the case now being considered it was dipped in this water of purification and dashed on the objects.

Verse 19. The attention to the third and seventh day is explained in 12 above.

Verse 20. Provision for the use of this water was made clearly known to them and the man who disobeyed would be subject to death.

Verses 21, 22. "Until even" is another indication that the uncleanness being spoken of under this law was formal or ceremonial, and not literal.

NUMBERS 20

Verse 1. The location of Kadesh or Kadesh-barnea is somewhat indefinitely pointed out in the geography and history of those times. In general we are sure that the people are in the last stages of their wandering for the deaths of Miriam and Aaron are soon to be recorded.

Verses 2-5. This is another of the famous murmurings of the children of Israel. It is again for water. Once before, they made the same complaint recorded in Ex. 17. On that occasion they were in the beginning of their wandering while this time they are nearing its end. The means used by the Lord at the former time was different from those used this time, as we will see below.

Verse 6. It is significant that both Moses and Aaron went to the tabernacle to prostrate themselves before the Lord. That would mean that both of them realized the need for relying on divine help, which thus contradicted their conduct later.

Verses 7, 8. This is the passage made famous by public speakers, but which is so generally misused. It is true that the Lord commanded that Moses "speak" unto the rock. A rock is an inanimate object and thus not subject to language intelligently. The word is used in the sense of subduing or taking charge of the rock, but to do so by the form of language that would be heard by the people. In other words, he was not to use any physical action on this occasion, but was to make it known to the people that here was to be another occasion where the Lord would supply their needs by means of this rock.

Verses 9, 10. Even to the end of this noted passage Moses has not yet performed the act that many speakers so often enlarge upon in their eagerness to have some instance to furnish them with an item of theorizing. Moses was commanded to take up the rod which he did. But the mere fact of holding the rod was a symbol of authority regardless of the particular use he should make of it. Let it be observed here that both Moses and Aaron acted in gathering the congregation to this place. In keeping with orderly manner, only Moses did the speaking while Aaron listened and sponsored. The offending circumstance in this whole transaction was the use of the word "we." The plural pronoun is what brings Aaron into the event on equal terms of guilt. The use of the first person pronoun deprived God of the credit that was due him for the miracle about to be done. That such was the basis of all the charges made against him in connection herewith is evident from Psa. 106: 33. It was what he said that was the cause of the condemnation and not the act of smiting the rock. This is further evident from the fact that Aaron was included in the guilt and had to die outside of Canaan for the same sin as Moses, yet only Moses smote the rock.

Verse 11. It was after all the performances of the previous paragraph, which was the cause of God's displeasure, that the physical act of smiting the rock took place. This shows that the act here was not the basis of the great downfall of Moses as to his privilege of entering the land of Canaan. He smote the rock twice, and the supply of water was abundant for the needs of the people and their beasts. This is a specific instance where the desired result was obtained, yet in direct opposition to the pleasure of the Lord. One of the most popular theories in the world is that "the end justifies the means." That if the result of any experiment is good then the means used to get that result must be considered lawful. The circumstance now under our consideration disproves that theory. The result was good. It saved a congregation and the beasts from death. Yet the guilty actors were condemned sorely. Men today may form their own plans for benefitting mankind. They may bring to them some real good by their human institutions. While the people may obtain some benefit from the transactions, God will reject the ones responsible for the unscriptural means.

Verse 12. The language of this verse is wholly conclusive that both Moses and Aaron are guilty alike. Their guilt is described as unbelief. The sin of unbelief can be manifested by failure to affirm faith in God just as surely as it would be by specifically denying his power. Since Moses and Aaron said "we" were the ones to bring this water from the rock, that ruled God out of the credit. To sanctify God in the sense used here meant to set him apart before the people as the one who was to bring about the result about to be seen. For this sin both brothers will be denied the privilege of entering the land of Canaan.

Verse 13. Many proper nouns in the scripture were given descriptive meanings. The name "Meribah" means "quarrel," used in this instance because the people strove or quarreled with Moses and Aaron. The passage says they strove with the Lord. That is the truth of course, but it is interpreted as being against the Lord when people oppose the Lord's constituted servants having charge of the Lord's work. The last sentence of the verse is explained by the fact that in spite of the self-praise of Moses and Aaron, the Lord actually caused water to come from the rock in the sight of the people. They would then realize God as being the one who gave them their great relief. In this way he was "sanctified in them." (The people.)

Verse 14. We have seen at the beginning of this chapter that the congregation has arrived in the region of Kadesh, which is variously described as to exact location. Its general site indicated that the land of the Edomites is near them and they are about to journey that way. We know that the Edomites occupied the country south of the Moabites. So that the Edomites were north and east of the Dead Sea just east of the wilderness of Zin. The address of "brother" which Moses uses with the king of Edom is in reference to the origin of the Edomites. They were of Esau who was physical brother to Jacob, the ancestor of the Israelites. On the supposed friendship that existed through this relationship Moses makes his plea to follow.

Verses 15, 16. He further prefaces his plea with a brief account of their many trials and other experiences, expecting that it would enlist sympathy and favor.

Verse 17. A group of people including many armed men would ordinarily be looked upon as invaders by any nation into which they entered. Recognizing this, Moses gives assurance that the sovereignty of the country of Edom will be solemnly observed and respected. A few of the areas were to be exempted from the general possession of the children of Israel. The land of Edom was one of such, based on the fact of the near relationship. Thus it was necessary to obtain permission from the king of Edom before passing through his country.

Verses 18-21. The king of Edom turned down the plea of Moses. He made further promises of peaceful march through the land but still the king of Edom refused and threatened to resist him with the sword. In thus opposing the descendants of Jacob, the descendants of Esau fulfilled the prediction of Isaac in Gen. 27: 40.

Verse 22. Mount Hor is north of Seir, the principal mountain of the people of the Edomites, and outside their country. This is enroute to the expected end of their wandering but will avoid going through the Edomite country.

Verses 23, 24. Addressing the two brothers God reminds them that "ye" had rebelled against him at Meribah. At present only Aaron is to receive his punishment. The Lord still has need for the services of Moses and thus he will be continued in the work for a while.

Verse 25. Both Aaron and his son are to be taken to the top of the mount. This is because the one is to take the place of the other.

Verse 26. The law had directed that the garments of the priest were to descend to his son. (Ex. 29: 30.) That was why the present command.

Verse 27. Exchange of clothing for the priest was made; they went to the top of Mount Hor. The people beheld the action.

Verse 28. In the top of the mount selected by the Lord for the sad occasion, the priesthood passed from father to son according to the law. Then Aaron was caused to die for his sin of unbelief at the rock.

Verse 29. The abitrary period of thirty days for the mourning shows that it was a formality and not a condition of sorrow in their minds. It is sometimes asked if the various exercises done at funerals are right. Of course all things can be abused. We have various indications that in olden times the people went through some form of ceremony at the occasion of death of a friend. Aaron had been with them for forty years and his services had been leaned upon. Now he is taken from them. It is true that genuine sorrow was present, which prompted the period of mourning, but it was carried out in accordance with some kind of formality.

NUMBERS 21

Verse 1. The spies had been through the territory of this king 38 years before. Now he hears that they are there in vast numbers and prepares to oppose them. This he does and succeeds in taking some of them prisoners.

Verses 2, 3. In this instance we have a concrete example of the ordinance recorded in Lev. 27: 29. The Israelites vowed these Canaanites to destruction upon condition of their success. The Lord granted the condition and then the complete defeat of the foe was carried out according to their vow.

Verse 4. Mention of the Red Sea here, takes the explanation already made at chapter 14: 25, which the reader should see. The congregation left Mount Hor and traveled on by this arm of the water and then went round (compassed) the land of Edom. This longer route was necessary in order to avoid conflict with that hostile people. (20: 14-21.) The people were discouraged because of having to take this way and gave vent to their feelings in murmuring.

Verse 5. This was the last recorded murmuring of the people referred to in the scriptures. The statement was made previously that when this place was reached in the work we are now doing, a chain of the various murmurings would be given the reader, whereby he might trace out all the instances by use of the chain. The first instance will be cited, then from that to the next and then the next and so on to the last one (the present verse), and then back to the first. This sort of endless chain of references will enable the reader to locate any of the occasions of the murmurings he is specifically interested in. Here they are: Ex. 5: 20, 21; 14: 11, 12; 15: 24; 16: 2, 3; 17: 3; Num. 11: 1; 11: 4, 5; 14: 1-4; 16: 41; 20: 2-5; 21: 5; Ex. 5: 20, 21.

Verse 6. As punishment for this murmuring the Lord sent fiery serpents among the people. This is referred to by Paul in 1 Cor. 10: 9.

Verse 7. The people now are repentant. Note the significant statement that they had sinned against both the Lord and Moses. They understood that when they opposed God's chosen person of authority it is the same as having opposed him. They then ask Moses to pray for them which he did. Again we see the office of mediator.

Verses 8, 9. In this place we have another instance where the Lord sees fit to use some visible means in connection with his miracle while bringing about the desired result. It should be observed that the means used had no logical or physical bearing on the thing to be accomplished. The conclusion would be that, after all, the whole transaction was the work of God and thus should strengthen the faith. Any person would know that looking at a thing of brass could have no effect on one who had been bitten with a poisonous snake. The Lord did the work of cure. He would not have done so had the people not had faith enough in him to obey and look at the object raised upon the pole. The lifting up of this serpent on the pole was a type of Christ, who was to be lifted up on the cross. (John 3: 14, 15.)

Verses 10-13. This paragraph puts down some of the stops the children of Israel made in their further journey toward the final goal. It brings them to the border of the land of Moab where such noted experiences are destined to be had.

Verse 14. This verse is a general citation of the records that were being made of the actions of the people of the Lord. It is mentioned here to indicate the fact that such events were well established. There are numerous places in the Bible where a statement will be made and then reference cited to some corroborative record.

Verses 15, 16. A simple association of their movements now, with a former instance in their experiences with the Lord at a time of need.

Verses 17, 18. On different occasions of prosperity the children of Israel would express their sentiments by singing a song. This they did soon after crossing the Red Sea. (Ex. 15: 1.) The sad thing about it is that they so often forgot the goodness of the Lord and went lusting for other experiences.

Verses 19, 20. The congregation is getting nearer and nearer their goal. They are now in the region of Pisgah which will figure prominently with them before long.

Verses 21, 22. Before proceeding further into outside territory they make application for permission to pass. Assurances of peaceable conduct are made to Sihon, the king of the territory.

Verse 23. Not only did Sihon refuse the permission asked for, but mobilized his people and made an attack upon the children of Israel. He thus became the aggressor.

Verse 24. The general conduct of the nation of the Israelites was that of defence since the land had been given to them at the time of Abraham their ancestor. Now in the specific case at hand, the battle is even locally one of defence.

Verse 25. The success of the Israelites is indicated by the fact that they not only defeated the enemy on the battlefield, but also occupied his cities.

Verses 26-28. These heathen peoples had previously been at war with each other. Now the former victors have become captives.

Verses 29, 30. Israel rejoices in victory over these people who had conquered over others before this. To be able to defeat a champion is better than victory over ordinary foes.

Verses 31, 32. "Amorites" was the name of a specific people, but they were so outstanding in their iniquity that the term came to be used to indicate wicked people in general. See Gen. 15: 16 and comments at that place. Thus we have the Amorites mentioned twice in this paragraph.

Verses 33-35. A noted heathen king is here encountered, Og of Bashan. But the Lord gives Moses assurance of victory which came accordingly. The victory was so complete that no one was left for the opposing king.

NUMBERS 22

Verse 1. The Israelites have now arrived at a very noted place in their journeys. A glance at the map will show the exact location since it is opposite Jericho. This area in general is occupied now by the Moabites and the Jordan river flows between it and the land of Canaan. The children of Israel will be in this same locality practically all the time until they cross over.

Verse 2. Balak was the king of the Moabites at this time. He had learned all about the success of the children of Israel against the Amorites as the report of their operations had preceded them. (Josh. 2: 10.)

Verse 3. The great numbers of the people caused the Moabites to dread their presence and determined them to attempt some kind of defence.

Verse 4. The Midianites occupied the territory just south of the Moabites and were on friendly terms with them. The ancestry of the two peoples made them akin in blood as well as in mutual hostility to the pure stock of Abraham's descendants. The Midianites sprang from one of the sons of Abraham by his second wife and the Moabites came from a son of Lot, nephew of Abraham. While each of these groups had the blood of Abraham, yet as a people they were considered aliens from the direct line. In the situation of distress surrounding Moab they confer with Midianites.

Verse 5. This verse is worded as if it was only the king of Moab who sent to Balaam. But verse 7 shows that after conferring with the Midianites they both agreed to oppose the operations of the Israelites. According to Josephus (4-6-2) Balaam was a prophet of the true God, who had become corrupt and mixed his prophecies with the arts of sorcery and other means of deception. The same idea is held by the Schaff-Herzog Encyclopedia. I shall quote a few words from this work: "Balak * * * called upon Balaam, who had a great reputation in the East as a sorcerer and prophet, and who withal was a worshiper of the God of the Israelites, to curse them, thinking that the curse of a fellow-worshipper would be more efficacious than that of a heathen * * * Balaam was a bad man, though a true prophet. He had no sincere convictions of the superiority of Jehovah. He followed him because it suited his interests."—Article, Balaam. Both these citations to the secular history agree with what we can learn from the Bible. We know that Balaam knew something about the true God although he could not have learned it from the Israelites. He lived in Mesopotamia while the Israelites have just now come into the region of Moab and have hitherto been farther away than that. But we will remember that the Patriarchal Dispensation is and has been in force and there have been some individuals all along who paid some attention to God through that system. In fact, this very region where Balaam lived is the same from where the father of the great nation of Israel came. So it is altogether clear why Balaam could be classed among the prophets of God. And yet also, that he would have become so corrupted through his personal ambitions as to take on the superstitions of sorcery and divination that we know God's people were so often corrupted with.

Verse 6. Balaam had acquired the reputation of being able to pronounce either a curse or blessing and that such would come to pass. A soothsayer or sorcerer often deceived the people in some way and caused them to attribute the unusual circumstance to the prophet. With this opinion of Balaam the king of Moab sends for him and offers an inducement in the form of a compliment for his ability to accomplish his schemes.

Verse 7. Some elders of both the Midianites and Moabites were selected to form the commission to Balaam. *Rewards of divination.* This refers to the payment they would offer to Balaam for his services. They arrive at the home of Balaam and relate to him their mission and the words of Balak.

Verse 8. Balaam would not give them an immediate answer but told them to prepare to lodge with him over night and he would see what the Lord had to say about it. The men agreed to this and lodged with him.

Verses 9-11. Sometime in the night God spoke to Balaam. He asked him as to the men lodged with him, and their mission. Balaam gave the Lord a true report.

Verse 12. The Lord then forbade him to go with the people. He must not curse the Israelites because they were a blessed nation.

Verse 13. Balaam was true to God at this time and refused the elders their request.

Verse 14. The princes, or elders, of Moab then departed for their home land. They reported their failure to their king.

Verse 15. Balak persists in his design. He thinks to overcome the refusal of the prophet by increasing the gifts; also by the presentation through men of higher rank than the ones sent on the first mission.

Verses 16, 17. The commission arrived at Balaam's home and delivered their new proposition. They assured the prophet that their king would promote him to great honor if he would come and curse the people. This was supposed to be a strong inducement and perhaps it would have been, had the Lord not interfered in the matter.

Verse 18. All the offers made to Balaam could not alter his determination to be obedient to God as he professes. He states that he cannot go beyond the word of the Lord. That was a true statement but not exactly in the way he pretended.

Verse 19. He does not close the conversations abruptly. He bids them remain with him over night again, and see if the Lord will change his decree in the case. They agree to this and now we find them lodged with Balaam for another night.

Verse 20. God did say something "more" to Balaam that night. It is important to note carefully the proviso which the Lord placed under the order to go with the men. That was, "if the men come to call thee." That would mean that the men might become so eager to see the wish of their king succeed that they would not wait till morning but would come to him in his slumber and insist on his going with them. If that takes place, then he might go. Even if that were to happen, he must still not say anything different from what the Lord directs him to say.

Verse 21. The princes did not come to him before morning. Instead, it was

Balaam who was not willing to wait until morning. He omitted the condition which the Lord had connected with his going, and prepared for the journey. He thus took it upon himself to go with the princes of Midian and Moab.

Verse 22. God's anger was kindled against Balaam. He had not waited for the men to come to him as was told him. He seemed so eager to comply with the request of the king of Moab that he jumped over the proviso in the case and went on his own authority. One meaning of "adversary" is "opponent." It means one who opposes the action of another. God sometimes uses angels for this purpose as well as for a favorable one. The whole setup was miraculous. God is able to complicate a miracle in the manner that suits his aims.

Verses 23-27. The angels of God would ordinarily be invisible to either man or beast. Divine power does not halt at the greatness of a miracle. Thus, not only is the ass enabled to see the angel, but God manages it so that Balaam does not. The angel is here with a sword, and has it "drawn," which means that it presented a threatening appearance so that the beast was frightened. It endeavored to avoid the angel by turning from one way to another. Balaam tried to force his beast into the desired way by striking her with his staff. There was a path leading to a vineyard and hedged on each side with a wall. The angel stood in this place. The space was too narrow for the ass to avoid the sword by turning to one side. Neither did she dare go onward. In the panic of fear that overcame the beast, she thrust herself and rider against the wall in such a manner that it crushed Balaam's foot. Going still further the angel selected a narrower place that made it impossible to even try to turn to one side. Rather than face the angel the beast fell down under the rider. By this time the anger of Balaam arose and he smote the ass with a staff. One of the strange things about this circumstance is that Balaam went through all these details of his experience and did not seem to suspect that anything special was causing the actions of the beast. No animal naturally performs as this one has been doing, and he should have at least thought of some cause unusual as being the explanation. But when a human being is bent on doing his own will he is often so blinded by perversity that all evidences of rebuke escape him. It was so with Balaam in this case.

Verse 28. This is not the first time that a dumb brute was made to talk with man's speech. The serpent in the garden was one other instance. It will not be confusing to us when we recall the powers of the Lord in controlling the things he has made. Here the beast is made to ask an accusing question. And it is another illustration of Heb. 1: 1. In that formative period of the world's history God uses various means in carrying out his purposes, that he will abandon later.

Verse 29. Still blinded with perversity and anger, Balaam wishes for a sword by which to slay his faithful beast. Had she not done as recorded, it would have meant the death of her master. Yet he is minded to slay her. This, too, after she has spoken to him with man's speech and thus demonstrated that something entirely out of the ordinary is happening.

Verse 30. The question the ass put to Balaam was to the same effect as expressed in the verses above. After reminding Balaam that she had been serving him ever since he owned her she then asked if she had ever been accustomed to refuse serving him. He had to admit that she had not. But still he is so blinded that the unusual situation has not brought him to his senses.

Verse 31. Now another miracle is performed, this time on Balaam. He is made able to see the angel with the drawn sword. At this he falls down flat in a prone attitude of reverence and submission as was the custom in the East.

Verse 32. In this verse the statement is made that the way of Balaam was perverse unto the angel of the Lord. The word perverse means contrary. That certainly is a proper description of the actions of this man. While the Lord is going to suffer him to proceed in the journey, he deems it necessary to give him this chastisement.

Verse 33. The angel now informed Balaam that his life was saved by the actions of his beast; the animal at which he was just now so enraged.

Verse 34. Another strange demonstration of how a man's perversity can blind him. After all that has been going on Balaam now says, "if it displease thee," etc. He should have concluded before this as to whether his way was pleasing to the Lord. Now he proposes turning back if so directed.

Verse 35. Balaam is now informed that he was not dealt this experience in order to turn him back. Instead, he is directed to go on in his journey toward the chosen goal. A restriction was placed over him and that was that he was to speak only what the Lord told him to speak. Such statement indicates to us that Balaam is to be inspired in the forthcoming speeches. This also will not be the only time such a thing takes place. God used the woman of Endor, to chastise Saul, even though she was an evil person. He uses characters that are adapted to the service he wishes to have.

Verses 36, 37. Upon hearing that Balaam had come, Balak went out to meet him. This was according to the rule of courtesy. Besides, Balak was very much interested and seemed to think that the conduct of Balaam would be according to his own decision, regardless of what the Lord would have to do in the matter. Meeting Balaam he gives him a mild rebuke for hesitating to come to him. He then reminded him of his ability to promote him to honor. This evidently was a bribe in advance.

Verses 38-40. The king of the Moabites was then informed that the prophet could not go beyond the word of the Lord in his speeches. Proceeding on, they came to a city. Now if it is the Lord who must be pleased in this transaction it might be well to get him in a pleased mood. So Balak made an animal sacrifice of large beasts and informed Balaam of his action and invited Balak and his princes.

Verse 41. Since the prophet is expected to pronounce a curse upon the people of whom Balak is afraid, it would be in order for him to see them in their entirety. Perhaps when he sees how strong they are, and thus, how great a menace they are, he will be impressed to pronounce a fitting curse upon them.

NUMBERS 23

Verse 1. It should never be forgotten that the Patriarchal Dispensation was still in force at the time of which we are reading. All men, more or. less, know what the major item was, of that practice, and that altars and sacrifices would be required. In figurative language seven is a signal of completeness. Balaam wishes to offer a complete service to God in preliminary operations for the speech he wants to make. In the work of making this preparation he directs Balak to do the work.

Verse 2. Balak gladly did as Balaam had requested and each of them offered sacrifices on the altars.

Verse 3. Balak was told to stand by, holding watch over the offering, while the prophet went to have private consultation with the Lord. He is again given to understand that whatever God commands him to speak that is what will be said.

Verse 4. God met Balaam and was informed by him that seven altars had been prepared and sacrifices offered on each of them. This again in the way of placating the Lord.

Verse 5. It must not be overlooked, that the inspired writer is telling us that the Lord put the words in Balaam's mouth. That proves that he was inspired here.

Verse 6. Upon his return to the altar he found Balak and the princes in waiting, expecting to hear a discourse of cursing against the enemy.

Verse 7. "Parable" as used here is from a word meaning some kind of illustration, not necessarily an item by item comparison, as we would ordinarily think of a parable. It is to be a figurative speech, but mixed with some literal truth. Since it will be inspired we may expect it to be important.

Verses 8-10. This is Balaam's first speech. He cannot curse those whom God does not curse. Not that it would be literally impossible for him to go against the Lord's will, but as a prophet, he cannot do so. He then turned his speech into prophecy and declared that the people should "dwell alone." This referred to the residence of the children of Israel in Canaan and that was to come very soon. Such prediction would necessarily mean that the desired curse would not be forthcoming now. The speech closes with one of the most beautiful expressions of faith in God, and of the solemnity of preparing for the next life, that we have anywhere. No one but an inspired man would have uttered such wonderful words.

Verse 11. Of course Balak was displeased with this speech. It was displeasing to him from two standpoints. It not only did not curse Israel but instead it blessed.

Verse 12. The previous notice was again made to Balak that Balaam would have to speak just what the Lord bade him speak.

Verse 13. Balak imagines that Balaam has been overawed by the immensity of the multitude and that perhaps if he should see only a part of them he might despise them and thus be influenced to pronounce a curse upon them. He was still forgetting that Balaam was not saying what he personally would have liked, but was bound under the word of the Lord. Now he thinks to try the opposite of what he had in mind the first time. Then he thought to obtain his desired curse from Balaam under the influence of his being overawed by the size of the crowd. But that failed, and now he thinks to try the experiment of arousing his contempt for the group, and thus be disposed to curse.

Verses 14, 15. The seven altars and sacrifices were prepared again and in course of the offering, Balaam steps aside to consult with God.

Verse 16. As before, let it be noted that the Lord put the word in the mouth of Balaam, so that what he says will be inspiration.

Verse 17. Balak is faithful to his personal duty assigned to him in this program attempted by Balaam. Upon the return of the prophet he is asked to report.

Verses 18-24. This is the second speech and in abbreviated form, was a summons, first, for Balak to rise up and give ear. God does not lie, neither does he repent as man repents. God repents all right, but not as man does. When man repents he changes his will. When God repents he wills a change. God will make good what he speaks. Balaam had been commanded to bless and therefore cannot curse. Israel as a people has been beheld by the Lord for good and he is with them. Their great deliverance from Egypt was referred to, which is a very significant circumstance. The unicorn of the Bible was a fabulous animal supposed to possess great strength and referred to as a symbol of strength. The word "enchantment" in verse 23 means magic, or any other supposed superhuman spell. The word "against" is not in the original. The marginal gives the word "in" instead of this other word and the context both in word and thought will support that wording. The wisdom that is manifested in Israel is not from the source of enchantment; instead, it is from God. Hence the expression, "what hath God wrought!" It was God who did it and not Israel through some power of magic. Final victory over the foe, is the close of the speech.

Verses 25, 26. In a flourish of despair Balak makes as if he would drop the matter now. But Balaam again assures him of his inability to go contrary to the word of God.

Verses 27-30. This paragraph shows that Balak was giving way to rashness in his last remarks to Balaam for he now made one more attempt to get things in shape that perhaps the Lord would favor the scheme now being attempted by him and Balaam. The same preparation of the seven altars and sacrifices was made as before.

NUMBERS 24

Verse 1. Balaam is now convinced that God will continue to have Israel blessed. On this conclusion the verse says that he did not seek enchantments as before. That statement is evidence that no enchantments can prevail against the wishes of the Lord. Neither did he go again with the hope of obtaining any encouragement from God. Instead, he went toward the wilderness.

Verse 2. In this position Balaam was given a view of Israel in camp formation in their tents. Again the "spirit of God came upon him." We cannot be too insistent on the idea that these speeches of Balaam were inspired.

Verses 3-9. This paragraph was the third speech. The words "into a trance," in verse 4 are not in the original. The text should read simply "falling," and "having his eyes open." In other words, God wants Balaam to be inspired and at the same time have his eyes open to see for himself the greatness of the people of Israel. When he does he finds them in goodly tents. He sees further scenes of the beauty and prosperity of the nation of Jacob. *Higher than Agag.* This has no special reference to any literal height but means the supposed exaltation of the king of the Amalekites. He did exalt himself very much, but even had his greatest ambitions been realized he would not have become as truly high as was Israel. Reference is again made to the unicorn. See remarks on that at chapter 23: 22. The speech closes with the words of one of the promises of God to Abraham. (Gen. 12: 3.)

Verses 10, 11. At this speech Balak became disgusted and dismissed Balaam. As a parting shot he reminds him of what he missed by not cursing Israel. Had he done so he would have been promoted to honor. However, he acknowledges that the whole thing was caused by the Lord who had kept him back from honor.

Verses 12, 13. The same explanation is repeated, that even a house full of silver and gold would not suffice to secure the services of Balaam in cursing Israel. He had told the servants the same when they first were sent for him.

Verse 14. Balaam is about to return to his people. Before leaving he said he would "advertise" (advise) him what this people would finally do.

Verses 15-19. This is the fourth speech of Balaam. It was not asked for by Balak and no preparations were made for it, as was the case in the other three speeches. This speech is inspired as well as the others for while Balak has dismissed Balaam, the Lord has not. Thus he makes another speech which contains many important predictions. Falling with his eyes open, is the same as in the second speech. The pronoun "him" in 17th verse means Christ in his kingdom. That kingdom will be seen, is now in the prophet's vision but its fulfillment is not now. The present Israel is destined to become a mighty nation and have existence for many centuries. Finally there shall come a star out of Jacob. This is the same as the seed promised to Abraham in Gen. 12: 3. Mention of the outside peoples in this connection is his way of expressing the triumph of Christ over all others. The same is meant in the last verse of this speech, and must be considered as an inspired prediction made through this prophet.

Verses 20-24. In the prophesying strain, Balaam makes some statements about other inferior nations, whose detailed history is not here available. The gist of it is, that God knows and does something about the various nations, putting down some and exalting others according to their conduct or as the Lord sees fit otherwise.

Verse 25. This verse would leave us with the impression that after the four speeches which Balaam uttered by inspiration, he went immediately to his home without any further conversation with Balak. Other statements in the scriptures and in secular history will indicate to us that such was not the case. See next chapter.

NUMBERS 25

Verses 1-5. This will bring up the thought expressed at the close of the preceding chapter. It pertains to the conversation between Balak and Balaam after the Lord had dismissed Balaam. He is now released and free to act on his own initiative and in doing so he shows his true attitude toward God's people. After having arrived near the Euphrates he sent for Balak and advised him what to do that would result in some degree of curse on Israel although he was not permitted to bring such upon them himself. The history of this is given by Josephus, which I shall now quote in part. "O Balak, and you Midianites that are here present (for I am obliged even without the will of God to gratify you), it is true no entire destruction can sieze upon the nation of the Hebrews, neither by war, nor by plague, nor by scarcity of the fruits of the earth, nor can any other unexpected accident be their entire ruin; for the providence of God is concerned to preserve them from such a misfortune; nor will it permit any such calamity to come upon them whereby they may all perish; but some small misfortunes, and those for a short time, whereby they may appear to be brought low, may still befall them; but after that they will flourish again, to the terror of those that brought those mischiefs upon them. So that if you have a mind to gain a victory over them for a short space of time you will obtain it by following my directions: Do you therefore set out the handsomest of such of your daughters as are most eminent for beauty, and proper to force and conquer the modesty of those that behold them, and these decked and trimmed to the highest degree you are able. Then do you send them to be near the Israelites' camp and give them in charge, that when the young men of the Hebrews desire their company, they allow it them; and when they see that they are enamoured of them, let them take their leaves; and if they entreat them to stay, let them not give their consent till they have persuaded them to leave off their obedience to their own laws and the worship of that God who established them, and to worship the gods of the Midianites and Moabites; for by this means God will be angry at them." Josephus, *Antiquities* 4-6-6. In following sections of the same place in Josephus the account is carried out and shows that it turned out just as Balak had predicted. They procured these girls to go to the vicinity where the Hebrews camp was located. The natural thing happened. These girls were attractive to the masculine eye and lusts, and allured them to their intimacy. Before granting the young men the liberty they sought they were first demanded to comply with their idolatrous practices. This was agreed to and thus the men committed idolatry and fornication with these girls. In agreement with these facts I quote from Rev. 2: 14: "Balaam, who taught Balak to cast a stumbling-block before the children of Israel, to eat things sacrificed to idols, and to commit fornication." Idolatry has always been very displeasing to God. It provokes his jealousy and he will not tolerate it. Balaam knew this and therefore used the above plan to bring about the plague upon Israel. After the people committed the sins here described the divine wrath was poured out and many thousands were slain. This fact is referred to in 1 Cor. 10: 8.

Verse 6. It was bad enough to go after these heathenish women in their lust, but even that did not satisfy some. One man was so arrogant as to bring his Midianitish partner in lust into the camp of the Israelites in the sight of Moses. This was adding insult to injury. The bad conduct of the young men had already resulted in the death of thousands. Now this man insults the congregation by bringing the vile woman into the presence of the law-giver of the nation.

Verses 7, 8. The grandson of the first priest was filled with indignation about the insult and went after the guilty pair. He pursued them into the tent and pierced them both through the body with a javelin. This brought a stay of the active plague that was killing the people.

Verse 9. The difference between the number here said to have been slain and the account in 1 Cor. 10: 8 has sometimes caused uneasiness among Bible students. There is more than one possible explanation. One is that Paul says there fell "in one day" three and twenty thousand. An additional thousand fell later but as a final result of the plague. Another explanation is in the fact that numerical values were indicated by letters and not figures in those ancient times. In transcribing the text from the manuscript, a blotted or blurred letter could be mistaken for another. This raises the question whether all of the scriptures might not have gone through the same mistakes. The silence of Jesus on the accuracy of the scribes while severely condemning them for other evils is significant. Had they been guilty of unfaithfulness as scribes, he certainly would not have let that subject go by, since that would have been a fundamental error. His silence on the subject leaves us with the conclusion that errors of the kind mentioned here were not important, as no principle was at stake.

Verses 10, 11. This was a case where a man of the priestly family interceded to quiet the wrath of God against the offenders. Note the last word in the paragraph. Then consult Ex. 20: 5 where God mentions his jealousy in connection with the commandment against idolatry.

Verse 12, 13. As a reward of consolation for his good offices in the case, God directs that Phinehas be assured again of the perpetual life of the priesthood in his family. This ordinance had already been passed, but upon such signal service on behalf of the people it was fitting to repeat the assurance. In doing so, in connection with his service in preserving the people, it justified the choice of the family for the important post of the priesthood.

Verse 14, 15. The names of the guilty man and woman referred to earlier in the chapter are given here. The point of interest in giving us these names is in the prominence of the two. They were not mere insignificant beings with no responsibility. Sin is sin, whether with the high or low, but mention of it with these important persons is an outstanding declaration of the principle that "God is no respecter of persons," as the New Testament tells us.

Verses 16-18. Because of the persistent wickedness and enmity of the Midianites, God ordains that they are to be opposed constantly by his people. They had provoked the divine jealousy and must suffer the fate due all such.

NUMBERS 26

Verse 1. By consulting Chapter 20: 28 as well as Ex. 29: 29, 30 the reader will see that Eleazar is now High Priest. The priesthood was to descend from father to son.

Verse 2. This is the second occasion of taking the number of the men of war in the congregation of Israel. The first time is recorded in first chapter of the book. The age limit at induction was the same as at the first time which was twenty and up. Also, they must be of military qualifications. The nation is under military rule and will be until they have entered and taken possession of Canaan, the capital portion of the promised land. Hence the necessity of military preparation.

Verse 3. The ones supervising this were Moses and Eleazar. The congregation is located in the plains of Moab, near the Jordan river, just opposite Jericho.

Verse 4. Reference is made to the first numbering of the people soon after they left Egypt which was forty years ago.

Verses 5-7. This chapter will be treated in much the same manner as was the first one of the numbering. The principal persons will be mentioned with the number of the various tribes. Also, if any person of special interest is named he will be noted here. It will be noted that certain ones of the heads of the various tribes and families are named in this chapter. That was doubtless for purposes of identification in case of inquiry or dispute over their family register. Such a dispute did arise in after years. (Neh. 7: 64.) The present paragraph gives the register and numbering of the tribe of Reuben. The number was 43,730.

Verses 8, 9. This paragraph gives names of special interest. They are from the tribe considered in the foregoing paragraph, but are given this personal mention because of the prominent part they had in the notorious conspiracy against Moses and Aaron. The information is also given here that these sons of Reuben were a part of the company of Korah, the leader of the uprising. Also, let it be observed here that the writer considers their actions as being against the Lord.

Verse 10. This is a brief history of the events referred to above. The gravity of that occasion is so deep that the Lord does not want it forgotten. They became a sign of wrath of God against rebels.

Verse 11. The children of Korah were exempted from the general destruction of his family unit as they evidently did not engage in the conspiracy. The statement in Ex. 20: 5 sets out that the children of wicked parents will be also punished like the parents, provided they also hate the Lord.

Verses 12-14. This is the account of the second son of Jacob, Simeon. After giving names of members of the family the number is stated as 22,200.

Verses 15-18. The sons of Jacob are not named in the order of birth in this chapter. The present paragraph is on the number of Gad which is 40,500.

Verses 19-22. In giving the names of Judah the writer considers it necessary to explain the absence of certain ones from the roll of descendants. This he does by saying they died in the land of Canaan. That took place before the family of Jacob ever went to Egypt. The record of their deaths, 38th chapter of Genesis, explains why no descendants are attributed to them here. There were others and the tribe became the most numerous of all. At the present numbering it is 76,500.

Verses 23-25. The number of military men in this tribe was 64,300 at this time.

Verses 26, 27. The number here is 60,500.

Verses 28-34. The reader may consult Gen. 48: 5, 6 and he will be refreshed on the event when Jacob provided that two whole tribes were to be made from the two sons of Joseph. Hence, sometimes only Joseph is mentioned when the children of Israel are in mind of the writer. Again, just one or both of his sons will be named. At other times (such as we will have here) mention will be made of Joseph and his two sons, with explanation. Thus after the introduction to the family as stated the eldest of Joseph's sons is named and the number of his tribe given which is Manasseh, 52,700.

Verse 35-37. The second son of Joseph, Ephraim, is numbered 32,500.

Verses 38-41. Benjamin is next recorded and he was one of the small tribes. His number at this census was 45,600.

Verses 42, 43. Dan was the son of Jacob by (his wife) Rachel's maid, Bilhah. His tribe numbered 64,400 and was one of the larger tribes.

Verses 44-47. Asher was the son of Jacob by Leah's maid, Zilpah. He numbered 53,400.

Verses 48-50. The twelfth one of the congregational group of tribes given here is Naphtali and his number was 45,400. It is noticeable that all of these numbers of the tribes end in 0. This is obviously not the exact number and would not be considered as such since it would be highly improbable that each of twelve tribes would actually have such an even number of military men. It is the custom of the writers of statistics to give round numbers, frequently, and not exact numbers.

Verse 51. The sum of the twelve tribes is 601,730. This is slightly less than the number they had at the first which was 603,550. Yet, it was practically the same, which indicates that the congregation has held its own thus far.

Verses 52-56. This paragraph gives the general principles on which the land is to be divided when they get settled in Canaan. The specific directions will be seen in the book of Joshua and will be studied in more detail when we reach it.

Verse 57. This verse gives the names of the heads of the special tribe, Levi. The service about the tabernacle and the priesthood was divided between them. For more detailed information on this subject see chapter 3.

Verse 58. A few of the heads of the family of Levi are named and connected up with one of the most outstanding one, named Kohath, who was the father of Amram.

Verse 59. Amram was actually a grandson of Levi and he married a woman of the tribe of Levi, here spoken of as a daughter of Levi. The term is used of any near relation and not an immediate offspring. Mention is made of the relation to show that the tribal distinction has been preserved. The pair, Amram and Jochebed had the children, Aaron, Moses and Miriam.

Verse 60. A number of famous persons are given space in the record here. Thus the four sons of Aaron are named while recording the family.

Verse 61. As in the case of the sons of Judah, the fate of two of the four sons of Aaron is given here, which accounts for their being eliminated from the accounts of activities afterward.

Verses 62, 63. This paragraph shows a gain of one thousand of the Levites over the numbering the first time as recorded in chapter 3: 39. This enumeration was taken under guidance of Moses and Eleazar in the plains of Moab.

Verses 64, 65. The sad fact is recorded that all of the men-of-war who had been numbered the first time, were now dead, except Caleb and Joshua. This was because they sinned and made rash statements which God carried out among them. The two exceptions were preserved because they "wholly followed the Lord."

NUMBERS 27

Verse 1. In chapter 26: 33 we were told that Zelophehad had no sons, but did have daughters. Now those daughters are before the face of Moses with a difficulty.

Verses 2, 3. Their predicament is that their father having no sons, the property might be alienated from them and the family. This was because the custom was to transmit all inheritances through the male line. Now these women are not condoning any sin of their father. He died on account of sin, but it was not the sin of conspiracy. He died in his own sin. The daughters expect some consideration from that fact and plead for their share in the possessions of their father.

Verses 4, 5. Not only are these daughters concerned about their property rights but are afraid the name of their father will pass from the congregation. This presented a problem to Moses because it was a special circumstance, and he did not know what to do about it. He thus brought the case before the Lord.

Verses 6, 7. The plea of these daughters was approved by the Lord and he commanded that the property of their father should remain among them.

Verses 8-11. This specific instance opened the way for more extended directions as to the distribution of property. In the main, it was to pass from one owner to his immediate descendant or relative. If he had no near relative in the way of daughter or son, then it should fall to the next nearest kin, and so on and on. This was to become a statute unto the children of Israel.

Verse 12. Abarim was a community, or region, in general and some certain mount in that region was designated for the one on which Moses was to view the land across the river. Later we will learn the name of the particular mount was Pisgah, or Nebo.

Verses 13, 14. Moses is notified here that he must die without entering the land of Canaan and that it will be his punishment for the sin at the rock. In connection with Aaron, the sin was that of taking honor to themselves, that belonged to God.

Verses 15-17. Meekness and unselfishness were among the prominent traits of this great man of God. He was told that he could never enter the land toward which they had been journeying. Yet there is no indication of bitterness or resentment. Instead, the welfare of the congregation is uppermost in his mind. He pleads that the Lord will appoint some man to care for the people so that they be not like scattered sheep.

Verse 18. The request of Moses is to be granted and the selection is Joshua. He is said here to have the spirit now, and Moses' hand is to be laid on him.

Verse 19. There will be no reason to daubt the authority of Joshua, but all must know that his position as leader was not usurped. The ceremony will be before the priest and the whole congregation. This precaution will be for their mutual protection.

Verse 20. Note that Moses was to put *some* of his honor on Joshua. This agrees with the idea that Joshua was to take the place of Moses as leader, and not lawgiver.

Verse 21. While Joshua will be an inspired man in all that he speaks authoritatively to the congregation, yet specific information will be obtained through the service of the priest. It was expected of the priests to procure knowledge for the people of God in that age. (Mal. 2: 7.) The priest must attend to his office in the orderly manner, and that in connection with the Urim which was without any virtue except when in the hands of the designated officer.

Verses 22, 23. Moses obeyed the voice of God and appointed Joshua as leader in his place. He will not "take over" while Moses is living.

NUMBERS 28

Verses 1, 2. It is not only necessary to attend to certain offerings and ceremonies about the altar service, but it must be done "in their due season." One indication of disobedience is the disposition to use one's own convenience about when or where or how to do what is commanded. Children sometimes want to "wait a minute," when told to do something. The spirit of obedience requires that commands must be obeyed in the manner and at the time commanded.

Verses 3-6. This paragraph describes the "daily sacrifice" that came to be so well known in the history of the Israelites. The same ordinance was outlined in Ex. 29: 38-42. It was sometimes called the "continual" offering because it was to be attended to faithfully and daily, without intermittence. A lamb was to be offered in the morning and another in the evening. The margin reads "between the two evenings." This is explained on the basis that the hours of the time from noon till sundown were considered two evenings. And the middle of this period of six hours would be our three o'clock in the afternoon.

Verses 7, 8. The drink offering was so called, not because any one was to drink it in the ceremony, but because it was an offering of material that ordinarily was used for drink. In other words, it was a substance of value and thus was a sacrifice.

Verse 9. The reader is advised to make special note of this verse because it is an item of the Jewish practice that is often unknown or forgotten. On the sabbath day the daily sacrifice was always doubled.

Verse 10. One duty can never take the place of another. Just because a pious Jew had doubled his service on one certain day did not excuse him from the performance of duties on the other days. Thus, the doubling of the sacrifice on the sabbath day did not atone for any neglect on some other day.

Verse 11. The first of each month was a holy day and must be celebrated by the offering of sacrifices. The month was ushered in by the appearance of the new moon as can be seen by studying 1 Sam. 20: 24, 27. Also, the principle must not be lost sight of, that one act of service to God did not take the place of another. If some special duty of a personal nature happened to come on the first day of the month, the usual festivities of that day must not be taken to suffice for the personal duties.

Verse 12. The word "deal" is an indefinite amount, except that it is understood as a small amount. It was a portion of flour used in connection with the animal sacrifice, and called in the A. V., the meat offering. It was of vegetable material.

Verse 13. The "several" deal, etc., means that each animal was to be offered with this meat offering connected. The meat or meal offering was not to be used just once for all of the animals.

Verse 14. The directions for this celebration of the coming in of a new month were to be observed for each of the twelve months of the year. One celebration could not be counted on behalf of the other months.

Verse 15. In this and other verses certain animals and other products are named to be offered and simply called sin offerings or burnt offerings, etc. The details of how they were to be offered have already been described at the introduction of the "ordinance" and recorded in the first five chapters of Leviticus.

Verse 16. All that is found here is the date and name of the feast. The reader should see Ex. 12 for details of this memorable feast. It came immediately before another feast and was observed in connection therewith.

Verse 17. This means that the feast of unleavened bread began the fifteenth. It lasted seven days. As the passover day also was without leaven that made a group of eight days in which no leaven was to be found in their houses. The ordinance for this feast was given on the occasion of their deliverance from Egypt. The motive for and observance of the seven days will be seen afterward. Since they had to get out of Egypt that night before the bread had time to ferment or become leavened, the deliberate observance of a feast of seven days without leaven was done to celebrate the eventful night. See Ex. 13: 7-9.

Verse 18. The first of the seven days was to be holy convocation, which means that it was a sabbath day for them. That meant that no servile or manual labor must be done on that day. A close study of Leviticus 23 will show that when a day was called a convocation it was the same as a sabbath day, and was under all the restrictions that held good for other sabbath days.

Verses 19-22. This paragraph outlines the service required at the altar on the first day of the seven day feast. The particulars of how such offerings were to be handled have been already referred to.

Verses 23, 24. Again they are cautioned not to consider these special services as taking the place of the daily sacrifice.

Verse 25. The seventh day here, means the last of the seven day feast of unleavened bread. It, like the first one, must be a convocation or sabbath day. Let it be understood that each of the seven days must be without leaven and each must have the sacrifices as described. Only the first and seventh were sabbath days. The mere service of offering a sacrifice did not make a day, a sabbath, or holy day. It it did, every day of the year would have been a sabbath day since a sacrifice was offered daily.

Verse 26. This is the day that is called "Pentecost" in the New Testament. It is not called that in the O. T., because it is a Greek word (meaning fiftieth) and the Old Testament was not written in Greek. Here it is designated to come "when your weeks be out." That is why it is elsewhere called the "feast of weeks." More details of this are given in Lev. 23. After the day following the sabbath that followed the passover they counted seven weeks, and then on the day following the seven weeks, they had this feast now called Pentecost. On that day the Israelites offered a token out of their crops. This was offered to God before they appropriated any of the crop for themselves. That is why it was called the feast of "firstfruits." It was a fitting type of the Pentecost in the New Testament, for on that day the first fruits of the Gospel were offered to God, in the obedience of three thousand Jewish converts.

Verses 27-31. These verses give the same directions already described, that pertain to the altar services in connection with the second of the three annual feasts.

NUMBERS 29

Verse 1. Here is a feast coming on the first day of a month and called feast of trumpets. It is a holy day already, because every month began with a holy day. But this time is another special day.

Verses 2-5. The offering of the various animals is here set forth. The details can be seen in the beginning of Leviticus.

Verse 6. Again the reader is cautioned that the present offering cannot be put in place of another. In such connection, mention is made of the "offering of the month." That refers to the offering that every month was to have, regardless of other purposes. The offering is again said to be according to the "manner" which is a reference to the ordinance of the altar service established in beginning of Leviticus. Sweet "savour" means sweet odor. It was pleasing to God. The word would apply to either taste or smell, and either literally or figuratively, always depending on the connection in which it is used. The expression "made by fire" was to distinguish between offerings that were to be burned on the altar, and others. Some things were sacrificed or given up by the Israelites that were not to be burned. They would be given over for the use of the Levites and the priesthood family.

Verse 7. This verse pertains to the great day of atonement. It was the day on which the High Priest went alone into the Most Holy place of the tabernacle. It was the only day this place was entered for services. On this day, while the priest was officiating in this place on behalf of the congregation, all the males of the nation were assembled and in waiting. On this day they were commanded to "afflict" themselves. The word is from ANAH and defined by Strong "to depress, literally or figuratively. " It means they were to be concerned about the seriousness of the day. The nation has a High Priest entering the Most Holy place to act for the sake of the whole people and it is a day to be devoted to serious contemplation. Not a time for hilarity or frivolous pastime. They must abstain from all manual labor and spend the day in meditation on the great subject of their dependence upon God for grace and the benediction of the Ruler of the universe. It typified the great office of Christ who had to die a terrible death so as to be able to enter Heaven with the means of salvation for all mankind.

Verses 8-11. These verses outline the general activities of that great day. Some things took place at the altar of burnt sacrifices, and some otherwise. Not all of the services of that day occurred in the Most Holy place. Neither did all of the services of Christ take place in Heaven. The items performed while on earth came first. Again I cannot refrain from reminding the reader that this service was to be observed besides the daily sacrifice and other offerings. What the priest did on that day affected the congregation as a whole only, and did not take the place of any other duty.

Verse 12. The feast mentioned in this verse is elsewhere called the feast of tabernacles. (Lev. 23: 34.) On that occasion the Israelites were to leave their houses and dwell under booths made of boughs of trees. (Lev. 23: 40-43.) That was in celebration of their forty year experience in the wilderness when they could not live in houses because of the irregular and changeable locations. Here it is also stipulated that it must be a time of holy days.

Verses 13-16. This paragraph gives the sum of the various animals and flour that were to be offered on the days of the feast. That is, a general statement of the service, not the total of all the items. The number of bullocks would diminish as the number of the date of the feast increased. The number of lambs required for each day was the same. In all of the cases the articles offered must be without blemish and in each case the order is to offer according to the "manner" which has already been explained as meaning the ordinance given in beginning of Leviticus. While the information for each day is practically the same, it will be curiously interesting to note briefly for each day the numbers of the various articles. That will be done as follows.

Verses 17-19. Second day, twelve bullocks, fourteen lambs, one kid of the goats.

Verses 20-22. Third day, eleven bullocks, two rams, fourteen lambs, one kid.

Verses 23-25. Fourth day, ten bullocks, two rams, fourteen lambs, one kid of goats.

Verses 26-28. Fifth day, nine bullocks, two rams, fourteen lambs, one kid of goats.

Verses 29-31. Sixth day, eight bullocks, two rams, fourteen lambs, one kid of goats.

Verses 32-34. Seventh day, seven bullocks, two rams, fourteen lambs, one kid of goats.

Verses 35-38. After the feast of tabernacles proper has been observed, it was to be followed by another time of sacrifice. This is referred to as the eighth day. This has numerical meaning only here as the feast of tabernacles was confined to the seven days before. After having gone through that strange experience it was fitting in the mind of the Lord for them to assemble solemnly and finish up the importance of the season by the sacrifices described.

Verse 39. The importance of not substituting one ordinance for another is made even more emphatic here in that the writer itemizes the vows and various other offerings which they were to make at other times.

Verse 40. This short verse is informative in that the authority of Moses is again clearly set forth before the reader. Moses told the children of Israel the things recorded. He had been commanded to do so. Not that he was commanded to perform all the things named in the law. He had been commanded to tell the children of Israel those things. That made it identical with any word that God would have spoken directly to them. Again we see an unanswerable rebuke of the sabbatarians, who try to disparage the authority of Moses in the Old Testament.

NUMBERS 30

Verses 1, 2. Vows were not generally required of the children of Israel. Only at certain times or for special purposes did the Lord command a vow. A vow could be voluntarily made at any time with certain restrictions. When a vow was made, the Lord came into the situation with his directions. One thing required was that a vow not be arbitrarily broken even though made voluntarily, any more than if the Lord had commanded it.

Verses 3, 4. This paragraph concerns a woman unmarried and still in her father's house. She is subject to her father's authority. In his hearing she may make a vow. The vow might not be approved by the father. If so, and he objects, the vow is not binding and the woman is released from its obligations. If he says nothing against the vow at the time she made it, it is binding and neither he nor she can alter it afterward. It must stand as made.

Verse 5. This verse is explained in preceding paragraph except for the word "forgive." It is used in a technical sense and not a moral one. It means the same as cancelling a debt found to be unnecessary.

Verses 6-8. The same restrictions apply in the case of a married woman as that of a daughter at home. If her husband hears the vow and says nothing, the vow must be carried out and neither she nor the husband can lawfully cancel it. But if the husband disapproved at the time the vow was made, it is legally canceled.

Verse 9. The regulations in the vow of a widow, or divorced woman, were the same as with a single woman except that she is bound to the vow with a certain exception which will be noted below.

Verses 10-12. This paragraph pertains to the vow of a widow or one divorced, but who was not a widow at the time of making the vow. In that case, the restrictions are the same as with the wife still living with her husband. That is, a woman might make a vow in the hearing of her husband, yet the vow might be such as not to take effect for some time. If, when the time arrives for the vow to be carried out the woman has become a widow, or divorced, that fact will not alter her obligations. If the husband had let it stand at the time he heard it then it is still binding on her even though she afterward became divorced or a widow. The significant conclusion we should get from this whole law about vows is that "silence gives consent." This is an old saying, but well supported in this law just now being considered. The principle is taught that when a person knows of a circumstance including some principle of right or wrong, his silence commits him to that situation. Sometimes a person will not say what he believes concerning questions that come up regarding a human expedient. When asked how he stands concerning the so-called evil he will say he is neither for nor against. But that is not true in God's estimation. Jesus taught that he that is not for him is against him. When a man will not "take a stand" against any human institution formed against the Lord's institution, he must be regarded as being for it.

Verses 13-16. This paragraph teaches the principle of responsibility of a husband or father who heard and approved of the vow made by the wife or daughter. If that husband or father afterward interferes with the carrying out of that vow, he alone must bear the results of such breach. That is what is meant by the words in verse 15, that "he shall bear *her* iniquity."

NUMBERS 31

Verses 1, 2. The grievous offence of the Midianites in the matter of Balaam is still held up for divine vengeance and Moses is commanded to bring on an attack.

Verses 3-6. An army of twelve thousand men was raised and sent against the Midianites under the leadership of Phinehas, the son of Eleazar the priest. The army was sent out on the mission equipped with the intruments previously ordained to be used on such occasions. (Chapter 10: 1-9.)

Verse 7. In usual cases a military operation is directed against the soldiers of the enemy and the civilians are not supposed to be attacked even when the enemy has joined battle with the aggressor. In this case there is no evidence that the Midianites had engaged primarily in joint combat. The leaders performed the usual practice of attacking only the males in general.

Verse 8. The Midianites occupied a larger territory than the Moabites, yet the two peoples were joined in many interests. They had both united in the conspiracy against Israel when Balaam was employed in an effort to curse Israel. He belonged in the region of the Euphrates river, but evidently spent some time on various occasions with the Midianites, with whom he sympathized. By being associated with them at this time he suffered the fate of the others and was slain.

Verse 9. As stated in verse 7, the males only were slain. The women and children were taken captive together with the possessions of the people. Then Israel destroyed the cities.

Verses 10-12. After destroying the cities and castles they brought the captives home with them and had them in the presence of the congregation.

Verses 13, 14. Of course the preceding paragraph was not meant to say they brought these heathen captives within the camp, but near it. Then Moses and the priest went out to meet the group. When Moses saw whom they had, he was wroth because they had all the women alive with them.

Verses 15, 16. The reason for the wrath of Moses is given here. Among the women taken alive were the ones who had seduced the men of Israel to commit fornication with them and to worship their idols. That iniquity had been brought about through the counsel of Balaam. They had killed him in the battle but had allowed his accomplices to escape punishment.

Verse 17. Then Moses gave commandment that they should kill all the males among the little ones. This may seem harsh upon first consideration, but the whole nation or group at that place was to be destroyed and that would have left these children orphans. They will not be put at any loss spiritually by their death while it would be disastrous for them to be left in the wicked world without a country. The women who had been guilty of the wickedness under Balaam's advice were to be killed.

Verse 18. This verse is the object of unfair criticism by certain evil persons. It is represented as teaching that these men were given license to appropriate these virgins to their own lusts in the ordinary sense of the case. If the critics were sincere in their comments they would consider all that the scripture says on such a case. Let the reader turn to Deut. 21: 10-13 and read. There he will learn that when a virgin was taken in battle who pleased some man for a wife, he could so use her. Even then he must let her have respectful consideration and not be hasty in his enjoying of her. This gives the lie to the vile insinuations made in connection with this verse.

Verses 19, 20. This provision of the law would logically be called for at this time since they have just returned from a battle where they have slain many people. While the slaying was commanded, yet it did not release them from the necessity of going through the formalities of cleansing required by the ceremonial law.

Verses 21-24. Everything that had been in possession of the heathen would be considered as unclean. Before it can be appropriated to the use of God's people it must be purified. The metals could stand the fire and were to be cleansed in that way. The things that would burn were to be cleansed by using the water of purification that had been prescribed by the law. After all this had been accomplished, they were free to reenter the camp and be considered clean.

Verses 25, 26. The things taken in the battle with the Midianites were valuable and were to be dispensed among the people as described below.

Verse 27. A general classification was made of the active warriors and the congregation. Not all the people went to the battle. They were not asked to go. Instead, one thousand from each tribe went, but the ones at home are considered. The division was made equal in the first place, but the distinction will be made in the next handling of this prey.

Verses 28, 29. The half of the prey was distributed among the men of war, and of those souls, or men of war, one man out of five hundred was to give to the Lord out of his part including the animals taken in the battle. It was to be turned over to Eleazar the priest and would thus be used in the tabernacle service.

Verse 30. Of the children of Israel's half of the spoils, there was to be given one out of every fifty. Thus the per cent required of the congregation was ten times as great as that required of the soldiers. That would be fair considering the greater sacrifice they made in the conflict. Lest I leave a misunderstanding about the whole subject I will explain myself more fully. It was not that the person who might number 50, or number 500, must give over all his personal share. That would not be in keeping with any of the law. But the offering was to be made on that basis.

Verses 31-35. This paragraph is the sum of all that was taken by the men of war from the Midianites: 675,500 sheep, 72,000 beeves, 61,000 asses, and 32,000 virgins. All this was to be divided as already seen.

Verses 36, 37. Here one half of the whole booty taken is given, and in next verse the Lord's part of the half is given. The half was 337,500 sheep and the Lord's part was 675. This verifies the remarks made at verse 30 above, for the larger number here divided by 500 will give 675.

Verses 38-40. This paragraph is the rest of the division of the booty including the virgins.

Verse 41. We have previously learned that a special division of the sacrifices was made for the priests for their personal consumption. That is what is meant here.

Verses 42-47. This contains the same subject matter as in verses 36-40 except that the result of the division is not named. That would be only a matter of arithmetic if we wish to have the result tabulated.

Verses 48, 49. The officers appointed to handle the enumeration of the men and their gains in the war now made a report to Moses. They declared that not one man had been overlooked.

Verses 50-53. Besides the beasts and women taken in the battle, and which have been accounted for above, each soldier obtained personal spoils of jewels and other valuables. Now their appreciation is manifested by their making an offering to the Lord of the same.

Verse 54. Moses and the priest took these spoils and brought them into the tabernacle of the congregation to become a part of the congregational treasury.

NUMBERS 32

Verse 1. The whole congregation is still east of the Jordan. They are soon to cross over and enter upon the major military project that has been before them. The tribes mentioned here have noticed the condition of the land near them as being good for pasturage which was their concern.

Verses 2-5. The tribes of Gad and Reuben (and later half of Manasseh) came to Moses and requested that they be given their inheritance in that place. The land had already been subjugated before the children of Israel came up this far in their journey, and now these tribes wish it for their place of residence.

Verse 6. Moses did not understand their full purpose. He thought it was just a scheme of theirs to escape the hardships of the war in Canaan. He chided them for wanting to sit down now in the peaceable possession of their land while the rest of the men of war went over and fought for their inheritance.

Verse 7. The comment of Moses on the effects that would come from their refusing to go on with the war was that it would discourage the others. In modern language, it would weaken their morale, and thus defeat the whole plan of the Lord.

Verse 8. As evidence that such a result would be logical and to be expected he told them about their fathers in the case of the twelve spies. Here is where we learn that the place from where the spies were sent was Kadesh-barnea as well as Paran.

Verse 9. Here he recites the fact that the spies were overawed by the sight of the land and then discouraged the heart of the Israelites. This discouragement caused the congregation of warriors to give way to rash statements and to rebel against going over to take the land.

Verses 10, 11. The rash statements angered the Lord and he decided to grant them the thing they so imprudently called for. And the general principle on which he decided to reject them is stated in the words, "not wholly followed me."

Verse 12. This is a wonderful passage. In contrast with the preceding one let us note carefully that Caleb and Joshua are to be permitted to enter the land of Canaan; not merely because they had followed the Lord, (almost every person follows the Lord in some degree) but because they had *wholly followed* the Lord. The same service of wholeheartedness is required of us today.

Verse 13. The forty years of this service include the 2 years preceding their arrival at Kadesh-barnea. The 38 additional years wandering in the wilderness will result in the death of all the men of war who had made the rash statements referred to and thus their wish will have been granted. Moses' purpose of inserting that bit of history here was to give emphasis to his warning against their request.

Verses 14, 15. There is not the least indication that these tribes made any attempt to interfere with Moses in this severe speech although they knew it did not apply to them. They respectfully heard his speech and then offered their explanation.

Verse 16. Approaching near Moses they stated their first concern would be to build places of shelter for their cattle and children. That was a good idea in itself. They knew it would be somewhat of a burden to have all that encumbrance with them in the battles to be soon fought against the heathen. They did not want to leave them unprotected so that on their return they might find them gone, and they themselves a burden on the congregation.

Verses 17, 18. They promised to go armed with the rest of the brethren and to remain in the conflict until they had received each his place. They would not return to their homes until all the children of Israel had received their inheritance.

Verse 19. The wording of this verse must not mislead us. It does not mean to be a positive conclusion independent of the authority of Moses. It is made in connection with the previous wish that they be allowed to take their possession on this side.

Verses 20-23. This explanation satisfied Moses and he granted their request. He does so with strong provisos according to their promise and also according to their logical duty in the case. After they have served their people until victory had been won, they might return to their chosen possessions with a clear case before God. He further warns them that if they should think to evade their duty and promise, it will not avail them anything, for their sin would "find them out."

Verse 24. He then endorses their plan to build shelters for their cattle and children as they said they would.

Verses 25-31. The whole agreement is rehearsed in the ears of Joshua, and the priest, and made them understand the terms. Also the tribes were in hearing at the rehearsal and heard Moses say that if they did not go across to fight, they could not have this land on the east side. They would have to take their chances for land on the west side. To all this the tribes again agreed.

Verse 32. This language shows that the land of Canaan was restricted to the part across the Jordan. Since the promised land was greater than the land of Canaan, we can see the two and half tribes were clear of any ingratitude in wanting to have their inheritance on the east side. Besides, when Moses misunderstood their motive and was chastising them, he never intimated there was anything wrong in their wanting to reside over on the east of Jordan. See Gen. 15: 18 for description of the promised land.

Verse 33. The reader will recall that when the children of Israel were in their journey they encountered the lands of Sihon and Og, and were attacked by these kings. The Lord fought for them and gave them the lands of the heathen. (Chap. 21; 24; 35.)

Verses 34-42. After arriving at an understanding with Moses, these tribes went to work to build (rebuild) these cities for the use of their people, while they are with their brethren warring against the heathen on the other side.

NUMBERS 33

Verse 1. *These are the journeys.* This chapter as a whole gives the record of the journeys of the Israelites from Egypt to the Jordan. Not all of the places they stopped are named but enough of them are so that a person can trace their route on a map.

Verse 2. Moses wrote the log as here seen. He wrote it by inspiration, but also their journeys were "by the commandment of the Lord." It will not be useful in a work such as the present to make special mention of all the places. No other history is connected with many of them; the mere mention of the name would add no information. We will group a number of them together that will include places or persons of note.

Verse 3. Rameses gives the location of the Israelites, before departing from the land of Egypt. They left there on the fifteenth of the first month. The passover was kept on the 14th. We shall realize that several million people could not pack and get started very soon, after being commanded, at midnight, to do so. Therefore, by the time they got a good start out of the land it was the fifteenth. And the Egyptians saw them leave. They were too busy with the number of deaths in their own families to bother about trying to hinder them now.

Verse 4. The Egyptians must have about finished the major work of disposing of their dead and thus had opportunity to see them in their movements. They had but newly finished the distressing task and were not in position of body or mind to make any stir as yet.

Verses 5-7. After leaving Rameses their first important stop was Pihahiroth, a place not far from the Red Sea. The history of the events near, and in, the sea is not the subject of Moses here, so that is ommitted.

Verse 8. An interesting observation on the brevity of the Bible in some places may be made here. "Passed through the midst of the sea," is a short account of what it took the 14th chapter to detail. The first stop of importance after crossing, was at Marah. Again the distressing experience of the stop is not mentioned.

Verses 9, 10. The Red Sea was the name of the body of water in general; not just that of the small arms that project upward in northwest and northeast fashion. This will account for what might be confusion on the name and place.

Verse 11. Attention of the reader is invited to this name Sin. It must not be confused with Zin which was a different wilderness. The latter was nearer the end of their wandering and not far from the Midianite country. The former was near the mountain of Sinai.

Verses 12-14. Rephidim was the place where they complained for want of water. And Moses was here told to smite the rock which brought forth drinking water. This event is not mentioned here. It is recorded in Ex. 17th chapter.

Verse 15. The brevity of the narrative is certainly seen here in that only a short verse is devoted to this place of Sinai whereas they spent a year at the place. That history is to be seen in other places. The journeys of the congregation constituted the subject of this portion of the Mosaic writing.

Verses 16-35. This whole paragraph is put down in the manner explained in first and second verses of the chapter.

Verse 36. This mentions the wilderness spoken about in verse 11, and should be distinguished from the wilderness of Sin. It is obvious that the last named place has a significant name only by coincidence, and with no particular meaning.

Verse 37. They pitched in the *edge* of Edom. This is significant. Reference to chapter 20: 21 will explain it was because Israel was not permitted to go through that land.

Verse 38. Take note of the fortieth year, as the year of Aaron's death. That will impress the reader with the fact that they are very near their journey's end since we know that it was in the same year that Moses died. He will survive his brother some months, because the Lord has need of him a little while yet.

Verse 39. Readers who are marking their books should include this verse as it gives the age of Aaron and will be considered in connection with that of Moses later.

Verse 40. The brevity of this verse is another interesting instance of the method of the sacred scripture. Reference to chapter 21: 1-3 will show the circumstances as one where the children of Israel made a vow to God under the law in Lev. 27: 29 and how they carried out that vow.

Verses 41-47. This paragraph stops at the place where Moses was called to take a look at the land to which the congregation was traveling, but which he was not to enter.

Verses 48, 49. This paragraph brings them to the place where they are in our present studies of their experiences, and where they had so much to go through before being led across the Jordan.

Verses 50-53. Most of this paragraph had been delivered to them before, but the subject is so great and the people are so forgetful that repetition was necessary. The pictures mentioned here were figures carved on walls or stones or other surfaces and used as objects of worship. They were like the carving of a cameo in our times.

Verse 54. They were commanded to decide the division of the land as to the various tribes by the method of the lot. When this procedure is used by man today it is merely a "chance" performance and does not make any logical conclusion. When the Lord resorts to such method he will see to it that the proper conclusion is reached. Such is the meaning of the statement in Prov. 16: 33. This was simply another of the incidences mentioned by Paul in Heb. 1: 1.

Verse 55. The awful prediction and warning of this verse may be considered a history, in the form of prophecy, of the book of Judges. Their past experiences should have taught them that God always meant what he said and said what he meant. We will see that such lesson was missed by the nation and they had to learn it in pain.

Verse 56. While the threat in this verse had a variety of fulfillment yet the outstanding one was in their being taken into captivity. God had promised to drive out the heathen nations from the land. Instead, he drove out his people through the instrumentality of other heathen nations, the Assyrians and Babylonians.

NUMBERS 34

Verses 1, 2. The land of Canaan is here spoken of as an inheritance falling to the people of God. We always think of inheritance as being something actually being bestowed on a person to which he was already entitled. That is the case here. God had previously given this land to them through their great ancestor, Abram. (Gen. 12: 7.) Thus, when they go over and fight for the possession, it will be a warfare of defence, battling for the possession of property already rightfully theirs, but being occupied by people of foreign origin.

Verses 3, 4. "Quarter" and "border" are words meanng, in general, the limits or lines dividing off the land considered. The details of these various descriptions of said borders may be seen in any good map of the country.

Verse 5. Starting from the place last named in the preceding paragraph the line struck out in a curve (compass) until it joined with the "river of Egypt." This name should not mislead the reader. It was the name of a small stream flowing in a northwesterly direction, into the sea, and forming the southern boundary of the land.

Verse 6. The "great sea" here is the Mediterranean Sea, which formed the western line of the promised land.

Verses 7-12. As stated a number of times previously, a distinction must always be made between the "promised land" and the land of Canaan. Because of this distinctive fact, the two are sometimes confusing. Particularly so because the distinction is not specifically made by the writers in the scriptures. On a subject such as the geographical descriptions of the land the best information we can obtain is from some good map that has been made by men who have traveled in the country. See the Preface on this idea of consulting works of reference now in existence. Another observation that should be made in the present connection is that the land as a whole is being bounded in above description. The divisions among the tribes come later on.

Verse 13. The explanation that Moses gave the people in this verse verifies the remarks of the preceding paragraph, for it is explained here that the outline recorded, pertained only to the possession of the nine and a half tribes who were to settle on the west of the Jordan.

Verses 14, 15. The two and a half tribes are said here to "have received" their inheritance on "this side" or east side as they were still on that side. Since their operations had already brought the land under subjugation to the children of Israel, it might well be spoken of as having been received.

Verses 16-18. It is always practical to have work done in an orderly manner. That result can be accomplished by assigning to men their specific task. Thus in the matter of dividing the land among the tribes it was directed that a man be selected from each tribe for the work. The whole thing would be under the supervision of Eleazar the priest and Joshua their next leader.

Verses 19-29. This paragraph simply names the men from the tribes selected to do the work outlined in foregoing verses.

NUMBERS 35

Verse 1. It is always well to keep our "bearings" when following a narrative. Thus we note that the congregation is at its last stand before crossing Jordan. It is just opposite Jericho and in the plains of Moab.

Verse 2. It has already been learned that the tribe of Levi was not numbered with the other tribes because of their exclusive appointments concerning the tabernacle. Today the suburbs of a city are the outskirts of the unit or the residential districts. In other words, the edges of the city, but still a part of it. The word in the scriptures has a different meaning. It is from MIGRASHAH and defined "a suburb (i. e. open country whither flocks are driven for pasture), hence the area around a building, or margin of the sea."—Strong.

Verse 3. Since the Levites had no single unit or landed estate as a whole they must have cities in which to dwell. The suburbs were for the use of their cattle and beasts in general. Question might arise as to what use they had for such place for cattle since they were not to engage in gainful occupation. There is nothing said about their reproducing these things. The other tribes were required to give to the Levites a tenth of their increase and this included cattle. These were for the personal use and consumption of the tribe. They needed a place to keep them from one time of tithing to another, and these suburbs were for that purpose.

Verses 4, 5. Any person knows that one thousand cubits and two thousand cubits are not the same. The cities were not required to remain just the exact size they happened to have at the time of being possessed. If times of prosperity should come and the city needed to be enlarged, there must be room for expansion without having to encroach upon the pasture land immediately joining the walls of the city. Therefore, they were to measure a distance of one thousand cubits from the wall all around and there begin the pasture land. The strip of land for the cattle was to be a thousand cubits. That would make the total measurement all round, including the suburbs or pasture land, two thousand cubits from the walls on all sides.

Verses 6, 7. The total number of cities that were to be given to the Levites was forty-and-eight with their suburbs. Of these there were six set apart to be cities of refuge. These cities were scattered among the possessions of the twelve tribes and taken from them for the exclusive possession of the special tribe.

Verse 8. While these forty eight cities were taken from all the tribes and were scattered variously over the territory as a whole, the appropriation was made according to the extent of the possessions of any given tribe.

Verses 9-11. The system given under Moses is sometimes called a "theocracy." That means "governed by the Lord." The only government the Israelites had for either their religious or civil guidance was the law of Moses. For this reason some provisions of the system look more like a civil government with its penal and punitive statutes, than like a religious system. Among the conditions arising among men living in a community is that of death, caused by one man toward another. The law of capital punishment given in Gen. 9: 6 required that when one man killed another he must be punished with death. It is known that a killing might not always be deliberate and hence would not come under the heading of murder. Therefore, it was necessary to make some provision for the protection of the killer, who was not guilty of murder. That was the purpose of these cities of refuge.

Verse 12. The avenger of the killing was the brother or near kinsman of the man killed. (Gen. 9: 5.) Theoretically, he had the lawful right to slay any man who killed his brother. Yet the killer might not be a murderer and thus not deserve any punishment. As protection from the vengeance of the executioner the city of refuge was open to him. He must be admitted therein and held until he has opportunity to be heard before the congregation.

Verses 13, 14. The location of three cities on either side of Jordan was because two and a half tribes of the children of Israel would be living over there, and there were times when it would be difficult, if not impossible to cross the Jordan. Therefore, the merciful provision was made that a killer would have the easiest possible means of protection until he could have a fair trial.

Verse 15. It is the principle of all civilized governments that a foreigner who may be sojourning in the land must be obedient to the laws of that land. By the same token he should be entitled to the protection of that land. Hence these cities of refuge were for the benefit of all classes as to citizenship.

Verses 16-18. The reader will note a difference is made between a manslayer and a murderer. That distinction is just and should be observed today. All murder is killing but not all killing is murder. This distinction is ignored by the sentimentalists who cry out against capital punishment for murder. They try to make the law of God contradict itself because it condemns murder, yet commands the death of the murderer. This subject is treated at length at Gen. 9: 6.

Verse 19. As to who was to avenge the slaying, the reference has already been made to Gen. 9: 5. Note here that he was authorized to slay the other man "when he meeteth him." No opportunity was provided for explanation then. Therefore, the city of refuge was provided for his protection until the guilt or innocence had been determined by the congregation. Of course a man having killed another, whether deliberately or otherwise, would not lose any time trying to get to one of these cities for refuge from the avenger. That is why the word "flee" is used here and also why Paul used the word "fled" in Heb. 6: 18, when considering the refuge provided for the sinner if we will flee to the salvation offered in Christ.

Verses 20, 21. This paragraph describes a murderer. He is one who intended to kill the other and was prompted by the motive of hate. He is a murderer and not merely a manslayer. He was to be punished with death.

Verses 22, 23. Now the man who was killed under circumstances here described was just as certainly slain as was possible for a man to be, but the question of guilt is what was to be considered. If the killing was not deliberate, then it was not murder.

Verse 24. The court having jurisdiction in the trial of the slayer was the congregation, and he must be taken from the city of refuge to which he had fled, to the assembling place, and there tried by the officers in power. They must decide whether the killing was deliberate and therefore was murder, or was not deliberate and thus not murder. After reaching their conclusion they must deal with the case as follows.

Verse 25. Having found the man not guilty of murder, he must be escorted back to the city of refuge to which he had fled. This must be done under protection from the revenger of blood. The only means of safety from this revenger for the present is the protection of the city of refuge. The revenger of blood was never permitted to enter the city to hunt out the slayer, but there was a limit to the time he was required to remain in the city, and that was until the death of the High Priest that was in service at the time.

Verses 26-28. If at any time in course of the life of that High Priest the slayer should venture to go outside of the city he would endanger himself. If the revenger of blood found him out there he was authorized to kill him. This was regardless of the fact that he had been found not guilty of murder by the congregation. If the man were found guilty of murder by the congregation, he was to be turned over directly to the revenger of blood for execution.

Verses 29, 30. The special item in this passage is that it required more than one witness to prove a man guilty of murder. Two men might be out together, but with no one else in sight. One of them might kill the other. Afterward the revenger of blood would learn about it. Then he would have the power to slay the surviving one, if he caught him out, regardless of guilt or innocence. Even if the "brother" of the slain man were present on the occasion the killer might outrun him and reach the city of refuge. When brought to the congregation the revenger could be used as a witness. Since there would be no question of fact as to the killing the thing to be settled would be the motive. Here is where more than one witness must be required. Previous knowledge of threats or intimations of bodily harm might prove the guilty mind of the killer and that would prove him a murderer.

Verses 31, 32. Fines for petty offences may be regarded as just punishment. In the case of a murderer, no amount of money can be accepted in place of the punishment required, that is the death of the murderer.

Verses 33, 34. Here is a serious paragraph in the declarations of God. It is not merely an arbitrary law, or edict, issued by the Lord but a statement of a positive truth. The land that allows a murderer to live is a polluted land. It has the stain of blood on it. The only way that stain con be removed is by the blood of the one guilty of the murder. Hence, any court or jury that finds a man guilty of murder and then does not require that the murderer be put to death is itself guilty of murder. I could not conscientiously sentence a man guilty of murder, to any kind of punishment except capital punishment. Anything less is an insult to God, in whose image every man has been created, which fact is the divine basis of, and motive for, capital punishment for murder.

NUMBERS 36

Verses 1-4. In order to understand this paragraph the reader should turn back to chapter 27: 1-11 and read carefully the provision that was made then on behalf of these women who had been bereft of the men who should have inherited land. An addition was made in the provision for land by giving these women what would have been possessed by the men. Now a difficulty seemed to come to these later men of the tribe. They fear that the favor extended to the women to retain the land might become strictly a personal possession of theirs. Afterwards they might decide to marry outside of the tribe. In that case the property would become alienated from its original tribe and that was objectionable in their view of the matter. It was likewise objectionable to the Lord. Therefore, he now ordains that if these women wish to retain the property, they must marry within their own tribe so that the land would not pass from one tribe to another.

Verse 5, 6. This is the decree of God as referred to in close of preceding paragraph. God wished to keep the tribal distinctions intact and thus would not permit the lines to be interrupted through the intermarriages of the members thereof.

Verse 7. The fathers referred to in this verse meant the ones who were heads of the tribes at the time of distribution of the land. They must be respected in the matter of the land as well as in other matters.

Verse 8. This law was not meant especially as a curb on the choice of men with whom marriage might be contracted, but if they desired to retain their land they must marry within the tribe of their fathers. Otherwise, they would forfeit their land.

Verse 9. Nothing new in this verse, but the importance of the ordinance is seen in that it is repeated so frequently. That is a circumstance to be noted in numerous places in the scriptures.

Verses 10-12. It is gratifying to know these daughters obeyed the Lord in this matter. Many times we see people disregard the law of God when the subject of marriage is under consideration. However, since these women could carry out the natural inclination for marriage and at the same time do so in a way not to lose their property, perhaps the consideration was partly of personal motive as well as desire to please God.

Verse 13. Once more we see the important thought brought forth that the laws and commandments placed over the children of Israel were from the Lord. They were commanded "by the hand of Moses." This ought to settle the question of the authority of Moses in the Old Testament.

DEUTERONOMY 1

General remarks. The books of the Old Testament were written in Hebrew but the titles are Greek words, except when the names of the writers are used. The title of this book is from two Greek words. DEUTEROS which means "the second" and NOMOS which means "a law."—Liddell & Scott. Hence the popular definition, "repetition of law," is correct as a title. The contents of the book will justify the word. Although much new matter will be found in it, yet much also is practically the same as what the people had been told before. The first few chapters will be found to be a recital of the Jews' history after leaving Egypt and coming on down to their arrival in the plains of Moab.

Verse 1. The congregation is located near the Jordan and not far from the spot where they will cross when the time comes for their final move against the enemy.

Verse 2. The actual time they used in going from Horeb, or Sinai, to the place from which the twelve spies were sent was about a year. The time that would have been necessary at the ordinary rate of travel for those days was eleven days. Thus it can be seen that God wanted them to have some experience in wilderness travel before entering their final goal. Had they been submissive to God's will, they would have ended their journeys at Kadesh-barnea; however, after their sin at that place, the Lord decreed 38 years more of wandering.

Verse 3. Very definite date is given here and shows that it will be no more than two months until they cross over. Once again we have the significant statement that what Moses is about to say to the people is what the Lord commanded him to say.

Verse 4. As the congregation was approaching their last stand before the invasion, the people mentioned here disputed their advance and were repulsed. This bit of history is inserted to complete the narrative to the time and place of the speech which makes up this fifth book of the Bible.

Verse 5. According to Strong the word "law" here is from a word that is derived from still another which means "to teach." Thus the word as used in the scriptures is broad enough that it includes any kind of discourse that has teaching in it, whether the express commands for action or any other subject-matter that might be related to human actions. With that view of the word we can easily see why history is included.

Verses 6, 7. The time of the movement here mentioned was after their work and experience at Horeb had been completed according to God's will and he wished them to proceed to the completion of the great scheme laid out for them. The places mentioned in the verse just give a few of the spots they should have passed en route to the land that was their objective. Mention of the Euphrates is perfectly in harmony with the original plan that God had laid out for them had they been obedient.

Verse 8. The land to which they were traveling was given to their ancestors and now it is theirs by right of inheritance. They will have to fight for possession since it is being occupied by the heathen nations.

Verses 9-12. There is much involved in this paragraph that is not detailed here. The reader may refer to Ex. 18 and Num. 11 and read the more complex account of the situation. It includes the advice of Jethro and the acceptance by the Lord of the plan.

Verses 13-15. This paragraph recites the carrying out of the advice mentioned in preceding one. The plan of cooperation between Moses and the leading men of the congregation was arranged and finally became an integral part of the Mosaic system.

Verse 16. Though the work of caring for the various disputes was spread out among the leaders of the people, it must not be thought that authority was taken from Moses and divided among them. All of their work had to be under the jurisdiction of the inspired law-giver, Moses, and all disputes would finally have to be decided by him if not settled before. Also, it should be understood this referred to matters arising between persons as to their personal dealings with each other. It would have no bearing on any of the ordinances or statutes of the law. That was still vested in Moses as the law giver and mediator for the people. Even these personal matters were to be handled according to principles set forth by their earthly head, Moses.

Verses 17, 18. This passage is like the teaching in the New Testament that says God is no respecter of persons. (Acts 10: 34.) That means that one's decision in any matter should not be influenced by personal regard for either of the disputants but that it should be solely on the basis of what is right. *The judgment is God's.* This does not mean they were inspired in their judgment, but that they must act with regard to God. An excellent comment on this thought is worded in the text in 2 Chr. 19: 6 which will be quoted here: "For ye judge not for man, but for the Lord." If men would keep God in mind always when acting between brethren in disputes, their decisions often would be different from what they are.

Verses 19, 20. The wilderness here is the territory they traversed between Horeb and Kadesh. The word "mountain" is often used figuratively and also is used generally of the condition of the country. One meaning of the word is "hill country" and is so rendered in the R. V. Thus, in this paragraph, it does not refer to any special mountain. The Amorites were undoubtedly originally a specific people, but their characteristics of iniquity were so strong that the term finally came to be used to designate all or many of the wild clans occupying the country. The word is so used in Gen. 15: 16, and it is so used in the passage now under consideration.

Verses 21-23. This passage throws much light on Num. 13: 1, 2 and should always be considered in connection with that place. It is always proper to consider everything the scriptures say on any subject before forming a final conclusion.

Verses 24, 25. This is another instance of the brevity of the scriptures. The events of the return of the spies, their report, and following complaint of the congregation are here implied. That is recorded in Num. 13 and 14.

Verses 26, 27. One of their most far-reaching murmurings is the subject of this passage. See above references to scriptures for details.

Verse 28. Some cities in those days were walled as a fortification against the enemy. The walls of these cities are described as being "up to heaven," or the sky, which is to be understood figuratively. The thought is that they were occupied by the Anakims, a group of giants living in the country.

Verses 29-31. The use of the personal pronoun should not be misunderstood. It refers to the congregation as such and not personally to the people to whom he was speaking. The men who were personally guilty of the mistakes being told about here are all dead, but the congregation as a whole is still before Moses. It is in that light we should understand the assurances which Moses said he had given about their ability to conquer the country, because God would be with them.

Verse 32. Lest the reader have the wrong impression of the people to whom Moses is actually speaking, be sure to consider the thoughts offered in preceding paragraph.

Verse 33. The guidance of God by use of the pillar of fire by night and the cloud by day made their success a sure thing. In spite of all this evidence the congregation (as a whole) rebelled against the divine directions.

Verses 34-36. The men included in the decree of God not to let them enter the land of the promise were the men of war as well as the spies. There were two of them who were exceptions, Caleb and Joshua, who will be mentioned later. The reason given for these exceptions is that they "wholly followed the Lord."

Verse 37. We generally think of "sake" as meaning "on behalf of." It here means "on account of" and refers to the noted instance in which Moses made the great mistake of his life, which mistake cost him his entrance to the land of Canaan. The mistake was brought about by a circumstance caused by the people.

Verse 38. At the time the announcement was made to Moses that he should not be allowed to enter the land in the conquest, Joshua was a faithful servant under him. Then Moses was informed that this same Joshua would take his place as leader. Because of that he was told to encourage Joshua.

Verse 39. The very ones who the murmurers claimed would die in the wilderness were still alive, and the ones making the complaint were all dead. This shows the weakness of man's judgment, especially when he thinks to judge against the Lord.

Verse 40. After leaving Kadesh-barnea they are said to have traveled by way of the Red Sea. The reader will again be reminded that the larger body of water called the Red Sea had two arms projecting northward and either of these arms would be referred to under the name of the body as a whole. This should always be remembered when in doubt about locations of the congregation.

Verse 41. The people saw the mistake of their rashness and expressed desire to attack the land. They even made military preparations in that they girded on every man his war weapons. Often it happens that man will realize his mistake after it is done and then perhaps think he can remove all effects by some rash action.

Verse 42. It is too late now to change their hasty conclusions. The decree of God has gone out and he will not be with them in their attempt. It should have been evident beforehand that it would be a failure.

Verse 43. In spite of the divine injunction, they went up. Note the strange workings of humankind. Before, when it was God's will that they go up against the land, they feared it would be a failure. Now, when God positively tells them he will not be with them, they think they can succeed regardless. The word "presumptuously" means to go with the spirit of defiance, to be determined to go even though they knew they were forbidden to do so, to go insolently or daringly.

Verse 44. It turned out just as they had been warned. The Amorites, wicked people of the rough country, repelled them with destruction and great humiliation.

Verse 45. They vainly looked to the Lord for sympathy but received none. They were not entitled to it because of their sin of presumption.

Verse 46. This verse is worded very unusually but the meaning is this: The record of their journeys was already made (Num. 33: 1) and that record would be open for perusal in due time. Moses makes this statement which is as if he said, "The number of days ye abode in Kadesh is a matter of record."

DEUTERONOMY 2

Verse 1. After the events in connection with the spies' report, the congregation took up their long journey that was destined to continue thirty-eight years. They surrounded Mount Seir, the country belonging to Edom, since that name was applied to him, another name for Esau. They would not invade it because of his relation to Abram.

Verses 2, 3. As stated above, they have been occupying the country surrounding that of Seir. They have been in that place long enough.

Verse 4. Now they are directed to get nearer the actual land. The coast means the edge of his territory. They are informed that the Edomites, descendants of Esau, will be afraid of them. They are not to be disturbed by this fact. Nations sometimes attack the ones of whom they are afraid. God means for them to understand such fear will not cause any interference for them.

Verse 5. Notwithstanding, the Edomites will be in fear at the approach of Israel, yet they will not make any attack. Neither may the Israelites meddle with the land of the Edomites, for God has already given that area to Esau's descendants for possession.

Verse 6. They were allowed to be on friendly terms with them and trade with them, paying for what they obtained.

Verse 7. In this verse Moses breaks from the thread of his account and comes to their present date, which is at the end of the forty years. It is a sort of reflection over the facts as support of the claim made in verse 6, that is, the claim implied in that they were ordered to pay for what they got, which they could not have done had they not been prosperous.

Verses 8, 9. In their next move they came near the region occupied by the Moabites. Of course, they did not at that time enter the country. That took place at the close of their journeys. At the time now being considered they might have been prompted to enter it. The Lord charges them not to meddle with Moab nor to think of taking their land. It had been given to them in deference to their ancestor Lot.

Verses 10-12. This paragraph merely relates to some earlier history in which these heathen races had occupied the territory but had been subjugated by the people near to the Lord and had taken over that area by the Lord's encouragement.

Verses 13-15. This is another big jump in history. From Kadesh, the place of the spies, to the place near where the congregation is now located, the time consumed was thirty-eight years. That unusually slow progress of the nation was because of the hand of the Lord. It was to give time for the rebellious group among them to be consumed and strewn along the way in the wilderness.

Verses 16-19. The same reason was assigned for the warning of treatment of the Ammonites as in the case of Moab. Both peoples were descended from Lot, and God would not let the Israelites molest them.

Verses 20-23. This paragraph is similar to verses 10-12 and calls for like note.

Verses 24, 25. After passing near the land of the Ammonites, they came near that of Sihon. He was king of another group of heathen classed as an Amorite. Assurances are given from God that Sihon's territory will fall to the children of Israel. It is well to observe here that, when the two and half tribes requested their part of the possessions to be on the east of Jordan, they included this territory we are reading about. We should also understand that the present possession of the territory is that of military occupation, for they are passing on soon to other regions. As further encouragement for the congregation, God said he had caused the nations to be in dread of the approach of the Israelites.

Verses 26-29. Before taking over the country of Sihon, Moses sent messengers offering to pass through his territory peaceably and agreeing not to forage but to pay for all things used. This kind of bargain had been offered to the Edomites and a friendly pact had been formed.

Verse 30. Sihon refused to enter the agreement offered him. The Lord hardened his heart, with the result that he came out with an army to oppose the movements of the children of Israel. It was just from every standpoint for his heart to be hardened or made obstinate. He was already a wicked king and his moral character was not made any worse by being used in this way to open up more of the previously titled property of God's people. Therefore, when it is gone through with, the property which the Israelites got from the people of Sihon was the rightful spoil of war.

Verses 31-36. This paragraph is a recital of the operations against Sihon in which his territory was taken by the children of Israel after they had slain him and all his people. They did not destroy the cattle, because of their usefulness, but they took such for their spoils of war according to the word of the Lord.

Verse 37. Because of the nearness of the land of Ammon to that of Sihon, the writer considers it well to make the exception again of that territory. It was not taken over, because of respect for the memory of Lot, the nephew of Abraham.

DEUTERONOMY 3

Verses 1-4. Since Moses, in this memorable speech, is rehearsing the history of the nation, both its favorable and unfavorable experiences, we read of many incidences previously related. These heathen kings, Sihon and Og, were so outstanding that they are referred to frequently by both secular and religious writers.

Verse 5. In some places the cities are said to be fenced. In others they are said to be walled. In this place both words are used. Thus we are to understand that when we read of a city being fenced we are to understand it to mean it is walled and prepared to resist siege. All such cities of Og were taken besides many towns that were unwalled. There is no point in making much distinction between city and town, for the same Hebrew word is used for both. The context must be considered when we wish to learn the difference, if any, in some cases. The size of the place does not always matter. Rather its importance, from location or otherwise, as a military post will count most of all.

Verse 6. There would be no advantage to these women and children surviving the death of their men; therefore, it was logical to remove them all from the scene.

Verses 7-10. The two Amorite kings are the ones already named, Sihon and Og. All of their territory was confiscated by the children of Israel.

Verse 11. Since a man would not likely provide himself a bed far beyond his bodily needs it indicates the size of the giant to describe his bedstead. It needed to be made of iron for strength. Generally speaking a cubit in scripture is 18 inches. Therefore this bed was 13½ feet long and 6 feet wide. That does not give us the specific length of the giant's body but does give a significant suggestion. The fact that he was conquered by ordinary men is proof that human strength is no item in a conflict against the Lord or his people.

Verses 12, 13. The primary account of this gift is in Num. 32. They saw this land and desired it. The same was given to them on conditions named in that chapter.

Verses 14-17. When a particular territory was assigned to a unit of God's people, the actual taking of it would be supervised by certain individuals within that unit. Hence the lines of this paragraph.

Verse 18. Again we have the idea that the land had been given to the children of Israel, and now it was for them to take possession. These tribes were told to go over "before" their brethren. That word does not necessarily mean that they were to precede the others. But that they were to be in sight of them. This is significant, since there had been a question in the beginning as to their motive in asking for possession on the east side. Now if they are seen by the other brethren in an armed condition and going along with them, no doubt can be entertained.

Verse 19. Nothing would be gained by forcing the families and the cattle to go along in the march. They would be an encumbrance. Hence they were told to remain in the place where they were to be located at last.

Verse 20. Interest in the congregation as a whole is taught in this verse. "Rest" was to be given their brethren "as well as you." They must fight for the benefit of the common good.

Verses 21, 22. The preliminary experiences they had gone through in subduing the kings, Sihon and Og, are referred to by Moses as basis for encouraging Joshua in the task before him. He is thus commanded by Moses to go on in the leadership.

Verses 23-25. To the mind of the writer this is one of the most pathetic passages in the life of Moses. After all the years of faithful watching and leading, and after the many repetitions of the bright prospect held out to the congregation, now he is not to enjoy the fruit of it himself. But its very seriousness of sympathy should impress us with the further seriousness of rebelling against any one of God's laws. In spite of all the great work Moses had done, he placed himself ahead of the Lord at the rock. The first commandment of the decalogue forbade having any other god before the Lord. By taking honor to himself that belonged to God, that very sin was committed, and it cost Moses his right to enter the land of Canaan.

Verse 26. *For your sakes.* Not on behalf of them but on their account. They had clamored for water and that brought up the occasion in which Moses made the great mistake of his life. He is told to drop the subject and never mention it again.

Verse 27. Here is an informative passage. Moses is already east of the Jordan and thus in a part of the promised land. Yet he was told to look in the four directions. The purpose of climbing the mountain was that he might have sight of the territory. The idea should be noted that, while all of the domain in sight was included in the "promise," yet the capital part was west of the Jordan. Hence it was necessary for the congregation to reach that point in order to carry out their full duty in fighting for possession of their own.

Verse 28. There is no opportunity for sulking and no indication that Moses was inclined to. He was not only to charge Joshua, but to encourage him for the great work of completing the mission begun forty years before.

Verse 29. This is a general statement of their location at this time, and it is identified by saying it is against or near the place named in this verse. It was just east of the Jordan and opposite the place where they will finally attack.

DEUTERONOMY 4

Verse 1. In practical use there is very little difference between statute and judgment. But the distinction is that the former means an enactment. The latter is a verdict. That is, a statute is a fixed law and made independent of any specific instance of application. While a judgment is a decision that might have been occasioned by some crisis that had not been provided for. After having ruled over the people for forty years, which included so many and varied experiences, there would have accumulated by this time a great many of both kinds of law.

Verse 2. This command is like the one in Rev. 22: 18, 19. The sin of adding to or taking from the Word of God is not realized as it should be. It not only constitutes disobedience but implies that the One giving the command did not know his own business in forming a law. Not only that, but also that finite man can perfect what the Lord was not wise enough to do.

Verse 3. *Baal-Peor.* This is a compound word. Baal was the name of an imaginary god and Peor was the name of a mountain at which the idolatrous worship occurred.

Verses 4, 5. When the men of war sinned and were sentenced to linger in the wilderness to die, others were obedient to God and they are now with Moses and ready to go in and take possession of the land as promised. Here is another statement that what Moses taught the people had been commanded by the Lord. Hence the authority of the lawgiver is the same as that of God in these laws.

Verse 6. *Keep, and do.* Many times in the teaching given the Israelites they were told to observe and do, or observe to do. This is an important expression. Many people may observe the law far enough to memorize it and be able to quote it. That is not enough. It must be both observed and obeyed.

Verses 7, 8. The contrast is made, favoring the nation of the Israelites, and is based on the God who is near his people. Near enough to see and hear their needs and cries. And powerful enough to meet any emergency that could arise.

Verse 9. Forgetfulness is a common weakness of man. They are here warned not to forget what they have seen and heard. Not only so, but they must tell it to their children who have not had the experiences their ancestors have had. This same kind of instruction is given parents under the law of Christ. (Eph. 6: 4.)

Verses 10, 11. This passage takes

us back to the beginning of the stay near the mount of Horeb. The people were actually directed to come within audible hearing of the voice of God. The purpose for this action was to impress them with the awe and dignity of the Lord. And the appearances of fire alternating with darkness, etc., were to add to the impressiveness.

Verse 12. Let the reader be sure to note this verse and bear in mind what has already been mentioned to him (Ex. 20: 1), that the ten commandments were spoken orally by the Lord before they were written on the tables. Of course, no man can see God's face and live. Hence the voice was actually his, but his presence was veiled.

Verse 13. The chief idea we should have fixed in our minds here is that the ten commandments which God wrote on the tables are called "his covenant." But they are not said to be the whole of his covenant as the sabbatarians teach.

Verse 14. The same God who wrote the ten commandments on the tables is the one who commanded Moses to do some teaching. Not all of the law of God could be written on the tables of stone, which were so small that a man could carry both in his hands. Thus it was necessary to have numerous items of government in addition to the ten which were on the stones. God did not propose writing them, but employed Moses for that work.

When Moses did that writing and delivered same to the people, or whenever he spoke to them orally as repeating the law of God, it had the same weight and authority as the lines written by the finger of God on the tables. To make a distinction between the authority of one part of the law, and the other part, is to say that God has more authority at one time than he has at another. That is rebellion and infiidelity.

Verse 15. While they heard the voice of God at the mount, yet they did not see anything that indicated the form of the one speaking. Therefore, it would be pure speculation as well as arrogance to make an image and pretend it to be a likeness of the Lord.

Verses 16-18. This passage embraces one of the three forms of idolatory that prevailed in olden times, that of the artificial. They used wood and metals and stone and made the images in what they conceived to be the form of the gods. It was illogical to do so because they had never seen God and hence did not know what form to make for him, even were it right to think of doing so.

Verse 19. This is a reference to another of the prevailing forms of idolatry, that of the natural, or worship of things in nature. Only the inanimate objects are named here. This form of idolatry included worship of animals and fishes and trees.

Verse 20. The figurative expression "iron furnace" in reference to Egypt is doubtless in connection with the burning bush (Ex. 3: 2), where the unusual condition obtained of the fire burning, yet not consuming. The people of God were sorely tried in Egypt and were made to burn with persecution. Yet they were not consumed and the fact should have impressed them with the oversight which was caring for them. And the grand purpose the Lord had in all that wonderful oversight and deliverance was that they should be a "people of inheritance." This is another expression looking back to the promise made in Gen. 12: 7. Having given the land by promise, God wished to have a separate people to inherit the land already given through the great ancestor.

Verses 21, 22. In several places Moses told them the Lord was angry with him for their sakes or on their account. This was not in the spirit of a taunt as the disposition of meekness attributed to him would not allow it. But if God would so bitterly punish the lawgiver for an act occasioned by the people, he certainly will punish the people themselves if they be guilty of sin. Therefore, they should be careful and be able to go across, after Moses has died, and possess the land.

Verses 23, 24. The warning given in connection with the first commandment is repeated here with the specification that God is jealous. Because of his jealousy he will burn with indignation those who dare to put some other God between him and them. They might do this if they should forget the holy covenant.

Verses 25-27. This warning is a form of threat or prediction of the tragic end of the national greatness at the time of this prediction.

Verse 28. Another fact often overlooked is that while in captivity they were not allowed to worship God as a nation. Certain individuals, like

Daniel and his three companions, and others, were exempted from serving idols while in captivity. But the people as a whole were compelled to go right on while in captivity and follow the practice of idolatry which was the cause of their national downfall. This great fact will be pointed out more in detail when we get to the prophecies.

Verses 29-31. This promise of restoration to God's favor also applied to certain individuals and not to the nation as a whole. It also will be given detailed explanation at the proper place in the study of the prophecies.

Verse 32, 33. This is a general reminder of the partiality which God had shown this people in the past, and their memory is called upon to make the observation. They had been given experiences unequalled by any other people on earth.

Verse 34. This is a more specific citation of the experiences referred to in preceding paragraph. The two nations meant in this verse, are the Israelites and the Egyptians. The signs and other demonstrations refer to the plagues on Egyptians.

Verses 35, 36. By the coincidental facts of hearing God's voice orally, and then seeing the effects of the divine law among them, they should have been convinced that the God who spoke to them was unlike any other. It would be folly in the extreme to rebel against the divine word delivered to them.

Verse 37. The fathers here were Abraham, Isaac and Jacob. This is evident from the distinction between "thee" and the fathers. The twelve tribes with their twelve heads, the sons of Jacob, were the ones brought out from Egypt, therefore the fathers would have to mean ancestors before their time. This is the conclusion, then, that the love God had for the three patriarchs caused him to watch tenderly over the great people descended from them and see that they were released from their bondage.

Verses 38-40. With the foregoing facts and truths as motives they should surely be willing to adhere to the law given them and be obedient to all its requirements.

Verses 41-43. The purpose and use and location of these cities are explained in Numbers 35, which see.

Verse 44, 45. The word "testimonies" is added to the other two already defined. The principal idea of this word is something that had been established as true and right by some miraculous demonstration of power and authority.

Verses 46-49. This is simply a brief summing up of the places and persons the children of Israel subjugated at their approach to this domain of the country.

DEUTERONOMY 5

Verse 1. This verse might well be considered as an introduction to the chapter in which the ten commandments and other laws are going to be given. Here we have the importance of them indicated by the words "learn" and "keep" to "do."

Verses 2, 3. The fathers here are the same as in chapter 4: 37. This is significant. The ten commandments, which included the sabbath commandment, were not given to Abraham according to this passage. Hence those who claim the sabbath law to have been in force from the beginning are in error. That commandment was a part of the covenant which God made with the people represented by the ones to whom Moses was then talking, and originated after leaving Egypt.

Verse 4. To talk face to face as expressed here means that they heard the voice of God directly and did not merely have it relayed by Moses. (Ex. 20: 1.)

Verse 5. This verse has been properly enclosed in parentheses, for it refers to what happened after the voice of God had orally given the commandments that are soon to be recorded in this chapter. Hence this passage really should come after the reciting of these ten commandments. (Ex. 20. 19).

Verses 6-21. Since these ten commandments are commented upon in detail in Ex. 20, it is not necessary to take space here for repeating them. But as Josephus is an authoritative Jewish historian, it will not be amiss to quote here his version of the ten commandments as follows: "The first commandment teaches us that there is but one God, and that we ought to worship him only; the second commands us not to make the image of any living creature to worship it; the third, that we must not swear by God in a false matter; the fourth, that we must keep the 7th day, by resting from all sorts of work; the fifth, that we must honor our parents; the sixth, that we must abstain from murder; the seventh, that we must not commit adultery; the eighth, that we must not be guilty of theft; the ninth, that we must not bear false witness; the tenth, that we must not admit of the desire of any thing that is another's." *Antiquities*. 3-5-5. One helpful thing in this is the fact that Josephus wrote about the time of Christ. His works are many centuries old. Yet the enumeration of the ten commandments as he gives them is the same as in our Bibles, which shows that we have a true record of the old law as it existed at that time.

Verse 22. *And he added no more.* Of course the connection shows this means no more were added to the commandments that were to be written on the tables after being spoken orally to the people. Since any person can see that no detailed outline for their conduct could be seen in that list the conclusion is necessary that whatever further instruction they needed from God would have to be found in some place other than the tables of stone. This proves again that God did not intend the tables to be considered as the complete law for his people under that Dispensation.

Verses 23-26. This incident in their history has already been explained as being the reason why the ten commandments were placed on the tables of stone. The people were frightened at the audible voice of God and requested not to hear it again.

Verse 27. It was thus the request of the people to hear God through Moses and that was the manner of communication between God and the people after that. But it did not lessen the authority of the law any to be relayed by Moses.

Verse 28. *Well said.* This is from a word that means right or correct. The thought is that the agreement to hear the words of God even when spoken through the mediator is a right promise. Whether they keep the promise is another thing.

Verse 29. This is an implied doubt as to whether they will keep their word.

Verse 30. The foregoing conversations had taken place near the mount, to which place the people had been called from their tents. Now they are dismissed with the orders to return to their tents.

Verse 31. Standing near the Lord, Moses was to hear the things commanded of God for the conduct of the people and he was then to teach them.

Verses 32, 33. The preceding paragraph ended the present quotation and this is now the direct language of Moses to the people. In this he again makes the significant expression "observe to do." Merely observing will not suffice. They must also do. This would require them not only to learn and enter the ways of the Lord, but they must walk therein. To do so would bring them their well-being under the hand of God.

DEUTERONOMY 6

Verses 1, 2. They are here instructed to fear the Lord. This word has two shades of meaning. One is to be in terror, or be frightened at God, the other is to have respect for him. The latter meaning is used when the fear of God is commanded. A motive for their obedience in this passage is the promise of having their days prolonged. Not specially the length of their individual age in years, but their days being extended as a nation in the land promised to the fathers and now possessed by them.

Verse 3. Flowing with milk and honey meant that the land abounded therewith. The natural resources of the land were such as to encourage grazing and beekeeping.

Verse 4. Every great system of human activity or enterprise that sustains an existence has some fundamental fact or supposed fact (or truth) as its basis. On that basis everything in the system rests for support. On the existence or non-existence of that basis the whole system stands or falls. That basis for the Old Testament System was the fact stated in this verse. As long as the children of Irael believed and observed this statement, they had no time nor desire to worship other gods. Every instance of idolatry was an instance of disbelief in the truth of this basis. That is the reason that Paul in 1 Cor. 10 itemizes the various acts of disobedience of the nation, then sums the whole matter up in Heb. 3: 19 as unbelief. The corresponding basis for the New Testament system is in Matt. 16: 16.

Verses 5, 6. Very logically then, if they accept the fundamental fact of the preceding verse, they will love the true Lord wholeheartedly and will lay up in the heart the divine words.

Verse 7. If they have these words in their heart they will be prepared to teach them to others. It was specially important to teach them to their children. The copies of the law were scarce because written by hand. Hence the greater necessity of having them inscribed in the mind so as to transmit them to the other generatons. They were to talk about the laws of God in their homes and when they were journeying. Day and night they should be chiefly interested in the law of the Lord. This is what David said was the frame of mind of the righteous man. (Ps. 1: 1).

Verse 8. For comment on this language see Ex. 13: 6-10.

Verse 9. While the language of the preceding verse was figurative yet that of the present one is not. In view of the scarcity of copies of the law it was well to have parts of them inscribed in places of public observance for the benefit of those who needed the instruction.

Verses 10, 11. In this paragraph the writer leaves us in no doubt as to who are meant by the "fathers" for they are named in connection with the promise of the land.

Verse 12. Prosperity often blinds the eyes to the source of that very prosperity. So Moses here warns them against forgetting God after they take possession of a land of plenty and containing advantages upon which they have bestowed no labor.

Verse 13. Some things were allowed in the Old Testament that are even forbidden in the New. Swearing or making oaths was one. It is condemned in Matt. 5: 34-37 and in Jas. 5: 12. It is a sin for a Christian to make an oath.

Verses 14, 15. The prevalence of idolatry among the children of Israel was largely caused by their surroundings. All of the people were idolatrous and communicated that influence to those with whom they came in contact. That is the reason why the frequent warning against the practice; also the reason why the command was given to drive these nations from the country.

Verse 16. God cannot be induced to sin, for he cannot sin. But the word "tempt" here means "to test or try." It is a matter where the attributes of God are challenged, either as a direct motive of the action or as a logical application of it.

Verse 17. Diligence is a virtue necessary in all fields of activity. It is that quality of performance that requires both thought and action. To be active without thinking, is liable to serious results. To be thoughtful, and yet not active, is fruitless.

Verse 18. The all-important thing is to do that which is right "in the sight of the Lord." Man may approve of actions of which God would disapprove. Therefore it is necessary to consult the divine law in regard to all our conduct and if we do so and act accordingly the blessing of the Lord will follow.

Verse 19. One of the blessings to follow their obedience was the riddance of the enemy nations then infesting the promised land. And this blessing was to come on condition that they refuse to have fellowship with those nations.

Verses 20. 25. Even on the basis of obligation or gratitude, they should be willing to obey the Lord. Since the primary motive for these laws would be a matter of history occurring centuries before, it would be natural for the inquiring mind of the children to ask about it. Thus they were told to be prepared to inform them about their experience as a people in the land of Egypt. How the Lord brought them out with a mighty hand and gave them their freedom. This would obligate them to be obedient to the divine rule. And thus duty in the way of gratitude, also respect for the divine origin of true law, should prompt their obedience.

DEUTERONOMY 7

Verse 1. The nations mentioned were among the leading ones of the heathen then infesting the land but not the entire group. Seven, being a prominent signal for completeness, is used here to designate the idea that the people of God would be able to overcome all of their enemies. The word "nation" is from GOI and has been rendered in the A. V., by Gentile, heathen, nation, people. It thus does not necessarily have a political meaning but rather refers to a breed or race. The context must always determine whether it is used to refer to some particular group of people formed together into a government or political society.

Verse 2. This verse expresses in very strong language the conditions on which the Lord promised to give his people the land of Canaan and to drive out the foreign inhabitants. There was to be no compromise whatsoever.

Verse 3. Not only were they to have no diplomatic relations with these nations, but also no social ones, especially in the way of marriage.

Verse 4. The logical reason for God's severe edict against these nations is here given. It was not merely an act of hostility on the part of God from personal hatred, but because of their bad influence upon his people. That principle has always been a promnent item in the teaching of the Lord. In 1 Cor. 15: 33, with a revised rendering, Paul says "evil companionships corrupt good morals." When God's people associate with those who are not, the danger is, and the rule is, that the evil will overcome the good. For that reason the Lord's people should choose good people for their intimate friends.

Verse 5. This requires that they entirely destroy the instruments of idolatry. The groves were places where the idolaters frequently placed their idols, so that the very appearance of a grove or even one tree suggested the practice of the idol worship. Thus we often have reference made to idolatry by the mere mention of a tree or grove. The altars mentioned were built, on which to offer sacrifices to their heathen gods.

Verse 6. The word "special" is from an original that means "separate or exclusive." The thought is that God only had any claims upon this people and for that reason he demanded that they worship no other god but him.

Verse 7. One of the commonest motives of choice among human beings is that of numbers. Disregarding all principles involved, a person will frequently go to the side that has the greatest number. This might be true in some instances where no principle of right and wrong is at stake. But if mere success was the only thing in mind the larger numbers would be considered. That was not the motive for the choice God made of this people. At the time this people was laid hold of, and taken to himself, they numbered perhaps three million. That was a small number compared with many of the older nations then in existence.

Verse 8. The highest possible motive prompted the Lord to choose them: his love for them. Also his desire to keep the promise and oath that he had made to their fathers. For these considerations the Lord brought them out from Egyptian bondage.

Verse 9. *To a thousand generations.* Of course, we know that nothing like that many generations had literally passed between the time of the promise and its fulfillment. But God is so faithful that had that many have passed before the conditions required in the promise had come into existence, he would not have forgotten the promise. Surely then he will not forget it in the much fewer actual generations.

Verse 10. *To their face.* The last word in this group is from an original that means "before, in view of, in the presence of." The idea is that God would bring the punishment upon them in a manner to make them realize what it was and what it was for. *Hate.* This does not necessarily refer to that condition of mind that we generally regard as present when one hates. It also means to be a foe or enemy in one's conduct regardless of personal sentiments. All people whose manner of life is contrary to the wishes of God are considered as those who hate him.

Verse 11. In keeping with the thoughts expressed by the foregoing verse they were to keep the commandents of the Lord. In so doing their conduct would not be contrary to the wishes, but in harmony with those of God.

Verses 12, 13. The conditions on which all of the promises of God were placed were constantly kept before their minds. This left them no excuse for overlooking the duty which they were to perform in their life as a people. And it is a principle of mutual obligation, recognized by man generally, that when one party to a contract breaks the agreement, that releases the other party. Hence when the nation of Israel broke their part of the agreement that released the Lord and they then were losers.

Verses 14-16. Superiority over all other nations and freedom from the evils the other nations suffered were to be among the rewards enjoyed by the children of Israel provided they obeyed the voice of God. To have such blessings they must be unsparing in their opposition against these evil nations.

Verses 17, 18. The natural inclination to consider numbers might cause these people to shrink. But they should remember the experiences of Egypt. Also the fears expressed by the ten spies and thus banish all consideration of numbers.

Verse 19. This verse is a general

summing up of the transactions in Egypt at the time Moses was preparing to lead them out. "Temptations" is another word for tests. The power of God was put against that of the magicians and it stood the test; they failed.

Verse 20. The insect here called hornet was more like the wasp in its nature of sting. Also a wasp would be more inclined to assume a general flight of attack than the insect we know by the name of hornet. The idea we should get is that God uses such means as he sees fit in bringing about the result desired in given cases.

Verses 21-23. The presence of these native people would work somewhat against the prevalence of the beasts. Therefore they were to be driven out gradually so as to give opportunity for destroying the beasts also. To drive out the nations gradually did not mean to cease opposing them even for a day. It was to be a gradual, yet continual fight against them.

Verse 24. By getting the kings into their hand they would get the rulers of the peoples and thus wipe out the very name of the heathen.

Verse 25. Mention has already been made of the various forms of idolatry that were practiced. Among them were the imaginary and the artificial. These two were generally combined, because, since they carried an image in their minds of the gods they adored they also wished to have something visible to their eyes to correspond. Hence the images of those invisible gods. They must all be destroyed.

Verse 26. One reason they were commanded to destroy these images was that they might not bring them into their houses to be a constant snare unto them.

DEUTERONOMY 8

Verse 1. This verse introduces a memorable chapter. And the reader is again asked to note the significant expression "observe to do." It is not enough to observe. One might do that as an act of the mind only, or merely to memorize the command. But he must observe the command for the purpose of doing it. And this was to be necessary if that people expected to live as a people and finally take possession of the land that had been assured to their fathers.

Verse 2. *Humbled.* This is from a Hebrew word that has a variety of uses. The most practical meaning of the word is "afflict." Of course, we can understand how an affliction brought on a person in punishment would also humble or humiliate him. So that their forty years in the wilderness would be remembered chiefly through the many afflictions they suffered in the way.

Verse 3. First, they were caused to hunger where there was no natural means of supplying the food. That called for divine help. It came in the form of manna. For critical explanation of this word see Ex. 16: 15. There is something very significant in the fact that their hunger was satisfied with an article they did not recognize. It should cause them to understand that the help was from a source higher than man. The logic of this verse is that hunger (as well as other conditions) was provided for in the wilderness. In spite of such fact, they were punished with afflictions from time to time. Thus they should conclude that even when the needs of the body are satisfied so that man is comfortable, he needs something more. That is the need for the character. And when a man's character is not what God wishes he will punish the offender. The grand conclusion should be that man is a being composed of inner and outer parts. Bread will take care of the outer but something more is needed for the inner. This is the passage quoted by Jesus in Matt. 4: 4 in his encounter with the devil in the wilderness.

Verse 4. Among the things providing for complete bodily comfort was a supply of clothing. The word "old" means "worn out." The actual age in years would not be denied, but they would not be worn with age. So that their supply of clothing would always be "just like new." Also, their feet would be so well cared for that they would not swell, which means "blister." Their travel was on foot, but their shoes would always be perfectly adapted to their feet in spite of the long use and thus would always make them feel at ease in that way. Their appetite would be constantly satisfied, and their external bodily needs supplied, thus no excuse for wrong doing could be laid to the provocation along the line of personal comfort.

Verses 5, 6. If then, their bodily comforts were provided for, and at the same time certain afflictions came upon them in punishment, they must conclude that they were in the nature of chastisement from a father. Even a fleshly parent would not chastise his child except for wrong doing. And God would not punish except for the same reason. Thus again, if they are punished at the very time they are completely provided for as to their bodily needs, the wrong for which they are punished is not induced by the want of the outward body.

Verses 7, 8. If God provided the necessities of life in the wilderness where it was only possible through miracle, when they come into a land where those good things are already in existence in abundance, they should conclude that such abundance is also provided by the Lord and should serve him out of gratitude.

Verse 9. Iron ore is found in rock and the stones of this country were to contain this valuable metal. As brass is an alloy, of course, it would not be found in the hills. The better translation is copper.

Verse 10. The proper reaction to the condition of great plenty to be enjoyed by them will be one of gratitude. They should bless the Lord which means they should recognize him as the source of their blessings.

Verses 11-14. A solemn warning is the subject of this paragraph. A popular theory has been taught by certain political agitators among professed religious people. That theory is that man will be good if he is comfortable. And that he will be comfortable if his bodily needs are supplied. That we should abolish all penal laws and institutions and rather see that the citizens are given food for the stomach, clothing for the body and shelter for the head. That if such provisions are made then man will be naturally good without the use of restrictive laws and penal impositions. The factual history of humanity belies that theory. The rule is that mankind will not endure prosperity without becoming corrupt. Thus the warning here and always, is, beware not to let temporal prosperity blind us to the needs of something higher, and cause us to forget the very God who gave us all things that are good, for nothing we have that is worth having, whether temporal or spiritual, came from any source than the Lord. (Jas. 1: 17).

Verse 15. The terribleness of the wilderness is specially described by reference to the serpents and other pests that befell them, likewise to the scarcity of life's needs which had to be provided by miracle. Yet God led them safely through it all.

Verse 16. Again they were reminded that they were fed with a food that they did not know, and again the reader is reminded of the logic in the fact that if they got necessary results of good from a thing they did not understand, they should have concluded that God was the source of the blessing and should be served therefore.

Verses 17, 18. Man is apt to boast of his accomplishments. But a modern machine might as reasonably boast of its usefulness independent of the builder, as for man to boast of the wealth he has amassed. Instead, he should remember that he could not have accumulated the wealth had he not possessed the power to do so. And he would not have possessed such power had he not been given it by the Lord. Therefore, he should give God the credit for all his blessings and show his gratitude for them by using them in a way pleasing to the Lord.

Verses 19, 20. This is a serious warning of what will befall them as a nation if they allow themselves to forget God and serve the idolatrous nations around them. They will be driven from the land and perish as a nation. This awful calamity did come to them and the history of it will be found in the closing chapters of 2nd book of Kings. The subject will be given further attention at that place.

DEUTERONOMY 9

Verse 1. *This day.* This expression is figurative or comparative. We know in literal days there were several to pass before their crossing. But the time was not far off and the expression is used in that comparative sense.

Verses 2, 3. It was thought well to keep them reminded they were to go against a strong foe. Giants in stature and characteristics. Living in fortified cities and with human provisions for resistance. The assurance is in the fact of God's great power over all opposition. No strength can prevail against him and if the people will obey and rely on him they are certain of success.

Verse 4. For purpose of distinction it is well to score "righteousness" and "wickedness" in this verse. After their victory over the enemy they must not conclude it was given them as reward for their righteousness. Regardless of whether they were a righteous people, the nations against which they fought were wicked and deserved to be destroyed. God used his people as the instrument of said destruction hence they should not boast. A similar argument is in Rom. 11: 19, 20. Paul warns the Gentiles not to conclude the rejection of the Jewish nation was in order to give the Gentiles a place. Instead, the Jewish nation was rejected because of unbelief regardless of whether others were believers. Therefore, the Gentiles should not be boastful.

Verse 5. In addition to the reasons given in preceding verse for making the great change in the occupants of the land the oath made with Abraham, Isaac and Jacob is here given.

Verse 6. A stiffnecked people means they were a stubborn and perverse people. Yet God loved them for the sake of the fathers and will not forget his oath and promise.

Verse 7. All through the wilderness they had provoked the Lord to wrath. So that the success they are now promised is not in reward for their righteousness but in spite of their unrighteousness. Therefore, they should not be puffed up.

Verses 8, 9. Going back to the time prior to the wilderness wandering Moses reminds them of their provocation at Horeb. This referred to the sin of the golden calf. The danger of destruction that overshadowed them at that time is brought to their memory. That destruction was averted through the mediation of Moses. This will be noticed more particularly below.

Verse 10. The reader should note this verse as one to be consulted on the subject of the oral delivery of the ten commandments. That delivery was made before they were given to them on the tables, which God wrote with his own finger. See detailed comments on this at Ex. 20: 1.

Verse 11. This is another place where the tables were called "the covenant." The same force of expression will be used of other parts of the law as will be cited from time to time.

Verses 12, 13. Even while Moses was yet in the mount the Lord informed him of the sin of the people. It is described as a turning aside. Such is the case in all acts of wrong. It constitutes a varying from the right path. It should be noted here that no specific mention is made of the one man who did the forming of the idol. The thought is that all were to be held responsible for the sin.

Verse 14. This is the threat of destruction mentioned in verse 8 and for which the prayer of Moses was interceded.

Verses 15, 16. In obedience to God's command Moses came down from the mount. All the intervening conversations between the Lord and Moses were left out at this place. But the fact that he had the two tables in his hands, shows that the arrangement for the memorial of their expressed fear had been completed, and they were ready for deposit in the place designated had there not been any event to interfere.

Verse 17. By taking these tables before their eyes Moses provided them evidence of their great provocation by the sin of idolatry.

Verse 18. Between the close of preceding verse and beginning of this we should place all the event of the meeting with Aaron at the place of idolatry. Of the calling for the people and the response of Levi and the slaying of three thousand, etc. Since this book is largely one of review or repetition it will not always be necessary to give the details of the history referred to. The additional thought is given to us here that in the second period of Moses' stay in the mount his fasting was done as an expression of regret and anxiety over their sins.

Verse 19. This relates to the prayer of meditation which Moses offered to God when he threatened to destroy the people. See that threat recorded in Ex. 32: 10 and the prayer of Moses immediately following. As a type of Christ, Moses was to be the mediator between God and the people and as such would have proper authority to reason with the Lord on behalf of them. In the present paragraph the statement is made that the Lord hearkened to the prayer of Moses.

Verse 20. As the individual specially guilty of the great sin of idolatry the people committed, Aaron was threatened with death. And Moses made a special prayer of intercession for him and was heard so that the services of Aaron were continued all through to the fortieth year of their wandering.

Verse 21. The calf was the visible sign of sin that was in their heart even before the idol was formed. But since it was a present symbol of their sin it was well to remove it from their sight. Not only so, but by burning it so that it would be crystallized it could be ground into powder and washed away by the brook.

Verses 22-24. These verses recall the instances where they had provoked the Lord and roused the divine anger against them. The conclusion was that they had been rebellious against God from the start. This is not thrown into their faces merely as a taunt but to keep them from self-confidence of a dangerous degree.

Verse 25. This verse repeats the motive for Moses' fasting and conduct of penitence on behalf of the people. It was in concern for their great sins.

Verses 26, 27. A strong item injected into the mediatory prayer of Moses is the mention of the fathers, Abraham, Isaac, and Jacob. God had said so many times that he was acting in view of his respect for those fathers. Now it is perfectly in order for the mediator to use that as a leverage in his plea before God.

Verse 28. The boast of the enemy nations would be a shame and Moses wishes to prevent such by overruling the sins of the people for good.

Verse 29. After all, these people, sinful though they are, constituted the ones whom God had separated from Egypt and all others to be his inheritance. So that love for even a wayward child would prompt the preservation of the child. But that very love and preservation should cause the child to be grateful and react accordingly.

DEUTERONOMY 10

Verse 1. Much brevity has already been discovered in our study of the Great Book. From other parts of the record we know that the ark was not actually made until after the second period of forty days in the mount. But it is necessary to precede that chronology here so as to complete the instruction about these second tables. Also let this verse and the following one be carefully observed as to the antecedents of the pronouns used in connection with the writing on the tables. In this verse Moses is quoting the words of the Lord.

Verse 2. He is still quoting the Lord when he uses the pronoun "I" so that we are to understand that God and not Moses did the writing on the tables. Besides, in this direct connection the second person "thou" is used as the one who broke the former stones. Thus the conclusion is unavoidable that God did the writing.

Verse 3. The chronological mixup of this verse is explained in verse one above.

Verse 4. The subject not having been changed we must know the pronoun "he" here means the Lord. Also that agrees with the fact that the first personal pronoun "me" is used in the same verse as the one to whom the tables were given *after* being written.

Verse 5. This is another verse that must take the explanation offered at first verse of the chapter. Of course at the time Moses was making this speech all of the facts of which he was speaking had taken place so that the children of Israel needed not to be confused as to their special chronology.

Verse 6. Departing for a short space from his direct address to the people Moses recites in the third person some historical events of great importance. The original account of this is in Num. 33. After Aaron had served the purposes of the Lord he was to be taken out of the scene as a punishment for his sin at the rock. The office of High Priest descended upon his son Eleazar.

Verse 7. Just another brief insert of some of their journeys.

Verse 8. *That time.* This is the time referred to in chap. 9: 18. Levi responded when the call was made to come to the Lord's side. As reward for and recognition of this reverence for God this tribe was selected to have the exclusive care and service of the tabernacle to be produced soon among the people.

Verse 9. The exclusive position and work of the tribe of Levi made it out of the question for it to be settled in a regular inheritance as the other tribes were. They were to be situated near the tabernacle while in the years of wandering and then after settling in Canaan were to live in cities scattered over the territory in general.

Verse 10. The same as stated in chap. 9: 18.

Verse 11. This is another big jump in chronology for it did not take place until the tabernacle had been made and reared up which was about a year after the children of Israel had come out of Egypt. At the time Moses was making this speech it was a matter of history.

Verse 12. Now Moses drops his

reminiscent form of speech and directs his language into the channel of teaching and exhortation. This is a wonderful passage and sums up the entire duty of man toward his God. If a man fears and loves God and walks in the ways God shows him, there will be nothing more required of him. Nothing more will be needed or possible as that will occupy all his thoughts and actions. This passage is quoted by the prophet Micah, chapter 6: 8.

Verse 13. Keeping the commandments delivered to them was not merely a service without any result for them. It was to be for their good. So it has always been and still is the one thing on man's side as the object of the law. It is for his good.

Verse 14. The simple word "heaven" has but one original in the Old Testament which is SHAMEH. It is defined "to be lofty; the sky (as aloft; the dual perhaps alluding to the visible arch in which the clouds move, as well as to the higher ether where the celestial bodies revolve)"—Strong. Since the central idea of the word is something lofty, the context must determine in each case as to *how* lofty the place is. Thus the use of the word in this verse would be to the effect that God's place of importance and dignity is above all others.

Verse 15. Despite this great exaltation of God he had delight in the fathers who respected this exaltation of their great Maker. In deference to this delight in these God-fearing fathers he chose their descendants after them to be a people above all others, as they were at the time when Moses was speaking to them.

Verse 16. On the basis of the great favor shown to the people their gratitude should be shown by their outward conduct. The outward conduct will not be as it should, unless their inward condition of mind became what it should. Hence the command to circumcise their heart. When this word is used figuratively, it means that something unwanted and objectionable to the Lord should be cut off. Of course that means that their proneness to idolatry and other forms of iniquity must be cut off and the service to God be unmixed with the things that are wrong.

Verse 17. The word "god" means an object of devotion and the word "lord" means a ruler. But the true one to be worshipped and to rule is the God and Lord of Israel. Therefore they should worship him and be ruled by him only. He is said here to be a terrible God. This has the same force as the word fear. God is to be respected for his goodness and to be dreaded when guilty of rebelling against him. He has no respect of persons and cannot be bribed. Nothing but character will make any difference in his treatment of man.

Verse 18. In harmony with the foregoing verse God cares for the helpless and unfortunate and stranger even though humble in personal character.

Verse 19. Therefore, the Israelites should imitate the divine example and show favor to the stranger, remembering their long stay in a strange land.

Verse 20. It is not enough merely to profess love for God but they should cleave unto him. This means an attachment of close communion and faithfulness.

Verse 21. He is "thy praise," means he is the one who only deserves the praise of the people. This is because all their blessings have come from this divine source.

Verse 22. This is a brief but significant, and should be gratitude provoking reference to the great growth they made under the providence of God. After dwelling in a strange land four hundred years, and in spite of the many disadvantages thrust on them by the overlords, they had grown to a multitude of over 600,000 men of the age and qualifications for war. This could be explained only on the basis of God's great love for and care of the several tribes.

DEUTERONOMY 11

Verse 1. This verse states an oft-repeated command, but the word "charge" has been added to the language. That is from a word that means guard or watch. It conveys the idea that they were placed as a sentry to guard the cause of the Lord against the enemy. That is also a principle taught throughout the scriptures. In more than a dozen places in the N. T. we have the command to watch.

Verse 2. The children of the congregation to whom Moses was speaking had been born recently and did not know of the happenings to the nation. These parents had gone through the knowledge by experience. They were not of the age to be numbered when they started but were old enough to have remembered.

Verse 3. Since all persons may be said to know of things that can be thus a part of their information only through others, the children of these parents could know all these things. Therefore, he meant they knew these things by personal observation. So we have the conclusion that many persons in the hearing of Moses now, had been with the congregation from the night of the first passover.

Verses 4-6. This paragraph is a brief review of the works of the Lord among his people and their enemies.

Verses 7, 8. Since their eyes had seen and thus had direct testimony of the works and power of God, they had no excuse from doing their duty.

Verse 9. This assurance does not especially refer to the individual life of the persons but also to the extension of their stay in the land as a nation. This fifteen hundred years that passed from the arrival at Sinai and then the land of Canaan until the New Testament, would have all been spent by them as a strong nation in their own land had they been obedient.

Verses 10, 11. This passage is contrasting the means of watering the crops as used in Egypt and will be used in the land to which they were going. It is a description of irrigation. The very details of the statement of Moses are verified by secular history. A quotation from George Rawlinson on this point will be interesting. "The government (of Egypt) had a general control over the main cuttings, opening and closing them according to certain fixed rules, which had for their object the fair and equitable distribution of the water supply over the whole territory. Each farmer received in turn sufficient to fill his own reservoir, and from this by a network of water-courses continually diminishing in size the fluid was conveyed wherever needed, and at last brought to the *very roots of the plants*. The removal or replacing of a little mud, with the hand or with the foot, turned the water hither and thither, at the pleasure of the husbandman, who distributed it as his crops required." Rawlinson's *History of Ancient Egypt*, Vol. 1, p. 84. Of course we understand the river Nile furnished all this water. The circumstantial description of its application as seen in profane history is so corroborative of the inspired statement that it increases our respect for the statements of Holy Writ.

Verse 12. In contrast with the land where artificial watering has to be done they were journeying toward a land where the God of all sources did the watering.

Verses 13-15. The natural blessings referred to above were promised on the condition they obey the commandments of the Giver of those things. This principle of cooperation with God had to be constantly kept before their minds.

Verses 16, 17. The influence of idolatry was so deceptive. And that was the common sight to be expected as they came among the inhabitants of the land and they were repeatedly warned against mixing with them. If they did so then these blessings would be denied them. Like children who have to be taught through physical punishments, the people of old had to learn through providential experiences what it meant to please or displease God.

Verse 18. In this verse the actual and the figurative use of words appear. They could make the commandments a part of their mind and could figuratively have them always at hand and before their eyes mentally. The same idea is expressed by Peter in 1 Pet. 3: 15.

Verses 19-21. All copies of the law had to be made by hand. They were therefore scarce and it was necessary to transmit it by mouth to the children. Also they could have parts of it inscribed on walls and stones of buildings.

Verse 22. Diligence is again enjoined which means "thoughtful activity." And they were told both to keep and to do the commandments. Not enough merely to keep them in their memory but they must do them.

Verse 23. The promise to drive out the nations is again based on their obedience to the law of God. And we have the information here that the heathen nations then occupying the land of Canaan were greater and mightier than the children of Israel. Of course, this referred to their strength as nations and numerically and not to their strength of character. If Israel can see these mighty nations driven out before them they should be convinced that Israel's God is mightier than all gods.

Verse 24. Again we have the extent of the promised land indicated, which shows it to be far more than the land of Canaan. See Gen. 15: 18 and 1 Ki. 4:21.

Verse 25. Their success in overcoming the enemy will depend on their obedience to the Lord. Then no man will be able to withstand them.

Verses 26-28. To set before them the blessing and the curse does not mean for them to "take their choice" as a liberty from God, as sometimes taught. But God has always been fair in his dealings with man. He not only tells of the favorable result of doing right but warns of the unfavorable result of doing wrong.

Verse 29. These mountains had no moral nor any other characteristics either good or bad. Again the reader must keep in mind the primitive nature of all God's dealings with man. Object lessons to impress ideas on the mind were used in those formative years. So that when certain blessings or cursings were to be pronounced they were to be done from specified places. That fact would finally cause the impression that blessings and cursings were not the same. That they were separate from each other and that no man could be mixed with one while with the other. A good map of Canaan shows these two mountains to be near each other. Since the people were to respond to the pronouncing of the curses the indication would be that they were positioned in the valley between, and in hearing of the words pronounced.

Verse 30. Not only were these mountains in the land of Canaan but here described as being by the way "where the sun goeth down." The map verifies this statement also, for they are located in the western part of the land. The word "champaign" is from an original that means "a desert," and the map shows it to be such.

Verse 31. To go in to possess the land shows that it was already theirs as having been given them through their great forefathers. But they must defend their right by war with the enemy.

Verse 32. Let us not for one instant forget the importance of observing to *do* the commandments of God. Memory verses are all right, but fruitless unless obeyed.

DEUTERONOMY 12

Verse 1. This verse indicates that it might have been permitted the Israelites to dwell in the land of Canaan as long as the earth existed. That is true. Had they always been obedient they should never have been taken from that land. Of course, after the coming of Christ with the N. T. law, they would have been required to submit to the new system for their religious and spiritual guidance, but as a nation among nations they could have continued in that land. Their government as a people would still have been the law given them at Sinai. Only it would then have had but a political significance.

Verse 2. The places where the heathen were accustomed to practice their worship were to be destroyed. This included all the green or living trees where such conduct was had. It thus did not mean to condemn the existence of trees, for in other places they were instructed to preserve certain trees.

Verse 3. This takes the same comments as the preceding verse.

Verses 4-6. The "place" mentioned here would apply according to circumstances. While in the wilderness it would have meant simply whatsoever place was the site of the tabernacle at any given time. After reaching the land of Canaan there will be finally some specific geographical location for the tabernacle and that will be the place where they must bring their sacrifices.

Verse 7. Certain festivities of the nation of Israel included eating for religious observance. While the eating would be literal and physical, the significance would be drawn from some circumstance in their relation to God.

Verses 8, 9. This does not mean that man was ever permitted to "do as he pleased" in his conduct. But while journeying through the wilderness and under the many conditions of varying circumstances there would be frequent need for exercise of human judgment. When they get settled in their own land it will be more regular.

Verses 10, 11. This passage laps back over the one previous. The time was to come when the congregation would be settled in their own land. When that comes, there will be a specified locality where they will find the name of God formally recorded and thither they must assemble at stated times.

Verse 12. The Levite within their gates referred to the fact of the Levites not having any specific location for possession. Their cities would be scattered over the general territory and as a result the members of that tribe might be seen in various places.

Verses 13, 14. Certain activities of the Israelites required animal sacrifices and these could not be lawfully performed in just any place they wished. There was to be some provision made for that matter according to verses 10, 11 above.

Verse 15. The privileges of this verse referred to the eating for religious purposes as mentioned in verse 7. Only in this place more liberty is extended than in the other for here is meant such religious festivities as did not connect with the national feasts. Those required the presence at the proper place of assembly.

Verse 16. Men are but grown children in size, and often in disposition also. If certain liberties are granted it is natural to take still more without permission. So the freedom of eating at pleasure as set out in preceding verse might encourage them to forget certain restrictions that had been made elsewhere. So with the eating of blood. At no time or place could they eat that without displeasing God.

Verses 17, 18. If a portion (tenth) of their fruits was to be eaten in religious service to God they must not presume to do so "at home" or just any place they chose, but must come to the proper place for the occasion. This is the same injunction as described in verses 10, 11 above. All through this chapter as well as in many others we must keep the distinction before us between the religious activities that might be performed wherever they saw fit and the ones whose location was prescribed by the Lord.

Verse 19. God was always especially thoughtful of the Levites. They had responded to the call of Moses to come over to the Lord. Now they have been given sole charge of the religious phases of their congregational life. They were not permitted to have centralized possessions as the other tribes. So in respect to all this, the other tribes were required to treat the Levites as described in many places.

Verses 20-22. This is the same in meaning as in verse 15 above.

Verses 23-25. Once more the warning against eating blood is repeated and the thought is added that it will be well with them before the Lord to observe this law.

Verses 26-28. This passage has the same teaching as that in verses 11, 13, 14, 18.

Verses 29-32. Another repetition of the warning against imitating the idolaters. Among the abominable practices of the heathen was that of burning their children in service to their gods. While God has accepted the destruction of enemies as an offering to him yet he has never permitted the sacrifice of human bodies on religious altars.

DEUTERONOMY 13

Verses 1-3. There have been times when God used evil persons to carry out his plans. He has even used them to communicate his word to the people. Also he has enabled evil characters to perform supernatural deeds. The question then would arise here how were they to be protected against deception when these false teachers performed some sign and it came to pass? The key to the situation is in the use the prophet tries to make of his supposed superhuman power. If this prophet tries to induce them to practice idolatry on the strength of his successful feat, then that was to be evidence that God was not with the prophet except to use him as a test.

Verse 4. They were to indicate their rejection of the false prophet by being all the more faithful in following the Lord and walking in his ways.

Verse 5. Their duty did not stop with the affirmative practice. Many times we hear it said that it is our business to advocate the right and let the negative take care of itself. But such is not the will of God. He requires us not only to be outspoken in favor of the truth but to be outspoken also against error. We have this taught in the N. T. (Eph. 5: 11.)

Verses 6-8. Blood relationship is often allowed to influence the professed people of God to depart from the divine law. One of the commonest circumstances even today is to see the influence of husband or wife or child or other relative interfere with the set duty toward the Lord. And what is worse, not only is this permitted but some will even offer it as a reason for modified religious devotion. It will be said that God would not expect us to "break up a family" in our zeal to stick to the law so closely. Such is false reasoning and is against the positive teaching of scripture. Christ even says that he came to make such division between relatives (Matt. 10:

35), and Paul tells us that when he was called to the work of the Gospel he immediately dismissed the thought of fleshly relation. (Gal. 1: 16.)

Verse 9. This evil person must be put to death. Of course a man can be killed but once. Hence the language of this verse does not restrict itself to the literal use of the physical hand in the execution. That comes in the next verse. It means that the relative must be first and foremost in testifying, and the others if additional testimony should be needed.

Verse 10. This verse brings us to the actual execution. And notice it requires that he be stoned "that he die." Stones might be hurled at a man and yet he not be killed. So the act must be complete. Likewise, when a man becomes guilty of grave disobedience against the law of the Lord in the N. T. he must not merely be chastised and then let go, but he must be given the final and extreme cutting off. (1 Cor. 5: 5.)

Verse 11. The object of the foregoing execution is stated here, that it is to cause the living to be filled with fear of God. Punishment of an evil doer is not only for the benefit of the guilty one but for the object lesson it makes to the others.

Verse 12. *If thou shalt hear say.* The mere report of some evil must be taken into consideration as will be noted further below. Let it be noted here that we are not permitted to be indifferent to the reports of evil in other parts of the world from where we may be located. Almost all evil movements that come among God's people start locally and then may spread. We should be on the watch.

Verse 13. The word "belial" is improperly capitalized here. It is not a proper noun in the O. T. It is a descriptive word and means any one who is base, worthless, lawless. In the N. T. it came to be used as one of the names of Satan and would be a proper noun there.

Verse 14. They were commanded to follow up the report of the false teacher. So it is the duty of God's people today to be on the alert for unscriptural movements that might be reported to exist in some part of the brotherhood. When Peter commanded that we love the brotherhood (1 Pet. 2: 17), he meant that we should be concerned about what might be going on abroad. Elders especially are to watch and be on the lookout for false teaching and teachers, that may come in from outside the community.

Verses 15-18. Upon inquiry, if it be found that such evil persons are among them, they must be destroyed. Of course, we will not forget that the nation was under military as well as religious regulations. Therefore, they must literally remove from their fellowship any character who might endanger their national strength as well as their spiritual relationship with the Lord. The same principle is to be accomplished today by the act of final discipline as taught in 1 Cor. 5: 5 and 2 Thess. 3: 6.

DEUTERONOMY 14

Verse 1. This means not to mutilate the flesh by cutting it, and not to shave the skin between the eyes as a ceremony on occasion of a death. The chief motive for this restriction was the fact that the heathen nations practiced the things restricted.

Verse 2. A peculiar people means they were to belong to God and him only. The same thought is in 1 Peter 2: 9. Being the Lord's possession exclusively required they please him only and not imitate the idolatrous people around them.

Verses 3-5. Certain unclean beasts were considered abominable. Others were clean and might be eaten and some of them are named outright without any general description in this paragraph.

Verse 6. The beasts that they might eat are described in this verse as those that had two characteristics, parting the hoof and chewing the cud.

Verses 7-8. In this passage the characteristics required are listed and specific examples named. This would make it impossible for them to misunderstand what the Lord meant by the restrictions. The clean beasts must not have merely one, but both of the characteristics. We do not know why the Lord used such marks to designate the kinds of beasts. That is, as to why just the marks given were chosen. The reason why some arbitrary rules were given, was to teach them the lesson that they were to obey God, even if they saw no logical reason for his commands.

Verses 9, 10. If this law were in force today, we would not be allowed to eat the catfish which we know to be one of the most desirable of foods. Again we must recall the lesson that by giving such rules the impression was to be made that God's law is to be obeyed because he commanded it, and not because man can see the reason for it. After that principle had been sufficiently placed before the world, the arbitrary restrictions were removed. That is why we have such teaching as recorded in Rom. 14 and 1 Tim. 4: 4. If there had been any actual detriment in eating those creatures the law against them would have been continued.

Verses 11-20. No distinctive description of birds could be given, hence the ones they could not eat are named. The word "creeping" in verse 19 might confuse us. It is from a word that means "to swarm," and thus does not mean the act of creeping as usual.

Verse 21. This is another passage that would be hard to explain satisfactorily for the critic, did we not know that many of the restrictive laws were ceremonial and not based on physical facts. Thus it was with these objects. There was nothing morally or physically wrong in eating them. If there were then it would be inconsistent to offer them to others. Since it is based on judicial law, the alien or stranger would not come under it, and therefore it was all right to offer them to such persons. There is one physical principle involved in this passage, and that is based on another law that was established in Gen. 9: 4, that blood must not be eaten. If a beast had died independent of the hand of a man, the blood would not have been properly excluded from the carcass, therefore they must not eat of it.

Verses 22, 23. The tithe or tenth of all their products, whether of vegetable or animal, must be given to the Lord to be used as his service required. Part of it would be used in the congregational activities and part in the personal support of the Levite tribe as the special tribe of the Lord. Even some of the religious feasts could be provided for out of this tithe. The offering was to be made to the Lord in the designated place where his name was recorded.

Verses 24-26. The Lord did not say that if the way were too long then they might substitute their own home as a place, just as good as the one designated in the law. No other place would be accepted for this kind of offering. If the way should be too long to transport the things they had produced and owed to the Lord, they need not try to move the animals and things bodily. Instead, they could sell them in the home land, then reinvest the money after reaching the place where the service was to be rendered. This provision in the law is what made the occasion of which we read in John 2: 13 and like passages in the N. T. There was nothing wrong in selling oxen but they were doing it in the wrong place. Neither was there anything wrong in conducting an exchange of money, since the foreign money would not be good in the local market, but this too was being done in the wrong place. Not only so, but they were taking advantage of the situation to exact exorbitant prices and thus were called thieves.

Verse 27. God would not let them forget their special duty toward the Levite that was "within thy gates." He was denied general possessions in the land and hence was rather a permanent guest among the people in general.

Verse 28. *At the end of three years.* This means after the three years has passed. See Lev. 19: 23. When they had set out a new orchard and it began to bear, they were to regard the fruit of the first three years as uncircumcised, or unfit for use. Then beginning with the crop of the fourth year they were to consider a tenth of it as the Lord's. That is, they were to give a tenth of it to the Lord and the other nine-tenths could be eaten by themselves.

Verse 29. This is explained mostly in verse 27 and elsewhere. Only in this the addition is made of the fatherless and other unfortunates among them. They were to be permitted to eat of the prosperity of the more fortunate. This generosity of theirs would bring them the blessings of God.

DEUTERONOMY 15

Verse 1. This year of release is the same as the jubilee described in Lev. 25. In that chapter the effects of the ordinance as to land and the bodies of servants was considered while in the present one, the subject of money transactions is dealt with in more detail.

Verse 2. The words for neighbor and brother are practically the same in meaning and apply here to those composing the congregation. Since this year is called the Lord's release it was consistent to require that his people be given this advantage. We are to understand the antecedent of the supplied "it" is the interest that might have been charged. Or, if a pledge in the form of some tangible had been taken to secure payment, it must be returned in the year of release even if the other is not able to come up with the money borrowed.

Verse 3. The exception allowed to be made was in case of a foreigner or one of a different nation. The strict rules of business could be carried out in such cases. The same kind of discrimination is taught in the N.T. Paul makes a difference in the importance of helping those who are our brethren, and those not. (Gal. 6: 10.)

Verse 4. In the margin the word "save" is rendered "to the end," and the lexicon justifies the translation. The idea is that the tendency of the ordinance about the money transaction would be toward prosperity and against poverty. It did not mean that any time would come when there would not be poor people for that would contradict a verse later on in the chapter. It is much like the efforts at sanitation imposed by law and practiced by medical institutions. They are for the purpose of reducing sickness although no one thinks to avoid all illness.

Verses 5, 6. They must be careful to observe to *do* all the commandments and in doing so as to this financial regulation, they would bring to themselves all the more prosperity. Even to the extent that they would be able to be the lender and not a borrower.

Verse 7, 8. The requirement of this passage is similar to what is taught in Jas. 2: 15, 16; 1 Jn. 3: 17. The Lord has been gracious to all mankind although they are undeserving. Therefore, it is reasonable that the more fortunate among us should share with the others, especially those whose relation to God is the same as ours, spiritually.

Verse 9. A covetous man might be tempted to think of the nearness of the year of release at which time the obligation of the borrower would be automatically cancelled. With that in mind he would be held back from helping his poor brother. This verse is a warning against such attitude.

Verse 10. This is another passage similar in teaching to that in the N.T. In 2 Cor. 9: 7, Christians are forbidden to give grudgingly. In the sight of the Lord a man who makes a gift outwardly but has regret over it at the same time, is as guilty as if he had refused to give at all. The receiver of the gift might get the same benefit from the money regardless, but the giver will not be blessed of the Lord.

Verse 11. This should always be considered in connection with verse 4 above and thus help to understand it. Jesus taught the same truth in Matt. 26: 11. Therefore, any theory that claims to banish poverty entirely, is only visionary and false.

Verses 12, 13. This is part of the same teaching found in Lev. 25. When the servant was to be let go in the seventh year, or year of release, he must be given something to carry him over until he finds some other source of living.

Verse 14. In this verse is a brief but interesting reference to the three principal sources of income in Canaan, the cattle, the grain and the vine. The word "floor" refers to their grain, from the use of the floor on which to beat out the grain from the chaff, before fanning it.

Verse 15. Over and over again the children of Israel were reminded that they had been strangers and bondmen in Egypt and had been released. This was not done in the spirit of boast or taunt. It was in order to impress them with the call, for showing appreciation for their blessings. Thus they might conclude that persons in a state of helplessness must rely on some more able and fortunate person or source. Had it not been for the mighty hand of God they would not have been released from their slavery. Now they should express their appreciation by releasing their debtors.

Verses 16, 17. This law is commented on in Ex. 21: 5, 6, which see.

Verse 18. In case the servant refuses to submit to this ceremony of flesh and chooses to take his liberty, the master must let him go willingly. In other words, he must give his servant his liberty with the same frame of mind as was commanded in the matter of giving money to an unfortunate. If he does this he will have a right to look to the Lord for a blessing upon his righteous act.

Verse 19. Not only must they count all the first born of the sheep and cattle as the Lord's, but they must not make any personal use of them before turning them over to the tribe entitled to them. This property was strictly the Lord's.

Verse 20. We have seen that certain religious activities were arranged in the Mosaic system whereby the participants would eat of the devoted things. The significant fact in this is that even while being given credit for service to God they were receiving personal benefit from the circumstance. So it is now. The Lord does not require Christians to turn all their money bodily over to the church treasury or into a common fund. Such an idea is purely of human origin and got people into trouble. (Acts 5.) While we are eating and wearing the blessings God has given us, we can be thankful and make such use of the strength derived from those blessings as will serve the wishes of our great Benefactor.

Verses 21, 22. While no animal with a blemish could be offered on the altar, such could be used in certain of these religious feasts; the kind that were permitted to be observed in their homes.

Verse 23. The danger of going too far with privileges was constantly kept before their mind. Thus, while thinking of the great freedom of eating these otherwise restricted animals, they were liable to take more for granted than intended. In that frame of mind they might think it permissible to eat the blood. So they are again reminded not to do so but to pour it on the ground. The blood of Christ was poured out on the ground at the foot of the cross, and no further use made of it physically. So the Lord intended that the item that symbolized the cost of salvation should in all ages be restricted from a common use.

DEUTERONOMY 16

Verses 1, 2. In this chapter the three yearly feasts of the Jews will be referred to again. In connection with these specific festivities there were others that came in that same time of the year. Hence the inferior or secondary ones may be the ones named instead of the primary ones. In this paragraph the major feast is the one named first. This ordinance was instituted in Egypt the night they were released from bondage. The animal that was to be used in direct connection with the passover was the smaller one, of the sheep or goats. In the present passage we see the herd mentioned. This is the larger animal, the beef. The explanation is in the fact that directly following the passover they were to keep the feast of unleavened bread and in that period the larger animal was used. (Num. 28: 18, 19.) In our present verses this seven day feast is anticipated and thus the herd is mentioned.

Verses 3, 4. The feast of unleavened bread was a period immediately following the passover. While it was described and arranged on the night of the slaying of the first born, its observance could not be had then, since they were to be thrust out at once. They were hastily driven out before the bread could take on the effect of the leaven deposited in the mass and hence was really unleavened. As this was done on this memorable night, the night that was to end their years of affliction, and was the occasion of their being forced to eat unleavened bread, God designed that it should be done purposely each year to celebrate the fact.

Verses 5-7. Since the passover was one of the national feasts they could not make a private or personal use of it by attending to it in their homes. It must be done at the place of assembly for the congregation.

Verse 8. This mention of eating unleavened bread six days should not confuse us. The idea is, that beginning with the first of the period they would be required to eat unleavened bread. After the first one of these days the only special requirement was to eat this kind of bread. After six of the days had passed and the last or seventh day came, they were again to have a holy day and not only eat unleavened bread, but also have a sabbath in which they must do no work.

Verse 9. Here is a practical example of how the indefinite statements of the scriptures may be explained by referring to the definite. Here they were told to begin numbering the weeks from the time of starting the use of the sickle. It would be hard to make a definite date out of this. But in Lev. 23: 15, 16 it was set specifically to begin on the morrow after the sabbath after the passover. It so happened that the beginning of some harvests came at that time of the year.

Verse 10. This is the second of the three yearly feasts. It is called Pentecost in the N.T. from the Greek word meaning five or a multiple. It is called the feast of weeks here because it called for a certain number of weeks. At that time they were required to make another offering to God. Likewise in the N.T. on the day of Pentecost a new offering was made to God, that of three thousand souls converted from sin.

Verses 11, 12. This was to be a day of rejoicing. Not one of frivolous hilarity but one of serious gladness for all the goodness of God, and of grateful remembrance of their deliverance from Egyptian bondage.

Verses 13-15. The third of the yearly feasts is directly referred to here by describing the feast of tabernacles. This is because it came in the same month as the day of atonement which was actually the third day of the annual festivities. This feast of tabernacles is minutely outlined in Lev. 23: 40-43. It was to celebrate the fact of their dwelling in temporary structures through their forty years wandering. It consisted of seven days of solemnity and rejoicing in the blessings of God.

Verse 16. This verse tabulates the three annual feasts. At these times the males were required to assemble at whatever place would be the established one. Others of the congregation could and usually did assemble at those times as well as the males. That was purely voluntary. None but the males were required to come.

Verse 17. The basis on which giving was required then, was the same as it is now and that was, according to the ability to give. Not according to what some one else gave. (2 Cor. 8: 12.)

Verse 18. These judges were subject to the authorized officers already in the congregation. This arrangement was first suggested in the days of Jethro and afterward made a permanent part of their government. They did not have any power to originate or limit the inspired law but were to act in cases of judgment in the petty affairs arising between man and man.

Verse 19. This verse supports the thoughts offered at the preceding one, that the work of these judges was with the personal affairs of the people. Therefore, they must be unbiased in their decisions and not be influenced by personal regard for the men in the disputes.

Verse 20. Even their right to maintain possession of the land to be given them was to be on condition of their honesty in dealing with their fellowmen.

Verse 21. There was nothing wrong with the trees as such, for they were God's work, but at that time and place the idolaters had made such general use of groves, and even single trees, as places of image worship that God did not wish any suggestion to be made in the way of these groves. Hence the command of this verse.

Verse 22. *Image.* This is from MATSTSEBAH and defined by Strong: "something stationed, i. e., a column or (memorial stone); by analogy an idol." It would be not only wrong to form an image of some false god, but to rear a commemorative pillar to the honor of such god would be abominable to the Lord. Likewise, we may not engage in the direct or actual service of an unscriptural kind. If we do anything that would tend to honor or keep in memory that kind of thing we are guilty. (Eph. 5: 3.)

DEUTERONOMY 17

Verse 1. In a general way any gift of valuables is rightly regarded as a sacrifice. But as the word was used in connection with the Mosaic system it had special application to the things burned on the altar. This was the climax of their actions as worshipers of their God. And for this service none but the perfect animals would be accepted. They must offer not only the best they had but it must be a perfect animal. If they did not happen to have such in their flock or herd at any given occasion, they must make arrangements to procure one.

Verses 2-4. A rumor that certain people were practicing idolatry among them could not be ignored and passed by. They were required to make inquiry to see if the report were true. Failure to do so would make their negligence as bad as the thing reported.

Verse 5. If the report was found to be true, the guilty persons were to be stoned *till they died.* Mere punishment or chastisement will not suffice, but the execution had to be completed.

Verses 6, 7. Life is so precious that it must not be taken unless the guilt can be established beyond a doubt. Hence, more than one witness was required. The word "hand" here is figurative and refers to the fact of having initiated the prosecution of the case and then followed by others in support of the execution. It was on this principle that Jesus required the accusers to be the first to cast a stone at the guilty woman. (Jn. 8: 7.) In that instance, it meant literally casting a stone for that would be possible, since the casting of one stone would not necessarily cause the death. The form of command was based on this idea of the ones first accusing, to be the ones to initiate the execution.

Verses 8-11. This paragraph is in the class of disputes mentioned previously where human judges were used. It includes cases that were more serious than mere petty subjects, but might involve blood. In that circumstance they must not rely altogether on the uninspired judges. They must bring the matter in conjunction with the priests that are in active service. They were the ones designed by the Lord to be the executioners of the law after the system had been established. In order that they could be dependable, they were given special help from the Lord in the exercise of the service. (Mal. 2: 7; Lev. 10: 11; Num. 27: 21.)

Verses 12, 13. To reject the word given through the priests was the same as to have rejected the Lord and the one guilty of doing so was to be punished with death.

Verse 14. We do not know why the Lord would practically predict the very thing that was done that was displeasing to him. We are safe in observing that God knows the future of man's conduct and has made provision for his proper conduct if he will accept the provision. Furthermore, it is well to know that it was several hundred years after this passage until the demand for a king was actually made. It would therefore be only a matter of the record and not from personal memory of the scripture that they clamored for a king. Since not the least reference was made by them to this place in the scripture, it proves that it was no encouragement to them for their rebellious act.

Verse 15. While the call for a king would not be based on any prompting from this scripture, it would give the leaders of the Lord's people a place of appeal in their effort to obtain the proper kind of king. Hence, the propriety of inserting here the instructions on the subject.

Verse 16. The horse is a noble animal and one of the most wonderful of God's creation. The use of the beast is therefore not wrong. At the time in mind of the Lord, he knew that Egypt would be a prominent source of these creatures, and he did not wish any pretense to exist that would turn the attention to that country because it had such an unfavorable history in the divine estimation.

Verse 17. The special reason for banning a multitude of wives was the evil effect they would have on the king. The moral right to more than one wife was not different in the case of a king from that of a private person. The extent of evil influence would be greater, therefore, it was forbidden to multiply wives. Also he was not to use his position as king to amass great wealth.

Verse 18. Copies of the law could not be purchased from some printer as can be done today. They had to be made by hand. So important was it that a king should have the correct copy that he was directed to make his own copy. Besides, there is a great advantage in copying the law. The very act of writing a thing impresses it on the mind more firmly than merely reading it.

Verse 19. While it would so impress his mind, time can act as an eraser, so he was to be required to read in the law constantly. Neither was he to permit it to be carelessly deposited in some unfrequented place, but must have it with him.

Verse 20. The end to be accomplished by his constant reading of the law was that he be not filled with the importance of his position. It is one of the common weaknesses of man to become inflated over any position of greatness. Or one that seems great. The kings of earthly nations are tempted to take undue advantage of their authority because of their supposed greatness. That is why Jesus taught that true greatness in his kingdom was to consist in humility of mind and life. (Matt. 20: 26.)

DEUTERONOMY 18

Verses 1, 2. This is the same ordinance that has been described previously and is based on the fact that the Levites responded to the call of Moses. (Ex. 32: 26-28.)

Verses 3-5. The Levites, as a tribe, were to receive a tenth of all the products of the other twelve tribes. In addition, the family of Aaron that had the office of the priesthood was to have certain portions of the animals brought to the altar in sacrifice. (Lev. 7: 30-34.)

Verses 6-8. After settling in the land of Canaan the nation will be scattered, and these Levites will also be scattered abroad among the people. Therefore, they will not all be stationed near the tabernacle as they were while in the wandering. There would be some not in active service although qualified for the service. Then, if some of them were to come to the place of the tabernacle and volunteer to do the service that belonged to such special classes they were to be regarded in the same light as the ones who were there in that service all the time. When they did so they were to be given the same consideration of support as the other Levites. They were not to be denied this, on the ground that they already had property they had inherited from their fathers, here called their patrimony.

Verses 9, 10. A precaution is given against imitating the abominations of the nations then infesting the land to which they were headed. Those abominations included sacrificing the children to the gods and patronizing persons with seducing spirits.

Verse 11. *Necromancer.* This is from two original words which when taken together, means one who pretends to make inquiry through the dead. The woman of Endor would be classed as such. (1 Sam. 28: 7-14.) In her case the Lord actually took charge of her, and used her to perform the actual thing that she had previously only pretended to do.

Verses 12-14. Many things are wrong in their very nature. These evils here condemned had a special ill favor to God in that they were the practices of the wicked nations then living in the land promised to the fathers. The Lord does not wish his people to be like the wicked people around them.

Verses 15-20. So inseparable are the thoughts connected with this noted prophecy that I have grouped these verses into one paragraph. One of the outstanding requirements of the prediction is that the new prophet was to be of their brethren and, therefore, he must be an Israelite. Then he was to be like Moses. That means that he will be a lawgiver and mediator. He was to be like Moses in that the Lord would put his words into his mouth and not speak to him through a third person. Instead, Jesus, like Moses, would himself be the third person and one between God and his people. And again, as the person who disregarded the word of Moses died physically, the one who disregards the word of the last prophet shall die spiritually. (Heb. 10: 28, 29.) Any man who will pretend to speak the law of God who does not speak according to the word of the predicted prophet, shall die eternally.

Verses 21, 22. The predictions of true prophets always come to pass, but there have always been men pretending to be inspired prophets, yet their predictions will fail. That fact does not seem to impress the public with their deception but they will go right on and swallow their false teachings afterward. This fact justifies the teaching of Christ on the matter of being misled. (Matt. 15: 14.)

DEUTERONOMY 19

Verses 1, 2. This chapter will give instructions about the cities of refuge that have been already considered. (Num. 35.)

Verse 3. *Way.* When this is used literally it means a road to be traveled. That was a hilly country and prevented speedy progress unless something were done to remove the obstructions. The necessity of reaching a city of refuge without unnecessary delay brought this requirement, to prepare a way so that the avenger of blood would not have the advantage of distance in overtaking the slayer as stated in verse 6.

Verses 4, 5. All killing is not murder. This describes a case where one man killed another and yet would not be guilty of murder. Yet he might fall under the wrath of the lawful executioner, unless protected in some way. These cities of refuge were provided for this purpose. There would need to be time and opportunity to investigate as to whether it happened by accident or otherwise.

Verse 6. By reference to Gen. 9: 5 it will be learned that the "avenger of the blood" is the brother (or nearest other relative) of the one slain. If such relative should be near, or even afterwards should learn of the incident, and find the slayer outside the city of refuge he was authorized to execute him.

Verses 7, 8. The aforesaid provision was for three cities and had reference to three cities on the west side of Jordan, to serve the tribes located in that part of the promised land. Note the significant words "all the land which he promised" as applying to territory other than west of Jordan. All this adds up to the fact often mentioned in this work, that the "promised land" was a more extensive domain than just the land of Canaan. This expression was looking toward the subjugation of more of the land than was situated west of the part, including the capital river line.

Verse 9. The addition of land intimated in foregoing paragraph was to be on condition they obey the commandments of the Lord.

Verse 10. The word "innocent should be scored here. The Bible makes a fundamental difference between innocent blood and guilty blood. To execute a man for a slaying that did not constitute murder would be shedding innocent blood. By the same token to execute a murderer would *not* be shedding it and would therefore be lawful killing. Opponents of capital punishment always ignore this principle of penal prosecution. See comments at Gen. 9: 6 on this subject.

Verse 11. If the killing was preceded by malice and intention, then it would be murder. Yet such a one would naturally try to protect himself by flying to one of these cities of refuge. That was to be expected.

Verse 12. This verse is a short cut to the proceedings. Verse 24 of Num. 35 shows that the man must be tried before the congregation, before being turned over to the revenger of blood.

Verse 13. The word "pity" is from an original defined as "to cover." Thus it does not mean the mere act of the mind but is a stronger word. The man found guilty of murder must not be shown any leniency regardless of what might be one's personal feeling toward him. Usually, if not always, those who oppose capital punishment do so as prompted by sentiment and not logical reasoning on the law. Any person who would spare the life of a murderer through sentiment or sympathy would have been regarded as a breaker of the law in the days of Moses.

Verse 14. The principle set forth in this verse is a part of law in about all civilized countries today. If a mark has been in existence for some time it has become a recognized limit or boundary of property. When a transfer of property is made it would be in view of what was supposed to be the bounds thereof. After the transfer has been made it would be unreasonable to object to the boundary.

Verse 15. The mention of sin and iniquity indicates this stipulation for more than one witness concerned cases of supposed crime and not merely a property dispute. While the life of another is sacred and should not be forfeited unless guilty, yet an enemy might also wish to injure the one accused otherwise, either in body or assets.

Verses 16, 17. *If a false witness.* This proviso is inserted by the inspired writer because it would not have been shown as yet that the witness, or accuser, or complainer, was a false witness until the cause was tried. Note that the expressions "before the Lord" and "before the priests" here are used in the same connection. This is very significant. It gives us one of the established principles of the entire dealing of God with man in all ages. God has always had some system of life for his creatures, and that system will be carried out through the instrumentality of certain officials or leaders. In all cases, when a person opposes or recognizes said official or leader it is counted as being done toward God.

Verse 18. The authorized judges in the case must not decide the dispute on their personal opinion, regardless of the facts. They must investigate. Not only so, but it must be a diligent investigation until the facts have been learned and it is proved that the complainant had made false statements.

Verse 19. Upon conviction of falsehood in the complaint, the accuser is the one to be punished. These cases might be as numerous and varied as the number of citizens in the land and thus it would be out of the question to stipulate in every instance, beforehand, just what the penalty should be. Since no law is complete without a penalty something must be provided along that line. Hence the Lord decreed that in all such cases of unjust intention of doing personal or property injury the false accuser should be punished with the very kind of treatment he sought to accord his would-be victim. In this way it could be truthfully said that the law was complete, since a penalty had been provided against violation.

Verses 20, 21. One great object in punishing wrong-doers is to furnish a warning to the spectator as well as punishment of the evil doer.

DEUTERONOMY 20

Verse 1. Assurance of victory when serving God, regardless of appearances, is the subject of this verse. Had the ten spies and the congregations borne this in mind at Kadesh-barnea they might have been saved from the disastrous experiences. Human strength and numbers do not count for anything when arrayed against the Lord.

Verses 2-4. It should be kept in mind that under the Mosaic system the priest was the established teacher orally for the people. If any special communication were necessary at any given time the priest was the one to administer it, after the days of personal service of Moses and his successor in leadership.

Verses 5-8. The morale of men in an army means much for the success of the battles. Hence, certain facts and conditions are set out as exemptions from military duty. They may be tabulated briefly as follows: Built a new house, planted a vineyard, betrothed a wife, fearful and fainthearted. But it should be noticed that none of these conditions is wrong in itself and the last named one could not be avoided. Hence, all the conditions mentioned would be regarded as hindering a person from rendering full service in the operation. Furthermore, it is understood that all such conditions mentioned must have been genuine and not pretended, and not things that were used or brought about deliberately as a means of avoiding military duty. It would be like the proverbial "ox in the ditch" on the sabbath. It is often said that such law of the Lord did not mean to encourage one's pushing his ox in the ditch in order to have excuse for breaking the holy day. Also, the present provisos do not apply to one who would deliberately bring them about for the purpose of avoiding an unpleasant duty.

Verse 9. After the men fit for battle service have been selected, an orderly attack was to be assured by appointing captains as leaders. The benefits and necessities of such are recognized by nations today.

Verses 10, 11. All cities situated in the land of Canaan were considered as in hostility against the people of the Lord, since they were occupying territory that had been given to them from their ancestors. Notwithstanding, they were to be given the opportunity of life if submitting to the aggressor. Then they were to become the servants of the congregation. All of this provision of peace for them was subject to another condition to be noted before the end of this chapter.

Verses 12, 13. If this besieged city resists, its inhabitants must be taken in hands and the men slain, which would put a stop to all military opposition.

Verse 14. This is one of the passages of scripture that are slandered by the enemies of the Bible. It is made to mean that the women were to be taken over, by the soldiers of the Lord's army, to be used as mistresses. The honest reader will first try to find all that is said on a subject before forming a conclusion. So in this case let the reader consider next chapter, verses 10-13.

Verses 15, 16. This passage contains the proviso mentioned at verse 11 above. All the cities that were near those of the Israelite territory would be considered as dangerous for their spiritual safety, and hence, they were commanded to destroy them. The ones far off would not have such effect on them and they were permitted to grant their inhabitants their lives, but to serve under tribute. This is the section of the law that was involved in the case of Joshua and the Gibeonites. (Josh. 9: 7.)

Verse 17. These nations so frequently mentioned were in the immediate vicinity of the nation of Israelites and were therefore considered as dangerous foes and were to be utterly destroyed.

Verse 18. The evil effect that was feared as coming from these heathen nations is here specifically stated. It pertained to the worship, and these idolaters would spread their evil teaching among the people of God. For this reason they were to be removed from the scene of action.

Verses 19, 20. The words which the A. V. has in parentheses read as follows: "for is the tree of the field man, that it should be besieged of thee?" The thought is that although they feel justified in besieging the people of a community, that did not give any reason for so treating an inaminate object like a tree, and one that may be used afterward for food. Trees not having such use for man, were the ones to be used in forming the arrangements for a siege.

DEUTERONOMY 21

Verse 1. The system given through Moses was a civil or political as well as religious government. As such it was necessary to provide for the various emergencies that would arise and certain formalities must be observed. So here is the case of finding a dead man in a field. Foul play is suspected but the guilty person, or persons, is not known as yet. Something must be done formally to settle the case.

Verse 2. The ceremony started by measuring from the dead body to the surrounding cities and the one nearest was held responsible theoretically.

Verse 3. Knowing this arbitrary action might enclose innocent parties the Lord provided a means of clarifying it. The elders of the city, being representative citizens, were to start by selecting a heifer that had never been used in any way.

Verse 4. Like the law of sacrifices to be burned on the altar (Lev. chap. 1-5), the persons to be benefited by the offering were to do the killing of the animal.

Verse 5. Also, as in the same instances, the priests were the ones to come into the case to officiate.

Verse 6. The manual action in this ceremony was that of washing their hands over the dead heifer. The signified result of washing one's hands, is that of cleansing.

Verses 7, 8. The oral action consisted of declaring their innocence of any guilt or knowledge of the sad affair. In connection, they were to pray to God and the statement is that "the blood shall be forgiven them." It would be asked how a man can be forgiven of something of which he is not guilty. Well, if a lawful provision is made for the detection of guilty persons and the clearing of the innocent, a person who would not make use of that provision would be considered as admitting his guilt. In the present case, the tentative conclusion is that these elders were the ones responsible for the death. Seeing they might not be, this arrangement is made for their protection. Until such arrangement is made use of, the elders are considered guilty, theoretically at least. So here is at least one circumstance where it is not true that a man "is innocent until proved guilty" which is a favorite saying among lawyers and defenders of criminals. The ordinance being here considered is that resorted to by Pilate in Matt. 27: 24 when he wished to evade his responsibility about the condemnation of Jesus. He was "between two fires" and wished to escape them both, and thought to take this means of accomplishing it. He overlooked the fundamental principle involved. Had those elders been really guilty all the washing of their hands would have availed them nothing. In other words, Pilate, a guilty man, sought to invoke a provision of the law intended to protect an accused but innocent man.

Verse 9. The significant remark about *innocent* is again made, which is of great importance and should not be forgotten by the reader of the Bible.

Verses 10-13. This is the passage referred to at Num. 31: 18 and at verse 14 of this book, preceding chapter. The last word of verse 11 is the key. It has always been moral to take a woman to one's self as a wife. If all instances of captivating the female sex were those with marriage in view, there would be far less confusion in the social world. In the present passage the Lord has in mind only such a case. Even though the captor intends to make the woman his wife, he is required to deal very considerately with her. He may not rush into intimacy with her as one would in cases of mere fleshly lust. He must allow her opportunity to make proper alterations in her personal appearance that had been imposed by previous servitude. She must be given time to wean herself from the immediate association with her parents and this must last for a month. After all that, he may become intimate with her. All this is far from the conduct of one who merely kidnaps a woman to be used as a mistress, as has been intimated by the slanderers of the scriptures. A very significant statement further is made in this paragraph. That it was after the man had "gone in unto her" that he is said to be her husband. That was in agreement with the original basis of marriage. (Gen. 2: 24.)

Verse 14. If the man finds that he had misjudged the desirability of the woman thus taken and decides to put her away he must not take any advantage of her. She must be turned free, although a captive of war, as well as of the social relation. But in deference to her misfortune of having been humiliated through no fault of hers she must be given her liberty without any encumbrances.

Verse 15. It is not correct to say that in ancient times God permitted plurality of wives. To permit a thing means to consent to or endorse it. God never endorses wrong. He does sometimes tolerate or suffer evil for the time being. Thus in the old time he tolerated this plurality of wives. As long as such was endured or suffered among the people, God makes certain regulations about the same. It could happen that a man would be partial to one of his two wives. Jacob was a man in that state of mind, for he loved Rachel more than Leah. The natural tendencies would be to mistreat or slight the offspring of the wife not preferred.

Verses 16, 17. The law required that if the first born happen to be the son of the woman not loved the father must not let that fact influence him in the disposal of his property. The financial manner by which he was to recognize the first born was by giving him a double portion of the estate over what the others received. The conduct of Jacob recorded in Gen. 48: 22 and fulfilled in Josh. 17: 17 and 1 Chr. 5: 1 must not confuse us here. Jacob did not violate this law. It is true that Joseph personally was the son of his favorite wife and he here promises him a "portion above" his brethren. That did not refer to the personal estate of Jacob, instead it referred to the subduing of land to be occupied as a tribe or tribes. Besidés, since Joseph was to form two tribes by using each of his sons as a complete tribe, that would make it right and equitable for him as the head to be considered as having a double portion of spoil.

Verse 18. This verse does not give any endorsement of parents who will not bother themselves to administer discipline to their wayward children as is so often observed among the people. In this case it is after the parents have chastened the stubborn son and learned that he is a "problem child" who requires and deserves some special treatment, that they are to take the other step.

Verse 19. They are not allowed to place him in the hands of some other private person, or appeal to some "feature writer" of some popular newspaper for advice. They must take him to the lawful authorities.

Verse 20. Notice that their accusations were not to be general for that is never fair in any case of accusation. They must specify the sins of which he is guilty and for which they have not been able to effect a cure.

Verse 21. Having now become a criminal under the law of the land the same must be executed according to that law. In this case, the penalty is death by stoning. It is stated furthermore here that one of the things to be accomplished by this execution is that evil will be put away. Another is, that others might be led to fear and behave.

Verse 22. The word "tree" here does not necessarily mean a live or standing wood in its natural state although it could be included. Any firm piece of wood could be meant. The hanging of one on the tree could be accomplished by any means that would suspend the victim on the wood, and in the air, in sight of the people. In later times the means of fastening the victim to the wood was by nailing the hands and feet. This was the method in use in the time of our Saviour.

Verse 23. Regardless of the method of fastening a man to the tree or wood, the sight of such a spectacle was horrifying to the eyes of the citizens. It was to be looked upon as a disgrace to the land even though an unavoidable one. Since it must be done to carry out the justice of an outraged law, yet for the sake of the land and its good name, the body must not remain on the tree overnight. It must be taken down and buried. Be sure to observe that the body must be buried the same day on which he was hanged, not after another day has started, as is sometimes argued in the case of the day of Christ's crucifiction. All this disgrace is the point made so much of by the writers of the N. T. in their accounts of the sacrifice of Christ. The great humility forced on his body was in harmony with the voluntary humility of his mind in offering himself as a redeeming sacrifice for the sin of the world.

DEUTERONOMY 22

Verse 1. We shall not forget that the Mosaic system was to regulate the people in matters of temporal interest between man and man, as well as in religious ones. The act brought up in this verse is only a due courtesy for a fellowman. One's personal loss would not be threatened by the straying of the animal, but he is his brother's keeper in principle, when a circumstance like this presents itself.

Verse 2. Not knowing from whence the animal had strayed it would not be possible to conduct it to its home. The finder must give it a place in his "house," which is from a word of various meaning. Any kind of shelter for either man or beast was called a house in that language. In specific language it would mean a barn or fold. Then when the owner comes round and proves his claim to the animal, it must be restored.

Verse 3. The same law applied to all kinds of animals and also to the personal property lost and found by another. So it is another instance where "finders are keepers" is not a just practice. A lost article does not belong to the finder until it becomes evident that the owner cannot be found. He is not even permitted to "keep still" about it for that is forbidden by the injunction, "not hide thyself."

Verse 4. The law in this verse is similar to that of the preceding ones except in this, the animal at hand has not strayed or been lost. The owner is present but has had the misfortune of having his beast of service fall. It is the duty of the passerby to stop and offer assistance. That is a good law and one to commend itself to all.

Verse 5. The N. T. teaches us to observe certain principles. The O. T. gives specific examples or descriptions of the principles. During that formative and educational period, man was like a child. He needed not only to be told what to do and what not, but was often shown in detail what it meant. So that when we are given a commandment in the N. T. to observe certain principles we may refer to the O. T. to learn what God meant by the teaching. (Rom. 15: 4.) Now the N. T. commands that women use modest apparel. (1 Tim. 2: 9.) By considering the present verse we may get a view of God's mind on the subject of modesty. It does not mean anything here for the purpose of the lesson at stake to mention the indefinite modes of dress that "might have been used" by the sexes. We do not have to know or consider a single item on that. What we do know is that at the time the law was written there was a recognized form of clothing for women that was distinguished from that of man. These must not be exchanged. The same principle applies today. When women appear on the streets, or in other public places, wearing the form of clothing that is always regarded as the kind belonging to man, they are guilty of immodesty and are violating the language of Paul.

Verses 6, 7. This is not to be considered as a law of the so-called humane society. If anything, it would be rather a cruel thing to take the mother from her nest and make use of her bodily product. Yet that was what was commanded. It was a conservation proposition. It is something like the idea of killing the fabled goose that laid the golden egg. That would stop all further production. If the eggs or young birds are taken for food, the mother is still left for future production. Or it might be compared to the thought of not running the soil to death for the sake of present crops, but use the crops in a way not to impair the future production.

Verse 8. The houses of ancient times had flat roofs and they were used to walk on, and otherwise be occupied. That was so generally the custom that no objection was to be made against it. In view of that, the requirement was made for the safety of the public. Knowing that persons would be walking upon the roof of the house the owner was required to place a battlement or banister there for safety and if not then the bad results that might come from its absence, would be charged against the owner. All this is on the principle that we are "our brother's keeper" even if Cain said he was not.

Verse 9. This does not necessarily mean that two kinds of crops must not be raised in the same vineyard. The word "diverse" is used in the sense of variance. A seed that would work against the other would mutually destroy both. God had promised that the new land to which they were journeying would be one of great plenty. In keeping with that promise he does not want them to practice anything that would make against the satisfactory crops, for that might look bad for his promises.

Verse 10. We have no intimation of what specific reason the Lord had for this commandment. We know it was not because either of the animals was regarded as unfit for service, because we have numerous instances where both were used. It was under that law where God had so many arbitrary regulations that were not based on any moral or other evident reasons, that we find this strange stipulation. Just what God had in mind in this case I am unable to say.

Verse 11. This verse is in the same class as the preceding one as far as I know.

Verse 12. See comments at Num. 15: 37-38 for explanation of this passage.

Verses 13, 14. This case concerns a woman who claimed to be a virgin, not a widow. A woman could be a widow and yet be chaste, but she would not be a virgin. In this case the woman took the man with the understanding that she was a virgin, and then claims that he found her not to be upon his first relations with her.

Verses 15, 16. In ancient times especially, it was the custom for parents to give their daughters in marriage. Therefore, if any question of propriety arose as to her character the parents were first to be concerned, and the ones to act in her behalf. Thus it will be their privilege and duty to produce the evidence of the innocence of their daughter, she having been given in marriage in their home where the union was formed. The evidence of the woman's chastity consisted in the bed clothing that had been used on the occasion of the consummative act of the marriage. When all the normal conditions of body are intact the female possesses a membrane, called the hymen, that partly closes the entrance to the reproductive organs. This will be ruptured by the first relation with the man and the discharges therefrom would be seen on the bed clothing. Of course, this is now a disputed subject because many deformities have crept into the bodies of both men and women so that the absence or presence of this organ is not to be considered as positive evidence either way. While the absence of the membrane might not be positive evidence of unchastity, yet the presence of it would certainly be at least a strong presumptive evidence of chastity.

Verse 17. In the case of a woman's innocence, the parents could present the cloth that had been used in the nuptial bed with its stain, and thereby argue the damsel's innocence. This was to be done in the presence of the elders of the city.

Verses 18, 19. Then the husband must be chastised. Also he must be "amerced," which means to be fined. The amount of his fine was a hundred shekels of silver. The fine was to be paid to the parents of the girl. She would not need the money since she is still to be under the support of the husband. The parents being thus injured, the money was to be given them. Then the couple must continue to live together as man and wife as long as both live.

Verses 20, 21. If the evidences of her virginity are not found, then the men of the city shall stone her to death and thus put away folly from Israel. It is here said that she had played the whore. This man is not guilty of that evil, for he was ignorant. If a woman who was not a virgin would impose herself on an innocent man as one who was pure, she would do the same to others and that would convict her of being a harlot. It may be suggested that the above physical test of the woman is not always a reliable one. To some extent that may be true. But it is a universally recognized fact that many laws intended for the general public will seem to work a hardship on innocent persons. That cannot always be avoided except by the detection by miracle and God does not always see fit to work a miracle. Also, if a person who is innocent is punished even to the extent of losing his life, that will not deprive him of his spiritual standing with the Lord, so that in the end he will not be any real loser.

Verse 22. This concerns a married woman detected in the act of adultery. Since there would be no doubt of guilt, the parties must both be killed. In the case of the woman brought to Jesus (Jn. 8: 5), they brought only the woman. Yet they could have brought the man also since they claimed to have taken them in the very act. Their hypocrisy was apparent and was condemned by Jesus.

Verses 23, 24. It will help to appreciate this passage to remember that in Bible times, an espousal was spoken of and regarded in the same light as an actual marriage as far as moral obligation is concerned. (Gen. 19: 14; Matt. 1: 20.) Thus in the case at hand the engaged woman allowed the man to seduce her and that was as sinful as if she had actually become the wife of the man to whom she was promised. Therefore, she and the man must die. The damsel was inexcusable because she did not resist the man. Further, the fact that it was in the city precluded the excuse that it would be of no use to call for help. This made her guilty with the aggressor, and both must be punished with death.

Verses 25-27. The moral obligation incurred by the promise of marriage explains much about the regulations of the O. T. The woman in the case here was not free from the man to whom she was engaged. Therefore, when a man used force against her in the way described it was a form of highway robbery. A case of robbery where it would be impossible to make it right by restoring the thing stolen. That is why the comparison is made to the act of murder. Since a murderer cannot make the wrong right by restoring the thing, it is used for comparison here and the man must pay with his life.

Verses 28, 29. There were many things suffered in olden times that are not allowed in the present. (Acts 17: 30). Marriage in God's sight is based on the fleshly relation. When a man leaves his father and mother and cleaves (makes a fleshly union) to his wife they become one flesh. So in the case of this paragraph. The damsel was free and not the claim of any other man. Therefore, when the man had relations with her, he did not interfere with the tie or promised tie between her and another. Hence, they are one flesh, and not at the moral expense of another. Therefore the circumstance can be atoned, by retaining the woman and giving her the protection of the marriage relation.

Verse 30. The second half of this verse is the same in meaning as the first. It would refer to the father's second wife and this relation was condemned in Lev. 18: 8, and was the iniquity that was being practiced at Corinth. (1 Cor. 5: 1.)

DEUTERONOMY 23

Verse 1. At that time the Lord was planning to make his nation a strong one and one that could cope with the enemies around them. Therefore the citizenship of recorded men must be such as could transmit their kind on down and so keep the nation strong as to their man power. Hence a man who had been deprived of his manhood was not listed.

Verse 2. *Bastard.* This is from MAMZER and Strong defines it "from an unused root meaning to alienate; a mongrel, i. e. born of a Jewish father and a heathen mother." Thus the word does not mean an illegitimate child as the term is used today. As in the case of the preceding verse, God wants the strain of the nation's man power to be kept pure. After the tenth generation the heathen blood would have been so nearly run out that the limitation was lifted.

Verses 3, 4. The person mentioned here would be a "distant relation" of the Jews, but too distant to be admitted to the census until the tenth generation. After that the foreign blood would have become so thin that the objection could be overlooked. Especially was their blood objectionable from their disposition of enmity against God's people as seen in the incidents referred to.

Verse 5. Having brought in the history of the sad affair the writer deems it well not to leave the wrong impression in the mind of the reader, so this verse is added to the present narrative as a completion of the account.

Verse 6. This would not apply to the personal treatment accorded to one of that nation, but to them nationally. God's people must not do anything that would lend support to the propagation of that foreign race.

Verses 7, 8. Even with the restrictions required as to these races their personal feeling does not need to be one of detesting. The Edomite was too nearly related and the Egyptian had too much of kindly remembrance for them to be abhorred. And because of these facts the children of either could be admitted after the third generation.

Verse 9. When engaged in military operations there seems to be a tendency of soldiers to take much for granted. They think it their privilege to impose on the civilians, sometimes on pretense that they are military men. Also, they take the liberty of ravishing the women and otherwise engaging in the sinful practices of the people.

Verses 10, 11. While actual defilement of the body would occasionally take place in course of a man's slumber, yet the seriousness of it was mostly of a ceremonial nature as we have previously observed a number of times. That truth is indicated here by the arbitrary hour of the sunset as the termination of the state of uncleanness.

Verses 12, 13. Mechanical or structural devices for sanitation were not known in those days, so the great outdoors had to be their place to retire to attend to the calls of nature. Even in attending to the necessary actions imposed by the law of their bodies, they must be careful, and maintain a condition of decency.

Verse 14. Certainly no personal injury could possibly come to the Lord by the sight of conditions here considered, but it would be offensive to him to behold his creatures manifesting carelessness even in the matter of cleanliness.

Verses 15, 16. There is nothing said here as to how the servant effected his escape. If he had not done any injury to his master's person or property, he was to be allowed his freedom since the master had let him escape. If this principle were in force today, the act of "jail breaking" could only be punished where the prisoner had committed some injury to the person or property of the prison keeper. If a prisoner should escape without doing any harm to the surroundings, his continued freedom should be allowed as a penalty for the negligence of the prison keeper. This idea was present in the case of the Philippian jailer. (Acts 16: 27.)

Verse 17. Let this verse be considered as a preface to the verse following.

Verse 18. There is such a thing as natural immorality and unnatural immorality. The first item now under consideration is the natural form. Not only does this verse have to do with the two kinds of immorality as to its performance but refers to the practice done for the money gained thereby. Here the "hire" of the whore is not hard to understand since that is common practice. The word "dog" is from KELEB and defined: "from an unused root, meaning to yelp, or else to attack; a dog; hence (by euphemism) a male prostitute."—Strong. If one man wishes to practice sodomy in preference to ordinary adultery, of course he must find another man willing to serve him thus. There are men willing to serve the sodomite in place of a woman provided they are paid money. And this money (here called price) is what was not to come into the treasury of the congregation.

Verses 19, 20. The word "usury," means simply the interest taken for money loans. There is nothing wrong in the transaction from a business standpoint. It would be wrong to take it from a brother because of social or sentimental reasons. No such reasons exist in the case of a stranger, hence it is all right to take interest from such, since there is nothing wrong in the act itself.

Verses 21, 22. No general law was made requiring men to make vows. When one was made, the Lord required it to be kept. There were occasions of special aims when the Lord called for vows, but no set law was included in the regular system.

Verse 23. This is practically the same as preceding paragraph, only it specifies an instance such as promising to make some certain offering to the Lord. If so, then the offering must be kept.

Verses 24, 25. This might be called a form of "eminent domain." The earth is the Lord's and the fullness thereof, and on that basis it was considered that the Lord's people should have a right to use what was necessary for the sustenance of life. The fact that they were not allowed to take anything from the vineyard or field proves that the necessity of life only, made it right for the individuals to help themselves. This privilege was still recognized in the case of Matt. 12: 1. It will be noticed that the disciples were not accused of stealing, which certainly would have been done had there been any chance for the accusation. So they had to fall back on the formality of the sabbath law, which they claimed was being broken.

DEUTERONOMY 24

Verses 1, 2. Let it be kept in mind that we are studying the law and customs of the O. T. in which certain things were suffered (not permitted), that were finally shut out by the stricter law. Among those was that of plurality of wives. Also that of putting away a wife that had become objectionable. The ordinance here was not looking so much to the idea that a man was putting his wife from him, but rather, to the justice due her of having a paper from him, that would show to the public that she was not a deserter. The bill of divorce might not be very complimentary for her as to her general conduct, but it would protect her from the accusation of desertion. Then if, in spite of the objection her husband had to her, some other man were willing to take her, he would know that he was not taking a man's wife from him.

Verses 3, 4. For some reason that we are not told this woman cannot return to the former husband. For one thing though, it would be inconsistent for him to take her back if he was sincere in his objection to her in the first place. The word "defiled" does not necessarily mean any actual uncleanness, but refers to the fact that she had become contaminated with the blood of another man after being put from the first. The Lord did not wish to have the promiscuous exchange of blood in this manner.

Verse 5. This is a repetition of ch. 20: 7 which the reader will please see.

Verse 6. These were the stones used to grind grain and they were not permitted to be used as a pledge. The theory would be that if a man were brought to the point of offering such personal assets for a pledge he certainly must be very poor. Therefore, he must be helped without any pledge since he would be one of the poor who the Lord said would never cease out of the land. (Ch. 15: 11.)

Verse 7. Stealing of human beings is called kidnapping today and in some states is punishable with death. We here see it was in such a class under the Mosaic law. The special phase of the crime is that of making a commercial use of a person.

Verses 8, 9. The grave situation when leprosy was present, or thought to be, called for one of the long passages in the law. (Lev. 13 and 14.) It was so serious that the sister of Moses was the occasion of holding up the journey of the Israelites for a week. (Num. 12:10.)

Verses 10, 11. It is not right to suspect any man of wrong without evidence. If a man says he will go into his house to get the pledge there is no need to follow him therein, since he could not defraud the lender by merely entering the house. If the reasonable time for making the transaction were allowed and the man did not appear, that would be soon enough to accuse him of bad faith. The extension of confidence to another is one of the surest means of encouraging him to honesty, and vice versa.

Verse 12, 13. This transaction has to do with a case where the exchange of money or other tangible is for a poor brother who is borrowing for his needs and not as a financial investment. Not that any usury or interest is charged in the case, for that has already been forbidden. As an evidence of good faith on the part of the borrower he makes a pledge in the form of some valuable. The very fact of tendering the pledge for even a few hours shows his confidence in his benefactor. On the other hand, after having made that much of an advancement of faith the lender should also show his confidence in the integrity of the poor brother by restoring the pledge before night.

Verses 14, 15. Let it not be forgotten that the law made a distinction between hired servants and bond servants. The former is in hand here. A man agreed to work because he was in need of income. That would indicate that he must have wherewith to purchase necessities of life and thus must have his money for the present. Therefore the pay day would come daily for him. Were he in better circumstances financially, he would not have been brought to engage himself to another as a servant.

Verse 16. Personal responsibility for conduct is the teaching of this verse. The second commandment said that God would visit the iniquity of the fathers upon the children, but it was confined to "them that hate me." Thus, if the children did not hate the Lord, then they were not to be punished on account of the sins of the fathers.

Verses 17, 18. Gratitude is the principle in view here. To pervert judgment means to deprive a man of the decision due him through some feeling of partiality or bribe. Thrown into this decree is the consideration that must be shown a widow. Her very widowhood was an indication that she was an object of charity.

Verses 19-21. This ordinance is based on the principle like that in ch. 23: 24, 25. The earth is the Lord's and therefore all mankind have some right to its products. No man was permitted to go into a field and cut down the grain for purpose of removing it. However, all grain overlooked or missed in the harvesting must be left for the poor of the public. This privilege was extended to include a sheaf that had been cut by the owner, but not to be cut by the gleaner.

Verse 22. Their personal experience of helplessness in that foreign land must always keep them in mind of others with a like situation, so that gratitude should cause them to act according to the commandment of God in such cases.

DEUTERONOMY 25

Verse 1. It might be said that all understood that the righteous were always the ones to be justified and the wicked to be condemned. Yes, but people need to be reminded of fundamental principles lest they forget and be influenced by wrong motives. It might be reasoned in certain cases that one man is poor and needy, or that he was a good man in other respects, or that his importance to the community was great, or for some other such consideration he should be given the favorable verdict even though in the controversy he seemed to be in the wrong. The verse means that regardless of all considerations the decision must be made on the basis of merit of the case.

Verses 2, 3. Corporal punishment for certain offenses was decreed by the law which we remember was both temporal and religious. The limit of stripes was forty. Paul said he received this form of punishment on five different occasions except that it was one less than the lawful limit each time. This is explained by secular history which it will be well to quote here: "This punishment among the Jews was not to exceed forty stripes (Deut. 25: 3), and therefore, the whip with which it was inflicted being made with three thongs, and each blow giving three stripes, they never inflicted upon any criminal more than thirteen blows, because thirteen of those blows made thirty-nine stripes; and to add another blow, would be to transgress the law, by adding two stripes over and above forty, contrary to its prohibition. And in this manner was it that Paul, when whipped of the Jews, received forty stripes save one (2 Cor. 11: 24) that is, thirteen blows with this threefold whip, which made thirty-nine stripes, i. e. forty save one."—*Prideaux's Connexion*, An. 108 and note. The word "vile" in this passage does not mean in a moral sense. It means low or trifling or disrespectful. A man might be considered as in the wrong and thus worthy of punishment. Yet he should not be regarded as not deserving of some consideration. If my brother were convicted of being in the wrong in the controversy between him and me, I would expect him to be given a just punishment. If the executioner of the punishment were allowed to go on and on to excessive degree it would make the action look is if he were beating a dog to death, or threatening to do so.

Verse 4. Machinery for separating grain from the chaff was not in existence then. The bulk was thrown down upon the grain floor and either beaten out with a flail, or trampled out by oxen. Naturally, the beast would be inclined to help himself unless hampered. This law forbade the owner hindering him with a muzzle. While the consideration of dumb brutes was actually required, yet the Lord had a future use to be made of this law. (1 Cor. 9:9.)

Verses 5, 6. This rule was invoked by Judah (Gen. 38: 8), and became a permanent feature of the law of Moses. The proviso in the ordinance was that the brother left no child. Otherwise it would be unlawful to take the widow since it would violate Lev. 18: 16. This would have made the act of Herod unlawful, as accused by John regardless of whether his brother had been living or dead, because he had left a child, a daughter. (Matt. 14: 6.)

Verses 7-10. A penalty in the form of public humiliation was to be inflicted on the man refusing to comply with this law. Just why a severer fate was meted out to Onan in the case cited above is not stated. However, we can see this difference in the circumstances. Onan made the pretense of obeying the order, in that he approached the woman in the fleshly relation. When he considered how the offspring would be credited he interrupted the proceeding. That showed that personal gratification was really the motive for beginning the act, which made his sin greater than that of merely refusing to have anything to do with the case.

Verses 11, 12. In the first place this struggle between two men should be considered as one of equal contest since it is between parties of equal class. For a woman to violate the principle of modesty and also to take an advantage of a man, which the merits of the controversy did not include would be an act of severe injustice. Therefore, the punishment due her would be the loss of her guilty hand.

Verses 13, 14. The civil as well as religious purposes of the law can be seen in this paragraph. The same standard used for buying should be used for selling.

Verses 15, 16. The principle of justice is universally recognized as due every one. The basis on which it is determined in any given case is that both parties to a transaction shall receive all, but no more than is coming to them by the law of equity. If one scale were used for selling and another for buying some one must be cheated.

Verses 17, 18. The first military encounter the children of Israel had with the enemy after being released from Egypt was with the Amalekites, as recorded Ex. 17. That was the occasion when the hands of Moses were supported by those of Aaron and Hur. The principle on which the grievance was estimated as being so great at that time, was the weakened condition of a part of the congregation. Amalek took advantage of that misfortune and oppressed them, which aroused the wrath of God.

Verse 19. The decree is here repeated that was made at the first instance. The fulfillment will be found in Est. 9. The word "remembrance" does not have the meaning of ordinary memory because the record of the event is inscribed in the book that was destined to be read by all generations. The word has the force of a memento; some visible trace of the thing considered. When the last member of that tribe was destroyed, there would not be left anything as a reminder of their existence.

DEUTERONOMY 26

Verses 1, 2. Throughout the dealings of God with man the right of the first has always been considered as belonging to the Giver of all good. So in this instance, when the children of Israel shall have entered and possessed the land so long ago promised to the fathers, their gratitude should be shown by this offering of the first of the land. It must be taken to the place where God's name would be recorded. This is somewhat indefinite, since we already know that the tabernacle was the thing in which the name of God would be recorded. The particular location of that structure was not as yet indicated, and hence this indefinite statement.

Verses 3, 4. *Priest that shall be in those days.* Not that some man would newly be made priest, for that was settled when God ordained that all the sons and descendants of Aaron were by that relationship qualified for the priesthood. They finally became so numerous that all were not used for active duty. This verse means that the man who was in active service as priest was to officiate in the reception of this offering of the first fruits.

Verse 5. The historical connection of this verse shows that Jacob is the father referred to, and at the time of the famine. He is here called a Syrian. Another name for that word is Aramean. It does not refer to an inhabitant of the country immediately north of Palestine. This word, Syria, is an abbreviation of Assyria, which lies in the country of Abram's birthplace. Aram is a name derived from the fact that it was like Mesopotamia, which means between the rivers. For information on this subject consult *Britannica*, Vol. 2 p. 307; and *Rawlinson*, Origin of Nations. The speech directed for the Israelite to make, was in appreciation of the providential care that the Lord had bestowed on the nation.

Verses 6, 7. This statement of their cry unto God, even before Moses was told to go unto them, agrees with Ex. 3: 7 and Acts 7: 34.

Verses 8-10. Paul asked the question "What hast thou that thou didst not receive?" (1 Cor. 4:7.) We know that had special reference to the spiritual gifts. The same fact applies to other gifts since we did not bring anything into this world. It is fair even from a view of justice that appreciation for the benefits be expressed by the return of the first fruits to the great Origin thereof. And since the land they will possess aboundeth (or floweth) with milk and honey they would not be deprived of any necessity of living, by making a contribution to God.

Verse 11. Rejoicing in iniquity would always be wrong (1 Cor. 13: 6), while it would always be right to rejoice in good. Since these things mentioned had come from God they would be good things and worthy of rejoicing.

Verse 12. For explanation of this third year of tithing see ch. 14: 28 and note.

Verse 13. God always knows the heart. Should the Israelite make these claims falsely, he would be detected and punished. Therefore, the command has the force of meaning that they should so conduct themselves that they can truthfully make them.

Verse 14. He must declare he has made proper use of the good things provided for him and that use included the gifts to the Lord. He had not eaten of that which should have been given to God. Not even in his "mourning" which is from a word that means a condition of extreme need or want. Not even such considerations were allowed to lead him to eat that which belonged to God's appropriation.

Verse 15. This is both an acknowledgement and plea. Acknowledgement that God lives in a holy habitation and a plea for him to look down on the people to bless.

Verse 16. Once the command to keep and twice to *do* is found in this verse. It cannot be made too emphatic that doing is necessary to acceptance by the Lord. Any other attitude taken with reference to the law of the Lord will be rejected.

Verse 17. *Avouched.* This is from a Hebrew word that is rendered variously in the A. V. but the outstanding principle of the expression is a very strong assertion in the form of a promise. The verse means they have made a strong promise to recognize the Lord as their God.

Verses 18, 19. The same strong promise is used in this verse. God has thus given his promise that he will accept the children of Israel as his peculiar (exclusively personal) people. The Lord never breaks his promise, and now he expects the Israelites to keep theirs.

DEUTERONOMY 27

Verse 1. The elders were associated with Moses and all the authority they had was subject to that of Moses. They were the experienced men and leaders of thought and judgment, but the final decision of all matters rested with Moses.

Verses 2, 3. The scarcity of the copies of the law has been already mentioned a number of times. That was because all copies had to be made by hand and with very crude instruments compared with what we know. Therefore, copies of it were to be written in public places in the same manner as our public bill boards. That would give many people access to the Lord's government.

Verse 4. Mt. Ebal was the mount called "the cursing." Therefore we must conclude that on the stones raised into a wall here, would be written that part of the law which pertained to the curses.

Verses 5-8. For a time after crossing the Jordan, God knew they would not be entirely settled in their religious headquarters. So the use of this altar made of stones was commanded. The legal use of an altar is that of burning sacrifices. Their gratitude for the blessings of God would be expressed by this demonstration. In Josh. 8: 30-32 is an account of the fulfillment of this order.

Verses 9, 10. *This day when thou art become the people.* We know that even from the bondage in Egypt, and very definitely at Sinai, they became the people of God and were declared to be the nation that had been redeemed from Egypt by a mighty hand. So we must look for some other significance in the statement. There can be but one, and that is, that God again repeated or recognized them as his people. Every time a blessing of God is bestowed on man in reward for worth or faithfulness that is equivalent to public declaration of the fact. Just as the N. T. teaches the principle that while Jesus was crowned, once for all, as king, when he took his seat at God's right hand, yet each time a human being recognizes him as king, it amounts to the same as crowning him.

Verses 11-13. In this paragraph the special position of Levi as a tribe is not recognized and thus we have the mention of twelve tribes. That is why Joseph is mentioned but neither of his two sons, who really formed two tribes. This classification is a general one and takes no account of any special official position. That will be done in following verses. For this there are six of the original twelve number on each of the mounts.

Verse 14. Here the Levites are mentioned as the ones to pronounce the curses on the people. This now is a different viewpoint of that tribe than considered above. It has already been learned that the tribe of Levi has been separated from all the other tribes as far as property holdings are concerned and more especially concerning authority. (Num. 3: 5-12.) Therefore, when any public work was done that pertained to instruction and enforcement of the law, the Levites were to do it. In this present matter the Levites were to pronounce these curses, and nothing is said about any of the other tribes in connection with the blessings either.

Verse 15. *Cursed.* This is from a word that means to threaten, warn, or wish an evil experience of some kind to come upon the person opposed. The word would mean the same, whether pronounced by the Lord or by uninspired man. The difference would be that when God makes the wish or threat he is able to enforce it, while man would not be able actually to bring the curse to pass, yet the motive of it would make the one pronouncing it as guilty in principle as if he could enforce it. In the present verse the curse is pronounced against the idol maker. In some cases the particular curse threatened is described in other parts of the Bible. Thus the curse for making idols is death. (Ch. 13: 15.)

Verse 16. The curse for making light of, or disregarding, the parents was death, as seen in Ex. 21: 17.

Verse 17. No particular penalty is prescribed for this wrongdoing but the law against it is found elsewhere. (Ch. 19: 14.)

Verse 18. The nature of this wrong is to take advantage of the unfortunate to mislead him. The result of such a sin in spiritual matters is taught by Jesus. The leader as well as the misled will fall into the ditch. (Matt. 15: 14.)

Verse 19. This is the sin of depriving the weak, or uniformed, of the righteous judgment due them in any matter.

Verse 20. This crime is condemned in the N. T. (1 Cor. 5: 1-5.)

Verse 21. The curse for this crime was death. (Lev. 20: 15, 16.)

Verse 22. The penalty for this wrong was death, or cutting off. (Lev. 20: 17.)

Verse 23. The curse for this iniquity was death by burning. (Lev. 20: 14.)

Verse 24. The penalty for this crime was death at the hand of the revenger of blood. (Deut. 19: 11, 12.)

Verse 25. No specific penalty is named as to this curse. The principles of the scripture require that those guilty of murder must suffer death. In this verse it is clearly set forth that the murder of another is the object of this bribe money.

Verse 26. This is a general curse and might mean whatever was the judgment of the Lord in any given case. The striking phase of this line of decrees is the requirement that the people must say "amen" at the pronouncement of the curses, thereby making them their own. That is, they must confirm the righteousness of the curses by saying "amen." That would commit them to the performance of their part in the various cases. Where the penalty was stoning, they must take the guilty one out and stone him. If it were burning then they must use the fire. It will always be understood that when men perform these various forms of punishment according to the stipulations of the scriptures, it is the Lord doing it and it is not by authority of men.

DEUTERONOMY 28

Verses 1, 2. As usual, the Lord bases his promises of good things on their doing the commandments. Then they will become a mighty nation above all others. The word "blessing" here means prosperity when bestowed by the Lord on man. It means praise for said prosperity, when bestowed by man on the Lord. No specific form of the blessing or prosperity will be mentioned but the various relations of life that will be blessed will be named in the several verses.

Verse 3. This is a pair of words to indicate two extremes, the city and country.

Verse 4. They will be happy with regard to their children, the young of their stock, and also the produce of the ground. The crops will not be disappointing.

Verse 5. They will bring the products of the soil home in their baskets, or any means of carriage, and will be happy in the use of the same.

Verse 6. The only significance of the terms here is in the fact of their being expressions of the two extremes. Since "in and out" would take in the full extent of whatever would be under consideration, this verse would simply mean that they would be blessed at all times, and in all conditions of life.

Verse 7. The enemy will be organized in a unit and in good order when he makes his attack upon the Lord's people, but will be so utterly defeated that he will be repelled with great loss and in complete (seven) disorder.

Verse 8. This is practically the same blessing promised in verse 5.

Verses 9-11. The nations around them will fight against them, but God will fight for them and exalt them as a people above all their enemies. That is, if they will be obedient to the divine command. All this will be fulfilling the promises made to the fathers and established with the oath of the Lord.

Verse 12. "Heaven" here means the first of the three heavens recognized in the Bible. The place of the atmosphere and clouds and the place from whence rain comes.

Verses 13, 14. It was the ambition of nations generally to be in the lead, and this was one thing promised to the children of Israel provided they obeyed the statutes of God.

Verses 15-19. It is not necessary to make detailed comments on this passage. It covers the same subjects as the verses on the blessings above. Instead of being prosperous and successful in the various relations of life as promised before, they will have the curse of God in them if they refuse to obey the law of God.

Verses 20, 21. This is a sort of summing up of the results to come from the curses threatened. They will finally be destroyed as a nation and driven from the land. This last was fulfilled in last two chapters of 2 Kings.

Verse 22. God could destroy in a moment the entire nation without the use of any visible means, but he will not see fit to do so. Instead, he will resort to various agencies in the form of disease and pests, and the sword of the enemy. The "consumption" here is not what is popularly meant as pertaining to the lungs. It is a word that means emaciation. It is the general shrinking and falling off of the flesh, and a sinking of the features of the body.

Verse 23. This is figurative, and it means that instead of the heaven dropping the rain for their ground, it will be as unyielding of the necessary moisture as if it were a canopy of brass. The ground will be as sterile as if it were iron.

Verse 24. Just another figure meaning a lack of moisture, as if the rain had turned into dust.

Verse 25. This is verse 7 in reverse.

Verse 26. Their helplessness is imaged here, as a carcass left on the open field. It will become the food of the birds of carrion, and there will be no one taking pity to fray (frighten) them away.

Verse 27. "The botch" was an inflammatory ulcer. "Emerods" was the same as what is now termed hemorrhoids, commonly called piles. Scab was a disease similar to the modern itch. This itch was slightly different from the preceding word in that it meant specially a condition of severe redness as if from sunburn, and so malignant that they would not be able to discover any remedy for it.

Verse 28. This verse had more direct application to their condition of mind that would be brought on by the various curses of God.

Verse 29. This verse is a specification of the general conditions mentioned in preceding verse. Although it may be bright noon time they will be in such a state of confusion that it will make them feel blind and in the dark.

Verses 30, 31. A general failure in all their enterprises, both social and commercial, will result from the curses of the Lord.

Verse 32. They will have to give up their children to the enemy nations and have nothing left but the heartache of a parent longing for his loved ones.

Verse 33-35. Very little added here to what has been threatened; only repeated for the sake of emphasis.

Verse 36. This is a direct prediction of their national captivity and the condition that will prevail, that of idolatry. This subject will be treated at length in the study of the prophecies.

Verses 37-41. Another summing up of the calamities to be placed over them, which will include the disappointments concerning their families. They will not get to enjoy them because the enemy will make servants of them.

Verses 42-44. Chief of the sorrows referred to here is that of being abused by the enemy nations. That would be a humiliation of the severest kind.

Verse 45. Here they are forewarned that the curses will not only vex them, but will pursue them until they are destroyed as a nation, and all because they refused to hearken to the voice of God. "To hearken" is the same as *doing*, which we have seen emphasized so often.

Verse 46. So evident will be these curses upon the nation that the world will observe it and be filled with wonder. That will add to the humiliation of them.

Verse 47, 48. Since they were not willing to serve the Lord he will suffer them to serve their enemies in the foreign land.

Verses 49-52. This paragraph is a prediction especially of the captivity at the hands of the Assyrians and fulfilled in 2 Kings 17.

Verse 53. This awful prediction was fulfilled in 2 Kings 6: 28.

Verses 54, 55. Even the normal sensibilities of the human being, will be dulled by the terrible condition into which they will be thrust in their disobedience.

Verses 56, 57. Modesty will give place to immodesty, and womanliness will be supplanted by coarseness. The affections intended to bind the members of the family together will be severed; general confusion will reign. The lowest ebb of love and mutual consideration will be reached, and the crying needs of the body will seek for gratification at the cost of human flesh, and all of this will be brought upon them through the means of the enemy with the siege.

Verse 58. They must observe to *do* all the words. Note that it does not insist merely on their doing the words that are written on the tables of the covenant, but the ones written in the book. Moses was the one who did that writing. Moreover, one result of observing these things written in the book was that they would come to fear the name of God. Hence, we must conclude that divine authority was recognized by them as being vested in what Moses wrote in the law.

Verses 59, 60. A spasmodic visitation of plagues would be bad enough, but the conditions being threatened here are to be of long continuance.

Verse 61. After mentioning by name a number of diseases the Lord adds that he will add to them the numerous plagues not written in the book. This idea is similar to that of Paul in Gal. 5: 21. After having named many works of the flesh he adds the expression "and such like." Here they were to be impressed that if such evil things as named are to be brought upon them, things which they know to be terrible; then what must be the awful nature of the ones not named!

Verse 62. The general population of the nation while in their full strength ran into the millions, while the remnant that remained after these terrible things had come to them was 42,360. (Neh. 7: 66.)

Verse 63. Being plucked off the land was a prediction of the captivity of the nation and fulfilled in 2 Kings, last two chapters.

Verse 64. While the nation as a whole will be confined in the land of the captivity and from there be brought back to their own land, there will be scattered ones of the race throughout the countries of the world. That threat was fulfilled as seen in John 7: 35.

Verses 65, 66. Even down to our day this awful condition exists as a terrible sign of the power of God in bringing about the fulfillment of his predictions.

Verse 67. This verse describes a general state of mind that will not let them have any rest. At every turn of the day they will have the feeling that something else would be preferable.

Verse 68. There are two predictions as to the captivity of part of the people given in this verse. One is the fact that they will be brought into the land of Egypt and the other is about a condition when they are there. Both of these predictions are fulfilled in the writings of Josephus. The former in Ant. 12-1-1, the latter in Wars, 6-8-2. After all the long list of things threatened against the nation of Israel that God recorded in this chapter we would think that nothing should have influenced them to depart from the divine law. But their grevious backslidings go to prove the general fickleness of the human mind, and, therefore, the necessity for it to be under constant regulation from a higher source than man.

DEUTERONOMY 29

Verse 1. The sabbatarians try to restrict the term "covenant" to the laws as written on the tables of stone. But here, as elsewhere, the word is used also with reference to that which Moses wrote. Lest we be misled into thinking he was speaking of the same things written on the tables, he specifies here that he means the words *besides* those made with them at Horeb. It is not claimed by any one that the tables were reproduced after leaving the holy mount. Therefore, we have the unavoidable conclusion that what God directed Moses to write was to be regarded as being of equal authority with that written on the tables.

Verse 2. It has now been only forty years since they had left Egypt and thus many of the present generations could remember what happened, for only the men twenty years old and up were slain miraculously after the affair at Kadesh.

Verse 3. The word "temptations" means "tests and judgments." When the Egyptians refused to release the Israelites, God brought various plagues upon them and thus the test of God's power as against the Egyptians was proved in many instances.

Verse 4. In spite of the advantage such recollection should have meant to them, they seemed to underestimate the significance of it all. The expression "Lord hath not given you," etc., is Biblical method of saying, they simply did not have such eyes, etc.

Verse 5. This wonderful fact is commented on at chapter 8: 4, which please see.

Verse 6. This means they had not depended on these articles from their own production. They had been provided by miracle which should have taught them the lesson of God's power and goodness, in spite of their waywardness and weakness.

Verses 7, 8. This is just a brief reminder of what they knew, that the heathen forces that came against them were overthrown by the superior force of God's people.

Verse 9. The logical, as well as authoritative, conclusion they should draw from these facts was that they should keep and *do* the words of "this" covenant.

Verse 10. The members of the congregation were in good order, having officers in their places, and thus ready for the invasion.

Verse 11. The wives and little ones were there present, the ones who they said would be a prey. That is, the congregation as a whole made that complaint. However, the ones actually making the complaint are dead and strewn along through the wilderness. The hewers of wood and drawers of water meant the ones who served the needs of the laver and altar.

Verses 12-15. By grouping these verses into one paragraph it is to bring about the interesting lesson that what Moses was then saying to the hearers was to be general in application, not only for the ones actually standing before him but also for those yet to be produced among them.

Verses 16-18. While the ones then standing before Moses had not been guilty of the grievous idolatry that had brought the judgments of God, it was worth while to remind them about it for their own admonition. They should profit by the history of the others of their congregation and thus not bring upon themselves the wrath of God which is here compared to gall (bitter or poisonous herbs) and wormwood.

Verse 19. Were it not for the concrete evidence of God's wrath against idolatry as seen in these judgments, some perverse man might be arrogant and boast that he personally would have peace in spite of these past histories, and in his arrogancy would "add drunkenness to thirst." It is bad enough to have the thirst for drink, but it is worse when that thirst is gratified, and drunkenness brought about.

Verses 20-22. This is another general summing up of the things that will come to them if they disobey the divine commands. God is jealous and will not suffer his authority and title to adoration to be trampled upon and replaced by idols. In the fire of his jealousy he will cause the guilty ones to feel the heat of his anger.

Verse 23. This verse is a reference to the general condition that is to result in the land of Israel after the threatened plagues have been brought. In this passage, a figurative comparison is made to the condition that had existed for centuries in the region of the Dead Sea. Incidentally we have some information about that interesting subject. The cities that were so wicked in the days of Abram and Lot were destroyed and the place of their former existence was finally one of salt and brimstone. There can be no mistake as to what he is talking about, for he mentions by name Sodom and Gomorrah, two of the outstanding cities involved.

Verses 24, 25. The demonstrations of God's wrath will be so evident that heathen people around will see and understand that it is a result of divine wrath. Not only that, but it will be demonstrated in such a way that all will understand the condition to be the judgment of God in punishment for their departures from his law.

Verses 26-28. We should note that the nations will not merely understand that God's people had displeased him and brought on the punishments, but will have knowledge of the specific phase of the law they had violated, that concerning idolatry.

Verse 29. This verse contains a fundamental principle regarding divine revelation. The world should bear in mind that God does not hold back from man anything that would be of any benefit to him. Therefore, no effort should be made to delve into the unseen for information which God has not seen fit to impart to man. This disposition has always been displeasing to God and is today. (Col. 2: 18.) Thus when there is something about a subject introduced in the Bible which seems to have mysteries about it, we must remember that what belongs to the Lord only, is not our business. We should therefore trust him for his grace and manifest a child-like faith in him.

DEUTERONOMY 30

Verses 1, 2. Not until the nation has been driven into captivity will it come to realize the awful mistake it made in departing from the law of God. That change of mind will come about, and when it does, the Lord will also change their situation and reverse their fallen condition.

Verses 3-6. This paragraph is a prediction of the return of the Jewish nation from Babylonian captivity. This great event is the subject of much of the major prophecies and will be commented on in detail at the proper place in this work. As for the scripture account of the fulfillment of the prediction, the reader may consult the books of Ezra and Nehemiah. The secular histories showing the fulfillment will be cited in connection with the various predictions made in the prophetic books. The expression, "circumcise thine heart" is a figurative reference to the consecration of the heart to God, after the purifying caused by the captivity.

Verse 7. The accounts of God's dealings in the past concerning his people and the heathen nations are significant. If God concluded his people needed a certain form of chastisement he would often use some heathen king and nation as the instrument of his wrath. Then after his work for his rebellious people had been completed, he would in turn punish the heathen instrument for the personal motive he showed in the affair.

Verse 8. This does not mean that the Israelites became and remained a nation of angels after the captivity, for they have always been a perverse and rebellious people, but on the subject that was the immediate cause of their captivity, idolatry, they never again were guilty of that. This fact will also be shown from secular history, later.

Verses 9, 10. This passage promises to reverse all the evils that had been visited upon them in punishment for their unrighteousness. Again the promise is based on their obedience to the divine laws. They must turn to the Lord wholeheartedly, and not merely in a partial degree as they had so often done before.

Verses 11-14. This language is cited by Paul in Rom. 10: 6-8. He did not mean to say that Moses was making a prediction in his utterance of the words. Rather, just as the law then being delivered to the Israelites was coming to them direct from the lawgiver, so the Gospel was brought right to the minds of the persons intended to be affected thereby. The general force of the passage is that no excuse is left for the disobedience of the people on the ground that the divine law was inaccessible, for it was brought to their "very doors," so to speak.

Verse 15. Not that the Lord invites us to "take our choice" between good and evil, between right and wrong, as is sometimes taught. He tells us about the two kinds of life and their fruits. Then we cannot be excused if we take the wrong side and come into the punishment of it.

Verse 16. This agrees with the teaching in the preceding paragraph, that God does not encourage the human choice unless that choice is the right one. Instead, the divine command is to love the Lord and walk in his ways.

Verses 17, 18. Even as God foretells the good results of obeying his law so he foretells the evil ones of disobeying. No pretense of ignorance will count.

Verses 19, 20. The angels in heaven and the inhabitants of earth will all know that God has given his human creatures all the instruction needed to keep them in the way of righteousness, and the way that would bring them the greatest amount of happiness.

DEUTERONOMY 31

Verse 1, 2. This is another place to mark as it states the age of Moses. We should not mistake his meaning when he said he could no more go in and out. That was not a reflection on his age; that he was becoming weak and infirm from age. The statement in chapter 34: 7 would disprove such a conclusion. The very last words in the verse constitute a comment on the other expression. He meant that his activity for the congregation was over, and that he would no longer go about looking after them, and supervising their various movements.

Verse 3. This is in keeping with foregoing paragraph. Moses was to cease his leadership and Joshua would then serve God as the leader of his people.

Verses 4-6. Citing the victories of the people over the heathen by the hand of the Lord, they are here encouraged to proceed in their assigned duties.

Verses 7, 8. Nothing was omitted that would tend to insure proper repect for the new leader, Joshua. Moses delivered his commission to him in the presence of the people and assured him of the blessings of God in his great work.

Verse 9. Not even the sabbatarians will deny the complete authority of the tribe of Levi in administration of the law of the O. T., yet we see in this verse that they operated under the law that Moses wrote and delivered to that tribe. Another rebuke for the modern Judaizers who would desert Christ and drag us back to the law.

Verses 10, 11. We are so frequently reminded of the scarcity of copies of the law in those days of manual reproduction of them, so that on the occasion of the great sabbath year when the people would be in general assembly, the law was to be read in the hearing of the people.

Verses 12, 13. At the time of this great celebration the stranger as well as the direct member of the congregation should be made acquainted with the law of the land. While there were some items of the system that only pertained to the Israelites, yet that which applied as man with man would have bearing on all within the limits. Even as we would expect a foreigner to respect and obey our laws while amongst us.

Verses 14, 15. The solemn hour for the departure of Moses is approaching. The Lord had his special place of representation and that was the tabernacle. Thus he commands that Moses and Joshua meet him in that place. The Lord did not appear directly in person since man could not endure that. He appeared in a cloud.

Verse 16. For "sleep" the margin has "lie down," and the lexion justifies that rendering. Also note that it says Moses was to sleep with his fathers. This could not apply to his body, for he was not buried with any other person. This shows that man is composed of something more than his body, and thus, that materialism is a false doctrine. Moses is told that after his death the people will go after the gods of the land and thus break his covenant with them.

Verses 17, 18. All this passage of threatening has been recorded previously and is here repeated on the eve of the change of administration in the leadership.

Verse 19. The song mentioned here is in the following chapter. A song is not always a rhyme. It is not confined to mere sentiment, but may include the more serious literature of teaching. It was so with this song of Moses.

Verses 20, 21. The song was to serve as a warning to the people, and prepare them to make the proper use of the great prosperity that was to come upon them after taking possession of the land that had been promised to the fathers. Even the punishment that was to come upon them for their disobedience was to be written for their warning.

Verse 22. The song was written, and then taught to the people. There having not been a copy of the song before, they had no way of knowing it, or of learning it. That made it necessary for them to be taught it, which Moses did.

Verse 23. The pronoun "he," has to refer to God since he it was who had made the oath of promise concerning the land. He it was who here gave the solemn charge to Joshua to take courage and go onward in leading the people.

Verse 24. This is the book that is referred to by some as the "ceremonial law" and such is true, if used properly. That is, the writings of the hand of Moses were the details of the system which God had in mind when he first gave the ten commandments. We have already learned that the decalogue in itself was not a complete law at all, since it did not contain a single specific penalty. What the Lord commanded Moses to write, was to complete the system and show the children of Israel how they were to carry out the several ceremonies, but to refer to the "ceremonial law" in the sense of its being less binding than the tables, is one form of rebellion against God.

Verses 25, 26, 27. Sabbatarians make a great ado over the fact that this book was put in the side of the ark, whereas the tables were in the ark. This means, they say, that it was of less importance and authority than the tables. It is a shameful use to be made of the scriptures, and only coincides with the spirit of rebellion possessed by such people. For the sake of the sincere inquirer on this subject it will be noted here that God had a purpose for this placing of the law, that it was to be a witness against them. The fact that this book was more accessible than the tables would prove it to be more important than the tables, if anything, but it does not prove that. There was really no difference in the importance of what God gave to them through the hand of Moses.

Verses 28-30. Moses is still talking directly to the Levites and commands them to call an assembly of all the people. The assembling was to be done under their elders and officers. After the assembly was formed he spake to them the song to be found in the following chapter. The word "spake" is not to be taken as meaning the opposite of sing. It is a more general word. Even the N. T. tells Christians to "speak" in song. (Eph. 5: 19.) What we should get here is that Moses delivered the words of this composition to the people from his mouth and to their ears.

DEUTERONOMY 32

Verse 1. This is the beginning of the "song of Moses" that is frequently referred to in the speech of God's people. It is also referred to in the N. T. (Rev. 15: 3.) It will contain much history and other teaching. The importance of the passage is indicated by the supreme call to attention. The heavens and earth are called upon to give ear to the words of the song. While they were written in a book, yet the whole congregation was to hear, therefore, they will be delivered by word of mouth.

Verse 2. Doctrine means teaching, and as the showers and dew of the sky bring blessings upon the earth so will the great truths of the song bring spiritual good.

Verse 3. The surety of the blessings just mentioned is in the fact that the name of the Lord will be invoked and all greatness is to be ascribed to him.

Verse 4. "Like a rock," would be as a basis for material greatness, so God is a Rock of support for all them who wish to follow truth and righteousness.

Verse 5. The noun for "they" is in the following verse and described as the "foolish people" which means the wayward among the nation. That is why it is now so important that they listen to this great classic to be delivered to them.

Verse 6. The accusation implied in this verse is that they had been ungrateful for the blessings of God. Not only had been indifferent about them but had returned to God their lives of disobedience and seemed to forget their close relationship to him.

Verse 7. A call to memory. They could read some of it in the written pages extant, and could further learn through the lips of their parents. From whichever source of information, they should profit by the record.

Verse 8. In one brief verse a great historical scope is covered. God separated the sons of Adam in the 11th chapter of Genesis and predicted the several possessions of the tribes of Israel who were at that time about to invade the land of the possessions.

Verses 9, 10. Jacob is a composite name for the nation of Israel and declared to be the possession of the Lord. That was in mind when he called Abram from his home in Chaldea and directed him out. (Gen. 12.) When the time of fulfillment of the promise was drawing near, God took special care of the founder of the nation and brought him safely through the perils of want and other weakness.

Verses 11, 12. This passage uses the object lesson seen in dumb creatures as to care for the dependent ones, to illustrate God's care for the nation while it was young and tender. At the time Moses is speaking to them, they are a strong people compared with what they were at one time.

Verses 13, 14. The providential sustenance of the people when no natural means could be relied on, is the subject of this paragraph. Often when all other help seems impossible the power and goodness of God intervenes to redeem the situation.

Verse 15. According to Strong's lexicon, Jeshurun is a symbolic name for Israel. Thus the verse teaches that Israel became rich or prosperous, and then rebelled. It is the history of man that he will generally allow his material prosperity to crowd out the importance of spiritual prosperity. See the comments on this thought that are offered at chapter 8 of this book.

Verse 16. When people begin to forsake God they usually become active in some other direction. So when the children of Israel started in their downward course away from God they became interested in false gods and thus provoked him to jealousy.

Verse 17. The word "devils" is from SHED and Strong defines it as "daemons." The descriptive form of them is by the word "malignant." Since the very principle of idolatry is one against the true God it would be proper to regard the whole of the system of idolatry as being like things malignant, with the Creator. Paul comments in the same line of thought on the subject. (1 Cor. 10: 20.)

Verse 18. If an earthly child were to forget his father or mother, he would be regarded as very ungrateful. How much more grievous was the indifference of the people of God to their divine origin.

Verse 19. The word "abhorred" is from an original that is not as severe as the present rendering makes it. The word means to "think little of." So it would be in the case of an earthly parent. A man would be bound to have a very humiliating estimate of a child who had turned away from him.

Verse 20. Sometimes a son or daughter will come to hold the parent in dishonor, yet wish to have them accessible for their own selfish wants. If the parent will turn from the ungrateful child for the time being and throw him out on the world on "his own," it might bring him to his senses. That is what God did to his people.

Verse 21. This is a noted prediction and connected with the condition of unfaithfulness of the ancient people. They had turned from the true God to the worship of idols. That roused the jealousy of the true God. Then he determined some day to give them something to be jealous over. It would be when they saw him take a "foolish nation," (the Gentiles) into his bosom. (Rom. 10: 19.)

Verse 22. Taking a future look at the waywardness of the people who had received so many favors from God, the threat is made that the fire of God would burn to the lowest depths. Even to the lowest "hell." This is from SHEOL and defined by Strong as follows: "hades, or the world of the dead (as if a subterranean retreat), including its accessories and inmates." It is the only word for "hell" in the O. T. It is rendered in the A. V.; by grave 31 times, hell 31 times, and pit 3 times. Thus, in the verse now being considered it is a figurative showing of the depths to which he will reduce those who come under the fire of the divine wrath.

Verses 23-25. The depths of degradation to which God will plunge his disobedient people will be brought about through such conditions and experiences as here described.

Verse 26. This is the captivity and general dispersion noted in ch. 28:68.

Verse 27. This means that the threat made in preceding verse would be made complete were it not for the boasting that would be done by the enemy. Because of that consideration, God will show more leniency toward his unfaithful nation than their conduct deserves.

Verse 28. They had been advised and offered counsel but would not accept it. Now they must be made to learn the lesson by painful experiences.

Verse 29. God grieves over the misdoing of his people. He warns and pleads for them to heed his teaching and profit by the mistakes their former brethren have made. It is significant to note that in this short verse the words "understood" and "consider" are used in connection. The same thought is found in Isa. 1: 3. The people did not know because they did not consider. Much of the so-called ignorance that exists among the professed children of God in all ages has been through their own indifference to the opportunities for learning.

Verses 30, 31. The successes of the children of Israel against all odds can be explained only on the theory that God had intervened. The pronouns "their" and "them" in verse 30 are to be connected to mean the Rock of the Israelites had sold or delivered them, the enemies. Even the enemy acknowledges the superiority of the God of the Israelites. An instance of this may be drawn from Ex. 8: 19.

Verses 32, 33. These articles are used figuratively of the wrath of God against his enemies. While he sometimes suffers these enemies to afflict his own people, he will finally turn against them. How foolish then for God's people to serve the very people whom God will finally destroy.

Verses 34, 35. The teaching in this paragraph coincides with Rom. 12: 19.

Verse 36. "To judge" often means to bring punishment or affliction. Here it means to avenge the people of God by judging the enemy who had oppressed them.

Verses 37, 38. God will call upon these heathen nations to explain the helplessness of their gods; the beings they had pretended to believe in, and on whom they were supposed to lean for help.

Verse 39. When the comparison is made, the conclusion will be forced on them that no god in the universe is like the God of Israel. As evidence of it, his ability to kill or make alive is cited, which had been fully established as historical fact.

Verse 40. This means that God always was and always will be; he is self-existent.

Verses 41, 42. Since the sword was a common weapon of warfare in ancient times, the figure of God's success in battle is indicated by the whetting of the sword. He declares the arrow will be drunk with blood. Not necessarily intoxicated as we commonly use that word. The original here means, "being satiated or gorged." The Lord will be so effective in his slaying of the enemy that such a description was given of it, as here stated.

Verse 43. The nations are called upon to share the rejoicing of the people of God. Those who do so instead of rejoicing at their downfull will be blessed of God.

Verse 44. Hoshea here is the same as Joshua, who was associated with Moses.

Verses 45-47. After reciting the entire song to the people, Moses admonished them to set their hearts on it and observe to *do* all the words of the law. It is so important a matter that life itself is involved.

Verses 48-52. This passage announces to Moses what he will be expected to do in the end, but a few more words will be revealed which he committed to the congregation before leaving them for the place of his death. Abarim is really not the name of any certain mountain. It is a more general area and the particular mount on which Moses will stand to get a look at the land is Nebo. The reason for his punitive death is given to him; that he failed to sanctify the Lord or give him the credit for the supply of water at Kadesh.

DEUTERONOMY 33

Verses 1-3. Moses, as the inspired writer of the book, will speak of Moses as the servant of God and teacher of the people under God. This speech will contain figures of speech and some direct reference to history, and repetition of some law. The great power and goodness of the Lord will run through the address. Some of the places will be mentioned where the greatness of God was manifested, such as Sinai, Seir and Paran.

Verses 4, 5. He speaks his own name in the third person as explained at beginning of preceding paragraph. Being called a king is indefinite. The word did not have as definite or strong a significance then, as it often does now. It sometimes is used in the scriptures as a designation of one who is at the head of a people. This was his position with the children of Israel. He was the mediator between them and God, and was second in command of all the forces after the Lord.

Verse 6. This and the following verses will be practically along the line of the discourse Jacob made to his sons in the 49th chapter of Genesis. The short benediction on Levi was in deference to the fact that he was his father's first born.

Verse 7. Several verses in Genesis are devoted to Judah while the one is given him here. But the few lines cover the superiority of this tribe over the others that is so elegantly described in the former place.

Verse 8. Levi was given the service of the tabernacle and the priests were of this tribe. They were the only ones who had authority to consult the objects named here that were placed in the ephod and worn by the priests in consultation with God.

Verse 9. This verse refers to the faithfulness of Levi when Moses called for the ones so disposed to come over to the Lord's side. This tribe alone responded. In so doing, he separated himself from the other tribes and preferred the Lord to fleshly kin. It is the same in thought as expressed by Paul in Gal. 1: 16.

Verses 10, 11. This paragraph also treats of the exclusive right of Levi to the work of authoritative teaching. (Mal. 2: 7.) The smiting called for, for those who oppose Levi, and especially the family of Aaron, is given a clear instance in Num. 16.

Verse 12. The specific fulfillment of this promised blessing is not at hand. But we shall learn in the last part of Judges how that an unexpected favor will be shown him.

Verse 13. Much tender regard is expressed for Joseph. The same was done by his father as recorded in Gen. 49. The blessings of God for him were numerous and great in more than one respect. For one thing, God permitted him to become two tribes and thus come into two portions of the promised land.

Verses 14, 15. The word "moon" in verse 14 is made plural in the margin. The months of the Jewish calendar began with the new moon. When used figuratively, as is done here, it would mean to convey the thought of monthly prosperity.

Verse 16. *Dwelt in the bush.* This is a reference to the experience of Moses at Horeb when the angel of God spoke to him from therein, and called him to go to Egypt to deliver his people from their bondage. Reference is made in this verse to the sad chapter in the life of Joseph when he was apart from his brethren after they had sold him to the traders.

Verse 17. The honor and advantage given to Joseph through his two sons have been already commented upon in verse 13. This advantage is here likened to the strength of a fabulous beast that was reputed to have gigantic horns of equal strength.

Verses 18, 19. What the public press calls "honorable mention" is about all that I have to say about Zebulun's place here.

Verses 20, 21. This is a reference to the military success of Gad. Mention of the arm, means the wielder of the sword; and the crown of the head indicates he will be able to dethrone kings and take their position of power. Gad was one of the tribes that subjudated the kings of Canaan and surrounding territory. By the same use of language it is stated that he had a portion of the lawgiver which refers to his overcoming the rulers of the heathen nations.

Verse 22. The activity of the young of the lion is the sum of this comparison.

Verse 23. *Satisfied with favor.* This does not mean, necessarily, that he will be actually satisfied with his portion although he may be. But the thought is that he will be given sufficient that should satisfy him.

Verse 24. Numbers counted for more in those days than they do now. That was a military nation and depended on its man power for success against the enemy. Therefore, it was wishing a blessing on a man to wish for him abundance of children. Oil of olive was the only source of that product with that ancient people. It was used for light, for food, for anointing, for many formal ceremonies. Therefore, a reference to it meant an indication of much provision.

Verse 25. The words of this verse are used in some religious songs today. It means here the same as expressed in 8: 4, except there it was specially applicable to their past experience in the wilderness, while here it is a promise of continued care.

Verse 26. "Jeshurun" is figurative for Israel and the God of Israel is without an equal. He is Lord of heaven and the source of "thy" (Israel's) help.

Verse 27. God is the refuge of Israel and his everlasting arms are underneath the children of Israel. The second personal pronouns here refer to Israel. The promise is made that the enemy will be subdued before Israel by the help of God.

Verse 28. The exclusive occupancy of Canaan was the plan of God, and what was promised to the descendants of Abram. That promise was on condition of their obedience to the commandments of God. In proportion as they complied with those conditions they acquired what this verse predicted.

Verse 29. This is practically the same outlook as described in preceding verse.

DEUTERONOMY 34

Verses 1-4. Not much comment is necessary on this chapter. From the mount before mentioned, Moses was permitted to see the land of Canaan with all its attractiveness, but was again told that he could not go over to enter it.

Verses 5, 6. Moses died in the mount (ch. 33: 50), in the land of Moab but was buried in a valley in a place unknown to any man. The Lord buried him. For this see last word of verse 5, and second word in verse 6.

Verse 7. Although 120 years old Moses did not die of "old age," for none of his vitality was gone. His was a miraculous death as punishment for disbelief in God.

Verse 8. This was a ceremonial mourning since it was for a set number of days and then the mourning was ended. Of course they could be, and doubtless were, sincere.

Verse 9. Joshua had already been commissioned to take the place of Moses. He did so and the people accepted him as their new leader.

Verses 10-12. Moses had no successor as a lawgiver and prophet. His place in the government of the O. T., was perpetuated through the law and no change was made in that law until the prophet came who was to take the place of Moses. That had been predicted by Moses himself and recorded in the 18th chapter of this book.

JOSHUA 1

Verse 1. When the twelve spies returned from their commission and reported on the case, Joshua was one of the two men who maintained faith in the Lord and encouraged the people toward their duty. When the death of all the men of war had been decreed at that time, Joshua was excepted for the reason that he had "wholly followed the Lord." Later when a successor was needed as leader of the people he was the one chosen and qualified. (Num. 27: 18-20.) Now that Moses is dead, the Lord calls on Joshua to take up his charge. He is here called Moses' minister. That is from a word that means "an attendant."

Verse 2. Many times we have had occasion to say that God had given the land to the fathers by promise, and to their seed after them. That made the whole conduct of the congregation one of defense. Now we have the subject brought down to date for in this verse the Lord says "I do give to them," the children of Israel, this land. If any doubt had existed before on this subject it should be dispelled now and remain clearly in the mind of the reader that as the congregation moves against the heathen in the land they are conducting a war of defense.

Verse 3. The subject of the preceding verse is made even more definite and emphatic in this. Every place on which they place their feet has been given to them. Thus in every action of the army they are not only fighting a war of defense but are fighting it on their own homeland.

Verse 4. The bounds of the promised land are again stated and can be seen to include a vastly wider extent than just the land of Canaan. This territory was first promised to Abram. (Gen. 15: 18.) The word "river" here is from NAHAR and has been rendered 18 times by "flood," as in Josh. 24: 2, 3, 14, 15; Psa. 66: 6.

Verse 5. God never did fail in his support of Joshua. When there seemed to be an exception to this promise the fact was explained by the conduct of the people in which they had broken some commandment of the Lord, but Joshua was always successful in the operations that depended soley upon his own conduct.

Verse 6. Not only will he be able to take over the land from the hands of the usurper but will finally be able to settle the tribes in their individual allotments.

Verse 7. Joshua is personally charged to observe to *do* according to the law. Not merely the part on the tables of stone but that which Moses had commanded. The authority of Moses is again set forth very clearly.

Verses 8, 9. The sabbatarians say that what God commanded is one thing, and what Moses commanded is another. But in these two verses the book of the law is mentioned and in direct connection the Lord says "I commanded." Thus, to all fair minded persons there can be seen no difference between the authority of the book and the tables.

Verses 10, 11. The narrative will soon disclose that three days will have been used by the men sent over as spies and of course the congregation would not move until their return. But Joshua makes that stipulation before hand. This shows that he was inspired for the great task set before him.

Verses 12, 13. It is here said to these 2½ tribes that the Lord "hath given" them rest. Since it is understood that the invasion for conquest has not yet been made, it might be confusing to read such words. It is explained by the fact that the possession allotted to them was on the east side of Jordan and that land had at the very time been taken over while Moses was with them, upon their approach to that territory. Hence they personally had been given rest from war for their own sake.

Verse 14. The wives and children as well as their livestock would be an encumbrance in warfare and no help. Therefore they were to remain on the east side of Jordan in the places prepared for them in the lifetime of Moses. But the men of war must go over prepared for battle. The word "armed" is from CHAMUSH and is the same word that is rendered "harnessed" in Ex. 13: 18.

Verse 15. They were not merely to go over and make a flourish as if they would do something great and then retire and leave the work in the hands of others. Instead, they were to engage in the conflict until the other tribes had won the possession of the land which God had already given them provided they fought for it.

Verse 16. The response was noble and complete. They were ready to do what Joshua commanded them to do, and go wherever he told them to go.

Verse 17. At first thought it might seem that these people were making false claims of their obedience to Moses because of what we know of the sad instances in which God punished the nation for disobedience. The explanation is in the observation that the men who had been responsible for those occasions are now dead and the ones who are making the guarantees of obedience now had not been implicated in those acts of rebellion. The very fact of their being alive and present is evidence of it.

Verse 18. The principle of delegated authority was well understood by these men. Certainly they understood that God was the only source of all authority. And yet they stood ready to punish capitally those who rebelled against the commandments of Joshua. All of which shows that rebellion against God's chosen representatives is the same as rebellion against God. This principle is taught in Rom. 13: 4.

JOSHUA 2

Verse 1. The place named here was situated near the Jordan and just across from Jericho. In civilized countries a spy is subject to death if detected while in the land he is spying on. But these men are really spying in their own land although that fact will not be recognized by the enemy. That is why they must maintain secrecy. Much criticism has been offered on the fact of this harlot and the connection she was allowed to have with the plans of God's people. Space would forbid any lengthy discussion of the subject here. It is safe to remember that the standards of life had not been raised as high among the heathen as they are now. Also, no person is so low but the grace of God can bring him up. If this woman had taken the wrong attitude toward the men of God then, or had manifested a desire to continue in wickedness afterward, we have no reason to think that God would have favored her. Another thing to consider here is the fact that she lived on the wall of the town and that would serve the purposes of these men of God better than a house down within the city.

Verses 2, 3. Following the custom of countries as to spies the king sought to take in hand these men reported to have entered his city as spies. Learning that they were supposed to be in the house of this woman, he demands them at her hands.

Verse 4. This is another feature of the incident that is criticized. The woman told a falsehood and yet the N.T. says that Rahab was justified. But it does not say she was justified because of her falsehood. It was because of her faith in God and because she was willing to show her faith by doing something on behalf of God's servants. She was justified because of her good traits and actions and in spite of these other things that were not desirable or right. It is a principle accepted by civilized countries even today that when military conditions are present, men expect to be treated with strategy and actions that would mislead. This woman is helping the cause of God by assisting the servants of God and opposing the enemies of the Lord's people.

Verse 5. The cities of ancient times were in two classes; those walled or "fenced," and those considered as open cities. The former were supposed to be prepared for defense against enemies of all kinds. Thus it was the practice to shut these gates at the approach of night. This is the time of day she represented the men as having escaped out into the open country. With this story as background she advised the king to pursue the men. In this way she diverted the attention from the men whom she recognized as being from the God of the Israelites.

Verse 6. We have already seen that the roofs of houses were used for other purposes than shelter. (Deut. 22: 8; Acts 10: 9). So this was a fitting place to take these men for hiding. Another thing, it will be more convenient to provide their escape if they are on the roof of the house. They can come down directly onto the wall surrounding the house and thence on the outside of the wall and escape. This was made possible by the peculiar condition and use of such roofs. (Matt. 24: 17.)

Verse 7. Having let the king's men out through the gate they closed it again. Then these men pursued the spies, as they thought, going in the direction of the Jordan to intercept them in their return to their own company.

Verse 8. The movements of the characters in this drama are swift. Before the spies had retired Rahab went up to them upon the roof. This being the same as some other place of public appearance there was nothing unusual in her coming to them here.

Verses 9-11. The account of the deliverance through the Red Sea had preceded the march of the people and it had caused consternation. The significant expression of the woman concerning the land is that the Lord "hath given" that to his people. That is what has been held forth all along. She regards the children of Israel as the rightful occupants of the very ground on which she was living.

Verses 12, 13. The woman makes no plea of personal merit and no professions of righteous living. No attempt is made to condone her past life. For that matter, we have no evidence that she was practicing her usual trade at the time of which we are reading. If she had been known to have used the business as a regular profession in her lifetime she would have retained the title even after she had ceased activity of it. But the request she now makes is based on the act of friendliness which she had just shown these men. That is another feature of recognized relations between nations interested in military affairs. Reference is often made to "friendly" countries as the basis for reciprocity in like favors. So it was a logical plea she made of them.

Verse 14. An agreement of mutual friendliness and assistance was entered into. The pact was on the condition of her keeping confidentially the knowledge she had of the situation.

Verse 15. The escape was effected through a window and is explained as being necessary because she dwelled upon the wall. This would indicate that no margin was left between the house and the edge of the wall. That would be a reasonable conclusion since a wall would not be so spacious as to provide any waste space.

Verse 16. There is something interesting in the coincidence of the three days. That is the exact period that Joshua set in his instructions to the congregation. All of which shows the hand of God in the matter and explains the success of a strategy that might otherwise have been fruitless.

Verses 17-20. This repeats the agreement already made between the woman and these spies, but it includes additional conditions. She must manifest the signal of the same thread (rendered in A.V. by "cord, fillet, line, thread") by which she let them down to the ground. This will insure her identification when the time comes for their fulfilling of the agreement. A condition of their promise to spare her people was that they be with her at the time and in her house.

Verse 21. The woman agreed to the conditions and immediately after letting the men escape she bound the cord in the window. No use for delay in so important a matter.

Verse 22. The period of three days was observed by all the actors in this performance. Which indicates the hand of God in its direction. A wonderful lesson is possible here. Not all of the actors were conscious of the unison of action, yet their respective actions perfectly harmonized. Which proves that when a common head is recognized as the source of authority, the conduct will be uniform regardless of whether all the parties to the scheme are acquainted with the others. Thus today, if all men who profess to be following the Lord actually do so, they will all act in harmony with each other, regardless of what might have been the personal differences between their former manners of life. See 1 Cor. 11: 1 along this line of thought.

Verses 23, 24. The men returned after the allotted time and reported to their chief and gave an encouraging picture of the prospect.

JOSHUA 3

Verse 1. The congregation was moved from the immediate vicinity of the city where they had been and got nearer the Jordan at the place where they will make the crossing. This move was made pending the return of the spies.

Verse 2. The three days period is again mentioned. After it had passed the officers begin immediate preparations for the journey and among the people.

Verse 3. A large crowd of people would need some visible signal for their movements and the object designated for that purpose was the ark. After being informed of the arrangement it would be expected that they would be always on the alert and thus be ready to march as soon as the ark was seen moving.

Verse 4. A distance of two thousand cubits must be allowed between the ark and the people. The reason assigned for this provision was that they had not passed that way before. The way being new, it was all the more necessary that they have clear and uniform means of guidance. The ark must be visible to all the people all the time and that would not have been likely were they jammed up against it. But the ark in the hands of the priests would be cautiously moving ahead to search out the way and the people at a convenient but respectful distance could follow in unison.

Verse 5. "To sanctify" means "to consecrate or be devoted." They are about to start on the last lap of the momentous journey started forty years ago. Drop all subjects of interest not helpful for the crisis on hand and be ready to start.

Verse 6. The ark had been provided with means of handling when being carried. (Ex. 25: 14, 15.) Now the authorized men, the priests, must take up the holy piece and proceed to lead out the way.

Verse 7. One meaning of the word "magnify" here is "to honor." God's honor for Joshua was to be made manifest to the people by the miraculous demonstrations soon to follow in their movement toward the land of their objectives.

Verse 8. The march was to continue until a certain point had been reached and then they must halt. That point is here called the "brink" of the water. This word means "edge, brim, border, limit"; and such like. As soon as the feet of the priests bearing the ark entered the edge of the water they were to pause.

Verses 9-11. Notice is again given to the people of their impending movements. The assurance is repeated of the victory over the heathen nations then occupying the land on the other side of Jordan. They must march under the orders given to follow the ark that is to precede them.

Verse 12. A special "chore" is to be performed in connection with the march and for that purpose there must be selection of a man from each tribe for this service. The nature of that service was not told them yet, only the selection was now made.

Verse 13. The miracles of God are not uniform, and of course, not according to what we would expect to see from nature. Some passage over the Jordan must be provided. Thus the feet of the priests having entered the edge of the water, that will be the signal, and the apparent means of providing the aforesaid crossing. Their feet would seem to be a barrier thrown across the stream and cause the water to cease flowing but stand up in a heap as if by a physical wall. The rest of the opening would require no miracle. As soon as the flow of water was stopped at the given point the water from there on would naturally run away in the usual course of a stream.

Verse 14. *And it came to pass.* This is a prelude to several things that will be seen in the following verses after the priests went forth bearing the ark.

Verse 15. Most of the active facts are still pending in the narrative through this verse. But for this paragraph the comments will be on the sentence which the A.V. edition has placed in parentheses, because the facts stated therein will be significant as to the various conditions and happenings on this occasion. The river Jordan is normally not a wide stream and not deep. Much helpful information about the river may be obtained in Schaff-Herzog Encyclopedia, article "The Jordan." The stream was often crossed in the ordinary pursuits of life of the inhabitants. And it had fords at various places so that it would not need to have miraculous help to cross over it, as a rule. But that the supernatural feat about to be done may be understood, the statement here referred to says that the river overflowed all its banks at the harvest time which was the time now reached. The word "banks" is a word meaning "a border." Hence it does not especially mean a steep wall of ground usually seen to enclose the main channel of a stream, but what we call the "bottomland" extending quite a distance beyond the banks proper. It means that at this time of year these bottom lands were overflowed and thus the stream would be several hundred feet wide. The depth would also be greatly increased. Then, since the stream was always a swift one, we can see that it would be impossible to ford or otherwise cross the stream at this time, without some miraculous assistance.

Verse 16. The general purport of this verse is that all of the tributaries of the river were backed up by this miraculous dam and made to stand as a heap so as to let the bed of the stream become dry for the passage.

Verse 17. Ordinarily the word "midst" would mean the center or middle. But it also means any place within the limits of a thing. In this place we know it means this, because verses 8 and 15 expressly state the point at which the priests stopped in their march, which was the edge of the water.

JOSHUA 4

Verse 1. The last verse of preceding chapter states that the people passed on across the Jordan after the priests bearing the ark paused at the edge of the water. When that had been accomplished the Lord gave Joshua further orders.

Verse 2. These were the men already designated in Ch. 3: 12. Now the congregation as a whole has crossed, but these twelve men having been chosen for some special use, are still at attention and ready for orders.

Verse 3. This verse gives the orders. Each of the twelve men was to take up a stone from the immediate spot where the priests had stopped and carry them over to be left at the place where they were to spend the night.

Verses 4, 5. The priests were still standing in the place where they stopped and will continue to be there until the men have gone over. The stones to be selected would not be mere pebbles for they were to carry them upon their shoulders. The use to be made of them explains why so large stones were to be taken.

Verse 6. This is a general statement of the object of these stones. It was for a sign to the future generations who would naturally be curious for information.

Verse 7. The explanation was then to be made to the children that once these same stones had been on the other side of Jordan, and that it was possible to have them on this side because the Lord had dried up the river for their passage. The way in which they would be of significance will be seen in verse 9 below.

Verse 8. This is still concerning the twelve men selected who each took up a stone and carried it over to the western side of the river and laid it down.

Verse 9. This verse is often overlooked or else confused with the previous ones on the subject of the stones. In addition to the twelve stones taken up by the twelve men, Joshua also gathered twelve stones from the same spot and piled them up in form of a pillar right on the spot. That pile was standing when this book was being written. Now the significance of verse 7 can be seen. These 24 stones having been taken up from the same spot they would naturally be similar in appearance and give evidence of having been at one time together. Hence, when the generations of children would have their eyes drawn to the two piles of stones, one on the west and the other on the east side of the river, and see that they were from the same source, it would signalize to them that it was true that their fathers had once been on the other side. Moreover, since they were piled up on the spot where the priests had paused, and since that was on the far border of the bottom land, they would be some distance from the main channel. Also, the stones would not be just like those that were constantly being washed by the water but would bear marks of being submerged only at times. And that would be logically concluded to be at a time when the water reached out to that extremity. They would know the history of the overflowing at harvest time and would know that no ordinary efforts could bring them across. The grand conclusion would be that the Lord had brought the deliverance to their fathers and thus the Lord would be praised.

Verses 10, 11. The constant leadership of the Lord through the priests with the sacred instrument in hands is indicated by this performance. They did not move from their position until all that company had time to cross to the other side.

Verse 12. In fulfillment of their promise the 2½ tribes went armed across the river prepared thus to do their part in the possessing of the land.

Verse 13. That is, these forty thousand soldiers were from these tribes.

Verse 14. Everything that Joshua had predicted or promised to the people came to pass. Since that included many superhuman feats they were forced to believe that God was with him and thus he was magnified as the verse states.

Verses 15, 16. The use of the ark in the hands of the priests having been completed it was then in order for them to come out also so that the river may be returned to its normal condition. Hence Joshua received orders from the Lord for them to come up out of the Jordan.

Verses 17, 18. The instructions of the Lord were carried out by Joshua and the priests. As soon as all parties were safely on the dry land the river was allowed to resume its condition and to fill the area that included the bottom land, as before.

Verse 19. Please note the date, tenth day of first month, on which the people came up out of the river for it will be an important point for a certain calculation. The place where they lodged was Gilgal. This should be marked also.

Verses 20-24. This passage is commented upon at length at verse 9, which the reader will please see again.

JOSHUA 5

Verse 1. One meaning of the word for "melted," is to become discouraged and faint. The demonstration of drying up the Jordan was evidence to the nations that no god of theirs was like the God of the Israelites and that meant utter defeat for them. Such a state of weakened morale was part of God's plan for giving his people the victory over the nations occupying their promised possessions.

Verses 2, 3. The form of language in this paragraph is in the nature of emphasis and not as an example of grammatical construction. No male was ever circumcised the second time. That would be impossible. But the idea is a second occasion of circumcising mankind. It could be said that a man washed the filth from his hands the second time. Not the same filth twice but the same man was washed the second time. This does not exactly illustrate the case but will answer in that the word "second" can be seen to have a figurative meaning.

Verses 4-6. The ordinance of circumcision was first given to Abraham. It was then incorporated in the law of Moses. So strict was the ordinance that if it were neglected the guilty one was to be put to death. See Ex. 4: 24-26 for an instance showing the exactness of the Lord in this command. In the case of the children of Israel, their being constantly on the march, and the irregularity of the length of stay in any one place made it out of the question to attend to this rite. The condition of physical disability that the operation would cause would hinder their activity. A case showing that such disability would follow said operation, can be seen in Gen. 34: 25. In a congregation of several million people there would scarcely be a day that some male child and even many of them would not come to the age for the rite. It could be thought that an eight day old babe would not be marching but would be carried anyway. That is true, but the condition brought on by the operation would add so to the incumbrance that it was deferred during the march. It must be remembered that this march was ordered by the Lord, hence the omission of the circumcision would not be charged up against the people.

Verses 7, 8. This passage again verifies the remarks as to the physical effects of the rite on the victims.

Verse 9. The reproach referred to here is the shame of having been in bondage to the Egyptians for so many centuries. Now that they have reached the place to which they have been journeying they are entirely free from any possible hindrance from the former enemy. Two great bodies of water, Red Sea and Jordan, have been crossed successfully and they are in a position to carry out the ordinance of the founder of the nation. That could not have been done in Egypt because of the condition of servitude surrounding them. Now that hindrance has been removed and full compliance with the original ordinance made with the head of their race has been effected.

Verse 10. Attention of the reader was called to the date given in Ch. 4: 19. That was the date the selection of the passover lamb was to be made. (Ex. 12: 4-6.) So they had crossed just in time to make this selection on the proper day, which made it possible for them to keep the feast on the lawful date as here stated.

Verse 11. Let us keep the dates clear in our minds. The passover was on the fourteenth day. They ate this old product of the land on the morrow after the passover which would be the fifteenth. The fact that they ate of this product of the newly found land proved that it was indeed a land of plenty and that no miraculous provision would need to be made for their living.

Verse 12. Very logically, then, the manna would not be needed and would cease. This was stopped on the morrow after their first day of eating of the old corn which would be on the sixteenth.

Verse 13. The angels of God often appeared on earth in the form of man. This fact is abundantly proved by various passages. A few of them will be cited in this connection: Gen. 32: 24 with Hos. 12: 4. Gen. 19: 1, 8. Heb. 13: 1. This circumstance was a fitting introduction for the great drama of conflict into which Joshua and the children of Israel are about to be plunged. A challenge to combat was indicated by the drawn sword. When a servant of God is confronted with a force of any kind that indicates a dispute, either physical or spiritual, he would meet that challenge squarely and compel the opposing force (or man) to take a stand either for or against. That is what Joshua did in this place. Being in the form of man, Joshua would not know that he was an angel of God. He already knew that the invasion into that land was to be followed by an armed conflict, hence it might be that the first encounter is to be experienced by him personally. He did not flinch. Neither did he wait for the other person to make the attack. He went up and prepared to meet the occasion.

Verse 14. The "man" then gave direct reply indicating that he was on the Lord's side, and was a captain in that army. This brought Joshua into an attitude of reverence and, following the custom of those times, he fell prostrate with his face toward the ground and asked for instructions.

Verse 15. We should not conclude from the statement, that the ground was holy because it was the "promised land" as is sometimes suggested. We have already seen that the promised land included much more territory than the present portion. It was on the same principle as occurred in the case of Moses (Ex. 3: 5), and must be understood to mean that the presence of the Lord renders any place holy. A church house or residence or public hall or shade tree or any other place where scriptural services are being conducted would be a holy place.

JOSHUA 6

Verse 1. Jericho was one of the fenced or walled cities. In times of war, or threatened war, such cities would keep their gates closed both night and day. A state of siege would be declared so that there would be no entrance nor exit permitted. This gate was brought about here because of the report concerning the Israelites.

Verse 2. This city was just across the Jordan opposite where they had been in camp, hence was to be the first place of attack.

Verse 3. Only the soldiers were mentioned in this verse, but later we will see the people mentioned with the march. The first lap of the plan was to make a daily circuit of the city for six days. Nothing more was done on those days.

Verse 4. The order of march is given more detail in this verse. Seven priests will take the lead and those bearing the ark will follow next. The leading priests were to be provided with ram's horns. These were instruments provided for the purpose of producing a long and continuous blast and its quality of tone would be such as to demand attention. It is significant that in this one verse the expressions "ram's horns" and "trumpets" are used in the same connection.

Verse 5. Here the people are introduced, and they had just one part to perform in the great event, which was to shout. The order of the whole procedure may be summed up thus. Surround the city once, daily, for six days. Surround it seven times the seventh day. The priests to make a long blast with the horns or trumpets. The people to give a shout. That completes the human part of the great attack. The Lord's part comes next which was the sinking of the wall. The word "flat" is from TACHATH and is defined "the bottom (as depressed); only adverbially, below (often with prepositional prefix underneath), in lieu of, etc."—Strong. This definition of the word indicates that the walls sank into the ground and that accounts for the statement that every man went "straight before" him into the city. There would not be even the presence of debris to hinder the attack.

Verses 6, 7. This is the order of God being relayed by Joshua to the priests and people; only an additional item is mentioned, that of armed men.

Verse 8. Attention is to be called to the idea that passing before the ark is the same as passing before the Lord. That is because that sacred piece always was to be symbolical of the presence of God.

Verse 9. More details of the order of march are given here. The armed men went first, the seven priests next, the ark next and the "rereward" (rear guard) next.

Verse 10. The only noise allowed was that of the trumpets while in the actions of the march.

Verse 11. The ark being the most important object among them it is said to have compassed the city once and then returned to camp. Of course all the rest of the combination went with it.

Verses 12-14. The same procedure was followed daily for six days.

Verse 15. The final day had dawned and they arose early, alert for the great climax of their attack on the enemy, and proceeded. Since this day was to require seven circuits of the city, there was reason for arising early.

Verse 16. This states the final act in the great performance. The shouting did not take place until Joshua had made some final statements and given instructions and warnings.

Verse 17. The word "accursed" means "devoted." It has many times been seen that God claims and deserves the first of everything. In this sense, the present statement is made. Jericho will be the first city attacked and its spoil will therefore belong to the Lord and not to be personally appropriated. This same principle of devotion to the Lord included the sacrifice of things or animals or persons that would not be fit for retaining as assets. The living creatures in this city must be killed. But exceptions will be made of the harlot and her company which was the contract made with her on the occasion of the two spies' visit with her.

Verse 18. A free use is made of this word "accurse" here, and can be clearly understood if its meaning is considered, that it means to be devoted to the Lord, either in the form of sacrifice or as an item of worth. So that if the people take to themselves that which has been devoted to God they will make themselves an object to be devoted or sacrificed to God. Hence the warning.

Verse 19. These items can be of practical use in the Lord's service so they were to be taken whole and put into the treasury of the Lord.

Verse 20. This verse might be inserted directly at the end of verse 16 as has already been explained at that place. Upon the final act of the people, the shouting, the wall fell down "flat." See comments at verse 5 on this word.

Verse 21. This is a statement of the general conduct of the congregation, without the exception, that will be mentioned next.

Verse 22. The words "had said" are very significant here for they are reflective. Since this woman lived on the wall which sank into the ground we must understand that previous to the final act the rescue of the woman was made and here is announced.

Verse 23. The same men who had been in the woman's house before were the ones sent to bring her out. They would make no mistake about it since she had fixed the cord in the window for their signal. And it is well to observe that she lived on the wall. She had given the men their escape directly through the window and down on the outside of the wall. By some similar means they could reenter her house without going through the gates to the inside. Since she was delivered before the walls were overthrown, the gates would have been closed to them.

Verse 24. After all of the items of the attack had been performed and the wall had been removed the next thing was the destruction of the houses and the inhabitants. The articles of value mentioned they put into the treasury. The exception of which we will read in next chapter does not contradict this verse for it describes faithfully the conduct of the true men and their intentions. Nothing was spared by their knowledge or consent.

Verse 25. Joshua respected the agreement the spies had made with the woman. Of course we do not understand that he would have been bound to it had it been wrong. But the writer says she was saved because of her service to the men of God. And this woman became a permanent resident among the children of Israel and finally married one of the men in the blood line. (Matt. 1: 5.)

Verse 26. This verse makes a very unusual threat and some indefiniteness seems to exist as to some of its expressions. The R.V. makes it mean that when the man is starting to rebuild the foundation his oldest son will die, and when he is ready to hang the gates his youngest will die. Our A.V. does not say the sons will die. My idea is that he was to start the work "in" the days of his firstborn and hang the gates "in" the days of his youngest. Had the man suffered the loss of his oldest son in connection with laying the foundation he naturally would have been impressed with the truth of the divine threat and nothing but blind perverseness would have led him on to complete the work. But the whole idea is that such a man would have so much trouble in the progress of the work that it would require practically all the prime of his life for the work. This would be indicated by the fact that he had begun the work of rebuilding in the beginning of his family group and was still at it at the time of birth of his last child. This was done as recorded in 1 Kings 16: 34.

Verse 27. Joshua had been designated by the Lord as the successor of Moses in the leadership of the people. Therefore he would be with him and cause his greatness to be reported throughout the country. Hence, there would be no excuse for any to oppose his movements on pretense they thought him an impostor.

JOSHUA 7

Verse 1. For the information of the reader the inspired narrative states what had been done, which is to be the factor in the sad affair about to happen. For the time being, Joshua as a man does not know of the sin here mentioned.

Verse 2. The number of armed men in the congregation was so great that not all of them might be needed in given movements against cities. Hence the commander orders a reconnaissance of the next proposed point of attack, which was the city of Ai.

Verse 3. The men returned and reported to their chief that the place was few in number and that two or three thousand men would be sufficient for the attack.

Verses 4, 5. The attack was repulsed with the loss of 36 men. No indication is made that a false estimate had been made of the strength of the city. They had been successful in their previous movements against the enemy. Also the Lord had given assurance that he would be with them, but now they have met shameful defeat in that they were put to flight.

Verse 6. Joshua now knows that something is wrong. He and the elders fell before the ark. That was where God was to be met in ceremonial formalities.

Verses 7-9. Joshua was an inspired leader and spoke with authority when delivering messages from the Lord to the people. But he was human, and now is overcome with astonishment and disappointment and confusion at the turn of matters. The defeat of his men was regretted for more than one reason. The immediate effect of it on his men was bad. But the humiliation of the nation in the eyes of their enemies was what grieved Joshua most. The same thoughts had impressed Moses on various occasions. (Ex. 32: 11, 12; Num. 14: 13, 14.)

Verses 10-12. Joshua now was informed by the Lord as to the cause of the defeat. No person is named as yet, but the fact that Israel had sinned by taking what belonged to the Lord, was explained to Joshua as the cause of the disappointment.

Verse 13. Joshua was commanded by the Lord to make certain statements to the people, the address to be made to them as a whole, and they were to be informed that they could not withstand their enemies until the evil was removed from the camp. The same principle is taught in the N.T. which will be dealt with in full in the proper place. But one general reference may well be cited here which is the case of the fornicator in 1 Cor. 5. There it is plainly taught that the service in general of the congregation will not be acceptable to God as long as that congregation retains within its fellowship the sin of its participants.

Verses 14, 15. The gist of this passage is that the sorting out to find the guilty party was to be done through group by group. Again we see a sample of God's methods in carrying out his will. He could have named the guilty person outright but chose to proceed in this other way for reasons of his own.

Verses 16-18. The various units of the people were approached in turn and in some manner eliminated one by one until the guilty one was left present. We are not told just here how the designation was effected. Some times such matters were decided by the lot. But whatever the means, the Lord was directing the whole procedure. So far the only thing that was decided was the identity of the guilty person.

Verse 19. Achan was the man left standing after all innocent ones had been eliminated. Then he was called on by Joshua to make a confession of what he had done. And the basis on which he was thus admonished and on which he should make his confession was the glory of God.

Verse 20. This verse gives the general confession of Achan. That he had sinned. Not only so, but had sinned against the Lord. That is a significant idea. Some men are more willing to acknowledge wrong done against their fellow men than against God. Any sin at all is against the Lord regardless of how many men are involved.

Verse 21. A general confession is not enough and should never be accepted from a person today when proposing to confess. It is unfair in that it leaves the complainant no ground of action justly and also leaves the guilty person a means of escape from just punishment afterward, if he tries to void his confession. So Achan specifies his sin and tells what he had done. He had taken certain things of value. These things were the Lord's, and thus, he was guilty of robbing God. And to show evidence of good faith in the confession he tells where they might find the stolen goods.

Verses 22, 23. Joshua made the search and found it as Achan had said and brought out the stuff in the presence of the people and before the Lord.

Verse 24. The guilty man and his entire family, together with all the things he had stolen as also his own cattle and other possessions are brought down to the valley of Achor (so named because of the circumstance taking place in the trouble that had been caused by Achan).

Verses 25, 26. The whole group was stoned and burned. The question will arise about the family in the guilt. Since the stuff was hid in the tent where the family would be present they would have guilty knowledge of the transaction. That would make them guilty with him. Another question that arises here is this. We see that Achan made a full and humble confession of his wrong, also restored in full the property damage he had done. What more could a man do? Why should he be lost when he did all that could be done to make his wrongs right? Here is another place where we must remember that both civil and religious government were administered through the Mosaic system. If a man violates a law of the land he must pay the penalty prescribed by that law. Even though he might be a disciple of the Lord, he must meet the demands of the civil government. His acknowledgement of wrong before the assembly of the Lord's people will not exempt him from his obligation before the law. If he makes his standing before God right, then the blessings he should receive from the Lord will come, even though he must go ahead and pay the penalty of the law. When Achan paid with his life for the thing he had done he was satisfying the penal laws of the government. When he made his full confession of wrong before God he made satisfaction for his religious relation to God, and whatever spiritual enjoyment he should have been entitled to before God would allow regardless of his other fate.

JOSHUA 8

Verse 1. The affair about Achan has been settled and the Lord has been satisfied. Now Joshua is encouraged to proceed with the campaign of attacking the enemy in the promised headquarters. The assurance of victory is made to them.

Verse 2. The same success will follow them in this attack on Ai that came in the attack on Jericho. But a change was made in the privileges of the soldiery. In this instance they may take the spoil. Not that it was any less valuable or desirable than that in the former city. But the Lord claimed only the spoil of the first city, so they are permitted to take this to themselves.

Verses 3, 4. Joshua is using what is called strategy in warfare. This detachment of warriors was instructed to be near the city, but of course not in sight.

Verse 5. Another part of the strategy is for the leader to take other men and approach the city. When the inhabitants therein come out, then Joshua and his men will flee from them which will mislead them into thinking they are being victorious.

Verse 6. Joshua and his unit will continue to flee so as to draw the inhabitants from their city. The previous experience in which the Israelites had been forced to flee will be fresh in the memory and they will conclude it is to be a repetition of that victory. With this delusion in their minds they will rush headlong from the city.

Verse 7. The situation will be one of advantage for the Israelites who had been sent out at the beginning of this movement. The city being deserted of its soldiers, this detachment would be given opportunity to attack it.

Verse 8. The instruction is given here that when the opportunity arrives now being described and predicted, they are to set fire to the city. This will accomplish two purposes. It will destroy the property of the enemy and will also attract the attention of the soldiers who had been in pursuit of the Israelites with Joshua.

Verse 9. With these instructions from the commander the men went to lie in ambush on the west side of the city while he remained with the people.

Verses 10, 11. The soldiers of the host were selected by Joshua and took up a position on the north of Ai.

Verse 12. This seems to be an extra detachment of five thousand, besides the ones mentioned in verse three. A glance at the map will show that Bethel was north and west of Ai. That would agree with the idea of the ambush being between the two cities, yet on the west of Ai.

Verse 13. We can see the array of preparation. Joshua and his main army are on the north of the city while the two detachments of the ambuscade are on the west and all set for the movement. All this being done, Joshua advanced as far as the valley spoken of that was near the city and came in sight of the men of the city.

Verse 14. The king of Ai saw the approach of the Israelites. He gathered the citizens of the city and went out to meet the enemy, unconscious of the men in ambush behind or west of the city.

Verse 15. At this juncture Joshua made a feint by performing as a defeated army and started to flee towards the wilderness, that being a place of advantage for the action expected on the part of the Israelites.

Verse 16. It had the desired effect. The men of the city, with the feeling of victory, hastened out of the city and after the fleeing Israelites. In this way they were decoyed from their city and left it open.

Verse 17. Bethel now entered the action through sympathy for the "victorious" ally city and both groups pursued the fleeing enemy, the very thing desired by Joshua.

Verses 18, 19. There were no special signals as perfect as are available today to communicate army orders. Thus, the Lord intercedes with miraculous effect. He commands Joshua to stretch out his spear toward Ai with the promise that the city will be given into his hand. He did so and simultaneously the men in the ambush arose and attacked the city. We know this was a miraculous demonstration since the human eye could not have seen the instrument in the hand of Joshua at the distance there was between them.

Verse 20. The great billows of smoke caused by this fire attracted the attention of the inhabitants of the city and threw them into a panic. In their excitement they turned back and came upon the host of their pursuers.

Verse 21. Joshua could also see the smoke, and knew that his men of the ambuscade had made their appointed movement; also it could be seen that the men of Ai had started a retreat, hence he also reversed his movement and began slaying the people.

Verse 22. In unison with this movement on the part of Joshua and his men, the men of the ambush attacked the citizens and thus they were thrown into a helpless huddle.

Verse 23. To take a notable foe "dead or alive," is considered a signal victory as a rule. But to be able to capture him alive is the greater one. This was done here.

Verse 24. Apparently this verse disagrees with verse 17. But the situation is open to a reasonable explanation. Although the entire citizenry had deserted the place, when the retreat took place it was but natural that a part of them would infiltrate through the mass and get back into their city. These were the ones that were here slain with the edge of the sword in the hands of Joshua's men.

Verses 25, 26. This passage gives us a report of the complete destruction of the people of this city. Such was a fulfillment of what had been commanded for their conduct of the campaign against all the heathen cities of that country.

Verse 27. The spoils of the various cities were not objectionable as to their quality. The ban on taking that of Jericho was not on the principle that they were "tainted" goods, but because the Lord claimed the first of everything and that was the first city they attacked. Now that other attacks are to be made, the people will be permitted to appropriate the spoils to themselves.

Verse 28. The word "forever" means "age-lasting" as we have previously seen. As used here it means that no specific term of years was decided upon when the city could be restored, for it was made so completely desolate that it continued, even up to the date of the writing, as a heap.

Verse 29. The king had not been allowed the honor of being killed in action. He was taken alive, then slain. Not by the "honorable" method of the sword, but by the disgraceful method of hanging. While the king was to be dealt the dishonor of such execution, the land must be spared the disgrace as much as possible. Therefore the body of the king was taken down at the end of the day, which was here determined by the setting of the sun.

Verses 30, 31. This altar was not for the regular tabernacle worship for that must be done on the altar built for that purpose. This is a special performance as on the field of battle and was a military action.

Verse 32. Since the system given through Moses was both temporal and religious, the actions just now concluded as to temporal interests would be authorized by this law, and hence it was appropriate to inscribe it on the spot of this military success.

Verse 33. Let it be borne in mind that the conquest of Canaan is only in the beginning. Until it has been completed there will be more or less unsettled conditions as to the tabernacle and its articles of furniture. So here we read about the ark as being in the presence of the people and all in connection with the priests. Also were they situated with reference to the two mounts previously selected upon which to stand for the blessings and cursings. Of course, in the present occasion the blessing of God is manifested in that the Israelites have been successful against the enemy.

Verses 34, 35. While the immediate condition is one of blessing, it is well not to forget the possibility of the curses. Hence both parts of the law are now recited in the hearing of the people. Mention is made of the strangers that were conversant, or visiting among them. While the provisions of the system were for special benefit of the children of Israel, when others saw fit to be among them they must be made to understand that obedience to the law will be expected of them. Otherwise, they will receive the same curses that disobedient Israelites would get.

JOSHUA 9

Verses 1, 2. The great success of Joshua against Ai was reported generally and the various groups of people then occupying the land expected a similar fate. As a result they formed a confederacy against the oncoming Israelites.

Verse 3. Among the cities which were aroused by the report was Gibeon. It was an important city not far from the site of the Israelite army at that time. Also that city had evidently learned something of the stipulation that had been given to the children of Israel on the subject of peace pacts. (Deut. 20: 15, 16).

Verse 4. It says they worked wilily, which means with trickery. Among the tricks, they prepared some of the indications of those who were authorized to act as ambassadors. Such an official would naturally be from an outside community and hence "very far off" as the stipulation referred to above required.

Verse 5. This verse is a continuation of the plan started in the previous one. They put clouts (patches) on their shoes and found some bread that was mouldy and also procured some old clothing. It has always been a strange circumstance that such a scheme could have been so deceptive. The sight of old articles would give not the least information as to when or where they had become such in condition. Since most people would have articles of clothing about their homes of such description, it ought to have occurred to the mind of the Israelites that after all the conclusion had to be based on the assertions of the Gibeonites. And if they would believe their word as to when and where these articles were changed from new to old, why not just take their word directly as to where they lived? But such is the usual nature of an institution of deception, that its most obvious inconsistencies will be overlooked. No doubt that is the reason for so many warnings in the Bible against being deceived.

Verse 6. Our main point of interest at this verse is to note the location of the camp of Israel. It would be well to mark the place here for future reference.

Verse 7. This statement was made in view of the stipulation in Deut. 20: 15, 16.

Verses 8-10. They acknowledged they had become disturbed by the reports of success of the Israelites. And in their reference to this report they used the word "fame" which would indicate that the report was not so much a direct sound from the immediate actions of success. That would be the case with an occurrence taking place near them. The reason they heard about it, though "far away," was that the Israelites had become famous. The whole procedure was one of grand strategy on the part of the Gibeonites.

Verses 11-13. The grand scheme was rounded out by the respectful attitude of their elders who instructed their "ambassadors" to make an official journey to communicate with the "distant" but victorious foe. They then repeat the falsehood already stated.

Verse 14. The word "took" is from an original with so much variety of meaning that the context must determine its special application in any given case. In the present one we know it did not mean they partook of the victuals since they were mouldy and unfit for consumption. Hence, the meaning is that the men of Israel took or accepted the men of Gibeon on the strength of the appearance of the victuals. The mistake they made was in relying on such flimsy evidence and not even consulting the Lord on the matter.

Verse 15. On the basis of the foregoing conclusions the Israelites made a league with the Gibeonites. And since this league was legalized by an official and national oath that made it binding. On the general principle of righteous obligations a promise obtained through force or deception is considered void. Evidently the Lord wishes his people to be taught a lesson by painful experience and thus here holds them to the faithful performance of all that a league implies, as we will see.

Verse 16. The original thought in the word "neighbor" was evidently that of physical nearness as seen here. That gave rise to the work of moralizing on the subject as was done in Luke 10: 29. That, as the man nearest to another physically would be his neighbor in that sense, so the man in need would be a neighbor to him who had first opportunity for helping him, and vice versa. After three days the word "got out" that they had been duped. To ascertain the truth they took a journey and found that within three days' travel, they reached the cities of the ones with whom they had made the league. Now any one would know that fresh bread would not become stale in three days nor would new shoes become worn in that time. So the truth now breaks upon their minds that they have been deceived.

Verses 17, 18. Although they discovered their mistake they were faithful to their league and did not attack the Gibeonites. But the leaders of the people had made the league and now the congregation at large complains at the princes.

Verses 19, 20. The league did not guarantee to them any further benefits than their lives. Hence, they are standing by the league to let them live. While they are thus bound to the agreement to let them live, that includes with an ally, the service necessary to help them live as we will see before long.

Verses 21-23. While their pact required them to grant them life it did not obligate them any further. Hence, as a penalty for their deception they will be put under servile tribute. The service they will be required to perform is preparing wood for the altar and water for the congregational use. All of the animals to be offered on the altar had to be washed with water. The altar fire had to be kept up with wood humanly provided. This double service will now be placed on the Gibeonites.

Verses 24-27. The Gibeonites were so relieved at not being subject to destruction that they gladly accepted the service thus imposed on them by Joshua. They even agreed in general terms to accept whatever service he might see fit to charge upon them, but the only penalty put on them was the one concerning the wood and water as stated.

JOSHUA 10

Verses 1, 2. In the realm of national and military interests one nation always fears and looks with jealousy upon any coalition between a neighboring nation and a foreign one that is a foe. That was the situation after this league with Gibeon. If that city and its colleagues have formed a pact with Israel then it means that in any conflict with either, the other would be linked up against them.

Verses 3, 4. With the situation as described, the strategy was to attack and overcome Gibeon while only it would be against them and before their newly formed alliance could be of any assistance to them. The king of Jerusalem, being one of the outstanding powers interested at that time appealed to the others near him to join him in the attack upon Gibeon because of this league they had with Israel.

Verse 5. In answer to the call, the friends of the king of Jerusalem responded and mobilized their forces for the attack on Gibeon as their common foe.

Verse 6. This brought a call from Gibeon to Joshua to respond.

Verse 7. True to his word of honor Joshua prepared to go to the assistance of his ally. And he did not make merely a pretended movement that might have been used as a pretext while reserving the best of his forces for his personal use. The record says he took all his men of war.

Verses 8, 9. The league formed with the Gibeonites was accepted by the Lord, for we here see that he encourages Joshua and assures him of success. With this encouragement Joshua proceeded toward the encounter and spent the night in the journey. In so doing he was enabled to make a surprise attack.

Verse 10. This first attack was a complete success against the enemy and resulted in a rout of their forces.

Verse 11. These stones were hailstones in the ordinary meaning of that word except as to size or weight. These were great enough to cause many deaths and thus were a weapon against which the enemy had no defense. The Lord helps those who help themselves. Had Joshua been negligent and depended exclusively on the miracle of God he would have been defeated in the action.

Verses 12, 13. Much has been said by both the friends and foes of the Bible upon this passage of scripture. And much of it has been unnecessary. The whole subject is involved in one question. Is there a supreme creator of the universe? If we say no, then a more fundamental basis of subject matter should be considered than the incidental item of managing this portion of the universe as here reported. If it is admitted there is such a Being, then all questions into the how or why of this circumstance are off the point. If God is, and can create the sun and other planets, then it is a small matter to control them as he sees fit. The maker of a machine certainly would know how, and have the power, to manage it as desired. To say that any power could bring the heavenly bodies into being, hold them in space in harmonious relation for centuries, yet could not alter their actions for a short time—to say this, is the poorest kind of a position. As to the quibble about whether it is the sun or the earth that moves that is foolish dodging of the issue. It is accommodative language. The sun appears to move and hence language is based on appearance. Even our "scientists" who have learned the truth about the relation of the heavenly bodies will speak of the sunset which would be unscientific were we to hold them to strict fact in their form of speech. The fact is that whatever may be the actual movements of these bodies to alternate the light and darkness, those movements were interrupted on this occasion for the length of time stated, so that the amount of sunlight wanted for the action would be increased. Furthermore as to the moon. What difference would it have made in the light Joshua would have whether the moon was acted upon or not? It would have made no difference at all. The Lord can perform any miracle that is right. Thus he could have permitted the moon to go on in its movement at this time without any disadvantage to Joshua in this battle. But that would have thrown the relative rate of travel of the moon to the sun out of order unless another miracle were performed upon the entire arrangement of the luminary system. So God preferred to avoid necessity of that miracle by performing this one of stopping the sun and moon at the same time. A man might be standing on a moving vehicle. Outside force is exerted on the vehicle to stop it without applying the force to the man. The tendency then would be to throw the man into bodily confusion. If that outside force were applied alike to both vehicle and man, both would stop together without any undue disorder. That is why both sun and moon were acted upon in this case. Reference is made to the "book of Jasher." This was a literary production in existence at that time, but since lost. It is one of the instances where an inspired writer or speaker confirms his inspired statement by reference to some uninspired but truthful writer outside. Paul did the same thing in Acts 17: 28. Such circumstances as these justify us in our reference to secular materials as long as we do not try to use them as authority.

Verse 14. The adverse critic of the Bible says this verse contradicts 2 Kings 20: 11 because that was another time when God favored a man's wish by interfering with the time. But this statement in Joshua was made in the fifteenth century before Christ, and that in Kings the eighth century before Christ. At the time Joshua wrote his statement this other instance had not yet happened. Thus once again the shaft of bitterness shot by the enemy of divine revelation rebounds as a well-deserved boomerang.

Verse 15. The present campaign having been completed, Joshua returned to his headquarters at Gilgal and will prepare for further operations.

Verses 16-18. The five kings who had

formed the forces against Gibeon for this war had escaped personally with their lives. They hid in a cave and Joshua ordered the cave closed as a present war prison for the kings, until other disposition could be made of them.

Verse 19. Having secured the kings against escape Joshua commanded his men to pursue the fleeing enemy and attack the rear of their number as they overtook them.

Verse 20. The portion of the enemy's forces that was at the rear was attacked and destroyed as commanded in previous verse. The others were suffered to escape this movement and enter some walled cities.

Verse 21. The field headquarters of Joshua being at Makkedah, the army returned to him there in peace. That is, the success of the children of Israel was so evident that no one even ventured to offer a protest.

Verses 22, 23. The prison made of the cave was then ordered to be opened and the five kings therein brought out before the commander.

Verse 24. *Put your feet upon the necks.* This statement is often used in a figurative sense, but it had its origin in a literal fact. Much of the killing in those days was done with the sword and thus it would be an advantage in beheading a man to have his body prone on the ground and his neck stretched out. On this account it was a frequent expression that referred to victory over the enemy by saying the hand would be in the neck. (Gen. 49: 8; 2 Sam. 22: 41; Ps. 18: 40.)

Verses 25, 26. The aforesaid action was a signal of their triumph over the foe and not to actually slay the kings. Joshua did that afterward. After they were slain they were disgraced by being hung on trees all day.

Verse 27. The command was given to take the bodies down at the time of sunset. This was according to the law previously given. (Ch. 8: 29.) These kings were not only given the shameful treatment in their deaths that they deserved, but were not accorded a respectful burial. They were cast into the very cave where they had crouched in hiding from their pursuers. That place became their final tomb.

Verse 28. Makkedah was used as temporary headquarters only, during the local campaign. When it had ended, he then attacked the place and destroyed the people therein.

Verses 29, 30. There are still some cities to be attacked and Libnah is one of them. Joshua attacks the place, and with the help of the Lord destroys it.

Verses 31, 32. One by one the cities must be attacked and destroyed. This was because there was no very well concentrated army of the enemy to be opposed but they consisted of the scattered remnants of the heathen resting behind walled places. The city of Lachish was one of these places.

Verse 33. If a person offers to assist an enemy of God that makes him also an enemy of God. Hence when this Gezerite king thought to help Lachish he brought himself into hostility against the Lord's forces and he was therefore destroyed.

Verses 34, 35. Let it be noticed that Joshua not only slew the people of these cities but the cities also were destroyed or laid waste.

Verses 36, 37. The attack upon Hebron included more than just one city for it says they destroyed Hebron "and all the cities thereof." That would include the suburban places around the city proper. The destruction must be so complete that all surrounding territory must be included in the purge.

Verses 38, 39. This was another place of centralized force for it was necessary to take the place with all the cities thereof. Nothing was suffered to remain.

Verses 40-41. This paragraph is more general as to location and intends to take in all the various spots formerly occupied by the enemy and extending over all the land of interest to the children of Israel. Mention is made of Kadesh-barnea because it was the southern boundary of the promised land.

Verse 42. The significant thought in this verse is that success came to the arms of Joshua because the Lord fought for him and all Israel.

Verse 43. This was the end of another general campaign and thus Joshua with his entire forces returned to the general headquarters located at Gilgal. This was the same place where they had paused after crossing the Jordan. It became and remained the camp of the Israelites for some time and will not be changed until 18: 1.

JOSHUA 11

Verses 1-5. In this paragraph we have another confederacy formed against the children of Israel. It was headed by Jabin, king of Hazor. He was a leader among the Canaanites. He was not the only Canaanite king with that name hence should not be confused with the man of the same name whom Barak overthrew in Judges 4. In the present case this was a strong coalition against the Israelites and appearances might have been considered as invincible from any mere human source.

Verse 6. As usual, the Lord gives assurance of victory for his forces because the whole war is one of defense on the part of his servants and is being fought in their right to the land that had been given to them through their great forefather Abram. Hence the whole series of operations will have the blessing of God. Among the actions done to hinder the enemy was to hough the horses. That means to cut the tendon or leader in the leg of the horse just above the hock joint. This would have two very great disadvantages for the enemy. If the horse were carrying a rider it would cause him to fall backwards upon the rider. Besides, it would disable the animal for further duty, yet leave him as an encumbrance to be cared for, provided they had such a humane feeling for dumb brutes which many certainly would have.

Verses 7-9. Joshua accomplished all that the Lord promised. He overthrew the men coming against him and also disabled the war horses as described above. Some of these horses were those used to draw the war chariots. They would be forced out of service by this injury done to their limbs. Lest other horses might be procured to draw these chariots Joshua burned them in the action.

Verses 10-12. Hazor is here said to have been the head of the other kingdoms. This is stated at verse 1. It will be noted that in general the people of a city were slain but also the material of the city was burned. There were some exceptions to this rule as will be seen in next paragraph.

Verse 13. Referring to previous paragraph we will here understand this to refer to the material of the city, not to the inhabitants. They were all slain. The act of slaying the people would not necessarily destroy the material of the city in every case. And when that was done, that the city stood still in its strength, which means the walls withstood the actions of the bodily conflicts. Those which did so were spared the fire except the city of Hazor. The reason for the exception is not given

Verse 14. After proper distribution had been made of the spoils of Jericho the soldiers were permitted to appropriate to themselves those of the other cities. Such is the meaning of this verse.

Verse 15. Let sabbatarians again please sit up and take notice. The inspired writer takes the care to tell us that the Lord commanded Moses. Then Moses commanded Joshua. That is not all. But *as* the Lord commanded Moses, *so* Moses commanded Joshua. Not one iota of difference between the authority of the command in the cases.

Verses 16-18. This is another generalization of the territory won by the arms of Joshua and thus a fulfilling of the assurances God had made to his people.

Verse 19. This exception is explained in chapter 9 where these people misled Joshua with their tricks. Having made a league with them Joshua would not break it.

Verse 20. By not destroying those nations at once, miraculously, which God could have done, those nations were encouraged to attempt battle for their own existence. So the Lord hardened their hearts in the same manner he used to harden the heart of the king of Egypt. It was done by giving him the opportunity and he then embraced it. And after generations could not say that had these people been given a chance they would have saved themselves from destruction at hands of the Israelites. They were given the chance and were not able to take care of themselves.

Verses 21, 22. The Anakim were a race of giants who were rather coarse physically and threatening in appearance. That was why the spies were impressed with the awfulness of the country. Joshua makes a special attempt after these creatures and about exterminates them. Doubtless the Lord will have occasion to use some of them later on so they were suffered to remain in a few cities of the Philistines.

Verse 23. Joshua gave the conquered land to the children of Israel "for an inheritance." This again agrees with the idea that prior to this the land had been earmarked for them and it was theirs. This is what made their war a war of defense. For the time being there was a cessation of war.

JOSHUA 12

Verse 1. This verse is to introduce the account of conquests of the children of Israel before crossing the Jordan. The territory referred to will be found shown on the map as extending from a point east of the Dead Sea and upwards. Also eastward into the desert.

Verses 2, 3. The conquest of Sihon is originally recorded in Num. 21: 21-25. That king had refused Israel a passage through his country even though assurance was given him that no damage would be done. Instead, he attacked the children of Israel. He was overcome and his country made a possession of the others. "Sea of Chinneroth" is another name for Galilee.

Verses 4-6. This account is found in Num. 21: 33-35. The territory formerly occupied by Sihon and Og was thus taken over by Moses while he was still with the people and given to the two and a half tribes that requested to have their possessions on the east of Jordan. It was thus accurate to refer to the conquests of the Lord's people in this general manner since part of the victories were accomplished under the leadership of Moses and the rest under Joshua.

Verses 7, 8. Having described the conquests of the congregation under Moses on the east of Jordan, the writer now gives that major accomplishment over all the principal territory west of the river under Joshua. The mention of the limits would have included of necessity all the conditions of the land therein. It was deemed well to cite the great variety of geographical conditions and thus show the fulfillment of the assurances so often made to the Israelites while journeying towards their goal. So we see mentioned mountains and valleys, plains and wilderness. Also the victory over the leading heathen nations, the Hittites and Canaanites, etc.

Verses 9-24. The nature of comments needed or desired over this group of verses is such that it is thought well to place them in one paragraph. It will be noticed that thirty-one kings are tabulated in this group. Previously it was common to read of seven nations of greatness. There is no disagreement in the two accounts. It will be also recalled that usually the qualification "greater and mightier than thou" was named in connection with those seven. Thus we understand that the outstanding forces which were overcome by the children of Israel were particularly pointed out. In the present paragraph the writer gives a more detailed list of the conquests. Many times the authority of a king was confined to his own individual city with perhaps some surrounding territory adjacent. Mention of a few of the most important cities attacked and overcome with reference to the original account will suffice here. Jericho, (Ch. 6); Ai, (Ch. 8); Jerusalem, (Ch. 10: 3, 23).

JOSHUA 13

Verse 1. The statements in foregoing chapter as to the conquests of the nation should not be misunderstood as conflicting with the present passages. The principal war is over. The victory has been established. After the major conflict has been ended in victory for one side, there often remains a period of "occupational" actions. Thus, it is common to read today about the "army of occupation" even long after the war is supposed to have been fought and won. It is not strange that enemy nations show the "die-hard" disposition even though having raised the flag of surrender. So it was in the case of the children of Israel. They found it necessary to enforce the victory already won and formally acknowledged, and that is why we read of further operations that resemble military actions. Now that Joshua is in his declining years the Lord reminds him of the work yet remaining to "cash in" on the conquests already made and thus take possession of the land rightfully theirs.

Verses 2, 3. Sihor is doubtless a reference to the Nile and was not specifically included in the promised land. But here it is indirectly included on the basis that it was "counted to the Canaanite." And since the Canaanites were among the principal nations occupying the western part of the promised land to be taken by the Israelites, and also since that heathen nation claimed some jurisdiction over the territory reaching to the borders of Egypt, we have the statement here recorded. The prominence of the two great heathen nations, Canaanites and Philistines, is explained by their location in the western portion of Palestine and thus their close contact with the Israelites.

Verses 4-6. If the reader will consult any good Biblical map of Palestine he may see the territory taken in by this paragraph. Find the place called Beersheba at the southern boundary, then run the eye upward as far as Lebanon. Now go over to the head water of the Jordan, thence down along the western shore of that stream and also the western shore of the Dead Sea to its southern terminal. This circuit will include the territory meant in the present paragraph and thus include Palestine or Canaan.

Verse 7. Mention of nine and a half tribes coincides with the two and a half tribes already located as to possessions on the east side of Jordan.

Verses 8, 9. This account of territory is the same as chapter 12: 1-3.

Verse 10. Notice this states a limit, the border of the children of Ammon. This is explained in Deut. 2: 19. The relation of Ammon to Abraham caused God to show them some favor and he would not permit his people to disturb the Ammonites' possessions.

Verses 11, 12. This territory has already been named as having been won. But the actual taking possession is what is here being considered. See comments at verse 1.

Verse 13. At the time of the present writing these people had not been driven out. The same kind of circumstance will be found to apply to other peoples and the explanation will be more definitely found in Judges 2.

Verse 14. Since the tribe of Levi was to be exclusively engaged in the religious activities of the nation it was not necessary nor appropriate for them to be encumbered with landed estates. Instead, they were assigned cities that were interspersed throughout the whole country occupied by the twelve tribes.

Verses 15-21. This territory has also been named before as having been conquered by the children of Israel. Here it is again mentioned as territory that had to be occupied or taken into possession.

Verses 22-28. The same remarks here would apply as in the preceding paragraph as to the necessity of engaging in the activities of the occupation of the land. Those activities will make it necessary to engage in the use of arms in many if not all cases. Thus while in this process they took in hand their enemy Balaam. This indicates that he had come among the children of Israel from his personal place of residence in the country of Mesopotamia. Having once been recognized as a prophet of God, who had become corrupted by the practice of soothsaying, he still desired to mingle with the people in various territories. He is now found to be in the territory assigned to the children whose brethren he once professed to be his own. So he at last met his fate.

Verses 29-31. There is no revealed explanation of why half of one tribe took this liking to the territory east of Jordan. When the request was made and explained to be properly based, in the eyes of Moses, the request was granted. Now it will be necessary for them to occupy the inheritance.

Verses 32, 33. The assignment of this whole territory above described by the authority of Moses was to be recognized. The actual taking of the possession remains to be accomplished under Joshua the military leader of the nation of the Israelites.

JOSHUA 14

Verses 1-3. Let it be noticed that "land of Canaan" in first verse is used in opposition to "other side Jordan" in third verse. The main reason I call attention to it is that the reader may not forget the fact that Canaan was not all of the "promised land." The particular method by which the decisions were to be rendered concerning the individual assignment of the land was called the "lot." There were various methods or manners of resorting to the lot and no very definite form can be settled on as the one used in any given age. For the information of the reader I shall quote from Smith's Bible Dictionary, Art. "Lot." "The custom of deciding doubtful questions by lot is one of great extent and high antiquity. Among the Jews lots were used with the expectation that God would so control them as to give a right direction to them. As to the mode of casting lots, we have no certain information. Probably several modes were used. Very commonly among the Latins little counters of wood were put into a jar with so narrow a neck that only one could come out at a time. After the jar had been filled with water and the contents shaken, the lots were determined by the order in which the bits of wood, representing the several parties, came out of the water. In other cases they were put into a wide open jar, and the counters were drawn out by the hand. Sometimes again they were cast in the manner of dice. The soldiers who cast lots for Christ's garments undoubtedly used these dice." Whatever might have been the method in use at certain times, if the Lord chose to resort to it in deciding a matter it would result in an infallible answer. (Prov. 16: 33.) As we think of this and numerous other means of communication of God's will to mankind, we should always remember Heb. 1: 1.

Verse 4. Mention is made of the two tribes coming from one man. Then of the fact that Levi received no inheritance. The two facts are connected with "therefore." This is the explanation. Knowing that some day the need would arise for a tribe to be entirely occupied in the religious work of the nation the Lord decided to provide for an extra tribe. This was done by taking the two sons of the man who would otherwise have made but one tribe and making a whole tribe of each of the sons. Since that was done there would be no need for the temporal provision for the religious tribe. They could be segregated from the nation and yet leave the complete unit of twelve tribes intact through the arrangement of the two sons of Joseph.

Verse 5. The children of Israel regarded the authority of Moses to the extent that they obeyed what God commanded him, and of course, through him to them.

Verses 6, 7. Caleb was one of the two spies who were faithful to the Lord. The principal information for us in this passage is to note the age of this man when he was sent from Kadesh-barnea to spy the land. Forty years.

Verses 8, 9. There is nothing vain in the statement of Caleb that he wholly followed the Lord for he immediately quotes the Lord on the point. And there is a logical reason for mentioning it which would save the statement from the charge of pride. It had to do with the possession of some territory. Further statements on this will be seen soon.

Verse 10. An interesting bit of chronology may be settled here. In verse 7 Caleb is 40 when sent from Kadesh-barnea. In Deut. 2: 14 we learn it was 38 years from this to the end of the wandering. This would make him 78 at the end of the wandering. In our present verse he is 85. This proves that the period covered by the wars of the conquest under Joshua was seven years.

Verses 11-13. Caleb evidently understands that while the war of conquest is over, the operations necessary for occupation must still be performed. Thus he assures Joshua of his confidence as to his ability for such duty. As a special request for his personal possession, certain territory is named and the request is granted.

Verse 14. Hebron as a permanent possession of Caleb is here settled and the significant reason given, that he had wholly followed the Lord.

Verse 15. The statement that the land had rest from war is indefinite in the same sense as in Ch. 11: 23. It means a temporary pause in the operations.

JOSHUA 15

General remarks. This chapter gives the boundaries of the lot that was to fall to the tribe of Judah. The general territory of the nine and a half tribes to inherit on west of Jordan has been described in 13th chapter. For supplementary information on these various territories the reader is advised to consult any reliable map.

Verse 1. Mention of the wilderness of Zin calls attention to the other place with similar name, wilderness of Sin. The two should not be confused. The latter is near the mountain of Horeb and was passed in the beginning of the wandering, while the former is up and farther over and passed at the end of the wandering.

Verse 2. The Salt Sea is the same as the Dead Sea and formed one of the "corner stones" of the possessions of Judah.

Verses 3, 4. Proceeding from the Salt Sea westward, the line includes the stream called "river of Egypt," which was a small body of water flowing north and west and into the sea mentioned here, which meant the Mediterranean. This formed the south line of the possession allotted to Judah.

Verse 5. An interesting expression here is that the Salt Sea is said to be at the end of Jordan. Not much new information perhaps, yet it is always refreshing to see the corroboration between statements of the Bible and the facts of geography.

Verse 6. Many cities of ancient times had various names. Therefore, their identity on present day maps is not always possible. But it is sufficient to point out some of the ones named that have a setting in the history in the scriptures and such will be done in the following passages.

Verse 7. Beginning at the northern

extremity of the Salt or Dead Sea we recognize the valley of Achor as the place where Achan was destroyed for his sin at Jericho. From there we are pointed toward Gilgal, which was the location of the national camp at the time of which we are reading.

Verse 8. *Hinnom.* This was a place just south of Jerusalem, here called Jebusite. The special interest we have in this place is the fact that the name of this valley is the source of the Greek name for the lake of fire spoken about in various places in the New Testament and which will be explained in the proper place. The present verse is giving us the boundaries of the possession of Judah. At the present date it has the line drawn south of this valley and thus south of Jerusalem. That would leave that city outside of Judah, whereas we know that in later years the capital city of Palestine was located in the possession of Judah. (Verse 63.) According to Rand McNally Bible Atlas the change of the line was made after the building of the Temple.

Verse 9. Passing on westward from Jerusalem we see mentioned the place called Kirjath-jearim. This was one of the cities included in the league with the people of Gibeon. (Ch. 9: 17.) It afterward became famous as the place where the ark was kept for twenty years. (1 Sam. 7: 2.)

Verse 10. Leaving Baalah or Kirjath-jearim and going on westward, the next city or place mentioned is mount Seir. This must not be confused with the place of that name made prominent through the location of the Edomites. It is another place and only named here in identifying the northern boundary of Judah's possessions. Another place named in this section of the boundary line was Timnah, elsewhere spelled Timnath. This was the place where Judah, founder of this tribe, had his flocks and to which he went for the shearing mentioned in Gen. 38: 12.

Verse 11. The place of later renown mentioned in this section is Ekron which was one of the stops made in the circuit of the ark. (1 Sam. 5: 10.) Going onward the line is described as reaching to the sea, which means the Mediterranean.

Verse 12. The western border was the line of the sea down to the place of beginning and was the shortest line on the boundary of this tribe's possessions.

Verses 13-15. Referring to Num. 13: 6 we learn that Caleb was of the tribe of Judah and thus very properly had any special possessions allotted to him within the general territory belonging to the tribe. Mention was made in previous chapter (v. 14) that Hebron was given to Caleb as a special possession. But, as in most of the cases, in order to complete the arrangement he had to dispossess the present occupants.

Verses 16, 17. Approaching the city of Kirjath-sepher, Caleb decides to procure its subjugation through the services of another. As an inducement to this end he offered as a reward for the feat the hand of his daughter in marriage. With this as the inducement, his nephew Othniel made the attack. We will read of this man later as one of the judges. (Judges 3: 9.) Having succeeded in his attempt, the daughter, Achsah, was given to him for wife.

Verses 18, 19. The arrangement has all the appearances of one that was agreeable to the parties concerned. The wife seeks through the husband for a dowry in the way of a field. She was successful for she received a southland territory. This encouraged her to make a personal request. As she approached her father she dismounted and indicated that she had some request to make of her father. Upon this he asked what was her desire and was told she wished the watering place. The request was granted and she received the springs situated at two different sites, one lower and the other higher.

Verse 20. The foregoing parts of this chapter describe the boundaries of the possessions of Judah as to the land or general territory. This was then to be distributed again among the various families or social groups within the tribe.

Verses 21-62. This long paragraph is a list of the various towns or cities that belonged to the members of the tribe of Judah. I shall try to point out some of the most noted ones as connected with some historical fact. Beersheba, which means well of the oath. (Gen. 21: 31.) Ziklag which became the special possession of David from the Philistines. (1 Sam. 27: 6.) Eshtaol, which was the place where the spies procured the large cluster of grapes. (Num. 13: 23.) Lachish, one of the cities joining in the confederacy against Gibeon. (Ch. 10: 3.) Eglon, which also joined in the group mentioned in preceding verse and was one of the cities that oppressed the children of Israel in the time of the judges. (Judges 3: 14.) Ekron, one of the border towns. (v. 11.) Ashdod, a Philistine town and the place where the ark was taken first after being captured in battle with the children of Israel. (1 Sam. 5: 1.) Gaza was a Philistine town with incidents of importance too numerous to mention here. We will read about it in the general histories of the Israelites. It was located at the southwestern boundary of the territory of Judah and included a considerable amount of land, extending to the river of Egypt (see Gen. 15: 18) and the "great sea," which is the Mediterranean. Hebron, already mentioned as the possession of Caleb. Carmel, another place made famous by the events concerning Saul and the various prophets and also of too numerous occurrence to relate here. Kirjath-jearim, one of the border cities and mentioned in verse 10. Engedi, a place where David took refuge from Saul. (1 Sam. 23: 29.) In many of these places the city will be named and then also reference to its towns or villages. That means the surrounding territory adjacent to them.

Verse 63. The explanation for this failure will be found in Judges 2.

JOSHUA 16

Verses 1-4. A reference to Joseph as a tribe here, means to his two sons combined. The land possessed by them had its south line as described in this paragraph.

Verses 5-8. This paragraph is practically the same as a description of the boundary line with the one in previous paragraph. Only in this the statement is made that it is the boundary of Ephraim. The significance of the passage is that of the two sons of Joseph the younger, Ephraim, was located south of the older, Manasseh.

Verse 9. The tribes of Ephraim and Manasseh sprang from one common head, Joseph. Some special nearness would naturally exist between the two. In harmony with such an idea there was a more or less intermingling of the two. This was exhibited by the fact that Ephraim had some cities in the territory of Manasseh. The rendering of this verse in the R.V. will help us in grasping this situation. For the information of the reader I shall quote that version of this verse: "together with the cities which were set apart for the children of Ephraim in the midst of the inheritance of the children of Manasseh, all the cities with their villages." Now let the reader go back and read the eighth verse, going directly to the ninth as rendered by the R.V., and the language of the passage as a whole will be clarified.

Verse 10. This verse will be explained in Judges 2.

JOSHUA 17

Verse 1. Manasseh was the older of the sons of Joseph and formed one of the whole tribes but only half of it took possessions on the west of the Jordan. As seen in preceding chapter (vs. 5-8), this tribe possessed immediately north of Ephraim. This group was efficient in warfare and in the occupational actions won Gilead and Bashan. However, the half of the tribe possessing on the east of Jordan is specified here, for that is where Gilead and Bashan were situated.

Verse 2. Having told the reader of the possession of Manasseh's descendants on the east of Jordan this verse comes to refer to that on the west and which was located just north of Ephraim.

Verses 3-6. The transaction mentioned in this paragraph is recorded in Num. 27: 1-11. Joshua respected the proclamation of Moses and gave to these women the land. As an explanatory piece of information the writer states that some of Manasseh's descendants had their possessions on the other side of Jordan. The rest were on the west side.

Verses 7, 8. This mentions some cities on the border of Manasseh's territory. Few of them are shown on the present day maps but the general description will enable one to locate the possession. Notice that mention is again made of the possessions of Ephraim within that of Manasseh. (Ch. 16: 9.)

Verses 9, 10. This paragraph takes us to the western boundary of the possession of Manasseh. A river is referred to. Such a stream is shown on the maps. It was located at about the dividing line of the tribes of Ephraim and Manasseh. Then a jump is made to the eastern limits of Manasseh where he joins us with Issachar.

Verse 11. It is evident that the boundary lines were not always exclusive of some particular local interests. In this verse it is seen that

Manasseh "had" some cities in the territory allotted to these two other tribes. The fact is explained to some extent by the seeming partiality that was to be shown to the sons of Joseph. In the latter part of this chapter will be seen some information along this line. The town of special interest mentioned in this verse is Endor. It was made famous by the incident of Saul and the woman with the familiar spirit. (1 Sam. 28: 7.)

Verses 12, 13. From the language in this paragraph it will be understood the cities mentioned in previous one were offered to the use of Manasseh on condition that he occupy them in force. However, he was not able entirely to overcome them. This fact will be explained in Judges 2.

Verse 14. *Children of Joseph.* This expression as used here is a reference to representatives of both Manasseh and Ephraim. (Gen. 48: 5, 22.) In this view of the case the request for more than one lot would mean that two tribes should have more allotment than just one tribe. Their claim would have merit in view of the prediction of Jacob in the passage in Genesis referred to.

Verse 15. There was a district of wild or wooded character that had not been especially taken over as yet. It was located in a rather south and westerly section of country. The suggestion made by Joshua was that these people should clear out the forest in this "open" district and thus enlarge their possessions. *Mount Ephraim.* Although this expression would seem to indicate some mountain yet the use of it is to include a more extended district. (See 1 Sam. 1: 1; 2 Chr. 13: 4, 19.) The expression will be found in various other places in the scriptures. It was in the possession of the tribes descended from Joseph, or at least within their use. Now if that is not enough territory for these sons of Joseph they are offered the suggestion of enlarging themselves as here stated.

Verse 16. The children of Joseph formed the impression that Joshua meant too small a portion of the mentioned territory and complained accordingly, that it was not enough, especially in view of the obstacles they would have to overcome.

Verse 17. Joshua is favorable to their demands for more territory than would be considered "one lot" since they were a great people. And in thus assuring them of more he is carrying out the noted prediction made by Jacob. (Gen. 48: 22.)

Verse 18. Notwithstanding their feeling of uncertainty (v. 16), Joshua gives them the prospects of overcoming the obstacles and taking the territory. Again we must bear in mind that all such promises were made on the condition that they perform their part of the contract as to driving out the usurpers.

JOSHUA 18

Verse 1. The camp of the Israelites has been at Gilgal since their entrance to the land of Canaan. Now it has been moved to Shiloh where it will remain for a long time. Its next location is indicated in 1 Chronicles 16: 39.

Verse 2. This means the actions necessary for occupation of the allotted territories had not been performed. For comments on this phase of the subject see ch. 13: 1.

Verse 3. Human beings like to have what is pleasant and desirable but often are negligent in the exercises required to have them. Thus Joshua chides these tribes for their indifference concerning this matter.

Verse 4. In chapters 13 to 17 the boundaries of various tribes are described. The inspired writer could put this description down independent of any survey. Now a more minute reconnaissance is thought necessary.

Verses 5, 6. After the survey has been made and description of the land brought to Joshua he will proceed to settle the titles thereto.

Verse 7. The special duties about the tabernacle made it impractical for the Levites to possess or occupy any general landed estate.

Verses 8, 9. The instructions of Joshua were obeyed. The description was made "by cities" which means that the cities were referred to as land marks by which to designate the legal boundaries.

Verse 10. It is significant that it states Joshua cast lots "before the Lord." This is in harmony with the information given at ch. 14: 1.

Verse 11. A look at the map will show the possession of Benjamin to be located between Ephraim (a son of Joseph) on the north, and Judah on the south.

Verse 12. Some of the possessions of tribes to be described joined those of other ones already considered. And the cities were usually used as landmarks and since that would put them on the line it follows that many of these cities are mentioned more than once in this book of Joshua. The possession for Benjamin started at the northeast corner at the river Jordan. From Jordan the line ran north of Jericho and onward through the mountainous section and further to the wilderness of Beth-aven.

Verse 13. The exact location of Luz or Bethel is an unsettled question among geographers, but the line of Benjamin is declared here to have run near it toward the west and then southward as far as Beth-horon.

Verse 14. The sea mentioned in this verse does not mean a body of water. One of the definitions of the original word is "west" and in harmony with that the R. V. here says "west quarter." Coming on down to the general region of Kirjath-jearim the west line is described.

Verses 15, 16. Continuing from the point described in preceding verse the line passes unto the mountain near the noted valley of Hinnom which was situated south of Jebusi, which is Jerusalem.

Verses 17-19. Continuing the south line of Benjamin it comes to end at the north bay or prong of the Salt Sea. This is the same as the Dead Sea.

Verse 20. The Jordan river formed the entire eastern line of the possession of Benjamin.

Verses 21-28. Having described the boundary lines of this possession the writer names some particular cities included. One of them is Jericho, too well known to call for further comment at this place. Another group of twelve cities is mentioned in verse 24. Verse 28 names Jebusi, and immediately explains it to mean Jerusalem.

JOSHUA 19

Verse 1. This verse should be considered in connection with 9th verse. The territory at first intended for Judah was regarded as more than the one tribe should have. Therefore it was subdivided so as to give Simeon a share. It was located at the southern extremity of the land of Canaan. Since the general assignment for Judah was described in chapter 15 no further description is given here, but certain towns will be mentioned.

Verses 2-8. Beer-sheba was noted as the well of the oath. (Gen. 21: 31; 26: 28, 33.) Ziklag was afterward made noted by the settlement of David there. (1 Sam. 27: 6.)

Verse 9. This is commented upon at verse 1.

Verses 10-16. The possession of Zebulun was one of the small ones and not many familiar landmarks will be read about. The "sea" in verse 11 is a brook as the original word has various definitions, such as quarter and brook and coast. Some small stream not of great importance generally was one of the line marks.

Verses 17-23. The possession of Issachar was just south of Zebulun. The only town of note mentioned within this lot was Shunem. It came into history in connection with the young woman chosen as a companion for David in his declining and final days, recorded in 1 Kings chapter one.

Verse 24-31. When Jacob was making his predictions of his sons (Gen. 49: 13) he said "Zebulun shall dwell at the haven of the sea." The description given in this paragraph as well as on the maps, shows that Jacob was inspired in his prediction. The possession was bordered along the coast of the Mediterranean with the heathen country of Phoenicia. But much of its own territory also bordered on the same body of water. The cities of Tyre and Zidon are mentioned in this paragraph. They were Phoenician cities but had so much connection with the history of the Israelites that it was very proper to name them in this description. Especially since the country of the Phoenicians was so narrow as to make these cities practically connected with the land of Israel.

Verses 32-39. This lot ran parallel with that of Asher. One peculiar fact in connection with this lot was that it extended beyond the Jordan at its northeastern extremity. But the major portion was on the west of that river and thus would be counted as among the possessions on the west side. With above exception, the eastern line was composed of the Jordan river and the lakes Merom and Galilee. Not much importance is attached to any of the cities mentioned. The Adamah in verse 36 should not be confused with Admah which was destroyed with Sodom. (Deut, 29: 23.)

Verses 40-46. It has doubtless been observed that the order of descriptions of the various possessions has not been according to the continuous junctions of the land. Thus the present one is further down the line and borders on the great sea. Among the cities linked with the boundary line were Zorah (Judg. 13: 2), Eshtaol (Judg. 16: 31), Ajalon (ch. 10: 12), Ekron (1 Sam. 5: 10.)

Verses 47, 48. The history of this verse is recorded in 18th chapter of Judges.

Verses 49, 50. This was given to Joshua as a personal possession and was used as his burial place. (ch. 24: 30.)

Verse 51. Eleazar was the High Priest and Joshua the leader of the people, hence it was appropriate that they have charge of this allotment of the possessions. It was decided by lot at Shiloh because that was the headquarters of the nation then.

JOSHUA 20

Verses 1, 2. These cities of refuge are the ones already written about in Ex, 21: 13 and Num. 35: 6.

Verse 3. The word "unwittingly" means "not knowing." Not that a man would kill another and not know it. But he did not know beforehand that he was going to kill him. The killing was done either accidentally or on the spur of the moment and was not premeditated. The avenger of blood was a brother or near relative. (Gen. 9: 5.)

Verse 4. Regardless of the conditions under which the killing was done, the killer could flee unto one of these cities for safety for the time being. Those cities were all walled or fortified ones and entrance to them must be had through the official gate. The elders of the city, which means the leading citizens thereof, were to admit the slayer and receive his story. They must also give him the right to reside in that city for the time being.

Verse 5. For the time being these elders must shield the slayer from the hands of the avenger because it has not yet been determined whether he is guilty of murder.

Verse 6. Of course the writer is here considering only the slayer who was not guilty of the kind of slaying that constituted murder. This fact had been learned by his standing before the congregation for trial. After that was done and he had been declared innocent then he was able to be returned to the city of refuge for protection from the revenger. And he was required to remain in that city until the death of the high priest who was serving at the time. In average cases that would give sufficient time for the wrath of the near relative who was the official executioner to cool off. Then the slayer could return to his home city and be safe with his life.

Verses 7-9. There were six of these cities of refuge. Kedesh, Shechem and Hebron on the west side of Jordan. Bezer, Ramoth and Golan on the east side. The reason for locating the cities on the two sides of the river was the fact that the two and a half tribes already mentioned had their possessions on the east side. When it would be necessary for one of those tribes to take refuge in a city of refuge he might not be able to reach one of the cities on the west side in time. That would be particularly true at the harvest season because of the overflow of Jordan (ch. 3: 15.) As the names and other information concerning these cities are given at length in next chapter no further comments will here be made on them.

JOSHUA 21

Verses 1, 2. The tribe of Levi was not given possessions in the same way as the other tribes. Because of the exclusive work of the tribe they could not make use of the landed estates. Yet they must be furnished places in which to live. The provision had been made while Moses was living. (Num. 35.) Now the leaders among the Levites come to Joshua and the high priest at the headquarters and remind them of this provision. The Levites being the tribe thus separated for the special service of the Lord it was appropriate that they should live in the cities to be used as cities of refuge since they were to serve in the administration of the government. Also, as the twelve tribes were required to give a tenth of all their increase to the tribe of Levi, it would be necessary for this tribe to be furnished with room to keep the cattle thus given them. They would use these cattle for food and for their personal sacrifices to the Lord. This room is what is meant here by the suburbs. This was not the outlying parts of the cities as we use that term, but the pasturage and other open land immediately surrounding the cities.

Verses 3, 4. The reader should remember that the entire tribe of Levi was separated unto the Lord and not given a local possession as were the other tribes. Therefore the cities that were to be their homes were scattered throughout the entire nation. A special allotment was made as pertained to the three sons of Levi and their families. It will be recalled that assignment of special service was made to these three sons. (Num. 3.) One of those sons was Kohath. Part of the assignments to him is named in this paragraph and seen to be located within the regular possessions of the tribes of Judah, Simeon and Benjamin.

Verse 5. The tribes of Ephraim, Dan and Manasseh were called upon to assign cities to the rest of the families of Kohath.

Verse 6. Another son of Levi was Gershon. He was given cities within the regular possessions of Issachar, Naphtali and the half tribe of Manasseh that was on that side of the river Jordan.

Verses 7, 8. The cities of Merari were on the east side of Jordan.

Verses 9-12. In the foregoing paragraphs the general location of the cities given to the Levites is named. In this and following paragraphs the names of the six cities of refuge and their suburbs will be given. However, in the present paragraph the description is still general except that special mention is made of the personal possession of Caleb. His assignment was the fields and small towns around one of the cities of refuge which will be named presently. This special gift to Caleb was according to the arrangement made through Joshua recorded in chapter 14.

Verses 13-19. From here on to nearly the end of the chapter the six cities of refuge with their suburbs, also the other cities, will be named and thus the only thing necessary in this part of our work will be to point out the refuge city so that the reader may mark his book accordingly if he desires. In the present paragraph the one named is Hebron and in direct connection with the name is the word "refuge."

Verses 20-26. Same general comments as on preceding paragraph. Here it is the city Shechem with "refuge" mentioned in connection.

Verses 27-31. Here it is Golan with "refuge."

Verses 32-35. This is the city of "refuge" called Kedesh.

Verses 36, 37. This paragraph names Bezer but is not here named as one of the cities of refuge for some reason. By consulting ch. 20: 8 it is seen to be such.

Verses 38-42. The sixth and complete list of the cities of refuge is given here which is Ramoth and "refuge."

Verses 43-45. The promise of complete possession of the land was made on condition that the children of Israel do their part in the covenant. That was their duty to oppose the heathen nations then occupying the land. They were to drive them out and have no dealings with them. And in proportion as they carried out their part of the covenant the Lord carried out his part. This paragraph is to be understood in light of these considerations.

JOSHUA 22

Verse 1-3. The tribes of Reuben, Gad and half of Manasseh had requested to have their possessions on the east side of Jordan. (Num. 32.) After explaining their motive and that they would fully share with their brethren the burdens of the war until final and complete victory had been won, Moses granted their request. Now the war is over. Joshua therefore calls these tribes to him and commends them for their faithfulness in carrying out their agreement.

Verse 4. Since the Lord has blessed the joint services of all the tribes it is proper for these two and a half tribes to be released from military duty and permitted to go to their own possessions. Joshua thus gives them leave by honorable discharge.

Verses 5, 6. Joshua blesses these tribes as he sends them to their own possessions, but admonishes them to be obedient to the law as given by Moses.

Verses 7, 8. The entire group of Israelites that was to settle east of the Jordan received blessing from Joshua. But here seems to be a specific reference to the half tribe of Manasseh that was to be on that side. With his good wishes he bids them divide the spoils they had taken in the war just ended with their brethren. After all, the ones who had remained at home and "kept the home fires burning" contributed quite a bit to the success of the whole victory.

Verse 9. This verse keeps us in mind that the headquarters of the nation were still at Shiloh at which place they will be for much time. Also in this verse we are shown that not all of the promised land was in Canaan.

Verse 10. The only description we have of this altar here is that it was great to see to or was great in appearance. And the misunderstanding that it caused makes a significant instance of how unwise it is to "jump" to conclusions, as we shall see.

Verses 11, 12. Attention is now called to the words "heard say" which was the only basis revealed for the action of going to begin war against the two and a half tribes. So many times in the affairs of mankind the mere assumption of a few perons and that based on a mere rumor has caused untold grief. How much better for all concerned it would be were the facts learned before coming to a conclusion. However, in the present case we are glad that no actual attack was made until further investigation was had.

Verses 13, 14. Having decided to investigate, the children of Israel sent men who were powered to speak on the subject at hand, the son of the priest and ten other leading citizens. This not only indicated the seriousness of the issue in the estimation of the congregation, but also let the tribes about to be called to account see that they would have opportunity to deal with representatives of authority.

Verses 15, 16. Upon arrival at the land of the two and a half tribes they claim their credentials by saying they spoke for the "whole congregation." They were somewhat premature in that they expressly accused them of trespass.

Verses 17-20. The commission still speaks in terms of accusation and even supplement their charges by comparison to others who had so grievously rebelled against God. It has been a matter of wonder to me that nothing was said in correction of these men for their false accusations. And false they were as the event proved for there was never a word of criticism uttered against the two and a half tribes afterward as to why they did not at least counsel the congregation before making this altar. Perhaps we may pass this phase of the case by with the thought that God's divine institutions are so sacred that the least threat of violence should be "nipped in the bud." Also that an innocent man will not be injured by ever so strict an investigation.

Verses 21, 22. When Moses misunderstood the motives of these tribes in their request about their possessions (Num. 32: 6-15) on the east side, they replied with humility and respect and gave a satisfactory explanation. Now when their motives have again been misunderstood and falsely accused they again manifest humility and respect. Not the slightest sign of resentment, but a complete willingness to make all things plain. A general denial of the accusation is made.

Verse 23. They realized that no lawful sacrifice could be offered in worship to God except on the altar and at the place designated by the Lord without bringing the curse of God. In this they manifest proper attitude toward the Lord's institutions.

Verses 24-29. The writer deems it best to group these verses together in one paragraph so as to keep the thought intact. It is a wonderful speech offered by the two and a half tribes. The purport of it is the very opposite to what was in the accusation. Instead of wanting to be factious and rebel against the lawful congregation their motive was the exact opposite. In order *not* to appear in the eyes of the coming generations to be rebellious they wished to have this pattern of the official altar to prove the common interest of all the tribes. No service was intended on this pattern but only a visible sign of their interest in the one that was located in the lawful place and to which they would journey at the appointed seasons.

Verses 30, 31. The answer of the tribes was entirely satisfactory to the commission sent by Joshua. Not only was it acceptable as a proper explanation but was pleasing to them. That is, unlike some false accusers, they were not anxious to be able to make their accusations "stick" by some means, but were glad that the accusations had proved untrue and that the wrath of the Lord would not need to be put upon them.

Verses 32-34. Canaan was west of the Jordan. The men sent to attend to the affair of the altar returned and made their report. The account given of what they learned pleased the children of Israel, who blessed God or praised and thanked him for the good news. "Did not intend" is worded in R. V. "spake no more." The meaning is that, whereas, they at one time intended to make war, they are now satisfied with the situation and so dropped the intention of war. After the affair was settled the two and a half tribes adhered to their original purpose of considering this altar as a witness of their unity with the congregation. The name here inserted into the text is not in the original. It is a word meaning "witness" and its insertion might be suffered on the basis that such was the avowed motive of the altar.

JOSHUA 23

Verse 1. The description of a man waxing old and stricken with age must be considered in the light of comparison. For instance, David is said to be old and stricken in years (1 Sam. 1: 1), when he was only 70 at death. (2 Sam. 5: 4.) Also, this is said of Joshua, although he was 110 at death. (ch. 24: 29.) Moses at the age of 120 was said to be unabated in his vigor. (Deut. 34: 7.) So we are to understand such conditions to be due to the experiences and other circumstances in connection with the men.

Verse 2. Joshua called for his men of all ranks to hear him. He informed them of his physical condition.

Verse 3. Not only did these men know of the success that had attended their arms against the nations, but he wanted them to bear in mind that said success was due to the help from God. The wonderful Lord had fought for them.

Verse 4. The actual war was ended as Joshua spoke to these men. But the work of taking possession of the land allotted was yet to be done. And that would include whatever occupational activities were necessary to rout the remaining occupants of the land.

Verses 5, 6. The help of God is still assured them. Also they were exhorted to be courageous. That indicated they must cooperate with God in the actions. Otherwise, no personal courage would be occasioned. That is, they were not merely to have faith that God would help them but must also be courageous in the matter; they would certainly know that they must also be in the actions. A practical method of manifesting the courage was stated in that they were to do all that was written in the book of the law of Moses, the man whose authority is slandered by the sabbatarians.

Verses 7, 8. They will have to oppose these heathen nations, even with arms. But they must not "come among them" which means not to associate with them. They must have no fellowship with their gods nor in any way participate with them. Instead, they must cleave unto the Lord their God. These and such like instructions and warnings have been spoken to the children of Israel all along and were the grounds on which the promises concerning the land were based. The omitting of them was the reason for all their disappointments.

Verses 9, 10. Had the Lord made promises only, without demonstrating his power it might have been thought to be the reason for their shortcomings. But he had already driven out some of the strongest of the heathen. This was done regardless of the great difference in their numbers.

Verse 11. It is not enough to give casual assent to the declarations of God. They must give heed. This word means to "observe to do" as is so often stated.

Verses 12, 13. The remnant of the nations mentioned here means those not yet dispossessed even after the major war has been won. They must be cleared out or else they will be suffered by the Lord to be pests. Figuratively, they will be thorns and traps and snares. The book of the Bible to be studied next will demonstrate how true this threat proved to be.

Verse 14. *Going the way of all the earth.* This statement was made also by David. (1 Ki. 2: 2.) The same thought is expressed by Paul in Heb. 9: 27. Since the sin of our first parents and their expulsion from the garden and from the tree of life, the only consequence to follow is that of physical death. All the people of the earth must die. That is why the statement is used referred to above. The strong statement Joshua makes here of the fulfillment of God's promises is a repetition of what has been repeated many times. See comments on this line of thought at the verses of chapter 21: 42-45.

Verses 15, 16. God is faithful to carry out all his promises when the conditions on which they are made are properly met. He is just as prompt to carry out all his threats against those who violate his laws and who do not make the necessary amends for their shortcomings. To transgress the covenant means to go beyond it or to disobey its restrictions. In the case of the children of Israel this transgression would especially consist in their going after the heathen gods of the land. God is a jealous God and will not tolerate this dividing of service to him. If his people become guilty of idolatry they will be punished severely. This punishment will extend unto the exile of the guilty nation into a heathen land.

JOSHUA 24

Verse 1. The national encampment was not at Shechem, but at Gilgal. But it was the place where Joshua assembled the tribes of Israel to hear his farewell message. This city was of such great importance that I shall quote from Smith's Bible Dictionary a few lines. Incidentally, the reader will see in the quotation an interesting statement of the nearness to each other of the mountains Ebal and Gerizim which were used in the peculiar ceremony of the curses and blessings. (Deut. 27: 12, 13.) Here is the quotation: "Shechem. 1. An important city in central Palestine, in the valley between mounts Ebal and Gerizim, 34 miles north of Jerusalem and 7 miles southeast of Samaria. Its present name, *Nablus*, is a corruption of Neapolis, which succeeded the more ancient Shechem, and received its new name from Vespasian. On coins still extant it is called Flavia Neapolis. The situation of the town is one of surpassing beauty. It lies in a sheltered valley, protected by Gerizim on the south and Ebal on the north. The feet of these mountains, where they rise from the town, are not more than five hundred yards apart. The bottom of the valley is about 1800 feet above the level of the sea, and the top of Gerizim, 800 feet higher still." What a wonderful spot for Joshua to choose at which to make this classical speech.

Verse 2. The word "flood" is from NAHAR and is the same as rendered "river" in ch. 1: 4, and means the Euphrates, since that was the river separating the ancient place of residences for these fathers from the land of the desert and Canaan. It is a singular fact that the ancestors of the children of Israel were idolaters. Not that they did not offer sacrifices on behalf of God, but they mixed the two. The images of these gods were in evidence among their descendants long afterward. We read of Rachel's stealing those of her father on their departure from Mesopotamia. (Gen. 31: 19.)

Verse 3. We understand that Abraham is to be included in the "fathers" of the preceding verse, for he is here so called. The word "flood" in this verse is from the same original as that in preceding verse. The verse makes a big jump in history, going from the call of Abraham to the birth of his son Isaac.

Verse 4. Not all of the branches of Abraham's seed are mentioned here as Joshua is not concerned at present with them. However, since the two sons, Esau and Jacob, were from the promised son of Abraham, mention is made of both. A short disposition is made of the history of Esau here by reference to an established site, Seir. The more important of the two sons, Jacob, went down into Egypt. This is a pursuing of the family history of the people of God whose descendants are now before Joshua.

Verse 5. This brief verse involves the history taking up Exodus 2 to 14 and gives us an indication of the brevity often used by the inspired writers.

Verses 6, 7. This is some more of the brevity of history. In the short passage here cited is couched the account of the final departure of Israel from the border line of Egypt, their experiences at, and in, and across the Red Sea and their dwelling in the wilderness, which covered 40 years.

Verse 8. While there was a specific race called Amorites, their unusual wickedness was such that the term came to be used with reference to many of the others then infesting the land to which the Israelites had to come. In this verse, reference is to the nations occupying the territory east of the Jordan and against which they first came. It especially here applies to Og and Sihon, whose land was taken from them and given to the people of God in the lifetime of Moses.

Verses 9, 10. Another concentration of history is seen here. The entire story of this passage requires the chapters 22, 23, 24 of Numbers to cover.

Verse 11. The reader should not forget that verse 2 of this chapter introduces the speaker of these several verses as the Lord. Joshua is relaying the speech, of course, but the pronouns of the first person refer to God. In this verse the Amorites are again mentioned, as they were, with reference to the territory on the east side. This is in agreement with the idea mentioned a few times that the Amorites, while a distinct people to themselves, were so outstanding in wickedness that the term came to be used generally of evil people.

Verses 12, 13. The hornet or wasp was simply one of the visible means which the Lord used to accomplish his purpose. Of course the Israelites were expected to do their part but their sword and bow unaided by the Lord would not have accomplished the desired result. This is proved by the fact that their efforts failed after God withdrew his help later. While this paragraph is chiefly about the events on the west of the Jordan it incidentally reverts to the case of the two Amorite kings on the east, (Og and Sihon) to include them in the matter of the hornets.

Verse 14. The quotation from the Lord is dropped for the time being and Joshua directly exhorts the people to their duty. He tells them to put away the gods which their fathers had served on the other side of the flood (Euphrates), and in Egypt. The tendency toward idolatry was still manifest among them and some strong language is used.

Verse 15. A careful reading of this verse is necessary to avoid serious misunderstanding. Before telling them to take their choice between gods, he lays down the supposition that they do not intend to serve the Lord. Now then, if they decide to reject the Lord it is taken for granted they intend to serve idol gods. If so, then take their choice between the gods their fathers served the other side of the flood (Euphrates) and the gods of the Amorites or wicked nations in the land where they are now. That would be logical. If they are determined to be idolaters, then it would not make any difference as to which gods of the heathen they chose. But Joshua did not tell them to "take their choice" between good and evil, as it sometimes erroneously taught.

Verses 16-18. The people responded favorably and agreed to serve the Lord. They furthermore gave him credit for their successes in Egypt and the present country.

Verses 19, 20. These two verses must be considered together to avoid another misunderstanding. The central thought of the whole passage can be seen at a glance by segregating the words as follows: "Ye cannot serve the Lord," "*if*" "ye serve strange gods." This doctrine is exactly the same as Jesus taught when he said "Ye cannot serve God and Mammon." (Matt. 6: 24.)

Verse 21. The people again insist on their determination to serve the Lord.

Verses 22-25. As visible evidence of their sincerity Joshua demands they put away the strange gods. They agreed and then he made a covenant to that effect with them.

Verses 26-28. Of course this covenant was a special agreement between the people and Jashua and attested by recording in a book and by erecting a stone or pillar. Upon the conclusion of this agreement the assembly was dismissed and the people returned to their various possessions.

Verses 29, 30. Some time after the events of the preceding paragraph the time came for Joshua to die. He was 110 years old at death. His burial took place in the spot having been assigned to him. (ch. 19: 50.)

Verse 31. The main thought we may get from this verse is that people seem to need the immediate influence of teachers and leaders to keep them in line. Hence, it can be understood why God has always had some lawful representative between him and his people, in all of the Dispensations.

Verse 32. The request made by Joseph is recorded in Gen. 50: 25 and is here being fulfilled. Paul refers to this subject in Heb. 11: 22.

Verse 33. High Priests served until death. (Num. 35: 25.) Now that Eleazar is dead his son, Phinehas, will serve in his stead.

JUDGES 1

General remarks: On numerous occasions the children of Israel were told that God would give them success over the nations then occupying the land they were to possess. That promise was based on the condition that no mixing would be done with those idolatrous people. Persistent opposition against them must be maintained and no covenants were to be made. God would not do all of the work miraculously, but they must cooperate by fighting the enemy. It was also stated to them that if they failed to do their duty along this line, the nations would be suffered to remain in the land to become thorns and pests to them. This warning was overlooked and the children of Israel allowed the heathen nations to remain in the land. True to his warning, the Lord used these heathen tribes as instruments of chastisement for his people. He would permit them to fall under the oppression of some one or more of these nations and they would be thus penalized for a time. When the punishment had gone as long as God deemed wise he would raise up some man among the Israelites to champion their interests. That man would be empowered to wage battle or other form of opposition and rescue them from their oppressor. He would rule and lead them for a period until they got "on their feet" so to speak. Soon they would forget the Lord and it would be necessary again to let them fall into the hands of an oppressor nation, and again some one would need to be raised up to deliver them. This kind of national experience went on for 450 years according to Paul in Acts 13: 20. The men thus raised up to deliver the children of Israel were called "judges." The book we are now beginning to study is the history of this period and hence the name used as title of the book.

Verses 1-4. See comments at Josh. 13: 1 for light on this passage. The "battle of occupation" is now before the children of Israel and that is why they ask for special instructions from God. The means of communication between the Lord and the people does not appear here. The priests were supposed to act in such capacity. For this information see Mal. 2: 7; Lev. 10: 11; Deut. 17: 9. We have previously seen that Simeon had his possession allotted to him out of the territory originally assigned to Judah. (Josh. 19: 1-9.) In harmony with that it is here stated that Judah called upon Simeon to join him in this action, for occupying their joint lot.

Verses 5, 6. The treatment here given this wicked king was in reprisal for the way he treated others, as will soon be seen.

Verse 7. This wicked man had taken 70 kings into his grasp. It should have been understood by him that captives deserved to be treated humanely. He had been cruel to them and had mutilated them as described. Not only this, but instead of feeding them even in an ordinary manner he compelled them to find their sustenance by gathering (gleaning in the margin) what they could under the table of their captor. When he was given a like treatment as to his body, he understood the reason and stated it so. After this, he succumbed at the headquarters of his captors.

Verse 8. This verse accounts for the statement at close of preceding one.

Verses 9-11. The tribe of Judah is proceeding to carry out the actions of occupation and this paragraph is a mention of some of the particular spots they attacked.

Verses 12-15. Some of the history of those times was somewhat distributed without strict regard for chronological order. Thus the events of this paragraph have been already recorded in Josh. 15: 16-19 which see.

Verse 16. The father-in-law of Moses was a Midianite as to his general blood. But the Kenites were a smaller unit of that race hence the mention of the name here. These people were more or less associated with the children of Israel all along on account of the friendliness that had been shown God's people by their common ancestor. The city of palm trees was Jericho. (Deut. 34: 3.)

Verses 17, 18. Judah and Simeon are allies in the work of occupation and thus are here said to have attacked these cities located among the Canaanites and Philistines.

Verse 19. It is generally understood that God's power is unlimited as far as ability is concerned. He was supposed to assist the Israelites in overcoming their enemies. Then why was there an apparent failure in one place on account of some human obstacle? This must be explained by consideration of the condition on which God promised to help his people overcome. See general remarks at beginning of this chapter. Since the obedience of his people was partial, God's help would be partial only and thus the Israelites would be the ones limited, not the Lord. To illustrate, should a father penalize a wayward son by cutting down on his allowance, then the son would be limited in the purchasing power he would have. Things desired that cost more than others would have to be done without. So here, since the help God extended to the people was cut down on account of their lack of full obedience, they would be unable to overcome the enemies who were the best fortified.

Verse 20. Hebron was a desirable site and had been given to Caleb. (Num. 14: 24.) Like the others, he must occupy it. The sons of Anak were giants' sons and would be strong foes, but there is no indication of failure. All this agrees with the statements in preceding verse, for Caleb "wholly" followed the Lord and hence the help given him from the Lord would be complete.

Verse 21. See general remarks at beginning of this chapter and those at verse 19.

Verses 22, 23. "To descry" means "to spy out." Before taking this place the men of Joseph's descendants sent spies to learn the conditions.

Verses 24-26. Most of the important cities were walled against invasion. Therefore it would be an advantage to find some secret way of entrance. The spies here saw a man emerging from the city and would know he understood the conditions. On promise of personal liberty he gave them information which led to the overthrow of the city. True to their promise they let the informant go and he went to the community of the Hittites and built a city which he called Luz. We will remember this was the original name of the city of Bethel, from which this man was now expelled.

Verses 27, 28. For explanation see general remarks at beginning of the chapter and the ones at verse 19.

Verses 29-35. All of these verses are here grouped into one paragraph because the explanation of the whole passage is to be found as above. The general remarks at beginning of the chapter and at verse 19 should be carefully read in connection with this.

JUDGES 2

Verse 1. Bochim was a town not far north of Gilgal and got its name from the circumstance of weeping recorded below. The statement is here made of God that he would never break his covenant with the people. As already learned many times, that covenant was based on their obedience to the Lord's requirements. If these are disobeyed then the covenant would automatically be void.

Verse 2. The requirements mentioned were that they make no league with the inhabitants of the country. They must throw down the idolatrous altars and have nothing to do with the evil practices. But they had not obeyed the commands of the Lord and were not able to give satisfactory explanation of their disobedience.

Verse 3. Because of this disobedience God will carry out his warning to let the heathen remain as snares to his people, to punish or oppress them.

Verses 4, 5. Upon hearing this sad announcement from the angel the people fell to weeping. The word "Bochim" is from a Hebrew word that means "the weepers," and hence, the name applied to this place. The immediate effect as to actions upon the people now was to offer a sacrifice to God. Whatever favorable acceptance this tardy action may have had at hands of God, it did not change the grand decision to penalize the nation for their general attitude of disobedience so long practiced.

Verses 6-9. This is another one of the passages out of chronological order. See Josh. 24: 28-31.

Verse 10. This verse is also a reflection on the conduct of the people after the death of Joshua and the elders who outlived him. It is another statement as an introduction to the general history about to be started.

Verses 11-13. *Baalim, Baal, Ashtaroth.* As critical explanation of these words I shall quote definitions from the lexicographers: "Baal, Baalim. The chief male deity of the Phoenicians and Canaanites, as Ashtoreth was their chief female deity. Both these names have the peculiarity of being used in the plural."—Young. "Baal, a Phoenician deity: Baal, (plural) Baalim."—Strong. In proportion as the Israelites served these heathen deities they forsook the true God. This again is according to the teaching of Jesus in Matt. 6: 24. This idolatrous conduct of the Israelites led them into disobedience of the commandments of God which brought them the divine judgments extending into final downfall of the nation.

Verse 14. A spoiler is one who takes from another his chief possessions. Thus these idolatrous nations took from the children of Israel their property and fruits of their fields and other labors.

Verse 15. *Evil.* This does not always nor even usually mean bad morally. It is from RAH and defined by Strong "bad or (as noun) evil (naturally or morally)." The word has been rendered in the A.V. by adversity, affliction, calamity, distress, grief, hurt misery, sorrow and others. God never entices man into sin but he does sometimes visit affliction on him in the days of special providence, as a punishment.

Verse 16. As proof that God did not bring these afflictions on his people in the spirit of spite or hate he raised up judges to deliver them, after they had received the necessary amount of punishment.

Verse 17. Sometimes even the judges had difficulty in getting the people to reform. They were bent on following after the gods of the enemy nations around them. When immorality is used figuratively it means the worship of false gods. Hence this verse says the people went a whoring, or lusting, after other gods.

Verse 18. *The Lord was with the judge.* This proves that when we read later in this book about the judges and their teachings and conduct of the situations it is the Lord inspiring the movements. That does not mean that none of the judges did any wrong or that everything without exception was favored by the Lord. When that was the case the situation will not be left without indicating plainly to the reader the fact. *It repented the Lord.* One item is always in the word "repent," whether referring to God or man, and that is "change." Unless a change has been made, the word repent cannot be properly used. Therefore when man repents he must change his wrong conduct, to right. When God repents he changes some condition or some plan or prediction that he had made. In this case, after the children of Israel had been punished enough, God would change their afflicted condition into a more agreeable one.

Verse 19. The frequent backslidings of the children of Israel, followed by the mercy of God make up the book of Judges and this verse is thus a brief preface.

Verses 20-23. The preface suggested in preceding verse is extended in this paragraph and outlines the general national history to be delineated in the following pages.

JUDGES 3

Verses 1, 2. Many of the Israelites who had been engaged in war with the people of Canaan are dead now. Those wars had been for the purpose of dispossessing them of their usurpation of the promised land and also to destroy their idolatry. The history of that period was written in a book and was open to the information of the later generations. They should therefore have profited thereby and been led to serve the Lord. But the lessons were often unheeded by them, so it was necessary to use the remaining heathen as rods of chastisement for them. Hence the words of this verse.

Verses 3, 4. This paragraph is a general listing of the enemy nations left to try or "prove" the Israelites.

Verses 5, 6. This more closely specifies the tribes or clans of the heathen nations infesting the land. The people of God not only mixed their worship with that of the heathen, but also mixed their blood by their marriages. It was then, as it always has been and always will be, that when God's people marry into those not his people, much trouble results. The social and fleshly interests created in the marriage relation often outrun those of spirituality. Therefore, it is extremely dangerous to say the least, for such intermarriages to be practiced.

Verse 7. It is there, and many times elsewhere, said that the people served the groves. Sometimes the same idea is worded by simple reference to trees or oaks, etc. This is because idolatrous nations so generally erected their altars and idol temples in the groves or near some prominent tree, that the system of idolatrous worship was identified in literature by the mere mention of these objects in nature. Sometimes in this day we hear people trying to connect the physical fact of a tree used for ornamental or mechanical purposes with the heathen worship. The conditions of mankind in the general ways of life are so changed that the comparison is entirely fanciful. It is as much off the subject as to forbid Christians eating certain animals today, because God at one time forbade such food to be eaten. We know that such restrictions are condemned by the N.T. (Col. 2: 16.)

Verse 8. It is worth while to keep a tabulation of the years mentioned in this book related to the period of the judges. Thus in this verse we note 8 years stated. This time the people were delivered into the hands of the Mesopotamian king.

Verses 9-11. The judge raised to power against this enemy king was the son of Kenaz, brother of Caleb. We read about him in Ch. 1: 13. He had already proved his courage in battle in the matter of securing a wife. Now he is helped by the Lord in his aggression against Chushan. This state of relief lasted 40 years. (Another place to mark.)

Verses 12-14. After a period of forty years the children of Israel broke over from their reformation and again did evil, which called for another chastisement. This time the instrument of God's wrath came from the other side of Jordan. The descendants of Lot, Moabites and Ammonites, together with the Amelekites all rallied to the support of the Moabite king, Eglon, and came against them. This oppression lasted 18 years.

Verse 15. Once more the people of God turned to him in their distress and once more he was moved with compassion toward them. The deliverer this time was Ehud, of the tribe of Benjamin. He was lefthanded. This does not mean merely that his habits of life were to use the left hand instead of the right. The original language here indicates that something had deprived him, or at least hindered him in his use of the right.

Verse 16. This dagger was about 18 inches long. Whether he personally knew the physical size of his enemy we do not know, but the event will show that he did wisely in making this weapon of such a length.

Verses 17, 18. The word translated "present" also means tribute. It was a familiar custom in old times to express one's recognition of another, especially a king or other person of dignity, by making a present. Not for the material value of the thing presented but as a token of regard. By using this custom Ehud obtained admission to the presence of this king. The usages of war which are universally permitted, made it rulable for Ehud to act as he did here. After the formalities of greeting had been performed the attendants were sent away.

Verse 19. The word "quarries" is so rendered because of its relation in thought to stone which comes from such places in the earth. The original really means a carved image and is here used with reference to the idols carved from stone that had been obtained from the quarries. Having finished the immediate business of greeting the king and dismissing the attendants, Ehud takes a little time looking over the situation and viewing these idols. Now, he turns from them again and addresses himself to the king, announcing that he has a confidential message to give him. In respect for his announcement the Moabite king indicated to those present to keep still. On this order they left the presence of the two men.

Verse 20. This summer parlour was a kind of comfort-room used for the general purpose of resting and cooling off, which contained provisions for caring for the requirements of the body. It was usually open and accessible to the public as to its material form but would be respected when occupied by a dignitary. Ehud now comes to the king of Moab as he was sitting in this apartment. He states that he has a message from God. This was another military action, at which the king arose.

Verses 21, 22. Ehud thrust the dagger into the body of the king with such force that the handle went in after the blade. Being a fat man with thick abdomen the flesh would have great pressure. It thus closed in upon the weapon and held it. Of course this wound would pierce through the intestines and cause great disturbance in that part of the body and force the excretions to be discharged.

Verse 23. By locking the doors of this parlor it would give it the appearance of being now used for privacy. This would give Ehud time to escape while the true state of affairs was being discovered.

Verse 24. It had the desired effect. *Covereth his feet.* This is rendered in the margin "doeth his easement." In other words, they supposed he was answering the calls of nature and hence did not feel disposed to intrude upon his privacy.

Verse 25. They waited so long, that at last they concluded their impression was wrong and they felt that an unusual delay had been caused. After concluding thus, they secured a key and opened the place. Doing this they found their lord dead.

Verse 26. As stated in verse 24 this plan of Ehud had the effect he sought. As the people were passing this time learning the true state of affairs, he had escape from their sight, passed beyond the quarries or images, and reached the place Seirath.

Verse 27. It will be well for us to keep our "bearings" as to the location of the actions of which we have been reading. Moab was just east of Palestine, across the Jordan. The Moabites had extended their oppression of Israel from their headquarters. That made it necessary for the Israelite judge to invade their territory and attack the king in his palace. That was accomplished and the judge escaped and came back into his own country as seen in preceding verse. Here he is reported blowing a trumpet to call attention of his people. Mount Ephraim was the name of a general territory in the southwest of Palestine.

Verse 28. Ehud now called for his people to follow him that they might complete the victory over the Moabites already begun in the slaying of their king. In pursuance of this plan, they seize the fords of the Jordan to prevent the escape of any of the men of Moab.

Verse 29. The populace of Moab generally speaking did not suffer death in this action, for the race as a whole existed afterward. But of the special classes, the lusty or fat men (those like their king, verse 17) and the men of valour, not a man escaped, because the fords had been taken by the Israelites.

Verse 30. This is another numeral to mark. Fourscore years of peace passed.

Verse 31. Very little is said of this period and no term of years mentioned. We therefore must understand it to have been a local situation that did not affect the history of the country as a whole.

JUDGES 4

Verses 1, 2. History is repeating itself again. After the oppression had been quelled and peace was enjoyed for a time, the children of Israel again forgot God and did evil. This time the chastisement came through the Canaanite king, Jabin. The man who commanded his military forces was Sisera, so that whatever operations will be necessary in the work of deliverance must be directed against this man.

Verse 3. This verse supplies the term of the oppression, twenty years. And the rigor of the oppression is indicated by the fact that Sisera had almost a thousand iron chariots. This means war chariots. This terrible oppression brought the cries of the children of Israel to the Lord.

Verse 4. The judge at this time was Deborah. But she had also been serving God's people in another capacity, that of a prophetess. *Prophetess.* This is from NEBIYAH and defined "feminine of NABIY; a prophetess or (generally) inspired woman; by implication a poetess; by association a prophet's wife." —Strong. *Judged.* This is from SHAPHAT and defined "a primitive root; to judge, i. e., pronounce sentence (for or against); by implication to vindicate or punish; by extension to govern; passively to litigate (literally or figuratively)." — Strong. We know that in the New Testament a woman is not permitted to teach authoritatively. But since this woman was inspired she would be qualified to teach or do anything else that God wished to have done.

Verse 5. The children of Israel would have good reason to rely on Deborah for judgment in view of her qualifications as seen in preceding verse.

Verse 6. While Deborah was qualified for the work of judge she did not propose taking active charge of the military operations. Hence she called into that duty and charge, Barak. And she did not assume the role of dictator as a human commander but informed him that "God of Israel commanded." On this order she directed him to mobilize ten thousand men of the tribes of Naphtali and Zebulun.

Verse 7. While Deborah is the mouthpiece we should bear in mind that it was God who was to cause Sisera to be drawn out into the desired place of the battle.

Verse 8. Since Deborah was an inspired woman it was natural for Barak to desire her cooperation in the great movement before them. It was on condition she go with him, that he agreed to take over this command.

Verse 9. Deborah agreed to go, but she warned Barak that the honor of the campaign would go to a woman, as a result of the capture of the leader of the enemy forces. The purpose of predicting this is not stated. The reader can see without any speculation that Barak was unselfish and loyal. Although he was informed beforehand by this inspired woman that he would not receive the honor of the success, he proceeds to carry out faithfully his charge.

Verse 10. Barak called for the men according to the instructions of Deborah and together with her they went up to the territory of the action.

Verse 11. In Ch. 1: 16 this Heber was given friendly farewell by the Israelites and he went to dwell among his people. In the present verse he has severed his association with them and was residing in the vicinity of the operations about to take place.

Verse 12. The Kenites now showed their sympathy for the Canaanites by giving information to Sisera about the movements of his enemy.

Verse 13. Acting upon the advice from the Kenites, Sisera mustered a mighty force of iron chariots and people and marched to the attack.

Verse 14. Here we can see an advantage of having Deborah along with the army of Barak. Speaking by inspiration she not only could instruct him to move forward but could predict the complete victory. Barak thus advanced with ten thousand men.

Verse 15. The attack resulted in the complete overthrow of Sisera's forces. He, like a cowardly leader, fled from his chariot and escaped on foot. While he thus made his escape from the heat of the battle he was not destined to escape finally.

Verse 16. In the meantime Barak is pursuing his victory until he has destroyed the last man among his enemies, except Sisera.

Verse 17. In verse 11 we learned that Heber had become the friend of this king of the Canaanites who was now in war with the Israelites. Therefore, Sisera considered it a safe place of hiding to flee into his vicinity. Being confident in his safety he comes to the tent of the Kenite himself.

Verse 18. This is not the first time that God used a supposed enemy to carry out some project favorable to his people. So in the present case, this friend of the enemy of God will be used to overthrow that enemy. Thus, in the manner of military procedure the wife of the Kenite invited Sisera to enter her tent, and even gives him false assurance of safety.

Verse 19. Being encouraged by this assurance, he asks for a drink of water. In response to the request the woman gave him milk and butter. (Ch. 5: 25.)

Verse 20. Sisera was now fully assured of his safety. With such a feeling of security he requested his hostess to direct all passing inquirers to go on because there was no man in the tent. There is no report of her reply to this request or whether she made any reply. However, Sisera then gave way to sleep of exhaustion.

Verse 21. We would ordinarily not think of a nail as being long enough to reach through a man's head, much less to go on into the ground far enough to become a fixed stake as it did here. But the word "nail" is from YATHED and defined "from an unused root meaning to pin through or fast; a peg."—Strong. The word elsewhere has been rendered in the A.V. by paddle, pin, stake. Hence we see it was one of the stakes used to fasten a tent that was used in this case. That shows how he was held fast to the place. His head was impaled to the ground even as the cord of a tent would be thus fastened. Since a hammer could be an instrument of any indefinite dimensions or weight, and also since in this case a tent stake was used, we must conclude that the hammer the woman used was the kind used to fasten a tent cord. As the man was in a deep sleep from his exhaustion of both body and mind, that would give her an opportunity for making the proper aim and location on his head to direct the stroke. Above all these natural considerations, the fact that God was in this act (verse 9) would explain her success in directing this stroke. The simple statement "so he died," leaves out any particulars of the incident. They will be considered in verse 27 of next chapter.

Verse 22. Barak had been following up his chase of Sisera, and Jael was watching for him. As he came in sight she went out and invited him to her. He came at her invitation and found the leader of his enemy fastened to the ground, dead.

Verses 23, 24. The military successes recorded in this chapter are here ascribed to God. The children of Israel needed punishment and these Canaanites were the instrument in the Lord's hands for the chastisement. The motives of these instruments were always disrespectful to God and hence he always returned the punishment upon them.

JUDGES 5

Verse 1. The original word for "sang" is defined in the lexicon as "sing." This is an English word and the same is defined by Webster as follows: "5. To relate or celebrate something in poetry." Poetry is described in English definitions as "beautiful or high thought," etc. Therefore, a song need not always be expressed by musical tones. Neither does it require to be expressed in rhyme, since poetry does not always have such a characteristic. The composition expressed by Deborah and Barak has all of the qualities of song as defined here.

Verse 2. Note the significant idea that God avenged his people when they willingly offered themselves. That was a condition previously placed with the promises.

Verse 3. Deborah being the inspired person in this duet, it would be appropriate for her to use the first person singular as seen in this verse.

Verse 4. Seir, which is Edom, is mentioned simply as one of the locations where the Lord had shown his might.

Verse 5. The majesty of mountains in nature is called to our attention in connection with God's majesty and the awe-inspiring effect of his presence.

Verse 6. Conditions were so oppressive that public travel was largely shut off. The names mentioned in this verse point out some of the times when this suppressed activity of travel was present.

Verse 7. These conditions had continued in Israel up to the time of Deborah. It is pleasing to read the title she takes to herself. No boasting of her official post, or of her inspiration. She is presented as a mother in Israel. This is a dignified, but gracious, expression of relationship.

Verse 8. The children of Israel chose these new gods. They were the gods of the nations about them. The choosing of these gods brought the wrath of God and the war with these same idolatrous nations. The war was made more bitter to the people of God by the absence of war materials made scarce by the enemy. (1 Sam. 13: 19, 22.)

Verse 9. At all times there were men among the children of Israel who were moved with faith in God and interest in the general welfare. As an instance, her colleague Barak, who was her chief officer in the conflict just ended.

Verses 10, 11. Riding on white asses indicated some prominence, and sitting in judgment denoted importance. All such were indebted to God for their deliverance from the foe. These are all exhorted to "speak" or meditate on the good fortune now turned toward them. To go down to the gate indicated a condition of peace whereas a state of war would have caused them to shrink back into the recesses of the city, for fear of the enemy at the gate.

Verse 12. This verse is in the form of rejoicing over their joint victory in the fight against their common enemy. The heathen who had been holding the people of God in captivity are now taken captive by Deborah and Barak.

Verse 13. The Lord is the antecedent of "he," and is the one who gave Deborah and Barak their dominion over the enemy.

Verses 14, 15. This paragraph is an acknowledgment of various ones associated with Deborah in the operations against the enemy.

Verses 16-18. The general state of anxiety, alternating with conditions of unrest, is here referred to by the prophetess.

Verse 19. This verse is a statement that was true from two standpoints. The kings of the nations did not gain anything finally by the war. Also the people of God were interested in delivering their nation from the foe and fought for that purpose, not for the sake of obtaining money.

Verse 20. The "stars" were the leading men among the people, otherwise called princes. Just as a leading player or actor is called a star, so these men were also.

Verses 21, 22. The river of Kishon was the spot used as the encounter (Ch. 4: 7). Here the forces were overthrown, including the horse and his rider.

Verse 23. Meroz was a place near the river where the issue was joined with the enemy. The people of this place refused to join in the fight against the common foe, hence Deborah was instructed to curse its inhabitants. Refusing to fight and work with God's people is the same as fighting against them. (Matt. 12: 30.)

Verse 24. Although Jael was supposed to be one of the enemy's forces yet she came to the service of God's people and now she receives the blessing of God's prophetess. This is similar in principle to the case of Rahab. (Josh. 6: 25; Heb. 11: 31.)

Verses 25, 26. This paragraph relates the event that entitled Jael to the praise of the preceding one. Smiting off the head of Sisera is figurative, of course, since his head was not actually cut off. His destruction was accomplished by driving the tent stake through his temples.

Verse 27. This is the verse that is charged by the foes of the Bible with being a contradiction of Ch. 4: 21. they say that if he fell down at her feet then he was not killed as reported in the former account. A more critical study of the language will make it not only agreeable but very plain and evident. The word "fell" is from a word that is translated "die" elsewhere. The word "bowed" is also defined by Strong as "sink" and in the R.V., it says he "swooned and died." "At her feet" is rendered in the margin as "between her feet." Now the whole event is plain. The woman found the man in a deep sleep. She wishes to make every surety of her action. Taking a tent stake in her left hand and the heavy hammer in the right, she takes a position straight over him by placing one foot on each side of his body. Then with one mighty stroke she drives the stake through his head and into the ground. So vital was the place where the instrument was driven that the man swooned and died here between her feet just as the verse indicates.

Verse 28. Whether her inspiration enabled her to report a literal action of this woman we know not. It could be a statement based on the obvious behaviour of the mother of the military leader. It would be perfectly natural for one woman to exult over the misfortune of another woman. Especially would this be true in a case where the exulting woman was on the righteous side of an issue.

Verse 29. This is another picture true to nature. The long delay of her son in showing up left no doubt in her mind, or those of her ladies as to the explanation.

Verse 30. This statement is in contradiction of the facts and of what the mother of Sisera really believed. The wish was father of the thought. So that in the desperation of her mind she paints a picture of her son's conquests when she had very much assurance that the battle of her people had been lost.

Verse 31. This verse expresses the good wishes of Deborah and Barak for the people of God, and is a statement upon the chronology of the times of rest.

JUDGES 6

Verse 1. The Midianites were the next instrument in the hand of God for the chastisement of his people, and these people afflicted them seven years.

Verse 2. These dens and caves are referred to by Paul in Heb. 11: 38.

Verse 3. The Midianites and Amalekites had long been enemies of God's people and the children of the east were the heathen nations in general who were located in that territory east of the Jordan. They afflicted the Israelites especially by destroying their crops.

Verses 4-6. Although these oppressors were living east of the Jordan, they entered the territory of the Israelites to destroy their crops. The destruction was very general and made possible by the vast numbers of their people.

Verses 7-10. God always heard the cries of his people. But he frequently gave them severe chastisements for their evil doings. Here he reminds them of the former deliverances he had wrought for them, beginning with the terrible experiences in Egypt. They were reminded that warning had been given them not to give any attention to the gods of the Amorites. They had not obeyed the voice of God. Thus, a prophet of God reproved them for their sinfulness even though God intends to come to their rescue again as he has done before.

Verse 11. In preparation for the next judgeship an angel is sent into the vicinity of a man named Joash. This man was an idolator (v. 25), but had a son whom the Lord wished to use as the next judge. This son's name was Gideon and he recognized the Lord. He had felt the weight of the oppression of the Midianites on account of his difficulty in retaining the products of the field. *Threshed wheat by the winepress.* The R.V. says he was beating out the wheat *in* the winepress. This was a vat commonly used to hold the grapes while being pressed for extraction of the juice. Wine was not considered as much of a necessity as wheat and hence would not be as liable to be confiscated as wheat. Hence Gideon was disguising his real work by doing this hand threshing of the wheat in this vat. This would mislead the Midianites.

Verse 12. No charge is standing against Gideon personally, and thus the angel gives him a favorable greeting. He also assures him that God is with him.

Verse 13. Although Gideon personally was a brave man and true to God, yet he was being made to share with his brethren in the misfortunes befalling them at the hands of the Midianites. He complains and wonders why so much evil had come upon the people if God still regarded his people. Gideon had not yet learned the lesson of God's manner of dealing with a nation. The righteous life of a man or a few men cannot always head off a punishment due the nation as a whole. That sad lesson was one the nation had to learn to their great sorrow later, in the times of the national captivity.

Verse 14. No detailed answer is given to the complaining inquiry of Gideon, but he is given assurance that his people will be delivered, also that he is to be the instrument in God's hands for the deliverance.

Verse 15. Thinking of mere human strength, Gideon cannot understand how a man of humble means and lowly standing would be able for so important a work.

Verse 16. This verse is an indefinite guarantee that he would succeed because the Lord would be with him, but no particulars are given as yet.

Verses 17, 18. Some people might call Gideon another "doubting Thomas." But it is not a bad trait to be unwilling to accept a fundamental declaration without some evidence of authority. It would be a good thing if all people were more careful along this line than they are. They would not be so free to accept just any kind of approach without a careful investigation. Joshua might have been saved the humiliation in the affair of the Gibeonites had he investigated. (Josh. 9: 14.) Request is made for time to procure an offering to be used on the occasion and the request is granted. This meat offering was to be in the way of a present which was one of the customs in old times. Recognition of a dignitary of any kind was often expressed by a "present."

Verse 19. Acting solely in the manner of this custom of respect, Gideon came with the offering all ready for the use of the angel.

Verse 20. Instead of using the offering as food, the angel directed Gideon to place the articles on the rock near by and to pour out the broth.

Verse 21. Gideon had asked for a sign by way of evidence that he was to be used as an instrument in the hand of God. This transaction answered his request.

Verses 22, 23. Had Gideon realized before this moment that it was an angel of the Lord he might not have thought of providing literal food. This was one of the instances referred to in Heb. 13: 1. When the truth was evident to him he was overcome with surprise and awe and felt doubtful of the outcome. His humility made him feel unfit to be present with an angel of God and he expressed that feeling in words. He was given the comforting assurance that no harm would come to him here.

Verse 24. As a token of his joy and reverence for God, an altar was built by Gideon. It was an altar in the way of a memorial and was named by a word meaning "peace."

Verse 25. The first act Gideon was commanded to do in his work of reform and destruction of the enemy was to confiscate the animal his idolatrous father had in keeping. Also to throw down the altar he had built near a grove. These groves were the ones connected with idol worship so generally in those times. See comments on this subject at Judges 3: 7.

Verse 26. Instead of the altar of Baal that is to be thrown down Gideon was to build an altar in an orderly manner, and for the Lord. He was then to take the bullock his father would have sacrificed to Baal and offer it here on this altar to God.

Verse 27. Gideon associates ten of his men with him in this action. Since his father's household might be incensed against him he chose the night time for it. This was a matter of good judgment because the time was not ripe for open opposition to the evil practices around him.

Verses 28, 29. Morning disclosed to the men of the place what had been done but they did not know who was the doer of it. Inquiry was made and they learned the truth.

Verse 30. It was natural to make their complaint and accusation to the father of the man who had destroyed the altar. They demanded that Gideon should die.

Verse 31. We should be greatly interested and pleased at the reply of Joash. It was not only different from what we would expect if viewed from a natural standpoint but was consistent and logical. If Baal is a true god he ought to be able to take care of himself. It should not be necessary for a human being to plead his cause. Thus Joash argues the point. He further demands that a man who will plead for a god that is not able to defend himself is not worthy to live and must be slain before morning.

Verse 32. Because of the meaning of the word Jerubbaal, "Let Baal plead," Joash attached the name to his son who was the cause of the present controversy.

Verse 33. These are the people mentioned in verse 3, now gathered to oppose the children of Israel.

Verse 34. Gideon accepted the challenge and blew a call to arms. Then Abiezer, the community of his father's people, responded to his call.

Verse 35. Gideon made further calls and specified the men of the tribes of Manasseh, Zebulun and Naphtali. These people also came at his call and now he has a vast number of men collected.

Verses 36-40. See comments at verses 17, 18. We do not have to explain such a request of Gideon on the ground of doubt as to God's power or willingness to help. He could have some uncertainty as to whether he understood clearly the Lord's will. If God will make this specified demonstration it will satisfy him of the Lord's will. By reversing the operation it makes the element of accident, or "happen so," impossible.

JUDGES 7

Verse 1. Gideon, with the host of people mobilized, encamped by the well of Harod which was on Mt. Gilboa, while the Midianites were encamped in a valley not far off and near the hill of Moreh.

Verse 2. If the visible means used in accomplishing an end seemed to be sufficient to the purpose it would tend to the impression that natural and not supernatural power had done the work. That would have encouraged the people to boast of their success, which God did not wish to be done.

Verse 3. The first reduction of the numbers was made on the basis of those who were "fearful and afraid." There is very little difference in the meaning of these words and either could be used without the other. The technical meanings of them are, "to be inclined to fear and thus easily startled"; and, "to be at the present time actually trembling over the prospect of danger near." Either defect would render a man unfit for military duty. When this qualification was designated it took 22,000 from the group thus far collected.

Verse 4. There are still too many people to leave the Lord the likelihood of glory and Gideon is told to move the host down near the water for further instructions.

Verses 5, 6. The ones who lapped in this instance were those who reached down with the hand and dipped up the water in the palm, then drinking from the hand as from a drinking vessel. The ones who bowed down to the water would penetrate the water with their mouth and drink directly from the water source. The action of the former would leave them in position to be watchful for the enemy, at the same time they were supplying their wants. Such would be the kind of men best suited for battle.

Verse 7. While these men will be employed in the attack, yet it was stated that by them the Lord would deliver the enemy into their hand, thus showing that the Lord would be the power that would accomplish the victory.

Verse 8. Now the selection is made. They supply themselves with things necessary for the sustenance and the other men are sent back to their homes.

Verses 9-11. God wishes Gideon to have his confidence made as strong as possible, so directs him to take his servant with him and go down near the Midianite camp. He will there see or hear something that will give him this added encouragement. The order was obeyed and Gideon went near the camp of the enemy.

Verse 12. The number of the enemy forces was so great that comparison is made to swarms of grasshoppers and to the sand of the seaside.

Verse 13. Gideon got near enough to do some eavesdropping. A man was relating his dream in which he saw a cake of barley bread tumble into the midst of the Midianites and overthrow them. A cake of bread would be an insignificant object to accomplish so decisive a result, and its meaning here was not lost in the minds of the people.

Verse 14. The man to whom the dream was related gave his interpretation of the picture. He said it meant the defeat of their forces by the hand of Gideon.

Verse 15. Having overheard this conversation Gideon was greatly encouraged and worshipped God for the revelation. Returning to the camp of his men, he reported to them what he had heard, and directed them to arise to the conflict.

Verse 16. The next thing he did was to make three divisions of the three hundred men already selected for the battle. Strong defines these pitchers as jars of earthenware. We know that such would be nontransparent. These lamps or torches being placed inside the jars would be out of sight.

Verses 17, 18. The value of united action is proved in this instance. If each man should be left to his own jugment as to when and how to act there would be great confusion and the object desired would be missed. By all having the same example to follow, their action would be the same as of one man.

Verses 19, 20. The "watch" was a period of the night during which certain men were placed on duty as a guard. In Old Testament times the usual arrangement was to divide the night into three watches of four hours each. They would thus run as follows: First watch from 6 P. M. to 10. Second watch ran from 10 to 2 A. M. Third watch from 2 A. M. to 6. So the beginning of the middle watch would be at 10 P. M. and that was the time that Gideon and his men approached the camp of the Midianites. When the signal was given by the action of Gideon the three companies acted simultaneously. The first made a blast with the trumpets, then broke the jars. When this was done all at once, there would be three hundred torches flare out in the night. And just as the nerves were rendered tense by this sudden appearance they would be made more so by the united shout of the crowd announcing the presence of the sword of the Lord and of Gideon. The effect of this action would be electrical.

Verse 21. It had the desired effect. The host of the enemy broke rank and sent up a cry, then fled.

Verse 22. This verse is a more detailed account of the preceding one. In their startled confusion of mind the Midianites attacked each other and thus helped to bring about the result desired by Gideon.

Verse 23. The men mentioned here are the ones already designated as composing the army of the attack upon the Midianites. After the rout of the enemy, the army of the Lord pursued the enemy to further victory.

Verses 24, 25. We have already learned that "Mount Ephraim" was the name of a general territory in southwest part of Palestine. Now that the enemy has been generally defeated Gideon calls upon the people of this territory to take advantage of the situation and seize certain places against the fleeing Midianites. They did so, and in the action took captive two prominent men of the enemy, Oreb and Zeeb.

JUDGES 8

Verses 1-3. About the time these men of Ephraim (Mount Ephraim) had taken the two princes mentioned in preceding chapter, they learned of the general success that Gideon had in the original attack. It is natural to wish for the honor following general success against an enemy. Now that such success has been accomplished, these men who had been called into the service at the last, felt that Gideon should have called on them at the same time he called on the men of the tribes mentioned in verses 24, 25 in chapter 7. Gideon thus feels it necessary to pacify them. He does so with an illustration. In general practice the gleaning of a vineyard gets only the leavings after the main crop has been taken. Yet, if one had choice of gleaning in a better vineyard or of taking the first crop even in a less desirable vineyard, he would certainly choose the former. So Gideon likens his general victory to the gathering of grapes in an ordinary territory and that of these men of Ephraim to the gleaning in a better one. In other words, they had at least taken two prominent men that he had not succeeded in taking and that was really more of a victory than his capture of many thousands. This illustration satisfied them.

Verses 4, 5. While much success has already been enjoyed, the follow-up work is still necessary. While in pursuit Gideon asks for food of the people of Succoth so that his men may be supported in their march after other men of the enemy. But the men of Succoth were like men often are today. They want to be on the winning side and will not give any support until they know which is that side. Their refusal brought a threat from Gideon.

Verses 6, 7. The attitude of the men mentioned in preceding paragraph was shown by the question whether the men were yet in the hands of Gideon, but their refusal to help did not hinder Gideon from proceeding in his march against the enemy.

Verses 8, 9. Coming to the vicinity of Penuel, Gideon made a request for support as at Succoth and received the same kind of rebuff. He also made a threat against them which was to be carried out after his victorious return.

Verse 10. There had been a hundred

and twenty thousand men slain, but a remnant of fifteen thousand were still left and were being led by the two men, Zebah and Zalmunna. These had taken refuge in Karkor, a place east of the Jordan.

Verse 11. The army was resting in tents and "was secure" which means they felt safe and thought the danger was over. Taking advantage of this condition, Gideon came upon them and routed them again and smote many of them.

Verse 12. The two men mentioned before, escaped from the present encampment and fled. Gideon overtook them and terrified the rest of the people with them.

Verses 13, 14. The battle having been completed in favor of Gideon he starts on his return homeward, and all this while it was yet night. When he got into the region of Succoth he seized on a young man of that community and demanded information leading to the identity of the leaders of that place.

Verses 15-17. Coming into the presence of these chief men, Gideon chided them for their former attitude toward him and also reminded them of his threat made at that time. Then he carried out his threat. With thorns gathered from the wilderness he taught ("made to know," in the margin) these men. This means that by this painful punishment they were made to learn an important lesson. After this corporal punishment he beat down their fortification and slew the men of the city.

Verse 18. It should be remembered these men were the principal leaders of the invasion made by the Midianites into the land of the Israelites. In their first operations they had slain a great many people. In this verse Gideon is making "post-war" investigation into the commission of "war crimes" and thus asks them the question recorded. They described the men whom they had slain in a certain place in such a way that Gideon recognized them as being his near blood kin. Also, as being men who were of the civilian population and should have been spared from death. Their deaths was the act of murder and so now the guilty men must be made to suffer.

Verse 20. These guilty men are sentenced to death and the executioner designated for the act was the oldest son of Gideon. In executing these men, Jether would be slaying the murderers of his uncles and in an act of war, which would have been right. The young man hesitated from a feeling of personal awe, not that he was unwilling to obey the orders of his father.

Verse 21. This verse states an unusual speech. It is perhaps not so mysterious considering the real situation. These men know they are doomed to death at best. Then if an inexperienced youth were depended on for the execution, with his feeling of hesitancy he might make an imperfect attempt that would be more tortuous than if done by a more practiced man. Thus they prefer to have Gideon do the act of execution. He does so and also confiscates the valuables on the camel's necks as being spoils.

Verse 22. Gratitude was now running high. The deliverance from the hosts of Midian brought such great relief that the Israelites offer to make Gideon their ruler.

Verse 23. The reply of Gideon was wonderful and filled with reverence toward the Lord to whom he owed all of his victory. In this view he denies the offered place of rulership to both himself and his son and declares that the Lord would rule.

Verse 24. Since the victory over the enemy had been won through the human instrumentality of Gideon he felt desirous of receiving the temporal spoils of the conflict. These would be especially prized because of their material and form, since they were taken from Ishmaelites. This statement reminds us of the circumstance in Gen. 37: 25. In that place it was seen that both Midianites and Ishmaelites mingled with each other in the matters of trade, and costly jewels of silver and gold composed the chief articles of trade with them. Hence the words in this verse.

Verses 25, 26. As would be expected, the people were very willing to comply with the request. They spread a garment to be used as a receptacle and on it they cast the metals and also many precious pieces of woven materials.

Verse 27. According to Strong, the word for "ephod" sometimes means an image. That would be made of metal. In the spoils mentioned in preceding verse we find mention of purple raiment which would furnish material for a girdle which was the original form of an ephod. Thus we might not be able to settle definitely on the specific nature of this thing that Gideon made. The thing that is clear is the fact that whatever it was the people made an improper use of it. Doubtless Gideon only intended it to be a trophy of war in which God had given him the victory. As such he would expect the people to be reminded of their dependence upon God for victory. But they were not inclined to take that view of the article. Relic worship is much akin to ancestor worship which has long been a weakness of mankind. Hence in this case the good intention of Gideon was turned into occasion of grief for him. The word for "whoring is ZANAH and defined by Strong as follows: "to commit adultery (usually of the female, and less often of simple fornication, rarely of involuntary ravishment); figuratively to commit idolatry (the Jewish people being regarded as the spouse of Jehovah)." This thing became a snare unto Gideon and his house. The word has both a literal and figurative meaning. The present sense is that Gideon was taken by surprise and thus trapped by the circumstance and humiliated. It cannot mean that he was personally led to commit idolatry for nothing elsewhere is found that even intimates such a thing.

Verse 28. The complete subjugation of the Midianites was accomplished by the valorous work of Gideon, and the land had peace for forty years.

Verse 29. Jerubbaal was the other name of Gideon. He now retired from active duty as a soldier and returned to his home.

Verse 30. *Of his body begotten.* Frequently in olden times a man's household would be composed of servants and others brought in and made heirs. These persons were sometimes given the name of sons. Hence the specification here so that we will know that Gideon had the seventy sons in the primary sense of the word.

Verse 31. As a general rule the main difference between a concubine and a wife was in the matter of property rights. The moral stigma that would be attached to the term today did not apply then because men were suffered to have plurality of wives. On account of the rights of legal wives over the concubines there was somewhat of an aversion against them by the rest of a man's family. The objection that would be made would not be on moral grounds but mainly from a social standpoint. In the present case the concubine had a separate place of residence from the immediate one of Gideon. The son of this concubine soon to figure in our study was located in Shechem.

Verse 32. Honorable report of the death of Gideon would be in order because of his valiant services for his God and people.

Verses 33-35. History repeated itself. After the death of Gideon the children of Israel not only fell to idolatry again but even became unmindful of the good work of Gideon so that they did not even accord his family the proper treatment. Of course we will expect to read of more trouble for the nation before long. The circumstances surrounding the proceeding will be unlike what have been shown to us before.

JUDGES 9

Verse 1. It should not be forgotten that Abimelech was that son of the concubine living at Shechem. Thus the people to whom he makes his appeal are those not related by blood to Gideon. Only Abimelech was related to him in that manner. But while they were not blood kin to Gideon yet the indirect relationship would imply that he would have authority over their community. This phase of the subject furnished Abimelech with a pretext for his theory and appeal.

Verse 2. If these Shechemites recognized the authority of Gideon that would mean an oppressive rule over them, since Gideon had seventy sons directly of his own. Thus there would never be any end to their subjugation and the rule might be torn with much unrest because of the jealousy and contentions of the many heirs to the throne. So why would it not be better just to disconnect themselves entirely from the whole brood of Gideon? Especially since he, Abimelech, though an apparent heir through Gideon was also related to them, the Shechemites, by blood.

Verse 3. This appeal was received by the family of the concubine. They made their position of mind known to the citizens of Shechem and induced them to espouse the cause of Abimelech. They recognized the relationship also of Abimelech to them.

Verse 4. All movements of any account that involve land and government require money. Having accepted the cause of Abimelech as their own the Shechemites will wish to contribute to the expenses. This was raised by drawing from the treasury of Baal-berith. This was a god specially classed as one for the Shechemites but belonging generally to the idolatrous worship of Baal. With this money Abimelech bribed a crowd of unprincipled persons who joined in the usurpation. The first objective of the usurpation is to get rid of the men who would be in the way of this ambition of the son of the concubine.

Verse 5. With the backing of these hired men, Abimelech went to the city of Ophrah and slew his father's sons in a mass murder. That is, he intended to, and thought he had slain all of them, but the youngest one had succeeded in his attempts to hide. The fact that he thus escaped and that no indication is seen of a search for him, indicates the wholesale nature of the murder.

Verse 6. *House of Millo.* This was a family or clan among the people in the days of Gideon. This group joined with the men of Shechem, the place of Abimelech's family, and together placed him up as their king or ruler. It must be borne in mind that while the three years of Abimelech's rule are allowed to figure in the chronology of the period of the judges (see comments at 1 Kings 6:1), the whole transaction was illegal and to be considered as a usurpation. It was somewhat connected with the process of opposing the oppressors of the Israelites. When the use of Abimelech was finished he was himself brought to degradation for his crimes.

Verse 7. Jotham was the one who escaped the murderous hand of the usurper. After the affair had been settled for Abimelech to rule over the people, Jotham went to a place of prominence among the Israelites and made a speech to the men of Shechem. We will recall that the two places were near each other, and hence, Jotham could be heard.

Verses 8, 9. The figurative speech Jotham used in this case would be technically called a fable since that word properly means a narrative in which either animals or inanimate things speak and act like human beings. The first section of his fable says the trees invited the olive tree to be their ruler, but this tree considered its value as an article of service to God and man, too great to be interrupted by a place of rule.

Verses 10, 11. The next invitation was made to the fig tree. The response of this tree indicates that when anything that has been qualified for a specific service takes up some other kind of life it loses its original use and purpose. Hence the fig tree is faithful to its mission in nature and refuses to become king over the trees.

Verses 12, 13. The trees that were approached refused the invitation to be ruler, hence the next approach was to the vine. It likewise refused the offer of prominence, preferring to maintain its intended service of cheer to God and man. The word "cheereth" is rendered by such expressions as rejoice, and make glad, etc. So we can see how it could cheer God. We would not think of the Lord as being in need of cheering in the ordinary sense of that word. But when man makes proper use of the gifts of nature it pleases God and in that sense cheers him. It is noted that the objects that would have been worthy of the position of rule over the trees, were not willing to take on the special honor. That is often the case among men. Also it is often the case that the most unworthy are the ones most forward in taking a place of such special favor. It will prove so in this case.

Verse 14. The next invitation was to the bramble. This is from ATAD and Strong defines it: "a thorn-tree (especially the buckthorn)." Having asked the more worthy trees to become their ruler and being rejected, the trees next appeal to that which should have been considered unworthy, the thorn tree.

Verse 15. The thorn tree accepts the call on condition that the other trees put their confidence in it and its shadow. But, anticipating possible treason, this tree threatens that it will discharge a fire that will consume even the cedars of Lebanon, which were the most prized trees of the country.

Verses 16-19. The fable was completed and Jotham then makes the application and shows that he was talking about the action of the people toward Gideon's house and the son of the hand-maid, or concubine. In his speech here he reminded them of their service his father had done for them against the Midianites which had been repaid with the murder of his lawful sons in mass slaying. He makes the challenge that they should prove their sincerity in the movement by mutual rejoicing in each other, they in Abimelech and he in them.

Verse 20. Jotham had challenged their mutual sincerity by demanding mutual respect between Abimelech and the men of Shechem. Now he predicts that if the whole thing is based on insincere motives, mutual distrust and harm will be practiced against each other.

Verse 21. Jotham knew he would be in danger after speaking the fable and making the application. After his speech he ran away to Beer, a place among the Israelites where he would be safe from attack by Abimelech.

Verse 22. This verse is noted mainly for the period of years stated so as to keep track of the chronology. While Abimelech was a usurper and not one of the lawful judges, his time must be considered in making up the required length of the period as accounted for elsewhere.

Verse 23. God does not force anyone to be evil morally who would otherwise be good. The word here means a spirit of unfriendliness. He caused the former state of friendship between Abimelech and the men of Shechem to be turned to the opposite.

Verse 24. The reason for the act of God stated in preceding verse is given here. It was in punishment for Abimelech's cruelty in slaying his brothers, and for the aid the men of Shechem gave him in that cruelty. Thus from here we will see these former allies in crime fighting each other, and thus fulfilling the prediction in Jotham's fable.

Verse 25. The Shechemites put men to lie in wait in the mountains and rob the people who were passing. This news reached the ears of Abimelech which was the thing they wished to happen.

Verse 26. Gaal was an Israelite who came to Shechem with a force of brethren and offered to take their side against Abimelech and his offer was accepted.

Verse 27. Hostilities against Abimelech were started by destroying the crops of the field and vineyards. They also made merry and entered the house of the idolaters in disrespect of the place.

Verse 28. Care needs to be exercised in this verse, not to be confused over the pronouns. Gaal is an Israelite, as is Abimelech on his father's side. This was recognized by Gaal in his saying that he is the son of Jerubbaal (Gideon). Yet Gaal advises that Hamor and the men of the city of Shechem be served, and not "him," meaning Abimelech.

Verse 29. Gaal makes a plea for the people of that place to trust his leadership and he would remove Abimelech from their midst. His offer was accepted and then he challenges Abimelech to strengthen his army and come out.

Verse 30. Zebul was ruler of the city and naturally wished to be true to Abimelech, whom he considered a friend of the place. Thus he was aroused by the action of Gaal and considered him an enemy.

Verses 31-33. Zebul now sends secret information to Abimelech of the movements of Gaal and urges him to do something about it, giving him suggestions how to act.

Verse 34. Acting upon the advice of Zebul, Abimelech rose up and laid siege against the city of Shechem.

Verse 35. Gaal saw the approach of Abimelech and went out to the gate of the city.

Verses 36-38. We should not forget that the forces on both sides of this struggle are in ill-favor with God. They are here placed in opposition to each other by the Lord in fulfillment of Jotham's fable. The multitudes of people now forming the siege of Shechem are exciting Gaal, and he exclaims to Zebul, the ruler of the city, that he sees these multitudes from the various sources. It is then that Zebul chides Gaal for his stand against Abimelech and reminds him of his words when he came to the city, and in the spirit of challenge urges him to go out and fight.

Verse 39. Gaal accepts the challenge and joins battle with Abimelech.

Verse 40. It is "six of one and half a dozen of the other" as to the right and wrong of the two sides of this conflict. Abimelech was wrong in usurping the judgeship after murdering the rightful candidates. The Shechemites and their leaders were wrong in their encouragement of the murderer. Now they are influenced by the Lord to oppose Abimelech so as to receive the judgment they deserve. The whole operation will be unfavorable for both sides.

Verse 41. After this skirmish, Abimelech went to a place named Arumah. Then Zebul, the ruler of the city of Shechem, expelled Gaal and his brethren from the city.

Verses 42, 43. Gaal and his forces were now exposed to danger after being thrust from the city. Abimelech was informed of this and made another forward movement by raising three companies of the people in sympathy with him. They arose and attacked those in sympathy with Gaal and smote many of them.

Verses 44, 45. The success of this action encouraged Abimelech and his men, so they came nearer to the city, even to the gate. At the same time the other two divisions of his forces attacked the people on the outside and in the fields and slew them. At last Abimelech stormed the city and took it. After killing the citizens therein, he beat down the city and sowed it with salt. The significance of this action is expressed in an interesting manner in the Schaff-Herzog Encyclopaedia as follows: "But salt was also strewn over a cursed place to indicate that nothing could any longer be allowed to grow there, because there can be no vegetation where the ground is saturated with salt (Deut. 29: 23; Judg. 9: 45; Zeph. 2: 9), hence 'a salt land' was a barren land (Job 39: 6; Jer. 17: 6)"—Article, SALT.

Verse 46. News of this disaster reached the ears of certain men of the tower or castle of Shechem, a unit of people who escaped the former destruction. Upon hearing this they fled to a place of supposed safety in the house of the god Berith.

Verses 47-49. Abimelech heard of this gathering of the people and prepared to attack the place. He ordered the men with him to imitate his example. Each man cut a branch from a tree and carried it with him to the hold where these other men had taken refuge after the affair of Shechem. Here they piled the branches they had taken and set fire to the place, destroying all who had fled there, and a thousand besides.

Verse 50. Thebez was another city not far from Shechem. After his success there, Abimelech next went to the former city and laid siege to it.

Verses 51, 52. Within the city of Thebez there was a strong fortification in the form of a tower and into this place the people of the city fled for refuge. Abimelech then came to this tower and was making preparations to burn it.

Verse 53. Being in this tower and above the men on the ground, a certain woman took advantage of the position and let a piece of stone fall down on the head of Abimelech, which broke his skull but left him conscious for the moment.

Verse 54. While death was bound to be the end soon, yet while still conscious Abimelech wishes to escape the shame of having been slain by a woman. Upon this he directed his armorbearer to thrust a sword through him. It was done and Abimelech died.

Verse 55. This ended the war and the Israelite confederates returned to their own places.

Verses 56, 57. The writer informs us that all the foregoing actions were in fulfillment of the predictions made by Jotham. Both Abimelech and the forces at first encouraging him were to be punished for their wrongs against God's authorized judge.

JUDGES 10

Verses 1, 2. The only definite thing that is said about this judge is the length of his work which is important in keeping the chronology in the record.

Verses 3-5. The rule of Jair was 22 years and that fact should be noted which is about all that needs to be said at this place.

Verses 6-8. After a period of rest the children of Israel again forgot the Lord and fell to serving the various gods of the nations. Thus the Lord again brings the punishment in the form of oppression from the Philistines and Ammonites. This period lasted 18 years.

Verse 9. The scope of the oppression is the subject of this paragraph. The Ammonites dwelt on the east of Jordan while the Philistines were on the other side and near the Great Sea. They both joined to oppress Israel.

Verse 10. The confession of the Israelites is significant as having two phases. It would be very wrong to forsake God even had they then remained idle. In addition to having forsaken the true God they had become active in serving the false gods. This kind of double guilt was committed later by the nation. (Jer. 2: 13.)

Verses 11-14. God reminded the children of Israel of the many times he had delivered them from their enemies. In spite of these deliverances they had forsaken him and served the heathen gods. Now then, in taunt for their sins he bids them appeal to these gods for help.

Verses 15-18. The mercy of God is

great. His people cried unto him in their sore distress and proved the present sincerity of their plea by putting away their idols and serving the Lord. Then God had compassion for them and encouraged them to resist the enemy. Upon this the forces on each side began mobilization for conflict. The Ammonites collected in Gilead a region east of Jordan and inhabited by Israelites. This presented a direct threat to the peace of the children of Israel. They encamped in Mizpeh, a city of Palestine. In their distress the princes of Gilead called for a volunteer leader against the Ammonites with promises of military honors.

JUDGES 11

Verse 1. There was a territory called Gilead and also a man by that name. We should not confuse the two, as they have no special relationship. This man had a son born to him by a harlot, and the son's name was Jephthah. No fault should be laid against him because of his "irregular" birth, although such is often done.

Verse 2. The sons of Gilead's legal wife grew to manhood, then resented the presence of Jephthah in their home and expelled him. They said he was the son of a strange woman. That word means one from outside. The mother of Jephthah being a harlot, she was not a part of the immediate family of Gilead.

Verse 3. Jephthah fled to the land of Tob, a region east of the Jordan but above the general territory of the one called Gilead. Of course, all men will have some sympathizers. Jephthah had his and they assembled round him after he had been rejected by his father's family.

Verse 4. The Ammonites were the first to start active hostilities.

Verses 5, 6. In their distress the elders or leaders of the region of Gilead sent a call for help from Jephthah, who was in the land of Tob.

Verse 7. Of course, we would expect Jephthah to remind them of their previous ungrateful attitude toward him in expelling him from his father's house. After all, Gilead was as much kin to Jephthah as he was to any of his other sons. Now that they are in distress they call for help from him. This shows that something unusual was evident in the life and characteristics of Jephthah since they now feel as if they can rely on his ability and faithfulness.

Verse 8. The elders of Gilead make an urgent reply to ask him for leadership against the Ammonites with the promise that he will be their head.

Verses 9-11. Jephthah requires further guarantee of respect and authority. They grant his request and together form a pact with an oath before God to bind it.

Verse 12. Having been made commander-in-chief of their forces against Ammon he now makes formal protest against the enemy and charges that he has aggressed against the people of the land.

Verse 13. For answer to this charge the children of Ammon accused the children of Israel of having taken their land while en route from Egypt.

Verses 14-23. To the accusations of the children of Ammon, Jephthah made general denial. He also detailed the history of the years covering the journeys of the Israelites from Egypt. In this account was seen that Israel offered the fair thing in every case as to the countries through which it was necessary to go. Only when the kings and rulers of the various lands resisted the fair offers of Israel did the Lord help them to defend themselves and thus obtain the land of the aggressors as spoils. The conclusion of this line is stated, that it was the Lord and not Israel who had given the territory to them.

Verse 24. The Ammonites would have considered it right for them to hold in possession anything that their god Chemosh would give them and claim it to be theirs as rightful possession. In that case they would deny that any personal or private robbing had been done. On the same principle the Israelites can justly claim the property that their God gave them and should not be accused of unlawful spoliation of land.

Verse 25. Jephthah reminds them of the case of Balak and asks the significant question in ironic inquiry if Balak ever strove against the Lord. It was expected that Ammon would answer in their own minds and see their own "handwriting."

Verse 26. Jephthah next asked Ammon why, if it were right and necessary to recover this territory, they had let all the centuries go by without doing so.

Verse 27. Concluding the general account of the facts of history Jephthah makes final denial of all accusations. Also he accuses Ammon of wrong in the aggression and appeals to the Lord as his judge of his own righteous course.

Verse 28. Notwithstanding the fairness and truthfulness of this message from Jephthah the children of Ammon refused to desist from their hostility.

Verse 29. The war must now be prosecuted, so Jephthah advances to the attack.

Verses 30, 31. On his way to the immediate vicinity of active war against the Ammonites, Jephthah made the vow that has been much misunderstood and thus incorrectly interpreted. The marginal reading gives us "or" instead of "and" in verse 31. That would make the vow read "shall be the Lord's, or I will offer it," etc. This makes the vow have a two-fold bearing. That is, it has two alternatives, either of which would be the fulfilling of the vow. These two were that he would let it be the Lord's for his exclusive service, or that it would be burned in sacrifice. Thus the vow does not require that the thing affected be burnt necessarily. But there will be more on this subject near the close of the chapter.

Verses 32, 33. After making the vow discussed in preceding paragraph Jephthah proceeded against the Ammonites and the Lord showed his favor for him by giving him complete victory over the enemy. Thus it may be inferred even from this fact, that God is holding Jephthah in his good will. Had he been against the practice of Jephthah he certainly would not have given him this victory without criticism. The case of Moses and his neglect of circumcising his son (Ex. 4: 24-26) may be compared at this place. As important as Moses was for the matter at hand, God would not accept his further services unless the law of righteousness were obeyed. Certainly, in the case of Jephthah, the issue is no more important. He is given complete success even though that very success was the condition on which he made his famous vow.

Verses 34-36. After his successful campaign, Jephthah returned homeward. Upon his approach, his only child, a daughter, came to meet him with musical instruments and other indications of merriment and joyfulness. We are not told just how detailed was the information that her father gave to her as to his vow. Whether he had gone over all the items or not, we know that she finally came to know the nature of his vow. She did not even protest or try to dissuade him from it. Instead, she urged him to carry out his obligation in gratitude for his victory over the enemy through God's help.

Verse 37. The daughter made one request and that was for two months time in which she would bewail or bemoan her virginity. Had her fate been that she was to be burnt in sacrifice, there would have been nothing significant in her virginity. In that case it would have been appropriate to bewail her untimely death. Or, even had she been a mother at that young age, it would still have been a matter of lament for her to die so young. So that the tragic death would have been the thing to bewail. Yet, that is not what she wished to lament. It was her virginity that was to be regretted. Yet a death and burning on the altar would have been the same tragedy whether a virgin or a bride. The circumstance will be all the more appreciated when it is remembered that motherhood in those days was considered far more desirable than it often is today. A woman who was unable to be a mother was considered as being reproached. (See Gen. 30: 1, 22; 1 Sam. 1: 5, 6, 16.) Thus it was the prospect that she was never to be a mother that she was lamenting.

Verses 38, 39. Her father gave her leave to do as requested. Thus she took some companions and spent two months in the mountains bewailing her *virginity*, which was the thought that grieved her. After the period of absence granted had expired she returned to her father. Then it is stated that he did to her according to his vow. See comments at verse 31 as to the requirements of this vow. In direct connection with this statement it says "she knew no man." All Bible students know this is a common expression of the scripture referring to the relation of the sexes. It means she was devoted to perpetual virginity and thus to spend her entire life as a virgin, without the joys of motherhood and under the constant occupation of service to God. This circumstance established a custom among the Israelites which will be described in following verse.

Verse 40. The custom mentioned in preceding verse was a practice carried on by other daughters of Israel.

The words "to lament" are rendered in the margin by "to talk with." This is more reasonable and agrees with all the facts and phases of the circumstance. People do not talk with a dead girl. Besides, if it were merely a time of lamentation in memory of the unfortunate girl it would not have been necessary to go to her. There are some general considerations that should be had in thinking over this subject. No law of God ever called for or authorized any voluntary sacrifice of a person on an altar of fire. Such would have been repulsive to God, and had any man presumed to do so he would been condemned. In all the Bible, not a word of criticism even can be found against Jephthah. On the other hand, he is mentioned as one of the great men of faith in Hebrews 11: 32. This is very significant.

JUDGES 12

Verse 1. When some great achievement has been made it is often the cause of envy. Jephthah has come off with such great honors in his war against the Ammonites that the men of Ephraim are bitter against him. In their bitterness they make a false accusation against him and threaten his life and property.

Verses 2, 3. Jephthah denied their charge and replied that the very opposite was the fact. He had called upon them without response and they left him to take care of himself. And in his speech he gives the Lord the glory for the success.

Verse 4. So Jephthah is again forced to engage in battle and gathers the forces of the men of Gilead. We should remember these people are east and somewhat north of the central portion of Palestine. The men of Ephraim as here mentioned were west of the Jordan and somewhat south. Hence the statement in first verse that they went northward. In this war Jephthah called the Gileadites over to him for service. One incentive for the intensity of the battle was another false accusation of the men of Ephraim. They charged that the men claiming to be Gileadites were really Ephraimites who had deserted. This was soon to be tested out as to their identity.

Verse 5. As would be expected, the Ephraimites were put to the worst in the battle. The ones who escaped the heat of battle thought to flee to their own country by crossing the Jordan. This was also expected by the Gileadites, hence they seized the passages of the river. The personal identity of all who might come to these established crossings of the river would make it necessary to proceed cautiously. They would not want to injure an innocent person. The first thing in the examination was to give the men opportunity for surrender by asking if they were Ephraimites. If they denied being so, the test would be put.

Verse 6. *Shibboleth: Sibboleth.* There is practically no difference between the meaning of these words. They mean something that is flowing or extending out and hence in the lexicon the definition of ear of corn, and of a river, or branch, is given. But the slight difference does call for the injection of the rough breathing sound in the pronunciation. The local vernacular of the Ephraimites had left out this sound and so their usage had trained their tongue against expressing it. This fact proved their undoing and exposed the attempted deception. As a result another 42,000 of them fell.

Verse 7. This short account of the death of Jephthah is characteristic of the language of the Bible. We should note another term in the years of the judges.

Verses 8-10. We have before noticed that some of the judges are barely mentioned with the length of their rule. But that is important in our tabulation of the years of the period of judges. In this paragraph we have seven years.

Verses 11, 12. Elon was of Zebulon, and judged ten years.

Verses 13-15. According to the information in the margin this and the two preceding judges were civil judges only and their territory was restricted to the north and eastern part of the country. This may be true. It would account for the brevity of the history. Evidently during these judgeships there was not much disturbance from the enemy in general and so no great amount of activity would be called for on the part of a judge. Yet the years of their rule must be counted since they go to make up the whole period. In this last one we have eight years. The word "nephews" is from a word of indefinite meaning, including grandsons. That is clearly the meaning in this place, since the number of sons is given in direct connection.

JUDGES 13

Verse 1. In some cases the writer gives us the term of years to include the time of oppression and that of the judge. But in this instance we are to understand that God allowed 40 years of oppression to go by as punishment for the nation before raising up their deliverer. So we are about to study the life and actions of one of the most noted judges.

Verses 2, 3. In so many instances recorded in the Bible the couples destined to figure prominently in the plan of the Lord were childless and the wife barren. In the case at hand it is thus. The couple chosen lived in the tribe of Dan. The angel of God appeared and promised the woman should bear a son.

Verse 4. Conditions of a Nazarite required that the hair be allowed to grow long (Num. 6: 2-5), but no mention of this was necessary here since women already left their hair long.

Verse 5. The son promised to this woman was to be a Nazarite from his birth. That would mean that he must not eat anything that came through the vine when he would have attained the age of eating such food. Since he was to be under such a vow from the time of his birth it would mean that the parents must never cut his hair. This son will grow up to become the deliverer of the people from the Philistines.

Verses 6, 7. The whole thing was astonishing to the woman and, of course, she told the matter to her husband. Her expression that the countenance of the person speaking to her was terrible, means that it was one to fill her with awe. We have also the definite information that this woman was intended to be under the Nazarite vow for she was told not to partake of the fruit of the vine. This was a specific symbol of that vow. Also, the child was to be a Nazarite from the womb, which agrees with the idea that he would be born of a Nazarite mother.

Verse 8. What a wonderful attitude this man showed. Concern for the proper training of the child was the subject of his prayer. Since he and his wife had been childless they did not have any experience. The unusual mission of this son to be born was such that it would be unwise to wait for the painful experiences of parenthood to bring the information. Thus it was logical to ask for instruction.

Verses 9, 10. In response to the prayer of Manoah the Lord sent the angel again to the woman who was alone in the field. Upon this she goes to bring her husband. Here is a fact that belies the intimated accusation sometimes made by enemies of the Bible that this whole occurrence was one of improper conduct and that it was not an angel who appeared to this woman, and that a man in the guise of an angel appeared and that he was intimate with the woman. Had that been the case she would not have gone at once to bring her husband while the angel was still present.

Verses 11, 12. Upon direct information as to the identity of the angel, Manoah repeats his inquiry as to the training of the child.

Verses 13, 14. Again notice that the course of procedure begins with the woman which shows that she was under the Nazarite vow as well as the promised son. See comments on this subject at verses 4 and 7.

Verse 15. Gratitude would suggest the hospitality here offered. Besides, Manoah did not know that it was an angel who was before him. This is one of the instances referred to by Paul in Heb. 13: 1. Sometimes angels even partook of material food. In the present one the angel will not do so although he will remain for a while.

Verse 16. While the angel declines to eat, he agrees that an offering to the Lord may be made. This will give the angel opportunity to demonstrate his supernatural power.

Verse 17. Gratitude again manifested itself with Manoah in asking for the name of his benefactor. He wished to be prepared to repay the favor to the proper person.

Verse 18. The request of Manoah was denied since the thing asked for would have been beyond his comprehension. We do not know why, since we do have the names of angels given in other cases. It is another place to read Deut. 29: 29.

Verse 19. There was no indication of bitterness of disappointment with Manoah, but instead he went on with his performance of offering the kid and meat offering. The angel in the meantime did some wonderful things which we are not informed about. They were done in the sight of the man and his wife and continued until the events of the following verse.

Verse 20. The prophet Elijah went up to heaven by a whirlwind (2 Kings

2: 11). The angel here disappeared in a flame that had been on the altar. After his departure the man and his wife were filled with awe and became prone on the ground.

Verses 21, 22. The demonstrations of the angel were ended and left in the mind of Manoah the belief that it was a real angel of God who had visited them. Being the most unusual experience they had ever known, the man is overcome with concern and feels that he is in danger from the exposure. Just how much he had learned on the subject of the presence of God we do not know. But we are sure of this, that the feeling of unworthiness of man for the company of a being from heaven was present with Manoah.

Verse 23. The reasoning of the woman here is wonderful. It would be well for the reader to consult Matt. 5: 23, 24. In that place Jesus taught that the performance of an offering at the altar would not take the place of another duty. Especially if that other duty pertained to the individual conduct of the one making the offering. So in the instance at hand. The acceptance of the formality of the sacrifice was evidence in the woman's mind that their standing before God was favorable.

Verses 24, 25. True to the promise from God the son was born and named Samson. In the time used for his physical maturity he was exercising himself in the camp of his family, that of Dan. The spirit of the Lord produced certain demonstrations of power in Samson even while still among his people. We are not told just what they were like, but the idea is that he was destined to be one of the great men of Israel.

JUDGES 14

Verse 1. Many of the incidents to be read about in the following chapters will be easier understood by remembering that the Philistines are now the enemies of Israel. They figure in the experiences of God's people in this period more than any other of the heathen and many unusual measures will be taken in dealing with them. For instance, God will suffer the present judge to take certain actions that would have been frowned upon in the life of a private Israelite. Neither does Samson always realize that the Lord is really using him in these various relations to bring about the defeat of the Philistines. For some reason, Samson made a journey to Timnath, a place shown in the map to be in the possession of Ephraim. While there he saw a woman of the Philistines who pleased him.

Verse 2. Customs of the times now being studied were different from those of ours. It was a common matter for parents to take action in securing a wife for a son. This was especially true when the woman sought was from a different community than that of the interested man. See for instance the case of Abraham and Isaac in Genesis 24.

Verses 3, 4. The parents of Samson did not realize that God was in all this affair and was taking such means to get their son in a position of advantage with the enemy. They protested his choice of a woman for a wife. He insisted on the choice because she pleased him well. Neither did he realize what it might mean to the cause of the people of Israel for him to be thus connected with the Philistines.

Verses 5-7. The trio went down to Timnath to attend to the matter of engaging the woman for Samson. On the way the strength of the young man was demonstrated by his encounter with a lion. This took place at a time that he was temporarily not in the company of his parents and he did not tell them about it. Going on down to Timnath he obtained a visit with the woman and was confirmed in his first impression made on the previous visit to the town. The language of the following verse indicates that an agreement was reached between him and the woman to become husband and wife soon.

Verses 8, 9. When the time drew near the trio again started to Timnath. When they reached the spot where Samson had killed the lion he "turned aside" as he evidently had done the other time for his parents had not known of his experience with the beast. Finding some honey in the carcase of the animal he took some and ate. Coming to the presence of his parents he gave them of the honey but still did not explain it to them.

Verse 10. The matter was settled for the woman to become the wife of Samson. It was a custom for a groom to treat his bride by giving a seven-day feast to the guests who might be present. This was what Laban required of Jacob in Gen. 29: 27. Samson does this for the woman who was to be his wife.

Verse 11. It was to be an interesting occasion for they invited thirty friends to be present and be companions to Samson.

Verses 12, 13. As one means of diversion Samson propounded a riddle to these companions and gave them the entire period of the seven days to guess it. The stake was thirty sheets. This word is from CADIYN and defined by Strong "from an unused root meaning to envelop; a wrapper, i. e., shirt." The R. V. says "linen garments," which is doubtless justified by the lexicon. Whichever lost in the proposition was to give these articles of clothing to the other. Whether the companions expressly agreed to the bargain is not stated. But they called for the riddle and in absence of any other conditions they would be honorably bound to the terms stated by Samson.

Verse 14. As the reader will know, the riddle was formed from his experience in the matter of the honey in the carcase of the lion. He must have had such a thought in his mind all along since the affair of the lion, since he kept the account of it from his parents although it was a very indifferent matter as to being confidential. He wished to know that he alone would have knowledge of it. Since we know they never did guess the riddle themselves the last statement of this verse must be taken to mean that they did not begin to surmise until the third day that the riddle would be too much for them.

Verse 15. They kept on trying at the riddle. Finally the seventh day arrived and now they have just the one day to win the prize. In their desperation they appeal to his wife to learn the answer. They accompany their request with threats to burn her and her father's house. They further accuse her of conspiring with her husband to take their possessions from them and put the question direct to her if such is not the case. This is what they meant by the last words, "is it not so?"

Verse 16. She resorts to a strong weapon of a woman, her tears. This she adds to the complaint that he had told some things to others that he had not told her. He tries to quiet her by telling her that he had not told it to his own parents.

Verse 17. His reply did not quiet her. She wept before him "the seven days." Since this weeping did not begin until the seventh day we see the explanation in the margin which says "the rest of the seven days." The entire seven days will not be over until the present one closes. Thus it means that from the beginning to the end of the seventh day she besieged him with her tears so that on this seventh day, the last day of grace for the riddle, he was overcome by her persistence. In this condition of mind, he told her the answer to the riddle. As yet, we know not that he expected it to go any further than to her. Neither does the text state whether she relayed it to the men of the city. That remains to be brought out.

Verse 18. Just in time for the conditions stated the men gave the answer to the riddle. Samson knew he had not told any one the answer but his wife and that she therefore had betrayed his confidence on that subject. One of the meanings of the word for "plowed" is to devise or work with secrecy. A heifer would be used figuratively as referring to his partner in the intimate relationship of this life. The whole sentence means that they had secretly devised with his young partner and in that way had obtained the answer to his riddle.

Verse 19. However, Samson will fulfill his promise although it will be to the sorrow of the Philistines. God helped him in the matter by giving him success in the encounter. By killing the thirty Philistines he obtains the articles of clothing to pay off the riddle. Also we may learn that since the articles were taken from the bodies of the men slain, it shows that the "sheets" of the stake were as already explained and not articles for the beds. In his anger over the whole affair it seems that Samson departed from the place and went back to his father's house. Evidently this was an act of hasty temper although it, too, might have been part of the Lord's plan.

Verse 20. The closing words of preceding paragraph were suggested by the statement of this. In the absence of Samson from his wife's home where he had left her for the time being, she had been given by her father to another man. It was one whom Samson had befriended, but ingratitude is a common trait.

JUDGES 15

Verse 1. In course of time Samson cooled off from his anger and decided to go on a visit to his wife. It was customary to express good will by making a gift of some value and so Samson decides to present his wife with a young goat. Now that he had already received the woman as his wife he is entitled to her intimate company and decides to avail himself of it. One meaning of the word for "chamber" here is bed chamber. It means that he proposed to enter his wife's bed chamber where he was supposed to have right to enter. But the father of the woman barred him from the apartment.

Verse 2. The father offers his explanation and says he thought that Samson hated her. We may justly infer that such conclusion was based on the angry conduct of Samson in taking his departure for his former home instead of remaining with his new wife. Especially might he so conclude since Samson had been absent a considerable time. Now that another man has been given possession of the young woman she cannot be claimed by Samson. Instead of her, the cold bargain is offered that he may have the younger sister of his wife. The inducement is suggested that she is fairer (better or more beautiful) than the one he had married. There is no indication that Samson even made any reply to this insulting proposition.

Verse 3. Samson plans to do the Philistines a disfavor but he will bring it about in such a way that they will not blame him for it and hence will not take any vengeance on him.

Verses 4, 5. Enemies of the Bible scoff at the idea that a man could catch three hundred foxes when it usually takes several men to catch one. For one thing we are not compelled to suppose that these foxes were the same as the animal by that name today. Even if they were, let it be remembered that Samson is now the instrument in the hands of God for the subjugation of the Philistines and he would enable Samson to do whatever was necessary for the work. By tying the foxes together in pairs and in the manner described with the torches attached to their tails, they would be incited to struggle for release. In the contrary pulling of the animals their speed would be interfered with and all the while the fire would be burning down the grain. This would result in much more destruction to the crop than would have been done had the foxes been left apart even though there would have been double the number of torches. But the hasty exit of the foxes from the place would have left less destruction in their wake than as done by Samson's wisdom.

Verse 6. Of course, this drew the attention of the Philistines with the inquiry as to the perpetrator thereof. Being informed that it was Samson and also as to the reason for it, they laid the blame all on the father-in-law of the man and the woman who was to have been his wife. Being a party to the fraud it was just that she suffer with her father. She had not only betrayed the confidence of her husband by exposing the answer to the riddle, but now, in the alienation from his companionship, she was guilty along with her father. Hence, it was right that she suffer with him. By looking over Samson and pouring their effective wrath on the cause of the situation the thing came to pass referred to by Samson in 3rd verse.

Verses 7, 8. While the aforesaid actions avenged Samson for his disappointment in the matter of his wife, he is not satisfied with the present evils inflicted on the Philistines. He attacked them in the hip and thigh. The last word refers to the groin and includes consideration of the generative parts. Thus the slaughter which Samson inflicted on them was not instant death, but a prolonged one. Having accomplished this revenge he went to a place in Palestine called Etam, which had a sort of resting place on a rock. There he prepared to dwell for a time.

Verse 9. The Philistines pursued Samson and assembled at a place called Lehi, the exact location of which was uncertain. It was in the same general territory as Judah.

Verse 10. On seeing the hordes of the enemy the men of Judah inquired their aim in coming there. They said it was to bind Samson and return vengeance on him.

Verse 11. The speech of the Philistines seemed to be a surprise to these men of Judah. They considered them as their rulers and did not realize that movements were being made for their release. Now they address themselves to Samson in a kind of critical mood.

Verse 12. Having been informed that it was Samson alone whom the Philistines wanted they think to appease them by delivering him into their hands. Samson is not afraid of the Philistines but asks for guarantees of security from his own brethren.

Verse 13. The assurance desired was given and then he was bound as if to prevent his escape. In this condition they brought him from his place on the rock at Etam and to the place called Lehi.

Verse 14. When he reached Lehi the Philistines gave a shout preparatory for an attack. The spirit of the Lord came to his rescue and the cords around him became as weak as if they had been burned in the fire and he was thus released.

Verse 15. He had not come to this place with any weapon. A moist jaw bone of an ass was nearby and that became his only weapon. With such a weapon he slew a thousand of the Philistines. We will understand, of course, that such a weapon, unaided by the Lord, would have been far too short to accomplish what was done at that time.

Verse 16. Here is where Samson forgot to give credit properly for the success of his deed. The first personal pronoun used exclusively got him into trouble with God.

Verse 17. According to Smith's Bible Dictionary the name Samson gave this place means "hill of the jawbone." And in the margin of the text we have "the lifting up of the jawbone." Not only did he take the credit to himself of killing the great number of men, but named a place by his personal feat.

Verse 18. The great thirst that came upon him must have been sudden in its attack and very depressing inasmuch as he felt the threat of death. It sometimes needs a thing like that to impress a person with his shortcoming. It had the desired effect on Samson, for he cried out in his misery that "thou hast given this great deliverance" and then pleads for help.

Verse 19. God never punishes his servants beyond what is necessary. After the penitent plea of Samson a fountain of water was made to flow from the very object by which he had accomplished, through the Lord, his great victory over the enemy. Then he gave a name that was different from the one just bestowed on the place. That name was in view of his feat in handling the jawbone. This one was in memory of his penitence. The word is defined in the margin as "the well of him that called or cried," and the lexicon agrees with the definition.

Verse 20. This passage not only gives us another term of years to be added to the chronology, but also states the particular people who oppressed Israel at the time.

JUDGES 16

Verse 1. Gaza was a prominent town in the land of the Philistines. The incident of his going down to that place and patronizing a harlot was not a very uncommon thing then any more than it is today. But it occasioned another demonstration of the power of Samson in the presence of the enemy as will be seen.

Verse 2. He had been seen coming into the city but his exact location would not be known. The principal cities were walled and going and coming had to be done through the gate. The men of the city planned to capture him in the morning, supposing that after passing the night in the place he would go out. Of course they were sleeping near the gate and not aware of his plan to go on after his visit with the woman. The word for "lay" is SHAKAB and defined by Strong "a primitive root; to lie down (for rest, sexual connection, decease or any other purpose). There is no evidence that they knew his purpose in the city or they would have watched at the house of the woman. It is the inspired writer who tells us of his actions there.

Verse 3. See comments on the word "lay" in preceding verse. After ending his visit with this woman he was ready to leave the city but found the gate closed since it was still night and those walled cities were thus fortified at night. Here is where Samson showed his physical might again by carrying away the very parts of the city that were supposed to be protection for the citizens on the inside. He was able not only to pull the parts down but carried them to the top of a hill near Hebron. Nothing more is said about this circumstance and we do not know how much effect it had on the Philistines except that it gave them to understand that he was a mighty man and that they would never be able to deal with him in an ordinary manner. This will be brought out in the following part of the narrative.

Verse 4. The word "loved" is from AWHAB and defined "a primitive root; to have affection for (sexually or otherwise)"—Strong. This shows us that the attachment between Samson and Delilah was more than mere physical gratification. Had that been the only sense in which he loved this woman the word would not have been used since it was not used just previous to this case. When the writer told us of his visit to the harlot nothing was said about his loving her. Moreover, we are not to forget that the Lord is in all of this matter and using all the various means to get Samson in a position of advantage over the Philistines. That can be accomplished by bringing about the intimate association of this judge with this outstanding woman of the enemy.

Verse 5. This verse indicates that something more than mere physical relations existed between Samson and Delilah. The leading men of the Philistines recognized this close attachment beween them, else they would not have hoped to overcome him through her help. It is true the word "wife" is not used in the story but there were no definite ceremonies that we know of in force in those days for making a woman a wife. All the elements of such a relationship were present in this case and we have reason to think of them in that light.

Verse 6. Being influenced by the vast amount of money promised her, Delilah asked Samson to explain the secret of his great strength. There could have been no indication of it by his personal appearance even though he might have been one of unusual muscular form. That could not have accounted for the ability to carry away the gate of a city.

Verse 7. The "withs" were cords, and being green, meant they were moist or new. It might be that such an article would be secure against rending.

Verse 8. The Philistines were willing to cooperate so they furnished her with the articles suggested by Samson. It might be asked why he permitted her to even tie him with these cords as he was strong enough to resist her had he wished to do so. Again we should keep in mind that the Lord is in this whole strange thing.

Verse 9. One meaning of the word for "chamber" is an apartment. Delilah admitted these men into her apartment but in a hidden manner, to be unknown to Samson. After binding him with the cords she announced that the Philistines were upon him. But they had no opportunity to take him because he broke the cords as if they were charred.

Verses 10, 11. She accused him of lying to her which was the case. Yet she was willing to trust him again and all this according to the plan of God referred to above. This time he explained that new ropes that had never been used would make him helpless. A rope would be heavier than a cord and so perhaps they would hold him.

Verse 12. The suggestion was followed and she bound him with the ropes. Also she had the men concealed and ready to take Samson if he were found to be really trapped. Again he tore them from him as if they were thread.

Verse 13. To the reader who knows the "secret" of his strength this theory of Samson might seem to come nearer the truth since the hair of his head was involved. The web was the warp in a loom and thus was a series of threads similiar to the series of filaments composing the hairs of his head which were long, being a Nazarite. It might be that by joining the two systems of these filaments he would be held fast. The seven locks would mean his entire growth of hair since the word indicates the idea of completeness when used figuratively.

Verse 14. The suggestion was followed, and again the presence of the Philistines was announced to him. Again his strength was exhibited by his leaving with all the parts of the loom adjoining the web, to which his hair had been fastened.

Verses 15-17. Delilah is not entirely discouraged. She continues her pleas from day to day until he is practically worn out. It is natural to ask why he kept on answering her as long as he did when he knew her motive for all the instances. We should also remember that the whole proceeding is of the Lord. So he told her the truth this time. His long hair was in evidence and had been since she had known him. What she did not know was that it had never been cut. He explained why that was the case and that his strength was a supernatural gift on condition of his special vow. The mere telling her of the secret of his strength would not have been wrong for any man under a vow could lawfully relate that fact. The text does not say that he gave her permission to have the hair of his head cut. He could have prevented her from doing so had he determined to do so. It is reasonable to conclude that he needed a lesson of confidence for others as well as for himself.

Verse 18. After being deceived three times why would Delilah conclude that he had told her the truth this time? Well, the three explanations Samson offered would at least have the appearance of being physical cause for overcoming his strength. Thus she could logically conclude that in some mysterious way such material obstacles to his exercise, might overcome him, hence she was decoyed the three times. But the explanation he gave her this time was fundamentally different. There could be no logical or physical connection between long hair and this phenomenal strength. Were the fact of long hair the physical cause of strength then all women of that day would have been strong because they had such hair. She rightfully concluded that indeed some hidden (to her) cause of his strength was connected with the locks of his hair. With such assurance she called for the lords of the Philistines once more and they came with the money in hand to reward her for her treachery.

Verse 19. Samson submitted to the plan of Delilah and allowed himself to fall asleep on the knees of this woman. In that condition the hair of his head was shorn and thus his vow was broken. When that was done the Lord took his strength from him because the vow was broken which was the condition, or one of the conditions, of his vow upon which the special favor of God was bestowed.

Verse 20. Delilah gave an arousing call to Samson and he awoke. We will recall that he had been vexed almost to the point of death before going to sleep. It was natural that awaking thus suddenly he would not miss his long hair at once. So he thinks to do as he had done on the three previous occasions. He proposes to go out and "shake" himself. This word is from NAWAR and defined by Strong "a primitive root (through the idea of the rustling of mane, which usually accompanies the lion's roar); to tumble about." The idea is that as the lion would roar and shake his mane in his great and majestic strength, so Samson will shake his strength as connected with his long hair like the mane of a lion. Being just aroused from the deep sleep he did not realize that he was minus his hair and hence did not realize that the Lord was gone.

Verse 21. The lords of the Philistines were on hands to take advantage of the situation. Without hindrance they took Samson into their grasp. They began their persecution of him by boring out his eyes. They are not forgetting the former disappointments they had and so are taking no chances this time. They took him to the important city of their country and there bound him with brazen fetters. Also they put him in prison and compelled him to do servile labor for them. They made him grind while in the prison house. The word is from TACHAN which is defined, "to grind meal."—Strong. According to the information of history it was always women who were compelled to do this work. The exception is made in this case, and its very significance is that he has been humiliated to the strength and position of women.

Verse 22. Samson has had his first lesson of chastisement for breaking his vow by losing his strength. Since another purpose of God in this proceeding is to get vengeance on the Philistines the strength will gradually return. That will be necessary for the accomplishing of the downfall of these enemies. It can be seen in numerous instances of the history of the Israelites that God would use heathen nations to punish his own wayward people. After the punishment had been inflicted, then the heathen nation would be punished. Thus in the present case Samson needed punishment for breaking his vow and the Philistines were the instrument by which the punishment was inflicted. Now that such has been done it remains for the enemy himself to be given the justice his motives deserved.

Verse 23. Citizens are permitted to visit their public prisons especially when a noted prisoner is there. So the Philistines came to the prison and beheld their hated foe in custody. In this situation they gave credit for their good state to their idol god, Dagon.

Verses 24. Chronologically this verse should be prior to verse 23. The people came to the prison and there saw Samson in slavery. When they saw him in that condition they proceeded to assemble in their temple used for the worship of their god. When assembled in that place they engaged in praises to their heathen god and gave it the credit for the overthrow of their common foe. They here acknowledge that Samson had slain many of their fellow citizens.

Verse 25. In the midst of their festivities and joyfulness over their supposed victory they thought of having further entertainment at Samson's expense. They sent to have him brought out of the prison and into this public building where they were gathered in so great numbers at the occasion of their triumph. The word "sport" is from an original, that means to laugh or to be laughed at. Thus they did not expect Samson to act for them as a sportsman would act, but that he might be the object of their jests and derisive laughs.

Verse 26. Samson is blind, hence asks for the services of a lad in finding the pillars of the house. His purpose as stated to the lad was that he might lean on them which would seem a very reasonable explanation.

Verse 27. Great buildings that were used for public activities were based upon tall and heavy pillars in olden times. So much so that a single pillar would support much of the building and hence the perpetuity of the building would depend often on one or two central posts. (See 1 Tim. 3: 15). At the time we are now considering this great building was filled with happy men and women with the lords of the Philistines. As the roofs of buildings were then used for personal occupation there were three thousand of them on this roof. We do not know how many more were on the inside.

Verse 28. The personal afflictions of Samson moved the Lord to compassion. A prayer was sent up to heaven. It was not overlooked that not only were the eyes of the servant of God destroyed, but in reprisal for them the great enemies of God would be punished. This interest in the cause of God on behalf of his people was very commendable for Samson.

Verse 29. Mere faith as exists in the assent of the mind is not enough. Some action on the part of man must be forthcoming. In confidence, Samson took hold of the two middle pillars on which the house was supported.

Verse 30. Continuing his prayer, Samson asks to die with the Philistines. Also continuing his own actions in cooperation with the Lord, he applied his strength against the pillars and the building collapsed, killing the people therein. The number of the slain is not given except in a comparison. He slew more at the time of his death than he had killed in all his life previously.

Verse 31. His relatives came for his body and buried it in the family burial ground. The statement of his twenty years of judgment must not be added to the term mentioned in ch. 15: 20. It is merely a repetition of the same fact and given here as a final summing up of his remarkable life. It might be inquired as to what benefit it was to the Israelites for Samson to have all these personal conflicts with the Philistines. It will appear clear when we reflect that all this had a detracting effect and that while these things were going on, the general oppression from the enemy would be hindered and the children of Israel encouraged.

JUDGES 17

Verse 1. Mount Ephraim has already been seen to refer to a general territory in the south and west part of Palestine. Somewhere in this district, this man Micah lived. He was an Israelite but had become interested in idolatry as did his mother.

Verse 2. This idolatrous mother had been saving some silver for an unlawful purpose which was unknown to the son. He had spied it and stolen it. When the mother missed it, not knowing the identity of the thief, she had given way to cursing in the hearing of her son. Now he confesses to her that he had taken it. Instead of reprimanding him for stealing, she asked the Lord's blessing on him. This evil attitude is explained by the fact that she was not concerned in the moral life of her son, but was glad that the silver was at least "kept in the family."

Verse 3. The son turned the silver over to his mother for the time being. She protested, since it had been saved for his use anyway. She had intended it to be made into images for idolatrous worship by him and hence he might as well have it again in his possession. On this explanation she handed it back to him.

Verse 4. We cannot consider it an unselfish act when the son turned the silver back to his mother this time. He had been informed that she would use it for his benefit and hence he would get its value appropriated to himself at last. Not only so, but he would be relieved of the trouble of having the articles made. He would thus let ner have that responsibility. So the silver was taken by the mother who procured the services of a workman, made a cast, and also a chiseled image, and they were placed in the house of the son Micah.

Verse 5. Not satisfied with these two images his mother had procured for him, Micah added these articles. They were similar to the sacred articles that were used by the priests in the tabernacle services. Thus this man Micah mixed the two kinds of worship, the idolatrous and the imitation of the true one in the tabernacle. He was a man somewhat along in years for he had sons, one of whom was acting as his priest.

Verse 6. There was no man in civil authority who would also be interested in seeing the true laws of God carried out. Hence each man became a law unto himself, and thus the independent conduct of Micah. No endorsement is intended for this man's evil ways, but just an account of conditions in that age of many upsets.

Verse 7. There is no apparent connection between the foregoing verses and those to follow. The relation will appear before the chapter is finished. Bethlehem is a town situated in the possession of the tribe of Judah. This young man who was a Levite as to his tribe was sojourning in this town of Bethlehem. We are not told why he had been there but evidently it was temporary, as will be seen in the next verse.

Verse 8. The words "a place" are not in the original. But the context shows them to be correctly inserted for the young Levite was said to have been only sojourning in Bethlehem which was outside the territory of his tribe. Now he is going away from Bethlehem to sojourn again wherever he can find a place to spend some time. In his rounds he comes upon that spot in mount Ephraim where the house of Micah was.

Verse 9. Micah asked this newcomer about his former whereabouts. In response, the young Levite informed him as desired, and also told him of his purpose in going about over the country, that he was looking for a place.

Verse 10. That was just the kind of man Micah was interested in. He invited him to dwell with him and be to him a father (figuratively, as an overseer) and a priest. Micah knew that the priests under the law were to be teachers also. So the young man engaged himself to this man on a stipulated sum of money and other temporal things.

Verses 11, 12. The contract having been agreed to, the young man was treated as one of the family. Micah also performed some sort of ceremony in consecration of the man to the priesthood over his house.

Verse 13. Another thing that Micah knew was that the lawful priests were to be of the tribe of Levi. Whether this particular young man was from the particular family of Aaron which alone of all the Levites could be priest is not stated. That much of the required qualification was present at least. For this reason Micah concluded that the blessing of God would be extended to him. He did not realize that no one can hope to have the favor of God in his wickedness just because he mixes some of the true items of service of God with his own unlawful actions. He was destined to learn at the last that his arrangement will not prove a permanent blessing to him.

JUDGES 18

Verse 1. For the first sentence in this verse see comments at ch. 17: 6. The tribe of Dan is not satisfied with the amount of land they possess at this time and we will see them making arrangements to enlarge the same.

Verse 2. Five men were sent on a mission of finding more territory that might be attached to what they already had. Going forth they came upon the general territory of mount Ephraim, to the particular spot containing the house of Micah.

Verse 3. This verse explains the one previous and why they lodged in the house of Micah. When they had come near this house they heard the voice of the Levite on the inside and recognized it. We do not know how they came to know him but the record says it was so. Upon hearing the voice they turned in to inquire why he was there and all about his business in that place.

Verse 4. The young man answered their questions and concluded with the most significant part of the contract, that he was the priest to the man employing him.

Verses 5, 6. These men doubtless understood the provisions of the law of Moses, that the priesthood was expected to be a means of communication between God and the people. (Lev. 10: 11; Deut. 17: 9; Mal. 2: 7.) Such would only apply regularly to the authorized priest and one in the faithful service of God. In the absence of any direct information in the record here, we are not able to say how much of this transaction was approved of by the Lord. We are able to say that what the priest predicted for them came to pass. Sometimes God used even unauthorized persons through which to give information to others (1 Sam. 28: 11-14), but whether that was done in the case at hand is not certain.

Verse 7. The men resumed their search for territory available for their tribe to acquire. Finally they came to the community of Laish as it was called at the time of this adventure; but which came to be called Dan. Bible students will recognize it by this name and will recall that it was located at the most northern extremity of Palestine. They found the people there to be unsuspecting and careless about their safety. In other words, so self-satisfied with their situation that they never seemed to realize that an enemy might slip in on them any time. With such an attitude they exposed themselves to attack without being prepared in mind, or otherwise, to defend themselves. This was the very kind of opportunity these men of the tribe of Dan were wanting.

Verses 8-10. This group of five spies returned to their home and made report of their discovery of a desirable land. They also urged their brethren to go at once to possess it and described the people as being careless and not watchful.

Verse 11. Acting on this advice they armed and sent 600 men.

Verses 12, 13. In their journey they retraced the same route the five men had taken on their mission of espionage and reached the place of Micah's house.

Verse 14. Of course these five spies were in the present group as pilots. Upon reaching the place of Micah's house they gave the company information about the articles that were in that house and suggested they do something about it.

Verses 15-17. The company now came to the immediate spot and the body of the army stood guard at the gate while the five spies entered the house and took the graven image and other articles that Micah had there for worship. In the meantime the priest looked on the company, standing with them at the gate.

Verse 18. Having confiscated the articles they came on out to the gate where the priest was standing and he asked them for explanation of their actions.

Verse 19. The priest was told to keep still and also offered a position like the one he had at present, only over an entire tribe.

Verse 20. This offer was pleasing to the priest and doubtless sounded like a better proposition than the one he had been holding. On this inducement he went with the company.

Verse 21. In the order of march they put the little ones in the front, also the cattle. The "carriage" here means their personal goods that had to be carried.

Verse 22. After the company had been gone some distance the people living near the house of Micah rose to his assistance and went with him in pursuit.

Verse 23. Upon overtaking them they made a cry of objection, or despair, or some other kind of expression that provoked the children of Dan. At this, the latter replied with the question as to what was ailing Micah and why he was pursuing with the company.

Verse 24. This seemed to be an unnecessary question in view of what they had done to him. He expressed the thought that he was left with nothing and that he had much on which to base a complaint.

Verses 25, 26. Micah was warned to keep still if he valued his life. The company then proceeded in their journey, while Micah, seeing his cause was lost, returned home.

Verse 27. The company of Danites arrived at the place that had been espied by the five on the previous trip. They found them still unmindful of any danger and not looking out for their own safety. In this state of affairs the city was easily captured. The people were surprised and slain and their city was destroyed. In thus taking sneak advantage of these quiet people, the children of Dan fulfilled the prediction made by Jacob in Gen. 49: 17. It was said that Dan should be "a serpent by the way," which was explained to mean he would make an unexpected attack.

Verse 28. The easy victory over this place is further explained by the fact that they had no one to fight for them. Zidon was too far off to furnish them any help and they were not allied to any other people by business or otherwise. The last part of the verse breaks into the matter of the Danites and their conquest just accomplished. They rebuilt the city they had just destroyed and established a colony thereat.

Verse 29. The language of this verse indicates that while the former city was the site of the present one, the name was changed in honor of the head of the tribe. It is here that we see one of the methods of recording facts in the Bible. As far back as Gen. 14: 14, we read of the city of Dan, yet we just now have read of the actual circumstance by which it got its name. The explanation is that when the events took place that are recorded in Genesis this history of which we just now learned had happened, so the writer uses the name that was then (at time of his writing) attached to it.

Verses 30, 31. This paragraph shows the fickleness of man. After practically kidnapping the priest of Micah and promising him a larger "pastorate" they now ignore all that, and instead place a man as priest over their institution who did not belong even to the tribe supposed to furnish priests. And nothing was ever said about the young Levite who had deserted Micah. Also, this illegal establishment here was along the same line of false worship that finally got the nation into serious trouble with the Lord, ending with the national captivity. When people once depart from the law of righteousness there is no logical stopping place. They seem more ready to imitate a bad example than the true one.

JUDGES 19

Verse 1. To avoid confusion, we must always remember that "mount Ephraim" is a term not restricted to a specific place, but to a territory of some general extent in the western part of Palestine. The Levites as a tribe did not have any possessions, thus the individual members of that tribe dwelled in various places. The one we are now reading about was sojourning on the farther side of this territory just named; and at Bethlehem, in the possession of Judah, he found a woman who became his concubine. A concubine in those times was practically the same as a wife in all moral senses, but differed as to her property rights. She was expected to be as true to her master in the intimate relationship, as the wife with legal rights.

Verse 2. The fact that this concubine was accused of playing the harlot proves that even in those liberal times a concubine was considered under obligations to one man, the same as the wife. This woman deserted her duty to the one man and began promiscuous relations with other men. In this sort of life she also deserted her new home and returned to that of her father.

Verse 3. After a period of absence, stated in the A. V. as four months, the husband went in search of his concubine and made a plea for the return of her affection. She evidently had repented by this time of her lapse of duty for she secured him entrance to her father's house. The meeting was also agreeable to the damsel's father.

Verse 4. The father-in-law expressed his friendship by giving three days of hospitality consisting in lodging and food.

Verses 5-7. On the morning of the fourth day the Levite prepared to leave, but his father-in-law persuaded him to remain another day and night.

Verse 8. On the morning of the fifth day he intended to depart, but his father-in-law persuaded him to remain till the afternoon and enjoy his hospitality.

Verse 9. Towards evening the Levite prepared to leave. His father-in-law used the approach of night as basis for pleading that they wait till morning and then go. The genuine nature of the friendship of this father-in-law is here proved.

Verse 10. The Levite would not be detained longer but departed and soon came to the vicinity of Jebus, which is Jerusalem. This was not very far from the place where they had been lodging.

Verses 11-13. As it was now getting late in the day the servant suggested they stop in Jerusalem for the night. The Levite objected because at that time the city was being held by a foreign class of people, called Jebusites. The possession of Benjamin was directly adjoining that of Judah and the Levite felt more at home there.

He therefore insisted that they proceed to one of the cities there.

Verses 14, 15. The sun had gone down by the time they reached Gibeah, a city in the possession of the tribe of Benjamin. As it was thus and they knew of no certain lodging place in the city they sat down in the street. It was now in the early hours of night or late hours of the day.

Verse 16. There was another man from this same general territory called "mount Ephraim," now staying in the city of Gibeah and finding work in that community. He had secured a lodging house for his own occupying. As he was coming home from his work, he came into the city, since his work was in a field. He was of another tribe than the one where he was now living for these natives were Benjamites.

Verse 17. Passing into the city he noticed this man sitting in the street and asked him about his situation.

Verses 18, 19. The information asked for was given. The Levite was returning to the house of the Lord. That would be an appropriate explanation to give this man who was a stranger to the Levite. The tabernacle was then at Shiloh (Josh. 18: 1), which was north of Jerusalem and in the general territory called mount Ephraim. He was now detained in his journey by night fall. He was in the street because no lodging place had been made available to him. He had sufficient provisions for himself and his beasts, hence, was not to be a burden on any one.

Verses 20, 21. Upon this, the old man invited the Levite and his group to lodge with him. Bringing him into his house the usual acts of hospitality were performed which included the washing of feet which was occasioned in those days by the fact of travel on foot and the wearing of sandals that subjected the feet to travel-soreness.

Verse 22. *Belial.* In Old Testament times this was not a proper noun. It was used as a descriptive word. It meant one who was base, worthless, lawless. It later came to be used especially with reference to Satan. In the particular instance before us the men were Sodomites. "That we may know him," meant they wished to commit sodomy.

Verses 23, 24. The protection connected with the obligations of hospitality caused the old man to protest their wicked demand. To quiet them he offered to bring out to them his own virgin daughter, as well as the guest's concubine. This was a strange proposition. For more complete comments on the subject see Gen. 19: 8 and note. Two wrongs never make one right. Yet of two evils, it is sometimes preferable to choose the less. Certainly natural immorality is less wicked than unnatural. This idea is recognized by the language of Paul in Rom. 1: 27.

Verse 25. *Would not hearken.* Since the men did use this woman we must understand this expression to mean only that they did not orally agree to the proposal. Still their attitude was threatening, so the Levite cooperated with his host to the extent that he exposed his concubine to the lust of the men of the city. They abused her all night so that her life was practically shut off by morning, at which time they let her go. In the case of Lot (Gen. 19: 8), the men would not use the women. In the present case they did not orally agree with a like offer although it states they abused the concubine. Thus, whether they used her in the same manner as in sodomy we are not told. The reasonable inference is that they so used her since that was their depravity.

Verse 26. The woman had just enough strength left to reach the door of the house where her husband was lodging but was unable to gain entrance.

Verses 27, 28. For the time being the Levite did not know what had become of his concubine since he had turned her into the hands of the men of the city. Hence he was preparing to resume his journey alone or at least to go out in search for her. When he opened the door there was his concubine prostrate with her hands grasping the threshold of the door in a desperate struggle for entrance. The husband thought her only resting and bade her arise that they might be on their way. Receiving no response he discovered that she was dead. Next he put her body on his beast of burden and went on to his home.

Verse 29. Upon arriving at his house he cut the body of his concubine into twelve pieces, a piece for each tribe, and sent the awful tokens out among the people.

Verse 30. The effect was what the Levite expected, no doubt. All who saw the gruesome articles were shocked. They stated that it was an action without parallel in all the history of their nation. A general call was made that the people hold consultations on the subject, and after doing so express themselves.

JUDGES 20

Verse 1. The act of the Levite recorded in previous chapter roused the entire people of Israel. *From Dan to Beer-sheba.* This was to signify that all of the nation had been aroused. Dan was at the northern and Beersheba at the southern extremity of the land of Palestine. Gilead was east of the Jordan. Thus we see that the whole population of the twelve tribes came together *as one man* which indicates the unity of feeling and of action. Mizpeh being an important city in Israel it was the general place of assembling to confer on action as to the case of the Levite.

Verse 2. Here they mobilized a group of four hundred thousand warriors.

Verse 3. When the army was assembled the Levite was asked to report more definitely on his terrible experience. The tribe of Benjamin in the meantime heard of the great assembling of armed men.

Verses 4-7. The Levite gave a full and true account of what he and his concubine had suffered. He concluded his speech with request for an expression from them.

Verses 8-11. The unity of mind and action is still manifest with this great throng of Israelites. Their decision was to divide their man power into relays and prepare for action. The first thing will be to advance to the city of Gibeah, the scene of the terrible mistreatment imposed upon the complainant.

Verses 12, 13. When they had gathered at Gibeah, representatives of all the other tribes sent men throughout the possession of the tribe of Benjamin. The whole tribe need not be charged with the guilt of one city unless they cause it to be so. Therefore, these commissioners offer to settle the controversy by punishing the men only who were guilty. That was fair and should have been agreed to by the tribe of Benjamin. But they would not accept the proposal made by their brethren.

Verses 14, 15. Having rejected the offer of peace made by the Israelites, the tribe of Benjamin knew that war was inevitable. They mustered an army from the various cities of their possession and assembled them at Gibeah. In that city they found others to add to the army. The forces of Benjamin now were 26,000 men from the outlying cities, and 700 from the city of Gibeah.

Verse 16. Among the forces of Benjamin were some special sharpshooters to the number of 700. *Lefthanded.* This word occurs only twice in the Bible. As a complete term it does not always mean that the person had adopted the use of the left hand instead of the right. It usually meant that something had impeded or deprived him of the use of his right hand and that he used the left of necessity. In the particular case of the Benjamites we have information in 1 Chr. 12: 2 that the Benjamites were skilful with each of their hands. That would give them certain advantages as to the angle desired for casting stones at the target selected. That fact accounts for the statement made here that they could sling stones at a hair breadth accurately. That would make them formidable antagonists.

Verse 17. The forces of Israel are numbered at 400,000. *Beside Benjamin.* This is said to agree with the idea that Benjamin is on the other side of the conflict.

Verse 18. As stated before, the Israelites divided their men into relays for the war. As to which group should make the first attack, they asked counsel of God by going to the house of the Lord. That was in recognition of the arrangement made by Moses that God was to be known in the place chosen to record his name. Upon their inquiry they were informed that Judah was to make the attack.

Verses 19-21. The first battle apparently brought defeat to the Israelites, but their knowledge of warfare and also their faith in the Lord prevented final defeat.

Verses 22, 23. Before making another attack, they again seek counsel of the Lord and are told to renew the battle.

Verses 24, 25. Again the children of Israel suffered loss of many men.

Verse 26-28. While they are not entirely discouraged, they seem to think that something may be lacking in their own preparation of mind. This time they put on a season of religious activities. After this they renew their inquiry. The inspired writer explains that the ark of the covenant was there, as was also the priest. These factors made it lawful to ask counsel of God. Again they were told to renew their battle against Benjamin. But the reader's attention will be called to a difference in the last response of God from the two previous ones. In them nothing was said as to the immediate outcome of the battle. In this they were not only told to go on with the battle, but that in it they would succeed over the enemy. The whole procedure agrees with the idea taught generally in the Bible that desirable results often have to be obtained through painful and expensive sacrifices.

Verses 29-31. Now the Israelites make the attack after arranging certain stratagems. In this battle the Benjamites slew thirty of the others. But this was for a purpose. It gave them false encouragement.

Verse 32. They concluded that the victory was to be theirs as in the previous battles and were thus prepared in mind to fall into the feint which the Israelites set for them by fleeing. This drew them from the city and into the highways where they would be open to the attack of the army of Israel.

Verses 33-35. The decisive battle was now about to begin. The ones lying in ambush joined the others and together they smote of the Benjamites, 25,000 and more. When we consider the small size of the army on that side, this number of slain will appear as a fundamental and fatal loss.

Verses 36, 37. The visible cause of the success was the stratagem practiced by the children of Israel. As the bulk of the army was fleeing and the Benjamites were thus encouraged to pursue, those in ambush arose unexpectedly and made the attack that resulted in the great slaughter of the pursuers.

Verse 38. This is an explanation of part of the strategy. At the proper time the signal to be used for movement was that of sending up a flame out of the city.

Verse 39. It was at this time that the Israelites in the larger unit made as if they were retreating and that decoyed the Benjamites on to their action.

Verse 40. To avoid confusion it is well to bear in mind that the scripture often makes a general statement of happenings and then gives more details. The total number of killed among the Benjamites was stated in 35th verse. From there on in the chapter some of the means used were explained specifically and the various stages of the day's actions outlined. This flame caused to arise out of the city was one of the ruses intended to throw the enemy into confusion, which it did.

Verses 41, 42. This paragraph sets forth that on account of the effect of the flame the Benjamites started to flee toward the wilderness and were slain in the flight.

Verses 43, 44. In this incident of the battle the Benjamites lost 18,000 men.

Verse 45. Still pursuing toward the wilderness and overthrowing all the stragglers along the highways they killed two thousand more of the enemy.

Verse 46. Here the writer sums up the total slain of the Benjamites except that it is given in round numbers instead of the specific hundreds as in 35th verse. Such an order of recording figures is common in both sacred and profane writers.

Verse 47. These six hundred men were usually swift in flight and thus escaped.

Verse 48. This verse is one of the details of the whole day's transactions and is to be considered as included with the account already referred to previously.

JUDGES 21

Verse 1. It was permitted by the law for women to marry into a tribe other than that of their fathers with the stipulation that no disturbance was to be made in the holdings of the land. But before starting into the war with the Benjamites the men of Israel were so hot in their indignation that they had made an oath not to let any of their daughters follow that practice. Whether they realized how completely the women of the Benjamites would be destroyed along with the men of war is not stated. But we can see from verse 16 below that about all of the available material for wives was slain. It is not considered ethical warfare to attack civilians, but if such mingle with the armed forces it is unavoidable that destruction of them will occur and hence the population as a whole will be reduced That is what took place in this battle.

Verse 2. After the war was concluded the men of Israel saw the awful condition of the tribe of Benjamin, that it was almost out of existence, at least as far as the prospects of future multiplying. If the marriage of their few remaining men to the daughters of the other tribes is prevented then the tribe will become extinct. This caused them to weep before the Lord in Shiloh.

Verse 3. In spite of the outrage committed by this one tribe, the Israelites were amazed at the very idea of losing one of the twelve tribes.

Verse 4. The enormity of their plight now brought upon them a feeling of remorse. In that condition of mind they instituted a season of sacrificial worship. After that it was determined to set about to find means of overcoming the situation. Of course those implicated in the vow mentioned in first verse were only the ones who had come together at Mizpeh at the general call referred to in ch. 19: 30 and ch. 20: 1. Now if any communities can be found who did not respond to that call, of course they would be free from the oath. Also they would be guilty of what would amount to desertion in time of war, in effect. This would give them a pretext for punitive action. With this sort of outlook they decided to make inquiry.

Verse 5. The decision arrived at was carried out. Inquiry was made as to whether any of the tribes of Israel had failed to respond to their country's call for service. It had also been determined with this plan of inquiry that if any were found to be guilty they were to be slain as "draft evaders."

Verses 6, 7. This paragraph repeats what has already been stated, that the men of Israel were very sorry for the situation and were eager to do something to repair the damage they had done to the future of this one tribe by their oath.

Verse 8. The inquiry is again stated and the information was obtained that the community of Jabesh in Gilead failed to respond. This was the chief city in the territory named and contained many people.

Verse 9. An examination of the enrollment was made and in this way it was found that the above mentioned units of the population were guilty of the breach of duty for not any of that community responded to the call.

Verses 10, 11. A detachment consisting in twelve thousand men was sent to carry out the decision of execution. The instruction was to kill all the men and also all the women except those who had never had relations with men.

Verse 12. After this was done they found four hundred virgins left from the lot.

Verse 13. The six hundred refugees mentioned in verse 47 were now contacted and given proclamation of peace. This was to let them know that the war was over and they could come out from their hiding.

Verse 14. These Benjamites were then given wives of the virgins saved from the slaughter at Jabesh. There were six hundred of these men needing wives while only four hundred of the virgins. Hence there lacked still two hundred without wives.

Verse 15. As used here the word "repented" means they were very sorry and filled with pity for the Benjamites. It is said that the Lord made this breach in the tribes of Israel. This is to be understood in the light of the binding nature of an oath. If an Israelite made an oath to the Lord he was bound to keep it.

Verses 16, 17. Still regretting the situation they declare that something must be done to preserve the inheritance of the tribe of Benjamin.

Verse 18. Even in their desperation they did not forget their oath and thus something must be done to remedy the sad affair without breaking their oath directly.

Verse 19. The law of Moses established three yearly feasts to the Lord and all males were required to assemble at the national headquarters to attend the services of the tabernacle. It was at this time located at Shiloh. While the males only were required to appear at those times, others were permitted to come and usually there were great numbers of others there out of interest in the Lord's institutions. And while the men would be engaged in the activities about the tabernacle the women and others not engaged in such work would be free to conduct themselves in various ways in the near community. This gave the Israelites an idea in the present emergency.

Verses 20, 21. The two hundred Benjamites yet without wives were now told to hide in the vineyards of the community. One form of activities practiced by people in old times was that of dancing in groups. Either the men would thus engage as a group or the women would do so. So while the men were engaged in the duties about the tabernacle the virgins would pass their time in this exercise of dancing. The instructions were for these men lying along the highway and in the vineyards to rise up and seize each man a virgin to become his wife.

Verse 22. No mention is made of complaint from the virgins. If any of them objected it is not revealed. It was natural to expect an objection from the fathers or brothers of the girls and hence an explanation was promised. They would make a plea to the men to be favorable toward the transaction for their sakes. That in the war the Israelites had not made any reservation from among the Benjamites for wives of the single men. Also that the fathers or brothers of these Israelite virgins were not guilty of having violated their oath on this subject and thus were not to be chided as being short of their duty to the nation. If they will all be quiet and let these remaining men of Benjamin find their own wives themselves the rest of the nation could be guiltless, at least as far as direct ceremony was concerned.

Verse 23. The counsel was accepted and the two hundred men secured each a virgin to be his wife and then returned home to repair the damage that had been done by the war.

Verse 24. The children of Israel of the other tribes also mustered out of military service and returned to their various homes.

Verse 25. This is explained in ch. 17: 6.

RUTH 1

Verse 1. *When the judges ruled.* This gives us the general period for the date of this book. But none of the works of reference that I have found can set the exact time. However, we know it was in the latter part of the reign of the judges because it concludes with the birth of the grandfather of David which brings us near the history found in the book of Samuel. The events of this very interesting and beautiful story occurred in the time of the period covered by the book previous to this and may be considered as an insert of that book. The immediate cause of the movements of the family concerned was a sore famine in the land of Canaan. This family belonged at Bethlehem of the tribe of Judah. In their distress they crossed the Jordan into the country of Moab which bordered along the river. The family now consisted of the man and wife, also their two sons.

Verse 2. The names of the members of this family respectively were Elimelech, Naomi, Mahlon and Chilion.

Verse 3. The first misfortune to befall Naomi here was the loss of her husband by death.

Verse 4. The entire time of sojourn in Moab of this family was ten years. In that time the two sons married women of the Moabites. Their names were Orpah and Ruth. Whether in the same order as named above we do not know.

Verse 5. The next misfortune for Naomi was the death of her sons, which left her with her two daughters-in-law only, of her own family.

Verses 6, 7 News now came to Naomi that the famine was over in Judah and thus she decided to return to her home land. In the first movements of leaving the land of Moab the two daughters-in-law were with Naomi with indications they intended going with her to her land.

Verse 8. These girls evidently were not sisters, for Naomi suggested they go "each to her mother's house." This would have been inappropriate language had they been of the same house. Naomi had nothing but a kindly regard for these women because of their respectful treatment of her. But they were foreigners to her native country and would naturally feel more at home where they had been born. So she bade them return to their former homes and wished the blessing of God on them.

Verse 9. She even wished that they might each again find a husband and have another home of rest or satisfaction. She kissed them which was a gesture of good-bye, for that act was generallly done only on meeting or parting. Since they had been with each other up to now, the kiss was one of parting. The immediate effect was one of sadness on the part of both for they wept.

Verse 10. The attitude of both women was favorable to going with Naomi and to joining with her among her people.

Verses 11-13. There are various thoughts suggested by this paragraph. One is that marriage was an important, if not the most important, objective of life. That is true in many senses. As such was the case, Naomi supposed the chief point of interest with these women was to find another husband with her. If that were the case, then it would indicate their love for and confidence in her and her family. Also that a husband obtained from her would be satisfactory and hence would also indicate that their married life with her sons had been satisfactory. She shows them that if that were their desire and expectation it would be in vain. She could not possibly offer them such a blessing. This was for two reasons. One, that she did not have a busband herself. Second, that if she did she would be too old to bear children again. And we might see a third reason and that was that even if she had overcome the two other obstacles to their wishes the sons would not be grown up in time to become the husbands of the women. All this sad prospect filled her with grief for the women.

Verse 14. This sorrowful speech of Naomi caused them to weep again. Orpah accepted the advice of her mother-in-law and kissed her farewell. Ruth would not bid her mother-in-law good-bye. She clave unto her.

Verse 15. Naomi calls Orpah the sister-in-law of Ruth which confirms the conclusion made at verse 8 that the two women were not sisters in the flesh. Ruth is urged again to follow her sister-in-law back to her people and to her gods. Since the women were Moabites and not of the nation of Israel it was supposed that when left alone without personal relationship with any Israelite they would not care to worship the God of Israel. On the principle of the language in Josh. 24: 15, (see notes at that place) they might as well go back to their own objects of worship. Naomi seemed not to realize the real motive Ruth had for clinging to her. It was not merely, or even chiefly, to obtain another husband. Through the years of association with the family of Naomi and her son, Ruth had become convinced that such was the most desirable situation in life she could find. What a wonderful compliment this is to the influence of a godly woman. This mother-in-law had conducted herself after such a manner before Ruth that an inseparable attachment had been formed for her and the religion she represented. This is another proof of the effect of example.

Verses 16, 17. To the mind of the writer this paragraph records one of the sweetest declarations in all literature. The abiding confidence in her mother-in-law and her conversion to the religion of Israel's God stand out as the prime motive in all the intended actions of Ruth from now on till death. She is completely weaned away from her native people and their gods. The influence of Naomi on her has been to satisfy, so that come what may, in conditions of favorable or unfavorable home accommodations, or whatsoever place to which she might choose to go, and whoever might be found to be her particular people; whoever was her god and then wherever might be her resting place after death, she was determined to remain inseparable with this holy woman whose life had proved to be the great benediction of hers. With this in her mind she makes an earnest plea to be permitted to remain with her mother-in-law until death.

Verse 18. What kind of a heart could resist a speech so full of sweet and tender affection? Certainly not the kind possessed by this righteous mother in Israel. Thus she ceased her objection and resumed the journey with this fine young woman.

Verse 19. Bethlehem was the native home of Naomi and thither these two women came. The word "moved" is from an original that means the people of the city were agitated at the appearance of Naomi and Ruth. It had been ten years since Naomi left the community and the years of trials had made changes in her appearance of person. So they exclaimed in surprised inquiry, "Is this Naomi?"

Verse 20. Proper nouns in Bible times often had a descriptive meaning. Thus the name of Naomi meant "pleasantness or agreeableness," coming from NOOMEE. Under her changed circumstances she considers that an inappropriate name. Not that she intends discarding it as a personal designation for she did not do so, but only offered the remark as a comment on the circumstances. On that principle she considered the name of Mara, a more suitable description, for her sorrowful reverses in life. Strong says the original word for Mara is the same in meaning as for Marah in Ex. 15: 23, where we recall the place was so named because of the literally bitter water there.

Verse 21. Her use of the words "full" and "empty" was figurative, of course, but was her way of describing the reduced condition she had come under.

Verse 22. The time of year in which these women reached the community of Bethlehem is not important apparently at present. Its significance will appear as we proceed.

RUTH 2

Verse 1. The word "kinsman" here merely means an acquaintance, without necessary reference to relationship otherwise. If such relation exists it must be gathered from another word later on. This particular acquaintance of Elimelech was a wealthy man and his name was Boaz. The word "family" brings in the idea of relationship since one meaning of the original word here is "circle of relatives," according to Strong.

Verse 2. A special provision was made in the law of Moses that poor people had the right to go into fields of grain after the main crop was taken and glean from what had been left. (Lev. 19: 9, 10.) Of course, this God-fearing woman, Naomi, had instructed her daughter-in-law in the word of the Lord and hence she understood it was her right to go out for this purpose since they were among the poor. Now we can begin to see the significance mentioned in last verse of preceding chapter. The provisos which Ruth stated were her way of saying she wished to glean in whatever field was favorable to her. She could not have referred to anything about Boaz, because at this time even Naomi did not know into what field Ruth might find opportunity for gleaning. She gave her daughter-in-law her approval.

Verse 3. The word "field" is from SADAY and defined by Strong "from an unused root meaning to spread out; a field (as flat)." The word has been rendered in the A. V. by "country, ground, land, soil." So the word refers to the farming districts in general and a gleaner would seek out the portions growing grain. This general portion of the country would be used by various citizens who had the personal title to any certain section of it. "Her hap," means that it so happened that Ruth stopped to glean in that place belonging to Boaz. Of course the writer means that as far as Ruth knew, it was just a happen so. But the reader will understand that the "happening" was caused by the Lord who is in all this wonderful story.

Verse 4. The city residence of Boaz was Bethlehem, another coincidence. He went to look after the work going on in his field and greeted his workers with a friendly word and they returned in the same kind of friendship. How much better it would be in all cases, if worker and employer manifested this sort of attitude toward each other. Too many times the feeling seems to be as if each were the enemy of the other, or, that it might be so and that a mutual need for watchfulness was present. The world could not move along as it ought without the labor of man. Neither could it accomplish what it should were it not for those who are financially able to support the "man with the hoe."

Verse 5. There was nothing surprising in the mere fact that some one was gleaning in the field since the law made provision for such practice, but something about this damsel attracted the attention of Boaz and thus the inquiry.

Verses 6, 7. While it was customary for people to glean in a field that had produced a crop of grain, it was not altogether the practice to follow up so near the workers who were still engaged in the main crop. This was probably part of the cause of the inquiry of Boaz. And the inquiry or request made by the damsel that she be permitted to glean not only near the reapers but even among the sheaves was also an unusual thing. Permission to do this would indicate much confidence in the honesty of the gleaner. The provision of the law as to a gleaner did not include any such special privilege. Again the reader will see the evidence that God is in all this.

Verse 8. Boaz confirmed the privilege the men had given Ruth. He gave her even further privilege, that of remaining near his maidens which means the young damsels of his employ who were obtaining part of their living by gleaning among the sheaves.

Verse 9. The antecedent of "they" in both instances is the same since the young men were the ones charged with the work of the direct harvesting. The charge he gave to his young men was appropriate in view of the fact that the damsel would be near them. The instruction that they were not to "touch" her, meant not to do her any harm either as to ordinary violence or as to her rights of moral security. Ruth had been married some years before this, yet Boaz considered her a damsel which is from a word that mean's "a young girl." This would indicate that she was married comparatively young. All of these special favors offered Ruth, manifested an interest on the part of Boaz that was more than mere courtesy. So we are sure that God is in all this. However, that does not mean that the attitude of this man was forced against what would have been his personal one. God always chose the kind of character he needed for any particular kind of service desired. We are sure that Boaz was naturally a man of refinement.

Verse 10. All of this kindness impresses Ruth so that she does the customary act of those times in recognition of friendship and greatness. She makes a low bow and seems filled with surprise at the attention being shown her. Being a "stranger" means that she was from another place and people from the ones here belonging.

Verse 11. The answer Boaz gave Ruth proves to us that in the meantime he had made further inquiry and had learned the history of the case. The reasons he stated to her for his attitude toward her are gracious. While we are sure that he had an interest in her even now, that was more than mere courtesy, yet there is not the least indication of flattery or personal complications. This will be clear to us when we consider that regardless of his inclinations toward her, he considers himself as outside the rights of a lover and therefore is too much of a gentlemen to make any advances toward her that could not honorably be carried out to the desired conclusion. Yet he does not need to reserve any courtesy that would be proper toward a virtuous girl.

Verse 12. What beautiful words these must have seemed to be to the mind of this trusting young woman. She had already come to believe in the God of her mother-in-law and that trust had brought her away from her own mother's people and family and attached her to her new relation in life with an inseparable tie. Now that same God is commended to her by this man who is showing such gallant friendship toward her.

Verse 13. Ruth acknowledged the comfort she had obtained from the treatment that Boaz had accorded her. She recognized that a difference existed in class between her and the other maidens gleaning and thus her words of appreciation are logical and true.

Verse 14. There was not a word in all the law of Moses that made provision for such attentions as Boaz was showing Ruth. It did provide that the poor of the country might glean after the main crop had been harvested, but nothing else was mentioned. In this special privilege Boaz here gave Ruth we see that an attachment of genuine love is forming in the case. We would not ordinarily think of vinegar as a desirable article of drink as a beverage. It was used as a special cause of reducing the strain of the physical exertions being made by mixing it with the bread of the diet. Such an item of bodily service would not be so easily procured at large, hence it was another special privilege to be allowed to partake of these provisions in common with him. He even shared his food with her to her full desire.

Verses 15, 16. Boaz now added another special privilege to that already given her. The young men are directed to drop some of the handfuls purposely for her and then to say nothing to her when she gathered them up. It would not be difficult to recognize the hand of Cupid in all this. Such fact, notwithstanding the evidence of God's hand underneath all the rest, makes the story one of the most beautiful in all literature.

Verse 17. An ephah was between a half and a whole gallon and this was the amount of barley that Ruth gathered by gleaning this day after it was threshed.

Verse 18. After consuming what her personal appetite required, Ruth turned over the remains of her gleaning to her mother-in-law who placed it with the family store.

Verse 19. Up to now Naomi only knows that Ruth has been fortunate in finding a good field in which to glean and one under circumstances that were unusual since the damsel has come in with such a bountiful supply of grain. She calls for the blessing on the person who had extended such favor to her daughter-in-law. Ruth told her mother-in-law the name of the man who had been so kind to her.

Verse 20. In mentioning the kindness which the Lord had shown she included the dead with the living. This indicated that Naomi saw the hand of God as acting in a more serious manner than merely that of food for the present. All she said for the present was that the man was a near kinsman. That meant a great deal under the provisions of the law. (Lev. 25: 25.) When the famine struck the land mentioned in ch. 1: 1, it forced this family to encumber their land with debt. Even after that was consumed it became necessary to leave the country to find a living. Now the land is still under the debt and will be until, and unless, it is redeemed. It was the duty of the nearest kinsman of the dead man to take over the family and financial obligation of the same. This fact is what Naomi had in mind with her statement to Ruth. But she does not try to explain as yet because much remains to be done before the case will be settled.

Verse 21. Ruth gave her mother-in-law further information about the privileges offered her by the man where she had gleaned. The mention of her being a Moabitess is to explain to the reader why this whole procedure was somewhat of a mystery to her, which will be made clear as the case advances.

Verse 22. Naomi does not know just how far Boaz will care to go in this circumstance of the property and family but she plans to cooperate with him and the Lord in it all; hence the instructions here given to Ruth. Should the other maidens observe her in company with the people in other fields it might discourage Boaz against pressing his own interests.

Verse 23. The same sweet trust in her mother-in-law that had bound her to her and caused her to desert her native land now continued to show itself. She carefully observed the instructions her mother-in-law gave her all through the harvest of that crop.

RUTH 3

Verse 1. Let it not be forgotten that Naomi was a Jewess and acquainted with the law of Moses and in the situation now at hand would be especially interested in that part of the law applicable to their conditions. In her view of the case Boaz is the man who would lawfully be the one to take the place of Ruth's dead husband. Acting on that impression she gave Ruth the announcement worded here, but it was her plan to let her learn as much of the procedure as possible from the experience she was to have. All this was because the young woman was of another country and did not know the law of the Jews that would apply in this case. The word "rest" here is from MANOWACH and defined "quiet, i. e. (concretely) a settled spot, or (figuratively) a home."—Strong. Hence we see that Naomi plans to obtain for Ruth a home of her own so that she can be settled again in the normal surroundings of a wife and housekeeper. Under the provisions of the law she considers that Ruth has legal claim to Boaz. It is in view of the law and what she thought to be the relationship between her dead son who had been the husband of Ruth, and the family, that she was giving all these instructions. While she considered that Ruth had the right under the law to lay claim to Boaz, she desired the whole problem to be completed at the voluntary performance of the one involved. Yet it would be proper to follow up her rights by keeping near Boaz, since he might not be fully acquainted with all the facts. Her confidence in the principles of Boaz was such that she fully believed he would carry out the law as fast as he was brought to realize the situation. All this explains her directions.

Verse 2. Little by little, Naomi acquainted Ruth with the nature of the situation as she thought it to be. Until she learns the full truth of the relationship we must interpret all her instructions to Ruth on the basis of what she thought it to be. So the next item of information given to Ruth was that Boaz was of their kindred and hence came under the provision of their law as to redemption of land and of marriage. Had she known the full particulars of the relationship she might not have felt it so necessary to press their claim upon Boaz as persistently as she was doing. And, had the true state of relationship been as Naomi thought it was it would not have been thought necessary thus to press it for he would have proceeded promptly, as we know he finally did. The gathering of the crop has been completed and now the next thing is to winnow or thresh it. Naomi is acquainted with the work connected with caring for the crops and understands that on that night the threshing would take place since there was generally a breeze in the evening, according to Smith. After the work of threshing which would require some physical exertion there would be occasion for refreshment in the form of food and then for rest in sleep. All this was in her mind.

Verse 3. The instructions in this verse mean that Ruth was to make herself attractive to the man who was intended to be her husband, also to be so clothed as to be ready for his advances, if and when they were made. More will be said on this particular phase of this case at 4th verse. "Raiment" here must be understood in a special sense for we know that Ruth was already clothed as her mother-in-law was talking to her. The word here is from SIMLAH and Strong gives the following definition and explanation: "Perhaps by complete alteration of thought for the feminine of CEMEL (through the idea of a cover assuming the shape of the object beneath); a dress, especially a mantle." The thought is that Ruth was to be attired in a manner suitable for the passing of the night with a man. In this condition she was to go to the threshing floor, but remain unseen through the activities of the evening just following the threshing, and before reposing for the night's rest.

Verse 4. When Ruth sees Boaz lie down for the night she is to approach the spot and lie down at his feet and take the covering over his feet and cover her as far as that would reach. After this, whatever the man directed, Ruth was to comply. Of course Naomi expected that Boaz would carry out the provisions of the law as set forth in Deut. 25: 5. Had he been the near kinsman that Naomi thought him to be, no doubt he would have done so and would have been in perfect legal and moral order in doing so. The critics of the Bible tried to make much out of this circumstance as being an instance of irregular conduct. When the stipulations of the law are understood the attempts of the criticisms will be seen to be based on ignorance and evil surmise. Let us suppose that a wife has been separated from her husband by circumstances beyond them both. Then she is informed that he is in a certain place but that her whereabouts are not known to him. Under such circumstances she would be wholly within her legal and moral rights in seeking his private company and in reminding him of their close relationship. That is what Ruth is doing in all these actions in which she is carrying out the instructions of her mother-in-law. In asking for his intimate recognition of their relationship, she is doing exactly what any wife would be doing if seeking the intimacy of her husband. The fact that her mother-in-law was uninformed on the exact state of the case does not change the principle here stated. The moral error that might have been committed was prevented by the more complete information of Boaz and his high principle of conduct.

Verse 5. All of this is new to Ruth but she is still the trusting and obedient daughter-in-law and is sweetly obeying and promising still to obey all that is told her.

Verses 6, 7. The hour arrived. The word "merry" is from YATAB and means that he felt well and good from a satisfactory meal. Not that he was under influence of the wine as sometimes such expression might mean. Having concluded the work of the evening and also the repast called for by such activity, he is retiring for the night and Ruth follows instructions and quietly comes to his presence.

Verse 8. Any person being awakened at an unusual hour might be in a kind of daze for a few seconds. If at the same time he realized that someone was near him who was not there when he lay down to sleep he would be startled, which was what was meant by being afraid. Then he "turned himself" which means that he grasped himself when he realized that a woman was lying at his feet.

Verse 9. He recovered himself sufficiently to speak and asked who it was lying at his feet. A frank and unabashed answer was given him by this pure minded woman. Then, acting on the information given her by her mother-in-law she bids him carry out the provisions of his law, and recognize her as his kinsman with the legal and moral right as well as obligation of the marriage relation. See comments at verse 4 on this.

Verse 10. One meaning of "kindness" given by Strong is "piety." So Boaz looks upon the actions of Ruth as those of devotion to the principles of the Lord rather than as merely the outward signs of fleshly desire. It was especially commendable for her, in that she, being a young woman, might have had the society of young men had she been interested along that line only. In the beginning of her life she had married a young man in accordance with the usual practice. But now at the latter part of her experience along that line she considers piety ahead of fleshly desire. For all of this Boaz calls the blessing of the Lord upon her.

Verse 11. For the moment Boaz promises to comply with her request and acknowledges her to be a virtuous woman whose character is recognized by people in general.

Verse 12. This verse tells of the information that Naomi did not have, but which Boaz did have. The law required that the nearest kinsman was the one to redeem the land and family of the dead husband. Boaz knew that another Jew was closer in kin to Elimelech's family than he, and therefore should have priority in the case.

This knowledge was what kept him from advancing toward Ruth when he came to recognize her lying at his feet. Here is one of the finest instances of pure manhood on record. Boaz saw that Ruth was unaware of the true state of affairs. She was at his feet in a pose to invite intimacy. He could have proceeded according to the natural inclinations of the flesh and Ruth would not have been the wiser. Yet Boaz was too much of a gentleman and had such regard for the moral as well as legal law, that he would not take advantage of her simple reliance on his integrity. Not only did he not take immediate advantage of the opportuninty for fleshly gratification, but he will not proceed to make her his bosom companion legally, while another has privilege before him. Were all men in the world as righteous as this man, what a vast amount of sorrow and sin could be avoided in the social world!

Verse 13. It is still night and no time yet to change lodging places. He bade her tarry until time to go home. He then promised that if the man who had first right to her were agreeable to the transaction, he would agree with it all. In case the other man refused to do his part then he, Boaz, would do so.

Verse 14. She lay at his feet until morning. That is, the night was practically gone, yet was still dark enough to disguise one's identity. After she was gone Boaz gave instructions that it was not to be made known that a woman had been there. It may be complained that Boaz did not act as if he had been doing the right thing or he would not have given these instructions. The reason is clear. While he knew all the facts in the case yet others did not. Not all of the people would know the error of Naomi's information and hence might misconstrue the conduct of Ruth under the instructions of her mother-in-law. Therefore, an injustice would be done to her reputation were the mere fact of Ruth's presence known. So Boaz acts in a precautionary way according to the principle taught in Rom. 14: 16; 1 Cor. 10: 32.

Verse 15. Before letting Ruth depart for her home he gave her a supply of barley. This would be the grain after being threshed or winnowed. The exact amount is uncertain since the word is in italics. But whatever vessel Boaz used to handle the grain he filled it six times. And it was an amount sufficient to be carried on the shoulder.

Verse 16. Of course Naomi recognized her daughter-in-law. And she had not been away except over night. Neither was her absence any surprise to Naomi since she had done according to her request. But the R. V. makes the question of the elder woman clear by the words "how hast thou fared?" She was eager to learn the success of the daughter-in-law with her marital adventure. In answer to the question Ruth told her the full story of the experiences of the night.

Verse 17. The gift of barley was not only a substantial expression of the respect Boaz had for Ruth but also the mention of her mother-in-law indicated he had received information of her worth. It showed further that Ruth and Naomi were understood to be mutually interested in the whole proceeding.

Verse 18. There is no doubt that Naomi was acquainted with the practices of the Jews and their expressions of mind. She knew that the persistence with which Boaz has been pressing his suit meant more than a mere compliance of the legal requirements of the law. When a man of the character exhibited by this godly individual manifests his interest by the way reported by Ruth it may be concluded that he wishes the whole matter to be decided as soon as possible. *Sit still.* This expression was one of assurance and had the force of saying "be at ease" or "be assured of success."

RUTH 4

Verse 1. The important cities of those times were walled as a means of fortification and often referred to as "fenced" cities. Hence the gate of the city would be the place where one would go when desirous of meeting a certain person. Boaz wished to contact the kinsman mentioned before, and for that purpose took a position at the gates of the city. The fact that these men were both near relatives of the same man indicates they were residents of the same city and that Boaz had selected the proper place at which to meet the other man. He was not disappointed in this, for the expected person came by. On seeing him Boaz called his attention. The man stopped and sat down near him.

Verse 2. The selection of these ten leading citizens of the city was a cautionary measure as we will see presently. Sitting down by these two men they would be witnesses to what was being said.

Verse 3. It has already been shown that Naomi was poor and that the land that bore title to Elimelech will have to be offered for sale in order to satisfy the financial demands of the creditor. Under such circumstances the land may be purchased or "redeemed" by near relative. In fact, the law made provision to that effect and the one designated to perform such an act was the brother or nearest relative. See Lev. 25: 25 on this point. The word "brother" is from ACH and defined by Strong "a primitive word; a brother (used in the widest sense of literal relationship and metaphorical affinity or resemblance)."

Verse 4. *Advertise.* This is from a word that means "to reveal." The R. V. gives us "disclose" which is a correct rendering. The statement as used here means that Boaz thought he should inform this near kinsman of the transaction about to take place. The peculiar circumstances of Ruth's gleaning in the field of Boaz caused him to have the information on this subject ahead of the other relative. Again we see the fine and unselfish disposition of this man. He will not take advantage of the ignorance of the other man who really has first choice. It was taken for granted that he knew the law on the subject and that the nearest kinsman was the one to buy or procure or redeem the land. *None to redeem it beside thee.* This meant that there was none any nearer to Elimelech in relationship than this man and that Boaz came after him. So the proposition was made that if he was willing to redeem the land, well and good. We note the reference to the elders who had been selected in 2nd verse and before whom the transaction was to be made. This relative said he would redeem the land.

Verse 5. There was another section of the law of which Boaz made no mention as yet, and that was concerning the wife of a dead brother or near relative which required that the surviving one should marry the widow and raise up children that would be enrolled in favor of the dead brother. (Deut 25: 5.) We cannot say that Boaz was taking any advantage of the other kinsman by not mentioning this at first. There would have been no chance of his being injured at last anyway because he would have been bound to learn of all the facts in course of the transaction. Hence we must conclude that no injustice was done. But by mentioning the property phase of the case only at first it would give opportunity for exhibiting the main point of interest by having this relative commit himself. Then if he goes on and accepts all the obligations of the case cheerfully, it would indicate the proper feeling of loyalty to the law and to a dead brother. We have seen that sometimes this test was denied (Gen. 38: 9), and a selfish attitude manifested. This will be found in the present case. After this near kinsman had committed himself as to the property settlement, Boaz informed him of the other angle in the matter and made reference to the law on that subject. We are to understand that where both the childless widow and an encumbered property were involved, the relative assuming the duties toward one phase would be obligated to take the other. The claim of right to the land would be the same as admitting the obligation on the part of the dead man's widow.

Verse 6. The fact of procuring more land would have no objectionable effect on any previous holding, hence that was not the basis of his objection. But by taking an additional wife into his intimate life, the new heirs might interfere with his own previous arrangement in some way. At least he feared it might be so. With this in mind, the near kinsman declined to accept the entire obligation and gave his consent to the next man. It is interesting to note the differences in the attitude of these two men. The one was not willing to accept the woman in order to acquire the land because he did not have any love for the woman. But the love of Boaz for Ruth was such that he was willing to assume the financial obligation connected with the case in order to secure to himself the woman he loved. This whole matter is a beautiful story.

Verses 7, 8. All systems of law have more or less formalites connected with the transactions of their citizens. There may be little or no logical significance in the forms, further than to make a record of the deed and to make it binding. In the case of assuming the obligations imposed regarding a dead relative a provision was made to take care of the exchange. That is, when one person was first in line but declined to perform his duty he was to be treated according to Deut. 25: 7, 9. If he wished to lessen the shame of his refusal he could voluntarily go through the formality. In the case before us the near kinsman was perfectly willing to let Boaz take his place. Also, Boaz was perfectly willing to take the other man's place for the reason that is now clear to the mind of the reader. So this formality was done as a "testimony."

Verse 9. Again we see the service of the elders chosen in the first of the chapter to be witnesses. Since the exchange of the shoe was the recognized sign of the legal transaction, this formality gave notice to the public that the exchange had been made by the agreement of both interested parties.

Verse 10. We do not like to think of purchasing a wife, especially in the case of such pleasant circumstances as the one at hand. The whole procedure of this very interesting experience shows a state of the purest love between the contracting parties, and one free from all taint of worldliness. So on examination of the word "purchased" it is found that one part of the lexicon definition is "to procure" which is the more agreeable word. Boaz did not have to expend money to obtain Ruth as a wife. Had there been no property involved at all, still it would have been the provision of the law for him to take her on behalf of the dead relative. Indeed it could be said that Boaz procured the young woman in that he did not have the lawful right to her in the beginning. That was the reason for his gallant attitude toward her at the threshing floor. He did his full duty. Having the information the other kinsman did not have and offering him the first chance, he laid the way open for the full and legal performance of the matter. Then the near relative declined to assume the obligation so that put Boaz next. This was all the more evident by his voluntary exchange of the shoe without requiring Ruth to do so according to Deut. 25: 7, 9. By doing everything he could to let the kinsman into the deal, Boaz made himself entitled to all that the other man should have made use of. So that it was a proper word to say he had "procured" Ruth to be his wife. We know that Boaz was in love with Ruth and that it was his chief personal motive for the performance of the law. It makes a fitting case of application for the statement "Happy is that man in whom the love of a woman and the sense of duty impel in the same direction." He did not need to say anything about the sentimental feature of the case for the public was not concerned about that. The people did understand the requirements of the law, hence he cites the ideas set forth therein on this subject. Boaz closed his statement on the matter by calling on the witnesses to agree to his declarations.

Verse 11. The witnesses, including the elders and the people, testified to the transaction. They moreover added their good wishes to the case by comparing Ruth to Rachel and Leah. The mention of both wives of Jacob indicates that no reference was being had to the personal characteristics of those two women since the differences in them would exclude a comparison to one woman. The wives of Jacob produced the members of the family of Jacob and that was the outstanding desire of the people of God in those times. The people also wished him financial success as well as a good name in the city. The two names given here refer to the same place, the former being more ancient.

Verse 12. This verse is just an additional citation of a case where a wife honored her master by giving him seed for future generations.

Verse 13. Nothing previously has been said in the text as to the fertility of Ruth, and whether her being without children was due to any defect. If she were barren the Lord overcame that defect by miracle. Of course, we have seen that Boaz was a righteous man and his high principles of life make us know that he would have done his duty toward her under the law regardless of any sentiment. But it is a beautiful thought that Boaz and Ruth loved each other and on that ground would come together in the consummation of their newly acquired privilege. What a complete and satisfactory instance of the law of marriage instituted by the Lord in the beginning. (Gen. 2: 23, 24.) A son was the fruit of this match.

Verse 14. In congratulating Naomi, the women referred to Boaz as the redeemer of the lost fortunes in both property and family. Their explanation of the good fortune was in attributing the matter to the Lord, which was a true consideration.

Verse 15. In the preceding verse the women gave credit to Boaz for the favors coming to Naomi. In this they also pay fitting tribute to Ruth. It is interesting to note their connecting the special joys to come to Naomi in the son with the fact that he had been born by the daughter-in-law. Now of course a grandson through the name of a son would necessarily be born by a daughter-in-law, hence we know that mere idea is not all there was in their language. But the proviso "which loveth thee" is what makes the story all the more significant. It also confirms the statement made above that Ruth loved her mother-in-law.

Verse 16. *Become nurse unto it*. This means that she cared for it as if it were her own child in the matter of attending to its bodily wants, also by bringing it up in the proper manner.

Verse 17. From various sources it seems that friends in old times often suggested a name for a new baby. (Luke 1: 59.) Such was done in the present case and the name given was Obed. The writer completes three generations in this verse by naming David.

Verses 18-22 The entire story of Ruth is beautiful, and exhibits all of the best and dearest sentiments of family ties and conjugal love, but the special use of the story is to show the reader a connecting link in the chain of Christ's ancestors. So in the conclusion of the book the writer goes back to the generations starting with Judah and brings them down to David who became the famous ancestor of Christ through two of his sons, Nathan and Solomon. One of these sons produced the line that came down to Mary, the mother of Jesus, as recorded in Luke 3. The other, Solomon, produced the line that came down to Joseph, the husband of Mary.